AUDITING CONCEPTS AND METHODS
A Guide to Current Theory and Practice

AUDITING CONCEPTS AND METHODS

A Guide to Current Theory and Practice

SIXTH EDITION

Douglas R. Carmichael, Ph.D., CPA
Baruch College

John J. Willingham, Ph.D., CPA
University of Texas at Austin

Carol A. Schaller, CPA

Boston, Massachusetts   Burr Ridge, Illinois   Dubuque, Iowa
Madison, Wisconsin   New York, New York   San Francisco, California   St. Louis, Missouri

Irwin/McGraw-Hill

A Division of The **McGraw·Hill** Companies

AUDITING CONCEPTS AND METHODS: A Guide to Current Theory and Practice

This book is printed on acid-free paper.

4 5 6 7 8 9 10 DOC/DOC 0 9 8 7 6 5 4 3 2 1 0

ISBN 0-07-011058-1

This book was set in Times Roman by GTS Graphics.
The editors were Alan Sachs, Terri Varveris, and Linda Richmond;
the production supervisor was Paula Keller.
The interior design was done by Amy Becker.
R. R. Donnelley & Sons Company was printer and binder.

Cover photo: Comstock.

Library of Congress Cataloging-in-Publication Data

Carmichael, D. R. (Douglas R.). (date).
    Auditing concepts and methods: a guide to current theory and
practice / D.R. Carmichael, John J. Willingham, — 6th ed.
      p.   cm.
    Includes bibliographical references and index.
    ISBN 0-07-011058-1
    1. Auditing. I. Willingham, John J. II. Title.
HF5667.C2766 1996
657′.45—dc20   95-33427

About the Authors

Douglas R. Carmichael, Ph.D., CPA, CFE, is an internationally recognized authority on auditing. He has a Ph.D. in Accountancy from the University of Illinois and has been a CPA for over 30 years and, more recently, has become a Certified Fraud Examiner. He spent over 13 years at the American Institute of Certified Public Accountants developing auditing standards and was Vice President, Auditing, in 1982 when he left the AICPA and joined Baruch College. Dr. Carmichael is the Wollman Distinguished Professor of Accountancy and teaches auditing at the undergraduate, master's, and doctoral levels. He is also a consultant to CPA firms on audit policy matters and has served as an expert witness on accounting and auditing matters in litigation proceedings. He has written 16 books, numerous articles, monographs, and continuing professional education courses, and is the accounting and auditing editor for the *CPA Journal,* a national professional periodical.

John J. Willingham, Ph.D., CPA, is a professor at the University of Texas at Austin. He was previously a partner in the Executive Office of KPMG Peat Marwick in charge of audit research and the firm's Research Opportunities in Auditing program. After a career as a professor on the faculties of Penn State University, the University of Texas and the University of Houston, he joined KPMG Peat Marwick in 1978. His committee responsibilities have included membership on the AICPA Auditing Standards Board (1976–1978). Dr. Willingham has written numerous articles that have appeared in accounting journals in three countries and is the coauthor of six books.

Carol A. Schaller, CPA, is an independent consultant in auditing and forensic accounting. She was previously the Director of the Computer Security group for Ernst & Whinney's New York region. Before joining Ernst & Whinney, she spent six years on the staff of the American Institute of Certified Public Accountants. She has written numerous articles and has authored or coauthored several books, including *Auditing and EDP,* published by the AICPA.

We wish to dedicate this book to Thelma Carmichael and Jennie Schaller, our mothers.
Both are petite, wiry women who have recently suffered some medical problems.
Each has more courage, strength, and determination than
an entire battalion of marines, and inspires all who meet her.

CONTENTS

CHAPTER 9 The Effect of Computers on the Audit 334

PREFACE

The two underlying premises of the sixth edition of *Auditing Concepts and Methods* are the same as the preceding editions:

- An understanding of concepts makes the methods of audit practice more meaningful and provides a foundation for continuing study.
- An explanation of how concepts are implemented in auditing practices, policies, and procedures is essential to achieve an understanding of auditing concepts.

The sixth edition is an up-to-date and practical guide to auditing theory and practice. This edition has been expanded to reflect the changing environment of auditing. There is a new chapter on legal liability as well as a separate chapter on professional ethics. In addition, other changes have been integrated into each chapter. This edition incorporates all the new Statements on Auditing Standards (SASs) issued up to and including SAS No. 73. The new SASs have been fully integrated into all relevant chapters of the book. A risk assessment emphasis and current terminology are woven into the discussion rather than grafted onto existing material. New discussion questions and problems have been added to the chapters.

This book is designed to provide an introduction to auditing for accounting students who do not have significant auditing experience. It may be used for a one-semester or one-quarter course at the undergraduate or graduate level. Coverage of topics is sufficient to permit use of this book without supplemental materials. However, it may also be used effectively with the AICPA *Codification of Auditing Standards and Procedures* and a large variety of supplemental materials. Use of supplemental materials is explained in detail in the companion Instructor's Manual.

SIGNIFICANT FEATURES OF THIS EDITION

This edition has several significant features related to both content and format.

- *Learning Objectives.* Each chapter begins by identifying several important matters that students should understand after studying the chapter.

- *Relevant sections of SASs.* Each chapter lists the relevant AU sections of the Statements on Auditing Standards for the chapter or other relevant authoritative literature, such as the AT sections of Statements on Standards for Attestation Engagements. The lists are useful as optional supplemental reading assignments.
- *Objective questions.* Each chapter includes true/false questions prepared specifically for this book and multiple-choice questions from the Uniform CPA Examination that provide a comprehensive review of important points and topics in the chapter.
- *Discussion questions.* Each chapter includes discussion questions classified by major topic in the chapter. Some questions are from the Uniform CPA Examination, but many were prepared specifically for this edition of the book, particularly those related to materiality, audit risk, audit sampling, legal liability and the audit environment, and audit efficiency.
- *New chapters on ethics and legal liability.* New chapters have been prepared to describe the auditor's ethical and legal responsibilities and liability to others. However, the effects of the changing audit environment are not limited to the chapters on ethics and on legal liability; they permeate the entire book.
- *Audit sampling chapter.* There is a separate chapter on audit sampling that uses the terms and concepts of SAS No. 39, as modified by SAS No. 55, as a base for explaining both *statistical* and *nonstatistical audit sampling.* The emphasis is on the rationale that underlies all audit sampling. An appendix on estimation sampling using a hypothesis testing approach has been added in this edition.
- *Computers and auditing.* Consideration of the computer is an integral part of an audit. Every chapter has included discussion of computer-related topics and examples. There is a separate chapter on the effect of computers on the audit that highlights computer-related effects on the internal control structure and computer-assisted audit techniques. This edition includes such topics as workpaper considerations when microcomputers are used as an audit tool, use of expert systems, electronic data interchange, and the effects of LANs and other network-based computer systems. An explanation of basic computer processing concepts is included as an appendix.
- *Internal control structure chapter.* This edition explains the five components of the internal control structure as defined in the COSO Report (Report of the Committee of Sponsoring Organizations of the Treadway Commission) and integrated into the SASs.
- *Planning tests of details chapter.* There is a separate chapter that explains the concepts of *audit risk* and *materiality* and illustrates how these concepts are actually used to make decisions on the nature, timing, and extent of tests of details. This chapter also explains *audit efficiency* as a concept of auditing theory and illustrates how efficiency considerations influence the direction of testing and coordination of tests of transaction classes and direct tests of balances.
- *Emphasis on objectives.* The chapters on internal control structure, tests of transactions, and tests of balances emphasize objectives. These chapters explain how the auditor develops *specific control objectives* and *specific audit objectives* and how the objectives are used in the planning and performance of audit tests.
- *Background information.* This edition briefly reviews topics that are necessary to understand auditing but that should ideally be covered adequately in other courses in

accounting or business. For example, basic concepts of computer processing and fundamentals of accounting systems (including source documents and flowcharting) are explained sufficiently to provide a background for understanding related auditing considerations. These topics are either being squeezed out of the curriculum or are compartmentalized by students to the extent that an understanding of them cannot be assumed in the first auditing course.

- *Coverage of auditing income taxes.* The chapter on direct tests of balances includes an explanation of the specific audit objectives and common audit procedures for examining income taxes in a corporation's financial statements. Given the importance of income taxes to a business and the materiality of the provision for income taxes to a corporation's income statement, it is difficult to justify failing to provide students with at least an introductory explanation of the auditing issues and normal audit approach for income taxes.

- *Comprehensive coverage of pronouncements.* This book covers specifically all significant Statements on Auditing Standards through SAS No. 73, as well as changes in related areas and all fundamental aspects of Statements on Accounting and Review Services through SSARS No. 7 and the Statements on Standards for Attestation Engagements through SSAE No. 3. Today, more than ever before, authoritative pronouncements are, for all practical purposes, the equivalent of statutory law for the practice of auditing. This book emphasizes the "how and why" of pronouncements rather than reproducing or paraphrasing long passages from the pronouncements.

- *Operational auditing chapter.* There is a separate chapter on operational auditing. This chapter covers both the theoretical base and the practice methods of operational auditing. It is not merely an explanation of internal auditing and governmental auditing with operational auditing tacked on. An explanation is given of both the framework of this type of auditing and the major steps in the conduct of an operational audit engagement.

ORGANIZATION

This edition is not divided into formal parts. Logically, however, the book could be viewed as consisting of the following parts:

Part 1: Chapters 1–4   An introduction to auditing as a subject of study, the environment of auditing, and the basic building blocks for understanding the next parts on the planning and performance of an audit of financial statements.

Part 2: Chapters 5–7   An explanation of audit planning. These chapters cover the planning phases of the audit, including general planning, understanding the internal control structure including the accounting system and related controls, and planning detailed preliminary audit programs. Materiality and audit risk, including assessment of control risk, are covered as an integral part of audit planning.

Part 3: Chapters 8 and 9   An explanation of the specialized planning considerations for use with audit sampling and the effect of the computer. These subjects are an integral part of audit planning, but their complexity warrants separate coverage.

Part 4: Chapters 10–12   An explanation of the performance of auditing procedures in the phases of the audit concerned with tests of transaction classes, direct tests of balances, and the general procedures and related matters dealt with near the completion of the audit.

Part 5: Chapter 13   An explanation of the modifications of the standard audit report that may be necessary in specific circumstances. The standard audit report and the various types of reports other than an unqualified opinion are introduced in Chapter 1. Chapter 13 explains these types of reports in more detail and discusses how the auditor decides the type of report that is appropriate.

Part 6: Chapters 14 and 15   A review of attestation standards; compilation or review of the financial statements of a nonpublic company; specialized reporting circumstances, such as special reports and forecasts; compliance attestation; and operational audit engagements as conducted by independent CPAs, governmental auditors, and operational auditors.

Organizational Variations   The most common variations in arrangement are to cover all aspects of the standard audit report and modifications of it at the beginning of the course (i.e., assign Chapter 13 immediately after Chapter 1) or to delay coverage of self-regulation (ethics, peer review, etc.) and external regulation (SEC, legal liability, etc.) to the end of the course (i.e., assign Chapters 2 and 3 as the last or next to last topics).

Another variation is to eliminate the topics of sampling and computers (Chapters 8 and 9) from the first course because they are covered in a second course on auditing. We discourage this variation. Chapters 8 and 9 introduce sampling and computers from the perspective of a general auditor. There is still a great deal that can be presented on these topics in an advanced course without serious duplication. Also, the knowledge in Chapters 8 and 9 is an integral part of current auditing practice.

Chief Organizational Feature   One organizational feature of this edition remains unchanged from the first edition published in 1971. The central part of the book is organized around the logical phases and sequence of an audit of financial statements. To our knowledge, auditing textbooks before 1971 were all organized either by balance sheet account order or transaction cycles.

After 1971, several auditing textbooks adopted the general organizational approach of *Auditing Concepts and Methods* and many other textbooks adopted the underlying premise of emphasizing concepts and theory rather than merely describing existing auditing practices and procedures.

In recent years, the trend started by our first edition in 1971 has accelerated far beyond the modest goals we envisioned approximately 25 years ago for a better integration of auditing theory and practice.

SUPPLEMENTS

Instructor's Resource Manual
0-07-011059-X

This resource manual is an Instructor's Manual, Solutions Manual, and Test Bank all in one. It begins with a section that provides suggestions on course presentation and coverage, so that instructors can design a course that is tailored to their individual needs. It then presents lecture suggestions for each chapter, solutions to end-of-chapter material in the text; a Test Bank with solutions, and transparency masters, some of which include figures from the text. The Test Bank consists of over 400 multiple-choice questions; many of which have been modified from the last edition.

Computerized Instructor's Manual

A computerized version of the above-described Instructor's Resource Manual will be made available to instructors on an on-demand basis.

MICRO, INC.: A Computerized Audit Practice Case, Second Edition
3.5" IBM Disk: 0-07-841989-1
5.25" IBM Disk: 0-07-841985-9

. . . by Joyce C. Lambert (University of New Orleans), S. J. Lambert III (University of New Orleans), and James G. Hruska (Nebraska Wesleyan University). This computerized practice case is to be used as a supplement for Auditing courses. It is a highly interactive simulation, placing students in the position of auditor. Upon completion of this practice case, students will gain experience with the major audit systems and understand the role of microcomputers in the audit process. This package requires access to a commercial spreadsheet package, such as Lotus, Excel, or Quattro Pro. **Available Instructor's Manual: 0-07-842823-8**

SCAD III: A Simulated Case for Audit Decisions
3.5" IBM Disk: 0-07-840385-5

. . . by William L. Felix, Jr. (University of Arizona), Robert J. May (University of Texas), Marcia S. Niles (University of Idaho), Jon M. Andrus (University of Arizona), and Janet D. Gillespie (University of Texas). This case combines a realistic scenario that describes a wholesale appliance company's accounting system and a comprehensive set of computer generated accounting data. **Available Instructor's Manual: 0-07-840391-X**

ACKNOWLEDGMENTS

We would like to thank the many reviewers who have enriched our book with their comments and suggestions: J. E. Boritz, University of Waterloo; Eric Carlsen, Kean College;

Nahnhee Choi, Long Island University–C. W. Post; William Donnelly, San Hose State University; Austin Emeagwai, LeMoyne-Owen College; Leon J. Hanouille, Syracuse University; Thomas J. Hogan, University of Massachusetts; William E. Huntley, Monmouth College; Malcolm H. Lathan, Jr., University of Virginia; Heidi H. Meier, Cleveland State University; Philip H. Siegel, University of Houston–Downtown; and Ira Solomon, University of Illinois.

We acknowledge the debt to the American Institute of Certified Public Accountants owed by any authors of an auditing textbook for permission to quote extensively from authoritative pronouncements and other publications.

We would also like to thank the Canadian Institute of Chartered Accountants for allowing us to use problems from Canadian CA examinations and the Institute of Management Accounting of the National Association of Accountants for use of CMA problems.

Finally, we wish to thank the staff at McGraw-Hill: Alan Sachs, Linda Richmond, Terri Varveris, Paula Keller, Chuck Carson, and Amy Becker.

Douglas R. Carmichael
John J. Willingham
Carol A. Schaller

AUDITING CONCEPTS AND METHODS
A Guide to Current Theory and Practice

CHAPTER

1

The Audit Function—
An Overview

CHAPTER OUTLINE

Learning Objectives

After studying this chapter you should be able to:

- Define auditing generally and distinguish an audit of financial statements from other types of audits
- Explain the need for an audit of financial statements
- Describe the essential features of the standard audit report and the meaning of generally accepted auditing standards and generally accepted accounting principles
- Identify the characteristics of an independent auditor and CPA firms engaged in public accounting practice
- Outline the types of audits other than an audit of financial statements, the auditors who conduct them, and the national organizations of such auditors

Relevant Sections of Statements on Auditing Standards

AU 110 — Responsibilities and Functions of the Independent Auditor

AU 150 — Generally Accepted Auditing Standards

AU 201 — Nature of the General Standards

AU 210 — Training and Proficiency of the Independent Auditor

AU 220 — Independence

AU 230 — Due Care in the Performance of Work

AU 410 — Adherence to Generally Accepted Accounting Principles

AU 411 — The Meaning of "Present Fairly in Conformity with Generally Accepted Accounting Principles" in the Independent Auditor's Report

AU 508.01 to AU 508.10 — Reports on Audited Financial Statements

AU 801 — Compliance Auditing Applicable to Governmental Entities and Other Recipients of Governmental Financial Assistance

HISTORY OF THE AUDIT FUNCTION

Audits have been performed at least since the fifteenth century. The exact origin of audits of financial reports is in dispute, but it is known that as early as the fifteenth century auditors were called on to ensure the absence of fraud in the records kept by stewards of wealthy household estates in England. Although its origins are ancient, development of the audit function has occurred most rapidly in the last century.

Independent Audits Prior to 1900

The origin of the audit function in North America is decidedly British. Accountancy as a profession was introduced on this continent by the British during the second half of the nineteenth century. North American accountants adopted the British form for audit reports and British procedures for carrying out examinations.

In the United Kingdom then, as today, public corporations were formed under a national law known as the Companies Act. All public companies must abide by this law. When the audit function was exported to the United States, the British form of reporting was adopted even though there were no comparable United States statutes. In addition, while British public companies were required to have audits, American companies were not. Even today, the state laws under which United States corporations are formed generally do not require audits. Rather, audit requirements generally arise from requirements of stock exchanges, regulations of the Securities and Exchange Commission (SEC), and general acceptance of the usefulness of an independent auditor's opinion on financial representations.

The absence of statutory requirements for audits to be submitted to stockholders resulted in nineteenth-century audits that varied from audits of only balance-sheet accounts to full, detailed examinations of all accounts of corporations. An auditor was engaged usually by management or the board of directors of a corporation, and the report was addressed and directed to these insiders rather than shareholders. Reports to shareholders on the representations of management were not common. Instead, the corporate managers were interested in being assured by the auditors that fraud and clerical errors had not occurred.

Twentieth-Century Developments

By 1990 the industrial revolution was approximately 50 years old and industrial companies had expanded greatly in size. There were many more absentee stockholders, many of whom began to receive auditor's reports. Many of these new stockholders did not understand the significance of an auditor's work, and misunderstanding was widespread even among businessleaders and bankers. In fact, it was widely believed that the auditor's opinion was a guaranty of the accuracy of financial statements.

The American accounting profession developed rapidly after World War I. Continued misunderstanding of the independent auditor's function was so widespread that in 1917 the Federal Reserve Board published in the *Federal Reserve Bulletin* a reprint of a document prepared by the American Institute of Accountants [which became the American Institute of Certified Public Accountants (AICPA) in 1957] ostensibly dealing with uniform accounting, but in reality a treatise on how to audit a balance sheet. This United States technical pronouncement was the first of many to be issued by the American profession throughout the twentieth century.

During much of the current century, certified public accountants (CPAs) drafted their reports with little formal guidance. In the last 50 years, however, the profession rapidly developed common report language through the AICPA. Common report language is so well developed today that audit reporting is no longer a writing exercise; it is a decision process. There are a limited number of alternative types of reports from which an auditor can choose, and once the auditor has made a decision about the type of opinion to render in a specific situation, the auditor can select the report form designated to express that opinion.

AUDITING DEFINED

Broadly speaking, *auditing* is an independent investigation of some particular activity. Although auditing has a precise meaning only when used with a limiting modifier, such as tax auditing or financial auditing, one general definition of the term is as follows:

> A systematic process of objectively obtaining and evaluating evidence regarding assertions about economic actions and events to ascertain the degree of correspondence between those assertions and established criteria and communicating the results to interested users.[1]

The important parts of this definition are:

- *Systematic process*. Audits are structured activities that follow a logical sequence.
- *Objectivity*. This is a quality of the way that information is obtained and also a quality of the person doing the audit. Essentially it means freedom from bias.
- *Obtaining and evaluating evidence*. This is a matter of examining the underlying support for assertions or representations.
- *Assertions about economic actions and events*. This is a broad description of the subject matter that is audited. An assertion is essentially a proposition that can be proven or disproven.
- *Degree of correspondence . . . established criteria*. This means an audit establishes the conformity of assertions with specified criteria.
- *Communicating results*. This means simply that to be useful the results of the audit need to be communicated to interested parties. The communication may be oral or written.

Financial Auditing

This book focuses on audits of financial statements by independent auditors. These types of audits are the primary activity of independent public accountants or independent CPAs who are engaged by businesses to examine their financial statements.

When the focus is on a particular type of audit, the generalized definition can be restated in more specific terms. The authoritative definition of the purpose of an audit of financial statements has been stated in this way:

> The objective of the ordinary audit of financial statements by the independent auditor is the expression of an opinion on the fairness with which they present fairly, in all material respects, financial position, results of operations and cash flows in conformity with generally accepted accounting principles. The auditor's report is the medium through which he expresses his opinion or, if circumstances require, disclaims an opinion.[2]

A comparison of this definition of an audit of financial statements with the generalized definition highlights the essential aspects of financial auditing.

- The systematic process of objectively obtaining and evaluating evidence is an audit of financial statements in accordance with generally accepted auditing standards.

---

[1]Auditing Concepts Committee, "Report of the Committee on Basic Auditing Concepts," *The Accounting Review,* Vol. 47, Supp. 1972, p. 18.
[2]AICPA, *Codification of Auditing Standards and Procedures* (New York: AICPA, 1995), p. AU 110.01.

- The assertions about economic actions and events are the representations made in financial statements by the management of an entity about its financial position, results of operations, and cash flows.
- The degree of correspondence with established criteria is judged by whether the financial statements are presented fairly in conformity with generally accepted accounting principles.
- The results of this kind of audit are communicated in an audit report.

This correspondence between the general definition and the definition of a financial audit is no accident. The drafters of the generalized definition developed it by inductively reasoning from the specific characteristics of known types of audits to general propositions.

Other Types of Audits

The other types of audits are basically compliance audits, internal audits, and operational audits. The characteristics of these types of audits and the auditors who perform them are explored later in this chapter and in Chapter 15. Other types of audits share the same heritage as audits of financial statements and use many of the same methods or procedures. However, audits of financial statements have one outstanding distinguishing characteristic, that is, their influence on the allocation of resources among organizations in the economy.

The Need for Audits of Financial Statements

Organizations achieve their goals through the use of human and economic resources. Most often, economic resources are entrusted to the organization by groups or individuals outside it; frequently these outsiders are quite remote from internal operations. Thus, organizations must issue stewardship reports on resource administration—source, quantity, allocation, accumulation, and depletion.

Many different types of organizations render reports on the administration of their resources. A comprehensive but not exhaustive list would include commercial and industrial corporations, banks, railroads, airlines, electric and gas utilities, insurance companies, hospitals, and governmental bodies (such as municipalities, counties, and the federal government).

In spite of the diverse activities of these organizations, they all issue some type of report concerning their fulfillment of responsibilities to outside parties. Regulated companies (such as banks, gas and electric utilities, transportation, insurance, and communications companies) issue reports to regulating authorities to serve as a basis for regulation. Short-term and long-term creditors use financial reports for assessment of repayment ability before extending credit and as evidence of compliance with the loan agreement after issuance. There are many examples of such reports, and the audit function may be applied to all of them; but the type of report most commonly associated with the work of the independent auditor is the report to stockholders and creditors. These reports are the representations of management about its effectiveness in administering resources to the stockholders and creditors, the suppliers of resources. Organizations represented by management are clients of CPAs, but CPAs report to the public.

The auditor-client-public relationship is complicated and delicate. The client organization engages an auditor and pays the fee. Professions other than auditing confine their responsibilities almost solely to clients. However, independent auditors in the United States have for many years acknowledged responsibilities to several parties other than those who directly engage them and pay their fees.

One of the primary reasons for an independent audit is the inherent potential conflict between an entity's management and users of its financial statements. Management could have an incentive to bias the information presented in financial statements because financial statements are one of the means used to evaluate management's performance.

Management exercises a great deal of discretion in preparing financial statements and in using resources entrusted to it in operating the entity. An audit provides reasonable assurance that management's representations on these activities are reliable. Thus, an audit has value because management's representations on its performance and stewardship are examined and reported on by an expert outside management's control.

In an economy such as that in the United States, however, the auditor is selected and paid by someone affected by his or her work. Thus, total independence is impossible. In addition, an audit of financial statements requires a close working relationship with management. The auditor needs intimate knowledge of many of management's actions, decisions, and judgments because of their significant effect on financial statements. An independent auditor is subject to conflicting pressures. The auditor depends on fees from clients and necessarily has a close relationship with clients. Nevertheless, the auditor must often persuade a client to disclose unfavorable information in fulfilling the duties imposed by the audit function.

As a result independent auditors as a group have adopted ethical rules and professional standards to guide individual auditors in resolving the conflicts that inevitably arise. In audits of financial statements, two critical sets of standards are generally accepted accounting principles and generally accepted auditing standards. They are also key phrases in the standard auditor's report—the subject of the next section.

THE AUDIT REPORT

The current audit report, like any other report, is essentially a communication device. Through the report the auditor conveys, in summary form, a professional judgment on the client's representations in the financial statements. The auditor's task is to present clearly and concisely a highly technical subject to a variety of interested readers.

The Standard Report

The wording of the auditor's standard report usually follows the pattern recommended in Statement on Auditing Standards (SAS) No. 58 (AU 508) issued in 1988. The 1988 revised report represents the first significant change in the standard report since 1948. The currently recommended report form is used by almost all CPAs. Since the specific words and phrases in the report have an established meaning, use of the precise wording serves the ends of conciseness and clarity.

Independent Auditor's Report

We have audited the accompanying balance sheet of X Company as of December 31, 19XX, and the related statements of income, retained earnings, and cash flows for the year then ended. These financial statements are the responsibility of the Company's management. Our responsibility is to express an opinion on these financial statements based on our audit.

We conducted our audit in accordance with generally accepted auditing standards. Those standards require that we plan and perform the audit to obtain reasonable assurance about whether the financial statements are free of material misstatement. An audit includes examining, on a test basis, evidence supporting the amounts and disclosures in the financial statements. An audit also includes assessing the accounting principles used and significant estimates made by management, as well as evaluating the overall financial statement presentation. We believe that our audit provides a reasonable basis for our opinion.

In our opinion, the financial statements referred to above present fairly, in all material respects, the financial position of X Company as of December 31, 19XX, and the results of its operations and its cash flows for the year then ended in conformity with generally accepted accounting principles.

(Signature)

(Date)

FIGURE 1-1
Example of an auditor's standard report. (The standard report on comparative financial statements is illustrated in Chapter 13.)

A typical example of an auditor's standard report is shown in Figure 1-1. The standard report has the following basic elements:

- An introductory paragraph identifying the financial statements that were audited and briefly describing management's responsibilities and the auditor's responsibilities regarding the financial statements
- A scope paragraph indicating that the audit was adequate to form an opinion on the statements, and briefly describing what an audit is
- An opinion paragraph stating that the financial statements present fairly, in all material respects, the financial position of the company as of the balance sheet date and the results of the company's operations and its cash flows for the period then ended in conformity with generally accepted accounting principles

These paragraphs contain a number of key words and phrases that concisely express the responsibility assumed by the auditor in rendering the report.

The Introductory Paragraph In the introductory paragraph, the auditor's responsibilities are defined.

"We have audited. . . ." This phrase emphasizes the point that an audit was performed. An auditor cannot express an opinion on financial statements without first conducting an audit.

". . . the accompanying balance sheet of X Company as of December 31, 19XX, and the related statements of income, retained earnings, and cash flows for the year then ended." The auditor must clearly identify the statements covered by the report, including use of the exact titles and dates of the financial statements reported on. The financial statements accompany the auditor's report and should be securely bound under the same cover. The standard report applies to ordinary commercial organizations. For other types of organizations such as some financial entities, government units, and nonprofit organizations, appropriate modifications of the identification of the statements and related aspects of the report are required.

"These financial statements are the responsibility of X Company's management. Our responsibility is to express an opinion on these financial statements based on our audit." These sentences direct attention to the fact that the financial statements are the representations of the client, not the auditor. Management, not the auditor, is primarily responsible for the adequacy and accuracy of the statements. The auditor may draft the statements but does so on behalf of the client.

The Scope Paragraph In the scope paragraph an audit is briefly described, and the auditor indicates the audit performed was adequate to form an opinion on the financial statements.

"We conducted our audit in accordance with generally accepted auditing standards." In this sentence the auditor represents that an audit adequate to support an opinion on the financial statements was performed with professional competence by properly trained persons. Generally accepted auditing standards are listed and discussed later in this chapter, and a major portion of this text is concerned with the meaning of these standards.

"Those standards require that we plan and perform the audit to obtain reasonable assurance about whether the financial statements are free of material misstatement." This sentence attempts to dispel the misunderstanding that the auditor's opinion is a guaranty of the accuracy of the financial statements. It points out that the opinion is based on the audit, and that the audit provides only reasonable, not absolute, assurance that the financial statements—within the context of materiality—do not contain misstatements.

"An audit includes examining, on a test basis, evidence supporting the amounts and disclosures in the financial statements." An audit does not involve an examination of 100 percent of the accounting records. This sentence emphasizes the fact that an audit involves tests of selected underlying data rather than a complete review of all such data. It also indicates that the audit was centered on the financial statements. The accounting records and other data are examined because they represent data underlying the statements.

"An audit also includes assessing the accounting principles used. . . ." This phrase continues the brief description of what an audit is. Statement on Auditing Standards No. 69 (AU 411) explains the judgments an auditor makes in assessing the accounting principles used. The auditor's judgments include:

- The accounting principles selected and applied have general acceptance.
- The accounting principles are appropriate in the circumstances.

". . . . and significant estimates made by management, as well as evaluating the overall financial statement presentation."   This phrase points out that financial statements are necessarily the result of estimates and approximations. Their precision cannot be absolute. It indicates that in an audit, the auditor forms a conclusion not only on the freedom of the statements from material misstatement, but also on the freedom of the statements from material omissions in the presentation of the financial statements. Financial statements may be misleading if they do not contain the information necessary to interpret them properly. SAS No. 69 (AU 411) identifies the auditor's judgments regarding presentation, including the following:

- The financial statements, including the related notes, are informative of matters that may affect their use, understanding, and interpretation.
- The information presented in the financial statements is classified and summarized in a reasonable manner, that is, neither too detailed nor too condensed.
- The financial statements reflect the underlying events and transactions in a manner that presents the financial position, results of operations, and cash flows within a range of acceptable limits; that is, limits that are reasonable and practicable to attain in financial statements.

The last point emphasizes that the auditor's judgments are made within the context of materiality.

"We believe that our audit provides a reasonable basis for our opinion."   This sentence emphasizes the role of professional judgment in designing and performing the audit that is the basis for the opinion that follows, and reemphasizes that the audit provides only a reasonable, not absolutely certain, basis for the opinion.

The Opinion Paragraph   The opinion paragraph presents the auditor's conclusions.

"In our opinion. . . ."   An auditor's opinion is an expression of informed judgment. The auditor's conclusions are not the same as absolute certainty. The auditor is an expert in the fields of accounting and auditing. Therefore, the opinion carries substantial weight. Nevertheless, the auditor cannot ensure or warrant the accuracy of the financial statements.

". . . . the financial statements referred to above present fairly, in all material respects, the financial position of X Company as of December 31, 19XX, and the results of its operations and its cash flows for the year then ended in conformity with generally accepted accounting principles."   Court decisions and critics of the public accounting profession have at times raised the issue of whether the auditor's opinion includes a judgment on fairness separate from conformity with generally accepted accounting principles. Those who raise this issue confuse the broad concept of generally accepted accounting principles with specific pronouncements on accounting by an authoritative body. Unfortunately, there is some basis for the belief that the letter of some accounting pronouncements has been adhered to while their spirit has been violated. However, "fairness" is too loose a term to provide a practical basis for evaluating the presentation of financial information without some specific guide, such as generally accepted accounting principles.

Generally Accepted Accounting Principles

Generally accepted accounting principles (GAAP) include all the conventions, rules, and procedures necessary to define accepted accounting practice at a particular time. Thus, they are not limited to authoritative pronouncements. They also include practices that have achieved acceptance through common usage in business. Of the phrases in the audit report, "generally accepted accounting principles" is one of the most difficult to explain. Unlike auditing standards, accounting principles are derived from a variety of sources.

Beginning in 1939, the Committee on Accounting Procedures of the AICPA regularly issued Accounting Research Bulletins dealing with the appropriate treatment of specific financial transactions and events. This committee was replaced by the Accounting Principles Board (APB) in 1959. The pronouncements of the APB—called *Opinions*—were similar in scope and purpose to the prior bulletins. In 1973, the APB was replaced by the Financial Accounting Standards Board (FASB). The FASB is composed of full-time, paid board members and a research staff independent of the AICPA and all other professional organizations. It is charged with the delineation of accounting principles.

Rule 203 of the Code of Professional Conduct of the AICPA states that a member shall not express an opinion or state affirmatively that the financial statements or other financial data of any entity are presented in conformity with generally accepted accounting principles "if such statements or data contain any departure from an accounting principle promulgated by bodies designated by Council to establish such principles that has a material effect on the statements or data taken as a whole." The bodies currently designated by Council to promulgate accounting principles are:

- Financial Accounting Standards Board (FASB)
- Governmental Accounting Standards Board (GASB)

An auditor must have a thorough knowledge of accounting theory, which includes knowledge of the pronouncements of the AICPA, FASB, and, for governmental units, the GASB, as well as other accounting literature and industry practices.

If there is no pronouncement in an area, industry practice and other accounting literature is considered to be GAAP. SAS No. 69 (AU 411) lists the sources of established accounting principles and defines their "hierarchy." That is, it defines categories and states that the sources in the higher category should be followed when conflicting practices exist between categories. The hierarchy of GAAP that the auditor should follow in rendering an audit opinion is as follows:

CATEGORY A: Pronouncements of Bodies Designated by Council to Established Accounting Principles

- FASB pronouncements
  - Statements on Financial Accounting Standards
  - Interpretations
- APB Opinions
- Accounting Research Bulletins

CATEGORY B: Pronouncements of Bodies of Expert Accountants that Issued Exposure Drafts for Public Comment and Were Cleared by a Council-Designated Body

- AICPA Audit and Accounting Guides
- AICPA Statements of Position
- FASB Technical Bulletins (written by the FASB staff, and authorized and reviewed by the FASB)

CATEGORY C: Pronouncements of Expert Accountants that Were Cleared by a Council-Designated Body, but Not Exposed for Public Comment

- AICPA Accounting Standards Executive Committee (AcSEC) Practice Bulletins
- Consensus Positions of the FASB Emerging Issues Task Force

CATEGORY D: Prevalent Industry Practice

- AICPA Accounting Interpretations
- Implementation Guides ("Qs and As") published by the FASB staff
- Practices that are widely recognized and prevalent either generally or in the industry

ADDITIONAL SOURCES: Other Accounting Literature

- FASB Statements of Financial Accounting Concepts
- AICPA Issues Papers
- APB Statements
- International Accounting Standards of the International Accounting Standards Committee
- Pronouncements of Other Professional Associations or Regulatory Agencies
- Technical Information Service Inquiries and Replies Included in AICPA Technical Practice Aids
- Textbooks
- Journal Articles

SAS No. 69 (AU 411) also presents a second GAAP hierarchy for governmental entities, which mirrors the above categories, substituting "GASB" (Governmental Accounting Standards Board) for "FASB."

Report Title, Address, Signature, and Date

Statement on Auditing Standards No. 58 (AU 508) requires the auditor's report to have a title that includes the word "independent."

An audit report is normally addressed to the person or group who retained the auditor. In the case of corporations, the auditor should be appointed by the board of directors or the stockholders. This is true even though the auditor is paid directly by the client company. The address and the title emphasize the independent nature of the auditor's opinion as a report to the stockholders, or their representatives, the board of directors.

The signature of an audit report is normally that of a public accounting firm. Even though an individual auditor signs the report, the auditor does so in the name of the firm.

A report should be dated as of the last date on which significant auditing work was performed. Although the auditor has some responsibility for adequacy of disclosure of significant events taking place after the balance sheet date, that responsibility diminishes considerably after the audit of the statements is completed.

Departures from the Standard Report

The type of audit report discussed in this chapter contains an *unqualified opinion.* Such a report is issued when there are no material deficiencies in the audit or in the financial statements. However, for various reasons the audit may be inadequate or the statements may not be fairly presented in conformity with generally accepted accounting principles. Even though deficiencies exist, the auditor may still issue a report, but this report will not contain an unqualified opinion. The possible courses of action in such a case are the following:

1 Express a qualified opinion
2 Express an adverse opinion
3 Disclaim an opinion on the statements

A *qualified opinion* ordinarily would be issued when the auditor takes exception to one or a few material items in the financial statements because of departures from generally accepted accounting principles or because the audit is incomplete or deficient with respect to one or a few significant financial statement items.

An *adverse opinion* should be issued if there are departures from generally accepted accounting principles of a very significant and serious nature in the financial statements. These deficiencies would necessarily be of such overriding importance that a statement reader might be misled if the reader relied upon the financial statements.

A *disclaimer* of opinion would be expressed if the audit were incomplete or circumstances caused the audit to be deficient to the point where the auditor was unable to express an opinion on the financial statements.

In addition, there are two important situations that require the auditor to add a fourth explanatory paragraph to the report describing the matters. These two situations are the following:

- A material uncertainty
- A material lack of comparability caused by a change in accounting principle (a material inconsistency)

In these situations, the opinion paragraph remains unqualified.

This preliminary discussion of types of audit reports presents the basic alternatives available to CPAs today. Examples and further detailed discussion of the meaning of each of these types of reports and the circumstances under which they are issued are presented in Chapter 13.

Generally Accepted Auditing Standards

Standards are measures of an acceptable level of quality of professional activity. The professional practice of auditing in the United States is governed largely by the generally accepted auditing standards adopted by the membership of the AICPA in 1948 and 1949, revised by the Auditing Standards Board in 1988, and reproduced in SAS No. 1 (AU 150), as follows:

General Standards

1 The audit is to be performed by a person or persons having adequate technical training and proficiency as an auditor.
2 In all matters relating to the assignment, an independence in mental attitude is to be maintained by the auditor or auditors.
3 Due professional care is to be exercised in the performance of the audit and the preparation of the report.

Standards of Field Work

1 The work is to be adequately planned and assistants, if any, are to be properly supervised.
2 A sufficient understanding of the internal control structure is to be obtained to plan the audit and to determine the nature, timing, and extent of tests to be performed.
3 Sufficient competent evidential matter is to be obtained through inspection, observation, inquiries, and confirmations to afford a reasonable basis for an opinion regarding the financial statements under audit.

Standards of Reporting

1 The report shall state whether the financial statements are presented in accordance with generally accepted accounting principles.
2 The report shall identify those circumstances in which such principles have not been consistently observed in the current period in relation to the preceding period.
3 Informative disclosures in the financial statements are to be regarded as reasonably adequate unless otherwise stated in report.
4 The report shall either contain an expression of opinion regarding the financial statements, taken as a whole, or an assertion to the effect that an opinion cannot be expressed. When an overall opinion cannot be expressed, the reasons therefore should be stated. In all cases where an auditor's name is associated with financial statements, the report should contain a clear-cut indication of the character of the auditor's work and the degree of responsibility the auditor is taking.

General Standards   The general or personal standards concern the qualifications of the auditor and the quality of the auditor's work. They govern both the field work and the reporting thereon. The first general standard requires the auditor to have competence—through experience as well as formal education—to practice as an auditor. An independent auditor represents himself or herself as one who is expert in accounting principles and practices and in auditing methods. The auditor's professional authority covers only the area of expertise. For example, the auditor is not an appraiser of assets.

Independence, the subject of the second general standard, is the hallmark of the auditing profession. In other professions, such as law and medicine, the professional is concerned almost solely with the interests of the client. In addition to a concern for the interests of the client, the auditor must consider the interests of third parties who will rely on the financial statements on which the auditor expresses an opinion.

The auditor's opinion would have little, if any, value if he or she were in fact, or if he or she were believed to be, not independent of the management of a client corporation. If the auditor is independent of the persons who prepare and issue the financial statements, then the audit has value to both management of the client and outside users of the statements. Management can be assured that the auditor's opinion lends credibility to the financial statements in the eyes of the users. On the other hand, the users of the statements have the benefit of the objective opinion of an expert with respect to the reasonableness of the reported data.

The third general standard—due care—requires the auditor to exercise the degree of care expected of a professional. This standard of care is aptly described in the following paragraph from an authoritative legal source, *Cooley on Torts,* as quoted in SAS No. 1 (AU 230.03):

> Every man who offers his service to another and is employed assumes the duty to exercise in the employment such skill as he possesses with reasonable care and diligence. In all these employments where peculiar skill is prerequisite, if one offers his service, he is understood as holding himself out to the public as possessing the degree of skill commonly possessed by others in the same employment, and, if his pretentions are unfounded, he commits a species of fraud upon every man who employs him in reliance on his public profession. But no man, whether skilled or unskilled, undertakes that the task he assumes shall be performed successfully, and without fault or error. He undertakes for good faith and integrity, but not for infallibility, and he is liable to his employer for negligence, bad faith, or dishonesty, but not for losses consequent upon pure errors of judgment.

Standards of Field Work   Field work standards govern the nature of an audit and the extent and types of evidence to be obtained in order to render an opinion. The first standard of field work is necessitated by the internal structure of CPA firms as discussed in the next section. An audit team carrying out an audit requires proper supervision. An audit of a client's financial statements also requires planning before the engagement is undertaken.

Internal control structure, the subject of the second standard of field work, is a complex subject that is treated in detail in Chapter 6. This standard identifies a client's internal control structure as an important means of determining the tests necessary to form an opinion on the client's financial statements.

The final standard of field work requires an auditor to obtain valid evidence in sufficient quantity to provide a basis for an opinion regarding financial statements. This standard further indicates the importance of procedures through which evidential matter is to be obtained. These procedures and others are explained in later chapters.

Standards of Reporting   This group of generally accepted auditing standards governs the form and content of the auditor's report. The first reporting standard requires that the report state whether the financial statements are presented in accordance with generally accepted accounting principles.

The second standard of reporting requires that an explanatory paragraph be added when there is a material change in accounting principle, affecting the comparability with the financial statements of the preceding period. Before 1988, the standard report included an expression of opinion on consistency. The revised standard report does not mention the consistent application of accounting principles unless there is a material inconsistency.

The third standard of reporting concerns the informative disclosures that are made in the body of financial statements or in notes appended to them. The auditor must obtain reasonable assurance that disclosures are adequate to meet the requirements of this standard. If disclosure is inadequate, the auditor must qualify his or her opinion and include the information in the audit report.

The fourth standard requires the auditor's report to contain an expression of opinion on the financial statements taken as a whole or a statement to the effect than an opinion cannot be expressed.

The Auditing Standards Board (ASB), a senior technical committee of the AICPA, issues pronouncements that deal with technical auditing questions. These pronouncements represent authoritative interpretations of generally accepted auditing standards. Fifty-four Statements on Auditing Procedure (SAPs) were issued beginning in 1939, when a committee was established to investigate the ramifications for auditors of a gigantic case of fraud within the wholesale drug firm of McKesson & Robbins.

A prominent public accounting firm had audited McKesson's financial statements, but millions of dollars' worth of assets shown on the consolidated balance sheet were discovered to be attributable to a fictitious subsidiary. As a result of the investigation, SEC regulations were ultimately amended to require that each audit report filed with the commission state whether the audit was performed in accordance with generally accepted auditing standards. The first pronouncement of the Committee on Auditing Procedure, a predecessor of the ASB, adopted the two procedures critically lacking in the McKesson audit—observation of physical inventory taking and mail confirmation of accounts receivable. This position was adopted by a vote of the membership.

Early SAPs were consolidated in the booklet *Codification of Statements on Auditing Procedure* in 1951. In 1954, the committee revised a 1947 report with the objective of explaining the meaning of generally accepted auditing standards. The revision was entitled *Generally Accepted Auditing Standards: Their Significance and Scope.* Another codification in 1963, *Auditing Standards and Procedures,* SAP No. 33, superseded the 1951 and 1954 reports as well as preceding SAPs. In 1973, the Committee on Auditing Procedure issued a codification of all 54 SAPs, entitled *Codification of Auditing Standards and Procedures.* This statement was the first of a new series of Statements on Auditing Standards (SASs).

The ASB has 15 members. All are members of the AICPA and, traditionally, 6 of the members have been from the 6 largest CPA firms. The members serve part-time and normally serve for 3 years. The ASB is supported by a full-time staff, which provides research and writing assistance and which adds continuity and perspective to the work of a rotating, volunteer group.

The ASB publishes its views on auditing on its own authority, and the SASs are enforceable under the AICPA's Code of Professional Conduct. The SASs cover the form and content of the auditor's report in various circumstances, the evidence necessary to support an opinion, and the audit procedures appropriate for obtaining evidence. Thus, the work of the committee provides a continuing source of codified knowledge on the practice of independent auditing. An intimate knowledge of SASs is essential for a competent auditor.

Periodically, congressional committees have questioned whether the function of setting standards for independent auditors who audit financial statements filed with the Securities and Exchange Commission should not be transferred to a government agency. As discussed in Chapter 2, the present system of regulation of independent auditors, including standards setting, is a complex mix of government and private action. The SEC has substantial influence over the setting of both accounting principles and auditing standards. The auditing standards-setting process has worked reasonably well. Studies of the alleged failures of auditors have shown that in most cases actual failures were caused by departures from standards rather than deficiencies in the standards. Although the standards-setting process could be improved, transferring the process to a government agency has been regarded as unwarranted and unnecessarily costly and disruptive.

The AICPA also issues *audit guides* which explain the intricacies of auditing organizations of a specialized nature, such as banks, investment brokers, and construction contractors, and *auditing interpretations* which explain the application of SASs to particular problems. While the interpretations and guides do not have the same official force as SASs, they offer the best guidance in areas covered.

THE INDEPENDENT AUDITOR

The terms *independent auditor, public accountant,* and *CPA* are often used interchangeably to describe a professional accountant who offers services to the public and whose chief service is an audit of financial statements. Technically, a CPA is one who has obtained a license to practice from a state.

To obtain a CPA certificate from a state, an individual must demonstrate technical competence on a uniform examination prepared and graded by the AICPA. Candidates must exhibit an acceptable level of competence in the subjects of auditing, accounting theory, commercial law, and accounting practice. In addition, a candidate must meet a state's individual requirements of residence, education, and experience. Only those individuals who have attained a certificate from one of the states are allowed to practice under the title of "certified public accountant."

CPAs practice in the form of public accounting firms that vary dramatically in size.

Types of CPA Firms

If we consider the public accounting profession to be a special type of industry and individual CPA firms to be production units, a unique aspect of the audit profession is revealed. Most professions are composed of thousands of small units. Only recently have other professionals begun to develop large and extended practices. The composition of the public accounting profession has differed from many other professions since its inception in America. The profession as an industry is composed of three types of firms: (1) those that are national or international, (2) those that are regional, and (3) those that are local.

International and National CPA Firms   As corporations have grown in size and scope of activity, so have some CPA firms. In order to provide services to large, complex organizations, it is necessary to have large CPA firms with sufficient personnel to perform audits of their sizable and far-flung activities. Today there are perhaps 20 CPA firms in the United States that have several hundred or more professional auditors located in offices geographically scattered across the country. For at least the last 50 years, six CPA firms have been in existence that have overshadowed others in terms of scope of activities, geographical area, and influence on the profession as a whole. These six firms have become known as the *Big Six*.[3] All are international in scope and have thousands of clients, thousands of professional accountants, hundreds of offices, and client billings in the millions of dollars.

As would be expected, these extremely large CPA firms audit the financial statements of large public corporations. These include the large public utilities, oil companies, airlines, banks, automobile manufacturers, railroads, food companies, electrical products and appliance manufacturers, and retail store chains. These large firms are necessitated by the existence of huge corporations. However, large firms also provide accounting and auditing services to a variety of small or closely held companies.

Regional CPA Firms   Most regional firms serve a limited geographical area that may be as large as one or two states. They often have as many as 10 offices located throughout the region. As is the situation with the large firms, clients of regional firms generally will be similar to them in size. Regional firms maintain a professional staff necessary to audit the financial statements of corporations and other organizations who consider themselves to be regional in their scope of activities.

Local CPA Firms   While there are approximately 20 firms that are national or international in scope and 100 to 300 that are regional in scope, local firms number in the tens of thousands. Local firms range in size from individual practitioners with no professional staff to partnerships of five or more CPAs with 20 to 30 or more professional staff members. The determining factor is the scope of activity of these firms. Generally, they serve small businesses and individuals in a very restricted geographical area such as a city or county. However, in a major city, a one-office firm may be larger than the local office of an international CPA firm.

CPA Firm Groups   Local and regional CPA firms basically have the same problems as national CPA firms. They provide most of the same services, have the same

---

[3]The Big Six in alphabetical order are as follows: Arthur Andersen & Co.; Coopers & Lybrand; Deloitte & Touche; Ernst & Young; KPMG Peat Marwick; and Price Waterhouse & Co.

staff-development requirements, and must adhere to the same standards as the large firms. One fairly recent innovation in the profession has been the development of groups of CPA firms. A *group* is an organization of CPA firms which is formed to provide services to its member firms that they cannot provide themselves. Occasionally, a small CPA firm may be asked to undertake an audit which requires a portion of the audit to be conducted in a distant city. In this situation, a firm might get assistance from another member of its group located in that city. Also, large international CPA firms can easily afford to hold regular educational programs for the professional staff to make sure they keep abreast of current technical developments. A local or regional CPA firm may find the cost of such programs prohibitive. The group, however, can provide this service at a reasonable cost for its member firms. Finally, a CPA firm group organization can provide an interchange of ideas and techniques related to business and technical aspects of the profession.

Internal Structure of a CPA Firm

Although the public accounting profession includes a large number of individual practitioners, most auditing is done by CPA firms that include several professional staff members. These firms have many common features. Among them are the partnership form of organization and internal organization of professional staff positions and duties.

Partnership Form   In spite of the size to which many CPA firms have grown, most practice as partnerships. The corporate form of organization became available in 1970 through a resolution of the Council of the AICPA that subsequently was approved by the membership. The current requirements, as revised in 1992, permit firms to practice in any organizational form permitted by state law, including general corporations and limited liability companies. Most state CPA licensing regulations still require firms to practice either as a proprietorship, as a partnership, or as a professional organization, all of whose directors and officers with authority over professional matters must be CPAs. However, there is a growing trend for states to permit CPAs to practice as limited liability companies. The Big Six firms are now all organized as limited liability partnerships (LLPs) where state laws permit that form of practice.

Positions and Duties   There are four basic staff positions in CPA firms—partners, managers, seniors, and staff accountants. The duties of the occupants of these positions, as well as the ratio of the relative number of people typically employed in these positions, are depicted in Figure 1-2. The ratios between positions are explained on the right of the chart. For example, for each partner in a firm there will probably be two managers, and so on. Not all firms have these exact ratios, but the chart is a good general guide. Some firms have positions intermediate between the levels in the chart, such as semisenior and principal. The meaning of the terms used to describe positions and the number of intermediate positions vary from firm to firm.

The partners of a firm normally elect a managing partner to be chief executive officer of the firm. A large firm with many offices will also have a managing partner in each

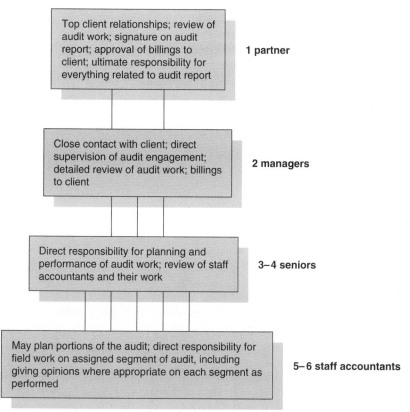

FIGURE 1-2
CPA firm—positions and duties. *(Adapted from Lewis C. Buller, "A Study of the CPA Firm and Its Implications for Members, Business, and Society," unpublished Ph.D. thesis, University of Illinois, 1966, p. 317.)*

office to administer the operating policies of the firm. To assist the managing partner in overall firm management, most firms have an elected executive or operating committee.

The pattern of firm organization is also influenced by the need to have such functions as personnel, finance, research, and practice development properly supervised and administered. In addition, the organizational pattern of some large firms reflect specialization in particular industries or services.

Audits are conducted by a team with differing levels of training and proficiency. Those with higher levels of training and experience are a smaller portion of the total staff for a given audit. The exact composition of the audit team will depend on the nature and size of the client. For example, an international conglomerate with several subsidiaries may require 8,000 hours for the audit and a large and complex audit team. On such an engagement a senior partner might have a staff of three to four partners, four to five managers, three to four seniors, nine to twelve staff assistants, and three to four specialists for computer and tax work. In contrast, a small manufacturer might require an audit of 300 hours with one partner, manager, and senior, and two staff assistants.

Nonaudit Services   CPA firms differ greatly in size and scope, but all offer similar basic services to clients. CPAs are experts in the broad field of accounting and have consequently been called on to provide many services related to the measurement and communication of economic data. Although the practice of many public accounting firms primarily involves audit work, other services are an important part of current practice:

1 *Tax services.* These involve tax planning and advice, preparation of tax returns, and representation of clients before government agencies.
2 *Consulting services.* These involve providing objective advice and consultation on various problems, such as design and installation of information and control systems, budgeting, cost control, profit planning, capital budgeting, and other quantitative analyses.
3 *Review services.* These involve performing inquiry and analytical procedures on financial statements to obtain a basis for issuing a report that expresses limited assurance that there are no material modifications that should be made to the statements for them to be in conformity with GAAP or, if applicable, with another comprehensive basis of accounting. CPAs provide this service to clients that want financial statements to give to others but wish to avoid the expense of an audit. Review services are less expensive because the testing performed is less than that performed for an audit. A review is suitable when a lower level of assurance than that provided by an audit is satisfactory for the client's needs.
4 *Accounting services.* These involve providing special investigations and analyses, such as investigations pursuant to the purchase or sale of a business; performing bookkeeping services; and preparing unaudited financial statements. When a CPA is associated with unaudited financial statements, a *compilation* report is attached, explaining that no audit or review was performed and that the CPA is not expressing any form of assurance on the statements.
5 *Other attestation services.* Audits and reviews are two types of *attestation services,* that is, services for which a CPA expresses a written conclusion about the reliability of another's written assertion. Other attestation services include reporting on forecasts and projections, reporting on characteristics of computer software, and reporting on investment performance statistics.

Accounting and tax services are often a substantial percentage of the work performed by small local firms. In contrast, accounting services are generally a very small percentage of Big Six firms' work. Large national firms often have large groups devoted to management services.

In order that services be provided for all types and sizes of organizations, it is necessary to have an auditing "industry" composed of units of varying sizes that offers a range of services. While the audit profession is different from any other profession, its structure has resulted from the unique aspects of the audit function and the complex organizations that demand it and other services.

OTHER TYPES OF AUDITORS AND AUDITS

In addition to independent auditors whose primary activity is auditing financial statements, other types of auditors may generally be classified as follows:

- *Internal auditors*—employees of organizations who function in a staff, rather than a line, capacity as a high-level control over organizational activities
- *Government auditors*—employees of government agencies who act as the auditing arm of the agencies employing them

Internal auditors and government auditors both have national organizations and professional standards that are explained more fully below.

Essentially, there are three other types of audits:

1 Compliance audits
2 Internal audits
3 Operational audits

Figure 1-3 illustrates types of audits listed by the type of entity receiving the audit. Figure 1-4 illustrates types of audits organized by the type of auditor performing the audit.

Compliance Audits

In our society the largest organization of all is the federal government. Government is truly big business, and there is a myriad of agencies both responsible for the administration of complex regulations and themselves subject to such regulations. Audits of governmental units (and of other entities subject to their requirements) are called *compliance audits* because the auditor checks for compliance with the laws, regulations, and other requirements of the relevant government program.

Agencies and departments of the federal government are audited by the General Accounting Office (GAO). In essence, the GAO is the internal auditing department of the government. As with internal auditing, the audit is an appraisal activity that measures the extent to which organizational objectives are met. The reports of the GAO highlight inefficiencies and make recommendations for improving the efficiency and effectiveness of operations. The GAO has issued standards for audits of efficiency, economy, and effectiveness and has pioneered in conducting such audits.

The auditing departments of some government agencies are concerned with the compliance of private-sector organizations with agency regulations. Tax agents, members of the staff of the audit agencies of the armed services, and bank examiners are auditors concerned with compliance aspects of the relationship between government and business organizations. Armed services audit agencies, for example, make audits of contracts between business organizations and the government. The auditors review the apportionment of costs between government and commercial products in accordance with prescribed regulations and the terms of the contract.

Some government agency audits are confined to ascertaining compliance with a defined range of regulations, and the agencies encourage organizations subject to their regulations to employ other auditors. For example, the Federal Home Loan Bank Board requires independent audits or internal audits in addition to its own examinations. In the Medicare program, independent audits have been used in lieu of establishing a government audit agency. The AICPA's guidance for the independent auditor performing a compliance audit is presented in SAS No. 68 (AU 801).

By type of client	Type of audit	Subcategories of type of audit	Examples of audit objectives
Governmental units and recipients of federal financial assistance	Compliance audit	Financial audit	Audits of financial statements to determine (1) whether they are presented fairly in accordance with GAAP, and (2) whether the entity complied with laws and regulations for those transactions and events that may have a material effect on the financial statements
		Performance audit • Economy and efficiency audit	(1) Evaluation of economy and efficiency in acquisition and use of resources (2) Determining the causes of inefficiencies
		Performance audit • Program audit	(1) Evaluation of compliance with laws and regulations applicable to the government program (2) Determining the extent to which the desired results are being achieved
Other entities (businesses and other nongovernmental entities)	Financial audit		Audits of financial statements to determine whether they are presented fairly in accordance with GAAP, in all material respects
	Operational audit		(1) Evaluation of economy and efficiency in acquisition and use of resources (2) Determining the causes of inefficiencies (3) Evaluation of adherence to company policies or procedures (4) Determining the extent to which the desired results are being achieved

FIGURE 1-3
Types of audits and auditors.

Government auditors generally belong to the Association of Government Accountants (AGA). The AGA is a voluntary member organization that provides a forum for all accountants in government to exchange information and pursue common goals. However, the GAO has taken the lead in setting standards that government auditors are expected to follow.

In 1972, the U.S. General Accounting Office issued *Standards for Audits of Governmental Organizations, Programs, Activities, and Functions* to set forth guidelines for the increased scope of governmental auditing. These standards were revised and reissued in 1981 and again in 1988. This publication is widely referred to as "The Yellow Book." The GAO standards define two types of governmental audits.

Financial Audits

- *Financial statement audits*, which determine (1) whether the financial statements of an audited entity are presented fairly in accordance with generally accepted accounting principles, and (2) whether the entity has complied with laws and regulations for those transactions and events that may have a material effect on the financial statements.

By type of auditor	Type of audit	Subcategories of type of audit	Examples of audit objectives
Independent CPA	Financial audit		Audits of financial statements to determine whether they are presented fairly in accordance with GAAP, in all material respects
	Operational audit		(1) Evaluation of economy and efficiency in acquisition and use of resources (2) Determining the causes of inefficiencies (3) Evaluation of adherence to company policies or procedures (4) Determining the extent to which the desired results are being achieved
Internal auditors	Internal audit	Operational audit	(1) Evaluation of economy and efficiency in acquisition and use of resources (2) Determining the causes of inefficiencies (3) Evaluation of adherence to company policies or procedures (4) Determining the extent to which the desired results are being achieved
		Financial-related audit	Examinations of financial and accounting matters
Government auditors	Performance audit	Economy and efficiency audit	(1) Evaluation of economy and efficiency in acquisition and use of resources (2) Determining the causes of inefficiencies
		Program audit	(1) Evaluation of adherence to laws and regulations applicable to the government program (2) Determining the extent to which the desired results are being achieved
	Financial audit	Financial-related audit	Examinations of financial and accounting matters

FIGURE 1-4
Types of audits and auditors.

- *Financial-related audits*, which include determining (1) whether financial reports and related items, such as elements, accounts, or funds are fairly presented, (2) whether financial information is presented in accordance with established or stated criteria, and (3) whether the entity has adhered to specific financial compliance requirements.

Performance Audits

- *Economy and efficiency audits*, which include determining (1) whether the entity is acquiring, protecting, and using its resources (such as personnel, property, and space) economically and efficiently, (2) the causes of inefficiencies or uneconomical practices, and (3) whether the entity has complied with laws and regulations concerning matters of economy and efficiency.
- *Program audits*, which include determining (1) the extent to which the desired results or benefits established by the legislature or other authorizing body are being achieved,

(2) the effectiveness of organizations, programs, activities, or functions, and (3) whether the entity has complied with laws and regulations applicable to the government program.

The purpose of audits of governmental organizations and programs is similar to that of audits of financial statements. An audit of a governmental organization or program provides an independent judgment of the credibility of public officials' representations about the manner in which they have carried out their responsibilities. The GAO standards follow the same general organization as the generally accepted auditing standards of the AICPA, and many of the standards related to financial audits are identical. However, a governmental audit may also be concerned with efficiency and economy of operations, compliance with both financial and nonfinancial laws and regulations, and program effectiveness.

In a financial audit, the auditor expresses an opinion on the financial statements taken as a whole. The auditor is able to judge whether the financial statements are fairly presented in all material respects in conformity with generally accepted accounting principles because the criteria—GAAP—are reasonably well codified in existing technical pronouncements and other literature.

In audits of efficiency, economy, and effectiveness, criteria for evaluating the level of performance of an organization have, for the most part, not been specified. Further, it is probably impossible to establish whether an organization has reached the maximum practical level of economy, efficiency, or effectiveness. Thus, an auditor is not expected to give an opinion as to the economy, efficiency, or effectiveness of a governmental organization as a whole, or to evaluate the overall quality of operations. The auditor's report should focus on specific areas of an operation or activity wherein improvements are possible or wherein performance has been notably good. The report should set forth the criteria on which the auditor's conclusions or recommendations are based.

Audits of efficiency and economy focus on whether an organization is achieving the maximum benefit given the economic resources it consumes. Audits of effectiveness focus on whether an organization has performed in a way that has enabled it to achieve its goals. In simpler terms, efficiency and economy mean "doing the thing right," but effectiveness means "doing the right thing."

Organizations of all types are concerned with operating efficiently and economically. Net income typically has been considered the measure of effectiveness of profit-making organizations. However, increasing concern with social responsibilities of all types of organizations has created a concern with the effectiveness of nongovernmental organizations that is not encompassed by the measurement of net income. Thus, the GAO standards have significance for nonfinancial audits of all types of organizations.

One important benefit of the GAO standards is greater uniformity in the terminology used to describe audits more extensive than financial audits. These audits have been described as operational audits, management audits, performance audits, and by a variety of other names. The terminology was confusing because generally accepted definitions did not exist, and each writer on the subject chose definitions to suit his or her own preferences. Standardized terminology and the explanatory material of the GAO standards improved communication.

Although audits of efficiency, economy, and effectiveness by independent public accounting firms can be expected to increase in the future, today most audits of this type are performed by government auditors, particularly those with the GAO. The GAO was established in 1921 by Congress to obtain better control of the already burgeoning federal budget. The GAO advises Congress on whether government programs are carried out in accordance with the intent of Congress. For example, the GAO was asked to make a comprehensive study of antipoverty programs. One of the findings was that placing ghetto youths in countryside camps did not help the youths. As a result, the camps were phased out with a saving of hundreds of millions of dollars.

Another term associated with audits of governmental units is *single audit*. Governmental units meeting certain criteria (too complex to cover here) are required to have a single audit, wherein the auditor tests and reports on "general and specific requirements" as listed in the Single Audit Act of 1984 and Office of Management and Budget (OMB) Circular A-128, and other specified laws and regulations. OMB Circular A-133 is similar to OMB A-128, only it applies to nonprofit institutions that receive federal financial assistance, and are therefore subject to the federal audit requirements.

Internal Audits

Internal audits are performed by employees of organizations functioning in a staff capacity and reporting to a high-level officer in the organization. Internal auditing is essentially an appraisal activity within an organization for the review of accounting, financial, and other operations as a basis for service to management. By measuring and evaluating the effectiveness of organizational controls, internal auditing, itself, is an important managerial control device.

While the independent auditor concentrates on an overall evaluation of the presentation of financial statements submitted to third parties, the internal auditor is more concerned with the effectiveness of detailed operating reports to management. The chief products of the internal audit are recommendations for improving the efficiency and effectiveness of operations and the influence exerted on people whose activities are subject to audit. Since operating personnel are aware that internal auditors evaluate their compliance with established policies, plans, and procedures, they are encouraged to conform to these prescriptions.

Internal auditors generally belong to the Institute of Internal Auditors (IIA). In recent years the IIA has attempted to follow the pattern of AICPA and create a professional structure for internal auditors. There is a certification program for becoming a certified internal auditor and standards have been developed for certain aspects of internal auditing practice.

The internal auditor may perform financial-related audits addressing accounting matters, or operational audits.

Operational Audits

Operational auditing began as an outgrowth of internal auditing. This fact has resulted in some confusion between the two terms. Both internal auditors and independent auditors perform operational audits. Essentially, *operational auditing* is a more comprehensive activity designed to analyze organization structure, internal systems, work flow, and managerial performance. In short, an operational audit is intended to provide a measure of the achievement of an organization toward its goals and objectives. The operational audit may address effectiveness of operating procedures and internal controls, performance of individual managers, and other nonfinancial aspects of the operation of an organization.

The products of an operational audit can range from reports recommending improvements in efficiency and effectiveness of current operations to general suggestions about the organization's use of resources to provide the greatest long-range benefit to the company. Operational audit reports may contain recommendations for restructuring of departments or divisions, recommendations for training and replacement of personnel, or results of cost-value analyses of internal controls of an organization. The operational audit is the broadest type of audit in scope and can encompass any of the major functions of an organization.

Operational auditing has developed rapidly in the last 40 years mainly because of the rapid growth and decentralization of corporate organizations. The concept of operational auditing is old, but the application of it to the almost limitless number of nonfinancial problem areas in organizations has come about only in recent years. Operational audits have been performed by all types of auditors. However, internal auditors and government audit agencies have been more active in this area than independent public accountants. As explained earlier, audits of efficiency, economy, and effectiveness are essentially operational audits. Chapter 15 explains operational auditing in more detail.

CHAPTER 1 ASSIGNMENTS

OBJECTIVE QUESTIONS

1-1 For each one of the following statements, indicate whether the statement is true or false.

T   F   **a**   During the early 1900s a statutory requirement for audits resulted in rapid development of the accounting profession in the United States.

T   F   **b**   Auditing in the United States was an extension of British practice, and in the early 1900s British procedures and reports were generally adopted.

T   F   **c**   In a financial audit the degree of correspondence with established criteria is judged by whether the financial statements are fairly presented in all material respects in conformity with generally accepted auditing standards.

T   F   **d**   One of the primary reasons for an independent audit is the inherent potential conflict between an entity's management and its employees.

T   F   **e**   An audit is primarily an examination of a company's accounting records and includes testing a substantial portion of such records.

T   F   **f**   The expression of opinion in the standard report means, among other things, that the auditor has concluded the information in the financial statements is classified and summarized in a manner that is neither too detailed nor too condensed.

T   F   **g**   A disclaimer of opinion would be issued if the auditor believed the financial statements departed from generally accepted accounting principles in a very significant way.

T   F   h Proper planning and supervision is one of the general standards of generally accepted auditing standards.

T   F   i Auditing is practiced primarily by CPA firms organized in partnerships that are regional in scope.

T   F   j Audits of efficiency, economy, and effectiveness were devised by the GAO and are still conducted primarily by the GAO.

1-2 The following questions relate to financial auditing and auditing standards. Select the *best* response.

   a The first general standard requires that a person or persons have adequate technical training and proficiency as an auditor. This standard is met by:

     1 An understanding of the field of business and finance

     2 Education and experience in the field of business and finance

     3 Continuing professional education

     4 A thorough knowledge of the Statements on Auditing Standards

   b The third general standard states that due care is to be exercised in the performance of the audit. This standard should be interpreted to mean that a CPA who undertakes an engagement assumes a duty to perform:

     1 With reasonable diligence and without fault or error

     2 As a professional who will assume responsibility for losses consequent upon error of judgment

     3 To the satisfaction of the client and third parties who may rely upon the audit

     4 As a professional possessing the degree of skill commonly possessed by others in the field

   c A CPA, while performing an audit, strives to achieve independence in appearance in order to:

     1 Reduce risk and liability

     2 Become independent in fact

     3 Maintain public confidence in the profession

     4 Comply with the generally accepted standards of field work

   d A CPA certificate is evidence of:

     1 Recognition of independence

     2 Basic competence at the time the certificate is granted

     3 Culmination of the educational process

     4 Membership in the AICPA

   e Which of the following standards requires a critical review of the work done and the judgment exercised by those assisting in an audit at every level of supervision?

     1 Proficiency

     2 Audit risk

     3 Inspection

     4 Due care

   f The first general standard requires that an audit of financial statements is to be performed by a person or persons having:

     1 Seasoned judgment in varying degrees of supervision and review

     2 Adequate technical training and proficiency

     3 Knowledge of the standards of field work and reporting

     4 Independence with respect to the financial statements and supplementary disclosures

AICPA

1-3 The following questions relate to audit reporting standards. Select the *best* response.

   a The first standard of reporting requires that, "the report shall state whether the financial statements are presented in accordance with generally accepted accounting principles." This should be construed to require:

     1 A statement of fact by the auditor

     2 An opinion by the auditor

     3 An implied measure of fairness

     4 An objective measure of compliance

   b The objective of the consistency standard is to provide assurance that:

     1 There are *no* variations in the format and presentation of financial statements.

     2 Substantially different transactions and events are *not* accounted for on an identical basis.

     3 The auditor is consulted before material changes are made in the application of accounting principles.

     4 The comparability of financial statements between periods is *not* materially affected by changes in accounting principles without disclosure.

1-4 The following questions relate to modification of the standard audit report. Select the *best* response.

   a When the client fails to include information that is necessary for the fair presentation of financial statements in the body of the statements or in the related footnotes, it is the responsibility of the auditor to present the information, if practicable, in the auditor's report and issue a(n):

     1 Qualified opinion or a disclaimer of opinion

     2 Qualified opinion or an adverse opinion

     3 Adverse opinion or a disclaimer of opinion

     4 Qualified opinion or an unqualified opinion

   b A CPA engaged to audit financial statements observes that the accounting for a certain material item is not in conformity with generally accepted accounting principles, and that this fact is prominently disclosed in a footnote to the financial statements. The CPA should:

     1 Express an unqualified opinion and insert a middle paragraph emphasizing the matter by reference to the footnote

     2 Disclaim an opinion

     3 Not allow the accounting treatment for this item to affect the type of opinion because the deviation from generally accepted accounting principles was disclosed

     4 Qualify the opinion because of the deviation from generally accepted accounting principles

   c Which of the following would *not* be required for the statements to be "presented fairly" in conformity with generally accepted accounting principles?

     1 That generally accepted accounting principles be followed in presenting all material items in the statements

     2 That the generally accepted accounting principles selected from alternatives be appropriate for the circumstances of the particular company

     3 That generally accepted accounting principles be applied on a basis consistent with those followed in the prior year

     4 That the generally accepted accounting principles selected from alternatives reflect transactions in accordance with their substance

AICPA

1-5 The following questions relate to other types of auditors and audits. Select the *best* response.

a Which of the following bodies promulgates standards for audits of federal financial assistance recipients?

1 Governmental Accounting Standards Board

2 Financial Accounting Standards Board

3 General Accounting Office

4 Governmental Auditing Standards Board

b Which of the following statements best describes how a detailed audit program of a CPA who is engaged to audit the financial statements of a large publicly held company compares with the audit client's comprehensive internal audit program?

1 The comprehensive internal audit program is substantially identical to the audit program used by the CPA because both cover substantially identical areas.

2 The comprehensive internal audit program is less detailed and covers fewer areas than would normally be covered by the CPA.

3 The comprehensive internal audit program is more detailed and covers areas that would normally *not* be covered by the CPA.

4 The comprehensive internal audit program is more detailed although it covers fewer areas than would normally be covered by the CPA.

1-6 Match the engagements listed in group 1 with the corresponding type of audit listed in group 2.

Group 1

_____ **a** Engagement to test adherence of Home Care, Inc., to the laws, regulations, and program requirements defined by the federal government, which provides the funding

_____ **b** Study performed by an assistant to the company president to consider whether travel expenses can be effectively reduced and to identify types of abuses and recommend new procedures to prevent abuses from occurring in the future

_____ **c** Study performed by a team composed of CPA firm personnel and client personnel to analyze the organizational structure and work flow in a subsidiary

_____ **d** Audit of financial statements by a CPA firm

Group 2

I Internal audit

II Compliance audit

III Operational audit

IV Financial audit

DISCUSSION QUESTIONS

Discussion questions require the application of the concepts explained in the chapter to specific facts, issues, or problems. They are classified by the primary chapter topic to which they relate. However, responses should not be confined to the primary topics, but should include all relevant implications.

Financial Auditing and the Need for Audits

1-7 List several reasons the following types of organizations would want to have an annual audit by a CPA.

Church	Labor union
Municipal government	National hobby association
Local United Fund organization	State society of CPAs

1-8 The following statement is representative of attitudes and opinions sometimes encountered by CPAs in their professional practices:

An audit by a CPA is essentially negative and contributes to neither the gross national product nor the general well-being of society. The auditor does not create; he or she merely checks what someone else has done.

Evaluate this statement and indicate:

a Areas of agreement with the statement, if any

b Areas of misconception, incompleteness, or fallacious reasoning included in the statement, if any

1-9 The following statement on one objective of an audit appeared in *Principles of Accounting* by William A. Paton and Russell A. Stevenson, published by The Ann Arbor Press in 1916:

A large number of enterprises feel obliged to have their records audited regularly to give authenticity to the statements issued to the stockholders. The annual report in such a case has a statement from the auditing accountants appended, declaring the condition of the company to be as represented. Too often such audits are only perfunctory and hence of no value.

Discuss the importance of this aspect of the audit function today.

1-10 The New York Stock Exchange, among others, requires an annual audit of the financial statements of companies whose securities are listed on it. What are the probable reasons for this?

1-11 In connection with current problems relating to audited financial statements it has been stated:

The bulk of the problems can be traced to a single crucial flaw in the basic structure (of the financial disclosure process): despite the fact that audited financial statements are meant to report on managerial operation of owner resources, it is management that controls the content of these reports.

The obvious question is: "What about the shareholders' auditor in this situation?" My hypothesis is that the auditor is just not sufficiently independent to overcome the power position of management.

Analyze and comment on the relative positions of and the causes of the potential conflict between management and the independent auditor.

1-12 It is recognized generally that an auditor does not guarantee the financial soundness of the client when the auditor renders an opinion as to financial statements, nor does the auditor guarantee the absolute accuracy of the statements. Yet the auditor's opinion is respected and accepted. What is expected of the auditor in order that he or she may continue to merit such confidence?

The Standard Audit Report and Related Responsibilities

1-13 The independent auditor issues a report at the end of the audit. Refer to the standard report in the chapter.

a What is the difference between "generally accepted auditing standards" and "auditing procedures"?

b Why is it important that the auditor state that the statements are "in conformity with generally accepted accounting principles"?

1-14 It has been observed that "there is a certain apparent similarity between notes to financial statements and qualifications in the auditor's report: both are means by which the auditor may be certain that necessary financial information not presented in the statements proper is nevertheless adequately disclosed."

Do you agree with this observation? Give reasons for your answer.

1-15 On page 32 is an actual auditor's report rendered in 1927 by Touche, Niven & Co., on the financial statements of The Studebaker Corporation. This historical report has similarities and differences from the current audit report.

a Explain what representations are made by the auditor.

b What implications might a reader of this opinion draw from the dollar amounts included in the report?

1-16 Discuss the following observation recently made by a business leader: "Published financial statements should be designed to enable the efficiency and skill of management to be evaluated."

1-17 The following statements refer to the standard auditor's report. List the letters of the statements that are *not* appropriate in the currently used report.

a We have examined the balance sheet. . . .

b In connection therewith, we examined or tested accounting records and obtained information from the officers of the company.

c We conducted our audit in accordance with generally accepted auditing standards. . . .

d . . . but we did not make a detailed audit of the transactions.

e . . . have reviewed the system of internal control. . . .

f In our opinion, the accompanying balance sheet. . . .

g . . . and to the extent we deemed appropriate.

h In our opinion, based upon such examination. . . .

i . . . and such other accounting procedures as we considered necessary in the circumstances.

j . . . in conformity with generally accepted accounting principles. . . .

1-18 Minker expresses an unqualified opinion concerning the financial statements of the Zee Company. In these statements, the basis of valuation of the fixed assets is not shown. She is aware of the fact that the fixed assets are valued on the statements at appraisal value, which is substantially above cost. She feels it is not her duty to divulge this information as long as she does not state any basis for the fixed assets. Is she correct?

1-19 Coleson is practicing on his own account and has audited the books of the Koltron Company for many years. This year, as a result of a press of duties, he is able to spend only enough time to read the statements prepared by the treasurer and the chief accountant of Koltron Company. From his many years of work for this client, during which time no fraud or defalcations had been discovered, he believes that is sufficient to permit him to give an unqualified opinion on this year's statements. Is this permissible?

1-20 In the *South African Chartered Accountant's Handbook,* the following statement appears:

The term "Auditing Principles and Standards" appears to connote or to suggest one proposition and it is perhaps unnecessary to attribute separate meanings to each word. As a general statement, however, it may be said that principles are the underlying con-

TOUCHE, NIVEN & CO.
PUBLIC ACCOUNTANTS
New York, Chicago, Cleveland, St. Louis, Minneapolis,
Los Angeles and Atlanta

10 South LaSalle St.
Chicago, February 2, 1927.

To the Board of Directors,
The Studebaker Corporation
South Bend, Indiana.

Gentlemen:

We have audited the books and accounts of The Studebaker Corporation and subsidiary companies for the year ended December 31, 1926, and hereby certify that the statements submitted by us are correctly prepared therefrom.

The notes receivable, cash on hand and on deposit and securities at the Home Office have been verified by examination or by certificates from the custodians. Full provision has been made for the anticipated loss on collection of accounts and notes receivable.

The inventories at the factories and branches have been taken by the company's officials and were valued at cost price, which was less than the current market value.

The property accounts have been increased during the year by expenditures amounting to $4,417,667.66, representing proper additions to capital account. Depreciation has been provided at adequate rates; the charges to current operations for this account during the year amounted to $1,520,437.92 and there has been deducted from the reserve the depreciation amounting to $164,190.00 previously set aside on the value of property dismantled. The net increase to the property account during the year is therefore $3,061,419.74.

So far as we are able to ascertain, provision has been made on the books for all unpaid bills and all known liabilities, including Federal income taxes.

And we certify that, in our opinion, the accompanying balance sheet with relative profit and loss and surplus accounts set forth a true and correct statement of the company's financial condition at December 31, 1926, and the results from the operations for the year then ended.

TOUCHE, NIVEN & CO.,
Auditors.

cepts which govern or should govern the auditor at all times irrespective of particular circumstances, and are the basic truths and personal codes of conduct inherent in all persons engaged in honourable work. Standards, on the other hand, are a general rule of measurement. If these are set up by and with the consent of a professional body, there is implied that a minimum standard of performance is being attempted.

Compare the American usage of the terms "principles" and "standards" with the South African interpretations above.

CPA Firm Structure and the Independent Auditor

1-21 Beth Jones & Co., has grown from a small firm that originally included only Ms. Jones and one junior accountant to a regional firm with seven partners and 21 professional staff members occupying four offices in two states. At a recent meeting all partners were in agreement that the growth of the firm has presented some problems, but that the financial and professional rewards far outweigh those problems. The partners are unanimous in their desire to see their firm grow to the size of one of the Big Six.
a Is the goal of the firm realistic?
b What steps can the firm take to advance toward this goal?

1-22 Until about 1945, staff accountants were hired at very low pay on a seasonal basis. They often worked only from December through the following March to become unemployed, at least as auditors, until the following December. After two or three "seasons" of auditing work, a staff accountant with promise might be given a permanent position with a CPA firm. Today, staff accountants are hired as permanent members of the professional staff by CPA firms. What effect has this change in the structure of CPA firms had on the audit function?

1-23 Technical accounting and auditing ability, supervisory ability, public relations ability, good judgment, and general decision-making ability are all important to the operation of an audit firm. Which of these personal traits is more important for:
a A partner?
b A new staff accountant?

1-24 Sidney Wells is an individual practitioner. In addition to himself, he maintains a professional staff of five auditors, and his firm is a member of a regional group of CPA firms. Wells is considering his alternatives to staff training. He is trying to decide whether to send his professional staff members to the programs offered by the state society and the AICPA, to send them to training programs offered by the regional group, or to attempt to offer in-house training himself. What factors should he consider in making this decision?

1-25 Large CPA firms take two different approaches to the scheduling of professional staff members to audit engagements. Some firms schedule staff members individually. Using this approach, a new staff accountant will be working with a different group of auditors on each engagement. Other large CPA firms use a *team,* whereby a new staff accountant is placed on a team of auditors and the team is scheduled to various engagements. Using this approach, a new staff auditor works with the same group of staff members on each engagement. List the advantages and disadvantages of each of these approaches to scheduling from:
a The standpoint of the CPA firm
b The standpoint of the new staff accountant

Other Types of Audits and Auditors

1-26 Independence is one characteristic that distinguishes independent auditing from internal auditing. The Institute of Internal Auditors, however, stresses the importance of independence in the following, which appears in the *Statement of Responsibilities of the Internal Auditor:*

> (1) The organization status of the internal auditor and the support accorded to him by management are major determinants of the range and value of the services which management will obtain from the internal auditing function. The head of the internal auditing department, therefore, should be responsible to an officer of sufficient rank in the organization as will assure a broad scope of activities, and adequate consideration of and effective action on the findings or recommendations made by him.

> (2) Since complete objectivity is essential to the audit function, internal auditors should not develop and install procedures, prepare records, or engage in any other activity which they normally would be expected to review and appraise.

Compare and contrast the above concept of independence with that of the AICPA.

1-27 The GAO has adopted standards for performance audits. The second field work standard states:

> Staff are to be properly supervised.

The fourth field work standard for government performance audits is:

> An assessment should be made of applicable internal controls when necessary to satisfy the audit objectives.

Compare and contrast those two standards with similar standards of generally accepted auditing standards.

1-28 Distinguish between a performance audit and a financial audit.

1-29 The U.S. Governmental Accounting Office "Yellow Book" states that the third field work standard for government performance audits is:

> An assessment is to be made of compliance with applicable requirements of laws and regulations when necessary to satisfy the audit objectives.

> In government auditing compliance with laws and regulations is important because government organizations, programs, services, activities, and functions are usually created by law and are subject to more specific rules and regulations than the same are in the private sector.

List the responsibilities this standard places upon the auditor.

1-30 The president of your company (a multidivision company) has been discussing the company's internal operations with several colleagues in the business community. She has discovered that most of them have an internal audit staff. The activities of the staffs at other companies include financial audits, operational audits, and sometimes management audits.

She has asked you to describe for her the meaning of the terms (1) financial auditing, (2) operational auditing, and (3) management auditing as they would relate to the internal audit function.

CMA adapted

1-31 G. Johnson, a local real estate broker, is a member of the Board of Directors of Pennset Corporation. At a recent board meeting, called to discuss the financial plan for 19X6,

Mr. Johnson discovered two planned expenditures for auditing. In the Controller's Department budget he found an internal audit activity, and in the Treasurer's budget he found an estimate for the 19X6 annual audit by a CPA firm.

Mr. Johnson could not understand the need for two different expenditures for auditing. Since the CPA fee for the annual audit was less than the cost of the internal audit activity, he proposed eliminating the internal audit function.

a Explain to Mr. Johnson the different purposes served by the two audit activities.

b What benefits does the CPA firm doing an audit of financial statements derive from the existence of an internal audit function?

CMA adapted

1-32 On pages 36 and 37 are the financial statements of the Anchor Manufacturing Corporation and the auditor's report for the year ended January 31, 19X4.

The audit was conducted by James Haas, an individual practitioner, who has audited the corporation's financial statements and reported on them for many years. List and discuss the deficiencies of the auditor's report prepared by James Haas. Your discussion should include justifications that the matters you cited are deficiencies. (Do not check the addition of the statements. Assume that the addition is correct.)

AICPA adapted

CASE

I am Carly Cairn, a CPA who has achieved a considerable level of success, if I do say so myself. Clearly, my duty was to provide guidance to my promising young nephew David before he left for Harvard. I cannot imagine how he managed to reach his age without developing any understanding of business and, in particular, about what *my* profession is. After all, he will have to become a useful member of society someday. After a brief but eminently clear, I believed, explanation of auditing and auditors, David unaccountably asked some questions evidencing his continuing confusion. I am rarely at a loss for words, but what do you think I should say to straighten out the misguided boy?

Required: For each of the following questions, help Ms. Cairn by identifying key issues to be used in her explanation.

Question 1

David: Aunt Carly, why do you work at a profession that just, well . . . double-checks things. Why, with your considerable talents, do you not choose a profession that actually serves the public interest?

Cairn: My dear boy, you must attempt to develop your heretofore untapped talent for listening. I have been saying. . . .

Question 2

David: I read in the *Times* that New Hope Widgets failed a few months after receiving a "clean opinion" on its audit report. Those auditors certainly must have done a miserable job. Do you think they are scoundrels or merely fools?

Cairn: No profession is immune to either scoundrels or fools, but a clean opinion followed by a business failure does not necessarily. . . .

Anchor Manufacturing Corporation Statements of Condition
January 31, 19X4 and 19X3

	19X4	19X3
Assets		
Current assets:		
Cash	$ 43,822	$ 51,862
Accounts receivable—pledged—less allowances for doubtful accounts of $3,800 in 19X4 and $3,000 in 19X3 (see note)	65,298	46,922
Inventories, pledged—at average cost, not in excess of replacement cost	148,910	118,264
Other current assets	6,280	5,192
Total current assets	264,310	222,240
Fixed assets:		
Land—at cost	38,900	62,300
Buildings—at cost, less accumulated depreciation of $50,800 in 19X4 and $53,400 in 19X3	174,400	150,200
Machinery and equipment—at cost, less accumulated depreciation of $30,500 in 19X4 and $25,640 in 19X3	98,450	78,560
Total fixed assets	311,750	291,060
Total assets	$576,060	$513,300
Liabilities and Stockholders' Equity		
Current liabilities:		
Accounts payable	$ 27,926	$ 48,161
Other liabilities	68,743	64,513
Current portion of long-term mortgage payable	3,600	3,600
Income taxes payable	46,480	30,866
Total current liabilities	146,749	147,140
Long-term liabilities:		
Mortgage payable	90,400	94,000
Total liabilities	237,149	241,140
Stockholders' equity:		
Capital stock par value $100, 1,000 shares authorized, issued, and outstanding	100,000	100,000
Retained earnings	238,641	172,160
Total stockholders' equity	338,641	272,160
Total liabilities and stockholders' equity	$575,790	$513,300

Note: I did not confirm the balances of the accounts receivable but satisfied myself by other auditing procedures that the balances were correct.

Anchor Manufacturing Corporation Income Statements for the Years Ended
January 31, 19X4 and 19X3

	19X4	19X3
Income:		
Sales	$884,932	$682,131
Other income	3,872	2,851
Total	888,804	684,982
Cost and expenses:		
Cost of goods sold	463,570	353,842
Selling expenses	241,698	201,986
Administrative expenses	72,154	66,582
Provision for income taxes	45,876	19,940
Other expenses	12,582	13,649
Total	835,880	655,999
Net income	$ 52,924	$ 28,983

To: Mr. Paul Young, President   **Anchor Manufacturing Corp.**

I have audited the balance sheet of the Anchor Manufacturing Corporation and the related statements of income and retained earnings.

These statements present fairly the financial position and results of operations in conformity with generally accepted accounting principles, applied on a consistent basis with that of the preceding year.

I conducted my audit in accordance with generally accepted auditing standards. Those standards require examining evidence and making assessments of the amounts, disclosures and presentation of the financial statements. I believe that the audit provides a reasonable basis for this report.

/S/ James Haas

Question 3

David: Charles said the accountants were responsible for the savings and loan crisis—at least the auditors could have prevented it.

Cairn: Outrageous! Charles' opinions are positively reckless. . . .

Question 4

David: Really, Auntie, the client company selects and pays the auditor. The company can hire someone else if the auditor objects to anything at all that management wants to put in the company's report. How can anyone think the auditor's opinion is objective?

Cairn: There are several inexorable forces at work to address that issue. . . .

CHAPTER

2

Professional Ethics and the Auditing Environment

CHAPTER OUTLINE

Learning Objectives

After studying this chapter you should be able to:

- Identify the attributes of professional status and describe to what extent they exist in public accounting
- Describe the primary features of self-regulation in public accounting, including the organizations involved
- Outline the parts of the AICPA Code of Professional Conduct and describe the individual rules
- Identify the elements of quality control within CPA firms and explain practice-monitoring programs and the related subjects of the AICPA division for firms and peer review
- Explain the regulatory role of the Securities and Exchange Commission as it relates to accounting and auditing
- Be aware of the legal liability of auditors to clients and to third parties under common law and statutory law

Relevant Sections of Statements on Auditing Standards

AU 110 — Responsibilities and Functions of the Independent Auditor

AU 161 — The Relationship of Generally Accepted Auditing Standards to Quality Control Standards

PROFESSIONAL STATUS—FRAMEWORK OF THE ENVIRONMENT

The audit function is carried out in a complex environment composed of interrelationships between governmental and professional organizations and individual auditors and CPA firms. These regular and enduring relationships form the structure of the profession. This structure, which has evolved over the last 150 years, was organized initially along British lines; today, it is decidedly American. The delicate auditor-client-public relationship results from this structure, as does the form of the modern audit.

The CPA is a member of a time-honored profession, and the status of the profession and the responsibilities that accompany this status affect the audit function and the structure of the profession. The independent auditor is subject to regulations imposed by the profession and by society.

The status of the public accounting profession can be measured by its acceptance and by its similarities to other recognized professions. The imposition of technical and ethical standards on members by a profession is one aspect of this measurement. Additionally, society tends to expect high standards from professionals as proof of the trust placed in them. This expectation is reflected in the legal responsibilities imposed on professionals.

The status of a profession can be determined by the extent to which the professional group exhibits certain attributes. Professional occupations possess certain common attributes which distinguish them from those that are nonprofessional. All professions seem to possess these five elements: (1) systematic theory, (2) professional authority, (3) community sanction, (4) regulative codes, and (5) a culture.[1]

Systematic Theory

One significant difference between a professional and a nonprofessional occupation is the underlying body of theory which supports the work of the professional. Although nonprofessional work may require procedural skill, that skill does not rest on a systematic body of theory. The underlying theory of the public accounting profession consists of accounting theory—generally accepted accounting principles and practices—and auditing theory—a science of validation. Public accountants share the underlying theory of auditing with internal and governmental auditors. Both groups are concerned with the systematic gathering of evidence of the financial and operating activities of organizations. The distinction between external and other auditors lies in the other aspects of professional status.

Knowledge in systematic theory can be achieved best through formal education in an academic environment. Today, therefore, a college-level education is considered a prerequisite for public accounting work. After the year 2000, AICPA members will be required to have at least 150 college-level semester hours, including a bachelor's degree.

Professional Authority

Expertise in the systematic theory of accounting and auditing is the basis for the public accountant's authority in these areas. The professional has authority within the area of expertise because clients, lacking the requisite theoretical knowledge, are unable to evaluate the calibre of professional service offered.

Community Sanction

Professionals normally attempt to formalize their authority by gaining community approval of certain powers and privileges. First and foremost among the powers for which professions strive is control over admissions to the profession. In the public accounting profession this has taken the form of establishment of a licensing system for those who desire to practice as certified public accountants. This licensing system is controlled by state boards of accountancy in each of the individual states. One of the first collective actions of public accountants in the United States was to press for such legislation. The first state CPA law was passed in New York in 1896.

Another privilege which professions strive for is *relative* immunity from community judgment on technical matters. Although professions are responsible to the community for their actions, it is generally accepted that a professional's performance should be judged by standards established by the profession itself. In the public accounting profession, setting of professional standards has been assumed primarily by the AICPA.

---

[1]Ernest Greenwood, "Attributes of a Profession," *Social Work,* July 1957, p. 45.

Among the powers and privileges for which professions strive, *privileged communication* stands out as perhaps the ultimate criterion of professionalization. Professional performance is facilitated if the client feels free to volunteer information that might not otherwise be divulged. Privileged communication is a right granted by the community to protect the client from legal encroachment on confidential communications with a professional. Although the professions of medicine and law have generally been granted this privilege, only a minority of the jurisdictions in the United States have changed the common law rule which denies the existence of privilege between a CPA and client.

Regulative Code

The powers and privileges granted to a profession by the community effectively constitute a monopoly. In the United States, CPAs have in effect been granted a monopoly on rendering independent opinions on financial statements. Since any monopoly is subject to abuse, a profession must take steps to assure the community that the profession will discipline its members. Professions, therefore, establish regulative codes.

Such codes are necessary because, if abuses were rampant, the community would revoke the monopoly of the profession.

A Culture

Another distinguishing feature of a profession is a well-established culture which applies to the professional group. Sociologists call this a *subculture*. A subculture contains specific behavioral prescriptions and proscriptions. For example, CPAs are expected to dress and behave in a rather narrowly defined fashion. A new entrant to the profession must learn what is expected or the entrant will not be accepted as a colleague by associates.

NATURE OF THE ENVIRONMENT

The auditing services provided by the public accounting profession and the regulation of independent auditors are influenced by a unique mixture of private and government action.

Part of the demand for audits is established by the requirements of the securities acts for audits of the annual financial statements of corporations whose securities are publicly traded. Other federal agencies have similar audit requirements. There is also a private demand for independent audits of the financial statements of smaller or privately owned companies. However, the government exercises substantial influence over all auditing practice through federal requirements for audits.

Financial statements filed under the federal securities acts must be prepared in conformity with generally accepted accounting principles and audited in accordance with generally accepted auditing standards. Development of the principles and standards is primarily by private action of the Financial Accounting Standards Board and the American Institute of Certified Public Accountants. However, these private groups must be responsive to the Securities and Exchange Commission, a government agency discussed later, because of its authority under the securities acts to specify both the content of financial statements filed with it and the form of auditor's report to fulfill the audit requirement. Also of significance is the SEC's authority to disqualify professionals from practicing before it. The SEC does not regulate the public accounting profession, but it does play a significant role in the disciplining of auditors.

One of the most important elements in the regulation of any profession is the means of disciplining practice by imposing penalties for substandard performance. Independent auditors are subject to both private and government discipline. Litigation, action by agencies such as the SEC, and action by the profession itself through professional associations all serve to exact penalties for improper conduct.

To gain an understanding of this complex environment, it is helpful to distinguish between self-regulation by the public accounting profession and external regulation by forces and agencies outside the profession. Also, because of the interrelationship between self-regulation and external regulation, it is necessary to consider areas of overlapping regulation. The remainder of this chapter is divided into the following areas:

- Self-regulation by the profession
- External regulation

In studying these aspects of the environment of auditing, one additional factor, caused by the fact that public accounting is often practiced by relatively large CPA firms, needs to be kept in mind. Some aspects of regulation relate only to individual CPAs, some aspects relate to CPA firms, and other aspects relate to both. Figure 2-1 summarizes the organizations, sets of standards, and enforcement mechanisms that regulate the CPA.

SELF-REGULATION BY THE PUBLIC ACCOUNTING PROFESSION

The form that self-regulation has taken in the United States has been influenced dramatically by the form of the organizations involved. Thus, this section begins with an explanation of those organizations. The important aspects of self-regulation are implied by several of the attributes of professional status explained at the start of this chapter. These are

- Development of *professional standards* related to the systematic theory and professional authority of auditors—accounting principles and auditing standards
- *Admission requirements* for entry into the profession—licensing of individual CPAs
- Establishment and enforcement of a *code of professional conduct*
- Establishment and enforcement of requirements for demonstration of *continuing competence* and maintenance of quality work

The last aspect of self-regulation requires some explanation. It results from one of the shortcomings of a code of conduct. A code of conduct applies to individuals, but users of audited financial statements rely on the standing and reputation of the CPA firm rather than the individual auditor responsible for the engagement. Several features of requirements to demonstrate continuing competence apply to firms. Also, experience has shown that screening entrants to the profession is not sufficient to assure continued competent performance. This has resulted in attempts to extend the regulative apparatus of the profession beyond admission requirements and rules of professional conduct.

Organizations	Standards and rules	Monitoring and enforcement
Self-regulation		
AICPA 　Individual membership 　Firm membership 　• SEC Practice Section 　• Private Companies Practice 　　Section	Code of Professional Conduct Generally accepted auditing 　standards Mandatory continuing 　professional education 　requirements Quality control standards	Trial Board—AICPA Ethics Division Audit failure inquiries by the Quality Control 　Inquiry Committee Public Oversight Board Peer review requirements
FASB GASB	Generally accepted accounting 　principles	Auditors
State societies of CPAs	State codes of ethics	State ethics enforcement is usually handled 　jointly with the AICPA Trial Board
External regulation		
SEC	SEC rules and regulations Financial reporting releases Staff accounting bulletins	Censure Disbarment from practice before the SEC
Courts	Civil law Criminal law Previously tried cases	Fines Damages to those injured Injunctions Imprisonment
State boards of accountancy	State licensing laws	Temporary or permanent loss of license

FIGURE 2-1
Organizations, sets of standards, and enforcement mechanisms that regulate CPAs.

The Organizations Involved

The following are the primary organizations involved in self-regulation within the accounting profession: the AICPA, the FASB, the GASB, and state boards of accountancy.

AICPA   Founded in 1886 and merged in 1937 with another national organization of accountants, the American Institute of Certified Public Accountants is the national professional organization of CPAs. Membership is voluntary, and the only power the institute has over its members is termination of their membership. Nevertheless, the AICPA has been the chief spokesperson in the United States on matters of auditing and financial reporting. To become a member, an individual must possess a CPA certificate from one of the states.

The purposes of the AICPA are (1) to unite the profession of accountancy as constituted by CPAs, (2) to promote and maintain high standards within the profession, (3) to prepare and grade the examination for CPA candidates, and (4) to encourage cordial relations among CPAs in this country and their equivalents abroad. The AICPA serves the public accounting profession by promoting the collective interests and objectives of its members.

Chief among the AICPA's functions are its policy-making activities. The power to make policy decisions rests with the Council of the AICPA. However, the Council has delegated authority to senior technical committees to issue pronouncements in the areas of auditing standards and procedures, ethics, taxation, management consulting services, quality control standards, and accounting and review services. The Governmental Accounting Standards Board has been given authority to set standards for governmental entities. The Financial Accounting Standards Board has been given authority in the area of accounting principles for other entities.

Another important activity of the AICPA is the publication of *The Journal of Accountancy*. Published since 1905, it contains technical articles, current events, and official releases by institute committees.

As mentioned earlier, the AICPA is a *voluntary* membership organization. There are over 300,000 CPAs who are members of the AICPA, but not all members practice as independent auditors. There are members in industry, government, and education; approximately half the AICPA membership comes from members in public practice. It is the members who serve on AICPA committees such as the Auditing Standards Board and other AICPA committees. The ASB and several other committees are discussed elsewhere in this book.

Individual CPAs are members of the AICPA. However, the AICPA has a division for firms, which was established in 1977 in partial response to congressional and SEC pressure for added assurance on the quality of audits of the financial statements of large public companies. The division has two sections:

- The SEC Practice Section (SECPS)
- The Private Companies Practice Section (PCPS)

The PCPS and the SECPS have separate objectives, membership requirements, peer review requirements, and governing bodies. In addition, the SECPS has two additional features—an independent monitoring group, the Public Oversight Board (POB), and the Quality Control Inquiry Committee (QCIC) to investigate alleged audit failures. For both sections, firms must adhere to the AICPA's Statements on Quality Control Standards.

A CPA firm may choose to belong to either section, both sections, or neither. However, firms who voluntarily choose to belong to the SECPS or PCPS must adhere to that section's quality control standards and other established requirements. Any CPA that audits one or more SEC clients must join the SECPS to remain an AICPA member.

One of the key features of the division for firms is that it provides a mechanism to be able to sanction firms rather than individual auditors.

FASB   The Financial Accounting Standards Board is an independent private organization charged with the development of accounting standards. The AICPA was one of several founding organizations of the FASB, but the two organizations are entirely separate and operate very independently of each other. Also, the FASB organization structure is decidedly different: It is not a membership organization.

The FASB consists of a seven member full-time, paid board assisted by a large research staff and a volunteer advisory council. The FASB issues Statements of Financial Accounting Standards and interpretations which are authoritative pronouncements.

The FASB also issues Statements of Financial Accounting Concepts, which present the fundamental concepts on which standards are based. However, the FASB has no mechanism for enforcing its pronouncements. As explained later, the FASB's authority comes from enforcement of its pronouncements by the AICPA and the SEC.

GASB   The Governmental Accounting Standards Board is the primary standards-setting body for accounting and reporting for governmental entities. The GASB is similar in organization to the FASB. The GASB has five members serving 5-year terms. Two are full-time, and all are compensated. It issues Statements of the GASB, Interpretations, and Technical Bulletins written by the GASB staff.

State Boards of Accountancy   State boards are independent agencies in state governments whose primary functions concern the issuance, renewal, and suspension of licenses to practice as an independent CPA. In some states, the licensing activities of the state board have been consolidated with agencies that license other professions and vocations.

In total there are 54 boards of accountancy—one in each state and in districts and territories. State boards are normally composed of five to seven members—usually CPAs—appointed by the state governor and are supported by relatively small staffs.

A state board administers the state accountancy laws which usually include requirements for a CPA license and an ethical code and, in most states, a requirement for continuing education.

State Societies of CPAs   State societies play a role in self-regulation at the local level similar to the role of the AICPA at the national level. State societies are voluntary membership organizations that are similar in structure, but smaller in scale than the AICPA.

Although the AICPA and the state societies have no legal relationship to each other, they cooperate in pursuing the objectives of the profession. A CPA normally can become a member of a state organization when a CPA certificate from the state is received. A chief activity of a state society is the promotion of state legislation beneficial to CPAs who practice in the state. Some state societies publish monthly or quarterly journals containing technical articles. Local chapters of CPAs are geographical divisions of the state society. They serve primarily as a meeting ground for the CPAs in a given locality.

The Code of Professional Conduct

Ethics are rules designed to maintain a profession on a dignified level, to guide members in their relations with each other, and to assure the public that the profession will maintain a high level of performance. Ethics are derived from fundamental values, many of which are held in common by all professions.

Practice as an independent auditor requires many decisions. These decisions include the type of report to be rendered on a set of financial statements as well as whether to approach another accountant with an offer of employment. Regardless of the alternatives from which to choose, a professional is guided in value judgment by the Code of Professional Conduct.

The subject of ethics is complex at best. Philosophers sometimes search for absolute imperatives—a luxury not afforded a practicing CPA who must make value judgments daily. To one who uses them, the rules in the Code of Professional Conduct must be relevant and allow use of knowledge in choice of alternatives. The ethical standards of the accounting profession have developed over time, and many present standards were accepted in practice before they were written into any code.

In making decisions, the goal of auditors always has been to make the best judgment possible in a given situation. As each situation is encountered, an auditor must apply an appropriate set of values to arrive at an ethical decision. Codes of ethics have developed as a result of many similar value judgments over a long period of time.

The AICPA has developed a Code of Professional Conduct for the guidance of its members. It was most recently amended in 1992. The Code has two sections:

- The principles
- The rules

Section I—Principles   Section I is an aspirational section that provides the conceptual foundations for the specific rules in section II. The section has the following components:

I *Responsibilities.* In carrying out their responsibilities as professionals, members should exercise sensitive professional and moral judgments in all their activities.

II *The public interest.* Members should accept the obligation to act in a way that will serve the public interest, honor the public trust, and demonstrate commitment to professionalism.

III *Integrity.* To maintain and broaden public confidence, members should perform all professional responsibilities with the highest sense of integrity.

IV *Objectivity and independence.* A member should maintain objectivity and be free of conflicts of interest in discharging professional responsibilities. A member in public practice should be independent in fact and appearance when providing auditing and other attestation services.

V *Due care.* A member should observe the profession's technical and ethical standards, strive continually to improve competence and the quality of services, and discharge professional responsibility to the best of the member's ability.

VI *Scope and nature of services.* A member in public practice should observe the Principles of the Code of Professional Conduct in determining the scope and nature of services to be provided.

Section II—Rules, Interpretations, and Rulings   The authority and nature of the other parts of the code are as follows:

- *Rules of the Code of Professional Conduct.* These are the enforceable standards that require approval of the full AICPA membership before they are adopted. These are specific rules that must be followed by all AICPA members. Some rules are applicable only to members in public practice, while others apply to all members.

- *Interpretations of rules.* These are guidelines on the scope and application of the rules. Interpretations are adopted by the AICPA's professional ethics executive committee after state societies and state boards have had an opportunity to review them. An Interpretation is usually issued when there are frequent questions in practice about the application of a particular rule to common circumstances.
- *Ethics rulings.* These are summaries of the application of rules and Interpretations to a particular set of factual circumstances. Like Interpretations, rulings are issued by the professional ethics executive committee after exposure to state societies and state boards.

The rules are broad prohibitions on conduct. The Interpretations and rulings are much more specific. The rules are listed individually below, each followed by discussion of some of the more significant aspects of the rule.

Independence, Integrity, and Objectivity   The rules of conduct in this area are as follows:

Rule 101—Independence
A member in public practice shall be independent in the performance of professional services as required by standards promulgated by bodies designated by Council.

Rule 102—Integrity and Objectivity
In the performance of any professional service, a member shall maintain objectivity and integrity, shall be free of conflicts of interest, and shall not knowingly misrepresent facts or subordinate his or her judgment to others.

Members in tax practice often resolve doubts in favor of a client. This practice is not in violation of Rule 102 in a tax advocacy engagement.

Since there are so many Interpretations and rulings under the rules of conduct, they are not all reproduced in this chapter. Interpretation 101-1 is presented because it establishes the requirements that define independence in an audit of financial statements. Interpretation 101-3 is presented because the issue covered—providing accounting services— is one that arises frequently in practice. An example of a ruling related to Interpretation 101-3 is also presented to illustrate the nature of rulings.

Interpretation 101-1
Independence shall be considered to be impaired if, for example, a member had any of the following transactions, interests, relationships:

A During the period of a professional engagement or at the time of expressing an opinion, a member or member's firm
   1 Had or was committed to acquire any direct or material indirect financial interest in the enterprise.
   2 Was a trustee of any trust or executor or administrator of any estate if such trust or estate had or was committed to acquire any direct or material indirect financial interest in the enterprise.
   3 Had any joint, closely held business investment with the enterprise or with any officer, director, or principal stockholders thereof that was material in relation to the member's net worth or to the net worth of the member's firm.

    4 Had any loan to or from the enterprise or any officer, director, or principal stock-holder of the enterprise. [A few exceptions to this rule exist—for small credit card balances, automobile loans, passbook loans, and "grandfather" loans that existed before the 1992 rule change.]

B During the period covered by the financial statements, during the period of the professional engagement, or at the time of expressing an opinion, a member or a member's firm

    1 Was connected with the enterprise as a promoter, underwriter, or voting trustee, as a director or officer, or in any capacity equivalent to that of a member of management or of an employee.

    2 Was a trustee for any pension or profit-sharing trust of the enterprise.

The above examples are not intended to be all-inclusive.

Prior to January 1988, Rule 101 related only to opinions on financial statements and prohibited a financial interest in the client or any relationship equivalent to employee status. The current rule is broader and applies to services other than audits of financial statements. Examples of other professional services that require independence include review of financial statements, examination of prospective financial statements, and other attestation engagements.

Interpretation 101-3—Accounting Services

Members in public practice may be asked to provide manual or automated bookkeeping or data processing services to clients. Computer systems design and programming assistance may also be rendered by members either in conjunction with data processing services or as a separate engagement. In addition, members may rent "block time" on their computers to their clients but are not involved in the processing of transactions or maintaining the client's accounting records.

    . . . A member providing such services to a client must meet the following requirements to be considered independent:

1 The client must accept the responsibility for the financial statements as his own. The client must be sufficiently informed of the enterprise's activities and financial condition and the applicable accounting principles so that the client can reasonably accept such responsibility, including, specifically, fairness of "valuation and presentation" and adequacy of disclosure. When necessary, the member must discuss accounting matters with the client to assist the client in understanding such matters.

2 The member must not assume the role of employee or of management. For example, the member shall not consummate transactions, have custody of assets, or exercise authority on behalf of the client. The client must prepare the source documents on transactions in sufficient detail to identify clearly the nature and amount of such transactions. The member should not make changes in such basic data without the concurrence of the client.

3 When financial statements are prepared from books and records which the member has maintained, the member must comply with applicable standards for audits, reviews or compilations.

When a client's securities become subject to regulation by the SEC or other federal or state regulatory body, responsibility for maintenance of the accounting records, including accounting classification decisions, must be assumed by accounting personnel employed by the client. The assumption of this responsibility must commence with the first fiscal year after which the client's securities qualify for such regulation.

Ruling—Payroll Preparation Services

Question—A member performs payroll preparation services for clients. A single bank account in the member's name is used to clear all checks. Individual employee checks are cosigned by the member as well as by an officer of each of the respective clients. The clients reimburse the member for the net amount of the payrolls. Would the independence of the member be considered to be impaired with respect to clients who avail themselves of this service?

Answer—Independence of the member would be considered to be impaired.

Independence essentially means taking an *unbiased* viewpoint. The rule recognizes that both independence in *fact* and in *appearance* need to be maintained. Interpretation 101-1 prohibits having a direct or material indirect financial interest in a client during a professional engagement or at the time of expressing an opinion. Also, holding a position with the client that is equivalent to officer or employee status is prohibited, and the period to which the prohibition applies is extended beyond that applicable to a financial interest to include the entire period covered by the financial statements.

General and Technical Standards   The rules of professional conduct in this area are as follows:

Rule 201—General Standards

A member shall comply with the following standards and with any interpretations thereof by bodies designated by Council.

A *Professional competence.* Undertake only those professional services that the member or the member's firm can reasonably expect to be completed with professional competence.

B *Due professional care.* Exercise due professional care in the performance of professional services.

C *Planning and supervision.* Adequately plan and supervise the performance of professional services.

D *Sufficient relevant data.* Obtain sufficient relevant data to afford a reasonable basis for conclusions or recommendations in relation to any professional services performed.

Rule 202—Compliance with Standards

A member who performs auditing, review, compilation, management consulting, tax, or other professional services shall comply with standards promulgated by bodies designated by Council.

Rule 203—Accounting Principles

A member shall not (1) express an opinion or state affirmatively that the financial statements or other financial data of any entity are presented in conformity with generally accepted accounting principles, or (2) state that he or she is not aware of any material modifications that should be made to such statements or data in order for them to be in conformity with generally accepted accounting principles, if such statements or data contain any departure from an accounting principle promulgated by bodies designated by

Council to establish such principles that has a material effect on the statements or data taken as a whole. If, however, the statements or data contain such a departure and the member can demonstrate that due to unusual circumstances the financial statements or data would otherwise have been misleading, the member can comply with the rule by describing the departure, its approximate effects, if practicable, and the reasons why compliance with the principle would result in a misleading statement.

These rules are the link between professional standards and ethics enforcement that make it possible to discipline substandard performance through a self-regulatory body. This has traditionally been a troublesome area for the accounting profession. To discipline a professional for improper performance, conduct that violates a standard needs to be clearly evident. These rules, in effect, bring technical standards within the code and make those standards enforceable.

As previously mentioned, the AICPA Council designates the bodies that have the authority to promulgate standards enforceable under Rule 202. For auditing, the primary body is the Auditing Standards Board. For review and compilation services, the Accounting and Review Services Committee of the AICPA has been designated. For management consulting services, the AICPA's Management Consulting Services Executive Committee is the designated standards-setting body. For tax services, no designated body has been named. The AICPA has a senior technical committee, the Federal Taxation Executive Committee, but it has not sought designation to have its pronouncements be enforceable under Rule 202. Under Rule 203, the FASB and the GASB have been designated to promulgate accounting principles. CPAs performing audits, reviews, or compilations must consider FASB and GASB Statements and Interpretations to be GAAP. Figure 2-2 summarizes the Council-designated bodies.

Rules 201, 202, and 203 apply to all members, if they provide the services described, whether or not the member is in public practice.

Responsibilities to Clients   The rules of professional conduct in this area are as follows:

Rule 301—Confidential Client Information
A member in public practice shall not disclose any confidential client information without the specific consent of the client.

This rule shall not be construed (1) to relieve a member of his or her professional obligations under Rules 202 and 203, (2) to affect in any way the member's obligation to comply with a validly issued and enforceable subpoena or summons, or to prohibit a member's compliance with applicable laws and government regulations, (3) to prohibit review of a member's professional practice under AICPA or state CPA society or Board of Accountancy authorization, or (4) to preclude a member from initiating a complaint with, or responding to any inquiry made by, a recognized investigative or disciplinary body of a state CPA society or Board of Accountancy.

Members of any of the bodies identified in (4) above and members involved with professional practice reviews identified in (3) above shall not use to their own advantage or disclose any member's confidential client information that comes to their attention in carrying out those activities. This prohibition shall not restrict the exchange of information in connection with the investigative or disciplinary proceedings described in (4) above or the professional practice reviews described in (3) above.

Service	Body	Standards
Rule 202—Compliance with Standards		
Audit	Auditing Standards Board	Statements on Auditing Standards
Review	Accounting and Review Services	Statements on Accounting and Review Services (SSARSs)
Compilation	Accounting and Review Services	Statements on Accounting and Review Services (SSARSs)
Management consulting	Management Consulting Services Executive Committee	Statements on Standards for Consulting Services (SSCSs)
Tax	None	
Rule 203—Accounting Principles		
Accounting	Financial Accounting Standards Board	Statements of Financial Accounting Standards (SFASs) and Interpretations
	Government Accounting Standards Board	Government Accounting Standards Board Statements and Interpretations

FIGURE 2-2
Council-designated bodies enforceable under Rules 202 and 203.

Rule 302—Contingent Fees

A member in public practice shall not

1 Perform for a contingent fee any professional services for, or receive such a fee from, a client for whom the member or the member's firm performs
  a an audit or review of a financial statement; or
  b a compilation of a financial statement when the member expects, or reasonably might expect, that a third party will use the financial statement and the member's compilation report does not disclose a lack of independence; or
  c an examination of prospective financial information; or
2 Prepare an original or amended tax return or claim for a tax refund for a contingent fee for any client.

The prohibition in (1) above applies during the period in which the member or the member's firm is engaged to perform any of the services listed above and the period covered by any historical financial statements involved in any such listed services.

Except as stated in the next sentence, a contingent fee is a fee established for the performance of any service pursuant to an arrangement in which no fee will be charged unless a specified finding or result is attained, or in which the amount of the fee is otherwise dependent upon the finding or result of such service. Solely for purposes of this rule, fees are not regarded as being contingent if fixed by courts or other public authorities, or, in tax matters, if determined based on the results of judicial proceedings or the findings of governmental agencies.

A member's fees may vary depending, for example, on the complexity of services rendered.

Except for the rule on independence and the rules on technical standards, the rule that has the greatest effect on daily auditing practice is the one on keeping client information confidential. The importance of confidentiality is deeply ingrained in the attitudes of practicing auditors.

The prohibition does not apply to information that must be disclosed in financial statements to conform with generally accepted accounting principles. Also, the prohibition does not apply to client information that might be reviewed by others as part of an AICPA-authorized quality control review or an ethics investigation by the AICPA, a state board of accountancy, or a state society.

An auditor's ethical and legal duty of confidentiality to clients should not be confused with the legal concept of privileged communication. Some professionals, such as doctors and lawyers, cannot be required to disclose information about their clients even in a legal proceeding. An auditor generally may not withhold information in the face of a valid subpoena or summons enforceable by order of a court. However, absent a formal court order, an auditor must keep client information confidential. For example, an auditor would not discuss a client's financial statements with a newspaper reporter or a shareholder of a client corporation without the client's permission.

The prohibition of contingent fees once applied to all professional services, but was challenged by the Federal Trade Commission and others. The rule was changed in 1991, to apply to clients where the firm performs an audit, a review, or other attest services or when compiled financial statements are expected to have third-party use.

Responsibilities to Colleagues   There are no rules of professional conduct in this area. At one time section 400 of the Code contained rules that prohibited competitive bidding, encroachment on the practice of other CPAs, and unsolicited offers of employment to the staff of other CPAs. However, all of these rules were eliminated as a result of legal challenge by the United States Justice Department or Federal Trade Commission, or concern by the AICPA that a rule would not hold up if challenged. The rules originated at a time when the accounting profession was struggling to distinguish itself as a profession and reflected values considered characteristic of professions. The fact that the rules might also serve to restrain competition was not seriously considered because entry to the profession was not arbitrarily restricted and all those who entered the profession were expected to live by the same rules. However, the Justice Department and Federal Trade Commission imposed a new set of values that made the dangers of restriction of competition paramount.

Other Responsibilities and Practices   The rules of professional conduct in this area include the following:

Rule 501—Acts Discreditable
A member shall not commit an act discreditable to the profession.

Rule 502—Advertising and Other Forms of Solicitation
A member in public practice shall not seek to obtain clients by advertising or other forms of solicitation in a manner that is false, misleading, or deceptive. Solicitation by the use of coercion, over-reaching, or harassing conduct is prohibited.

Rule 503—Commissions and Referral Fees

A *Prohibited Commissions*

A member in public practice shall not for a commission recommend or refer to a client any product or service, or for a commission recommend or refer any product or service to be supplied by a client, or receive a commission, when the member or the member's firm also performs for that client

a an audit or review of a financial statement; or

b a compilation of a financial statement when the member expects, or reasonably might expect, that a third party will use the financial statement and the member's compilation report does not disclose a lack of independence; or

c an examination of prospective financial information.

This prohibition applies during the period in which the member is engaged to perform any of the services listed above and the period covered by any historical financial statements involved in such listed services.

B *Disclosure of Permitted Commissions*

A member in public practice who is not prohibited by this rule from performing services for or receiving a commission and who is paid or expects to be paid a commission shall disclose that fact to any person or entity to whom the member recommends or refers a product or service to which the commission relates.

C *Referral Fees*

Any member who accepts a referral fee for recommending or referring any service of a CPA to any person or entity or who pays a referral fee to obtain a client shall disclose such acceptance or payment to the client.

Rule 504   There is currently no Rule 504.[2]

Rule 505—Form of Practice and Name[3]

A member may practice public accounting only in the form of a proprietorship, a partnership, or a professional corporation whose characteristics conform to resolutions of Council.

A member shall not practice public accounting under a firm name that is misleading. Names of one or more past partners or shareholders may be included in the firm name of a successor partnership or corporation. Also, a partner or shareholder surviving the death or withdrawal of all other partners or shareholders may continue to practice under such name which includes the name of past partners or shareholders for up to two years after becoming a sole practitioner.

A firm may not designate itself as "Members of the American Institute of Certified Public Accountants" unless all of its partners or shareholders are members of the Institute.

The rule on discreditable acts is certainly the broadest restriction in the Code. The most common violations disciplined under the rule are a CPA's willful failure to file his or her own tax return or attempted bribery of an IRS agent. Also, Interpretation 501-1 specifically identifies retention of client records when the client has requested return of the records as a discreditable act. These circumstances sometimes occur when a CPA provides bookkeeping services and would like to hold the records to force payment for services provided. In some state codes, this practice is directly prohibited. Under the AICPA Code the same result is reached by defining the matter as a discreditable act.

---

[2]Formerly, this rule prohibited incompatible occupations.

[3]As explained in Chapter 1, practice as a limited liability company is permitted under Rule 505.

Advertising was prohibited until 1978. Rule 502 was revised because of concerns similar to those affecting the former rules on encroachment and competitive bidding. When the legal profession's prohibition of advertising was struck down by court action, the members of the AICPA voted to voluntarily truncate the advertising rule to its current state. The present rule, as a practical matter, does no more than prohibit conduct that would be illegal anyway.

The rule on commissions previously applied to all clients of members in public practice, but was revised in 1990 after challenge by the Federal Trade Commission. The rule now applies only to clients having an audit, review, or other attestation service, or whose compiled financial statements are expected to have third-party reliance.

Quality Control within CPA Firms

Professional standards (AU 161) require that a CPA firm should establish quality control policies and procedures to provide it with reasonable assurance of conforming with generally accepted auditing standards in its audit engagements. Guidance on quality control is contained in a separate AICPA series of pronouncements called Statements on Quality Control Standards. Statement No. 1 in that series identifies and explains nine elements of quality control. These elements are summarized in the following list:

1 *Independence.* Persons at all levels in the firm maintain independence in fact and appearance.

2 *Assigning personnel to engagements.* Audit work will be performed by persons with the necessary training and proficiency.

3 *Consultation.* Auditors will seek assistance on accounting and auditing questions from persons having appropriate levels of knowledge, competence, judgment, and authority.

4 *Supervision.* Audit work at all levels in the firm meets the firm's standards of quality.

5 *Hiring.* Those employed possess the appropriate characteristics to enable them to perform competently.

6 *Professional development.* Personnel will have the knowledge required to enable them to fulfill assigned responsibilities.

8 *Acceptance and continuance of clients.* Minimize the likelihood of association with a client whose management lacks integrity.

9 *Inspection.* The other procedures designed to maintain the quality of the firm's auditing practice are being effectively applied.

For example, hiring policies might include specification of minimum academic results for new entrants and experience requirements for more advanced positions. Professional development policies might include required attendance at outside and in-house training courses.

The specific policies and procedures a CPA firm adopts will depend on matters such as its size and organization structure, its philosophy on the autonomy of individual partners and practice offices, the nature of its practice, and appropriate cost-benefit considerations. Standards on quality control are not directly enforceable under the Code of Professional Conduct. However, the AICPA membership approved a resolution requiring all members in public practice to enroll their firms in an AICPA-approved practice-monitoring program in order to retain AICPA membership.

A practice-monitoring program requires periodic study (generally every 3 years) and evaluation of a firm's quality control policies and procedures by an independent (outside the CPA firm) peer reviewer. The peer reviewer may be another CPA firm or a review team specially formed for the purpose. Most large CPA firms engage a firm of comparable size to conduct the peer review. A peer review includes review of compliance with the CPA firm's quality control policies and procedures at each organizational level within the firm and in selected audit engagements. The Statements on Quality Control Standards provide a framework for the peer review.

Mandatory Continuing Professional Education

The AICPA requires continuing professional education for all of its members as follows:

- For members in public practice, 120 hours of continuing professional education every 3 years, with a minimum of 20 hours each year
- For members not in public practice, 90 hours of continuing professional education every 3 years, with a minimum of 15 hours each year

In addition, individual states have their own minimum continuing professional education requirements that often exceed the AICPA minimum. In order to remain licensed to practice public accounting in the state, the CPA must meet the state's requirements.

Monitoring and Enforcement

The previous parts of this section have discussed ethical and quality standards and rules of the profession. This section addresses how those standards are enforced.

Peer Review and Other Practice-Monitoring Programs   AICPA individual membership, and membership in the SEC Practice Section or the Private Companies Practice Section all require periodic peer reviews or some other form of AICPA-approved practice-monitoring program. For the SECPS, a peer review is required every 3 years and the results are made available to the public. The peer review is documented by a peer review report, letter of comment, and a response from the reviewed firm that states its corrective action plan. The SECPS Peer Review Committee may require remedial measures, such as requiring specific continuing education courses, and may require active follow-up to ascertain whether the corrective action plan was implemented.

Ethics Enforcement   The bylaws of the AICPA and the state societies establish the criteria a member is expected to observe as a condition of continued membership. These bylaws also describe how a member who may have violated the requirements for continued membership will be investigated, judged, and, if found guilty, expelled or suspended from membership or otherwise disciplined.

The AICPA and the state societies have codes of professional conduct that members must observe as a condition of continued membership. The codes of the state societies are the same, or nearly the same, as the AICPA code and the AICPA and the state societies have joined together to establish a Joint Ethics Enforcement Plan (JEEP). This plan provides for mutual enforcement of the codes of the AICPA and state societies. The AICPA or the relevant state committee has the authority to take one of the following forms of disciplinary action:

- Issue a letter of constructive comment
- Close the inquiry if it is concluded no violation has occurred
- Based on the *prima facie* evidence, determine whether to
  a Impose administrative censure, which may include required continuing education
  b Refer the case to the trial board

If a trial board hearing is held, the trial board may censure, suspend, or expel a member. The names of all members found guilty of ethics violations are published in the *CPA Letter*—a biweekly newsletter of the AICPA.

Public Oversight Board   The POB is an oversight arm of the SECPS. It is composed of five part-time paid members from outside of public accounting practice and has a small full-time staff. The POB is charged with general oversight of peer reviews. In this capacity, it evaluates review teams' qualifications, reads the peer review reports, letters of comments, and the reviewed firms' response letters. The staff directly observes many reviews, especially those of firms with five or more SEC clients. The board may change the composition of the review team, change the scope of a review or revise the report or comment letter, or indicate alternative corrective measures for the reviewed firm.

The POB also oversees the work of the special investigations committee that investigates alleged audit failures. POB members are active participants in confidential meetings of the Quality Control Inquiry Committee with the firms involved in litigation. The QCIC also interviews firm personnel, reviews audit work papers, and evaluates the firm's quality control system. The results of a QCIC inquiry is a report. Many of the lawsuits against auditors are determined to be unfounded. Some result from isolated mistakes. Some result from a problem with the firm's quality control system. Some indicate a need for changes in accounting or auditing standards. The committee follows up to ascertain that any weaknesses in the firm's quality control system are addressed. The QCIC refers matters involving accounting or auditing standards to the standards-setting body for consideration.

The POB issues a report to the public annually on the activities of the SECPS.

EXTERNAL REGULATION

As noted at the beginning of this chapter, regulation of independent auditors is achieved by a mixture of private and government action. Regulation includes the day-to-day measures undertaken to assure adequate performance and the measures that apply only when inadequate performance is alleged.

External measures to assure adequate performance are established and administered by government agencies, and external remedies for inadequate performance are pursued primarily by litigation in the courts. The Interstate Commerce Commission and the Federal Communications Commission are examples of government agencies that have had an effect on the public accounting profession. For the most part, their influence stems from their power to prescribe accounting practices for the organizations which they regulate. Public accountants are sometimes requested to report on an organization's compliance with regulatory agency requirements. However, the primary government agency that, in effect, exerts regulatory influence in the accounting and auditing areas is the SEC, the subject of the next section.

The Securities and Exchange Commission

The Securities Act of 1933, which was administered initially by the Federal Trade Commission, has been called the *truth in securities* law. It has the objectives of providing investors with financial and other information concerning securities offered for public sale, and prohibiting misrepresentation and other fraudulent acts in the sale of securities. The principal provision of the act requires that a registration statement be filed with the SEC by an issuing company before securities may be sold to the public. The purpose of this registration statement is to provide assurance to the SEC that the prospectus (selling circular) contains factual information necessary for investors to appraise the merits of securities. Investors must be provided with a prospectus which contains all important data appearing in the registration statement. Both the registration statement and the prospectus become public immediately upon filing with the SEC; however, it is unlawful to sell the securities until the effective date, which is the 20th day after filing or earlier if the SEC, at its discretion, decides to allow it. Registration statements are available on request from the SEC, while prospectuses are distributed by brokers and dealers in securities.

Soon after the passage of the Securities Act, two things became evident: (1) a permanent office was necessary to administer the act and (2) current information on previously registered securities was needed for public trading through national exchanges. The Securities Exchange Act of 1934 was passed to meet these needs. In addition to the creation of the SEC to administer both the 1933 and 1934 acts, the Securities Exchange Act requires, following registration of securities, an annual report and other periodic reports to update the information contained in the original filing.

The SEC does not judge the merits of a security. The purpose of the Securities Act is to ensure fair disclosure of material facts regarding the initial public offering of securities to be sold in interstate commerce or through the mails. The purpose of the Securities Exchange Act is to require public distribution of significant information on corporations whose securities are listed on national securities exchanges.

A significant feature of the acts for the public accounting profession is the statutory requirements for *audited* financial statements. Registration statements must include financial statements audited by independent public accountants, and audited financial statements must be filed annually in addition to those filed with the registration statement. Audits had been performed in the United States for some time and the stock exchanges had encouraged listed companies to have annual audits, but the securities acts were the first legal recognition of the importance of independent audits.

Accounting and auditing matters relating to the acts are under the principal supervision of the chief accountant. The views of the SEC on these matters are communicated to the public accounting profession in SEC pronouncements such as *Regulation S-X,*

General Rules and Regulations, a series of interpretive opinions entitled *Financial Reporting Releases* (formerly *Accounting Series Releases),* and a series of staff views called *Staff Accounting Bulletins.* These pronouncements cover such matters as the form and content of financial statements, the content of the audit report, and the qualifications of the independent auditor. Although the SEC has broad authority under the acts to set accounting principles, the commission has urged voluntary action by the accounting profession and has cooperated with the profession to this end. However, the SEC has not hesitated to use its statutory powers when it felt voluntary action did not go far enough.

Of particular interest to accountants and auditors are reports that need to be filed with the SEC that include financial statements or financial information. The 1933 Act applies to the *original* sale of securities, and the sale must be registered with the SEC. When a sale of securities is registered, the proper registration form must be used, and there are many with each designed for specific circumstances. However, *Form S-1* is the generalized form. All the forms require incorporation of audited financial statements.

Under the 1934 Act, companies that have securities listed on a national securities exchange, such as the New York Stock Exchange, and companies that have assets exceeding $5 million and 500 or more shareholders must register the securities and file periodic reports with the SEC. The following are the primary periodic reports:

- *Form 10-K.* This is an annual report and it includes audited financial statements and related supplementary data.
- *Form 10-Q.* This is a quarterly report and it includes interim financial information. This information is not audited, but auditor involvement may be required if the company meets a size test.
- *Form 8-K.* This is a special events report and must be filed after the occurrence of reportable events such as changes in control, significant changes in asset composition, and bankruptcy. A change in independent auditors is designated as a reportable event.

When there has been a change of auditors, the Form 8-K must disclose whether the board of directors or an audit committee discussed disagreements with the former auditors, whether the company limited discussions between the former auditors and new auditors regarding the disagreement, and whether the former auditor resigned or was dismissed.

A reportable event would include situations such as an auditor's resignation or dismissal in cases like the following:

- After questioning internal control structure, accounting practices, or integrity in the preparation of financial statements
- After the client refuses to make a satisfactory material adjustment to the financial statements that the auditor believes should be made
- After advising the client that a matter needs to be investigated further because it might materially affect the financial statements, but the investigation is not completed before the auditor's dismissal or resignation

The SEC, as noted earlier, has a significant effect on accounting and auditing. However, it should be recognized that a substantial part of auditing practice does not include

SEC involvement. The SEC has no regulatory authority over companies that do not sell securities publicly or certain nonprofit entities, such as municipalities, even if they sell securities. The term *security* is broadly defined under the 1933 Act and includes notes, stocks, bonds, debentures, and investment contracts. Nevertheless, there are important exemptions to registration requirements generally related to the size of the security offering and the number and type of investors. Generally, SEC practice is regarded as a specialized area by auditors, and most CPA firms with an SEC-related practice have SEC specialists who are thoroughly familiar with the forms and related regulations, particularly Regulation S-X.

The SEC does not regulate auditing practice even when the auditor's client has securities subject to SEC regulations, but the SEC's authority to influence the content of audited financial statements and to discipline auditors with SEC clients does give the SEC substantial influence in the regulatory framework. One of the features of this influence is legal liability under the securities acts—the subject of Chapter 3.

Legal Liability

CPAs meet professional standards for many reasons—to have pride in their work, to satisfy peer reviewers and maintain a good reputation, to avoid ethics inquiries and licensing problems. One additional reason has substantial importance—if the CPA's work fails to meet the profession's standards, he or she may face legal liability for that work.

CPAs are subject to all laws that govern general behavior. Additionally, auditors must take legal responsibility for their audits and the reports they render. As a result of his or her work as a professional accountant, a CPA may incur either criminal liability, civil liability, or both.

In the early 1990s, the number of civil cases against CPAs dramatically increased. The AICPA's Public Oversight Board stated in their 1992 annual report, ". . . the present flood of litigation assailing accounting firms and the multi-million dollar judgments and settlements constitute a grave danger to the continued viability of the accounting profession as it presently exists. . . ." The increase was not caused by a drop in the quality of CPA work. Based on peer review results and other measures, it appears the work quality continued to increase. The increase appears to have arisen from the general trend to litigate against professionals and an increasing awareness that the CPA is a valuable potential source of funds for damages. In some of the cases, the lawsuits were unfounded; in others the lawsuits had merit. Chapter 3 explores the CPA's legal liability.

CHAPTER 2 ASSIGNMENTS
OBJECTIVE QUESTIONS

2-1 For each one of the following statements indicate whether the statement is true or false.

T   F   a The essential difference between professional and nonprofessional work is the professional's need for procedural skill.

T   F   b A privilege that professionals strive for is relative immunity from community judgment on technical matters.

T   F   c The only direct power the AICPA has over its members is termination of their membership.

T   F   d The Financial Accounting Standards Board is the division of the AICPA that deals with the development of accounting principles.

T   F   e The groups that actually issue licenses to practice as a certified public accountant are state societies of CPAs.

T   F   f The ethical principles of the concepts of professional ethics must be adhered to and CPAs may be disciplined for violations of such principles.

T   F   g An auditor will not be considered independent of a company if the auditor has even one share of stock in that company even though the company has issued thousands of shares that are widely held.

T   F   h If a CPA provides a company with bookkeeping services, that CPA cannot be considered independent of that company.

T   F   i Adherence to generally accepted accounting principles or auditing standards are separate matters from adherence to the rules of conduct.

T   F   j The rule of confidentiality does not preclude a member from furnishing information related to clients to the AICPA Ethics Division.

T   F   k A CPA firm must adopt policies and procedures to minimize the likelihood of association with a client whose management lacks integrity.

T   F   l All members of the AICPA engaged in auditing practice must have a peer review periodically.

T   F   m Standards on quality control are directly enforceable under the Code of Professional Conduct.

T   F   n Peer reviews are performed within a firm, one CPA in the firm reviewing another in the same firm.

T   F   o SEC Form 8-K has to be filed only when certain types of events occur.

2-2 The following questions relate to compliance with the Code of Professional Conduct. Select the *best* response.

a The AICPA Code of Professional Conduct states that a member shall not disclose any confidential information obtained in the course of a professional engagement except with the specific consent of the client. This rule should be understood to preclude a CPA from responding to an inquiry made by:

1 The trial board of the AICPA

2 A CPA-shareholder of the client corporation

3 An investigative body of a state CPA society

4 An AICPA voluntary quality review body

b A CPA who is seeking to sell an accounting practice must:

1 Not allow a peer review team to look at working papers and tax returns without permission from the client prior to consummation of the sale

2 Not allow a prospective purchaser to look at working papers and tax returns without permission from the client

3 Give all work papers and tax returns to the client

4 Retain all work papers and tax returns for a period of time sufficient to satisfy the statute of limitations

c A CPA's retention of client records as a means of enforcing payment of an overdue audit fee is an action that is:

1 *Not* addressed by the AICPA Code of Professional Conduct

2 Acceptable if sanctioned by the state laws

3 Prohibited under the AICPA rules of conduct

4 A violation of generally accepted auditing standards

d The concept of materiality would be *least* important to an auditor in determining the:

1 Transactions that should be reviewed

2 Need for disclosure of a particular fact or transaction

3 Scope of the CPA's audit program relating to various accounts

4 Effects of direct financial interest in the client upon the CPA's independence

e Inclusion of which of the following statements in a CPA's advertisement is *not* acceptable pursuant to the AICPA Code of Professional Conduct?

1 Paul Fall
Certified Public Accountant
Fluency in Spanish and French

2 Paul Fall
Certified Public Accountant
J. D., Evans Law School 1964

3 Paul Fall
Certified Public Accountant
Free Consultation

4 Paul Fall
Certified Public Accountant
Endorsed by AICPA

f A violation of the profession's ethical standards most likely would have occurred when a CPA:

1 Compiled the financial statements of a client that employed the CPA's spouse as a bookkeeper

2 Received a fee for referring audit clients to a company that sells limited partnership interests

3 Purchased the portion of an insurance company that performs actuarial services for employee benefit plans

4 Arranged with a financial institution to collect notes issued by a client in payment of fees due

g An auditor strives to achieve independence in appearance in order to:

1 Maintain public confidence in the profession

2 Become independent in fact

3 Comply with the generally accepted auditing standards of field work

4 Maintain an unbiased mental attitude

h Which of the following acts by a CPA who is *not* in public practice would most likely be considered a violation of the ethical standards of the profession?

1 Using the CPA designation without disclosing employment status in connection with financial statements issued for external use by the CPA's employer

2 Distributing business cards indicating the CPA designation and the CPA's title and employer

3 Corresponding on the CPA's employer's letterhead, which contains the CPA designation and the CPA's employment status

4 Compiling the CPA's employer's financial statements and making reference to the CPA's lack of independence

i If requested to perform a review engagement for a nonpublic entity in which an accountant has an immaterial direct financial interest, the accountant is:

1 Independent because the financial interest is immaterial and, therefore, may issue a review report

2 Not independent and, therefore, may *not* be associated with the financial statements

3 Not independent and, therefore, may *not* issue a review report

4 Not independent and, therefore, may issue a review report, but may *not* issue an auditor's opinion

AICPA

2-3 The following questions relate to quality control and peer review. Select the *best* response.

a A firm of CPAs may use policies and procedures such as notifying professional personnel as to the names of audit clients having publicly held securities and confirming periodically with such personnel that prohibited relations do *not* exist. This is done to achieve effective quality control in which of the following areas?

1 Acceptance and continuance of clients

2 Assigning personnel to engagements

3 Independence

4 Inspection

b In connection with the element of inspection, a CPA firm's system of quality control should ordinarily provide for the maintenance of:

1 A file of minutes of staff meetings

2 Updated personnel files

3 Documentation to demonstrate compliance with its policies and procedures

4 Documentation to demonstrate compliance with peer review directives

c A CPA establishes quality control policies and procedures for deciding whether to accept a new client or continue to perform services for a current client. The primary purpose for establishing such policies and procedures is:

1 To enable the auditor to attest to the integrity or reliability of a client

2 To comply with the quality control standards established by regulatory bodies

3 To lessen the exposure to litigation resulting from failure to detect irregularities in client financial statements

4 To minimize the likelihood of association with clients whose management lacks integrity

d Williams & Co., a large international CPA firm, is to have an "external peer review." The peer review will most likely be performed by:

1 Employees and partners of Williams & Co. who are *not* associated with the particular audits being reviewed

2 Audit review staff of the Securities and Exchange Commission

3 Audit review staff of the American Institute of Certified Public Accountants

4 Employees and partners of another CPA firm

e Which of the following is *not* an element of quality control?

1 Documentation

2 Inspection

3 Supervision

4 Consultation

f A CPA firm's quality control procedures pertaining to the acceptance of a prospective audit client would most likely include:

1 Inquiry of management as to whether disagreements between the predecessor auditor and the prospective client were resolved satisfactorily

2 Consideration of whether sufficient competent evidential matter may be obtained to afford a reasonable basis for an opinion

3 Inquiry of third parties, such as the prospective client's bankers and attorneys, about information regarding the prospective client and its management

4 Consideration of whether the internal control structure is sufficiently effective to permit a reduction in the extent of required substantive tests

g A CPA firm evaluates its personnel advancement experience to ascertain whether individuals meeting stated criteria are assigned increased degrees of responsibility. This is evidence of the firm's adherence to which of the following prescribed standards:

1 Quality control

2 Human resources

3 Supervision and review

4 Professional development

h A CPA firm should establish procedures for conducting and supervising work at all organizational levels to provide reasonable assurance that the work performed meets the firm's standards of quality. To achieve this goal, the firm most likely would establish procedures for:

1 Evaluating prospective and continuing client relationships

2 Reviewing engagement working papers and reports

3 Requiring personnel to adhere to the applicable independence rules

4 Maintaining personnel files containing documentation related to the evaluation of personnel

i CPA firms should establish quality control policies and procedures for professional development in order to provide reasonable assurance that:

1 Employees promoted possess the characteristics to perform competently

2 Personnel will have the knowledge required to fulfill responsibilities assigned

3 The extent of supervision and review in a given instance will be appropriate

4 Association with a client whose management lacks integrity will be minimized

AICPA

DISCUSSION QUESTIONS

Discussion questions require the application of the concepts explained in the chapter to specific facts, issues, or problems. They are classified by the primary topic to which they relate. However, responses should not be confined to the primary topics, but should include all relevant implications.

Code of Professional Conduct

2-4 This question relates to the attribute of independence associated with the CPA's function of auditing and expressing opinions on financial statements.

Required:

a What is meant by "independence" as applied to the CPA's function of auditing and expressing opinions on financial statements? Discuss.

b CPAs have imposed upon themselves certain rules of professional conduct that induce their members to remain independent and to strengthen public confidence in their independence. Which of the rules of professional conduct are concerned (directly or indirectly) with the CPA's independence? Discuss.

c The Milton Company is indebted to Bradley, a CPA, for unpaid fees and has offered to issue unsecured interest-bearing notes. Would Bradley's acceptance of these notes have any bearing on independence or in relations with the Milton Company?

AICPA adapted

2-5 Bald Eagle Corporation was formed on October 1, 19X4, and its fiscal year will end on September 30, 19X5. You audited the corporation's opening balance sheet and rendered an unqualified opinion on it. A month after rendering your report you are offered the position of secretary of the company because of the need for a complete set of officers and for convenience in signing various documents. You will have no financial interest in the company through stock ownership or otherwise, will receive no salary, will not keep the books, and will not have any influence on its financial matters other than occasional advice on income tax matters and similar advice normally given a client by a CPA.

a Assume that you accept the offer but plan to resign the position prior to conducting your annual audit, with the intention of again assuming the office after rendering an opinion on the statements. Can you render an independent opinion on the financial statements? Discuss.

b Assume that you accept the offer on a temporary basis until the corporation has gotten under way and can employ a secretary. In any event, you would permanently resign the position before conducting your annual audit. Can you render an independent opinion on the financial statements? Discuss.

AICPA adapted

2-6 During 19X6 your client, Mark Corporation, requested that you conduct a feasibility study to advise management of the best way the corporation can utilize electronic data processing equipment and which computer, if any, best meets the corporation's requirements. You are technically competent in this area and accept the engagement. Upon completion of your study the corporation accepts your suggestions and installs the computer and related equipment that you recommended.

a Discuss the effect the acceptance of this management services engagement would have upon your independence in expressing an opinion on the financial statements of the Mark Corporation.

b Instead of accepting the engagement, assume that you recommend Roy Flack, of the CPA firm of Green and Flack, who is qualified in specialized services. Upon completion of the engagement your client requests that Flack's partner, Fenster Green, perform services in other areas. Should Green accept the engagement? Discuss.

c A local printer of data processing forms customarily offers a commission for recommending him as supplier. The client is aware of the commission offer and suggests that Flack accept it. Would it be proper for Flack to accept the commission with the client's approval? Discuss.

AICPA adapted

2-7 Winston Gould is the controlling shareholder of Gould, Inc., a closely held corporation. He has expressed dissatisfaction with his present auditors and informs Henry

Cramer, a CPA and member of the AICPA, that he will be appointed auditor if he agrees to the following proposals:

a Because Gould's present dissatisfaction is related primarily to fees, which he feels are too high in relation to the time the job should take and the services rendered, Cramer is to quote a fee in advance and detail the services he would provide. This quotation must, of course, be lower than the fee presently being paid by Gould, Inc.

b Because Gould feels quite strongly that the company's auditor should take an active part in the operation of the business, Cramer is to serve as a director of Gould, Inc. While Gould appreciates that Cramer must maintain a position of financial independence, he points out that the acquisition of one qualifying common share would not interfere with his independence.

c Because Gould, Inc., has experienced financial difficulty during the past several years, Cramer is to accept redeemable preferred shares in lieu of fees for the first year of the engagement. As these shares have no voting rights Gould feels that Cramer's independence will not be affected. Moreover, if conditions improve significantly, the shares will be redeemed.

d Because Gould has certain personal income tax problems, Cramer is to review his affairs. As the possibility of refund is uncertain, Cramer's fee is to be 40 percent of all recoveries.

e Because Gould is very impressed with a particular auditor who has been employed on the audit for 2 years by the present auditors, Cramer is to hire the auditor and retain him on the audit. Gould knows that the auditor would be amenable to such a suggestion.

With respect to each of the above proposals, what answers should Cramer give to Gould? Give reasons to support these answers.

CICA adapted

2-8 In each of the following unrelated circumstances, explain what course of action a CPA should follow in order to discharge his or her professional and ethical responsibilities:

a Nobles is employed by a firm of CPAs practicing in a small town. Early in 19X2, he reviews with the principal shareholder the draft of the audited 19X1 financial statements of Builders, Inc., a building contractor. Nobles notes that the company's deteriorating cash position is so serious that he believes that the company is facing bankruptcy.

Nobles subsequently reviews the draft of the audited 19X1 financial statements of Patton Corporation, also a client, and notes that the company has a large overdue account receivable from Builders, Inc., against which no allowance for doubtful accounts has been provided. When Nobles questions the owner of Patton Corporation on the collectibility of the account, he is convinced that the owner is not aware of the actual financial condition of Builders, Inc.

b Brenda George, a CPA, is in charge of the audit of Portland Corporation, a public company. George is asked by an economist, who is doing research for a thesis on the financial operations of firms in the same industry as Portland, if she would contribute any information or views on the financial operations of Portland. The economist promises to keep confidential any information received from George.

c Singing Mines, Inc., is a small mining company whose principal shareholders are actively promoting the company's stock. Peter Dunn, the auditor of the company for several years, is in the company's offices conducting interim audit tests before the year-end when he discovers a copy of a set of third-quarter financial statements recently prepared and apparently sent to the company's bank. These were prepared by the company's accounting staff without Dunn's knowledge. They are clearly marked "unaudited," and Dunn's name does not appear on them. A quick scrutiny reveals that the statements appear to overstate net income by a material amount.

CICA adapted

2-9 An auditor makes an agreement with a client that the amount of the audit fee will be contingent on the number of days required to complete the engagement.

   a What is the essence of the rule of professional conduct dealing with contingent fees, and what are the reasons for the rule?

   b Did the auditor violate the rule?

AICPA

2-10 A firm of certified public accountants is considering the use of an outside mailing service to handle confirmations of the accounts receivable of clients upon whose financial statements the firm is to render an opinion. The mailing service would mail the requests, receive the replies, remove the replies from the envelopes, and return them to the accountants. Would this proposed action be considered proper?

AICPA adapted

2-11 Carlson, a CPA, is engaged in a fee dispute with a client. Carlson has in her possession various client records and decides to withhold them until such time as the client satisfies her bill. She notes that statutes of the state in which she practices specifically grant her a lien. Is her action ethical?

Securities and Exchange Commission

2-12 A press release announcing the appointment of the trustees of the Financial Accounting Foundation stated that the Financial Accounting Standards Board "will become the established authority for setting accounting principles under which corporations report to the shareholders and others" (AICPA news release July 20, 1972).

   a No mention is made of the SEC in the press release. What role does the SEC play in setting accounting principles?

   b How have accounting principles been set over the past 25 years? In your answer identify the body performing this function, the sponsoring organization, and the method by which the body arrived at its decisions.

2-13 Legally, the SEC has the authority to specify accounting principles and practices and thereby completely regulate accounting practice. It has chosen not to do this, but rather to work with the AICPA and FASB. Why does the SEC not establish accounting principles?

CASE

Day 1

The firm of Sober & Snicker, CPAs, had fallen on hard times. They needed clients—needed them badly. Steve Snicker ran into the office. "We got it!!! We got the audit!!!"

Sam Sober smiled at him. "Congratulations. Which company?"

"Acme," Steve replied. "You remember—the public company that was firing the audit firm because they thought the partner was a straight-laced, unreasonable old goat. And so unprofessional that the auditors were demanding payment of the audit fee before they would finish the audit. They should have expected to get fired after that stunt. Well, the

Acme chief financial officer Mike Swindler said I was exactly the young, understanding, reasonable, modern, and flexible CPA they were looking for to head their audit."

"The old Snicker charm worked. When do you meet with the predecessor auditors?" Sam asked.

"Tomorrow."

Day 2

"How did the meeting with the predecessor auditors go, Steve?"

Steve looked down to avoid Sam's gaze. "Oh, there's a lot of sour grapes there. The old partner is jealous of any new auditors who take their place and straighten out the mess they are leaving. And talk about a story to justify their unprofessional behavior with the fees! You have to picture this stuffy old guy in a three-piece suit, glaring at me over his bifocals saying, 'We resigned because we felt it was in the best interest of our firm.'"

Sam frowned. "This sounds serious. Why in the best interest of their firm?"

"Something about no longer wishing to be associated with Acme management."

"What exactly was their story?" Sam pressed Steve to continue.

"He said they questioned some of the revenue transactions—Acme couldn't provide documentation to support them, and the auditors weren't satisfied. They requested the fees early after, he says, Swindler threatened him: 'You give me a bad opinion and I'll give you a bad check.' So he resigned. I tell you, Sam, he's a narrow-minded curmudgeon trying to make us squirm with a story of questionable client behavior because his firm lost the business."

"A client integrity issue. We don't want to accept the client if it's true, Steve."

"It's sour grapes, Sam. Hell hath no fury like a CPA scorned."

Sam sighed. "It's not worth having a client like that."

Steve scowled. "We don't exactly have so many clients that we can turn down a great fee at full billing rates based on the word of one jealous old auditor. We have to keep busy—we are having trouble meeting the payroll here in case you haven't noticed."

"What if what the old guy says is true?"

"What if it isn't and we are just so principled that we are turning it down for no reason except the whining of the loser?" Steve snapped back.

"What if it's true?"

"We can handle it as professionals. We are still going to do an audit. So we do the audit with a heightened sense of professional skepticism. We do more audit tests on those revenue transactions. We audit them every which way! We catch them if they misstate anything. We give a qualified opinion if they deserve it. Or an adverse. But why do we have to turn down the audit?" Steve asked.

Sam sighed. "Without even mentioning what it says in our firm's quality control procedures for client acceptance, consider this: Doing extra auditing requires lots of extra time which results in lots of extra costs for us. Will the client pay substantially more to compensate for the extent of audit work needed? How much will they be willing to pay for an audit? And if it isn't a clean opinion, will we have to refuse to continue the audit as the last firm did?"

"Let me talk to Swindler—I'll figure out a way to explain we need to do extra work. And I'll look at the Form 8-K to see what it says about any disagreements causing the change in auditors."

Day 3

Steve entered Sam's office. "It's all resolved. The Form 8-K Acme just filed indicates there were no disagreements about internal control structure, accounting practices, or integrity in the preparation of financial statements. The old auditors haven't responded yet. Swindler was great about the fees. He understands completely. He is willing to give us double what the last auditors got—I mean what they billed, since they never really got paid—because, he says, we are so clearly professional and superior to the others. I told him that as a small firm we have limited resources to cover the audit costs and we would prefer to receive the fee in a series of four payments (at the start of work, after completion of audit planning work, during tests of transactions, and the last one on delivery of the report). Swindler agreed without hesitating. The most we can lose is the last payment. We can start Monday."

"I don't know, Steve. Did you do the other client acceptance procedures? What were the results of those? The 8-K should have referred to that revenue matter that needs to be investigated further before financial statements are issued. Shouldn't we give the predecessor auditors a chance to respond to the 8-K as filed?" Sam worried.

Steve's temper flared. "I bring in a client who pays good fees, and you complain. This firm is a business. We need to bring in money, not theorize about standards. I satisfied your concerns about the revenue transactions by outlining a thorough and professional audit approach. Now I am making this decision. We are doing this audit." He walked out.

Required:

1 Is accepting an audit engagement while concerned about management integrity permitted under the Code of Professional Conduct? Under the Quality Control Standards? Under Statements on Auditing Standards?

2 Having decided to accept the engagement, what potential outcomes should Sober & Snicker be concerned about? What actions should they take to minimize risk of unfortunate outcomes?

3 Was requiring payment of fees before completing the audit permitted under the Code of Professional Conduct? Under Quality Control Standards?

CHAPTER

3

Legal Liability

CHAPTER OUTLINE

Learning Objectives

After studying this chapter you should be able to:

- Describe the legal environment in which the independent CPA practices
- Define ordinary negligence, gross negligence, negligent misrepresentation, and fraud, as they apply to accounting practice
- Explain the three approaches to liability to third parties under common law and list the criteria required for each
- Explain the accountant's liability under the Securities Act and the Securities and Exchange Act and the differences in liability for information used in initial public offerings versus ongoing annual reports
- Be aware of other criminal liability for accountants, and describe the punitive damage system
- Cite the most noted legal cases in the history of accountant's liability, recognizing both the name of the case and its significance
- Be aware of accountant's liability insurance and its limitations
- Understand the profession's movement to change certain aspects of the accountant's legal liability through legislation
- List some of the activities of a forensic accountant

Relevant Sections of Statements on Auditing Standards[1]

AU 230 — Due Care in the Performance of Work
AU 634 — Letters for Underwriters
AU 711 — Filings under Federal Securities Statutes

THE LEGAL ENVIRONMENT

This chapter reviews legal responsibilities of CPAs for their work. Most professionals performing work for a client owe a duty of due care to that client, but the professional does not have to worry about liability to unspecified or unknown others. The CPA's work, however, produces audit opinions or other reports that third parties may use. If the third parties rely on the CPA's report and thereafter have a financial loss, the third parties suing the CPA's client often also sue the CPA.

In some cases, such suits are merited. However, many accountants consider some suits against CPAs to be motivated largely by monetary incentives rather than attempts to redress the damages from inadequate audits. One reason some accountants suggest for this is that a client may no longer be solvent, but the CPA is. The tendency to sue the party with the capacity to pay monetary damages is called "the deep-pocket concept."

---

[1]AU 316, *Responsibility to Detect and Report Errors and Irregularities;* AU 317, *Illegal Acts by Clients;* and AU 341, *The Auditor's Consideration of an Entity's Ability to Continue as a Going Concern* are Statements on Auditing Standards that are often cited in auditor malpractice litigation. They are addressed in Chapter 5.

The AICPA Board of Directors has stated "Accountants should not pay for others' mistakes simply because they are the only one left standing after a financial collapse."[2]

In 1993, the Big Six presented a report to the SEC on the CPA's liability crisis in the United States, reporting that the total expenditures for settling and defending audit- and accounting-related lawsuits during 1992 were $598 million—which was 11 percent of audit and accounting revenues in the United States.[3] The trend toward limitless liability to nonclients threatens the viability of the public accounting profession.

Currently, most firms carry professional liability insurance (the Big Six deductibles are approximately $45 million per suit). Costs for that insurance are rising. Such costs ultimately are passed on to clients. The large firms fear several possible outcomes, among them: (1) The fees charged for audit and accounting services (including liability insurance costs) may rise higher than anyone would be willing to pay for such services, or (2) insurers may refuse to issue professional liability insurance. However, critics suggest that liability costs are a necessary incentive for greater care and more skeptical auditing.

The courts have historically decided the extent of CPA liability and the amount of damages. The noted legal cases that have defined the accountant's liability are covered in this chapter. Each state uses the precedents from cases tried within its own jurisdiction. If such suitable precedents do not exist, the state's courts consider cases tried in other states, which then become the precedents for the state. Thus, a discussion of three approaches to accountant's liability covers most of the issues relevant to all 50 states, with only minor variations.

The AICPA and other CPA groups are working with federal and state lawmakers to define liability and limit damages through legislation, and several states have begun to address this issue. The statutory laws governing accountant's liability are also addressed in this chapter.

As a result of his or her work as a professional accountant, a CPA may incur either civil liability, criminal liability, or both.

CIVIL LIABILITY

The accountant's civil liability may be either to the client or to third parties that rely on the accountant's professional work and reports. Liability to third parties may be defined either by previous legal decisions (called *common law*) or by statute (called *statutory law*).

Legal liability results when a standard of care imposed by society is disregarded. Society imposes a duty to exercise care or skill in relation to another person in two ways:

1 A duty in contract arising from an oral or written agreement between the parties. This is called *privity*.

---

[2]Board of Directors of the American Institute of Certified Public Accountants, *Meeting the Financial Reporting Needs of the Future: A Public Commitment from the Public Accounting Profession* (New York: AICPA, June 1993).
[3]*Big Six Report to the SEC,* June 1993. A more meaningful comparison is probably total revenues. Some observers estimate that total legal expenditures were from 5 to 6 percent of total revenues.

2 A duty imposed by law arising from a special relationship between the parties.

Generally, the party bringing the legal action (the plaintiff) must prove three things:

- Liability (that the CPA defendant was at fault)
- Causation (that the CPA's failure caused the damages)
- Damages (the amount of the resulting loss)

In addition, the plaintiff needs to establish that the CPA owed a "duty of due care and skill" to the plaintiff. There are several approaches to this issue, which are addressed below.

Liability to Clients

When an independent CPA is engaged to perform work for a fee, the relationship that arises depends on the contract. The auditor's duty of care and skill is rarely expressly defined in the contract, but the law always attaches to the contract an implied obligation to perform the work undertaken with reasonable skill and care. An action by the client against the CPA is an action for breach of contract and only the *client,* who is party to the contract, can sue for breach of it. Contractual liability (privity) arises under common law.

An example of breach of a specific contract provision would be failure to file on time when a CPA has agreed to file tax refund claims for the client. An example of breach of an implied obligation would be negligent failure to detect a material misstatement in audited financial statements caused by fraud on the part of a client's employee.

Responsibility to Use Due Care   There are distinctions in what the CPA is liable for. *Negligence* results when the auditor fails to conform to the standard of care that the law requires. The law reads: "Every one is responsible, not only for the result of his willful acts, but also for an injury occasioned to another by his want of ordinary care or skill in the management of his property or person. . . ."[4] In negligence actions, the plaintiff has the burden of proof; the client must prove the auditor's failure to exercise the necessary care. In defense, the auditor may prove the comparative negligence or contributory negligence of the client. The reasonable care which the auditor owes to the client is that degree of skill and care that would ordinarily be exercised by other members of the profession in similar circumstances. In essence, this means adherence to generally accepted auditing standards. Failure to exercise due care is *ordinary negligence.* Ordinary negligence is distinguished from *gross negligence* and from *fraud.*

- Ordinary negligence is an unintentional act, a thoughtless slip or blunder.
- Gross negligence is a flagrant or reckless departure from the standard of due care, or willful and wanton misconduct.
- Fraud is an intentional misstatement or concealment of a material fact.

The CPA is liable to the client for ordinary negligence; it need not be gross negligence or fraud.

---

[4]Civil Code, section 1714, subdivision (a).

The Comparative Negligence Defense   In some jurisdictions, the plaintiff's recovery of damages is limited if part of the negligence is attributable to the plaintiff. For example, a client with a weak internal control structure suffers an embezzlement. The client sues the auditor for failing to discover it. If the court finds that a portion of the overall negligence should be attributed to the client's poor management practices, the client's recovery of damages is limited.

Not all jurisdictions handle the limitation in the same way. Some reduce the damages by the percentage of the overall negligence attributed to the plaintiff. Some do not permit recovery if the plaintiff's share of the negligence was more than 50 percent. A few jurisdictions do not permit recovery if any portion of the negligence belongs to the plaintiff. Some permit full damages if any portion of the negligence is attributed to the defendant.

Confidential Relationship   The independent CPA also has an implicit confidential relationship with the client. During the course of an audit, the auditor ordinarily acquires a good deal of confidential information about the client. If this information were arbitrarily disclosed to others by the auditor, the confidential relationship would be breached and the auditor would be liable to the client for any damages resulting from the disclosure. The auditor would also be subject to disciplinary action by professional associations for violation of a rule of conduct.

Liability to Third Parties—Common Law

"Every person is bound, without contract, to abstain from injuring the person or property of another, or infringing upon any of his rights."[5]

"Third parties" are those not in a contractual relationship with the CPA. Liability to third parties may arise under common law or by statute. In this section, key concepts from common law cases are discussed.

Common law cases are decided primarily by state courts; it is difficult to generalize about the auditor's liability to third parties because it may differ somewhat from state to state. As one observer noted, "The courts do not speak with a single voice, and they always speak in the context of the particular cases before them." However, with minor variations, the common law for all 50 states substantially follow three approaches, traceable to a handful of landmark cases that have served as precedents. The key issue in these landmark cases is to what extent an auditor owes a duty of due care to those who are not, in the ordinary sense, clients (such as shareholders and creditors who use the audited financial statements).

Fraud or Gross Negligence   If, in rendering an opinion, the auditor intentionally deceives third parties for the purpose of inducing them to act in reliance on the deception, the CPA has committed a fraud and is liable to third parties who can prove that they relied on the information and were damaged thereby. Actual dishonest or deceitful misrepresentations by the CPA may result in either civil or criminal liability or both.

[5] Civil Code, section 1708.

Similarly, the CPA is liable to third parties for gross negligence. The third-party plaintiff must prove that the CPA's negligence was willful and wanton or reckless.

The plaintiff in a gross negligence or fraud action may be able to recover punitive as well as compensatory damages. Because the damage award is intended to be a punishment, the judge or jury can consider the financial resources of the CPA in deciding the amount.

One statute that has been used in accountant liability cases is the federal Racketeer Influenced and Corrupt Organizations Act (the *RICO statute*). Congress enacted the law to combat organized crime. However, plaintiffs wanted the RICO statute to apply in accountant liability cases because RICO permits the awarding of treble damages (three times the amount of actual compensatory damages). In some cases, the plaintiffs were successful in obtaining the inflated damage awards from accounting firms.

In a landmark case in 1993, the *Reves* decision, the Supreme Court held that accounting firms do not violate RICO unless they actually "manage and operate" an illegal RICO enterprise's affairs.[6] The CPA performing a typical audit, review, or compilation of financial statements is not managing or operating the business. Thus, this decision may reduce RICO claims against CPAs, but the decision is too new to predict its effect on future litigation.

Negligence   What is the auditor's liability to third parties when the auditor makes a negligent, but honest, mistake in rendering an opinion? In what circumstances, if any, should the auditor be liable to third parties for various degrees of negligence? The states have, in general, followed three schools of thought on this issue. These approaches are categorized by the relationship of the third party to the CPA's work:

- Primary beneficiaries of the CPA's work and near client equivalents
- Foreseen or intended beneficiaries
- Foreseeable beneficiaries

Primary Beneficiaries and Near Client Equivalents   In 1931 a landmark case in the development of the auditor's liability to third parties (*Ultramares v. Touche*) addressed three important issues:

- Is the auditor generally liable for ordinary negligence to parties with whom there is no contractual relationship?
- Can a special relationship with a third party be so direct that it is almost equivalent to that of a contractual relationship? An auditor is liable for ordinary negligence if there is a contractual relationship.
- Can the auditor's negligence be so gross that it is constructive fraud? An auditor is always liable for committing fraud.

In *Ultramares* the court decided to uphold the doctrine that auditors should not be liable to third parties generally for ordinary negligence. This decision was directed specifically at auditors and others who render professional opinions—at that time the

---

[6]*Reves v. Ernst & Young*, U.S. LEXIS 1940 (1993).

doctrine was *not* being upheld for others, such as automobile manufacturers. The court was careful in drawing a line around those to whom the auditor owes a duty of care rather than simply a duty of honesty:

> If liability for negligence exists, a thoughtless slip or blunder, the failure to detect a theft or forgery beneath the cover of deceptive entries, may expose accountants to a liability in an indeterminate amount for an indeterminate time to an indeterminate class. The hazards of a business conducted on these terms are so extreme as to enkindle doubt whether a flaw may not exist in implication of a duty that exposes to these consequences.[7]

In *Ultramares* the court also suggested that an auditor would be liable to the third party for ordinary negligence if the auditor knew that the audit was being performed for the *primary benefit* of the third party and that third party was specifically identified.

The *Ultramares* case extended the auditor's liability to third parties by holding that negligence can be so gross that it is constructive fraud. In the words of the court:

> Our holding does not emancipate accountants from the consequences of fraud. It does not relieve them if their audit has been so negligent as to justify a finding that they had no genuine belief in its adequacy, for this again is a fraud. It does no more than say that, if less than this is proved, if there has been neither reckless misstatement nor insincere profession of an opinion, but only honest blunder, the ensuing liability for negligence is one that is bounded by contract, and is to be enforced between the parties by whom the contract has been made. We doubt whether the average businessman receiving a certificate without paying for it, and receiving it merely as one among a multitude of possible investors, would look for anything more.[8]

In 1985 another landmark case was decided in the same jurisdiction. In *Credit Alliance v. Arthur Andersen & Co.*, the court upheld the *Ultramares* decision that only third parties that have a relationship so close that it approaches a contractual relationship should be able to hold the auditor liable for ordinary negligence.[9] However, the court established the criteria to determine if that close relationship exists:

- The accountants must have been aware the financial reports were to be used for a particular purpose.
- The accountants must have known a particular third party was going to rely on the reports.
- Some action by the accountants must link them with the third party and demonstrate the accountants knew of this reliance on the reports.

Cases that followed explored the issue of what action was sufficient to link the auditor with the third party. Some courts found linkage in very minor acts, such as mailing a copy of the report, or in one extreme example where no report had even been mailed, the sending of a confirmation to a creditor.

In 1988 there was a landmark case on this issue: *Iselin v. Mann Judd Landau.* The purported "linkage" actions were not obscure. Iselin had been the primary source of

---

[7]*Ultramares Corporation v. Touche*, 255 N.Y. 170, 174, N.E. 441 (1931).
[8]Ibid. "Certificate" was the common term at the time used to describe a standard audit report.
[9]*Credit Alliance Corp. v. Arthur Andersen & Co.*, 65 N.Y. 2d 536, 551, supra (1985).

financing of the company for years. The evidence showed a phone call and a face-to-face meeting to discuss the company's financial condition. The accountants had at least once mailed a report to Iselin. Mann Judd's engagement letter referred to providing the information to "Banks, factors . . . or any other source from whom you would expect to receive credit."

In *Mann Judd Landau*, the court found for the accountant. The court required substantial direct contact clearly relating to the creditor's intended reliance on a specific report for a specific transaction. Although the auditor may have anticipated reliance in some general way, there was no evidence that there was specific intended reliance for the particular loans. The court did not find general discussion with the creditor and general knowledge of the lending relationship sufficient to be linking actions. In the words of the court:

> . . . the single act of sending the Report at an undetermined time for an unknown purpose would not satisfy the burden of coming forth with evidence evincing Mann's understanding of Iselin's reliance.[10]

The report in question was a review report rather than an audit report, but the court's decision on the issue of whether privity existed is relevant to both types of reports.

In 1992 *Credit Alliance* and *Mann Judd Landau* were reaffirmed in *Security Pacific v. Peat Marwick*. A "single unsolicited phone call" by the third party was considered insufficient as a linking action.[11] The court found that the auditor must be aware of a "particular purpose" for the audit engagement and must act to further that purpose. "Multiple direct and substantive communications and personal meetings" were found to be a valid linking action.

This approach is sometimes called "the New York rule." States that use essentially the New York rule include Alabama, Arkansas, Idaho, Illinois, Kansas, Nebraska, New York, Pennsylvania, and Utah.

Foreseen or Intended Beneficiaries   From 1931 until the late 1960s, the *Ultramares* decision remained the common law without serious challenge in any state. Then, in some states, courts began to depart from *Ultramares*. In 1968, a Rhode Island court, in *Rusch Factors v. Levin*, decided against the auditor, holding that "an accountant should be liable in negligence for careless financial representations relied upon by an actually foreseen and limited class of persons."[12] In other words, the third parties may not be specifically identified to the auditor, but their general identity and specific purpose for relying on the financial statements can be foreseen.

This position was endorsed by the American Bar Association, in what is usually referred to as the *ABA Restatement Rule*.[13] In the rule, the ABA commented that one who is under a public duty to give information is liable for losses suffered by any of the class of persons for whose benefit the duty is created, and for any of the transactions in

---

[10]*William Iselin & Company, Inc. v. Mann Judd Landau*, 71 N.Y. 2d 420 (1988).
[11]*Security Pacific Business Credit, Inc. v. Peat Marwick Main & Co.*, 79 N.Y. 2d 695 (1992).
[12]*Rusch Factors, Inc. v. Levin*, 248 F. Supp. 85 (D.R.I. 1968).
[13]American Bar Association, *Restatement 2nd of Torts* (Section 552—Information Negligently Supplied for the Guidance of Others), 1977.

which the information is intended to protect them. The rule also observes that, as a general principle, one who negligently supplies false information "for the guidance of others in their business transactions" is liable for economic losses suffered by the users of the information in justifiable reliance on the information.

The criteria under this approach requires that the loss be suffered:

- By the person or one of a limited number of persons for whose benefit and guidance the auditor intends to supply the information or knows that the recipient intends to supply it
- Through reliance upon it in a transaction that the auditor intends the information to influence or knows that the recipient so intends to influence

Under the ABA Restatement Rule, when an auditor is engaged for no other specific purpose than the annual audit and is not informed of specific uses to be made of the financial statement, there is generally no duty to third parties. The Restatement Rule comments that the number and character of the persons to be reached and influenced and the nature and extent of the transaction for which guidance is furnished may be vitally important. The rule provides examples of this:

- If the auditor is told that the audited financial statements will be used to obtain a $50,000 loan, the auditor may be held liable to the third-party lender even though the lender was not named, or if a different lender than the one named makes the loan.
- If a third party is named and the purpose for reliance on the financial statements is to consider selling goods to the client on credit, the auditor is not liable if the named party uses the financial statements instead to decide to buy a controlling interest in the client's stock.

States that have been using the Restatement Rule include Florida, Georgia, Iowa, Kentucky, Louisiana, Michigan, Minnesota, Missouri, Montana, New Hampshire, North Dakota, Ohio, Rhode Island, Tennessee, Texas, Washington, and West Virginia. Precisely how many states actually endorse the Restatement Rule has been debated, but it is the most commonly used approach of the three, exceeding in frequency both "Foreseeable Beneficiaries" and "Primary Beneficiaries and Near Client Equivalents."

Foreseeable Beneficiaries   In 1983 a New Jersey court in *H. Rosenblum, Inc. v. Adler*[14] extended the auditor's liability further by finding the auditor liable for ordinary professional negligence to any foreseeable relying party. This was a more significant extension of liability than it may seem at first. Before, auditors could defend themselves by proving what they knew and foresaw. This case permits a court or jury to decide, with hindsight, that the auditor should have been able to foresee a transaction, even if the auditor did not do so. Courts have found "foreseeable" users to include all creditors and shareholders, both past and present, and potentially unlimited others. The court found no reason to distinguish accountants from other suppliers of products or services to the

---

[14]*H. Rosenblum, Inc. v. Adler*, 93 N.J. 324, 461 A. 2d (1983).

public and no reason to deny to third-party users of financial statements recovery of losses resulting from negligent misrepresentation.[15] The court stated:

> The auditor's function has expanded from that of a watchdog for management to an independent evaluator of the adequacy and fairness of financial statements issued by management to stockholders, creditors, and others.[16]

The court did restrict the auditor's liability to "all those whom that auditor should reasonably foresee as recipients *from the company* of the statements for its proper business purposes, provided that the recipients rely on the statements pursuant to those business purposes."[17] However, an auditor who delivers his or her report to the client has no control over its distribution and might "foresee" it going to anyone.

This approach was referred to as the "New Jersey rule" and has been used in Mississippi, New Jersey, and Wisconsin. However, in 1995, New Jersey adopted a privity statute. California also adopted it, but in 1992 created a new approach in *Bily v. Arthur Young & Co.*, using the New York rule for some things and the Restatement Rule for others.

The Bily Decision   The new approach divides negligence into separate parts:

- Ordinary professional negligence
- Negligent misrepresentation

The definition of *ordinary negligence* continues to be unintentional "thoughtless slip or blunder." For this, the California court limited the CPA's liability to the client.

The definition of *negligent misrepresentation* is "a separate and distinct tort, a species of the tort of deceit: 'Where the defendant makes false statements, honestly believing that they are true, but without reasonable ground for such belief, they may be liable for negligent misrepresentation, a form of deceit.' "[18] This simply means that the auditor provided inaccurate, misleading, or false information in performing professional services. The court considered negligent misrepresentation a more serious wrong, and stated that CPAs are liable not only to primary beneficiaries, but also to foreseen, intended beneficiaries, as under the Restatement Rule.

Liability to Third Parties—Statutory Law

Under the Securities Act of 1933 ("the Securities Act") and the Securities and Exchange Act of 1934 ("the Exchange Act"), the auditor's liability to third parties was extended, as discussed below.

Suits brought under the federal securities laws are often class action suits. One or a few plaintiffs sue on behalf of a large number of parties who have suffered losses, such as all investors purchasing stock of the company in the years in which the financial statements were materially misstated. The potential liability for claims in class action suits can be many millions of dollars.

[15]Ibid.
[16]Ibid.
[17]Ibid.
[18]*Bily v. Arthur Young & Co.*, 11 Cal. Rptr. 2d 51 (1992).

Initial Public Offerings   The Securities Act requires a registration statement to be filed with the SEC before securities may be sold to the public in an initial offering. The effect of Section 11 of the 1933 Act has been summarized by Levy as follows:

1 Any person acquiring securities described in the Registration Statement may sue the accountant, regardless of the fact that he is not the client of the accountant.
2 His or her claim may be based upon alleged false statements or misleading omissions in the financial statements, which constitutes his or her *prima facie* case. The plaintiff does not have the further burden of proving that the accountants were negligent or fraudulent in certifying to the financial statements involved.
3 The plaintiff does not have to prove that he or she relied upon the statement or that the loss suffered was the proximate result of the falsity or misleading character of the financial statement.
4 The accountant has thrust upon him or her the burden of establishing his or her freedom from negligence and fraud by proving that he or she had, after reasonable investigation, reasonable grounds to believe and did believe that the financial statements certified were true not only as of the date of the financial statements, but beyond that, as of the time when the Registration Statement became effective.
5 The accountant has the burden of establishing by way of defense or in reduction of alleged damages that the loss of the plaintiff resulted in whole or in part from causes other than the false statements or the misleading omissions in the financial statements. Under the common law it would have been part of the plaintiff's affirmative case to prove that the damages which he or she claims were sustained were proximately caused by the negligence or fraud of the accountant.[19]

In essence, the Securities Act shifts the burden of proof from the plaintiff to the defendant and raises the standard of care which the auditor owes certain third parties (purchasers of securities) for reports included in registration statements for original sales of securities. There are some limits on the accountant's liability under Section 11. First, it is limited to situations in which the accountant prepares or "certifies" (audits and expresses an opinion on) a portion of the registration statement and is accordingly aware that it is part of a communication to the public. Second, liability is limited to third parties who actually purchased the securities. And third, damages are limited to the out-of-pocket losses.

Ongoing Reporting   The Exchange Act, which concerns the ongoing filing of annual reports with SEC, does not expose auditors to a liability significantly different from the common law. In contrast to Section 11 of the 1933 Act, Section 18 of the 1934 Act:

1 Has no provision for extending liability to an "effective date"
2 Requires the plaintiff to prove that he or she relied on the financial statements and

---

[19]Saul Levy, "Liability to Third Parties—by Statute," in Robert L. Kane, Jr. (ed.), *CPA Handbook* (New York: AICPA, 1952), p. 39.

that such reliance was the cause of damages (this concept is called *proximate cause*)

3 Does not require the auditor to prove absence of negligence, but merely requires the auditor to prove that he or she acted in good faith and had no knowledge that the statements were false or misleading

However, Section 10(b) and Rule 10b-5 of the Exchange Act are sufficiently broad to serve as a basis of action against auditors, although auditors are not specifically mentioned in the section or rule. Clause (b) of the rule requires a plaintiff to establish that "any person" has made "any untrue statements of material fact" or has omitted "to state a material fact necessary to make the statements made, in light of the circumstances under which they were made, not misleading." Federal jurisdiction under the rule is supported by the use of the facilities of interstate commerce or the mails.

In *Drake v. Thor Power Company*,[20] a federal district court determined that auditors could be liable under Rule 10b-5 if they were negligent in expressing an opinion on financial statements. Rule 10b-5 was promulgated in 1942 for the specific purpose of allowing the SEC to reach corporate officers who committed fraud in the *purchase* of securities. The securities acts were aimed at fraud in the *sale* of securities. However, decisions such as *Drake v. Thor Power* indicated that the rule could be used by private plaintiffs to reach experts that were not a party to securities transactions. Thus, Rule 10b-5 loomed as a potential federal negligence statute that might obliterate the common law restraints on liability to third parties.

In 1976, however, the Supreme Court of the United States, in the *Ernst & Ernst v. Hochfelder* decision, rejected negligence as the measure of an auditor's culpability under Role 10b-5, writing:

> When a statute speaks so specifically in terms of manipulation and deception, and of implementing devices and contrivances—the commonly understood terminology of intentional wrongdoing—and when its history reflects no more expansive intent, we are quite unwilling to extend the scope of the statute to negligent conduct.[21]

A private plaintiff must now show an auditor's intent to deceive, manipulate, or defraud (this state of mind is called *scienter*). As a result, third-party negligence suits against auditors are brought as state civil actions rather than as federal statutory actions.

In summary, the plaintiff in a civil action under Rule 10b-5 now needs to prove the following:

- The CPA made one or more false representations.
- The plaintiff relied on the CPA's representations.
- The auditor knew or should have known that the representations made were false (scienter).
- The plaintiff's damages were proximately caused by the CPA's representations.

---

[20]*Drake v. Thor Power Company*, 282 F. Supp. 94 (N.D. Ill. 1967).
[21]*Ernst & Ernst v. Hochfelder*, 425 U.S. 185 (1976).

SEC Sanctions In addition to civil liability under the federal securities laws discussed above, which may be used by the SEC or private parties, the SEC has other disciplinary actions available to it: injunctive proceedings, administrative proceedings, and criminal penalties.

In *injunctive proceedings*, the auditor or firm is "enjoined" to restrain future violations of the federal securities laws. This may sound insignificant—merely promising not to break the law in the future, and perhaps improving quality assurance procedures in the firm. However, injunctions are tried without a jury, and the outcome depends on the decision of the trial judge. Once the judge grants an injunction, the plaintiffs in both civil and criminal suits can use that fact to support their claims.

Administrative proceedings are also called disciplinary actions under Rule 2(e) of the SEC's Rules of Practice. Rule 2(e) states that the SEC

> may deny, temporarily or permanently, the privilege of appearing or practicing before it in any way to any person who is found ... (i) not to possess the requisite qualifications to represent others, (ii) to be lacking in character or integrity or have engaged in unethical or improper professional conduct, or (iii) to have willfully violated or willfully aided and abetted the violation of the federal securities laws ... or the rules and regulations thereunder.

The SEC presents its allegations publicly in *Accounting and Auditing Enforcement Releases.* (These were formerly called Accounting Series Releases.) The suspension of practice before the SEC is often temporary (such as being prohibited from new engagements resulting in filings with the SEC for 60 days) and might involve agreements with the firms to institute improvements in their quality assurance programs, continuing education programs, firm audit approaches, etc. In most administrative proceedings, the audit firm or individual CPA agrees to a consent decree, without admitting or denying guilt. An administrative proceeding may result from ordinary negligence.

CRIMINAL LIABILITY

In most instances when CPAs have been convicted of crimes, these convictions have resulted from acts that are unrelated to independent auditing and that are popularly thought of as criminal conduct. For example, CPAs have been found guilty of bribing tax agents or filing false tax returns for clients. However, in some cases, CPAs have faced the threat of criminal action for audit failures when they were not alleged to have benefited directly from their wrongdoing.

Several auditors have now been convicted of willfully expressing unqualified opinions on financial statements that they knew, or should have known, were false in material respects. Failure to comply with professional standards was part of the evidence of the required "knowledge and willfulness" needed for a conviction. The alleged motivation for this conduct was a desire to avoid exposure of inadequacies in past audits. In these cases, the distinction between criminal and civil liability seems to rest entirely on a jury's assessment of the good faith of auditors in fulfilling their duties. Criminal actions of this type are usually based on alleged violations of state or federal statutes that prohibit fraudulent or false financial statements.

NOTED LEGAL CASES

For several decades a student of the independent auditor's legal liability could study a relatively small number of cases and be conversant with the subject. Then within the past 25 years, there have been literally hundreds of lawsuits against auditors.

This wealth of information is fertile ground for the study of both legal and professional issues. Sophisticated legal theories have developed concerning who should be able to bring suit and under what conditions. Comparisons can be made to developing law in other areas, such as what constitutes professional malpractice by doctors or lawyers. Lawsuits also direct attention to the technical accounting or auditing deficiencies alleged and their implications for presenting financial statements or conducting audits and other professional work. A hybrid subject for study is the interplay between professional standards and legal responsibilities. Legal decisions often lead to the modification of professional standards, and professional standards are interpreted by courts in evaluating the conduct of CPAs.

Comprehensive coverage of all the important cases regarding auditor liability would require a separate book. However, the following are a group of noted cases that auditors should be familiar with, each presented with a brief explanation of the issues involved.

Bar Chris[22]

This was the first important case decided under Section 11 of the 1933 Act. The decision, issued in 1968, held that independent auditors did not prove their due diligence in the audit of the financial statements of Bar Chris Construction Corporation. Bar Chris constructed and then sold or leased bowling alleys. Financing their operations was a continual problem for Bar Chris, and when the bowling industry slumped, Bar Chris defaulted on its debentures. It was found that current assets were materially overstated and current liabilities were materially understated.

The auditors were charged with failing to perform both an adequate audit of the annual financial statements and an adequate review, called an S-1 review, of the developments between the audit date and the effective date of the registration statement for the debentures.

In finding the auditors liable, the court observed: "Accountants should not be held to a standard higher than that recognized in their profession. I do not do so here." However, the CPA firm's program for an S-1 review went beyond professional standards and their performance was evaluated as lacking due diligence because they failed to follow their own program.

---

[22]*Escott v. Bar Chirs Construction Corp.*, 283 F. Supp. 643 (S.D. N.Y. 1968).

Yale Express

In this case, decided in 1967, the auditors of Yale Express Systems, Inc., during the course of a special accounting engagement unrelated to the audit of annual statements discovered material errors in the financial statements of the past year. However, the auditors did not disclose their findings for several months.

In denying the auditors' motion to dismiss the case, the court held that auditors could be held liable to third parties for failure to disclose the information they subsequently discovered that revealed the financial statements on which they had expressed an opinion were misleading.

The Auditing Standards Executive Committee, a predecessor of the Auditing Standards Board, then issued a statement on subsequent discovery of facts, now AU 561 which specifies the auditor's responsibilities in such circumstances.

Continental Vending

In 1969 two partners and a senior associate of a large public accounting firm were convicted of a criminal violation of the Exchange Act for expressing an opinion on misleading financial statements.

The president of Continental caused it to make loans to an unaudited affiliated company he controlled. The affiliate in turn loaned him the money, which he used for personal stock dealings. The financial statements disclosed the loan to the affiliate but did not disclose the affiliate's related loans to the president nor the fact that the collateral the president posted to secure the loan, at the auditor's insistence, was composed primarily of Continental stock.

Shortly after the lawsuit was started, the Auditing Standards Executive Committee began a study of the subject of detecting and disclosing material transactions with related parties. SAS No. 6, now AU 334, was issued several years later. However, the case is most noted for the judge's rejection of adherence to generally accepted accounting principles as a sufficient measure of an auditor's good faith.

When the case was decided, the standards for disclosure of related-party transactions were vague and ill-defined. The fact that no pronouncement specifically required disclosure of the details of the transactions among Continental, its president, and its affiliate did not relieve the auditors of their duty to insist on adequate disclosure. In particular, the auditors could not close their eyes to the fact that the net effect of the transactions was a looting of Continental for the president's personal benefit.

U.S. Financial

This case led to a large national CPA firm's undergoing a mandatory review of its quality controls by an outside group. The details of the case are reported in Accounting Series Release No. 153. The firm consented to review as part of an agreement reached with the SEC resulting from a disciplinary proceeding under Rule 2(e) of the SEC's rules of practice. The mandatory peer review is one of a number of innovative administrative sanctions the SEC has achieved using its authority over experts practicing before it.

The CPA firm was charged with failing to obtain sufficient evidential matter for several material real estate sales of U.S. Financial. The circumstances surrounding the sales and management's involvement in them called for greater professional skepticism.

This case gave impetus to the development of SAS No. 6, now AU 334, on related-party transactions, which was in process at the time and also caused the issuance of SAS No. 7, now AU 315, on communications between auditors when there has been a change in auditors. ASR No. 153 noted that the predecessor firm failed to communicate its doubts about the integrity of U.S. Financial's management. Communication with a predecessor before accepting an engagement is now a necessary auditing procedure.

National Student Marketing

A substantial amount of the revenue of National Student Marketing Corporation was derived from the sale of "fixed-fee" advertising programs, for example, a direct mailing to a specified number of addresses for a specified fee. The SEC contended that a large national CPA firm permitted recognition of income on the sales of such programs on a percentage-of-completion basis when none of the criteria for income recognition under that method had been met. It was alleged that the CPA firm relied solely on management's representations on the amount of work completed. The SEC also charged the firm with failure to disclose knowledge of deficiencies in unaudited interim information in a proxy statement used in connection with a merger agreement.

The details of the cases are reported in Accounting Series Release No. 173 along with information on four other cases involving the same CPA firm. One of the sanctions obtained was a mandatory peer review. The SEC required the review so that it could assess implementation of various quality control procedures that seemed to be lacking in the five cases involved.

1136 Tenants Corporation[23]

In contrast with many other noted cases, this one involved a small CPA firm that was engaged in providing an accounting service rather than an audit. A local CPA firm was charged with failure to detect the defalcations of the managing agent of an incorporated apartment cooperative. The CPA firm believed the engagement was simply to "write up" the accounting records and prepare unaudited financial statements. However, the scope of the engagement was an issue at trial. The CPA did not have an engagement letter with the client specifying the scope of services he was to provide, and his report was not a clear disclaimer of opinion. The case emphasizes the importance of an engagement letter and the need to exercise care both during an engagement and in writing a report.

Equity Funding

For 10 years, Equity Funding produced continued high earnings growth, but in early 1973 it was exposed as a gigantic fraud. Equity Funding described itself as an insurance

[23] *1136 Tenants Corp. v. Max Rothenberg & Co.,* (36 A. 2d 30 N.Y. 2d 804), 319 N.Y.S. 2d 1007 (1971).

company that specialized in funding programs. The funding programs involved sale of mutual fund shares that a customer pledged as collateral for a loan to pay premiums on life insurance. Several top officers, including the president, directed a scheme of falsifying accounting records and creating phony insurance policies to give a picture of spectacular earnings. To keep the fraud concealed they forged many documents, recorded fictitious assets, and incurred unrecorded liabilities.

Early publicity surrounding the fraud based on limited information led to speculation about its nature and causes. It was variously described as a sophisticated computer fraud, a complex insurance fraud, and a clever deception of independent auditors and regulators. However, the information produced by the investigation for the report of the bankruptcy trustee and related litigation showed it was none of these things.

Fictitious revenue was recorded manually in large, late entries without documentation. The computer was used to create some documentation, but its use was peripheral and the computer department was not involved. The three auditors from a small local firm who had audited Equity Funding for years were convicted of knowing complicity in the fraud. They were charged with disregarding accepted accounting principles and auditing standards, closing their eyes to wrongdoing, and candidly discussing false accounting entries with the perpetrators. Thus, the Equity Funding fraud has few, if any, implications for the conduct of audits, the effectiveness of auditing procedures, or the development of auditing standards. However, the small local firm, immediately before exposure of the fraud, had merged with a large national firm, and another large national firm was involved in the audit of subsidiaries. Implications do exist, therefore, for the obligations of large national firms merging with or relying on the work of smaller, lesser known firms. These relational aspects have always been troublesome for the profession and their resolution depends on social and political, rather than technical, considerations.

Fund of Funds[24]

In the late 1970s, Fund of Funds, a mutual investment company specializing in buying other mutual funds, decided to diversify and acquire oil and gas properties. Under an agreement with King Resources Company, Fund of Funds paid approximately $90 million for over 400 oil and gas properties. The agreement specified that the properties were to be sold at prices no less favorable to Fund of Funds than King Resources ordinarily received.

The same CPA firm audited both companies. During the audit of King Resources, the CPA firm learned that profits on the sales to Fund of Funds were considerably higher than for similar sales to King Resources' other customers. This information was kept confidential by the CPA firm and not disclosed to Fund of Funds' management. Considerably later, when Fund of Funds' management learned about the price discrepancies, an action was brought against the CPA firm claiming it had a duty to disclose the information about the violation of the agreement or withdraw from one of the audit engagements. The CPA firm cited the rule of conduct on confidentiality, but the court awarded damages of $80 million to Fund of Funds shareholders.

[24]*Fund of Funds, Ltd. v. Arthur Andersen & Co.,* 545 F. Supp. 1314 (S.D. N.Y. 1982).

Credit Alliance Corporation

As discussed earlier, the New York State Court of Appeals in 1985 upheld the basic tenets of the *Ultramares* decision disallowing a negligence action against an independent auditor brought by a plaintiff having no contractual relationship with the auditor.

Credit Alliance, the plaintiff, is a financial service company engaged primarily in financing the purchase of capital equipment through installment sales or leasing agreements. Credit Alliance provided financing to L. B. Smith of Virginia and required audited financial statements. Approximately 2 years later, Smith defaulted on several million dollars of obligations to Credit Alliance.

Credit Alliance brought suit for damages against the CPA firm that audited Smith's financial statement claiming negligence and fraud. The CPA firm moved to dismiss the complaint, but a trial court denied the motion. On appeal of the motion, the appellate division affirmed the denial, holding that the absence of a contractual relationship between the parties did not bar an action by a limited class whose reliance on the financial statements should have been specifically foreseen by the CPA firm.

The Court of Appeals reversed the appellate division and took the opportunity to reexamine and delineate the principles enunciated in *Ultramares* and related cases. It reaffirmed the basic rationale of *Ultramares* and specified the prerequisites discussed earlier in this chapter before an independent auditor may be held liable in negligence to noncontractual parties who relied on audited financial statements to their detriment.

Mann Judd Landau

In 1988, this case, as mentioned earlier, clarified the three conditions for third-party negligence suits as established by the *Credit Alliance* case. The case is also significant because the decision recognizes that a review engagement is not an audit engagement and an accountant performing a review is not held to the same standards as an audit.

William Iselin & Co. had been the major creditor of Suits Galore since the company was established. The CPA firm, Mann Judd Landau, issued a review report on Suits Galore's financial statements as of May 31, 1983. Suits Galore filed bankruptcy 6 months after the report was released. Iselin sued for simple negligence. (Causes of action for gross negligence and fraud were dismissed.)

The court decided that general discussions with Iselin, the act of sending a report to them at Suits Galore's request, and general knowledge that the review report might be used to obtain credit were not enough to provide the direct linkage required under the *Credit Alliance* criteria.

Iselin alleged negligence for such matters as errors in inventory valuation and failure to note in bank reconciliations that checks had been written to a jewelry store. However, Statements on Standards for Accounting and Review Services do not require tests of inventory valuation or bank reconciliations. The court found that accountants issuing review reports are not held to generally accepted auditing standards. They are held to review standards as set forth in the Statements on Standards for Accounting and Review Services. In the words of the court:

> . . . we note that a review report is not to be equated with the traditional certified audit.
> . . . The accountant's review is not performed under GAAS; no physical inventory is taken;

the review consists principally of inquiries of the client's management and analysis of financial information supplied by the client. The report offers only the limited assurance that the accountant is not aware of any material modifications that should be made to the client's financial statements in order for them to conform with GAAP.

ESM

ESM was a government securities dealer. It loaned money to savings and loan associations and received more than the loan amounts in municipal securities as collateral, which is a common practice. It also borrowed money from municipalities, using as collateral the municipal securities from the savings and loans. It did this by dealing in "repurchase and reverse repurchase agreements." It paid higher interest rates for its borrowings if the municipalities agreed to let it hold the collateral securities.

The problem was that ESM used the same collateral over and over, thus borrowing far more than the collateral it had. If no fraud had existed, the financial statements would have shown an approximately equal amount of borrowing and lending. ESM made the financial statements look proper by borrowing from municipalities and "lending" to affiliates. The fraudulent "loans" to unaudited affiliates were uncollectible. Eventually in 1979, a partner at the firm that audited ESM started to ask some questions indicating he was getting suspicious. He was a new partner, one of the youngest people ever to be made partner in the firm, although he had been the audit manager on the engagement for years. Two ESM officers told him about the scheme, indicating he better go along with it or his new partnership would be in jeopardy, and assuring him that EMS's investments would make up the losses in the future. The fraud continued. In 1980, the audit partner accepted $200,000—a loan that was not to be repaid.

In 1985 ESM collapsed. The lending municipalities lost nearly all the money they had loaned ESM. The borrowing savings and loans lost because the value of the collateral they had provided was much higher than the amounts they borrowed. Investors lost $320 million. One of the savings and loans, Home State of Ohio, lost so much that it failed. The state insurance fund of Ohio went bankrupt bailing it out. Depositors began a run on the Ohio thrifts, and 71 state-chartered savings and loans were temporarily closed (a new insurance fund was authorized by the Ohio legislature and the thrifts were required to obtain federal insurance). *The Wall Street Journal* blamed the EMS fraud for a brief decline in the dollar on the international markets. The audit partner was convicted and went to jail for 4 years. The audit firm settled ($80 million) with some plaintiffs and paid substantial sums under court decisions ($36 million).

Bily

The effects of the Bily decision on auditor's liability common law were discussed above. Osborne Computer Corporation was the maker of the first successful portable personal computers. Osborne sales skyrocketed, and underwriters had intense interest in a public offering. Within a year of the first shipments, sales had reached $10 million per month. The plaintiffs in the case were the sophisticated venture capitalists who acquired warrants to purchase Osborne stock from the company's founder, Adam Osborne. Soon after the warrant transaction, Osborne sales declined sharply because of manufacturing problems with a new model. Then IBM came out with its personal computer and software, and other competitors appeared. The public offering was never made, and the company filed for bankruptcy.

The plaintiffs charged that the audit report failed to disclose deficiencies in accounting controls and did not disclose a $3 million loss on revenue of over $68 million. (The financial statements showed a net operating profit of $69,000.) The plaintiffs claimed reliance on the audit report to make their investment decision. The California Supreme Court judgment was in favor of the auditors for the general negligence verdict, setting aside the jury verdict. A lower court jury rejected Bily's cause of action for negligent misrepresentation.

Crazy Eddie

"Crazy" Eddie Antar changed the way electronics are sold. He was known for "His Prices Are Insane" commercials, and his chain of discount electronics stores grew rapidly. It was a family-run business, and he made a fortune when the company went public. However, Eddie made sure he made more than he should have by "improving" the financial statements—by inflating inventory between $30 and $60 million, by artificially increasing store revenue deposits with funds skimmed from operations, and by understating accounts payable by recording $40 million in false debit memos.

Unfortunately, auditors were not the heroes of this story. They test-counted inventory, accompanied by Crazy Eddie personnel. Crazy Eddie then inflated the amounts for batches of inventory that the auditors had not selected for testing. They audited the $90 million in accounts payable credits—but not the $40 million in offsetting debits. They also did not pick up on the scheme to improve store revenue statistics.

The fraud was discovered because Crazy Eddie was a family business, and uncles, brothers-in-law, etc., were in on the fraud. When Eddie Antar's affair with another woman was leaked to his wife by a trusted family member, the hard feelings grew until they reached a point where the scheme fell apart.

Eddie fled the country, was extradited and returned, and was convicted on criminal charges of securities fraud. Other family members active in the fraud testified against him, and some also received jail sentences. The auditors settled out of court.

SELF-PROTECTION AGAINST LIABILITY

To protect against the risk inherent in the practice of public accounting, an auditor should secure liability insurance. If a CPA firm incorporates, the Board of Directors and the Council of the AICPA recommend that the firm acquire liability insurance or capitalization in the amount of $50,000 per shareholder and professional employee up to a maximum of $2 million. Insurance provides a CPA with reimbursement for direct monetary losses arising from claims and the costs of legal defense.

In addition to insurance, protection against claims brought by clients is provided by engagement letters which explicitly state the scope and responsibilities assumed by the auditor. A CPA can also reduce the risks of practice by adopting adequate policies and procedures for controlling the quality of audits, as discussed earlier. Particularly important are policies and procedures for the acceptance and continuance of clients. Client acceptance and engagement letters are discussed further in Chapter 5.

TORT REFORM

As discussed above, there has been a growing trend to sue CPAs. The AICPA's nation-wide survey in 1992 of approximately 5,000 firms indicated that the median claim in legal actions against CPA firms was $155,000. Thirty percent of the firms reported claims exceeding $1 million; the median fee for the professional service underlying a claim was $5,000. This trend is increasing audit costs, and some accountants suggest it might be damaging the profession's ability to attract highly qualified people. Some firms are refusing to audit start-up companies or entities in higher-risk industries, such as savings and loans. In 1992 the AICPA reported that 56 percent of small accounting firms were limiting the industries they served and avoiding banks, insurance companies, and credit unions, believing that the fees do not compensate for the risks of doing audits in those industries.

The AICPA and groups of firms are banding together to try to persuade legislators to change the liability system. One problem is restrictions on the form of organization of firms. Every partner may be held liable to the full extent of his or her personal assets for the actions of others working in that firm. Elimination of these restrictions is one of the main reforms sought.

Another problem is the relationship between liability and fault. The client is responsible for financial statements. The client disseminates the audit report, and enters into transactions. An audit report is only one source of information in investment and credit decisions. Nevertheless, under the doctrine of joint and several liability followed in many jurisdictions, a defendant found responsible for any portion of the fault can be held liable for the full amount of damages.

Accountants are encouraging legislation that increases the number of jurisdictions permitting the comparative negligence defense. For example, in 1992 the Illinois legislature passed a law that limits joint liability in negligence cases where the CPA is found to be less than 25 percent responsible for the total damages suffered by a plaintiff, and bars any recovery by a plaintiff who is more than 50 percent responsible for the total damages.

FORENSIC ACCOUNTING

The definition of *forensic* is "belonging or having application to courts of justice." The CPA helps establish the financial facts: what has happened, what exists, what took place, and what claims are in existence.

In some cases, forensic accounting work can be analogous to detective work or to a coroner's performance of an autopsy, but relating to accounting records and work papers. For example, how did an embezzlement scheme work and what were the weaknesses in the internal control structure that permitted it? How much was stolen? What is the amount of the damage from a breach of contract? Why did the auditor not note that material amounts of expenses were being fraudulently capitalized as fixed assets to inflate net earnings? How did the auditor miss large long-term liabilities not included in the balance sheet?

Other forensic accounting tasks relate to gathering and preparing the information needed in legal cases, such as preparing a projection of lost royalties resulting from a patent infringement, or preparing financial statements for a bankruptcy trustee. The CPA may also perform an accounting function in a legal matter, for example, in disbursing class action awards to many recipients.

Damage quantification matters arise from a variety of cases. An embezzlement case may find the CPA determining how much cash, inventory, etc., is missing. An antitrust violation or trademark infringement case may find the CPA using regression analysis and other statistical techniques to determine what the revenues would have been if the unfair practice had not occurred. Insurance companies often require quantification of economic losses, especially in business interruption cases. Investigation of false claims may require the analysis of cost of goods sold, allocation of labor and overhead, etc.

Bankruptcy cases typically include preparing financial statements for the trustee, and often require investigative work. Has fraudulent conveyance of assets occurred prior to or during the bankruptcy? That is, have assets been siphoned off? The CPA may also search for undervalued assets, or overstated or fictitious claims.

Business valuation arises in the sale of a business, the settlement of an estate, or a divorce action. The valuation may be based on anticipated earnings. Have past earnings been overstated? The tax considerations of a purchase payment agreement need to be addressed. The specifics of the accounting for postsale earnings need to be defined if additional payments are based on future earnings. The CPA can also explain the effect on the financial statements that a merger or acquisition will have.

The CPA is often called to testify in tax cases. The CPA is an expert in the field and testifies as to the taxability of income, the deductibility of expenses, the calculation of basis, or the suitability of a transaction for the tax treatment used.

Criminal matters may include such procedures as tracing laundered funds to their source or embezzled funds to their ultimate use, and often include an assessment of an entity's internal control structure as well as a damage assessment.

CPAs are sometimes used to assist in divorce cases, especially where there is a lack of cooperation in obtaining financial information and/or a possibility of hidden assets. The CPA may help determine available funds, locate assets, and trace the sources and disposition of earnings during the marriage.

In accountant liability cases, a CPA may be called upon to assist either the plaintiff or the defendant. The CPA may serve as an investigator and/or as an expert witness, providing his or her opinion in court on accounting, auditing, tax, and other business matters.

CHAPTER 3 ASSIGNMENTS

OBJECTIVE QUESTIONS

3-1 For each of the following statements, indicate whether the statement is true or false.
T   F   a The concept "privity," as it relates to the audit relationship, means that the inde-

pendent CPA must not arbitrarily disclose confidential information about the client to others.

T   F   b In civil actions under common law, the independent CPA is liable to third parties for ordinary negligence.

T   F   c In criminal actions, the independent CPA is liable to third parties for both ordinary and gross negligence.

T   F   d For privity to apply, a contract must be signed by both parties.

T   F   e Under the ABA Restatement Rule, the independent CPA would be liable for ordinary negligence to foreseen or intended beneficiaries.

T   F   f Under the *Mann Judd Landau* decision, the single act of mailing a report to a creditor establishes that the auditor knew of the creditor's reliance on the report.

T   F   g The auditor's liability to third parties under common law can be determined only by reference to recent decisions within the particular state where a case is litigated.

T   F   h The CPA's liability for ordinary negligence under statutory law differs depending on whether the audit report was included in a registration statement for an initial public offering or in a Form 10-K filed annually.

T   F   i "Forensic" means "belonging or having application to courts of justice."

T   F   j Under the "New York rule," the independent CPA is liable for ordinary negligence to foreseeable third parties.

T   F   k For the accountant to be liable to the client for ordinary negligence, the plaintiff must prove the alleged malpractice was a willful or reckless act.

3-2 The following questions relate to the accountant's liability. Select the *best* response.

a DMO Enterprises, Inc., engaged the accounting firm of Martin, Seals & Anderson to perform its annual audit. The firm performed the audit in a competent, nonnegligent manner and billed DMO for $16,000, the agreed fee. Shortly after delivery of the audited financial statements, Hightower, the assistant controller, disappeared, taking with him $28,000 of DMO's funds. It was then discovered that Hightower had been engaged in a highly sophisticated, novel defalcation scheme during the past year. He had previously embezzled $35,000 of DMO funds. DMO has refused to pay the accounting firm's fee and is seeking to recover the $63,000 that was stolen by Hightower. Which of the following is correct?

1 The accountants *cannot* recover their fee and are liable for $63,000.

2 The accountants are entitled to collect their fee and are *not* liable for $63,000.

3 DMO is entitled to rescind the audit contract and thus is *not* liable for the $16,000 fee, but it *cannot* recover damages.

4 DMO is entitled to recover the $28,000 defalcation, and is *not* liable for the $16,000 fee.

b If a CPA firm is being sued for common law fraud by a third party based upon materially false financial statements, which of the following is the best defense which the accountants could assert?

1 Lack of a contractual relationship

2 Lack of reliance

3 A disclaimer contained in the engagement letter

4 Comparative negligence on the part of the client

c Lewis & Clark, CPAs, rendered an unqualified opinion on the financial statements of a company that sold common stock in a public offering subject to the Securities Act of 1933. Based on a false statement in the financial statements, Lewis & Clark are being sued by an investor who purchased shares of this public offering. Which of the following represents a viable defense?

1 The investor has *not* met the burden of proving fraud or negligence by Lewis & Clark.

2 The investor did *not* actually rely upon the false statement.

3 Detection of the false statement by Lewis & Clark occurred after the audit report date.

4 The false statement is immaterial in the overall context of the company's financial statements.

d Gibson is suing Simpson & Sloan, CPAs, to recover losses incurred in connection with Gibson's transactions in Zebra Corporation securities. Zebra's Annual Form 10-K Report contained false and misleading statements in the financial statements audited by Simpson & Sloan. To recover under the Securities and Exchange Act of 1934, Gibson must, among other things, establish the following:

1 All of his past transactions in Zebra securities, both before and after the auditor's report date, resulted in a net loss.

2 The transaction in Zebra securities that resulted in a loss occurred within 90 days of the auditor's report date.

3 He relied upon the financial statements in his decision to purchase or sell Zebra securities.

4 The market price of the stock dropped significantly after corrected financial statements were issued by Zebra.

e Donalds & Company, CPAs, audited the financial statements included in the annual report by Markum Securities, Inc., to the Securities and Exchange Commission. The audit was improper in several respects. Markum is now insolvent and unable to satisfy the claims of its customers. The creditors have instituted legal action against Donalds based upon Section 10(b) and Rule 10b-5 of the Securities Exchange Act of 1934. Which of the following is likely to be Donalds' best defense?

1 They did *not* intentionally certify false financial statements.

2 Section 10(b) does *not* apply to them.

3 They were *not* in a contractual relationship with the creditors.

4 Their engagement letter specifically disclaimed any liability to any party which resulted from Markum's fraudulent conduct.

f The scope and nature of an auditor's contractual obligation to a client ordinarily is set forth in the:

1 Management letter

2 Scope paragraph of the auditor's report

3 Engagement letter

4 Introductory paragraph of the auditor's report

g An auditor's document includes the following statement:

"Our audit is subject to the risk that errors, irregularities, or illegal acts, including fraud or defalcations, if they exist, will not be detected. However, we will inform you of any such matters that come to our attention."

The above message is most likely from:

1 The explanatory paragraph of a "subject to" qualified auditor's report

2 An engagement letter

3 The explanatory paragraph of a compliance report on a governmental entity subject to GAO standards

4 A comfort letter

AICPA

DISCUSSION QUESTIONS

3-3 You inquired about a well-publicized auditor liability case that was just decided. The attorney told you: The relationship to the auditor defendant was not close enough for privity to exist. The court decided that the plaintiff had not shown proximate cause and, further, that scienter was not present.

a What is privity? Proximate cause? Scienter?

b What is the effect of each on the auditor's liability?

c Was the auditor found liable for damages?

d What are the considerations about showing proximate cause and the presence of scienter if a relationship that approaches privity exists?

3-4 Raymond was annoyed. "I don't understand these audit firms. They get paid to guarantee the accuracy of the financial statements and then complain when they have to pay up if the statements are wrong. If they checked everything properly, the numbers would be right. If they had a concern about the company's financial health, they shouldn't have given the company their stamp of approval. Plus, the attorney says I shouldn't bother to sue because I never saw a copy of the financial statements before I bought the stock. So what! The broker recommended it and I'll bet he looked at the financial statements, or his research department did. He said the stock had been stalled for a year at about 40, but that he expected the stock to skyrocket to 200 in 6 months. It went down to 5! I lost money because they relied on the faulty financial statements. The audit firm should pay!"

Required: Discuss Raymond's arguments, identifying weak points, if any, and contrast his position with the federal Securities Act.

3-5 a What is the legal relationship of an independent accountant (auditor) to a client? Explain.

b What is the legal duty of skill and care that the accountant-client relationship imposes upon the accountant? Explain.

c Compare the accountant's common law liability to clients and third parties for actual fraud committed by the accountant with the accountant's liability to them for ordinary negligence. Explain.

d In addition to the civil liability imposed upon the accountant, certain federal statutes impose criminal liability on those preparing financial statements. List three well-known statutes which have so imposed liability and with which accountants are frequently concerned.

e 1 What is meant by privileged communication? Explain.

2 Does the common law recognize the existence of a privilege insofar as the accountant-client relationship is concerned? Explain.

3 Assuming that the accountant-client relationship is privileged, who has the right to waive the privilege? Explain.

AICPA

3-6 Williams, a CPA, was engaged by Jackson Financial Development Company to audit the financial statements of Apex Construction Company, a small closely held corporation. Williams was told when he was engaged that Jackson Financial needed reliable financial statements which would be used to determine whether or not to purchase a substantial amount of Apex Construction's convertible debentures at the price asked by the estate of one of Apex's former directors.

Williams performed his audit in a negligent manner. As a result of his negligence he failed to discover substantial defalcations by Brown, the Apex controller. Jackson

Financial purchased the debentures but would not have if the defalcations had been discovered. After discovery of the fraud, Jackson Financial promptly sold the debentures for the highest price offered in the market at a $70,000 loss.

a What liability does Williams have to Jackson Financial? Explain.

b If Apex Construction also sues Williams for negligence, what are the probable legal defenses which Williams' attorney would raise? Explain.

c Will the negligence of a CPA as described above prevent him or her from recovering on a liability insurance policy covering the practice of his or her profession? Explain.

AICPA adapted

3-7 Factory Discount Prices Inc., was a chain store discount outlet that sold women's clothes. It had an excessively large inventory on hand and was in urgent need of additional cash. It was bordering on bankruptcy, especially if the inventory had to be liquidated by sale to other stores instead of the public. Furthermore, about 15 percent of the inventory was not resaleable except at a drastic discount below cost. Faced with this financial crisis, Factory approached several of the manufacturers from whom it purchased. Dexter Apparel, Inc., one of the parties approached, indicated a willingness to loan Factory $300,000 under certain conditions. First, Factory was to submit audited financial statements for the express purpose of providing the correct financial condition of the company. The loan was to be predicated upon these financial statements and Factory's engagement letter with Dunn & Clark, its CPAs, expressly indicated this.

The second condition insisted upon by Dexter was that it obtain a secured position in all unsecured inventory, accounts, and other related personal property. In due course a security agreement was executed and a financing statement properly filed and recorded.

In preparing the financial statements, Factory valued the inventory at cost which was approximately $100,000 over the current fair market value. Also, Factory failed to disclose two secured creditors to whom substantial amounts were owed and who took priority over Dexter's security interests.

Dunn & Clark issued an unqualified opinion on the financial statements of Factory which they believed were fairly presented.

Six months later Factory filed a voluntary bankruptcy petition. Dexter received $125,000 as its share of the bankrupt's estate. It sued Dunn & Clark for the loss of $175,000. Dunn & Clark deny liability based upon lack of a contractual relationship and lack of negligence.

Required: Answer the following, setting forth reasons for any conclusions stated: Is Dexter entitled to recover its loss from Dunn & Clark?

AICPA adapted

3-8 Smith, CPA, is the auditor for Juniper Manufacturing Corporation, a privately owned company which has a June 30 fiscal year. Juniper arranged for a substantial bank loan which was dependent upon the bank receiving, by September 30, audited financial statements which showed a current ratio of at least 2 to 1. On September 25, just before the audit report was to be issued, Smith received an anonymous letter on Juniper's stationery indicating that a 5-year lease by Juniper, as lessee, of a factory building which was accounted for in the financial statements as an operating lease was in fact a capital lease. The letter stated that there was a secret written agreement with the lessor modifying the lease and creating a capital lease.

Smith confronted the president of Juniper who admitted that a secret agreement existed but said it was necessary to treat the lease as an operating lease to meet the current ratio requirement of the pending loan and that nobody would ever discover the secret agreement with the lessor. The president said that if Smith did not issue her report by September 30, Juniper would sue Smith for substantial damages which would result from not getting the loan. Under this pressure and because the work papers contained a copy of the 5-year lease agreement which supported the operating lease treatment, Smith issued her report with an unqualified opinion on September 29.

In spite of the fact the loan was received, Juniper went bankrupt within 2 years. The bank is suing Smith to recover its losses on the loan and the lessor is suing Smith to recover uncollected rents.

Required: Answer the following, setting forth reasons for any conclusions stated.
a Is Smith liable to the bank?
b Is Smith liable to the lessor?

AICPA

CASE

The following events actually happened.

CPA X was Company A's auditor. Company B purchased the stock of Company A. CPA X performed some services on behalf of Company A (and without any involvement of Company B). For example, in an engagement letter, Company A hired the CPA to audit the Company A financial statements for the period ending December 31, 19X4. However, there is evidence that Company B used this information in its preacquisition financial analysis of Company A.

There is also evidence indicating that Company B hired CPA X to perform audits for the express purpose of using the financial information in connection with the purchase of the stock. Company B's president contacted CPA X for the purpose of requesting the CPA to perform some accounting work in connection with the purchase of the stock. This request resulted in two engagement letters, both of which were between CPA X and Company A. In one letter, CPA X agreed to perform another audit of the 19X4 financial statements. In the other letter, CPA X agreed to provide a "review" of Company's A's interim financial statements for the 3 months ending March 31, 19X5 (referred to in the letter as "the acquisition audit"). Both letters stated:

> It is our understanding that these financial statements constitute all the financial statements required by Company B to complete your requirements under the letter of understanding and the contract of sale.

The bill for services rendered in connection with the "acquisition audit" was sent by CPA X to both Company A and Company B.

Company B was unhappy with the CPA's work. They believed the financial statements understated the liabilities of Company A. They did not pay the CPA's bill. In the fall of 19X5, CPA X filed suit against both Company A and Company B seeking to recover amounts due under the unpaid bill for services rendered in connection with the acquisition audit. In the complaint filed in that case, CPA X alleged that it had a relationship with Company B which was the equivalent of contractual privity. CPA X also alleged "that all of the hours of work performed by the Plaintiff and/or his auditing staff pursuant to the acquisition audit were performed for the benefit of and in furtherance of the interest of the Defendant Company B." CPA X further alleged:

> During the period that the Plaintiff worked pursuant to the engagement agreement, the Plaintiff and his auditing, accounting and tax staff were authorized by the Defendant Company B even though the actual engagement agreement itself was not actually signed by any representative of Defendant Company B.

Company B filed suit against CPA X for negligent work.

Required:
1 Would a user of financial statements ordinarily be expected to be successful in such a suit? What defense would the CPA ordinarily use? Consider each of the three common law approaches to liability to third parties.
2 What actions of CPA X increased liability in the situation?

CHAPTER

4

The Elements of Auditing

CHAPTER OUTLINE

Learning Objectives

After studying this chapter you should be able to:

- Describe common auditing procedures used in an audit of financial statements
- Define evidential matter and its relationship to auditing procedures
- Explain the difference between accounting and auditing
- Outline the logical process of identifying financial statement assertions, developing specific audit objectives, and selecting auditing procedures
- Outline the audit risk model
- Define types of audit tests
- Identify the major steps or phases in an audit of financial statements
- Describe the general requirements and contents of work papers

Relevant Sections of Statements on Auditing Standards

AU 312 — Audit Risk and Materiality in Conducting an Audit
AU 326 — Evidential Matter
AU 329 — Analytical Procedures
AU 330 — The Confirmation Process
AU 339 — Working Papers

This chapter explains the basic elements of an audit of financial statements—the building blocks necessary to understand how such an audit is accomplished in conformity with generally accepted auditing standards. The most relevant standards are the three standards of field work:

- *Planning and supervision.* The work is to be adequately planned and assistants, if any, are to be properly supervised.
- *Internal control.* A sufficient understanding of the internal control structure is to be obtained to plan the audit and to determine the nature, timing, and extent of tests to be performed.
- *Evidential matter.* Sufficient competent evidential matter is to be obtained through inspection, observation, inquiries, and confirmations to afford a reasonable basis for an opinion regarding the financial statements under audit.

These standards are related and, in fact, the ultimate purpose of the first two standards of field work is to contribute to the "reasonable basis for an opinion" comprehended in the third standard on evidential matter.

Most of the auditor's work in forming an opinion on financial statements consists of obtaining and evaluating evidential matter about the assertions in financial statements by applying auditing procedures. Each of the elements—evidential matter, assertions, and audit procedures—is important to understand in order to comprehend an audit of financial statements. Since these elements are all related, it is difficult to talk about one of them without knowing about the others. For convenience, this discussion begins with the most rudimentary element—auditing procedures.

EVIDENCE, ASSERTIONS, AND PROCEDURES

Auditing standards are usually distinguished from procedures on the basis that *procedures* are acts to be performed and *standards* are the measures of performance of those acts.

Auditing Procedures

Four types of audit procedures are specifically identified in the third standard of field work—inspection, observation, inquiries, and confirmation. However, these are only examples, and it should be recognized that the names and descriptions of auditing procedures are not authoritatively established.

The names and meanings of specific audit procedures are part of the working vocabulary of auditors, but highly refined definitions are not necessary because the meaning is usually clear in context. The following, however, are some common terms and descriptions of auditing procedures.

Physical Examination   This procedure usually means identification of an item's quantity and sometimes its quality by physical inspection or count. Sometimes it is simply called *counting*. Examples are counting cash or securities on hand and making test counts of inventory items. The auditor can apply this procedure any time an item has a physical existence and is present.

Confirmation   SAS No. 67 (AU 330) provides guidance on the confirmation process. *Confirmation* is a type of inquiry by which an auditor obtains a written statement from outside companies or individuals on information which that person is qualified to give. The independent party questioned must be reliable and knowledgeable about a subject of interest to the auditor. Confirmation is often used as a substitute procedure for physical examination. In some cases the object of interest may be held by outside parties. For example, the auditor typically confirms cash on deposit in banks. In other cases, the auditor may need information concerning an item that does not have a physical existence, such as an obligation owed to the client. Thus, an auditor typically confirms accounts receivable.

A significant feature about the procedure of confirmation is that the statement of the outside party should be communicated directly to the auditor. The possibility of influence or change of information by client employees should be avoided. Steps must, therefore, be taken to maintain control over confirmations. Maintaining control is further complicated by the necessity of having the request for confirmation come from the client. The outside parties have engaged in transactions with the client and will not disclose information about their dealings to everyone who asks them. If the client makes the request, cooperation is much more likely. This necessitates the following control measures:

1 The letter is prepared by the client's personnel and given to the auditor for inspection and mailing.
2 The auditor inserts the confirmation requests in envelopes bearing the auditor's return address and mails them.

3 Included in the confirmation request is a stamped return envelope addressed to the auditor. If the confirmation reply is returned by another method, such as by fax, the auditor should call the outside party or otherwise make sure that the reply actually came from the outside party.

Inspection   *Inspection* is a general term for looking at documents. Examples are inspecting contracts, insurance policies, leases, and minutes. Usually, the auditor has to extract items of accounting or audit significance from these documents. Sometimes this procedure is referred to simply as *reading* or *reviewing* the particular document. Other terms for looking at documents are "vouching" and "tracing." However, sometimes these terms have more specific meanings as explained below.

Vouching   *Vouching* is the process of inspecting a document that supports a recorded transaction or amount. The direction is from the accounting record to the document. Examples are supporting recorded sales transactions by inspecting sales invoices and supporting recorded additions to property by inspecting manufacturers' invoices.

Tracing   The opposite of vouching is *tracing.* The direction of testing is from the source documents to the accounting record. An example would be tracing shipping documents to recorded sales.

Reperformance   Repetition of client clerical routines such as footing (adding) and posting are generally called *reperformance.* Sometimes repetition of a calculation is referred to as *recomputation.* Examples include determining that journal entries have been posted to the proper accounts and recomputing depreciation calculations.

Scanning   Visually examining accounting records and schedules to identify unusual items or inconsistencies is *scanning.* Sometimes it is called *scrutiny.* Examples include scanning the December sales journal for unusual and late sales and scanning expense accounts for anomalies. For example, rent expense would be scanned and anything more or less than 12 debits would be unusual.

Inquiry   Questioning management and employees about matters of accounting or auditing significance is called *inquiry.* The responses may be oral or written. Examples include asking whether consignment sales are made and obtaining a representation letter from client management. Usually, it is more efficient for the auditor to first ask management or employees and then corroborate the information rather than trying to find answers independently. Although inquiry is a useful procedure, the auditor does not accept unsupported responses.

Observation   Visually reviewing client activities or locations is called *observation.* Examples include observing clerical processing operations and touring the client's physical facilities.

Analytical Procedures   Making a systematic analysis or comparison of plausible relationships among information is generally referred to as an *analytical test.* For example, the auditor might compare gross margin percentages between accounting periods or the relationship between bad debts and sales. A descriptive term sometimes used for this type of procedure is *ratio and trend analysis*. However, the term used in authoritative literature [SAS No. 546 (AU 329)] is *analytical procedures.*

Evidential Matter and Its Relationship to Procedures

Audit procedures are not evidence, rather they are the means used to obtain evidential matter. The term *evidential matter* is authoritatively defined. According to SAS No. 31 (AU 326.14), evidential matter consists of underlying accounting data and all corroborating information available to the auditor.

The Audit Equation   Some auditors regard the following audit equation[1] based on this definition as being analogous in importance in auditing to the accounting equation of assets = liabilities + equity. The *audit equation* is

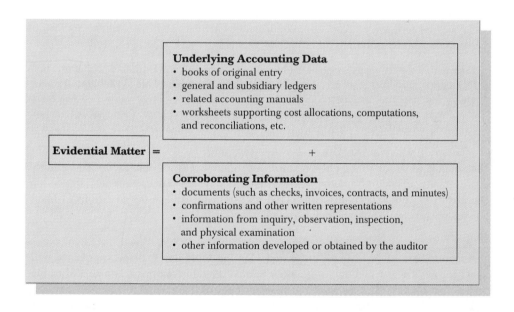

Underlying Accounting Data
- books of original entry
- general and subsidiary ledgers
- related accounting manuals
- worksheets supporting cost allocations, computations, and reconciliations, etc.

Evidential Matter =   +

Corroborating Information
- documents (such as checks, invoices, contracts, and minutes)
- confirmations and other written representations
- information from inquiry, observation, inspection, and physical examination
- other information developed or obtained by the auditor

The audit equation is fundamental because it captures the conceptual logic of an audit of financial statements.

The auditor needs to test the propriety and accuracy of the underlying accounting data to be able to express an opinion on the financial statements. However, accounting data alone are not considered sufficient support for the financial statements. The auditor tests

---

[1]The "equation" is a conceptual formulation, rather than a mathematical computation.

underlying accounting data by analysis and review. Procedural steps followed in the accounting process are retraced; allocations are recalculated; related information is reconciled. Common audit procedures used in this process are inspection, vouching, tracing, reperformance, and scanning. The logic behind this process is explained in SAS No. 31 (AU 326.17) as follows:

> In a soundly conceived and carefully maintained system of accounting records, there is internal consistency discoverable through such procedures that constitutes persuasive evidence that the financial statements do present financial position, results of operations, and cash flows, in conformity with generally accepted accounting principles.

Notice that this process is directed to the accounting system. The accounting records provide the link between the economic activity of a business—its exchange transactions—and the financial statements. The auditor's understanding of the accounting system, control environment, and control procedures—commonly called the *internal control structure*—may, as explained in Chapter 6, increase the auditor's confidence in the propriety and accuracy of the underlying accounting data and permit a reduction in the corroborating information that might otherwise be necessary.

Some corroborating information for material assertions in the financial statements, however, is always considered essential. This information is obtained by audit procedures such as physical examination, confirmation, inquiry, and observation. Sources of corroborating information are described in SAS No. 31 (AU 326.18) as follows:

> Both within the company's organization and outside it are knowledgeable people to whom the auditor can direct inquiries. Assets having physical existence are available to the auditor for his inspection. Activities of company personnel can be observed. Based on certain conditions as he observes them, for example, a low assessed level of control risk, he can reason to conclusions with respect to the validity of various assertions in the financial statements.

The sources of corroborating information are limited only by the auditor's ingenuity. However, the practice of auditing is also influenced heavily by custom and convention. The audit procedures generally considered necessary to validate the assertions in financial statements are explained in subsequent chapters.

Accounting and Auditing Contrasted   As the foregoing explanation clearly indicates, accounting and auditing are closely related. For this reason, it is essential to recognize that auditing is a separate, independent field of knowledge.

This point tends to be obscured by the close relationship between the two subjects. Auditing is taught at the college level as a course in the accounting department. An entrant to the profession aspires to become a certified public accountant, and the profession itself is often called the public accounting profession. The overlap of accounting and auditing also exists in the way an audit is conducted. A large part of the evidential matter obtained in an audit relates to the underlying accounting data produced by the accounting system. The criteria used to evaluate the presentation of financial statements are generally accepted accounting principles. To audit financial statements the auditor must first be a competent accountant.

Accounting and auditing are nevertheless separate fields. Accounting is essentially the process of accumulating, measuring, and communicating economic information about an entity. It is a creative process concerned with communication of financial information useful for decision making. In contrast, auditing is a critical and analytical process that controls and adds credibility to the information communicated by the accounting process.

An important aspect of this distinction is that an audit does not by design or function duplicate the accounting process. Through selective testing of the underlying accounting data and by obtaining and evaluating corroborating information, the audit of financial statements validates or substantiates accounting information.

Additional Classifications of Evidence   Some auditors identify additional subdivisions of audit evidence beyond the elements of the audit equation of underlying accounting data and corroborating information. For example, evidence might be classified as to whether it is internal or external to the company or developed by the auditor. Also, evidence might be classified as physical, documentary, oral, visual, or mathematical. These distinctions are not critical as long as the auditor recognizes the difference between audit procedures and audit evidence. Usually one is clear when the other is specified. For example, documentary evidence is obtained by inspection, tracing, and vouching; physical examination obviously produces physical evidence. However, the auditor cannot lose sight of the fact that evidence is not produced merely by applying procedures. It is essential to obtain and evaluate enough valid and relevant evidential matter. The characteristics of relevance and validity as they relate to substantiating assertions in financial statements are discussed in the next section.

Financial Statement Assertions and Audit Objectives

"Assertions," according to SAS No. 31 (AU 326.03), "are representations by management that are embodied in financial statement components." In effect, by presenting financial statements, management is stating, either explicitly or implicitly, certain things about the company's financial position and operations.

The broad categories of assertions and a brief explanation of each follows:

- *Existence or occurrence.* Reported assets and liabilities actually exist at the balance sheet date, and transactions reported in the income statement actually occurred during the period covered by the financial statements.
- *Completeness.* All transactions and accounts that should be included in the financial statements are included, or there are no undisclosed assets, liabilities, or transactions.
- *Rights and obligations.* The company owns and has clear title to the assets, the liabilities are obligations of the company, and the company was actually a party to reported transactions.
- *Valuation or allocation.* The assets and liabilities are valued properly, and the revenues and expenses are measured properly.
- *Presentation and disclosure.* The assets, liabilities, revenues, and expenses are properly described and disclosed in the financial statements.

The auditor needs to obtain evidential matter that supports each of the assertions for every material component of the financial statements. A component of the statements may be an account balance (or group of account balances) or a class of transactions, and the broad categories of assertions encompass both transactions and balances.

Developing Audit Objectives   The categories of assertions provide a framework for developing specific audit objectives. An auditor develops specific audit objectives for each material account balance or class of transactions. An audit objective is an assertion translated into terms that are specific to the particular balance or class, the entity's circumstances, the nature of its economic activity, and the accounting practices of its industry.

As an example of the development of specific audit objectives for the account balance of inventory of a manufacturing company, consider the following listing of assertions and objectives adapted from SAS No. 31 (AU 326):

Financial statement assertion	Illustrative audit objectives
Existence or occurrence	Inventories included in the balance sheet physically exist. Inventories represent items held for sale in the normal course of business.
Completeness	Inventory quantities include all products, materials, and supplies on hand. Inventory quantities include all products, materials, and supplies owned by the company that are in transit or stored at outside locations. Inventory listings are accurately compiled and the totals are properly included in the inventory accounts.
Rights and obligations	The company has legal title or similar rights of ownership to the inventories. Inventories exclude items billed to customers or owned by others.
Valuation or allocation	Inventories are properly stated at cost (except when market is lower). Slow-moving, excess, defective, and obsolete items included in inventories are properly identified and valued. Inventories are reduced, when appropriate, to replacement cost or net realizable value.
Presentation and disclosure	Inventories are properly classified in the balance sheet as current assets. The major categories of inventories and their bases of valuation are adequately disclosed in the financial statements. The pledge or assignment of material inventories is appropriately disclosed.

After the auditor has developed specific audit objectives for a particular account balance or class of transactions, the next step is to select audit procedures to achieve those objectives.

Selecting Audit Procedures   The selection of particular procedures to achieve specific audit objectives is influenced by the following considerations:

- The nature and materiality of the particular component of the financial statements (account balance or class of transactions)
- The nature of the audit objective to be achieved
- The assessed level of control risk
- The relative risk of error or irregularities
- The kinds and competence of available evidence
- The expected efficiency and effectiveness of possible audit procedures

The application of these considerations is explained in Chapter 7. The basic criterion, however, is simply stated. The procedures selected should produce evidential matter that is sufficient and competent for the auditor to form conclusions concerning the validity of the individual assertions embodied in the components of the financial statements. Competence and sufficiency are the characteristics of evidential matter identified in the third standard of field work.

Competence and Sufficiency of Evidential Matter   Evidential matter to be competent should be both *relevant* and *valid. Relevance* is largely a matter of the relationship between the evidential matter and the financial statement assertion involved. For example, if the related assertion concerns existence of an asset, the auditor may select items included in the account balance and physically examine or confirm the items. However, these procedures are not relevant to the completeness assertion. To achieve an audit objective related to completeness, the auditor must select from evidential matter indicating that an item should be included in the account balance and see whether it is included.

The *validity* of evidential matter is difficult to generalize about because the reliability of evidence is subject to important exceptions. However, the following presumptions, adapted from SAS No. 31 (AU 326.19), are generally regarded as useful:

- Evidential matter from sources outside a company is more reliable than evidential matter obtained solely within a company. (For example, a written confirmation directly from a customer is more reliable than a duplicate sales invoice indicating a customer was billed.)
- Accounting data developed under satisfactory conditions of control are more reliable than data developed under unsatisfactory conditions. (For example, prenumbered documents when the sequence of numbers is accounted for are more reliable than unnumbered documents.)
- An auditor's direct personal knowledge obtained through physical examination, observation, recomputation, and inspection is more persuasive than information obtained indirectly. (For example, observation of physical inventory taking is more persuasive than confirmation of inventory quantities at outside locations.)

The two aspects of competence have to be considered together because evidential matter may be highly valid but limited in relevance to achieving audit objectives. For example, footing an account provides direct personal knowledge but footing is of limited relevance in achieving an audit objective related to existence. The reverse is also true. Inquiry of management may produce highly relevant evidential matter but is of limited validity.

Sufficiency relates to the *amount* of competent evidential matter necessary to provide the auditor with a reasonable basis for an opinion on financial statements. The factors that influence sufficiency are discussed in Chapters 7 and 8.

OVERVIEW OF THE AUDIT RISK MODEL

SAS No. 47 (AU 312.02) defines audit risk at the financial statement level as:

> The risk that the auditor may unknowingly fail to modify his opinion on financial statements that are materially misstated.

Before issuing an opinion on financial statements, the auditor wants to reduce audit risk to a level low enough to justify issuing the opinion. The auditor reduces audit risk by performing audit procedures until sufficient competent evidential matter has been obtained for each assertion of each significant transaction class or balance to provide reasonable assurance that the financial statements are not materially misstated.

Performing an audit is essentially performing audit procedures until audit risk is low enough to issue an opinion. However, the nature of the audit procedures is important. Some audit procedures are more efficient than others for specific accounts and assertions. In planning the audit procedures in each area, the auditor has two approaches to choose from:

- Audit procedures designed to provide reasonable assurance that the inherent nature of the item and the internal control structure are such that the risk that the client has a material misstatement in the financial statements is low
- Audit procedures designed to directly validate an item so that the auditor has reasonable assurance that any material misstatement in the area would have been detected

The auditor's approach is almost always a combination of the two kinds of audit procedures.

SAS No. 47 (AU 312.20) describes three components of audit risk at the account balance or transaction class level as follows:

1 *Inherent risk.* This is the susceptibility of an assertion to material misstatement given inherent and environmental characteristics, but without regard to prescribed control procedures. For example, cash is more susceptible to theft than an inventory of coal. Complex calculations are more likely to be misstated in error than simple calculations.

2 *Control risk.* This is the risk that material misstatement in an assertion may occur and not be prevented or detected on a timely basis by prescribed internal control structure policies and procedures.

3 *Detection risk.* This is the risk that an auditor's procedures will lead the auditor to conclude that material misstatement does not exist in an assertion when the assertion is actually materially misstated.

Audit risk is a combination of inherent risk, control risk, and detection risk. The auditor cannot change inherent risk. To complete the audit, the auditor must reduce the assessed level of the other two kinds of risk. The auditor can obtain evidence of a reduced *assessed* level of *control risk* by obtaining an understanding of the control environment, accounting system, and control procedures and testing their effectiveness. If the evidence indicates that control is effective, the auditor can assess a lower level of control risk. If the evidence indicates control problems, the auditor's assessed level of control risk will accordingly remain high. The auditor can reduce *detection risk* by performing effective tests of the details of the account balance or other procedures.

TYPES OF AUDIT TESTS

An understanding of financial statement assertions, specific audit objectives, the audit risk model, and auditing procedures provides the background necessary to consider the general classes of audit tests.

The types of audit tests are part of the working vocabulary of auditors, and the conceptual distinction among types of tests is important to understanding the different phases or major steps in an audit of financial statements.

Classification by Purpose of Test

The basic classification of audit tests depends on the auditor's purpose in applying the test. The basic purposes of audit tests are:

- *Tests of controls*—to obtain evidence about either (1) the effectiveness of the design of the policies or procedures in the internal control structure, or (2) the operating effectiveness of those policies or procedures. These tests may produce evidence to support a lower assessed level of control risk.
- *Substantive tests*—to obtain evidence about the validity and the propriety of the accounting treatment of transactions and balances or, conversely, of errors or irregularities therein. These tests reduce detection risk.

The auditor performs tests of controls to see whether the internal control structure policies and procedures are effective. Substantive tests are performed of the specific transactions and balances to see whether the dollar amount of an account balance is materially misstated.

Types of Tests of Controls

There are two types of tests of controls:

- Tests of controls directed toward effectiveness of the *design* of the policies or procedures and whether they are placed in operation
- Tests of controls directed toward the *operating effectiveness* of the policies or procedures and how they were applied, the consistency with which they were applied, and by whom they were applied throughout the period under audit

What the auditor does to perform the audit test differs depending on whether or not the client's procedure to be tested leaves a visible trail of evidence that it was performed:

- *No trail.* This involves inquiries and observation of client personnel and routines to determine how internal control structure policies and procedures are performed and who performs them. For example, this approach would be used to see whether cash is handled by someone who does not record cash transactions.
- *Documentary trail.* This involves inspection of the documents to see whether an internal control structure policy or procedure, such as approval or other checking, was performed and who performed it as indicated by signatures or initials.

The subject of tests of controls cannot be explored until the control risk assessment process is discussed in Chapter 6, but the classification of audit tests is introduced here to identify the relationship to evidential matter and auditing procedures.

Types of Substantive Tests

There are two general categories of substantive tests.

- Analytical procedures
- Tests of details of transactions or balances

Analytical Procedures   Analytical types of tests were explained as an audit procedure earlier in this chapter. Essentially they involve study and comparison of relationships among accounting data and related information. They focus on the reasonableness of relationships and also identify unusual fluctuations for investigation. For example, an auditor might test the reasonableness of the revenue of a hotel by multiplying the average number of occupied rooms by the standard room rate by the number of days in the period.

Analytical procedures are used for three purposes:

- To assist the auditor in planning other audit procedures
- As a substantive test to obtain evidence about an assertion
- As an overall review of the financial information near the end of the audit

An important point to recognize is that analytical procedures are often substantive tests that may achieve specific audit objectives if the evidential matter is considered persuasive by the auditor.

Tests of Details   This type of substantive test involves obtaining evidential matter on the items (or details) included in an account balance or class of transactions. Thus, tests of details are also referred to as follows:

- *Tests of transactions.* These are tests of the processing of individual transactions by inspection of the documents and accounting records involved in processing, for example, tracing a sample of shipping documents to the sales journal to see whether shipments have been recorded as sales.
- *Tests of balances.* These are tests applied directly to the details of balances in general

ledger accounts, for example, confirming the balances of accounts in the accounts receivable subsidiary ledger with individual customers.

Some auditors refer to tests of balances as direct tests of balances to emphasize the substantive nature of the test as directly supporting an account balance. Note that tests of details of transactions (substantive tests) and tests of controls that leave a documentary trail may both involve the inspection of documents supporting transactions. For this reason, these tests are often applied together to the same group of documents. In that case, the test is referred to as a *dual-purpose test.*

OVERVIEW OF AN AUDIT OF FINANCIAL STATEMENTS

An audit of financial statements usually follows a logical sequence of major steps or phases. These are:

1 *Understanding the client.* The auditor must obtain or update an understanding of the client's operations and circumstances, including management policies, the company's position in its industry and the economy, and its legal obligations. The objective is to understand the events, transactions, and practices that may have a significant effect on the client's financial statements. Typical audit procedures for this step are inquiry of company personnel, analytical procedures, observation of operations and facilities, and inspection of documentation such as company manuals and legal documents. Much of the detailed planning for the audit can be done only after this step.

2 *Understanding the internal control structure.* The next step in the audit is to obtain an understanding of the internal control structure, which consists of the following five components:

- Control environment
- Risk assessment
- Information and communication
- Control activities
- Monitoring

This understanding is obtained through the auditor's test of controls directed toward the design of the policies and procedures. Typical audit procedures for this step include a more extensive and directed application of procedures used in obtaining an understanding of the client and, often, limited tracing and vouching of transactions. Based on this understanding, the auditor assesses the control risk and considers whether further tests of controls would yield evidence to support a lower assessed level of control risk.

3 *Tests of transaction classes.* After obtaining an understanding of the client and the internal control structure, the next step is application of audit procedures to the accounting record of transactions. This is the step in the audit with the most variation in practice. Virtually all audits have this step, but the auditor's objective and the emphasis and timing can vary from client to client. The audit procedures used are always similar. Transactions of each major class are selected, and the auditor examines the support for them with procedures such as tracing, vouching, and

recomputation. However, a test of transactions may be a test of the operating effectiveness of controls, a substantive test, or both (a dual-purpose test).

4 *Direct tests of balances.* This step consists of substantive tests of balances in the accounting records. The tests are of two types—analytical procedures and tests of details. They both provide corroborating evidence. Typical procedures include confirmation with outside parties, observation and counting of assets, recomputation and evaluation of related allocations between current and future periods, and comparisons of related accounting data.

5 *Completion and review.* The final step in the audit consists of following up issues raised in earlier steps; certain procedures, such as the subsequent events review, analytical tests of the final draft of the financial information, and review of work papers, which can be completed only at the end of the field work; and evaluating all the evidence obtained and forming an opinion on the financial statements.

When all five steps or phases are completed the auditor issues the audit report that accompanies the client's financial statement. Each of the five steps or phases is covered in a separate subsequent chapter of this book as follows:

- Understanding the client and general planning (Chapter 5)
- Understanding the internal control structure (Chapter 6)
- Tests of transaction classes and related balances (Chapter 10)
- Direct tests of balances (Chapter 11)
- Completion of the audit (Chapter 12)

The intervening chapters in this sequence (Chapters 7 to 9) are concerned with planning tests of transactions and balances, audit sampling, and the effects of computers on auditing.

WORK PAPERS

The auditor must prepare and maintain audit work papers, but the specific form and content of them is determined by the circumstances of the particular engagement.

The Function of Work Papers

Work papers, according to SAS No. 41 (AU 339.02), serve two main functions:

1 Work papers are a direct aid in the conduct and supervision of the audit.
2 Work papers provide the principal support for the auditor's opinion, including the representation that the audit was conducted in accordance with generally accepted auditing standards.

Work papers are an important physical aid in recording the results of audit tests. For example, when a sample is taken, the items drawn must be recorded and computations must be made. Work papers, in addition, are necessary for coordination of the work leading to an opinion. Final decisions concerning the opinion given on the financial statements are made by supervisors who perform few, if any, of the actual audit tests. There must be a means of reviewing the work performed. The supervisors use the work papers as a basis for evaluating the evidence gathered.

After an opinion has been given, work papers are the only physical proof the auditor has that an adequate audit was conducted. The auditor works with original documents and accounting records which must be left with the client when the audit has been completed. The auditor must include in the work papers a description of the work done and the results of the tests performed. There is always a possibility that the auditor will have to prove the adequacy of the audit in court.

The Contents and Requirements of Work Papers

Work papers normally include the audit plan and programs, documentation of the auditor's understanding of the internal control structure, the assessed level of control risk, account analyses explaining the composition of account balances, reconciliations of related records, letters of confirmation and representation, abstracts of company documents and other relevant information, recommended journal entries if necessary to correct the accounts, and trial balances and lead schedules which summarize the contents of other work papers.

Permanent and Current Files   There are two main divisions of audit work papers: the permanent or continuing audit file and the current audit file. The permanent file contains all those papers which are of continuing interest from year to year, such as the following:

1 Excerpts of the corporate charter or articles of copartnership
2 Charts of accounts and accounting procedure manuals
3 Documentation of the internal control structure, such as flowcharts and notes on the accounting system and related controls from prior audits
4 Continuing analyses of fixed assets
5 Terms of capital stock and bond issues
6 Organization charts and excerpts from job manuals
7 Excerpts of pension plans, patent agreements, profitsharing plans, labor contracts, and other contracts

The current work paper file contains all papers accumulated during the current year's audit. A listing of work papers found in the current file will include the following:

   I Original draft of the report
     A The financial statements
     B Draft of the auditor's opinion
   II A documentation of the auditor's conclusions about the assessed level of control risk for the current period under audit
   III The audit plan and programs
   IV Work papers concerning general matters, such as:
     A Excerpts from minutes of the meetings of the board of directors
     B Notes on conferences with client officers and employees

    C Excerpts from new corporate bylaws
    D Excerpts from important contracts
    E Memoranda about impressions of the tour of the client's offices and plant
  V Working trial balance
  VI Adjusting and reclassification journal entries
 VII Lead and supporting schedules prepared for all accounts from cash through operations

At the start of an audit the permanent file and the prior year's current work paper file are studied and used for reference purposes.

General Requirements   There are certain general requirements that the contents of work papers should meet. To support the auditor's representation that the standards of field work have been complied with, the work papers must show that:

1 The engagement has been planned (such as by use of audit programs) and the work of any assistants has been supervised and reviewed (such as by supervisors' initials indicating approval of the work).

2 An understanding of the internal control structure has been obtained in planning the audit and in determining the nature, timing, and extent of tests to be performed, such as by completed questionnaires, memos, and descriptions of test of controls.

3 The auditing procedures followed and testing performed in obtaining sufficient competent evidential matter indicate observance of the third standard of field work. The work papers supporting this may take various forms, but work papers should permit reasonable identification of the work performed by the auditor and the significant conclusions reached.

The work papers should also be sufficient to show that the accounting records agree or reconcile with the financial statements because the underlying accounting data is important evidential matter. Usually, this agreement is shown in the working trial balance which is sometimes called the backbone of the work papers.

Common Types of Work Papers   The quantity, type, and content of work papers necessary for a particular engagement depend on the auditor's judgment, and that judgment is influenced by the nature of the report to be issued, the financial statements or other information to be reported on, the condition of the client's accounting records, and similar considerations. However, some common types of work papers are part of an auditor's working vocabulary. These common types of work papers are described in the following list:

- *Audit program.* This is a list, usually in detail, of the procedures to be applied to a specific account balance or class of transactions. [An audit program or programs is one form of documentation of *planning* that is specifically required by professional standards (AU 311).]

- *Working trial balance.* This is a list of the accounts in the client's general ledger with columns that, as a minimum, include unadjusted amounts directly from the client's accounting records, proposed adjusting entries, and adjusted (audited) amounts. (A trial balance is often called the backbone of the work papers because it provides an

overall index of the work papers, is an aid in controlling and reviewing the audit as
it progresses, and serves as the base for accumulating and arranging account balances
for financial statement presentation.)

- *Lead schedule.* This is a grouping of related account balances. (When lead schedules
  are used, all the general ledger accounts that are combined into a line item on the
  financial statements and related accounts are put on individual lead schedules and the
  total on the lead schedule appears in the trial balance.)
- *Account analysis.* This is an analysis showing the activity during the period in a particular balance sheet account. It starts with the beginning balance, shows the transactions (additions and reductions) that occurred during the period, and concludes with
  the ending balance. If transaction volume is great, the analysis may combine transactions by type or below a specified amount. (This type of work paper schedule is
  often used for investments, allowance for doubtful accounts, property and equipment,
  debt, and equity accounts.)
- *List or trial balance.* This is a list that shows the detail making up an ending balance
  of an account. An analysis shows the activity during the year. A list, in contrast, shows
  only the items included in the ending balance. (This type of schedule is often used
  for accounts receivable, accounts payable, repair and maintenance expenses, miscellaneous income and expenses, and legal expenses.)
- *Reconciliation schedule.* A reconciliation relates an amount in the accounting records
  to another source of information. It supports an account balance but does so by showing that the balance agrees with other information. (This type of schedule is often
  used for reconciling: cash book balance with bank statement, or subsidiary accounts
  receivable balances with customer confirmation, or accounts payable balances with
  vendors' statements.)
- *Comparison schedule.* A comparison is a side-by-side presentation of amounts in the
  accounting records with relevant other information, such as prior year's amounts, budgeted amounts, related operating data, industry statistics, or a calculation made by the
  auditor to test overall reasonableness. It is the usual schedule for applying most types
  of analytical procedures. (This type of schedule is often used for various revenue and
  expense accounts.)
- *Procedure description or results.* This is a work paper limited solely to an explanation of auditing procedures applied or the results of applying procedures. (This type
  of schedule might be used for a summary of inventory observations or an explanation of procedures applied to supporting documents. It might also be documentation
  gathered by an auditor as a result of applying procedures, for example, confirmation
  replies, representation letters from client or lawyers, copies of client agreements.)

Examples of several of these types of work papers are presented in Figures 4-1 and
4-2 later on in this chapter.

Legal Aspects of Work Papers

Work papers are the property of the auditor, and a number of states have statutes which
designate the auditor as the owner of the work papers. Legal ownership of the work
papers, however, does not change the auditor's ethical responsibility not to violate the

confidential auditor-client relationship. For example, an auditor who sells a practice cannot turn over files of work papers to the purchasing auditor without the permission of the clients involved.

Mechanics of Work Paper Preparation

Certain matters concerning the mechanics of work paper preparation are so traditional in the practice of auditing that they require mention even in a general discussion. These matters are "tick" marks, indexing, and adjusting journal entries.

Tick marks are symbols used by the auditor to indicate the nature and extent of procedures applied in specific circumstances. Like all symbols, they are a shorthand for conveying information. For example, if the auditor has examined vouchers supporting disbursements for every item on a work paper listing the charges to an expense account, the auditor will place a tick mark (a symbol such as √) after each item. At the bottom of the work paper will be an explanation of the meaning of the mark in this manner:

√—Voucher with supporting papers examined and found satisfactory.

Indexing work papers requires coding the individual sheets of paper so that needed information may be found easily. The auditor prepares cross references creating a trail through the work papers. A variety of indexing systems are in use. These systems include (1) sequential numbering, (2) combinations of letters and numbers, and (3) digit-position index numbers. A short example of the third system should be sufficient to illustrate the general principle of work paper indexing:

1000 Draft of audit report
•
•
•
2000 Cash
2001 Count of petty cash
2002 Bank reconciliation
2100 Accounts receivable
•
•
•
3000 Fixed assets
•
•
•

Adjusting journal entries are the corrections the auditor believes may be required. The auditor does not make entries in the client's records. The auditor makes the entries on the work papers and reviews their recording by the client. The adjusting journal entry is the entry required to *correct* the accounts. For example, assume that an ordinary expense is incorrectly capitalized as follows:

Dr. Machinery and Equipment	$175	
Cr. Cash		$175

The adjusting journal entry necessary to correct the accounts would be:

Dr. Repair Expense	$175	
Cr. Machinery and Equipment		$175

(to record ordinary repair expense
incorrectly capitalized)

Illustrative Audit Work Papers

A typical audit program—list of audit procedures—for the audit of fixed assets is illustrated in Figure 4-1. Figure 4-2, consisting of five hypothetical work papers, illustrates the accomplishment of the procedures specified in this audit program. These illustrations

Client Palmwood Corporation

Audit Program for Fixed Assets

Audit Period 6/30/x4

Item no.	Audit procedures	Done by	Work paper reference
1.	Obtain or prepare a schedule of property, plant, equipment, and accumulated depreciation.	*RP*	*B*
2.	Trace additions and retirements from the accounts through records to supporting vouchers and examine support.	*RP*	*B/1, B/2*
3.	Examine supporting vouchers for repairs and maintenance to ascertain whether such charges should be capitalized or expensed.	*RP*	*B/4*
4.	Recompute depreciation calculations.	*RP*	*B/3*
5.	Trace depreciation to depreciation expense accounts.	*RP*	*B/3*
6.	Ascertain that depreciation rates and depreciable lives being used appear to be reasonably adequate.	*RP*	*B/3*
7.	Ascertain that depreciation rates and depreciable lives being used are consistent with prior years.	*RP*	*B/3*
8.	Recompute gains or losses on retirements and trace to gain or loss accounts.	*RP*	*B/1, B/2*

FIGURE 4-1

Example of an audit program for property, plant, and equipment (fixed assets).

present one possible format for work papers. The indexing system used is a combination system made up of letters and numbers. The lead schedule is indexed "B" while the backup work papers are number "B/1" through "B/4." A lead schedule is prepared for each major account classification and is used to summarize all final amounts that will appear in the financial statements. Cross-referencing individual items from one work paper to another and to the lead schedule and to the working trial balance is also illustrated.

On each work paper in the set, the procedures undertaken are indicated at the bottom. These procedures reflect the types of evidence obtained for each of the items comprising the balances of fixed assets and related accounts. By clearly indicating the work undertaken, an auditor's work papers reflect the types of procedures used, the timing of the procedures, and the extent of the procedures. Finally, the set of work papers illustrated in Figure 4-2 shows the interrelationship between accounts as well as the integrated approach to the audit of such accounts.

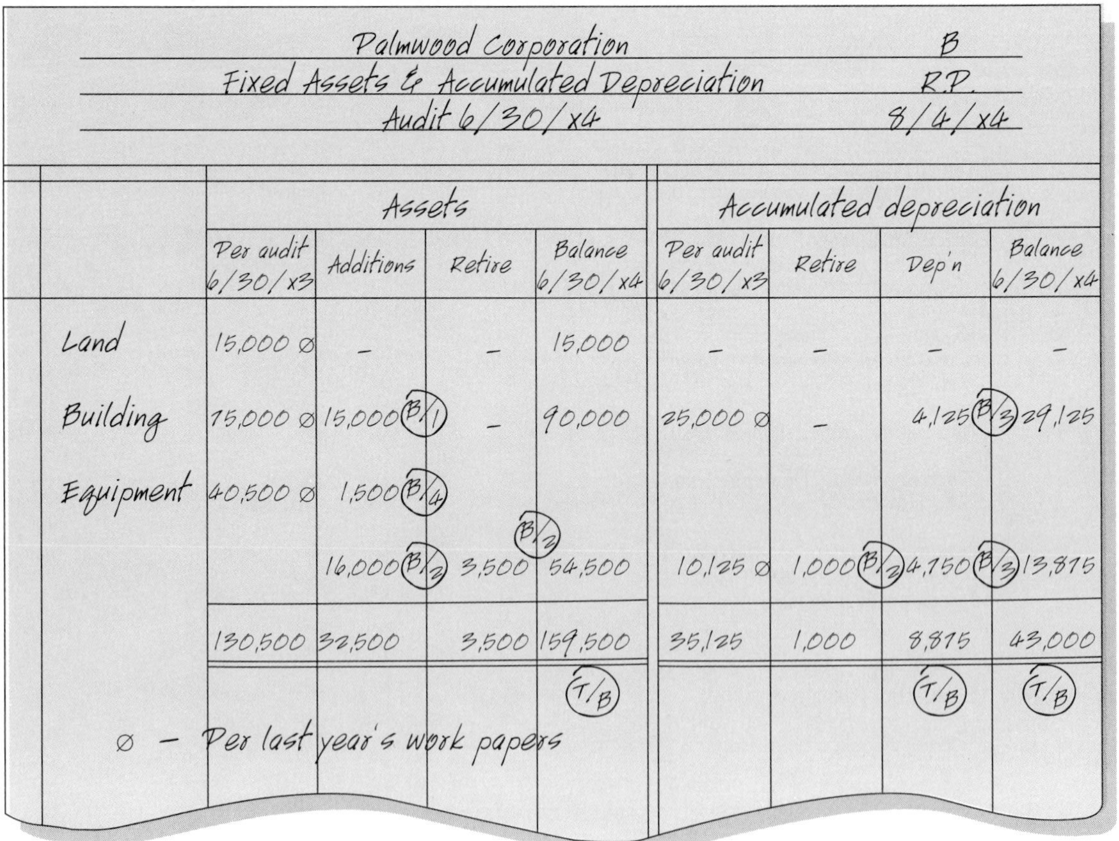

Palmwood Corporation — B
Fixed Assets & Accumulated Depreciation — R.P.
Audit 6/30/x4 — 8/4/x4

	Assets				Accumulated depreciation			
	Per audit 6/30/x3	Additions	Retire	Balance 6/30/x4	Per audit 6/30/x3	Retire	Dep'n	Balance 6/30/x4
Land	15,000 ⌀	–	–	15,000	–	–	–	–
Building	75,000 ⌀	15,000 (B/1)	–	90,000	25,000 ⌀	–	4,125 (B/3)	29,125
Equipment	40,500 ⌀	1,500 (B/4)						
		16,000 (B/2)	3,500 (B/2)	54,500	10,125 ⌀	1,000 (B/2)	4,750 (B/3)	13,875
	130,500	32,500	3,500	159,500	35,125	1,000	8,875	43,000
				(T/B)			(T/B)	(T/B)

⌀ – Per last year's work papers

FIGURE 4-2
Integrated work paper illustration.

Palmwood Corporation — B/1
Building & Accumulated Depreciation
Audit 6/30/x4
R.P.
1/29/x4

	Cost	Acccum. dep'n
Balance, 6/30/x3	15,000 v	25,000 v
12/15/x3 Bolivar Const. Bldg. add.	15,000 u	
6/30/x4 — JV 6-19 Depreciation provision		4,125 (B/3)
Balance, 6/30/x4, per Audit	90,000	29,125
v — Per last year's work papers	(B) (T)	(B) (T)
u — vouched to original contract & invoice, & examined cancelled check		
(T) — Footings checked OK		

Palmwood Corporation — B/2
Equipment & Accumulated Depreciation
Audit 6/30/x4
R.P.
1/29/x4

	Cost	Acccum. dep'n
Balance, 6/30/x3	40,500 v	10,125 v
11/1/x3 — Bolston Eq. Co.— Milling machine	−200 ∅	
3/3/x4 — Bagley Bros.— Casting machine	8,800 ∅	
JV 1-19 - Sale of milling machine punch. 1/1/x0	(3,500)u	(1,000)u
6/30/x4 — Depreciation provision		4,150 (B/3)
AJE #4	1,500 (B/4)	
Balance, 6/30/x4, per audit	54,500	13,815
	(B) (T)	(B) (T)
v — Per last year's work papers		
∅ — Traced & vouched to invoices and cancelled checks		
u — Traced, vouched, recomputed- OK- Loss on sale = $800 (E)		
(T) — Footings checked -OK		

FIGURE 4-2 (continued)

			Building	Equip.
Palmwood Corporation			B/3	
Depreciation Expenses			R.P.	
Audit 6/30/x4			1/29/x4	

computations:

Bldg

∅ 5% × 15,000 Ⓑ/₁ = 3,750

Ⓨ 1/2 (5% × 15,000) Ⓑ/₁ = 315   4,125

Equipment

∅ 10% × 40,500 Ⓑ/₂ = 4,050

Ⓨ 1/2 (10% × 16,000) Ⓑ/₂ = 800

Ⓨ 1/2 (10% × 3,500) Ⓑ/₂ = (175)

   New machine —

Ⓨ 1/2 (10% × 1,500) Ⓑ/₄ = 15   4,150

Balance, 6/30/x4, per audit   4,125 Ⓑ   4,150 Ⓑ

Balance, 6/30/x4, per books   4,125   4,615

   AJE #6   0   15

∅ Consistent with prior year's work papers

Ⓨ Company consistently takes
   1/2 year's dep'n on additions
   and retirements - OK

   (AJE #6)

   Depreciation expense   15—

   Accum. dep'n eq.   15—

   To adjust 19x4
   dep'n expense

FIGURE 4-2 (continued)

Palmwood Corporation   B/4
Maintenance & Repair Expense   R.P.
Audit 6/30/x4   1/28/x4

1/25/x3	Alto Equip. Repair Co.	625 ⅴ	
9/11/x3	Bolton Paint Co.	775 ⅴ	
11/15/x3	Minot Elec. Rep. Co.	350 ⅴ	
1/17/x4	Beardsley Equip. Co.	1,500 Ⓧ	Ⓑ/₂
4/13/x4	Manner Welding, Inc.	640 ⅴ	
	various items all under $200. — not examined	120 ⅴ	
Balance, 6/30/x4, per books		4,610	
	AJE #4	(1,500)	
Balance, 6/30/x4, per audit		3,110	
		Ⓖ/₁	

ⅴ — Traced and vouched to
      invoice — OK.

Ⓧ — Traced and vouched —
      Invoice indicates this is
      a purchase of a new 211
      casting machine
                Ⓐ̲J̲E̲ ̲#̲4̲

Equipment		1500-	
	Maint. & repair exp.		1500-
	To reclassify & capitalized cost of 211 casting machine		

FIGURE 4-2 (concluded)

CHAPTER 4 ASSIGNMENTS
OBJECTIVE QUESTIONS

4-1 For each one of the following statements indicate whether the statement is true or false.

T F a Each of the standards of field work is independent and describes a separate goal of the auditor in auditing financial statements.

T F b Two features of the procedure of confirmation are that the request for response is made by the auditor but mailed by the client.

T F c Tracing is a procedure in which the direction of the test is from the source document to the accounting record.

T F d In the audit equation, underlying accounting data does *not* include documents, such as checks and invoices.

T F e If the auditor is convinced that the underlying accounting data is proper and accurate, it is not necessary to obtain corroborating information.

T F f Accounting and auditing are related but essentially separate fields of knowledge.

T F g Assertions are representations by management that are embodied in financial statements, but the broad categories of assertions are used by the auditor to develop specific audit objectives.

T F h A specific audit objective related to the assertion of completeness is that inventories are reduced to net realizable value.

T F i A written confirmation from a customer and inspection of a sales invoice are equally reliable as evidential matter to achieve audit objectives related to existence of accounts receivable.

T F j The basic classification of audit tests depends on the auditor's purpose in applying the test.

T F k Analytical procedures and tests of details are two types of tests of controls.

T F l Work papers are often an important aid in conducting an audit, but are not essential if the auditor does not need that aid.

4-2 The following questions relate to types of audit tests. Select the *best* response.

a The auditor is examining copies of sales invoices only for the initials of the person responsible for checking the extensions. This is an example of a:
1 Test of controls
2 Substantive test
3 Dual-purpose test
4 Test of balances

b Which of the following would be *least* likely to be included in an auditor's test of controls?
1 Inspection
2 Observation
3 Inquiry
4 Confirmation

c In the context of an audit of financial statements, substantive tests are audit procedures that:
1 May be eliminated under certain conditions
2 Are designed to discover significant subsequent events
3 May be either tests of transactions, direct tests of financial balances, or analytical procedures
4 Will decrease proportionately with the auditor's assessed level of control risk

d Which of the following *best* describes the primary purpose of audit procedures?
1 To detect errors or irregularities
2 To comply with generally accepted accounting principles
3 To gather corroborative evidence
4 To verify the accuracy of account balances

AICPA

4-3 The following questions relate to evidential matter. Select the *best* response.
 a Audit evidence can come in different forms with different degrees of persuasiveness. Which of the following is the *least* persuasive type of evidence?
 1 Vendor's invoice
 2 Bank statement obtained from the client
 3 Computations made by the auditor
 4 Prenumbered client invoices
 b To be competent, evidence must be both:
 1 Timely and substantial
 2 Reliable and documented
 3 Valid and relevant
 4 Useful and objective
 c Evidential matter concerning proper segregation of duties ordinarily is best obtained by:
 1 Preparation of a flowchart of duties performed by available personnel
 2 Inquiring whether control procedures operated consistently throughout the period
 3 Reviewing job descriptions prepared by the personnel department
 4 Direct personal observation of the employees who apply control procedures

4-4 The following questions relate to work papers. Select the *best* response.
 a The current file of an auditor's working papers most likely would include a copy of the:
 1 Bank reconciliation
 2 Pension plan contract
 3 Articles of incorporation
 4 Flowcharts of the internal control structure procedures
 b An auditor ordinarily uses a working trial balance resembling the financial statements without footnotes, but containing columns for:
 1 Reclassifications and adjustments
 2 Reconciliations and tick marks
 3 Accruals and deferrals
 4 Expense and revenue summaries
 c Which of the following is *not* a primary purpose of audit work papers?
 1 To coordinate the audit
 2 To assist in preparation of the audit report
 3 To support the financial statements
 4 To provide evidence of the audit work performed
 d Which of the following eliminates voluminous details from the auditor's working trial balance by classifying and summarizing similar or related items?
 1 Account analyses
 2 Supporting schedules
 3 Control accounts
 4 Lead schedules

AICPA

DISCUSSION QUESTIONS

Discussion questions require the application of the concepts explained in the chapter to specific facts, issues, or problems. They are classified by the primary topic to which they relate. However, responses should not be confined to the primary topics but should include all relevant implications.

Assertions and Audit Objectives and Procedures

4-5 In the chapter there is an illustration of specific audit objectives for inventory developed from the broad categories of assertions. For the account balance *accounts receivable,* develop one specific audit objective for each of the broad categories of assertions. Which audit objective do you believe will be the most difficult to achieve?

4-6 In the chapter there is an illustration of specific audit objectives developed from the broad categories of assertions for inventory. For the account balance *accounts payable,* develop one specific audit objective for each of the broad categories of assertions. Which audit objective do you believe will be the most difficult to achieve?

4-7 Five broad categories of assertions apply to account balances and classes of transactions. Identify and explain the aspects of each assertion that apply to transactions and those that apply to balances. Organize your answer in the following format:

Broad category of assertions	Transactions	Balances

4-8 Using the illustration of specific audit objectives for inventory in the chapter, identify the general categories of audit procedures that could be used to achieve the audit objective and give at least one specific example of an audit procedure in each category. Organize your answer in the following format:

Specific audit objective	General category of audit procedure	Specific example of audit procedure

4-9 Listed below are misstatements that audit procedures may detect related to inventory. For each misstatement identify the broad category of assertion involved.

  a Some inventory items are out on consignment and were not counted during the physical inventory.

  b During the physical count the client's employees mistakenly counted some items twice.

  c The basis of inventory valuation is not included in the financial statements.

  d Included in the inventory counts are some items that are held on consignment.

  e Some inventory items are listed at cost, but replacement cost is lower.

Field Work Standards, Reliability of Evidence, and Specific Audit Procedures

4-10 You have accepted the engagement of auditing the financial statements of the Boeme Company, a small manufacturing firm that has been your client for several years. Because you were busy writing the report for another engagement, you sent a staff accountant to begin the audit, with the suggestion to start with the accounts receivable. Using the prior year's work papers as a guide, the staff accountant prepared a trial balance of the accounts, aged them, prepared and mailed positive confirmation requests, examined underlying support for charges and credits, and performed such other work deemed necessary to assure the validity and collectibility of the receivables. At the conclusion of the staff accountant's work you reviewed the prepared work papers and found that the prior year's work papers had been carefully followed.

The opinion rendered by a CPA states, "We conducted our audit in accordance with generally accepted auditing standards. . . ."

List the three generally accepted standards of field work. Relate them to the above illustration by indicating how they were fulfilled or, if appropriate, how they were not fulfilled.

AICPA adapted

4-11 Indicate which one item in each of the following groups of items of evidence you would consider to be of superior reliability, and briefly explain why.

  a In support of the recorded cost of purchased raw materials:
  1 Standard costs used by the company
  2 A supplier's quotation list on file in the purchasing department
  3 The actual invoices representing materials actually purchased
  b How would your answer to part a differ if you were attempting to support the ending inventory of raw materials rather than purchases?
  c In support of the valuation of a marketable security held by the company:
  1 The canceled check used to pay for the security
  2 *The Wall Street Journal* dated the last day of the company's fiscal year
  3 Both 1 and 2
  d How would your answer to part c differ if you were attempting to support long-term investments rather than marketable securities?

4-12 You have been instructed to audit the financial statements of Christi Manufacturing Company. You are furnished the following condensed balance sheet:

Cash	$ 100,000	Notes payable	$ 200,000
Accounts receivable—trade	300,000	Accounts payable—vendors	200,000
Deposits, due from officers, etc.	100,000	Rent, taxes, etc., payable	300,000
Inventory	400,000	Long-term debt	500,000
Plant and equipment	1,000,000	Capital stock	1,000,000
Investments and		Retained earnings	200,000
advances—subsidiaries	400,000		
Prepaid expenses and other			
assets	100,000		
	$2,400,000		$2,400,000

Your assistant will be carrying out most of the work. State for her guidance what information she should request third parties to confirm directly to her.

AICPA adapted

4-13 You are engaged to audit the financial statements of a central school district. The district has an elected treasurer and a clerk of the board of education who is appointed by the board. Each of these officers keeps independent accounts with regard to the monies received and with regard to disbursements authorized from the school bank accounts. During the course of your audit you learn that the treasurer of the school district is one of the principal employees in the same branch of the bank. You have sent to this bank, in which various accounts are carried for the school district, your regular form for confirmation of bank balances and for confirmation of liabilities, and they have been received back by you properly filled out and signed for the bank by its manager, who also is the treasurer of the school district.

All information in the confirmations appears to be correct in accordance with the records which you are examining.

Discuss the value of these confirmations in these circumstances. What further steps, if any, would you take with regard to these confirmations?

AICPA adapted

4-14 Listed below are specific audit procedures. For each procedure indicate the type of misstatement the procedure would be likely to detect and the broad category of assertion to which it is related.

a Reconciliation of interest expense with bonds payable

b Review of maintenance and repairs account

c Confirmation of selected accounts receivable

Types of Audit Tests

4-15 Substantive tests include (1) tests of the details of transactions, (2) tests of the details of balances, and (3) analytical procedures. Listed below are several specific audit procedures. Identify the type of substantive test—1, 2, or 3.

a Compare recorded travel expense with the budget.

b Vouch entries in the check register to paid checks.

c Recompute accrued interest payable.

d Calculate inventory turnover ratios by product and compare with prior periods.

e Reconcile the year-end bank account.

f Discuss uncollectible accounts with the credit manager.

g Count office supplies on hand at year-end.

h Vouch entries in the sales journal to sales invoices.

4-16 The following audit procedures may be used in tests of controls and in substantive tests. Give one example of use as a test of controls and one example of use as a substantive test for each procedure.

a Inspection

b Inquiry

c Observation

4-17 An auditor frequently makes comparisons. For each of the following comparisons indicate whether the audit test is a (1) test of controls, (2) test of details of transactions, (3) test of details of a balance, or (4) analytical procedure.

a Comparison of recorded amount of major disbursements with appropriate invoices

b Comparison of recorded amount of major disbursements with budgeted amounts

c Comparison of signatures on disbursement checks with board of director's authorizations

d Comparison of returned confirmation forms with individual accounts

Work Papers

4-18 To comply with generally accepted auditing standards a CPA includes certain evidence in work papers, for example, "evidence that the engagement was planned and work of assistants was supervised and reviewed." What other evidence should a CPA include in audit work papers to comply with generally accepted auditing standards?

AICPA adapted

4-19 Miller and Flood, certified public accountants, were employed for several years by the Retrograde Corporation to make annual audits. As a result of a change in control, the corporation discontinued the engagement of Miller and Flood and retained another firm of accountants. The Retrograde Corporation thereupon demanded Miller and Flood surrender all work papers prepared by the accounting firm in making audits for the corporation. Miller and Flood refused on the grounds that the work papers were their property. This corporation brought legal action to recover the work papers. Should it succeed? State briefly what the law is, in general, as to ownership of accountants' work papers.

AICPA

4-20 Day, a CPA who has been practicing alone, decides to "sell his practice" to Knight. As a part of the transaction Knight asks Day to turn over to her all his files and work papers. One client, John Doty, does not want Knight as his accountant and objects to the transfer of the files and work papers relating to his affairs. Would such transfer be valid or desirable? Discuss.

AICPA adapted

4-21 You are instructing an inexperienced staff accountant on her first auditing assignment. She is to examine an account. An analysis of the account has been prepared by the client for inclusion in the audit work papers. Prepare a list of the comments and notations that the staff accountant should make on the account analysis to provide an adequate work paper as evidence of her examination. (Do not include a description of auditing procedures applicable to the account.)

AICPA adapted

4-22 For several years Martin engaged Watson, a CPA, to prepare the financial statements for the construction business which Martin owned and operated in his own name. Franklin is the owner of a building which Martin built on a cost-plus-fixed-fee basis. Franklin sued Martin, alleging that Martin overcharged him by inflating the cost to construct his building. In preparing for trial, Franklin obtained a court order requiring Watson to turn over to Franklin all Watson's work papers and correspondence relating to Martin's construction business.

At the subsequent trial, Franklin's attorney sought to introduce in evidence the work papers and correspondence subpoenaed pursuant to the court order. Martin's attorney objected, claiming that the papers were inadmissible evidence.

a What is the legal basis for Martin's attorney's objection to the admission of the papers in evidence? Explain.

b Will the evidence be admitted? Explain.

c Who owns the working papers prepared by Watson? Explain.

AICPA adapted

CASE

Your assistant prepared the following two work papers. Review the work papers and prepare a list of questions and review notes for the assistant to address.

Karkas Implements, Inc.
Bank Reconciliation—General Account
12—31—x5

Balance per bank statement:						$18124981
Add: Deposits in transit						
	12—29—x5	$45120891	V			
	12—30—x5	65169222	X			
		101890113	7			101890113

Deduct: Outstanding checks							
6/x4	3060	$22,000.00		12/x5	9911	$6111893	+
1/x4	3303	20,435.41		12/x5	9964	1500000	+
3/x5	6213	13,692.40		12/x5	9963	25000000	
4/x5	6629	20,291.63		12/x5	9969	512181	
5/x5	7031	40,693.46		12/x5	9910	1830198	
8/x5	8309	2,031.99		12/x5	9912	11819300	p
9/x5	8510	62,981.44 +		12/x5	9913	500000	
9/x5	8599	18,981.00 +		12/x5	9914	189412	
10/x5	9021	40,603.19 +		12/x5	9915	1111189	
11/x5	9611	2,029.88		12/x5	9916	522000	
11/x5	9699	152.48					
12/x5	9803	916.64				90611930 7 ‹90611930 7›

Other:		
Misellaneous charge	tt	4000
Balance per books:	n	198466000
		7

T/M legend
7 — Footed
V — Agreed to validated deposit slip dated 12/28/x5
X — Agreed to validated deposit slip dated 1/3/x6
+ — Check number, amount and date agreed to cancelled check obtained with bank cut-off statement. Scope for review is $25,000
tt — Received debit memo for this amount received with bank cut-off statement. It is a charge for printing of new checks as their blank check supply was depleted near the end of the year. Appears reasonable.
p — This check was not returned with the bank cut-off statement, however, per Mr. Christopher, controller, the check was for inventory purchases.

WORK PAPER I

Karkas Implements, Inc.
Inventory Price Test—Raw Materials
12-31-x5

Part No.	Material	Inventory Listing		Invoices			Comments
		Quantity	Price	Quantity	Price	Date	
4192	Aluminum arms	496	17560	600	17560	11/10/x5	Priced correctly
2618	Electrical wiring strips— 20"	1342	2230	1400	2210	1/14/x5	Invoice was not received until after year-end. Price per inventory listing came from previous invoice. Audit difference passed due to immateriality of extended error. Priced correctly.
9021	Machine bolts and nuts	10080	985	5000	985	12/10/x5	Priced correctly
0386	Wooden handles	150	175	300	195	12/16/x5	Client indicated that price of $1.95 was a temporary price fluctuation. The cost listed on the inventory listing more properly reflected lower of cost or market
1024	Motors	30	111/200	30	111/200	4/30/x4	Priced correctly.

Conclusion:

Based upon the work performed, raw material inventory for EII appears fairly valued at 12-31-x5

WORK PAPER II

5

Understanding the Client and General Planning

CHAPTER OUTLINE

Learning Objectives

After studying this chapter you should be able to:

- Explain why the decision to accept a client is important and describe the primary features of client acceptance and continuance
- Identify the important aspects of the auditor's knowledge of a client's business
- Describe the decisions made by an auditor in preparing a preliminary audit plan, the knowledge on which the decisions are based, and the procedures used to obtain that knowledge
- Explain the factors that influence general planning decisions on audit risk, including control risk assessment, materiality, timing, involvement of specialists, and staffing
- Describe the auditor's responsibilities in the special risk areas of management fraud, related-party transactions, illegal acts, and business failure
- Outline the types and uses of analytical procedures and distinguish those that are useful in obtaining an understanding of the client

Relevant Sections of Statements on Auditing Standards

AU 311 — Planning and Supervision
AU 312 — Audit Risk and Materiality in Conducting an Audit
AU 315 — Communication between Predecessor and Successor Auditors
AU 316 — The Auditor's Responsibility to Detect and Report Errors and Irregularities
AU 317 — Illegal Acts by Clients
AU 329 — Analytical Procedures
AU 334 — Related Parties
AU 336 — Using the Work of a Specialist
AU 341 — The Auditor's Consideration of an Entity's Ability to Continue as a Going Concern

The auditor's planning and conduct of the audit are naturally influenced by the auditor's understanding of the client's operations, the trends within its industry, and the effect on the client of economic and political influences. The auditor uses this type of knowledge to identify existing or potential accounting and auditing problems and develop an overall strategy for the expected conduct and scope of the audit.

CLIENT ACCEPTANCE AND CONTINUANCE

The auditor's need to understand the client starts when the auditor first considers acceptance of an engagement and continues throughout association with the client.

Quality Control Policies and Procedures

A CPA firm needs to establish policies and procedures for investigating potential clients before acceptance of an engagement and for periodically reviewing continuance of clients.

The AICPA quality control review program for CPA firms (QC 200.28) suggests the following for client acceptance:

> A participating firm should establish policies and procedures for deciding whether to accept or continue a client in order to minimize the likelihood of association with a client whose management lacks integrity. The firm does not vouch for the integrity or reliability of a client, nor does it have a duty to anyone but itself with respect to the acceptance, rejection, or retention of clients. However, the firm should consider that the reputation of a client's management could reflect on the reliability of representations and accounting records and on the firm's own reputation. In making decisions to accept or continue a client, a firm should also consider its own independence and its ability to service a client properly with particular reference to industry expertise, size of engagement, and manpower available to staff the engagement.

Policies and procedures for client acceptance and continuance are important because a CPA firm needs to take precautions to avoid association with a client whose management lacks integrity. Also, a CPA firm needs to consider the effect of a client's reputation on its image in the financial community.

Communication with a Predecessor Auditor

Often, when an auditor accepts a new client, the auditor will be replacing another auditor. When an auditor is approached by a potential client, he or she should inquire about the client's present arrangements for accounting and auditing work. If the client's past financial statements have been audited, the auditor should obtain the client's permission to communicate with the other auditor. According to SAS No. 7 (AU 315.04), on such communications:

> Inquiry of the predecessor auditor is a necessary procedure because the predecessor may be able to provide a successor with information that will assist him in determining whether to accept the engagement.

The auditor's inquiry of the predecessor auditor should be reasonable and specific. A predecessor may need to respond to several potential successors. The auditor's inquiry, according to SAS No. 7 (AU 315.06), should include specific questions on:

> ... facts that might bear on the integrity of management; on disagreements with management as to accounting principles, auditing procedures, or other similar significant matters; and on the predecessor's understanding as to the reasons for the change of auditors.

Inquiries of the predecessor about matters that bear on acceptance of the client are required. Other inquiries may be made of the predecessor after acceptance. These inquiries are not required, but they are usually the most efficient means of obtaining evidence supporting the account balances at the beginning of the period under audit. Beginning balances can have a material effect on current financial statements. For example, beginning inventory usually has a material effect on cost of goods sold in current results of operations. Also, the auditor must consider the consistency of the application of accounting principles, and include an explanatory paragraph in the audit report if there is a material lack of comparability caused by a change in accounting principle.

The auditor could apply audit procedures to beginning balances and significant prior transactions. However, according to SAS No. 7 (AU 315.08):

> The successor auditor's audit may be facilitated by (a) making specific inquiries of the predecessor regarding matters the successor believes may affect the conduct of his audit, such as audit areas that have required an inordinate amount of time or audit problems that arose from the accounting system and records; and (b) reviewing the predecessor auditor's working papers.

The auditor would review the predecessor's work papers relating to matters of continuing accounting significance, such as the work paper analyses of balance sheet accounts and those relating to contingencies. A first audit will require additional effort in understanding the client and testing beginning balances and significant past transactions. If prior financial statements were not audited, the first audit would need to be even more extensive.

Engagement Letters

After accepting an engagement, the auditor ordinarily should document the arrangements made with the client and clarify matters that may be misunderstood. Most CPA firms use engagement letters for this purpose. An engagement letter normally includes the following matters:

1 *Scope*. This is a description of the services to be provided, particularly whether there is to be an audit in accordance with generally accepted auditing standards or a more limited accounting service is to be provided, and whether additional services are to be provided, such as preparation of tax returns or tax planning.
2 *Responsibility*. This is an explanation of the relative responsibilities of management and the auditor for assuring that financial statements are in all material respects in conformity with generally accepted accounting principles and other matters that often raise questions of responsibility such as fraud, illegal acts, deficiencies in the design or operation of the internal control structure, and related-party transactions.
3 *Procedural arrangements.* This is a specification of the schedules to be prepared by the client, the method and frequency of billing the auditor's fee, and similar matters.

Engagement letters are not a requirement of professional standards, but several legal cases, such as the 1136 Tenants' Corp. case explained in Chapter 3, have demonstrated their necessity. An example of an engagement letter is presented in Figure 5-1.

Conferences with Client Personnel

Soon after acceptance of an engagement the auditor should have conferences with key client personnel. The auditor will meet with principal administrative, financial, and operating officers, and with the chief internal auditor and EDP (electronic data processing)

CPA FIRM
555 State Street
Houston, Texas

October 23, 19X3

Board of Directors
Billings Corporation
12 Main Street, Houston, Texas

Ladies and Gentlemen:

This letter is written to confirm our understanding concerning the conference held October 20, 19X3, in our office between Billings Corporation, represented by Mr. L. C. James, and our firm, represented by Mr. Ben Green.

Our understanding is that we are hereby engaged to audit the balance sheet of Billings Corporation at December 31, 19X3, and the statements of income, retained earnings, and cash flow for the period then ended.

We will conduct our audit in accordance with generally accepted auditing standards. Those standards require that we plan and perform the audit to obtain reasonable assurance about whether the financial statements are free of material misstatement. An audit includes examining, on a test basis, evidence supporting the amounts and disclosures in the financial statements. An audit also includes assessing the accounting principles used and significant estimates made by management, as well as evaluating the overall financial statement presentation.

Our audit will be designed to provide a basis for expressing an opinion on the financial statements. We are aware of the possibility that such matters as fraud, illegal acts, or related-party transactions may have a material effect on the financial statements. Accordingly, our audit is planned and conducted with due consideration of such matters as specified in Statements on Auditing Standards of the AICPA. However, your management is responsible for the financial statements and for adopting sound accounting policies, for maintaining an adequate and effective system of accounts, for safeguarding of assets, and for devising an internal control structure that will, among other things, help assure the production of proper financial statements.

Our fees for this audit will be based on the time spent by various members of our staff based on our standard billing rates. These amounts vary on an hourly basis in accordance with the experience and expertise of our staff members.

In order for us to work as efficiently as possible, it is understood that your staff will provide us with as much information and assistance as we need.

Our work will commence within one week of your acceptance of this proposal.

This proposal, in duplicate, is submitted this 23rd day of October, 19X3.

CPA FIRM

By _____
                                                    Partner

Accepted at Houston, Texas, this_____ day of _____ , 19X3.

BILLINGS CORPORATION

By _____
                                        Chief Financial Officer

FIGURE 5-1
Auditor's engagement letter.

manager if applicable, to discuss matters expected to have a significant effect on the financial statements or on the conduct of the audit.

Good relations with client personnel are important. An audit usually causes considerable inconvenience and disruption for affected client personnel, and their assistance is often needed to obtain documents, records, and explanations of various matters. Effective early conferences can establish a foundation for a good working relationship with all client personnel.

Effective communications with top management are particularly important. The auditor should have an opportunity to consider the accounting implications of important planned transactions, such as merger negotiations or lease or purchase decisions. The chief executive officer should be informed on a timely basis of new accounting and disclosure requirements that may affect company plans. A good working relationship throughout the engagement helps to avoid a crisis conference at year-end over a potential qualification of the auditor's report.

KNOWLEDGE OF THE BUSINESS

According to SAS No. 22 (AU 311), on planning and supervision, the auditor's knowledge of the client's business "should enable him to obtain an understanding of the events, transactions, and practices that, in his judgment, may have a significant effect on the financial statements." The knowledge of a client's business which the auditor should obtain includes:

- Organization structure
- Operations and legal structure
- Industry and economic conditions

Organization Structure

In an organization of any size, a plan of organization is essential to specify the responsibilities and tasks of the various components of the organization. The structure of an organization divides tasks among individual employees, groups or departments, and locations. To control the work of an organization, procedural methods and measures are adopted which provide evidence that the tasks specified by the organization structure have been carried out.

The concept of structure is a behavioral one which bears elaboration. Behavioral scientists term human relationships that exist and remain fairly stable over a period of time, regardless of the individuals involved, *social structure*. In any social situation, there are things one should do and those one should not do. Sometimes individuals violate these rules, but nevertheless the rules themselves are generally known to everyone. Thus, we can say that buying and selling, receiving and giving, or teaching and learning are each carried on in about the same fashion regardless of the individual people involved.

Interactions between people in social situations are reciprocal. One can buy only if another sells, for example, and one can teach only if others learn. In fact, much if not all of human behavior is reciprocal. Social structure and resulting interaction patterns are of interest to all students of business organization, management, and auditing because formal organizations can be understood as patterns of relationships. To understand these patterns, it is necessary to know what determines behavior. Social scientists identify the guides to interaction as norms. A *norm* is simply a prescription or proscription—something one should or should not do in a given situation. These norms can be formal and explicit or informal and only implicit. Laws are examples of formal norms, as are written rules of any club, organization, or company. However, norms can be informal and may simply be generally known but unwritten. Patterns of dress and manners of speech fall into this category.

In a large, complex organization, formal determinants of behavior (norms) take the form of organization charts, charts of accounts, rules, office memos, manuals, contracts, and, in general, *all specifications developed and supported by most or all of the top personnel.* Informal determinants, though, influence the behavior of an employee or member of an organization.

The auditor reads the manuals and other specifications of formal structure, makes inquiries about the policies and procedures in effect, and observes the formal and informal actions of employees and top management. The auditor needs to understand the business purpose served by the various components of the organization structure to understand the business purpose of material transactions. For example, SAS No. 45 (AU 334.05) on related-party transactions, observes that:

> Normally the business structure and style of operating are based on the abilities of management, tax and legal considerations, product diversification, and geographical location. Experience has shown, however, that business structure and operating style are occasionally deliberately designed to obscure related party transactions.

Related-party transactions are discussed in more detail later in this chapter.

Operations and Legal Structure

The auditor needs to obtain an understanding of the client's operating characteristics, its legal structure, and related management policies and procedures. Operating characteristics include types of products and services, locations, and methods of production, distribution, and compensation. Some of this information is obtained in reading manuals and other specifications of formal structure and related inquiries and observations. In a continuing engagement the auditor can also review correspondence files, permanent files, and the work papers of last year. Once the auditor has a basic understanding of operating characteristics, efforts are directed to important changes in operations and current business and accounting developments.

Knowledge of Operations   An audit should begin with a sound knowledge of the operations and circumstances of the organization being audited. The auditor should prepare a brief description of the nature of the business activities, including all significant factors which have a bearing on operations. To intelligently interpret the evidence gathered throughout the audit, the auditor must be familiar both with the client's business and with the many factors which will have an influence on the client's operations.

A sound knowledge of the business not only assists the auditor in assessing the areas of importance and risk for purposes of gathering audit evidence but also increases the opportunity to be of service to the client by making suggestions for improving operations.

Consider the inventory area, for example. If the auditor determines that the client has a much lower profitability than other companies in the same industry, the problem of inventory valuation may deserve extra attention. A comparison of the production schedule with sales forecasts may reveal overproduction of some product lines and the corresponding need to give greater consideration to questions of inventory obsolescence. These same observations can be the basis for recommendations of corrective action to be taken by management. In any case, proper inventory valuation requires a sound knowledge of pricing methods and the marketing and distribution system.

A sound knowledge of the business has implications for the entire audit. Even in the examination of documentary evidence the auditor's background knowledge can serve as the basis for important observations and useful recommendations to the client. In tests of sales invoices, excessive back ordering indicative of poor inventory planning may be noted. By determining the lapse of time from receipt of an order to shipment, when examining sales orders, delays in the shipping department may be disclosed. Tests of purchase vouchers can determine whether the company is buying in economic order quantities.

Tour of Plant   Important knowledge about the client is also obtained by a tour of the client's physical facilities. A tour of the offices and plant can give the auditor background knowledge on such things as materials handling methods, the physical layout of facilities, and the general condition of fixed assets and inventory. During the tour the auditor can also meet key personnel in the organization.

Legal Documents   A review of legal documents is essential for intelligent interpretation of the accounting records and financial statements. The auditor will generally take excerpts from the corporate charter and bylaws or partnership agreements, the corporate minute book, tax returns of prior years, major contracts, such as pension and profitsharing plans, and important correspondence for inclusion in the audit work papers. This information will contribute to an understanding of the business and will contain information about specific items that should be compared with data in the accounting records.

The corporate charter contains information on the corporate structure, the authorized capital, and the powers granted to and the restrictions placed on the corporation by state law. A partnership agreement will contain similar information about the operating rules of a business organized as a partnership.

Minutes, Contracts, and Correspondence   The minutes of the meetings of the corporate board of directors contain an official record of the important transactions and agreements of the organization. By examining the minutes the auditor obtains information to be substantiated during the remainder of the audit. The declaration of dividends, authorization of fixed asset expenditures, purchases and sales of securities, and opening and closing of bank accounts are examples of the important information contained in corporate minutes.

Contracts and correspondence with customers, suppliers, personnel, labor unions, and various government agencies contain information that will enable the auditor to understand the business practices and problems of the client, as well as provide information for audit tests.

Importance of Information   This information is useful to the auditor in determining the propriety and reasonableness of the transactions recorded in the accounting records. Knowledge of the client's activities is a source of independent evidence. Many errors of omission can be disclosed only by acquiring independent evidence outside the accounting records. For example, an unrecorded liability for dividends payable cannot be discovered by a 100 percent examination of the accounting records. However, by reading the minutes the auditor can gain the knowledge that such a liability should have been recorded. Similarly, knowledge that the manufacturing process employed by the client normally results in large quantities of scrap creates an expectation of revenue from scrap sales in proportion to the level of production activity. In this manner, unrecorded revenue may be disclosed.

These procedures are so important that a restriction on the scope of the audit in this area, such as a client's refusal to allow the auditor to review the minute book, would normally result in a disclaimer of an opinion. Much of the independent evidence gained in this manner cannot be acquired in any other way.

Industry and Economic Conditions

The auditor should have a basic understanding of economic conditions, government regulations, changes in technology, and competitive conditions that affect a client's operations. Of particular importance is knowledge about accounting practices common to the industry in which the client operates.

Some sources of such information are trade journals, books of industry statistics, and, in some cases, AICPA industry audit guides and industry audit alerts, which are published annually. If government regulations are an important factor in recognition of revenues or expenses, the auditor may need to investigate the administration of those regulations and inspect contracts, noting pertinent conditions and terms. For example, in the Sterling Homex case the auditor permitted recognition of revenue on government contracts based on letters of intent that were not binding on the government agency involved. In general, the auditor should be aware of developments pertinent to clients in normal reading of financial and business magazines and newspapers.

The auditor's knowledge of the client's organization structure, its operations and legal structure, and relevant industry and economic conditions, according to SAS No. 22 (AU 311), on planning and supervision, can help the auditor to:

- Identify accounting or auditing matters that need special attention
- Assess the conditions under which accounting data are prepared
- Evaluate the reasonableness of management's estimates and other financial statement representations
- Make judgments about the appropriateness of management's selection and application of accounting principles

GENERAL PLANNING AND THE PRELIMINARY AUDIT PLAN

One of the really difficult aspects of understanding general planning is separating (1) the *decisions* the auditor needs to make, (2) the *knowledge* to be obtained as background information for making those decisions, and (3) the *procedures* that are ordinarily applied to obtain that knowledge. To clearly distinguish these matters, consider the following separate listings of decisions, knowledge, and procedures. These lists reconsider the earlier discussions of client acceptance and continuance and knowledge of the business from the perspective of their relationship to the preliminary audit plan.

General Planning Decisions to Be Made

1 *Anticipated* assessed level of control risk
2 Preliminary estimates of *materiality* levels for audit purposes
3 Financial statement items likely to require adjustment or other *risk conditions* that may require extension or modification of audit tests
4 *Overall timing* of audit work
5 *Extent of involvement,* if any, of consultants, specialists, and internal auditors
6 *Staffing requirements* and the expected assistance of entity personnel in data preparation

Result: A preliminary audit plan and time budget

Knowledge Obtained to Prepare Preliminary Audit Plan

1 *Business*—type of business, types of products and services, capital structure, locations, and methods of production, distribution, and compensation
2 *Industry*—economic conditions, government regulations, changes in technology, and competitive conditions
3 *Control environment, risk assessment, and monitoring*—including management philosophy and operating style, organizational structure, audit committee, methods of assigning authority and responsibility, management control methods, internal audit function, and human resources policies and practices
4 *Accounting system*—client accounting policies and procedures, accounting practices common in the industry, and unusual accounting matters likely to require more than ordinary attention, such as related-party transactions, unusual accounting estimates, complex or innovative accounting methods, significant classes of transactions, initiation of transactions, records, documents, and accounts used in the processing and reporting of transactions, accounting processing, and the financial reporting process
5 *Control activities*—control policies and procedures under which accounting data are produced, processed, reviewed, and accumulated within the organization
6 *Management integrity*—factors likely to create a predisposition on management's part to misstate financial statements

Procedures in Preparing Preliminary Audit Plan

I Procedures applied at the CPA firm using the auditor's records or other firm resources:

   A Reviewing correspondence files, prior year's work papers, permanent files, and prior years' financial statements and audit reports

   B Discussing matters that may affect the audit with firm personnel responsible for nonaudit services to the client and firm personnel familiar with the industry

   C Reviewing various sources of industry information, such as AICPA industry guides, industry or trade publications, and annual reports of companies in the industry

   D Considering the relevance of existing, and particularly any new, authoritative accounting or auditing pronouncements

   E Considering the reports to be issued as a result of the audit, such as SEC filings and special reports on contractual compliance

II Procedures applied on the client's premises:

   A Inquiring of management about current business developments

   B Reading current year's interim financial statements

   C Discussing the type, scope, and timing of the engagement with management and the board of directors or its audit committee

   D Touring the client's physical facilities and offices

   E Reading the corporate charter, bylaws, major contracts, and minutes of directors' and stockholders' meetings

   F Calculating general profitability, liquidity, and solvency ratios and trends and comparing to client experience and plans, and, if available, industry ratios and trends

III Completing a generalized questionnaire, checklist, or narrative memorandum that organizes and summarizes the information obtained by applying the procedures in I and II above

AUDIT DECISIONS IN PRELIMINARY PLANNING

The following discussion explains the auditor's considerations in making the general decisions that are usually necessary to prepare a preliminary audit plan.

Understanding the Internal Control Structure and the Control Risk Assessment

The auditor obtains an understanding of the internal control structure to plan the audit. The components of the internal control structure are:

- *Control environment, risk assessment, and monitoring,* including an awareness of such matters as management philosophy and operating style and organizational structure, among other things.

- *Accounting system,* including an understanding of significant classes of transactions, accounting processing, etc.
- *Control activities,* including knowledge of safeguards, authorizations, segregation of duties, etc., as needed to plan the audit.

The auditor uses the knowledge of the internal control structure to identify types of potential misstatements in the financial statements, consider factors that affect the risk of such misstatements, and design substantive tests.

The audit's understanding of the internal control structure is used initially to assess the auditability of the client company's financial statements. Auditability may be affected by doubts about management integrity or the adequacy of the records. If these doubts are serious enough, the auditor may conclude that an audit is not feasible.

The auditor also considers the internal control structure in assessing control risk. Assessing control risk is the process of evaluating the effectiveness of the client company's internal control structure policies and procedures in preventing or detecting material misstatements in the financial statements.

This assessment is used to determine the nature, timing, and extent of auditing procedures to be used to detect material misstatements in the financial statements.

These matters are explained further in Chapter 6 on the control risk assessment.

Materiality and Audit Risk

Since the generally accepted auditing standards were originally proposed in 1947, authoritative auditing literature has recognized that the elements of materiality and audit risk underlie the application of all the standards, particularly the standards of field work. SAS No. 47 (AU 312) was issued to provide a more explicit framework for considering audit risk and materiality in planning audit procedures and evaluating the results of those procedures.

Materiality and audit risk need to be considered at the financial statement level as part of general planning and at the account balance or transaction class level in planning audit procedures for specific balances or classes. The focus of this discussion is at the financial statement level. Use of materiality and audit risk in planning specific audit procedures for balances or transaction classes is discussed in Chapter 7 on planning substantive tests and Chapter 8 on audit sampling.

Materiality   The term *materiality* is used both often and loosely in accounting and auditing. The underlying concept is always essentially the same—it is the criterion for distinguishing the trivial from the important. The FASB, in Statement of Financial Accounting Concepts No. 2, defines materiality as:

> . . . the magnitude of an omission or misstatement of accounting information that in the light of surrounding circumstances, makes it probable that the judgment of a reasonable person relying on the information would have been changed or influenced by the omission or misstatement.

From this perspective, materiality judgments involve both quantitative and qualitative considerations.

In auditing, materality is used at the financial statement level and at the account balance or transaction class level, and it is used both in planning and evaluation. In all these uses, the underlying concept is the same, but the implementation is influenced by the auditor's purpose, practical necessity, and reasonableness in the circumstances. SAS No. 47 (AU 312.13) states that:

> The auditor plans the audit to obtain reasonable assurance of detecting misstatements that he believes could be large enough, individually or in the aggregate, to be *quantitatively* material to the financial statements. [Emphasis added.]

This means that in general planning the auditor wants to estimate a single dollar amount that would be material to the financial statements taken as a whole. At this stage, materiality is viewed as an allowance or "cushion" for misstatement in the financial statements. The auditor uses this amount as a guide to how effective audit procedures must be to result in a relatively low risk of failing to detect misstatements with a combined effect that exceeds this amount. Planning materiality has these components: detected known and likely misstatements that will not be corrected and an allowance for misstatements that will remain undetected because of the imprecision of auditing procedures. A *single* dollar amount is normally estimated because misstatements usually affect both the balance sheet and the income statement. For example, an overstatement of ending inventory will overstate both assets and net income. The only practical approach is to use the smallest aggregate amount that would affect one of the financial statements.

In all of its uses, materiality is a concept of relative significance. It depends on the amount of the item of interest and some relevant basis of comparison. Absolute dollar amounts are unworkable. An error of $10,000 might materially misstate the financial statements of a small business, but an error of $100,000 might not materially misstate the financial statements of a large business.

To estimate an amount for planning materiality, the auditor needs to select a base and a suitable percentage to apply to that base. This is a highly judgmental decision and not all CPAs do it the same way. Some CPA firms use a rule-of-thumb approach to estimating materiality for planning purposes. The following table summarizes one possible approach.

RULES-OF-THUMB FOR PLANNING MATERIALITY

Common bases	Range of percentages applied to base	Relative advantages
Income before taxes*	5 –10	Relevance
Total revenue	0.5– 2	Stability
Total assets	0.5– 2	Predictability and stability

*Income before tax is used rather than net income to neutralize the tax effect of transactions.

The table shows three constant percentage methods. Some auditors use a blend of these, making several calculations on a variety of bases and then taking the average of them. Others use a sliding scale, such as a declining percentage of total assets.

The choice of a rule-of-thumb depends on value judgments about relevance, stability, and predictability. Income may be the most relevant base for a company with publicly traded securities. However, because income can fluctuate significantly from year to year, it lacks stability, and it is not relevant to some entities such as nonprofit organizations. Generally in practice, size-related bases, such as total assets or total revenue are preferred because of their relative stability. Also, the information in the table is often combined in the rule-of-thumb. For example, another approach is to use the larger of 1 percent of total assets or total revenue.

Use of a rule-of-thumb as a decision aid in general planning is not universal in auditing practice. SAS No. 47 does not specifically require estimation or documentation of a single dollar amount for planning materiality. However, materiality has to be reduced to an explicit dollar amount as a practical necessity in conducting the audit. Making an explicit preliminary judgment is a useful planning tool. A CPA firm may adopt a specific rule-of-thumb, or the judgment may be left to the individual auditor in the circumstances.

The financial information used as a base may be taken from:

1 Financial statements to be audited (if available and not likely to be adjusted significantly as result of the audit)
2 Interim financial information (adjusted for expected seasonal or cyclical fluctuation and annualized)
3 Prior period's financial statements (adjusted for unusual matters and known significant changes, such as a new wage contract or a merger)

Making a preliminary judgment about the amount to be considered material to the financial statements taken as a whole is an important general planning decision. The auditor may use this judgment to identify components of financial statements to be emphasized, the locations to visit in a multilocation company, and, naturally, the size of a misstatement to be considered material in planning the nature, timing, and extent of specific auditing procedures. A smaller materiality amount results in more extensive testing and larger sample sizes for tests. Since different approaches to calculating materiality can lead to substantially different amounts, the auditor's judgment in the circumstances is key.

The amount considered material does not remain fixed after its initial calculation. The auditor may revise this judgment based on the results of audit tests and new information as the audit progresses, and the auditor's approach in *evaluation* at the completion of the audit may be considerably different. This means the amount estimated for planning materiality should not be confused with the amount used in the evaluation of the materiality of individual misstatements.

The auditor's use of materiality in evaluation will be influenced by qualitative considerations, additional information, and the nature of the decisions to be made. Qualitative considerations, for example, may include the nature of the transaction, such as related-party transactions or possible illegal acts. The use of materiality in evaluation is explained in Chapter 12 on completion and review.

Audit Risk   At the financial statement level, audit risk is defined, in SAS No. 47 (AU 312.02), as:

> The risk that the auditor may unknowingly fail to appropriately modify his opinion on financial statements that are materially misstated.

Naturally, the auditor wants to plan the audit so that audit risk will be limited to a low level that is appropriate for issuing an opinion on the financial statements. Another way of looking at it is that audit risk is the complement of audit assurance. The auditor wants reasonable assurance that the financial statements are not materially misstated. However, at the financial statement level, neither the degree of risk nor the degree of assurance can be precisely quantified as a percentage.

In general planning, the auditor considers audit risk from the perspective of whether this particular audit involves a higher than ordinary level of risk of material misstatement of the financial statements.

Audit risk is considered in general planning because it may specifically affect other decisions made at this time, such as staffing requirements, and other aspects of the preliminary audit plan. For example, some of the possible responses to higher than ordinary audit risk are to assign more experienced personnel, to increase the extent of supervision, and to conduct the audit with a heightened degree of professional skepticism.

Some matters that influence audit risk at the financial statement level also have a direct effect at the account balance level. For example, a company in a high technology industry would normally be judged to involve more than the ordinary level of audit risk for the entire audit, and the auditor would also expect particular problems with inventory valuation.

Some CPA firms use a questionnaire or checklist to assure an orderly consideration of conditions that may increase audit risk. A questionnaire on audit risk would include questions on:

1 *The environment in which the company is operating.* Have operations deteriorated recently? Do business conditions indicate future difficulties? Is there a likelihood of difficulty in meeting financial obligations? Is more than the usual significance likely to be attached to the financial statements, such as contests for control, other litigation, transfers of interest, or a public offering of securities?

2 *The attitudes or credibility of management.* Does management appear willing to take unusual risks? Does it unduly emphasize earnings-per-share or maintaining the market value of securities? Is a major portion of compensation derived from bonuses or stock options?

3 *Special problems in applying accounting principles or making accounting estimates.* Is a new accounting pronouncement applicable? Are there new transactions or conditions to be accounted for? Is a change in accounting principle to be made? Are there unusual transactions or adjustments, particularly near the end of the period? Are particular estimates of unusual significance because of the nature of operations or the industry?

The consideration of audit risk during general planning normally includes, among other matters, the following areas:

- The potential for management fraud
- The existence of related-party transactions
- The possibility of illegal acts
- The possibility of business failure

These matters are explored separately in the next section. However, it should be acknowledged at this point that these matters often involve both audit risk and business risk. *Business risk* is generally viewed as the risk of loss or injury to an *auditor's* professional practice from litigation, adverse publicity, or similar events. An auditor may expand the scope of the audit because of a higher than ordinary level of audit risk or business risk. The reverse is not necessarily true. A lower than ordinary business risk does not justify reducing the scope of the audit below what would ordinarily be necessary for conformity with generally accepted auditing standards. For example, a greater than normal potential for management fraud increases both audit risk and business risk. On the other hand, if a company's securities are publicly traded, there is increased business risk because of the expanded possibility of litigation, but not necessarily an increase in audit risk.

Special Areas of Audit Risk

The following special areas of audit risk are discussed at this point because of the influence the auditor's responsibilities in these areas has on audit planning. However, their influence naturally extends beyond planning to the performance of the audit, evaluation of the results of audit tests, and audit reporting.

Management Fraud   Statement on Auditing Standards No. 53 (AU 316.05) imposes a significant responsibility on the independent auditor to assess carefully the risk of management fraud in planning the audit. The SAS describes the auditor's responsibility as follows:

> The auditor should assess the risk that errors and irregularities may cause the financial statements to contain a material misstatement. Based on that assessment, the auditor should design the audit to provide reasonable assurance of detecting errors and irregularities that are material to the financial statements.

Errors are unintentional misstatements or omissions of amounts or disclosures in financial statements. *Irregularities* are intentional misstatements or omissions of amounts or disclosures in financial statements. Irregularities include *management fraud* (fraudulent financial reporting to make the financial statements misleading), and *employee fraud* (defalcations or the misappropriation of assets). Employee fraud is often referred to by a variety of terms with a legal origin, such as "embezzlement," and may also distort financial statements if the theft of assets is concealed in the accounting records. However, in discussions of the auditor's responsibilities, management fraud is usually stressed for the following reasons:

- Although employee fraud is a more frequent occurrence, the amounts involved are less likely to be material to the financial statements. If the employee fraud becomes material, auditing procedures directed to comparing or reconciling accounting records with counts or confirmations should detect it.

- In the area of employee fraud, there is no possible conflict between the auditor's and management's objectives, and management usually adopts control procedures and other safeguards, such as internal auditing and fidelity insurance, to minimize the consequences.

In the second respect, management fraud is considerably different. The auditor assumes that there is no necessary conflict of interest with management. However, the auditor must specifically consider the possibility that management may have made material misrepresentations or may have overridden control procedures. This is the reason that the initial phase of the audit—understanding the client—includes obtaining information relevant to management's integrity.

SAS No. 53 (AU 316) makes clear that the auditor should exercise an attitude of professional skepticism. This attitude requires an objective evaluation rather than a presumption of management honesty or dishonesty. An assessment that the risk of material irregularities is high is not a prejudgment that management lacks integrity. If the auditor really believed that management had no integrity, the auditor would probably regard the financial statements as unauditable. The auditor's risk assessment is used to design an audit that has no more than a relatively low risk of failing to detect the potential material misstatements. However, the auditor does not guarantee detection of all material misstatements.

The auditor's risk assessment is made by obtaining and evaluating information about the client company's characteristics and management. These characteristics are sometimes called risk factors or red flags because their presence is a warning of the need for caution. Examples of red flags that are indicators of a predisposition to material misrepresentations include:

Management Characteristics

- Management operating and financing decisions are dominated by a single person.
- Management's attitude toward financial reporting is unduly aggressive.
- Management (particularly senior accounting personnel) turnover is high.
- Management places undue emphasis on meeting earnings projections.
- Management's reputation in the business community is poor.

Operating and Industry Characteristics

- Profitability of entity relative to its industry is inadequate or inconsistent.
- Sensitivity of operating results to economic factors (inflation, interest rates, unemployment, etc.) is high.
- Rate of change in entity's industry is rapid.
- Direction of change in entity's industry is declining with many business failures.
- Organization is decentralized without adequate monitoring.
- Internal or external matters that raise substantial doubt about the entity's ability to continue as a going concern are present.

Engagement Characteristics

- Many contentious or difficult accounting issues are present.
- Significant difficult-to-audit transactions or balances are present.
- Significant and unusual related-party transactions not in the ordinary course of business are present.
- Nature, cause (if known), or the amount of known and likely misstatements detected in the audit or prior period's financial statements is significant.
- It is a new client with no prior audit history or sufficient information is not available from the predecessor auditor.

These same considerations also have a bearing on the attention given to related-party transactions, the subject of the next section.

Related-Party Transactions   The auditor must be concerned with two distinguishable, but connected, aspects of related-party transactions—adequate disclosure and management fraud. Accounting standards (FASB Statement No. 57) require disclosure of the nature and volume of transactions with related parties because this information may be essential to understanding the financial statements. For example, if 60 percent of a company's revenue is derived from sales to a party under management's influence, knowledge of the relationship is obviously essential in evaluating the company's future earnings prospects. However, the existence of significant transactions with related parties is no basis for presuming management dishonesty. There are many legitimate reasons for such business relationships and transactions. The connection to management fraud arises from the possibility that the fact that the other party to material transaction is related may be concealed from the auditor and may not be disclosed adequately, or the transaction may be a sham.

For these reasons, the auditor is concerned with identifying related parties and transactions with such parties. These matters require the auditor's considered attention because accounting systems are often not designed to accumulate transactions with related parties separately, and if the relationship is concealed from the auditor, the identification of related-party transactions is even more difficult.

SAS No. 6 (AU 334) as amended by SAS No. 45 describes the auditor's responsibility for identifying material related-party transactions and evaluating the adequacy of their disclosure. Generally, the auditor's approach is as follows:

- *Identify related parties.* Through inquiry and inspection of relevant data, determine the identity of related parties so that material transactions with them can be examined during the audit.
- *Identify material transactions.* Through scanning and other analysis identify transactions that materially affect the financial statements and evaluate the possibility of relationships with the other party.
- *Examine identified material related-party transactions.* Through normal auditing procedures, such as inquiry, vouching, and inspection, obtain an understanding of the business purpose of the transactions and their effect on the financial statements. If necessary, apply unusual procedures such as inspecting evidence in the other party's possession.

- *Evaluate the adequacy of disclosure.* Based on the evidence obtained consider whether the financial statements appropriately describe and disclose the nature of the relationship, the dollar amount and nature of transactions, and the amounts due to or from related parties.

Audit procedures normally applied to identify related parties at the start of the audit include:

- Inequity of the predecessor auditor
- Review of prior year's work papers
- Inquiry of management
- Reading or scanning stockholder listings, information on pension and similar trusts, and investment listings
- Reading minutes of stockholders' and directors' meetings

Note that these procedures are among those listed earlier as procedures ordinarily applied as part of preliminary planning. Identification of related parties is only one of several types of information obtained by these procedures.

Related parties include affiliates; equity investees; pension and profitsharing trusts for employees; principal owners, management, and members of their immediate families; and other parties subject to significant influence by management. Once related parties are identified, examination of related-party transactions is pursued during examination of relevant account balances or classes of transactions. Also, the auditor should apply procedures to give adequate consideration to the possibility that the other party to material transactions is related.

Illegal Acts   The term *illegal acts* means violations of laws or governmental regulations. They include acts performed by:

- The entity whose financial statements are being audited
- Management or employees acting on behalf of the entity

Misconduct by personnel is not included if it is unrelated to the entity's business activities.

The auditor's responsibility for detecting illegal acts in general needs to be clearly distinguished from responsibility for fraud detection. Management fraud or employee fraud may be illegal, but they are more directly related to distortion of the financial statements or underlying accounting data.

The auditor's responsibility for fraud detection is set forth in SAS No. 53 (AU 316), and the auditor's responsibility for illegal acts is covered in SAS No. 54 (AU 317). If an illegal act has a direct and material effect on the determination of a financial statement line item amount, the auditor's responsibility is the same as for detection of material irregularities and the auditor should follow the guidance in SAS No. 53. For all other illegal acts, the guidance in SAS No. 54 applies.

American business is affected by many laws and regulations including those related to securities trading, occupational safety and health, food and drug administration, environmental protection, equal employment, and antitrust matters such as price-fixing. Normally, the auditor does not design the audit to include any procedures specifically directed to the detection of such illegal acts. Even though violations of these laws and regulations could have consequences very material to financial statements, an independent auditor is not really equipped to recognize or detect such matters unless he or she is informed by the client or its lawyer. Determination of whether an act is illegal is usually beyond the auditor's professional competence. Also, many illegal acts are unrelated to accounting records and financial statements.

Violations of these laws or regulations have *indirect* effects on financial statements that usually arise from the need to disclose material contingent liabilities. If the auditor is aware of a violation, the need for disclosure must be considered. However, the auditor need not perform any procedures solely for the purpose of detecting such violations. On the other hand, many of the procedures the auditor applies for general purposes such as reading minutes, reviewing subsequent events, and inquiry of the client's lawyer may provide evidence of a government agency investigation or enforcement proceeding concerning violations of laws or regulations. Also, the auditor usually requests from the client a letter that includes management's representations concerning the absence of violations or possible violations that should be considered for disclosure in the financial statements, or as a basis for recording a loss contingency. The auditor is not required to perform any other procedures in this area if information concerning possible illegal acts does not materialize.

If the auditor does become aware of information concerning a possible illegal act, the auditor should obtain an understanding of the act and the circumstances surrounding it, and gather sufficient information to evaluate its effect on:

- The financial statements, including such matters as loss contingencies (e.g., fines, penalties, damages, litigation) and adequacy of disclosure (e.g., if material revenue is derived from transactions involving illegal acts or if the illegal acts create unusual risks)
- The audit, especially the reliability of management representations

The procedures to obtain this information would include inquiring of management at a level above those involved, if possible. If satisfactory information is not obtained that there has been no illegal act, the auditor should consult with the client's legal counsel and continue to perform additional procedures to obtain a sufficient understanding of the act. Additional procedures might include reviewing supporting documents such as checks and invoices, confirming the transaction with the other party or with intermediaries such as a bank, or considering whether similar transactions have occurred and identifying them.

The auditor should inform the client's audit committee (or its equivalent if there is no audit committee) about the illegal acts coming to the auditor's attention. However, the auditor continues to have an obligation of confidentiality, unless the matter affects the opinion on the financial statements. Circumstances that may arise that would result in a duty for the auditor to notify parties outside the client include disclosure:

- As a "reportable event" when the entity reports an auditor change on Form 8-K
- To a successor auditor under SAS No. 7 (AU 315)
- In response to a valid subpoena
- To a funding agency or other specified agency under the requirements for audits of entities that receive financial assistance from a government agency

Examples of laws or regulations that could have a *direct and material* effect on financial statement amounts (and therefore covered under SAS No. 53—*Errors and Irregularities*—rather than under the standards for illegal acts) are:

- Internal Revenue Code and other tax laws
- Applicable laws and regulations affecting the amount of revenue accrued under government contracts

The auditor's responsibility for detection errors and irregularities is discussed earlier in this chapter.

Business Failure   Auditors consider the likelihood of a client's filing for bankruptcy after the audit. A bankruptcy increases the chance that the auditor will have to defend the quality of the audit in court. In addition, an imminent business failure may have an effect on the appropriateness of the presentation of financial statements or may motivate management misrepresentations.

The auditor considers the risk of failure of the client's business at several points. Initially the auditor ordinarily would give some consideration to the matter as part of client acceptance and continuance. As a matter of prudence, because of the likelihood of litigation, many auditors would not accept a client who appeared to be headed for bankruptcy. However, this is a consideration of business risk rather than audit risk.

In preliminary planning, an auditor would also give some consideration to the possibility of business failure. However, an audit ordinarily is not planned to search for evidential matter to support a company's continued existence. In the absence of evidence to the contrary, continuation is a normal presumption under generally accepted accounting principles.

As part of preliminary planning, however, an auditor would consider whether there was information contrary to this normal presumption. For example, if a company has recurring operating losses, a working capital deficiency, negative cash flow, or similar severe financial or operating problems, the auditor would consider the significance of the contrary information and management plans or other factors that might mitigate the problems.

The reasons that the auditor has for considering the possibility of business failure during preliminary planning are as follows:

- The principal conditions that raise doubt about the company's ability to continue may need to be disclosed in the financial statements if the likelihood of failure is more than remote.

- The conditions that raise doubt about continued existence may also predispose management to misstate financial statements.
- If the conditions cause a significant uncertainty about the propriety of the amounts and classification of financial statement items, the auditor's report would have to be modified.

All these reasons might affect the audit plan and the nature, timing, and extent of auditing procedures.

SAS No. 59 (AU 341) describes the auditor's responsibility for evaluating whether there is substantial doubt about the client company's ability to continue as a going concern for a reasonable period of time.

The client's status as a going concern relates to its ability to continue to meet its obligations as they become due without substantial disposition of assets outside the ordinary course of business, restructuring of debt, externally forced revisions of its operations, or similar actions. To continue for *a reasonable period of time* means for a period of time not to exceed 1 year beyond the date of the financial statements being audited.

The auditor is not required to design audit procedures solely to identify conditions and events that taken together indicate there could be substantial doubt about the client's ability to continue as a going concern. SAS No. 59 (AU 341) requires that the auditor evaluate the results of audit procedures designed and performed to achieve other objectives for the purpose of considering whether there is substantial doubt about going concern status. Examples of procedures that may provide evidence of going concern problems include analytical procedures, review of subsequent events, inquiry of legal counsel, reading minutes, and reviewing compliance with the terms of debt and loan agreements. Some of these procedures are performed near the completion of the audit so the auditor cannot make an overall evaluation until then.

Some procedures that would identify going concern problems, such as preliminary analytical procedures, are performed as part of planning the audit. When the auditor identifies going concern problems during audit planning, the auditor can usually be more efficient in gathering evidence about management's plans to deal with the conditions or events that create substantial doubt.

If at the completion of the audit, the auditor has concluded that there is substantial doubt about the client's ability to continue as a going concern, the auditor needs to consider the adequacy of disclosure and the effect on the audit report. Uncertainty about going concern status is treated in the same way as any other material uncertainty. The auditor needs to add an explanatory paragraph to the report to describe the uncertainty, but the opinion paragraph is unqualified. Reporting when there is a material uncertainty is discussed in more detail in Chapter 13.

Overall Timing of Engagement

The overall timing of the engagement essentially relates to when the major steps or phases in the audit will be done and when principal substantive tests will be applied to specific account balances.

Basic Time Segments   The first thing to understand about timing decisions is the relationship between the financial statement period and the audit report date. This relationship for a calendar year company is illustrated in Figure 5-2.

The financial statement period is determined by the period of operations covered in the financial statements, and it ends at the balance sheet date. The auditor's opinion is expressed on the balance sheet *as of,* or *at,* this date and the income statement for the period ended *as of,* or *at* this date. While there is a free choice between "as of" and "at" in report language, it is important to recognize that, in talking about timing of audit procedures, timing relates to the application of audit procedures *as of* a particular date. For example, many audit procedures are applied to account balances as of the balance sheet date, but the actual time the procedures are done will depend on factors such as the specific audit objective, convenience, and practicality. An asset physically on hand might be counted on the balance sheet date, but an account receivable balance as of that date could be confirmed any reasonable period after that date.

The subsequent period is determined by the length of time necessary to complete the audit which, in turn, is determined by the time schedule of the audit plan and developments as the engagement progresses. The audit report is dated as of the completion of field work. This date is intended to establish a cutoff point for the auditor's responsibility to keep informed about subsequent events, that is, events after the balance sheet date that could materially affect the financial statements reported on.

In preliminary planning the auditor will establish a time schedule for the engagement based on pertinent client requests of legal requirements that establish audit report deadlines and based on planning decisions about the timing of audit procedures.

Efficiency and Effectiveness in Timing   The auditor's dilemma in making timing decisions is to strike an appropriate balance between efficiency and effectiveness. From an effectiveness standpoint, later is usually better. For example, an auditor could substantiate that accounts receivable were valid and collectible by waiting until all accounts

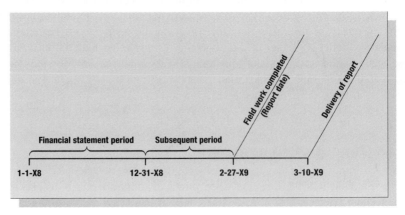

FIGURE 5-2

at the balance sheet date were collected. This is a very effective approach, but not a practical one for more than a portion of receivables, because of the need for current financial information. An auditor frequently does make effective use of the time lag between the end of the financial statement period and the report date, but practical considerations cause time pressures for earlier completion.

Outside pressures for efficiency are caused by things such as SEC filing deadlines and related considerations in selling securities or obtaining loans. CPA firms also have to consider difficulties in scheduling audit staff time. Many clients have calendar year-ends, and in many industries there is a traditional year-end for fiscal periods. This causes peak periods during the year and results in the so-called *busy season* for CPAs.

The chief method used for achieving a smoother work load during the year and meeting report deadlines shortly after year-end is to schedule audit tests earlier than year-end to the extent that it is practical and does not impair audit effectiveness.

Timing Decisions   In a new engagement, one important timing consideration is beyond the auditor's control—the date of appointment when the auditor is engaged. Both the auditor and client benefit when the auditor's appointment is relatively early. This allows the auditor to plan audit tests for optimal efficiency and effectiveness and give early consideration to things that may cause accounting or auditing problems. In some cases, difficulties can be corrected and audit problems avoided. For example, if the auditor identifies defects in client routines for closing the accounting records, correction can save considerable audit time.

In a continuing engagement, the critical timing decisions are as follows:

- *Tests of transaction classes.* Since the auditor reports on transactions that occur during a period of time, these tests can conveniently be applied during the year if that is desirable for efficiency. Audit procedures are applied to transactions that have occurred from the start of the year to the date of interim testing. A common approach is to do this type of audit test as of the ninth or tenth month of the period, that is, September or October for a calendar year company. (As explained in Chapter 7, these tests may be tests of controls, substantive tests, or a combination.)
- *Principal substantive tests.* Since the auditor reports on balances as of the balance sheet date, the ability to apply principal substantive tests at an interim date depends entirely on effectiveness considerations. As the length of time before the balance sheet date increases, the risk of extending the audit conclusion at the interim date to the balance sheet date also increases.

Principal substantive tests are tests of details of balance sheet accounts that are the principal, or primary, source of evidential matter for achieving specific audit objectives. For example, confirmation of accounts receivable with customers and observation of the client's taking of physical inventory are the substantive tests of details that provide the principal evidential matter for audit objectives related to the existence assertion for those accounts. Common interim testing dates for such account balances would be between 1 and 3 months before year-end. The audit effectiveness considerations in making this timing decision and the approach to extending interim audit conclusions to year-end are explained in Chapter 7.

Involvement of Specialists and Others

In the audit of a complex organization the auditor may require the assistance of specialists within his or her own firm, such as specialists in complex computer systems, mathematical techniques, SEC rules and regulations, or taxes; specialists within or serving the client's organization, such as internal auditors, engineers, or legal counsel; and independent specialists, such as consulting actuaries. It should be recognized that the auditor's responsibility for reviewing and understanding the work of specialists within a CPA firm differs dramatically from the outside experts identified above. They are mentioned together here only because consideration of the extent of their involvement is a part of preliminary planning. The considerations that relate to using the work of internal auditors are discussed in Chapter 6 as part of obtaining an understanding of the internal control structure and assessing control risk.

The first type of specialist considered here is one employed by or engaged by the client. In essence, the auditor views the work of such a specialist as a source of evidential matter, and the auditor must evaluate the competence and sufficiency of that evidential matter. The other specialists are part of the CPA firm and when they assist in an audit they become part of the audit team.

Specialists Engaged or Employed by Client   The specialists of this type are those with training or skills in fields unrelated to accounting. The auditor may sometimes need to use the work of a specialist in a field other than accounting or auditing. For example, the work of an actuary, appraiser, engineer, or geologist may be needed in a particular engagement. The reserves of life insurance companies require actuarial determinations; the quantity or condition of specialized assets, such as mineral reserves, may require studies by engineers or geologists; the valuation of specialized assets, such as works of art, may require appraisal.

The auditor may need to use the work of such a specialist because a specialist has determined a material amount presented in financial statements or because a substantive test of a material account balance requires specialized skill or knowledge. When the work of a specialist must be used, according to SAS No. 73 (AU 336), the auditor should evaluate the professional qualifications and reputation of the specialist by inquiry or other procedures as appropriate. For example, the auditor may consider the specialist's professional license, if appropriate, his or her membership in professional organizations, and his or her reputation in the view of those familiar with the specialist's work.

The auditor cannot be expected to have the knowledge or skill of a person qualified to engage in another profession, but the auditor should not accept a specialist's work based solely on the specialist's qualifications and reputation. SAS No. 73 (AU 336) indicates that although the appropriateness and reasonableness of methods or assumptions used and their application are the responsibility of the specialist, the auditor should obtain an understanding of the methods or assumptions used by the specialist. Ordinarily, the auditor would use the work of the specialist unless the auditor believes that the findings are unreasonable in the circumstances. The auditor, naturally, would test any data used by the specialist and, if the specialist had a relationship to the client, additional procedures might be necessary.

CPA Firm Industry Specialists   CPA firms often designate specialists in industries that have unique organizational or operating characteristics that raise special accounting or auditing considerations. For example, utilities, insurance companies, and retailers all have unique operating characteristics that create special problems in the application of accounting principles or the audit of accounting estimates.

Every auditor in charge of an engagement is expected to obtain an adequate understanding of the client and its industry. However, the industry specialist is available to consult on special accounting or auditing questions and to review the audit plan and programs, work papers, and financial statements and auditor's report for the first audit of a client in the designated industry. The industry specialist is also usually responsible for keeping abreast of current developments in the industry and recommending firm policies and procedures appropriate for the industry. Naturally, a CPA firm must have a number of clients in a specialized industry to make designation of a specialist worthwhile. The industries in which specialists are designated and the duties and authority of specialists are functions of the size and philosophy of the CPA firm.

CPA Firm Functional Specialists   Functional specialists are often designated for the areas of taxes, management consulting services, SEC practice, computers, and statistics and other mathematical applications. Specialists in taxes and management consulting services provide services to clients in separate engagements and consult on request on pertinent matters that arise in audits. SEC specialists are available for consultation on engagements that involve SEC filings, but their main function is to review plans, programs, work papers, and filings for every such engagement.

Specialization in computers and statistics often requires two levels of expertise. First, there are specialists in data processing technology and mathematics. These specialists are trained professionals in their own fields and may be in the management consulting services section of a firm. Their special skills are used from time to time in audit engagements when unique or sophisticated problems arise. They also usually participate in the development of firmwide policies and procedures for statistical or computer applications.

Second, there are computer audit specialists and statistical audit specialists. They are auditors, but specially equipped auditors with advanced training and experience in their specialized fields. They usually work as members of the audit team and plan and review the application of the specialized tools—use of the computer or statistical sampling—in an audit engagement. Staff auditors generally handle ordinary computer use and statistical applications. However, it is usually unreasonable to expect staff auditors to have the time or expert knowledge required to assure the valid use of the more complex applications of these tools. However, staff auditors must recognize when the assistance of a computer audit specialist or a statistical audit specialist is required and supervise their work. In a large firm, computer audit specialists and statistical audit specialists may also be supervised by coordinators in each respective area.

CPA Firm Technical Specialists   Some CPA firms have also designated technical specialists. The subjects of accounting and auditing in many ways can today be viewed as specialties. Every auditor is expected to be an expert in accounting and auditing. However, there are so many authoritative pronouncements in accounting and auditing and so many complexities that can arise in the application of pronouncements that some firms have found it advantageous to designate specialists in this area. These specialists are available to consult on questions that arise in particular engagements and to develop firm policies and procedures to assure uniform implementation and compliance with new pronouncements throughout the firm.

Assignment and Scheduling of Audit Staff

Based on the procedures applied during preliminary planning, the auditor is able to anticipate the assistance that will be available from client personnel and determine the size and broad qualifications of audit staff needed for the engagement.

Supervision of Staff   The first standard of field work requires both adequate planning and proper supervision. According to SAS No. 22 (AU 331.11):

> Supervision involves directing the efforts of assistants who are involved in accomplishing the objectives of the audit and determining whether those objectives were accomplished. Elements of supervision include instructing assistants, keeping informed of significant problems encountered, reviewing the work performed, and dealing with differences of opinion among firm personnel. The extent of supervision appropriate in a given instance depends on many factors, including the complexity of the subject matter and the qualifications of persons performing the work.

The instruction and review provided by a supervisor on an engagement are important for both assuring satisfactory completion of audit work and developing audit staff. A great deal about auditing can be learned only in the field, and the quality of this experience depends on the ability and effort of the supervisor.

Supervision is accomplished by observing staff, reviewing the results of audit work in work papers, and conferences among staff and supervisors. To achieve an organized approach to supervision and assure the control of field work, most CPA firms use checklists and specially designed memoranda for such things as appraising staff performance and identifying and resolving significant matters raised during the engagement. For example, some firms use a memorandum of matters for the attention of the partner. The memorandum identifies significant accounting or auditing problems encountered and is updated throughout the engagement.

Most of the field supervision in an audit is the responsibility of the accountant-in-charge, or senior. An overriding review of the senior's work is made by the manager and partner.

Time Budgets and Work Schedules   A time budget is an estimate of the total hours an audit is expected to take. It is based on the information obtained in the first major step in the audit—obtaining an understanding of the client. A time budget takes into consideration such things as the client's size as indicated by its gross assets, sales, number of employees, and so forth; the locations of client facilities; the anticipated accounting and auditing problems; and the competence and experience of staff available.

The total time must be allocated by the preparation of work schedules indicating who is to do what and how long it should take. Thus, total hours are budgeted by major categories and may be scheduled on a weekly basis.

Assignment of Competent Staff   The number and quality of audit staff needed on an engagement will depend on the complexity and extent of audit work anticipated. Most CPA firms rely on quality control practices related to hiring, development, and advancement to assure audit staff of the necessary competence. In addition, the assignment of staff to audit engagements to match the competence and experience of staff with the requirements of the various audit engagements underway at the same time is a specialized personnel function in a large CPA firm.

ANALYTICAL PROCEDURES

SAS No. 56 (AU 329.02) defines analytical procedures:

> Analytical procedures . . . consist of evaluations of financial information made by a study of plausible relationships among both financial and nonfinancial data. Analytical procedures range from simple comparisons to the use of complex models involving many relationships and elements of data. A basic premise underlying the application of analytical procedures is that plausible relationships among data may reasonably be expected to exist and continue in the absence of known conditions to the contrary.

Examples of analytical procedures include the following:

1 Comparison of the financial information with information for comparable prior period(s)
2 Comparison of financial information with anticipated results (for example, budgets and forecasts)
3 Study of the relationships of elements of financial information that would be expected to conform to a predictable pattern based on the entity's experience
4 Comparison of financial information with similar information regarding the industry in which the entity operates
5 Study of the relationship of financial information with nonfinancial information

Various methods may be used to perform these procedures. They may be made using dollars, physical quantities, ratios, models, or percentages.

Uses of Analytical Procedures

Analytical procedures may be used in the following different ways in planning and conducting an audit:

- *In planning the audit*—to assist the auditor in planning the nature, timing, and extent of other auditing procedures
- *As substantive tests*—to obtain evidential matter about particular assertions related to account balances or classes of transactions

- *In the overall review*—to assist in the final stage of the audit in assessing the conclusions the auditor has reached and in evaluation of the overall financial statement presentation

SAS No. 56 requires the auditor to apply some analytical procedures in planning the audit and in the overall review at the end of the audit, and provides guidance when analytical procedures are used as substantive tests.

Analytical Procedures in Planning the Audit

In preliminary planning, analytical procedures are used to gain a better understanding of the client, its business, and its industry, and transactions and events that have occurred since the last audit date. These procedures may also identify a risk regarding a component of the financial statements that requires more than normal audit attention. Analytical procedures useful in preliminary planning include:

1 Computation of ratios and percentage relationships for comparison with prior years, budgets, and industry averages
2 Comparison of current balances in the financial statements with balances of prior periods and budgeted amounts
3 Scanning the financial statements for unusual or significant transactions, events, or balances

Ratio and Trend Analysis   To gain a better understanding of the client the auditor may use common profitability, liquidity, solvency, and activity ratios. Examples are presented in the following list.

Ratios Commonly Used in Understanding Client

   I Profitability
     A Gross margin (net sales minus cost of goods sold over net sales)
     B Asset turnover (net sales over total assets)
     C Return on investment (net income over stockholders' equity)
  II Liquidity
     A Current ratio (current assets over current liabilities)
     B Quick ratio (cash, short-term securities, and net receivables over current liabilities)
 III Solvency
     A Debt to equity ratio (long-term debt over stockholders' equity)
     B Debt service coverage (net income, interest, depreciation, and similar noncash charges over annual principal and interest payments)
 IV Activity
     A Inventory turnover (cost of goods sold over average inventory)
     B Receivables turnover (net sales over average accounts receivable)

These or similar ratios may be compared to the following:

I *Industry data.* Information on average ratios in industries may be obtained from such sources as Dun & Bradstreet, Robert Morris Associates, trade publications, and computer data base services.
II *Internal data.* Internal information useful for comparison of ratios includes:
  A *Prior years.* Comparable ratios may be computed for the client for prior years, and trends may be analyzed.
  B *Budgets.* If the client has effective budgeting procedures, significant variations from the budget indicate activity that the client did not expect at the time the budget was prepared.

Comparisons of internal data (with prior periods or budgets) is most commonly used. Initially, comparison with industry data may seem appealing and may, in fact, be useful. However, the industry information may be difficult to compare because of differences between a client's characteristics and the industry due to different lines of business, accounting methods, and geographical influences.

An auditor may also compute percentage relationships among balances that are expected to be related (receivables and bad debts, equipment and depreciation, interest expense and debt) and compare them to prior experience and budget data.

Comparison of Balances The auditor can identify account balances that have changed significantly simply by comparing the amounts for the current and prior year on the working trial balance in the work papers. Similar comparisons can be made to budgeted amounts, or the client's internal reports comparing and analyzing budgeted and actual amounts may be reviewed.

Scanning The auditor can scan the financial statements and trial balance to identify unusual or significant matters. This procedure may also be applied to quarterly financial information.

Analytical Procedures as Substantive Tests

The use of analytical procedures to plan tests of details and to reduce or replace tests of details is explained in subsequent chapters. SAS No. 56 (AU 329) does not require the use of analytical procedures as substantive tests; it requires them only during planning and during the overall review at the final stage of the audit. SAS No. 56 simply notes that analytical procedures, in some cases, can be more effective or efficient than tests of details for achieving particular substantive testing objectives. How effective or efficient the analytical procedure will be as a substantive test depends on the following:

- The nature of the assertion
- The plausibility and predictability of the relationship
- The availability and reliability of the data used to develop the expectation
- The precision of the expectation

For example, if a popular hotel/resort maintained a 98 percent occupancy rate, a reasonable estimate of room revenue might be obtained by multiplying the number of rooms by the average rate times 98 percent. If room revenue on the books is significantly more or less than the estimate, the auditor should perform additional procedures to determine the reason.

When analytical procedures are used as substantive tests, the auditor must investigate any significant unexpected differences identified. *Significant unexpected differences* would include fluctuations that are not expected, the absence of expected fluctuations, and other items that appear to be unusual that are identified by analytical procedures and that the auditor believes indicate matters significant to the audit. Procedures useful to the auditor in evaluating unexpected differences include:

- Reconsidering the methods and factors used in developing the expectations
- Inquiry of management
- Corroboration of management responses with other evidential matter

The extent of investigation of significant unexpected differences depends on the circumstances but generally should go beyond inquiries of management. For example, if the auditor notes a significant increase in bad debts expense as a percentage of sales, the investigation should be more extensive than asking management about changes in credit policy. Also, if the auditor is aware that credit policy has changed, but there is noticeable change in the relation between bad debt expense and sales, investigation would also be necessary.

Examples of analytical procedures useful as substantive tests include:

1 Calculation of the approximate balance in a revenue or expense account
2 Scanning the details of an account balance
3 Comparing the details of an account balance to prior annual and interim amounts and budgeted amounts for similar periods
4 Calculating ratios based on the detailed components of a particular account balance

Analytical Procedures in the Overall Review

In the final stage of the audit, the auditor uses analytical procedures for one last look to evaluate the overall financial statement presentation and double-check the audit conclusions. The partner or manager, in the overall review, would generally read the financial statements and notes and consider the adequacy of the evidence gathered in response to unusual or unexpected balances identified and consider whether any unusual or unexpected balances were not previously noted.

The auditor also considers whether there could be substantial doubt about the entity's ability to continue as a going concern for a reasonable period of time. The auditor may note negative trends: recurring operating losses, adverse financial ratios such as a high debt-to-equity ratio, poor debt service coverage ratio, low return on investment, etc. The auditor's response when a "going concern" doubt arises is discussed more fully in Chapter 12.

Data Used in Analytical Procedures

In planning analytical procedures, the auditor should consider whether the data needed are easily available, and consider the audit time that will be needed to gather the particular information in determining whether other audit procedures would be more effective for the same effort.

The auditor also considers the reliability of the data used in the analytical procedures. More reliable data results in more effective audit evidence. Factors influencing reliability include the following:

- Data from an independent source outside the entity are generally more reliable than internal data.
- Data from a different department within the entity are generally more reliable than data whose source is the department responsible for the amount being audited.
- Data from a system with effective controls are more reliable than data from a poorly controlled system.
- Data audited in the previous year, or in the current audit, are more reliable than unaudited data.
- Data from a variety of sources that corroborate each other are more reliable than data from only one source.

The auditor also considers the plausibility, predictability, and precision of the analytical relationship. For example:

- Relationships in a stable environment are more predictable than relationships in a dynamic, changing environment.
- Relationships involving income statement amounts (transactions over a period of time) tend to be more predictable than relationships involving only balance sheet accounts (amounts as at a point in time).
- Relationships involving transactions that are subject to management discretion are less predictable.
- Direct relationships are more predictable than indirect relationships, e.g., the auditor's prediction of annual rental income (12 times the monthly rent per the lease) is more predictable than selling and administrative expenses as a ratio of sales volume.
- Disaggregated relationships are more precise and show clearer relationships than combined or aggregated relationships, e.g., comparisons by line of business will generally be more effective than companywide comparisons, and monthly comparisons will generally be more effective than annual comparisons.

CHAPTER 5 ASSIGNMENTS
OBJECTIVE QUESTIONS

5-1 For each one of the following statements, indicate whether the statement is true or false.

T F **a** A CPA firm should adopt adequate policies and procedures on client acceptance, but the only one that is specifically required is communication with a predecessor auditor.

T F b Since the assets and liabilities of most commercial entities are similar in nature, an auditor does not need to be concerned about obtaining a knowledge and understanding of the business except for specialized industries.

T F c The procedures used in preparing the preliminary audit plan are virtually all done at the CPA firm before visiting the client's premises.

T F d Determining a single dollar amount that is material to the financial statements taken as a whole during preliminary planning is a requirement of professional standards.

T F e Materiality, as used in planning, is a quantitative consideration, but, as used in evaluation, has both quantitative and qualitative aspects.

T F f Audit risk at the financial statement level must be quantified during preliminary planning.

T F g The auditor has a responsibility to search for fraud that could be material to the financial statements, and failure to detect a material fraud is clear evidence that the auditor has not satisfied this professional responsibility.

T F h The auditor's procedures in preliminary planning include identification of both related parties and material transactions regardless of the relationship with the other party.

T F i Violations of the Internal Revenue Code should be addressed by the auditor as "errors and irregularities" under SAS No. 53 and not as an "illegal act" under SAS No. 54.

T F j The auditor's responsibility is to search for evidential matter to support a company's continued existence.

T F k The audit report should be dated as of the date the report is issued.

T F l Analytical procedures are helpful to the auditor in planning other audit procedures, but are not required by professional standards.

T F m An example of an analytical procedure is comparison of a vendor's invoice with the recorded amount of equipment.

T F n An analytical procedure would never use nonfinancial data.

5-2 The following questions relate to client acceptance and communication with a predecessor auditor. Select the *best* response.

    a What is the responsibility of a successor auditor with respect to communicating with the predecessor auditor in connection with a prospective new audit client?

        1 The successor auditor has *no* responsibility to contact the predecessor auditor.

        2 The successor auditor should obtain permission from the prospective client to contact the predecessor auditor.

        3 The successor auditor should contact the predecessor regardless of whether the prospective client authorizes contact.

        4 The successor auditor need *not* contact the predecessor if the successor is aware of all available relevant facts.

    b Hawkins requested permission to communicate with the predecessor auditor and review certain portions of the predecessor auditor's work papers. The prospective client's refusal to permit this will bear directly on Hawkin's decision concerning the:

        1 Adequacy of the preplanned audit program

        2 Ability to establish consistency in application of accounting principles between years

        3 Apparent scope limitation

        4 Integrity of management

c The understanding between the client and the auditor as to the degree of responsibilities to be assumed by each are normally set forth in a(an):

1 Representation letter

2 Engagement letter

3 Management letter

4 Comfort letter

d Before accepting an audit engagement, a successor auditor should make specific inquiries of the predecessor auditor regarding the predecessor's:

1 Awareness of the consistency in the application of generally accepted accounting principles between periods

2 Evaluation of all matters of continuing accounting significance

3 Opinion of any subsequent events occurring since the predecessor's audit report was issued

4 Understanding as to the reasons for the change of auditors

AICPA

5-3 The following questions relate to several of the factors that affect the auditor's general planning decisions. Select the *best* response.

a Which of the following underlies the application of generally accepted auditing standards, particularly the standards of field work and reporting?

1 The elements of materiality and relative risk

2 The element of internal control structure

3 The element of corroborating evidence

4 The element of reasonable assurance

b The independent auditor's plan for an audit in accordance with generally accepted auditing standards is influenced by the possibility of material misstatements. The auditor will therefore conduct the audit with an attitude of:

1 Professional skepticism

2 Subjective mistrust

3 Objective indifference

4 Professional responsiveness

c With respect to errors and irregularities, which of the following should be part of an auditor's planning of the audit engagement?

1 Plan to search for errors or irregularities that would have a material or immaterial effect on the financial statements

2 Plan to discover errors or irregularities that are either material or immaterial

3 Plan to discover errors or irregularities that are material

4 Plan to search for errors or irregularities that would have a material effect on the financial statements

d An audit performed in accordance with generally accepted auditing standards generally should:

1 Be expected to provide assurance that illegal acts will be detected where control risk is minimal

2 Be relied upon to disclose violations of truth in lending laws

3 Encompass a plan to actively search for illegalities which relate to operating aspects

4 *Not* be relied upon to provide assurance that illegal acts will be detected

e Which of the following statements concerning illegal acts by clients is correct?

1 An auditor's responsibility to detect illegal acts that have a direct and material effect on the financial statements is the same as that for errors and irregularities.

    2 An audit in accordance with generally accepted auditing standards normally includes audit procedures specifically designed to detect illegal acts that have an indirect but material effect on the financial statements.

    3 An auditor considers illegal acts from the perspective of the reliability of management's representations rather than their relation to audit objectives derived from financial statement assertions.

    4 An auditor has *no* responsibility to detect illegal acts by clients that have an indirect effect on the financial statements.

f The concept of materiality would be *least* important to an auditor when considering the following:

    1 Adequacy of disclosure of a client's illegal act

    2 Discovery of weaknesses in a client's internal control structure

    3 Effects of a direct financial interest in the client on the CPA's independence

    4 Decision whether to use positive or negative confirmations of accounts receivable

g If specific information comes to an auditor's attention that implies the existence of possible illegal acts that could have a material, but indirect, effect on the financial statements, the auditor should next:

    1 Apply audit procedures specifically directed to ascertaining whether an illegal act has occurred

    2 Seek the advice of an informed expert qualified to practice law as to possible contingent liabilities

    3 Report the matter to an appropriate level of management at least one level above those involved

    4 Discuss the evidence with the client's audit committee, or others with equivalent authority and responsibility

h Which of the following statements concerning the auditor's use of the work of a specialist is correct?

    1 If the specialist is related to the client, the auditor is *not* permitted to use the specialist's findings as corroborative evidence.

    2 The specialist may be identified in the auditor's report only when the auditor issues a qualified opinion.

    3 The specialist should have an understanding of the auditor's corroborative use of the specialist's findings.

    4 If the auditor believes that the determinations made by the specialist are unreasonable, only an adverse opinion may be issued.

AICPA

5-4 The following questions relate to related-party transactions. Select the *best* response.

  a Which of the following would *not* necessarily be a related-party transaction?

    1 Sales to another corporation with a similar name

    2 Purchases from another corporation that is controlled by the corporation's chief stockholder

    3 Loan from the corporation to a major stockholder

    4 Sale of land to the corporation by the spouse of a director

  b Which of the following events most likely indicates the existence of related parties?

    1 Borrowing a large sum of money at a variable rate of interest

    2 Selling real estate at a price that differs significantly from its book value

    3 Making a loan without scheduled terms for repayment of the funds

    4 Discussing merger terms with a company that is a major competitor

 c An auditor searching for related-party transactions should obtain an understanding of each subsidiary's relationship to the total entity because:

  1 This may permit the audit of intercompany account balances to be performed as of concurrent dates.

  2 Intercompany transactions may have been consummated on terms equivalent to arm's-length transactions.

  3 This may reveal whether particular transactions would have taken place if the parties had *not* been related.

  4 The business structure may be deliberately designed to obscure related-party transactions.

 d After discovering that a related-party transaction exists, the auditor should be aware that:

  1 The substance of the transaction could be significantly different from its form.

  2 The adequacy of disclosure of the transaction is secondary to its legal form.

  3 The transaction is assumed to be outside the ordinary course of business.

  4 The financial statements should recognize the legal form of the transaction rather than its substance.

AICPA

5-5 The following questions relate to the use of analytical procedures in general planning. Select the *best* response.

 a Analytical procedures are:

  1 Statistical tests of financial information designed to identify areas requiring intensive investigation

  2 Analytical tests of financial information made by a computer

  3 Evaluations of financial information made by a study of plausible relationships among both financial and nonfinancial data

  4 Diagnostic tests of financial information which may *not* be classified as evidential matter

 b As a result of analytical procedures, the independent auditor determines that the gross profit percentage has declined from 30 percent in the preceding year to 20 percent in the current year. The auditor should:

  1 Include an explanatory paragraph in his audit report indicating the inability of the client company to continue as a going concern

  2 Evaluate management's performance in causing this decline

  3 Require footnote disclosure

  4 Consider the possibility of a misstatement in the financial statements

 c Analytical procedures used in planning an audit should focus on identifying:

  1 Material weaknesses in the internal control structure

  2 The predictability of financial data from individual transactions

  3 The various assertions that are embodied in the financial statements

  4 Areas that may represent specific risk relevant to the audit

 d An example of an analytical procedure is the comparison of:

  1 Financial information with similar information regarding the industry in which the entity operates

  2 Recorded amounts of major disbursements with appropriate invoices

  3 Results of a statistical sample with the expected characteristics of the actual population

  4 EDP-generated data with similar data generated by a manual accounting system

e Auditors try to identify predictable relationships when using analytical procedures. Relationships involving transactions from which of the following accounts most likely would yield the highest level of evidence?

1 Accounts payable
2 Advertising expense
3 Accounts receivable
4 Payroll expense

f Auditors sometimes use comparison of ratios as audit evidence. For example, an unexplained decrease in the ratio of gross profit to sales may suggest which of the following possibilities?

1 Unrecorded purchases
2 Unrecorded sales
3 Merchandise purchases being charged to selling and general expense
4 Fictitious sales

g Significant unexpected differences identified by analytical procedures will usually necessitate a(an):

1 Consistency explanatory paragraph added to the audit report
2 Review of the internal control structure
3 Explanation in the representation letter
4 Auditor investigation

AICPA

DISCUSSION QUESTIONS

Discussion questions require the application of the concepts explained in the chapter to specific facts, issues, or problems. They are classified by the primary topic to which they relate. However, responses should not be confined to the primary topics but should include all relevant implications.

Client Acceptance and General Planning

5-6 The CPA firm of Gleim & Co. has been approached by the following potential clients:

a Columbus Entertainment Inc., which recently made news in the financial press when its board of directors reinstated the chief executive officer who had misappropriated corporate checks totaling $15,000 (an amount that was immaterial to Columbus and the CEO's annual salary). The board said the CEO was essential to operations and that his theft was the result of mental problems rather than a sign of dishonesty.

b Harridan Press Enterprises, Inc., which publishes a magazine for women that features explicit male nudes and operates clubs around the country that feature male go-go dancers.

c Lansker Inc., which operates vending machines in several East Coast states and has part interest in a gaming casino in Las Vegas.

1 What procedures would Gleim & Co. use to investigate these three potential clients? (Would any unusual procedures be applicable to any of the three?)

2 Explain the considerations of Gleim & Co. in deciding whether to accept each of the three companies.

5-7 Gordon Howe was recently appointed auditor of Watts Ltd., a public company. He had been approached by the audit committee of the board of directors and had communicated with the company's previous auditor before indicating that he would be prepared to accept the appointment. He attended the shareholders' meeting at which he was appointed but has not yet visited the company's offices.

List the matters that Howe should attend to between the time of his appointment and the commencement of his audit work in order to plan an effective audit of Watts Ltd.

Canadian Institute of Chartered Accountants (CICA) adapted

5-8 The inspection of the minutes of meetings is an integral part of a CPA's audit of a corporation's financial statements. Discuss the effect each of the following situations would have on specific audit steps in a CPA's audit and on the auditor's opinion.

a The minute book does not show approval for the sale of an important manufacturing division which was consummated during the year.

b Some details of a contract negotiated during the year with the labor union are different from the outline of the contract included in the minutes of the board of directors.

c The minutes of a meeting of directors held after the balance sheet date have not yet been written, but the corporation's secretary shows the CPA notes from which the minutes are to be prepared when the secretary has time.

d The corporation's purchase of their principal product for resale are not mentioned in the minutes.

AICPA adapted

5-9 The Board of Directors of Lectosonic Corporation declared on June 15, 19X3, a dividend amounting to $400,000 payable on July 15 to stockholders of record July 1. An auditor who made an audit of the company for the fiscal year ended June 30, 19X3, did not include the dividend payable on the balance sheet of June 30, 19X3. If the auditor omitted the dividend not by design but by oversight, what audit procedure did the auditor probably neglect?

5-10 When a CPA has accepted an engagement from a new client who is a manufacturer, it is customary for the CPA to tour the client's plant facilities. Discuss the ways in which the CPA's observations made during the course of the plant tour would be of help in planning and conducting the audit.

AICPA adapted

5-11 In an initial engagement the CPA usually applies the auditing procedure of reviewing the client's federal income tax returns for prior years. What are the general purposes or objectives of this auditing procedure?

AICPA adapted

Materiality and Audit Risk

5-12 The concept of materiality is important to the CPA in an audit of financial statements and expression of opinion.

a How are materiality (and immateriality) related to the proper presentation of financial statements?

b In what ways will considerations of materiality affect the CPA in doing the following?

1 Developing the audit program

2 Performance of auditing procedures

c What factors and measures should the CPA consider in assessing the materiality of an exception to financial statement presentation?

AICPA adapted

5-13 Alpine Ltd. operates a machine shop. It does custom machining, welding, fabricating, and other metalwork for a large number of customers and also manufactures a line of metal utensils for camping and similar outdoor activities. Its customers for the custom work (which is about 80 percent of its business) are other businesses of many kinds; its customers for the utensils are wholesalers and retail chains. As at the fiscal year ended December 31, 19X9, the company's unaudited balance sheet showed the following:

Assets	
Cash	$ 40,000
Accounts receivable	230,000
Inventories:	
Raw materials	180,000
Work in process	410,000
Finished goods	240,000
Land	100,000
Building and equipment	2,600,000
Accumulated depreciation	(1,400,000)
	$2,400,000
Liabilities	
Bank loans payable	$ 300,000
Accounts payable	130,000
Equipment purchase contracts	60,000
Mortgage payable	740,000
Due to shareholders	110,000
Capital stock	200,000
Retained earnings	860,000
	$2,400,000

The company had been growing slowly until early 19X9, when the president, treasurer, and production manager retired, turning the management over to a group of younger managers, all of whom became minor shareholders. The new group embarked upon an ambitious expansion program. In July 19X9, A. Fernand, CPA, was appointed auditor.

On his short first visit to the company's offices, Fernand has determined the following:

1 The accounting and office staff of three clerks and a typist are supervised by the controller (one of the group of new shareholders).

2 The preparation of income tax returns, statistical reports to governments, and other

such documents had been done by the previous auditor, and the controller expects that Fernand will also prepare them.

3 Perpetual inventory records are maintained for raw materials, finished utensils manufactured for stock, and (on a job-order basis) custom work in process. Memorandum records are maintained on the shop floor for utensils in process; these records are not tied into the general ledger.

4 Custom work reaches its peak activity in the summer and is at a low point of activity in the autumn and winter. Therefore, most of the annual production of utensils is done during the winter. Finished utensils are sold in the spring and early summer.

a What factors would control the timing of Fernand's audit work on Alpine Ltd.?
b Assume the following:

1 The company wishes to have its audited financial statements as at December 31, 19X9, ready by January 20, 19X0.
2 Fernand has evaluated the company's control risk and found it to be low for accounts receivable and those inventories having perpetual records but high elsewhere.
3 Fernand has done no audit work other than to understand the internal control structure.
4 It is mid-September 19X9.

Outline in general terms the work Fernand could do prior to December 31, 19X9, to enable him to complete his work by January 20, 19XO. Specify the amount that Fernand would regard as material to the financial statements and explain how this amount would be used in planning the audit. Also, identify those factors that would affect Fernand's assessment of audit risk and explain their influence on the audit plan.

CICA adapted

5-14 "As increasing numbers of lawsuits against auditors are demonstrating, the public accountant incurs very real risks as auditor of a corporation. In his or her own interest, the auditor should be more aware of the factors that must be considered in any attempt to measure the risk of an audit engagement."

What factors affect the risk of a specific audit engagement? Explain each of them briefly.

CICA

5-15 During the audit of the Vernon Company, the existence of fraud was strongly suspected. Because of the limitations placed upon the engagement, the auditor could not pursue his suspicions. The desirability of further work in testing cash receipts from sales was mentioned to the treasurer of the company, who simply told the auditor to "skip it" and to confine himself to the engagement. Should the matter be mentioned in the audit report? Explain briefly.

AICPA adapted

5-16 You have been engaged to audit the December 31, 19X4, financial statements of the Frio Equipment Corporation, which was formed in 19XO and sells or leases construction equipment such as bulldozers, road scrapers, dirt movers, and so forth to contractors. The corporation at year-end has 50 pieces of equipment leased to 30 contractors who are using the equipment at various locations throughout your state.

The Frio Equipment Corporation is identified as the owner of the leased equipment by a small metal tag that is attached to each machine. The tag is fastened by screws so that it can be removed if the machine is sold. During the audit you find that the contractors often buy the equipment that they have been leasing, but the identification tag is not always removed from the machine.

The corporation's principal asset is the equipment leased to the contractors. While there is no plant ledger, each machine is accounted for by a file card that gives its description, cost, contractor-lessee, and rental payment records. The corporation's control risk is high.

You were engaged upon the recommendation of the president of the local bank. The Frio Equipment Corporation, which had never had an audit, had applied to the bank for a sizable loan; the bank president had requested an audited balance sheet.

You barely know John Frio, the principal stockholder and president of the Frio Equipment Corporation; he has a reputation for expensive personal tastes and for shrewd business dealings, some of which have bordered on being unethical. Nevertheless, Mr. Frio enjoys a strong personal allegiance from his contractor-lessees, whose favor he has curried by personal gifts and loans. The lessees look upon Mr. Frio as a personal friend for whom they would do almost anything. Often they overlook the fact that they are dealing with the corporation and make their checks payable to Mr. Frio, who endorses them over to the corporation.

a List the audit procedures that you would employ in the audit of the asset account representing the equipment leased to the contractors.

b Although your audit procedures, including those you described in answering part a, did not uncover any discrepancies, you have been unable to dismiss your feeling that Mr. Frio and some of the contractor-lessees may have collaborated to deceive you. Under this condition discuss what action, if any, you would take and the effect, if any, of your feeling upon your auditor's opinion. (Assume that you would not withdraw from the engagement.)

AICPA adapted

5-17 Audit procedures appear to concentrate on detecting overstatement of assets and understatement of liabilities—in other words, overstatement of shareholders' equity. Is an auditor not equally concerned with understatement of shareholders' equity? Explain.

CICA adapted

5-18 You are engaged in the audit of the financial statements of Oak Hill Company for the year ended December 31, 19X1. Oak Hill Company sells lumber and building supplies at wholesale and retail; it has total assets of $1,000,000 and a stockholders' equity of $500,000.

The company's records show an investment of $100,000 for 100 shares of common stock of one of its customers, the Custom Building Corporation. You learn that Custom Building Corporation is closely held and that its capital stock, consisting of 1,000 shares of issued and outstanding common stock, has no published or quoted market value.

Examination of your client's cash disbursements record reveals an entry of a check for $100,000 drawn on January 12, 19X1, to Mr. Leland Bouldin, who is said to be the former holder of the 100 shares of stock. Mr. Bouldin is president of the Oak Hill Company. Oak Hill Company has no other investments.

a List the auditing procedures you would employ in connection with the $100,000 investment of your client in the capital stock of the Custom Building Corporation.

b Discuss the presentation of the investment on the balance sheet, including its valuation.

AICPA adapted

Timing of Engagement and Assignment of Staff

5-19 An auditor of a public company is often required to issue an audit report very soon after the company's fiscal year-end in order to meet the client's deadline for publication of the annual report.

Explain briefly the audit problems caused by the deadline imposed by a client. What can the auditor do to minimize the problems?

CICA

5-20 You have been assigned by your firm to complete the audit of the 19X8 financial statements of Amon Manufacturing Corporation because the senior accountant and her inexperienced assistant who began the engagement were hospitalized due to an accident. The engagement is about one-half completed. Your auditor's report must be delivered in 3 weeks, as agreed when your firm accepted the engagement. You estimate that by utilizing the client's staff to the greatest possible extent you can complete the engagement in 5 weeks. Your firm cannot assign an assistant to you.

The work papers show the status of work on the audit as follows:

1 *Completed*—cash, fixed assets, depreciation, mortgage payable, and stockholders' equity
2 *Completed except as noted later*—inventories, accounts payable, tests of purchase transactions, and payrolls
3 *Nothing done*—trade accounts receivable, inventory receiving cutoff and price testing, accrued expenses payable, unrecorded liability test, tests of sales transactions, payroll deductions test and observation of payroll check distribution, other expenses, analytical procedures regarding operations, vouching of December purchase transactions, auditor's report, assessment of control risk, management letter, minutes, preparation of tax returns, procedural recommendations for management, subsequent events, supervision and review.

Your review discloses that the assistant's work papers are incomplete and were not reviewed by the senior accountant. For example, the inventory work papers present incomplete notations, incomplete explanations, and no cross-referencing.

a What field work standards have been violated by the senior accountant who preceded you on this assignment? Explain why you feel the field work standards you list have been violated.
b In planning your work to complete this engagement, you should scan work papers and schedule certain work as soon possible and also identify work which may be postponed until after the report is rendered to the client.
  1 List the areas on which you should plan to work first—say, in your first week of work—and for each item explain why it deserves early attention.
  2 State which work you believe could be postponed until after the report is rendered to the client and give reasons why the work may be postponed.

AICPA adapted

5-21 Kyle Boyd is an audit manger with Bell, Botts, and Bone, CPAs. He has been placed in charge of this year's audit of Zerone Plastics Corporation. After assessing his staff needs for the audit, he made the following request for staff:

1 A senior accountant with 4 to 5 years' experience
2 A staff accountant with 2 to 3 years' experience
3 A staff accountant with 1 year's experience
4 A new staff accountant with no experience

The firm is extremely busy at this time of the year, and there are many audits being undertaken concurrently. The partner in charge of scheduling made the following assignment of professional staff to the Zerone Plastics audit:

1 A senior accountant with 3 years' experience
2 A staff accountant with 1 year's experience
3 A staff accountant with no experience

Evaluate the adequacy of the following:
a The requested staff
b The staff assigned to the audit

5-22 CPAs budget time required to perform specific audits. Sometimes budgeted hours are exceeded in order to complete an audit.
a What factors might cause a CPA to exceed the time budget on an audit?
b Are the hours in excess of the budget charged to the client at the usual billing rate, or should they be absorbed by the CPA?

Analytical Procedures

5-23 Following are some ratios that a CPA might compute:

- Notes receivable to interest earned
- Notes payable to interest expense
- Net income to owners' equity
- Marketable securities to dividend income
- Accounts receivable to bad debts expense
- Unexpired insurance to insurance expense

a What do all these ratios have in common?
b Would the auditor be more likely to use them to compare current year with the preceding year(s), or to compare the client with other companies in the same industry, or both? Explain.

5-24 At the beginning of the annual audit of Hinse Corporation, wholesale distributor, Lynna Magnum, the auditor, was given a copy of the company's financial statements as prepared by the company's accountant. On reviewing these statements, Magnum noted the following abnormal conditions:

1 The accounts receivable outstanding at the year-end represent an unusually high number of average days' credit sales.
2 The inventories on hand at the year-end represent an unusually high proportion of the current assets.
3 The working capital ratio of the company is almost twice that of the previous year.
4 The percentage of gross profit on net sales is considerably in excess of that of previous years.
5 The rate of turnover of inventory is unusually low in comparison with previous years.

Taking all the above conditions together, what irregularities might Magnum suspect regarding sales and inventories?

CICA adapted

5-25 In connection with your analytical procedures of 19X8 operations, you are presented with a summary of certain data prepared by a staff accountant as follows:

	19X8 industry averages	North Slope 19X8	North Slope 19X7
1. Net profits on net sales (percent)	3.63	8.40	3.60
2. Net profits on tangible net worth (percent)	7.62	7.70	5.20
3. Net profits on net working capital (percent)	17.64	23.00	21.30
4. Net sales to tangible net worth (percent)	2.10	1.03	0.95
5. Net sales to net working capital (times)	5.23	2.70	2.84
6. Net sales to inventory (times)	8.80	7.84	6.93
7. Collection period (number of days)	53.00	50.00	52.00
8. Current assets to current debt (times)	2.46	2.39	2.60
9. Current debt to inventory (percent)	120.80	120.00	151.00
10. Inventory to net working capital (percent)	52.90	54.00	41.00

a Which of the listed ratios should be investigated further by you due to the fact that they are out of line with the preceding year?

b Which of the listed ratios should be investigated further by you due to the fact that 19X8 is out of line with North Slope's industry?

5-26 When a CPA discovers a significant change in a ratio when compared with the prior year's ratio, the CPA considers the possible reasons for the change. Give the possible reasons for the following significant changes in ratios:

a The rate of inventory turnover (ratio of cost of sales to average industry) has decreased from the prior year's rate.

b The number of days' sales in receivables (ratio of average of daily accounts receivable to sales) has increased over the prior year.

AICPA adapted

5-27 In auditing the financial statements of a manufacturing company, the CPA plans to place increased emphasis upon overall checks of the data under audit. The overall checks include the computations of ratios, which are compared with prior-year ratios or with industrywide norms. Examples of such overall checks or ratios are the computation of the rate of inventory turnover and of the number of days' sales in receivables. In addition to the computations given above, list the ratios that a CPA may compute during an audit as overall checks on balance sheet accounts and related nominal accounts. For each ratio listed name the two (or more) accounts used in its computation.

AICPA adapted

5-28 During the course of preliminary analytical procedures at Caroline Sales Company, a client, a CPA observed the following:

	Actual expense, 19X1	Budgeted expense, 19X2	Actual expense, 19X2
Rent	$12,000	$15,000	$15,000
Sales commissions	6,000	7,000	11,000
Advertising	4,000	5,000	9,000
Office supplies	400	400	350
Depreciation	1,700	1,800	2,700

    a Which of the expenses would probably not require any further investigation of over-all propriety?

    b If sales commissions expense were to be investigated further, what is the first pro-cedure the auditor would undertake to establish its overall reasonableness?

    c List the procedures the auditor should perform to further investigate the propriety of each of the expenses that need investigation.

5-29 In connection with your overall review of operations of Medina Company, you are presented with a summary of certain data prepared by a staff accountant comparing Medina with industry averages as follows:

	Medina Co.	Industry average
Current ratio	2.1 to 1	1.97 to 1
Net income to net sales	8%	4.2%
Net income to owner's equity	4%	2%
Acid test ratio	1.3 to 1	1.1 to 1
Inventory turnover	5	2.5
Receivables turnover	11	13
Earnings per share	$2.13	$0.14
Cost of goods sold to net sales	71%	80%
Sales returns and allowances to net sales	7%	1%
Book value per share	$53.25	$7.00

    a Explain the difference between earnings per share of Medina Company and that of the industry as a whole.

    b List one inconsistency between Medina and its industry you would want to inves-tigate. Briefly explain why.

CASE

"We had a fairly good year," said the president of Fannin Ltd. "Sales exceeded $2,000,000 for the first time in our history, though net income didn't keep pace with the sales increase because of higher labor costs."

    Fannin Ltd., is a Canadian manufacturing company; its factory and most of its sales branches are located in western Canada, but it also has sales branches and warehouse facilities in Toronto, Montreal, and Halifax. The company sells a number of industrial products, divided into "Product Line A" and "Product Line B." The industry is highly competitive, in both price and quality, and technological developments have been quite rapid, subjecting most products to a substantial obsolescence risk.

    The company's accounting functions are concentrated at the factory; the sales branches and warehouses maintain only payroll, petty cash, and inventory records, which are subject to review by the head office. The company's four principal officers (the pres-ident, the sales manager, the product development manager, and the factory manager) own substantially all its shares and manage the company in a highly individualistic man-ner.

    Assume that you are the partner in charge of the Fannin Ltd. audit. Following are the financial statements for the fiscal years ended June 30, 19X3, 19X2, and 19X1. (The

19X2 and 19X1 figures were those reported in the audited financial statements, but the 19X3 figures were as prepared by the chief accountant prior to the audit.)

Fannin Ltd. BALANCE SHEETS as of June 30			
	19X3	19X2	19X1
Cash	$ 148,000	$ 234,000	$ 210,000
Accounts receivable:			
Trade	387,000	263,000	219,000
Employees	8,000	6,000	5,000
Income taxes recoverable	10,000	...	...
Land sale	130,000	...	...
Allowance for doubtful accounts	(15,000)	(15,000)	(15,000)
Inventories:			
Raw material (cost)	69,000	72,000	78,000
Finished goods: (standard cost):			
Product line A	204,000	124,000	84,000
Product line B	166,000	156,000	149,000
Shop supplies (cost)	23,000	...	...
	$1,130,000	$ 840,000	$ 730,000
Land (cost)	$ 150,000	200,000	200,000
Plant and equipment (cost)	1,600,000	1,600,000	1,600,000
Accumulated depreciation	(870,000)	(800,000)	(685,000)
	$ 880,000	$1,000,000	$1,115,000
	$2,010,000	$1,840,000	$1,845,000
Bank loan	170,000	110,000	80,000
Accounts payable	374,000	304,000	241,000
Trade notes payable	97,000	34,000	21,000
Income taxes payable	...	9,000	8,000
Due to shareholder	...	12,000	100,000
Current portion of mortgage	75,000	60,000	60,000
	$ 716,000	$ 529,000	$ 510,000
Mortgage (6%)—less current portion	440,000	500,000	560,000
Deferred income taxes	71,000	68,000	63,000
	$1,227,000	$1,097,000	$1,133,000
Common share capital	$ 210,000	$ 200,000	$ 200,000
Contributed surplus	50,000	50,000	50,000
Retained earnings	523,000	493,000	462,000
	$ 783,000	$ 743,000	$ 712,000
	$2,010,000	$1,840,000	$1,845,000

Fannin Ltd. INCOME STATEMENTS for Years Ended June 30

	19X3	19X2	19X1
Sales	$2,100,000	$1,800,000	$1,700,000
Cost of sales	1,690,000	1,380,000	1,320,000
Gross profit	$ 410,000	$ 420,000	$ 380,000
Selling and administrative expenses:			
Advertising and promotion	$ 117,000	$ 77,000	$ 51,000
Bad debts	10,000	7,000	6,000
Depreciation	10,000	15,000	15,000
Insurance	7,000	7,000	7,000
Salaries	182,000	160,000	150,000
Sundry	28,000	12,000	11,000
Utilities and telephone	26,000	22,000	20,000
	$ 380,000	$ 300,000	$ 260,000
Operating income	$ 30,000	$ 120,000	$ 120,000
Other expense (income):			
Interest and bank charges	$ 63,000	$ 41,000	$ 38,000
Profit on sale of land	(80,000)		
Cash discounts and sundry	(1,000)	(3,000)	(4,000)
	$ (18,000)	$ 38,000	$ 34,000
Income before tax	$ 48,000	$ 82,000	$ 86,000
Income taxes:			
Current	$ (10,000)	$ 21,000	$ 20,000
Deferred	3,000	5,000	8,000
	$ (7,000)	$ 26,000	$ 28,000
Net income for the year	$ 55,000	$ 56,000	$ 58,000
Dividends paid	$ 25,000	$ 25,000	$ 25,000

Fannin Ltd. SCHEDULES OF GROSS PROFIT for Years Ended June 30			
	19X3	19X2	19X1
Product Line A			
Sales	$ 850,000	$825,000	$800,000
Cost of sales:			
Material (standard)	$ 417,000	$386,000	$378,000
Labor (standard)	231,000	160,000	156,000
Overhead (standard)	84,000	56,000	50,000
Standard cost variances	(22,000)	(2,000)	1,000
Depreciation	20,000	35,000	35,000
	$ 730,000	$635,000	$620,000
Gross profit	$ 120,000	$190,000	$180,000
Product Line B			
Sales	$1,250,000	$975,000	$900,000
Cost of sales:			
Material (standard)	$ 482,000	$347,000	$323,000
Labor (standard)	297,000	223,000	207,000
Overhead (standard)	173,000	113,000	103,000
Standard cost variances	(32,000)	(3,000)	2,000
Depreciation	40,000	65,000	65,000
	$ 960,000	$745,000	$700,000
Gross profit	$ 290,000	$230,000	$200,000
Total gross profit	$ 410,000	$420,000	$380,000

Note: The overhead standards shown above do not include depreciation; however, when the finished goods are transferred to inventory, a factor for depreciation is added to the material-labor-overhead standard to get the inventory carrying cost.

In planning the audit of Fannin Ltd. for the year ended June 30, 19X3, which specific matters shown by the financial statements would the auditor be particularly interested in investigating? Explain the significance of each item you mention. In making this analysis, specify the amount you would consider material to the financial statements being audited and the factors that would affect your assessment of audit risk and make use of this information and of analytical procedures.

CICA adapted

CHAPTER

6

Understanding the Internal Control Structure and Assessing Control Risk

CHAPTER OUTLINE

Learning Objectives

After studying this chapter you should be able to:

- Explain the audit logic of assessing control risk
- Understand the concepts of *reasonable assurance* and *inherent limitations* with regard to the internal control structure
- Describe the general objectives of internal control and how the auditor uses them to develop specific control objectives
- Define the internal control structure and each of its five components
- Explain the internal audit function's role in the internal control structure and how it may affect the audit
- Define the term "audit trail" and explain its use in the audit
- Identify the steps in the auditor's obtaining an understanding of the internal control structure and assessing control risk, and the methods and procedures used by the auditor in each step
- Explain the origin and basic requirements of the Foreign Corrupt Practices Act

Relevant Sections of Statements on Auditing Standards

AU 319—Consideration of the Internal Control Structure in a Financial Statement Audit

AU 322—The Auditor's Consideration of the Internal Audit Function in an Audit of Financial Statements

This chapter explains the importance of obtaining an understanding of the internal control structure in an audit of financial statements, and the methods and procedures used by the auditor to obtain that understanding and to assess control risk.

AUDIT STRATEGY AND THE INTERNAL CONTROL STRUCTURE

The importance of understanding the internal control structure has been recognized in professional standards at least since 1947 and is expressed in the second standard of field work, as revised in 1988, as follows:

> A sufficient understanding of the internal control structure is to be obtained to plan the audit and to determine the nature, timing and extent of tests to be performed.

Note three important points in this standard:

- The auditor obtains an understanding of the internal control structure *to plan the audit.*
- Based on the auditor's understanding of the internal control structure, he or she will *determine the nature, timing, and extent of tests to be performed.*
- The process of obtaining an understanding of the internal control structure is never

the entire audit. For example, the auditor's understanding may result in the auditor performing fewer procedures when the control risk is assessed as low. However, other audit procedures are *never entirely eliminated.*

The auditor's understanding of the internal control structure provides a basis for the *assessment of control risk.* The assessment of control risk is used to determine the nature, timing, and extent of other audit tests. Control risk is one of the elements of audit risk in the risk model introduced in Chapter 4.

Audit Logic and the Internal Control Structure

Evidential matter supporting financial statements consists of underlying accounting data and corroborating information available to the auditor. Thus, obtaining reasonable assurance of the propriety and accuracy of the underlying accounting data contributes to the basis for the auditor's opinion on the financial statements. The relation of the effectiveness of the internal control structure to evidential matter arises from its effect on the propriety and accuracy of accounting data.

To reach a conclusion on the accuracy and reliability of underlying accounting data, the auditor may test the accounting data itself (reducing detection risk) or perform procedures to understand and evaluate the internal control structure to see whether the accounting data was developed under conditions likely to ensure accuracy and reliability (assessing control risk).

As discussed in Chapter 4, to issue an opinion on financial statements, the auditor must address audit risk *for each assertion for each significant transaction class and account balance* to reduce it to an acceptable level. Control risk is one of the three elements of audit risk.[1] The auditor can assess control risk at the maximum level, or, alternatively, the auditor can perform tests of controls to obtain evidential matter that the control risk is below the maximum level (if the tests show that the design of specific control procedures is effective and that the procedures have been consistently applied throughout the period under audit).

The auditor's alternatives can be illustrated by considering the overview of the accounting flow of transactions for credit sales and collections depicted in Figure 6-1. To substantiate the accuracy and reliability of the accounting data for credit sales and collections, the auditor has the following alternatives:

1 Test sales and cash receipts transactions to establish the validity, completeness, and accurate recording of the recurring debit and credit entries to accounts receivable.
2 Identify and test internal control structure policies and procedures that ensure the validity, completeness, and accurate recording of these transactions. (The figure depicts only the accounting flow.)
3 Some combination of the above.

Note also, that the substantiation of the underlying accounting data is interrelated with the corroborating information the auditor will need to obtain for the balances. For example, the number of confirmations sent to customers on the amount owed at year-

---

[1] Audit risk is composed of (1) inherent risk, (2) detection risk, and (3) control risk.

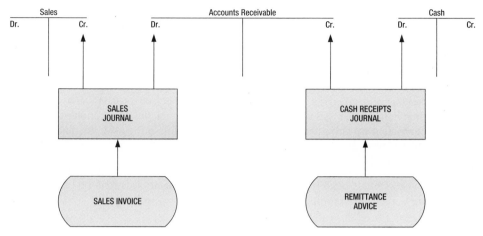

FIGURE 6-1
Overview of flow of transactions for credit sales.

end will be influenced by the auditor's confidence in the propriety and accuracy of the debits and credits to accounts receivable. Also, confirmations of the accounts receivable balance provide some assurance of the accuracy and reliability of the debits and credits recorded. Determining the mix of auditing procedures necessary to test the accounting data and obtain corroborating information is discussed in Chapter 7. The point to be emphasized here is that tests of controls can be performed to support the assessed level of the control risk. Obtaining evidential matter that the control risk is low for specific assertions for specific accounting data is an alternative to substantiating the data directly.

Internal Control Structure Concepts

SAS No. 55 (AU 319.6) states:

> An entity's internal control structure consists of the policies and procedures established to provide reasonable assurance that specific entity objectives will be achieved.

Reasonable Assurance   This definition speaks of reasonable rather than absolute assurance. As explained in AU 319.14:

> The concept of reasonable assurance recognizes that the cost of an entity's internal control structure should not exceed the benefits that are expected to be derived. Although the cost-benefit relationship is a primary criterion that should be considered in designing an internal control structure, the precise measurement of costs and benefits usually is not possible. Accordingly, management makes both quantitative and qualitative estimates and judgments in evaluating the cost-benefit relationship.

> The purpose of the internal control structure is to prevent or detect errors or irregularities, but absolute prevention or complete detection would be too costly and is probably a practical impossibility.

Inherent Limitations   In addition to the need to recognize that the internal control structure can provide only reasonable assurance, there are inherent factors that limit the potential effectiveness of the internal control structure. AU 319.15 enumerates the factors as follows:

> Mistakes in the application of policies and procedures may arise from such causes as misunderstanding of instructions, mistakes in judgment, and personal carelessness, distraction, or fatigue. Furthermore, the policies and procedures that require segregation of duties can be circumvented by collusion among persons both within and outside the entity and by management override of certain policies or procedures.

These limitations influence the extent of the auditor's assessment of control risk. The auditor never assesses control risk as so low for material transactions or balances that all substantive tests are eliminated for those transactions or balances.

Internal Control Structure Objectives

Appendix D of SAS NO. 55 (AU 319) lists four objectives that management should consider when establishing specific policies and procedures to record, process, summarize, and report financial data:

- Transactions are executed in accordance with management's general or specific authorization.
- Transactions are recorded as necessary (1) to permit preparation of financial statements in conformity with generally accepted accounting principles or any other criteria applicable to such statements and (2) to maintain accountability for assets.
- Access to assets is permitted only in accordance with management's authorization.
- The recorded accountability for assets is compared with the existing assets at reasonable intervals and appropriate action is taken with respect to any differences.

These objectives may conveniently be grouped as follows:

1 Execution in accordance with authorization
2 Transaction-recording accuracy
3 Safeguarding assets and accountability tests

These categories provide a general framework for considering the control procedures that are necessary in particular circumstances. However, in practice, auditors find a more detailed listing of objectives to be more helpful. For example, the following listing provides more detail but is still general in nature:

  I *Authorization and approval.* Transactions are executed in accordance with management's general or specific authorization.
  II *Validity.* Recorded transactions represent events that occurred (are not fictitious).
 III *Completeness.* All authorized transactions are recorded.
  IV *Recording accuracy.* Transactions are recorded accurately with respect to:
    A *Account*—classified properly in the general ledger
    B *Amount*—recorded at the correct dollar amount

C *Period*—recorded in the accounting period in which executed

D *Detail*—if applicable, summarized correctly in detailed subsidiary records

V *Safeguarding.* Physical access to assets is limited to assigned personnel, physical security precautions are taken, and responsibility for physical custody of assets is assigned to personnel who are independent of recording and approval functions (separation of incompatible functions).

VI *Reconciliation.* Accounting records are compared with related assets, or control accounts are compared with detailed subsidiary records, and differences are identified, investigated, and necessary adjustment recorded.

These objectives provide a framework for considering whether a particular company has control procedures for the processing of particular classes of transactions that provide reasonable assurance of the objectives being achieved.

Detailed Objectives of Internal Control

The auditor needs to develop detailed objectives of internal control for the processing of a particular transaction class.

Example of Detailed Objectives   For the processing of credit sales transactions, for example, the auditor might develop the following detailed control objectives using the objectives listed earlier as a framework:

1 *Authorization and approval.* Goods shipped (or services rendered) to customers do not exceed established credit limits.

2 *Validity.* Recorded sales are for goods actually shipped (or services actually rendered).

3 *Completeness.* All goods shipped (or services rendered) have been billed.

4 *Recording accuracy.* Billings have been recorded correctly as to account, amount, and period and summarized correctly in the detailed customers' (accounts receivable) subsidiary ledger.

5 *Safeguarding.* (This general objective is not directly relevant to this class of transactions because the related asset, the receivable, does not have a physical existence. However, shipping and billing would need to be kept separate.)

6 *Reconciliation.* The customers' (accounts receivable) subsidiary ledger is periodically reconciled with the control account in the general ledger.

Relation of Detailed Objectives to Substantiating Data   As explained earlier, the auditor's alternatives in substantiating accounting data are to test the accounting data itself, to test the operation of internal control structure procedures, or some combination. This means that the detailed control objectives for a particular class of transactions can conveniently serve as a framework for both assessing control risk and substantively testing the transactions processed.

Another way of looking at this is that the detailed objectives are things to be accomplished by the system and related controls for processing a particular transaction class.

Two ways of seeing whether the objectives are being accomplished are (1) to test the resulting transactions data or (2) to test the operation of the control procedures designed to achieve those objectives.

COMPONENTS OF THE INTERNAL CONTROL STRUCTURE

A company's internal control structure consists of five components:

- Control environment
- Monitoring[2]
- Risk assessment
- Information and communication
- Control activities

Control Environment

Management's attitude toward control sets the stage for the attitudes and actions of the entire company. If employees perceive that control is not important to top management, there is little hope for an effective, conscientious application of accounting and control procedures. The control environment sets the tone of an organization. It influences the control consciousness of all organization personnel and is the foundation for the other components.

The auditor obtains an understanding of the control environment because it influences the consistency of procedures and the general effectiveness of the accounting system and control procedures.

The auditor's understanding of the control environment includes consideration of the following factors:

- Management's philosophy and operating style
- Integrity and ethical values
- Commitment to competence
- Organizational structure
- Audit committee
- Methods of assigning authority and responsibility
- Human resource policies and practices

Management's Philosophy and Operating Style   This factor includes the overall control consciousness of management. This is a subjective, but critical, aspect of the auditor's consideration of whether the control environment is conducive to good control. Management's control consciousness is simply the combination of conditions and circumstances within the company that reflect management's attitude about controls. If management emphasizes the importance of maintaining reliable accounting records and

---

[2]The five components are described in *Internal Control—Integrated Framework,* published by the Committee of Sponsoring Organizations of the Treadway Commission (COSO Report).

adhering to established policies and procedures, then a company's personnel are more likely to have a high regard for these matters in performing their duties.

Other management characteristics the auditor may consider are: management's attitudes and actions toward financial reporting and management's emphasis on meeting budget, profit, and other financial operating goals, and whether management is dominated by one or a few individuals.

The auditor also considers management's actions to foster *integrity and ethical values* and engender a *commitment to competence* throughout the organization.

Organizational Structure   A company's organizational structure is the overall framework for planning, directing, and controlling operations. It includes the form and nature of the company's organizational units, and related management functions and reporting relationships. An effective control environment requires clear definitions of responsibilities and lines of authority for personnel. These features are also important at higher levels. There should be clear definitions of responsibility for the board of directors, the audit committee of the board, and senior management.

Audit Committee   All companies listed on the New York Stock Exchange are required to have an audit committee made up of outside directors with responsibility for communication with independent as well as internal auditors. Many other companies also have audit committees, or committees (such as a finance committee or budget committee) that serve the same purpose.

An effective audit committee takes an active role in overseeing the company's accounting and financial reporting policies and practices. The board of directors has fiduciary and accountability responsibilities which an effective audit committee will help fulfill. The committee should maintain a direct line of communication between the board and the company's auditors, permitting open discussion of sensitive issues like controversial accounting issues, disagreements with management, deficiencies in internal control structure design, failures in the operation of the internal control structure, and difficulties encountered in performing the audit.

The lack of an audit committee or an ineffective committee without direct lines of communication with the auditors or with members under the control of management influences the auditor's evaluation of the control environment.

Methods of Assigning Authority and Responsibility   Methods of assigning authority and responsibility influence how well responsibilities are communicated, how well they are understood, and how much responsibility personnel feel in performing their duties. Methods mentioned in Appendix A of SAS No. 55 (AU 319) include:

- Entity policy regarding such matters as acceptable business practices, conflicts of interest, and codes of conduct
- Assignment of responsibility and delegation of authority to deal with such matters as organizational goals and objectives, operating functions, and regulatory requirements
- Employee job descriptions delineating specific duties, reporting relationships, and constraints

- Computer systems documentation indicating the procedures for authorizing transactions and approving systems changes

Human Resource Policies and Practices   The competence and integrity of a company's personnel and its management are important factors in providing an environment conducive to an effective internal control structure. The best structure in the world will not function properly if the company's personnel or management are dishonest or incompetent. The auditor does not make an extensive investigation of these matters, but through general inquiry and observation obtains an awareness of policies and practices that influence the honesty and capability of personnel.

The following personnel policies and practices are generally considered desirable:

- Annual vacations required of all employees (This means that any irregularities that require continuing attention of concealment will be detected.)
- Bonding of employees in positions of trust to provide some background check and insure against losses
- A written conflict-of-interest policy or code of employee conduct to communicate the company's attitudes and expectations on proper conduct
- Systematic methods for personnel selection; training; supervision; performance evaluation, especially for key accounting personnel; promotion; compensation; and adequate resources for personnel to discharge their responsibilities

Monitoring

The process of assessing the quality of the internal control structure's performance over time is called *monitoring*. For financial reporting purposes, two important aspects of monitoring are *management control methods* and an *internal audit function*.

Management Control Methods   Management's use of budgets and other financial reports to monitor operations can be a significant factor in the control environment because of management's intimate knowledge of operations. Control is enhanced if management regularly compares recorded transactions and balances with expected results, based on sources such as budgets, standard costs, and prior experience. For example, if management routinely analyzes monthly sales reports by product and location and obtains satisfactory explanations of significant variations from expected results, the auditor can have increased confidence in the reliability and accuracy of accounting records of sales and receivables.

The effectiveness of this procedure depends on the thoroughness of management in investigating the variances between planned and actual results. Diligent use of budgets, responsibility reporting, and operating data by management to monitor operations can contribute to the achievement of specific objectives.

In obtaining an understanding of management's control methods, the auditor would consider:

- Procedures established to develop plans, budgets, forecasts, and responsibility accounting

- Methods used to measure actual performance and compare it to planned performance
- Procedures established to communicate the results to appropriate management personnel
- Management's attitude and response to variances from expectations (i.e., whether or not management investigates and takes corrective action effectively)
- Policies and procedures to modify the accounting system and control procedures to update them for a changing environment and to correct problems or enhance efficiency or effectiveness

Internal Audit Function   An internal audit function is identified as a factor in the control environment because it is one means management may use to monitor the accounting system and related control procedures.

An internal audit function is an individual, group, or department within a company that acts as a separate higher level of control to determine that the internal control structure is functioning effectively. Internal auditors and internal audits are described in Chapter 1. The term *internal audit function* is used here to emphasize the point that the independent auditor's concern is with the function actually performed and not personnel within the company that simply have the title of internal auditor. Internal auditors may make special inquiries at management's direction or generally review operating practices to promote increased efficiency. However, the independent auditor is concerned with internal auditors who act as a higher level of control—and additional layer in effect— to ensure that the accounting system and control procedures are operating.

The internal audit function may affect the independent audit in three ways:

- *The internal audit function is part of the internal control structure.* If a company has an internal audit function that acts as a higher level of control, it will influence the independent auditor's assessment of control risk, and as a result, will affect the scope of audit procedures.
- *The internal auditors may have descriptions and other documentation of the internal control structure.* This documentation may help the independent auditor obtain an understanding of the internal control structure.
- *The internal auditors may provide direct assistance to the independent auditor* by making substantive tests or tests of controls.

In an independent audit, the auditor first obtains an understanding of the internal audit function: What are its activities, and are these activities relevant to the audit of the financial statements? To rely on the work of the internal auditors, the independent auditor must follow a series of steps to evaluate the internal auditors' work. If the independent auditor decides that the internal audit activities are relevant to an audit area, he or she then compares (1) the substantive tests that would have been performed if no reliance were placed on the internal auditor's work to (2) the procedures to be performed to evaluate the internal auditors' work together with the revised planned audit tests in the area. The approach that is most efficient (the least total work for that audit area) is selected. In some cases, the independent auditor's own tests can be performed more easily and quickly than performing the steps required to use the internal audit work in the area.

If the efficient approach is to use the internal audit work, the independent auditor does the following:

- *Assesses competence.* The auditor inquires about the qualifications of the internal audit staff and company policies in hiring, training, and supervising internal audit staff.
- *Assesses objectivity.* The auditor inquires about the organization level to which internal auditors report; reviews recommendations made in internal audit reports; and considers the ability of internal auditors to act independently in light of reporting levels and report recommendations.
- *Evaluates the effectiveness of internal auditors' work in the area.* The auditor considers, for his or her own purposes, whether the scope of work is appropriate, audit procedures are adequate, work is adequately documented, and reports have appropriate conclusions and are consistent with work results. Some of the work performed is tested by examining some of the items (controls, transactions, or balances) that the internal auditors examined, or by examining similar items.

Risk Assessment

Risk assessment is the organization's process for identifying and analyzing the risks relevant to the achievement of its objectives. The risk assessment forms the basis for determining how the risks should be managed. For financial reporting purposes, risk assessment involves the identification, analysis, and management of risks relevant to the preparation of financial statements that are fairly presented in conformity with generally accepted accounting principles. The risk assessment process should consider external and internal events and circumstances that may occur and adversely affect the ability to record, process, summarize, and report financial data consistent with the assertions of management in the financial statements. Examples of circumstances that can cause risks to arise or change include new personnel, rapid growth, new technology, new products or activities, changes to information systems, and corporate restructurings.

Information and Communication

The information and communication component involves the identification, capture, and exchange of information in a form and timeframe that enables organization personnel to carry out their responsibilities. An organization's information system includes its *accounting system* and consists of the methods and records established to identify, assemble, analyze, classify, record, and report exchange transactions and relevant events and conditions and to maintain accountability for the related assets and liabilities.

For financial reporting purposes, the accounting system is the most significant aspect of the information and communication component. An effective accounting system gives appropriate consideration to establishing records and methods that will:

- Identify and record all valid transactions
- Describe on a timely basis the transactions in sufficient detail to permit proper classification of transactions for financial reporting

- Measure the value of transactions in a manner that permits recording their proper monetary value in the financial statements
- Determine the time period in which transactions occurred to permit recording of transactions in the proper accounting period
- Present properly the transactions and related disclosures in the financial statements

Thus, the *accounting system* consists of all the functions and procedures for recognizing transactions and recording, processing, and reporting the data representing them. The auditor obtains an understanding of the accounting system, for example, to learn the classes of transactions in the company's operations and how they are recorded and reported in the financial statements. This helps in determining where errors or other activity resulting in misstatements could occur in the accounting process. Obtaining this understanding permits the auditor to identify the accounting records and documents needed to perform the audit tests.

Nearly all businesses use a computer for at least part of their accounting system. The amount of computerization ranges from the use of a microcomputer to summarize transactions in a simple system to extremely complex systems. In this chapter, the examples use a relatively simple system to focus on the concepts of internal control. Chapter 9 explores in more depth the various types of computerized accounting systems and their variations in control procedures and audit trails. This chapter concentrates on the similarities of all types of data processing systems.

An important feature of an accounting system is the *audit trail.* This term developed because an auditor needs to be able to take individual transactions and trace them through each step of the accounting system to their inclusion in the financial statements, and similarly, be able to take the financial statements and trace the amounts back to the individual items making up each amount. However, the most important and frequent user of the audit trail is the company's management. A clear audit trail is needed to track down the specific sources of errors. For example, when a customer complains that a bill is too high, management must be able to determine whether an error has been made and identify specifically the cause and amount of the error (or explain in detail what goods or services were included in the bill that resulted in the "high" amount).

The audit trail consists of all accounting documents and records prepared as transactions are processed from origin to final posting. *Source documents, journals,* and *ledgers* are the main elements in the audit trail.

Source documents are the initial record of transactions in the system. Processing procedures usually provide for creation of a source document when a transaction is executed. For example, processing procedures usually provide for entering goods received on a receiving report and entering goods shipped on a shipping report. Source documents are evidence of the authenticity of a transaction. Some of the basic types of source documents are:

- *Invoice.* This is a billing statement for goods or services that are purchased or sold. A company receives invoices from suppliers or vendors and sends invoices to customers. Invoices are very important because they usually result in the initial recording of transactions in the accounting records and also usually ultimately result in a cash receipt (for a sale) or a cash disbursement (for a purchase). For a particular transaction, an invoice indicates the amount owed by the company (an account payable) or the amount to be received from a customer (an account receivable).

- *Memorandum.* This is an adjustment that reduces accounts receivable or accounts payable. A *credit memorandum* is issued if a customer returns goods sold on credit to reduce the amount the customer owes. It is a credit to a company's account receivable. A *debit memorandum* is issued if goods purchased on credit are unacceptable and are returned to the supplier. The debit memorandum reduces accounts payable. A copy of a memorandum is sent to the supplier or customer as a notification.

- *Order.* This is a formal offer for an exchange transaction. A *purchase order* is a document prepared by a company offering to purchase specific items from a specific supplier. A *sales order* is a document created when a company receives an offer from a customer. An order is often the first document created in a sequence of events that ultimately result in an exchange transaction being recorded. However, an order is only an offer and an order is not recorded in the accounting records.[3]

- *Slips, reports, and advices.* This is a catchall category for documents created to evidence a particular step or event in processing. Usually the meaning is clear in context. For example, a *receiving report* is obviously a document that is filled out when goods are received and a *shipping report* is a document created when goods are shipped. A *remittance advice* is a slip that a customer returns with payment that indicates the amount and source of the remittance. Usually a remittance advice is a perforated portion of the billing statement sent to the customer.

Other types of documents are introduced and explained at relevant points in this and following chapters.

Journals are summarizing and recording devices. They accumulate totals of similar transactions or posting to accounts in the ledger and they provide a chronological record of the essential elements of transactions.

Ledgers further summarize transactions by account classification for use in preparing financial statements. They provide a historical record of activity within the individual accounts.

Explanations and cross-references link together source documents, journals, ledgers, and financial statements. Figure 6-2 illustrates the audit trail in a simple system for collection of receivables. The trail begins with a source document, the remittance advice received with the customer's check. Related source documents include the duplicate sales invoice, the shipping report, and the duplicate deposit ticket. The collection is recorded in the cash receipts book or computer log, where it becomes part of the total debit to cash and credit to accounts receivable. The totals are recorded on a journal voucher, a common posting medium. The totals are then posted to the general ledger accounts cash

---

[3]Note that source documents are used in the accounting system but are *not* part of the accounting system. The sales order from a customer, for example, is eventually an input to the accounting system after the goods are shipped. Both the shipping report and order are matched and then enter the accounting system. The system to process sales orders before that point is part of operations rather than part of the accounting system.

REMITTANCE ADVICE

MAX PARTS SUPPLY CO.

Please include this portion with your remittance.

Palo Duro Corporation
6 Three Ponds Lane
Water Island, PA 16611

Amount Due $ 300.00

Amount Enclosed $300.00

DEPOSIT TICKET

MAX PARTS SUPPLY CO.

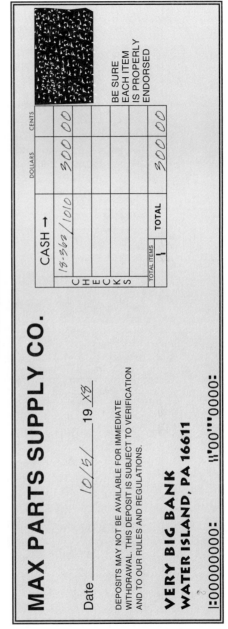

	DOLLARS	CENTS
CASH →		
C H E C K S	18-362/1010	300	00
TOTAL ITEMS 1	TOTAL	300	00

BE SURE
EACH ITEM
IS PROPERLY
ENDORSED

Date _____10/5/_____ 19 X8

DEPOSITS MAY NOT BE AVAILABLE FOR IMMEDIATE
WITHDRAWAL. THIS DEPOSIT IS SUBJECT TO VERIFICATION
AND TO OUR RULES AND REGULATIONS.

VERY BIG BANK
WATER ISLAND, PA 16611

I:000000000:   II"00""0000:

FIGURE 6-2

CASH RECEIPTS JOURNAL   Page 10-1

Date	Cash Acct Debit	Other Dr Acct	Other Dr Amount	Explanation	Sales Account Credit	Accts Rec Credit	Other Cr Acct	Other Cr Amount
10-05-x8	300.00			Palo Duro Corp.		300.00		
10-07-x8	174.50	401	25.50	NImity, Inc.	200.00			
10-21-x8	150.00	110	350.00	Northcross Co.	500.00			
10-23-x8	45.00			Warrior's Mark, Inc.			127	20.00
							601	25.00
10-29-x8	200.00			RMS Construction Co.	200.00			
10-30-x8	10.00			Wheeler Drug	10.00			
	879.50		375.50	J.V. 10-2	910.00	300.00		45.00

JOURNAL VOUCHER	DATE: 10/31/X8	JV NO. 10-2

Debit: Cash #100   819.50
    Accs. Rec. #110   350.00
    Cash Disc. #401   25.50

Credit: Sales #1000   910.00
    Accs. Rec. #110   300.00
    Inc. Rec. #127   20.00
    Inc. Inc. #601   25.00

Explanation:

To record totals from Cash Receipts journal for the month of October, 19X8

Source: CR Jul. p. 10-1

Prepared by: GRM

Approved by: CL.

FIGURE 6-2 (*continued*)

GENERAL LEDGER — ACCOUNTS RECEIVABLE				Acct	110
Date	Explanation	LF	DR	CR	Balance
9-30-x8	Balance Forward				1,142.50
10-31-x8		J.V. 10-2	350.00	300.00	1,192.50

GENERAL LEDGER — CASH				Acct	100
Date	Explanation	LF	DR	CR	Balance
9-30-x8	Balance Forward				1,720.44
10-31-x8		J.V. 10-2	879.50		2,599.94

FIGURE 6-2 *(concluded)*

and accounts receivable. The posting may be automatically done by the computer in an integrated system, or the totals from the journal voucher may be entered by accounting personnel. Note the vital part played by explanations and cross-references. Starting with the balances in the general ledger, the journal voucher number indicates the supporting document. The journal voucher explanation evidences the consistent performance of various internal control procedures. It indicates the person who prepared the posting media and/or entered the data, the propriety of the transactions, and proper approval of the transactions. From the journal voucher, the page in the journal listing the detailed components of the totals can be determined. Reference to the appropriate page in the journal supplies information for finding the pertinent underlying source documents. Notice that the tracing may begin at any point in the system: forward from the source document, backward from the ledger balance, or in either direction from intermediate records.

This depiction of the audit trail does not illustrate a related feature of accounting systems that helps to ensure recording accuracy—the use of subsidiary ledgers. The total of the control account, accounts receivable, in the general ledger should always equal the total of the individual accounts in the customers' subsidiary ledger.

Desirable features of a well-organized accounting system also include:

- *Chart of accounts.* This is a list of the account numbers and titles for all asset, liability, equity, revenue, and expense accounts along with a description of each and instructions on its use.

- *Procedures manual.* These are instructions on the operation of the accounting system and the treatment of the various types of transactions that can occur. Usually the chart of accounts is part of the procedures manual.

Control Activities

The term *control activities* encompasses both policies and procedures that management has established to help ensure management directives are carried out. Control activities relevant to an audit are often called *control procedures.*

Control procedures should be distinguished from the *accounting system* discussed earlier. A company needs an accounting system, for example, for billing shipments to customers, recording these individual transactions, and summarizing them for recording in the general ledger. Control procedures are added to ensure that the accounting system produces accurate and reliable data. For example, control procedures would be added to a billing system to ensure that all shipments are billed and that all billings are for the correct amount.

SAS No. 55 (AU 319.11) categorizes control procedures as follows:

- Proper authorization of transactions and activities
- Segregation of duties that reduce the opportunities to allow any person to be in a position to both perpetrate and conceal errors or irregularities in the normal course of his or her duties—assigning different people the responsibilities of authorizing transactions, recording transactions, and maintaining custody of assets
- Design and use of adequate documents and records to help ensure the proper recording of transactions and events, such as monitoring the use of prenumbered shipping documents
- Adequate safeguards over access to and use of assets and records, such as secured facilities and authorization for access to computer programs and data files
- Independent checks on performance and proper valuation of recorded amounts, such as clerical checks, reconciliations, comparison of assets with recorded accountability, computer-programmed controls, management review of reports that summarize the detail of account balances (for example, an aged trial balance of accounts receivable), and user review of computer-generated reports

The internal control structure may include many policies and procedures, but only some of these will be relevant to the audit of the financial statements. The following discussion of control procedures is organized by objective:

- Authorization and approval
- Validity
- Completeness
- Recording accuracy
- Safeguarding
- Reconciliations

Authorization and Approval   Effective procedures for processing transactions usually start with clear policies on authorization and approval of those transactions. A corporation's board of directors has the ultimate authority, but approval by the board is usually reserved for major acquisitions and dispositions involving real estate, debt, and capital stock and similar important financing and investing activities. The day-to-day authority of running a business is the responsibility of senior management who delegates that authority to operating personnel.

Management's authorization of transactions may be general or specific. General authorization applies to transactions that are recurring and have a high volume. Examples of the use of general authorization include the use of price lists and credit limits for credit sales transactions. Specific authorization is applied when management has decided that individual transactions must be approved, such as all purchases in excess of an established dollar amount. The term *approval* relates to the actual step of checking that the conditions established for authorization have been met. Examples of authorization and approval procedures include requiring a second signature on checks over a specified limit, and limiting certain error correction functions to persons who sign onto the computer with a manager's ID and password.

Validity   Procedures for authorization and approval also provide some assurance of validity. Authorization and approval steps help to ensure that only valid transactions are processed and that invalid transactions are rejected. Related procedures that provide assurance of validity concern the proper use of documents that serve as the original record of transaction execution, the source documents.

Source documents should be designed to reduce the risk that a transaction will be recorded incorrectly, recorded more than once, or omitted from recording. Desirable features of source documents include:

1 *Prenumbering*—to allow for physical control of the documents
2 *Preprinted instructions*—to indicate the steps to properly fill out the document and route it through the system
3 *Approval blocks*—to provide a designated space for necessary approval signatures, stamps, or initials
4 *Simplicity*—to make the document as easy to use as possible and to minimize the number of copies of the document

In some systems, source document information is recorded on a computer screen. The four features of the source document information are little changed:

1 *Numbering.* The numbering is generally assigned automatically by the computer system.
2 *Instructions.* These either appear on the screen or are available through a "help" function.
3 *Approval.* The person who signed on (with a password or other unique key) is generally recorded with the source document information automatically for each transaction.
4 *Simplicity.* This serves to make the screen as easy to use as possible.

A report of the source document information (the "journal") is generally printed as an audit trail, and the individual source document record remains available for display on the system for a designated period.

Control procedures that help ensure validity are concerned with the proper handling of such source document information. For example, control procedures would include comparing details on a receiving report, such as description and quantity, with details on the vendor's invoice. Another example of a control procedure is cancellation of supporting documents for a purchase when payment is approved. This prevents inadvertent or fraudulent reuse of the source documents to support a duplicate payment or fictitious purchase.

Control procedures designed into the computer data entry system can also help ensure validity. The computer system may reject invalid dates, requiring a month between 1 and 12 and a day between 1 and 31. Any entry in an amount field that is not numeric may be rejected. These are called *computer editing* controls.

Completeness   Proper handling of documents is also an aspect of control procedures to help ensure completeness. One central procedure involves subsequently inspecting prenumbered documents to see that all of them have completed processing. This procedure is often called *accounting for the sequence of prenumbered documents.* If documents are not prenumbered, they should be numbered when a transaction originates, but that is less effective in controlling completeness. Another control procedure for completeness is the use of *control totals.* If 10 documents totaling $500 in cash receipt transactions were supposed to be entered into the computer system, the system should report that it processed 10 entries totaling $500.

A third control procedure involves *matching related source documents* to see if related processing steps have been completed. For example, purchase orders or receiving reports can be matched with vendors' invoices to see that goods ordered or received have subsequently been recorded as accounts payable.

Recording Accuracy   An organized set of accounting records is an essential starting point for achieving recording accuracy. In all but the very smallest organizations a double-entry accounting system is essential. The requirement that debits equal credits is a built-in error-detecting feature. Also, as explained later, the debits and credits to ledger balances provide an effective record of accountability. The use of ledgers also contributes to recording accuracy. They do this in two ways: A trial balance prepared from the ledger proves the balancing of debits and credits, and, as explained later, the ledger contains control accounts for use in balancing subsidiary ledgers.

The use of control totals discussed above under completeness also contributes to achieving recording accuracy. If a cash receipt for $23 is mistakenly entered as $32, the system will report that it processed $509 for the 10 receipts, instead of the $500 control total.

All of the features of accounting systems described above provide the foundation for controls to help ensure recording accuracy. However, the actual control procedures are usually in the form of independent checks, reviews, and approvals established at the points in the processing of transactions and handling of related assets where errors or irregularities could occur. For example, the controller may review supporting documents for a disbursement before payment.

Safeguarding   Adequate safeguarding controls include physical safeguards, restricting physical access to assets and accounting records to assigned personnel, and separation of incompatible functions.

Physical safeguards include measures such as locked storerooms for inventory and fireproof safes for cash and securities on hand. Physical protection of accounting records and source documents is also important. The nature of the item usually dictates the extensiveness of physical precautions that are necessary. For example, an inventory of diamonds would be treated differently from an inventory of coal.

Restricting access to assets and accounting records to assigned personnel presumes a clear delegation of authority and responsibility. Personnel must know what they are to do and what others are to do. This means that authority and responsibility must be fixed on specific individuals. Measures to accomplish this include a plan of organization formalized in an organization chart and written job descriptions. Figure 6-3 presents an organization chart for a medium-size manufacturing company.

Segregation of duties is an integral part of the plan of organization. It is described in AU 319.11 as follows:

> Segregation of duties . . . reduce(s) the opportunities to allow any person to be in a position to both perpetrate and conceal errors or irregularities in the normal course of his duties—assigning different people the responsibilities of authorizing transactions, recording transactions, and maintaining custody of assets.

This concept is also commonly referred to as "separation of incompatible functions."

The discussion of segregation of duties quoted above stresses one of the realities of business. In order for a company to operate, some personnel must have access to assets. Restricting access to assets limits opportunities for irregularities but cannot prevent them. Control is achieved through segregation of duties by limiting the opportunities both to perpetrate and conceal the act.

Thus, the most basic segregation of duties is to have different individuals or departments responsible for custody of assets and the recordkeeping for those assets. This basic separation is reflected broadly in the organization chart presented in Figure 6-3.

The financing operations of a business are sufficiently dissimilar to the other operating activities, such as manufacturing and selling, that these activities normally are regarded as a separate function. Accountability for the financing operations of receiving and disbursing cash, granting credit, collecting receivables, planning for cash requirements, and custody of cash and securities normally is assigned to the *treasurer's department*. Accountability for the other operating activities of planning, administration, and custody of resources other than cash and securities is assigned to *operating management* (V-P Sales and V-P Manufacturing). The *controller's department* is made accountable for administering the accounting system, which involves keeping records of operations and maintaining the related internal control structure policies and procedures.

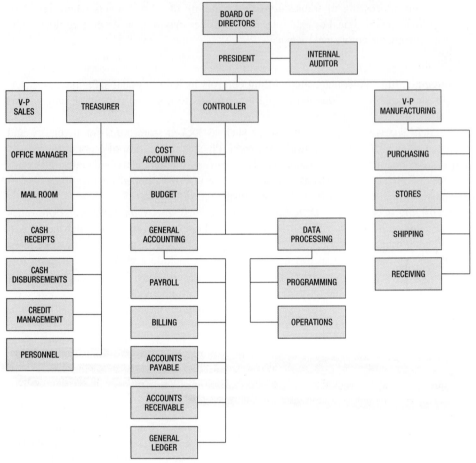

FIGURE 6-3
Organization chart.

Appropriate segregation of duties creates an interdependence of functions and responsibilities that permits tests of accountability. Thus, someone in the treasurer's department might attempt to make an improper cash disbursement, but the improper disbursement would be disclosed when the record of cash maintained by the controller's department is compared with the cash balance.

The debits to an asset account establish the initial record of accountability, and credits to the account indicate a discharge of accountability. As the asset is transferred from the control of one employee to that of another, the charges (debits) for accountability must equal the discharges (credits) relieving accountability until there is a proper charge against income. For example, within the treasurer's department the credit manager is normally responsible for granting credit and making collections, while the cashier (cash receipts) is responsible for the custody of cash collected. The record of accountability for these duties is maintained by the controller's department in the receivables records and the general ledger cash account. When cash collections of receivables are recorded, the credit entry to the receivables account discharges the credit manager's accountability and the corresponding debit entry to the cash account transfers accountability to cash receipts.

While this separation of custody and recordkeeping is basic, usually a more detailed analysis is necessary by transaction class. For this purpose, a transaction may be considered to pass through the following four phases:

1 *Authorization*—the initial authorization or approval for an exchange transaction
2 *Execution*—the actual act of committing the company to the exchange, such as placing an order
3 *Custody*—the physical act of accepting, delivering, or maintaining the asset
4 *Recording*—the entry of the transaction data into the accounting system

Ideally all four phases should be kept separate. However, for convenience and efficiency phases 1 and 2 are often combined without significant risk. Clearly, combining phases 2, 3, and 4 is incompatible and normally combining direct physical access (phase 3) and recordkeeping (phase 4) is incompatible. The risk of incompatible combinations, however, should be evaluated by considering specific circumstances in conjunction with the following general guideline: No one person should be in a position to misappropriate an asset or improperly record transactions without detection.

When control procedures are performed by persons having no incompatible functions these procedures are said to be performed *independently*.

Reconciliations   The control procedures that depend most heavily on independent performance for their effectiveness are reconciliations. The accountability tests referred to earlier are a type of reconciliation. A reconciliation occurs when an accounting record is compared with related assets, documents, or control accounts.

Control procedures commonly include the following types of comparisons of detailed accounting records to:

- *Asset counts*—periodic reconciliation of counts of inventory or securities to accounting records or reconciliation of bank balances with accounting records
- *Control totals*—periodic reconciliation of detailed postings to accounts receivable records to total cash received
- *Outside information*—periodic reconciliation of accounts payable to vendors' statements
- *Control accounts*—periodic reconciliation of accounts receivable subsidiary ledger to the control account in the general ledger

As mentioned earlier, the effectiveness of reconciliations depends on independent performance. For example, the person who does the bank reconciliation should not be responsible for handling cash or keeping the related accounting records; physical counting of inventory should not be the responsibility of the inventory storekeeper.

Effective reconciliations also depend on thorough follow-up of discrepancies detected. The nature and cause of the discrepancy should be determined and both the individual discrepancy and, if possible, the cause should be corrected.

THE AUDITOR'S CONSIDERATION OF THE INTERNAL CONTROL STRUCTURE IN A FINANCIAL STATEMENT AUDIT

In every audit, the auditor obtains a sufficient understanding of each of the five components of the internal control structure to plan the audit and determine tests to be performed.

The nature and extent of the auditor's consideration of the internal control structure can vary considerably from audit to audit. In all audits, the auditor must obtain an understanding of the internal control structure, particularly the accounting system. No matter what audit strategy is followed, substantiating the underlying data is important. The auditor must obtain an understanding sufficient to identify types of potential misstatements, consider factors that affect the risk of material misstatement, and design effective audit tests. On the other hand, for some assertions for some balances or transaction classes, an understanding of the control procedures element of the internal control structure may be minimal, depending on the audit strategy followed.

An Overview of the Auditor's Consideration

The second standard of field work, quoted at the start of this chapter, speaks of an understanding. "Understanding" in this context is a technical term that includes both obtaining knowledge and, as needed, performing tests of controls.

Basic Terms   The basic terms that must be understood as a starting point for understanding the auditor's understanding are as follows:

Tests of Controls   Tests directed toward the design or operation of an internal control structure policy or procedure to assess its effectiveness in preventing or detecting material misstatements in a financial statement assertion.

Control Risk   The risk that a material misstatement that could occur in an assertion will not be prevented or detected on a timely basis by a company's internal control structure policies or procedures.

Substantive Tests   Tests of details and analytical procedures performed by the auditor to detect material misstatements in the account balance, transaction class, and disclosure components of financial statements.

The logical process followed by the auditor is:

- Obtain an understanding of the five components of internal control structure.
- Assess control risk for each assertion for each significant account balance, transaction class, and disclosure component of the financial statements.
- Where the auditor believes control risk for an assertion may be assessed at less than the maximum, the auditor obtains evidence of the effectiveness of the design and consistent operation of the company's relevant policies and procedures in the area.
- Determine the nature, timing, and extent of auditing procedures to be applied.

The first step is usually accomplished through inquiry of client personnel; use of generalized materials, such as questionnaires, checklists, and other general practice aids;

inspection of documents; and observation of company activities and operations. This knowledge may also have been obtained in part through previous experience with the company.

The second step is accomplished by analyzing the results of the first step.

The third step, obtaining evidence, may be accomplished by performing tests of controls or may be the result of procedures performed to obtain the understanding of the internal control structure in the first step.

The fourth step is accomplished by analyzing the results of the third step, and its output is the design of substantive audit tests.

This is a logical process and not a routine that the auditor goes through step-by-step in the same manner in every engagement. For example, the auditor may decide that performing tests of controls is most efficient if done concurrently with obtaining an understanding of the internal control structure. Also, some of the auditor's knowledge of the internal control structure may be carried over from previous audits of the company and need only updating. All the procedures needed to obtain the information the first year need not be repeated every year.

Note that the outcome of the understanding is the assessment of control risk. A high control risk may result from deficiencies in any of the components of the internal control structure. A significant deficiency in the design or operation of the internal control structure is called a *reportable condition,* and communication of reportable conditions is discussed further in Chapter 13. However, the auditor is not required to search for reportable conditions. Thus, the purpose of assessing control risk is to plan the auditor's tests. If the internal control structure does not provide reasonable assurance that material errors or irregularities will be prevented or detected by the client, the auditor will need to apply more extensive auditing procedures designed to detect such errors or irregularities that could be material misstatements.

Figure 6-4 presents the steps in the auditor's consideration of the internal control structure in the audit of financial statements. The process presented in Figure 6-4 is discussed in this section. The following is an overview of the steps in outline form:

I Obtain an understanding of the internal control structure.
  A Obtain an understanding of the company's *control environment, risk assessment,* and *monitoring.*
  B For each significant transaction class or account balance, obtain an understanding of the *accounting system.*
  C For each assertion within each significant transaction class or account balance, if necessary, obtain an understanding of the *control activities.*
  D Document the understanding.
II Assess the level of control risk based on the understanding obtained.
  A The auditor may assess control risk at the maximum level for any one of the following three conditions:
    1 Internal control structure policies and procedures are unlikely to relate to the specific assertion (i.e., the client does not have controls for this assertion).
    2 The evidence that would be obtained by additional testing would probably not support a reduced level of control risk (testing would probably prove control for the assertion is weak).

3 Obtaining additional evidence to support the control risk level would not be the most efficient audit approach for the assertion (the substantive test is easier to perform than the test of controls).

B Consider whether further reduction in control risk would be an efficient audit approach and whether further evidence would be likely to support the reduced level.

III For each assertion within each significant transaction class or account balance for which the auditor plans to assess at a level less than maximum, consider whether sufficient evidence has been obtained to support the desired control risk level. Perform tests of controls directed to evaluation of the design or operation of the internal control structure policy or procedure to obtain needed evidence.

IV Document the basis for conclusions about the assessed level of control risk.

V Design substantive tests to detect potential material misstatements.

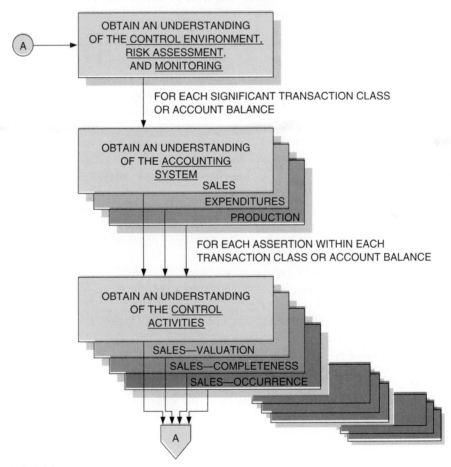

FIGURE 6-4

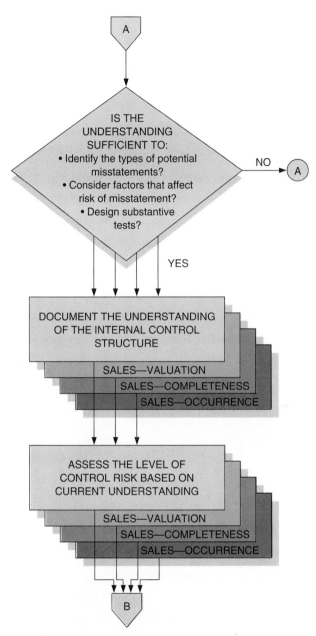

FIGURE 6-4 *(continued)*

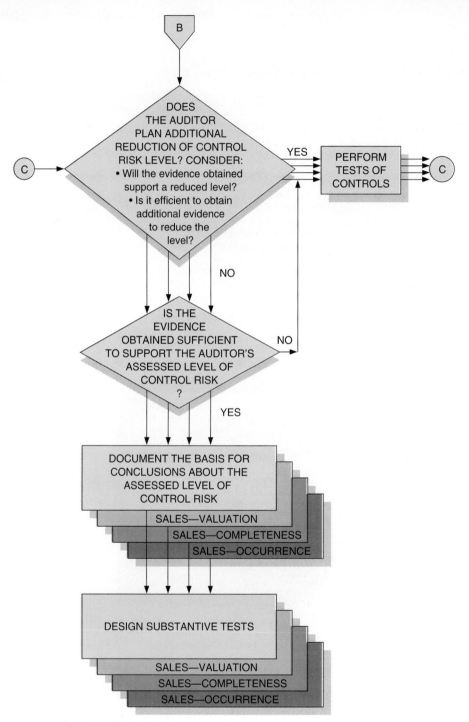

FIGURE 6-4 *(concluded)*

Organizing the Auditor's Consideration

The understanding of the control environment, risk assessment, and monitoring is obtained for the entire company. The understanding of the accounting system is obtained for each of the company's significant transaction classes or account balances. The understanding of the control procedures is obtained for each assertion within each transaction class or account balance.

Major Classes of Transactions   Every type of business engages in four major classes of transactions on a continuing basis.

1 *Sales*—selling goods or services to customers on credit or for cash
2 *Purchases*—buying goods or services from vendors or other suppliers on credit or for cash
3 *Cash receipts*—receiving cash from collection of receivables, cash sales, or other events
4 *Cash disbursements*—disbursing cash in payment of accounts payable or making other payments

These are all exchanges with parties outside the company. A manufacturing company engages in a fifth major class of transactions.

5 *Production*—conversion of purchased goods and services into products for sale

This is the primary example of internal transfers or use of assets that is considered a transaction for purposes of internal control structure. Certainly, businesses do engage in other types of transactions, but the types enumerated above are those that are continuously recurring and large in number.

Transaction Cycles   Although most transactions are recorded individually as they occur, a cycle of steps is contemplated. The following examples are for the cycle of steps for credit sales and purchases:

   I Sales
      A Acceptance of an order
      B Shipment and billing of the product
      C Collection of the billing
  II Purchases
      A Requisitioning of the material
      B Issuance of the order
      C Receipt of the material
      D Payment of the purchase price

Grouping Transaction Classes   Several considerations influence how an auditor goes about grouping transaction classes. The particular grouping used influences the organization of the auditor's consideration of the internal control structure. However, the particular grouping also usually influences the entire approach to the audit.

One of the considerations is the relation among account balances. For each transaction class there are related account balances in the general ledger. For example, one possible grouping for two major activities of any business—selling and buying—would be as follows:

- Revenue, receivables, receipts
- Purchases, payables, payments

These are sometimes called the sales cycle and the expenditures cycle. Each cycle enumerates two major transaction classes and one major account balance. For example, the sales cycle has the transaction classes of sales and cash receipts and the account balance–accounts receivable. Also, with this approach, related transaction classes and account balances would be included in the cycle. For example, the sales cycle would also include the transaction classes for uncollectible receivables, sales discounts, and sales returns and the related account balances.

A variation on this cycle approach is to separate the transaction classes of cash receipts and cash disbursements. Not all cash receipts, for example, originate from sales transactions. This means that cash receipts would also be a transaction class in a treasury or financing cycle with related transactions and balances for debt, capital stock, and investments. For this reason cash transactions are sometimes treated as a separate category so that all sources of cash receipts are considered together. With this approach, the sales and expenditures cycles might be considered without cash transactions and the following grouping might be used:

- Sales, trade receivables, and related accounts
- Purchases, trade payables, and related accounts
- Cash receipts
- Cash disbursements

Another consideration in grouping transactions is how comprehensive the groupings should be. Some CPA firms have adopted audit approaches with comprehensive groupings so that all of the transaction classes and account balances of a typical commercial or industrial business fit in a particular cycle, component, or segment. These standardized groupings provide a framework for the organization of the understanding of the internal control structure and the entire audit approach. They also provide a framework for understanding a particular business. For example, two possible comprehensive groupings are as follows:

I Grouping by activity:
   A Sales (marketing, distribution, billing, and collection)
   B Production or service (acquisition and conversion of resources into products or services)
   C Finance (management of financial resources)
   D Administration (control and support of operating activities)
II Grouping by transaction categories:
   A Revenue (resources sold and collected)
   B Expenditure (resources acquired)
   C Conversion (resources held, used, or transformed)

D Treasury (resources, received from investors and creditors and invested)
E Financial reporting, planning, and control

Another possible consideration in grouping transaction classes is the inherent likelihood of assessing the control risk at maximum. As explained more fully in Chapter 7, for some account balances the auditor anticipates assessing control risk for the assertion at maximum. Essentially this is because assessing the control risk at less than maximum is more likely to be an efficient audit approach when there is a large volume of repetitive transactions. Some account balances, such as debt and stockholders' equity, are typically affected by only a few large transactions. In this case, it is generally more efficient to substantiate the balance directly without performing procedures to test controls. For this reason, some auditors prefer to use a mixture of transaction cycles and account balances in organizing the consideration of internal control structure and the audit approach.

Organization Used in This Book   This book uses a mixed organization. Transaction classes and related balances are grouped for the sales cycle (revenue, receivables, receipts) and the expenditures cycle (purchases, payables, disbursements). These are the typical areas for which control risk may be assessed at less than maximum because they usually include a large volume of repetitive transactions.

Understanding the Internal Control Structure

The auditor obtains an understanding of the internal control structure for several reasons:

- To identify the types of potential misstatements that could occur and the factors that contribute to the risk that they will occur.
- To understand the accounting system sufficiently to identify the client documents, reports, and other information that may be available and ascertain what data will be used in audit tests.
- To determine an efficient and effective approach to the audit—the auditor's understanding of the internal control structure may even raise doubts about the auditability of the financial statements if there is a question of management's integrity or if the accounting records are so poor that it is unlikely that sufficient competent evidential matter can be obtained.

The auditor generally performs the procedures to obtain the understanding during the general planning phase of the audit as described in Chapter 5.
SAS No. 55 (AU 319.02) states:

> In all audits, the auditor should . . . understand the design of policies and procedures relevant to audit planning and whether they have been placed in operation.

The phrase "placed in operation" is different than "operating effectiveness." For example, an auditor may read a company's policies and procedures manual to help obtain an understanding of the internal control structure. However, not all those policies and procedures may still be used by company personnel. Some may have been phased out or never actually used for any length of time. In obtaining an understanding, the auditor learns both what the policies and procedures are and whether company personnel use them.

Operating effectiveness, on the other hand, is the manner in which company personnel apply the policies that are in place. Have the policies and procedures been used consistently throughout the year? Are they used by all the employees performing the job function? When the employee ordinarily responsible for a procedure is ill or on vacation, is the procedure still effective? Does the employee take the appropriate action when an exception is noted, or are overrides common?

When the auditor is obtaining the initial understanding of policies and procedures within the internal control structure, knowledge of the operating effectiveness is not necessarily obtained, and is not required by SAS No. 55. However, if the auditor decides that it would be desirable to reduce the assessed level of control risk below the maximum, then the auditor will consider operating effectiveness.

Understanding Control Environment, Risk Assessment, and Monitoring   The methods and audit procedures used in obtaining an understanding of these components are:

- Inquiries of key management personnel
- Inspection of company documents, to the extent the company has documented relevant policies and procedures
- Observation of company activities and operations
- Consideration of past experience with the client

Understanding the Accounting System   The audit procedures to obtain an understanding of the accounting system include inquiry of management, supervisory, and staff personnel; inspection of records, documents, and reports; reading client-prepared descriptions of the system or similar client documentation such as a chart of accounts or a procedures manual; observation of company activities and operations; previous experience with the client; and review of prior year's work papers.

The auditor is required to obtain knowledge of the accounting system sufficiently to understand:

- Major classes of transactions
- Initiation of transactions
- Records, documents, and accounts used in processing and recording transactions
- Accounting processing
- Financial reporting procedures

Understanding the Control Procedures   The audit procedures customarily used to obtain an understanding of control procedures are:

1 Inquiries of appropriate client personnel
2 Inspection of written documentation
3 Observation of the processing of transactions and handling of related assets

Many auditors use a technique called a *walk-through* to clarify their understanding of information obtained. Using this technique the auditor traces one or a few transactions of each type in the transactions class through the related documents and accounting records and observes the related processing and control procedures in operation. For example, the auditor might select a few transactions recorded in the sales journal and trace them back to the related source documents (invoice, customer order, shipping report) and trace them forward to posting in the accounts receivable subsidiary ledger and control account. In doing this, the auditor would actually walk the selected transactions through the system by visiting the departments involved in processing and talking to the personnel responsible for performing the various processing and control procedures.

The purpose of the walk-through is to clarify the auditor's understanding of how the system and the control procedures work. However, the audit procedures applied are substantially the same as those that would be applied to a larger number of transactions in doing tests of controls. The distinction is based on the auditor's purpose in applying the procedures.

The auditor is required to obtain an understanding of the control procedures to the extent needed to plan the audit. A sufficient understanding has been obtained when the auditor is able to identify types of potential misstatements and consider the factors that affect the risk of those misstatements in designing the substantive tests. An understanding of all of the client's control procedures is not needed for audit planning.

The nature and extent of procedures to obtain an understanding of the control procedures varies considerably from client to client. A key issue is the level of complexity and sophistication of the accounting system and operations.

In the case of a small business client, for example, the auditor may note a control environment in which there are too few employees to achieve an adequate separation of duties. In that case, knowledge of the control procedures sufficient to plan the audit may have been achieved while obtaining the understanding of the control environment and the accounting system, and additional work on specific control procedures will not be needed.

Documenting the Understanding

Documentation of the understanding of the internal control structure commonly includes:

- Questionnaires and checklists
- Narrative memoranda
- Flowcharts

Because this type of documentation can be time-consuming to prepare, the auditor wants to be careful to document only the understanding that is necessary to identify potential misstatements and design effective substantive tests. Unless the auditor believes that understanding of particular procedures is needed for audit planning, the internal control structure procedures need not be documented.

The auditor's goal is to identify and document the *minimum number* of specific control procedures that provide reasonable assurance of achieving specific control objectives. For this reason, the documentation the auditor prepares may be much less detailed than would be prepared by a systems analyst. For example, if a company's disbursement system provides for the controller's review and approval and cancellation of supporting documents before payment, the auditor may not be concerned with prior processing steps for individual supporting documents such as purchase orders. The auditor will document and test those specific control procedures that provide reasonable assurance of achieving specific control objectives for specific assertions.

Questionnaires and Checklists   Almost all auditors use some form of generalized materials such as questionnaires and checklists in obtaining an understanding of the internal control structure. The questionnaires and checklists act as both a memory aid and a convenient way to document the understanding obtained.

Generalized forms relating to the control environment vary from checklists that present virtually all the potential features of a control environment to simple forms that list broad categories of features, such as personnel policies and procedures and organizational structure, leaving space for the auditor to describe the client's relevant policies and procedures.

Questionnaires and checklists to document the understanding of the accounting system tend to be less detailed than the generalized forms for the control environment and the control procedures. They are usually organized with a separate section for each transaction class or cycle. They lead the auditor through questions (requiring a written answer rather than a "yes" or "no" check mark) requiring listing of each transaction type, the source document to initiate the transaction and the party responsible for the initiation, the approximate volume of each transaction type, the accounts and computer files in which the transaction is recorded, and what processing occurs, and where the transaction is summarized in the financial statements.

Questionnaires and checklists to document control procedures are widely used. Figure 6-5 presents a segment of an internal control questionnaire. Some are in the form of "yes" or "no" questions about whether specific control methods and features are in place. Others are organized by detailed control objective and the auditor writes in the client's control procedures that achieve the listed control objective.

Narrative Memoranda   A narrative is a written description of internal control policies and procedures. Narratives may be used to document all five components of the internal control structure. Figure 6-6 presents a narrative description of a segment of a sales accounting system. An auditor does not require exhaustive documentation of every step in all accounting systems or enumeration of all control procedures. The narrative provides the auditor the flexibility to write only what is significant to the specific audit. However, narratives have no memory-joggers to help ensure that all important aspects are adequately documented, and narratives are more dependent than questionnaires on the ability of the auditor to write understandably.

(Each question must be answered "Yes" or "No" or "N/A". If answer is "No" attach an explanation.)

Sales

___   1. Are sales orders approved by the credit department before they are accepted?

___   2. Is the credit function separated from other functions, particularly cash, sales, and accounting functions?

3. Are shipping documents—
___   (a) Used?
___   (b) Used on all items leaving plant?
___   (c) Prenumbered?

___   4. Are shipping documents checked to customers' orders for quantity and descriptions to determine that items shipped are those ordered?

5. Are invoices—
___   (a) Prepared on all sales?
___   (b) Prenumbered?

___   6. Is a check made to determine that there are notices of shipment for all invoices and invoices for all notices of shipments?

___   7. Are invoices checked to notices of shipment for quantity and descriptions to determine that items shipped are being billed?

___   8. Is a check made to determine that all invoices are recorded and all invoice numbers accounted for?

9. Are invoices checked for—
___   (a) Extensions?
___   (b) Footings?
___   (c) Terms?
___   (d) Prices?

___   10. Are partial shipments subject to the same procedures as regular sales?

___   11. Do miscellaneous sales follow the same procedures as regular sales, e.g., sales of equipment, sales of scrap, and sales to employees, etc.?

___   12. Are sales summaries prepared, independent of the accounting department, which may be used as a check on recorded sales?

FIGURE 6-5
Example of a segment of an internal control structure questionnaire. *(Adapted from AICPA "Case Studies in Interval Control, Number 2.")*

The *shipping department*, based on an approved sales order, prepares a three-copy shipping document when a shipment is made. The distribution of the document is as follows:

1 Sent to customer with goods as a packing slip.
2 Forwarded to billing department.
3 Forwarded to accounts receivable recordkeeping. The sales order is filed numerically.

The *billing department* uses the shipping document to prepare a two-copy sales invoice with the following distribution:

1 Sent to customer.
2 Forwarded to accounts receivable recordkeeping. The shipping document is filed numerically.

The *accounts receivable recordkeeping function* periodically matches sales invoices and shipping documents received.

1 Matched sales invoices are posted to accounts receivable detail.
2 Matched sales invoices and shipping documents are filed alphabetically by customer name.

FIGURE 6-6
Example of a narrative description of a segment of a sales accounting system.

Flowcharts   Flowcharting is a technique that uses graphic symbols to present a diagram of an accounting system and control procedures.

Both the manual and EDP portions of a system may be documented, and flowcharting has advantages even for purely manual systems. However, flowcharting is particularly useful for systems that mix manual and computer processing in significant accounting applications.

Figure 6-7 presents some of the common flowcharting symbols. Figure 6-8 presents a flowchart for a portion of a simple accounting system. Figure 6-9 presents a system flowchart for a portion of a batch computerized accounting application. One of the advantages of flowcharting is supposed to be that a graphic presentation of a series of related processing steps is easier to understand than a narrative description. However, if a flowchart includes all the document and information flows in the system, it often becomes too complex to be easily understood and the significant control procedures can be difficult to identify. For this reason, the emphasis in practice today is on flowchart simplification.

Several CPA firms have devised unique approaches to flowcharting that use a relatively few nonstandard symbols. These approaches are too diverse to illustrate, but they all emphasize exclusion of document flows that are not relevant to the understanding of

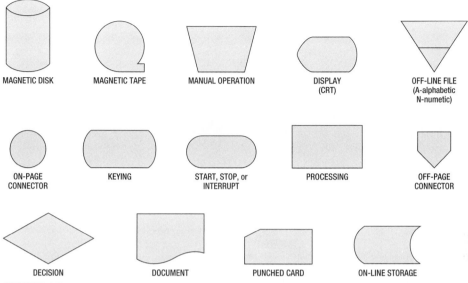

FIGURE 6-7
Standard flowchart symbols.

the internal control structure for the purposes of audit planning. The standardized symbols illustrated in this book are still useful because they are used in the computer industry and may be used in client documentation of systems and programs.

Assessing Control Risk

After obtaining an understanding of the five components of the internal control structure, the auditor assesses the control risk for the assertions embodied in the account balance, transaction class, and disclosure components of the financial statements. *Control risk* is the risk that a material misstatement could occur in an assertion and not be prevented or detected on a timely basis by the company's internal control structure policies or procedures.

The auditor's first decision is whether to assess control risk for a particular assertion at the maximum level, or at less than maximum. The auditor may assess control risk at the maximum because:

1 The company's internal control structure policies and procedures in the area are poor and will not support less than a maximum assessment.
2 The company's internal control structure policies and procedures in the area may be effective, but the audit tests to gather evidence of the effectiveness of the policies and procedures would be more time-consuming than performing direct substantive tests of the account balance or transaction class.
3 Internal control policies and procedures do not pertain to the particular assertion.

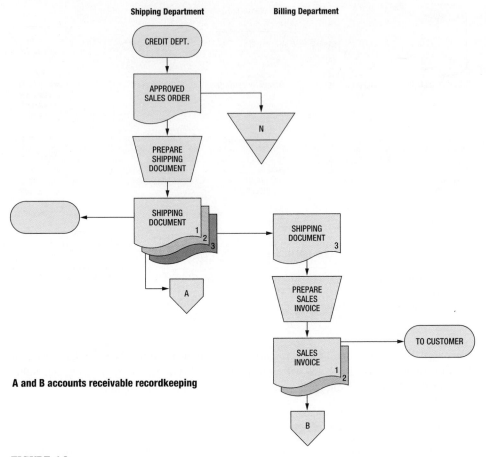

FIGURE 6-8
A flowchart of the first portion of the sales accounting system described in Figure 6-6.

If the auditor believes that assessing control risk at below the maximum level would be efficient and effective, the auditor's approach is as follows. First, the auditor identifies specific internal control structure policies and procedures relevant to specific assertions that are likely to prevent or detect material misstatements in those assertions. Next, the auditor performs tests of controls to evaluate the effectiveness of the policies and procedures identified. This process is followed for each account balance or transaction class that is material to the financial statements.

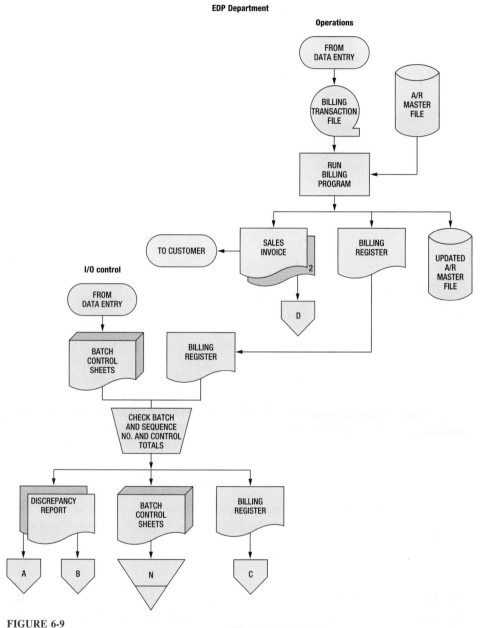

FIGURE 6-9

Segment of a flowchart on the billing function in a batch computerized sales accounting system. The flowchart shows the EDP department activities in operations and input/output (I/O) control involved in recording the sale, generating the invoice, and updating the

The following example involving sales illustrates the process in more detail.

Transaction class:	Sales.
Assertion:	Completeness.
Audit objective:	Recorded sales include all authorized sales transactions.
Control objective:	All goods shipped are billed.
Relevant internal control structure policies and procedures:	• The sales manager reviews a detailed summary of sales activity by location. • Shipping documents are periodically matched with sales invoices.

In this example, the auditor would design tests of controls to obtain evidence about the operating effectiveness of the policies and procedures identified.

The auditor is never required to assess control risk at lower than the maximum level. The auditor decides to do so only when it improves audit efficiency.

The assessment of control risk varies along a range from maximum to minimum, depending on the level of effectiveness of the company's internal control structure policies and procedures and on the evidential matter the auditor has obtained. When the auditor assesses control risk below the maximum level, the auditor must obtain evidence sufficient to support that assessed level.

Note that the auditor may have a different assessment of control risk for each material account balance or transaction class or assertions within the balance or class. For example, the auditor may assess control risk for inventory assertions as high and assess control risk for cash assertions as low or assess the risk for existence of cash as low but completeness as high. However, the auditor would recognize the interrelationships of account balances and transaction classes. For example, a low level of assessed control risk for sales and cash receipts would mean a low level of control risk for accounts receivable for assertions affected by the accuracy and reliability of recorded sales and cash receipts.

Tests of Controls

The auditor must obtain evidence sufficient to support the assessed level of control risk for an assertion. In assessing the control risk at less than maximum, the auditor has identified specific internal control structure policies and procedures that he or she believes will prevent or detect misstatements for the assertion. The evidence needed is to support that those identified policies and procedures are effective. The evidence should demonstrate both:

- The effectiveness of the design of the policies and procedures as placed in operation
- The operating effectiveness of the policies and procedures, that is, consistent and proper application of the policies and procedures

Some of this evidence may be obtained concurrently with obtaining an understanding of the internal control structure, or an audit procedure performed to obtain an understanding may also simultaneously yield evidence on the effectiveness of the design of a policy or procedure.

Types of Tests of Controls   Additional evidence is gathered by performing *tests of controls.* The two types of tests of controls are:

- Tests directed toward the effectiveness of the design of the internal control policy or procedure. These tests help evaluate whether the policy or procedure is suitably designed to prevent or detect material misstatements in the specific assertion.
- Tests directed toward the operating effectiveness of the policy or procedure. These tests are concerned with how the policy or procedure was applied, the consistency with which it was applied during the audit period, and by whom it was applied.

Tests of controls directed toward design generally include inquiries of company personnel, inspection of documents and reports, and observation of the application of specific internal control structure policies and procedures, including walk-throughs. These tests often involve the preparation of flowcharts or questionnaires if the internal control structure procedure is complex.

Tests of controls directed toward operating effectiveness generally include inquiries of company personnel, inspection of documents and reports indicating performance of the policy or procedure, observation of the application of the policy or procedure, and reperformance of the application of the policy or procedure by the auditor.

The methods and procedures the auditor uses for tests of controls depend on whether the control structure procedure leaves a documentary trail of its performance.

- *No trail.* This involves inquiries and observation of accounting personnel and routines to determine how control procedures are performed and, especially, who performs them; for example, this approach would be used to see whether cash is handled by someone who does not record cash transactions.
- *Documentary trail.* This involves inspection of documents supporting a particular type of transaction to see whether a control procedure, such as approval or checking, was performed, such as by noting signatures or initials, and whether the procedure was performed effectively.

Observing the client's personnel and processing routines and making corroborative inquiries of appropriate personnel are usually accomplished when the auditor is on the client's premises for other purposes. The inquiries and observations are done at this time, but the auditor is concerned with operations in the entire period covered by the financial statements. Thus, the auditor's inquiries extend beyond the immediate duties of the personnel being interviewed. The auditor will inquire about the employee's understanding of the duties of others; what happens when review and reconciliation procedures detect errors; who handles the investigation and resolution of errors; and what happens when employees with key assigned duties are on vacation.

When documentary support of consistent application of a procedure exists, the auditor inspects a sample of the documents to see whether they were approved or checked as prescribed and to see who performed the control procedures. Since the auditor will also usually apply substantive tests of details of transactions to the same type of underlying documents, these substantive tests and tests of controls are usually combined in what is called a *dual-purpose test.* A dual-purpose test is essentially inspection of the same sample of documents to test both controls and substantive aspects of the transaction class. Usually this type of testing is done at an interim date and covers the first 9 or 10 months of the year. This type of testing is explained further in Chapters 7 to 10.

Sufficiency of Evidence   The evidence necessary to support a specific level of control risk is a matter of audit judgment. The auditor requires stronger evidence of the effectiveness of a procedure if the assessed level of control risk is very low than if it is only moderately reduced. Other factors the auditor considers in determining whether the tests of controls have yielded sufficient evidence of effectiveness include:

- Type of evidence
- Source of evidence
- Timeliness of evidence
- Interrelationship with other evidence

Type of Evidence   The auditor recognizes that some audit tests provide stronger evidence than others. For example, inquiry and observation that the accounts payable manager appears to review invoices and receiving documents before checks are written provide some evidence, but inspection of written approvals for a sample of checks throughout the period would provide more assurance.

Source of Evidence   Evidence obtained by the auditor directly provides more assurance than evidence obtained indirectly or by inference. Inquiry of company personnel about the reconciliation procedure they perform provides evidence, but the auditor's personal inspection of a random sample of the daily reconciliation forms for the entire period under audit would yield stronger evidence.

Timeliness   Timeliness enhances the amount of assurance provided by the evidence. The two factors in *timeliness* are:

1 When the evidence was obtained. For example, the auditor may include in his or her consideration evidence obtained from prior years' audits, but the auditor must consider whether the procedure in place has changed, and consider that the longer the time elapsed since the test of controls was performed, the less assurance it provides.
2 Whether it applies to the entire audit period or only a portion of the audit period. Ideally tests of controls would demonstrate the effectiveness of the policy or procedure for the entire audit period. As discussed in Chapter 5, regulatory deadlines and other timing problems may make it impractical or impossible for the auditor to accomplish that ideal.

Interrelationship of Evidence   The auditor considers the combined effect of various evidence about a particular assertion. Included in the consideration are how the control environment, accounting system, and control procedures work together to affect risk for the assertion. There is generally a combination of evidence types, including inquiry and a variety of other audit methods that were discussed above. Individual pieces of evidential matter that, taken alone, would not be sufficient evidence may be sufficient when taken together. Conversely, evidence that is persuasive taken by itself may be relied upon less if, for example, there is evidence that the control environment is weak.

Documentation of the Assessment of Control Risk

The auditor must document the assessment of control risk for the various assertions for significant transaction classes and account balances. When the auditor assesses control risk at the maximum level, the basis for that assessment need not be documented. Only the assessment must be written.

When the assessed level of control risk is less than maximum, the basis for the assessment must be documented as well. This documentation is generally in narrative form, or on a generalized form with spaces to fill in for the assessment and the basis.

Effect on Design of Substantive Tests

The result of the auditor's consideration of the internal control structure is the assessment of control risk, which is then used in planning substantive tests for the various assertions within the transaction classes or account balances. As mentioned in Chapter 4, control risk is one of the three risks comprising audit risk, as demonstrated in the following equation:

$$\text{AUDIT RISK} = \text{INHERENT RISK} \times \text{CONTROL RISK} \times \text{DETECTION RISK}$$

Inherent risk, although it is an audit judgment, cannot be reduced by an action of the auditor. Accordingly, to have reasonable assurance that a material misstatement of the particular transaction class or account balance will be detected, the auditor must reduce his or her assessment of control risk or detection risk for its assertions. This chapter has explained tests of controls and how the auditor can reduce the assessed level of control risk.

If the auditor assessed control risk at the maximum, the result is that he or she must reduce the level of detection risk so that it is very low. Detection risk is reduced by performing substantive tests. The higher the level of assessed control risk, the more assurance the auditor must obtain from substantive tests. Chapter 7 explains how to plan substantive tests to reduce detection risk.

An ineffective internal control structure results in the auditor having to increase the quantity and effectiveness of the substantive tests because there is a general relationship between control objectives and audit objectives. Because it is not consistent, the relationship must be considered for each transaction class separately. For example, *approval* of credit sales (goods shipped to customers do not exceed established credit limits) is related to the specific audit objective of *valuation* of accounts receivable. On the other hand, approval of disbursements is related to specific audit objectives concerning *existence* or *occurrence*.

However, the following generalizations can be made about the effect of an effective internal control structure on the nature, timing, and extent of substantive tests.

- *Substantive tests related to existence.* Effective internal control structure policies and procedures may allow the auditor to modify the nature or reduce the extent of substantive tests of the existence of recorded assets or liabilities. For example, the number of confirmations sent to customers may be reduced when control procedures over the validity and recording accuracy of debits and credits to accounts receivable are effective.
- *Substantive tests related to completeness.* Effective internal control structure policies and procedures may allow the auditor to modify the nature or reduce the extent of substantive tests of the completeness of recorded assets or liabilities. For example, if processing and control procedures relating to the completeness of sales transaction (all goods shipped have been billed) are effective, the auditor's tests related to the completeness of receivables may be limited to analytical procedures. The relationship between completeness control structure elements and audit objectives related to completeness is a consistently direct relation for all transaction classes.
- *Substantive tests related to all audit objectives for income statement accounts.* Because of the relationship between income statement and balance sheet accounts, substantive tests of opening and closing balance sheet accounts substantiate the amount of net income for the period. When processing and control procedures for the major transaction classes that affect income statement accounts are effective, the substantive tests of these accounts often can be limited to analytical procedures.
- *Timing of substantive tests.* Effective internal control structure policies and procedures related to safeguarding may permit the auditor to conduct principal substantive tests of recorded assets at an interim date rather than at year-end. Usually, processing and control procedures that achieve specific control objectives related to validity, completeness, and recording accuracy must also be somewhat effective because the auditor uses the accounting records to compare the account balances at the interim date with the balances at year-end and needs to investigate significant fluctuations.

The relationship between specific control objectives and specific audit objectives is considered further in Chapters 7 and 10.

THE FOREIGN CORRUPT PRACTICES ACT

The Foreign Corrupt Practices Act (FCPA) resulted from a public scandal. Nearly 450 companies—including some of the biggest in the country—were determined to have made kickbacks, bribes, or other questionable payoffs. The so-called culprits ranged from Bell Helicopter, a subsidiary of Textron Inc., to giant oil companies such as Gulf Oil Corporation and Exxon Corporation. The litany of corporate misdeeds reported daily in the press shocked the public and toppled two foreign heads of state. Some secret payments were recorded and inadequately described; others were made from off-the-books funds set up for that purpose. A tire manufacturer listed payments as CDs for "crooked deals." The FCPA was a legislative solution to this problem.

The FCPA has been in effect since 1977 and it has two main parts. The first part makes it unlawful to bribe foreign officials or politicians to get or to keep business. This part is administered by the Department of Justice and covers all U.S. companies. Its subject, "antibribery," is what you would expect from the title of the law.

The other part, which the law calls the "accounting standards," establishes requirements for accurate accounting records and sound internal accounting control. These requirements apply to domestic as well as foreign transactions and locations *but only to public companies subject to the 1934 Act,* and they are administered by the SEC. Note that the law applies to both domestic and foreign transactions and, perhaps even more significant, no bribe (foreign or domestic) has to be involved for the SEC to invoke this part of the law.

The FCPA adopted a definition of internal control from the auditing literature. The broad objectives are asset safeguarding and reliable accounting records. More detailed objectives concern (1) transaction authorization, (2) transaction recording, (3) restricted access to assets, and (4) accountability comparisons of asset counts to records.

Under the FCPA the responsibility of compliance falls on the management of the company. No direct responsibilities are imposed on independent auditors. However, many CPA firms have adopted the policy that the audit of the financial statements of a company subject to the 1934 Act should include a comprehensive consideration of the internal control structure even if that is not the most efficient audit strategy under the circumstances.

CHAPTER 5 ASSIGNMENTS

OBJECTIVE QUESTIONS

6-1 For each one of the following statements indicate whether the statement is true or false.

T F a The relation of internal control to evidential matter arises from the expected effect of the internal control structure on the propriety and accuracy of underlying accounting data.

T F b The primary objective of the auditor's consideration of the internal control structure is to identify reportable conditions.

T F c The primary objective of the auditor's consideration of the internal control structure is to obtain sufficient understanding of it to plan the audit.

T F d The auditor must always document the basis for the assessment of control risk, no matter what level that assessment is.

T F e The fact that the cost of a control procedure may exceed the expected benefits is not sufficient justification for failure to adopt a control procedure necessary for effective control.

T F f The general objectives of internal control, such as validity, completeness, safeguarding, and reconciliation, are not intended to be applied to the internal control structure taken as a whole.

T F g Specific control objectives for a particular transaction class can conveniently serve as a framework for both assessing control risk and substantively testing the details of transactions processed.

T F h Accounting for the sequence of prenumbered documents is a control procedure intended to achieve specific control objectives related to validity.

T F i Control procedures related to recording accuracy usually take the form of independent checks, reviews, and approvals.

T F j Incompatible functions are those that place any person in a position to perpetrate errors or irregularities.

T F k Management's use of budgets to monitor operations may affect the auditor's judgment on whether there is reasonable assurance that specific control objectives are achieved.

T F l A walk-through is a technique used by auditors to clarify their understanding of information obtained through inquiry and observations about prescribed control procedures.

T F m When performing walk-through procedures of a portion of the client's accounting system, it is *not* necessary to follow the same item of information through the processing steps.

T F n The Foreign Corrupt Practices Act prescribes specific responsibilities for independent auditors related to internal control.

6-2 The following questions relate to the auditor's consideration of the internal control structure. Select the *best* response.

    a The primary purpose of the auditor's consideration of internal control structure is to provide a basis for:

        1 Determining whether procedures and records that are concerned with the safeguarding of assets are reliable

        2 Constructive suggestions to clients concerning improvements in the internal control structure

        3 Determining the nature, extent, and timing of audit tests to be applied

        4 The expression of an opinion

    b Which of the following is not a component of the internal control structure?

        1 Control activities

        2 Organizational structure

        3 Risk assessment

        4 Control environment

    c After obtaining an understanding of the internal control structure in an audit engagement, the auditor should perform tests of controls on:

        1 Those procedures that the auditor identified to reduce the assessed level of control risk

        2 Those procedures for which reportable conditions were identified

        3 Those procedures that have a material effect upon the financial statement balances

        4 A random sample of the procedures that were identified

    d After obtaining an understanding of an entity's internal control structure and assessing control risk, an auditor may next:

        1 Perform tests of controls to verify management's assertions that are embodied in the financial statements

        2 Consider whether evidential matter is available to support a further reduction in the assessed level of control risk

        3 Apply analytical procedures as substantive tests to validate the assessed level of control risk

        4 Evaluate whether the internal control structure policies and procedures detected material misstatements in the financial statements

e An auditor uses the knowledge provided by the understanding of the internal control structure and the final assessed level of control risk primarily to determine the nature, timing, and extent of the:
   1 Attribute tests
   2 Compliance tests
   3 Tests of controls
   4 Substantive tests

f When obtaining an understanding of an entity's control environment, an auditor should concentrate on the substance of management's policies and procedures rather than their form because:
   1 The auditor may believe that the policies and procedures are inappropriate for that particular entity.
   2 The board of directors may *not* be aware of management's attitude toward the control environment.
   3 Management may establish appropriate policies and procedures but *not* act on them.
   4 The policies and procedures may be so weak that *no* reliance is contemplated by the auditor.

g An auditor is *least* likely to test the internal controls that provide for:
   1 Approval of the purchase and sale of marketable securities
   2 Classification of revenue and expense transactions by product line
   3 Segregation of the functions of recording disbursements and reconciling the bank accounts
   4 Comparison of receiving reports and vendors' invoices with purchase orders

h A procedure that would most likely be used by an auditor in performing tests of control procedures that involve segregation of functions and that leave *no* transaction trail is:
   1 Inspection
   2 Observation
   3 Reperformance
   4 Reconciliation

AICPA

6-3 The following questions relate to basic concepts or terms concerning the internal controls structure. Select the *best* response.

a Which of the following would be *least* likely to be considered a control objective?
   1 Checking the accuracy and reliability of accounting data
   2 Detecting management fraud
   3 Encouraging adherence to managerial policies
   4 Safeguarding assets

b Which of the following is *not* a factor considered in assessing the control environment?
   1 Proper authorization of sales transactions and activities
   2 Personnel policies and procedures
   3 Management's philosophy and operating style
   4 The company's organizational structure

c The basic concept which recognizes that the cost of internal control should *not* exceed the benefits expected to be derived is known as:
   1 Management by exception
   2 Management responsibility
   3 Limited liability

      4 Reasonable assurance

AICPA

6-4 The following questions relate to possible responsibilities of the independent auditor concerning the internal control structure. Select the *best* response.

  a When the auditor assesses control risk at the maximum level for a specific assertion:

    1 The auditor need not document the assessment.

    2 The auditor must document the assessment but need not document the basis for that assessment.

    3 The auditor must document both the assessment and the basis for it.

    4 The extent of documentation is not related to the level of assessed risk, but rather to the complexity and sophistication of the company's operations and systems.

  b Which of the following statements regarding auditor documentation of the client's internal control structure is correct?

    1 Documentation must include flowcharts.

    2 Documentation must include procedural write-ups.

    3 No documentation is necessary although it is desirable.

    4 No one particular form of documentation is necessary, and the extent of documentation may vary.

  c Which of the following is not a reason to assess control risk at the maximum level?

    1 Internal control structure policies or procedures are unlikely to pertain to an assertion.

    2 Internal control structure policies or procedures are unlikely to be effective.

    3 The auditor has assessed detection risk at the maximum level.

    4 Evaluating the effectiveness of the internal control structure policies or procedures would be more time-consuming than another audit approach.

  d The Foreign Corrupt Practices Act requires that:

    1 Auditors engaged to audit the financial statements of publicly held companies report all illegal payments to the SEC

    2 Publicly held companies establish independent audit committees to monitor the effectiveness of their internal control structure

    3 U.S. firms doing business abroad report sizable payments to non-U.S. citizens to the Justice Department

    4 Publicly held companies devise and maintain an adequate internal control structure

AICPA

DISCUSSION QUESTIONS

Discussion questions require the application of the concepts explained in the chapter to specific facts, issues, or problems. They are classified by the primary topic to which they relate. However, responses should not be confined to the primary topics but should include all relevant implications.

Internal Control—General

6-5 As a part of understanding the control environment, an auditor studies the organization structure as it relates to the division of labor and responsibility. The auditor also studies the accounting system. How are the organization structure and the accounting system of a company related? Explain briefly.

6-6 Family Finance Company opened four personal loan offices in neighboring cities on January 2, 19X2. Small cash loans are made to borrowers, who repay the principal with interest in monthly installments over a period not exceeding 2 years. Ralph Minton, president of the company, uses one of the offices as a central office and visits the other offices periodically for supervision and internal auditing purposes.

Mr. Minton is concerned about the honesty of his employees. He came to your office in December 19X2 and stated, "I want to install a system to prohibit employees from embezzling cash." He also stated, "Until I went into business for myself, I worked for a nationwide loan company with 500 offices, and I'm familiar with that company's accounting system and control procedures. I want to describe that structure so that you can install it for me, because it will absolutely prevent fraud."

a How would you advise Mr. Minton on his request? Discuss.

b How would you respond to the suggestion that the new structure would prevent embezzlement? Discuss.

c Assume that, in addition to undertaking the systems engagement in 19X3, you agreed to audit Family Finance Company's financial statements for the year ended December 31, 19X2. No scope limitations were imposed.

1 How would you determine the scope necessary to satisfactorily complete your audit? Discuss.

2 Would you be responsible for the discovery of fraud in this audit? Discuss.

6-7 Jones, CPA, who has been engaged to audit the financial statements of Ajax, Inc., is about to commence obtaining an understanding of the internal control structure and is aware of the inherent limitations that should be considered.

Required:

a What are the objectives of internal control?

b What are the reasonable assurances that are intended to be provided by the internal control structure?

c When considering the potential effectiveness of any internal control structure, what are the inherent limitations that should be recognized?

AICPA adapted

Control Objectives, Control Procedures, and Identification of Deficiencies

6-8 Western Meat Processing Company buys and processes livestock for sale to supermarkets. In connection with your audit of the company's financial statements, you have prepared the following notes based on your understanding of procedures:

1 Each livestock buyer submits a daily report of purchases to the plant superintendent. This report shows the dates of purchase and expected delivery; the vendor; and the number, weights, and type of livestock purchased. As shipments are received, any available plant employee counts the number of each type received and places a check mark beside this quantity on the buyer's report. When all shipments listed on the report have been received, the report is returned to the buyer.

2 Vendors' invoices, after a clerical check, are sent to the buyer for approval and returned to the accounting department. A disbursement voucher and a check for the approved amount are prepared in the accounting department. Checks are forwarded to the treasurer for signature. The treasurer's office sends signed checks directly to the buyer for delivery to the vendor.

3 Livestock carcasses are processed by lots. Each lot is assigned a number. At the end of each day a tally sheet reporting the lots processed, the number and type of animals in each lot, and the carcass weight is sent to the accounting department, where a perpetual inventory record of processed carcasses and their weights is maintained.

4 Processed carcasses are stored in a refrigerated cooler located in a small building adjacent to the employee parking lot. The cooler is locked when the plant is not open, and a company guard is on duty when the employees report for work and leave at the end of their shifts. Supermarket truck drivers wishing to pick up their orders have been instructed to contact someone in the plant if no one is in the cooler.

5 Substantial quantities of byproducts are produced and stored, either in the cooler or elsewhere in the plant. Byproducts are initially accounted for as they are sold. At this time the sales manager prepares a two-part form; one copy serves as authorization to transfer the goods to the customer and the other becomes the basis for billing the customer.

For each of the numbered notes 1 to 5 above state:

a What the specific internal control objective(s) should be at the stage of the operating cycle described by the note

b The deficiencies in the design of the present procedures, if any, and suggestions for improvement, if any

AICPA

6-9 A company's internal control structure is strengthened by including procedures that have specific functions or purposes. For example, the control procedures may include a voucher system that provides for all invoices to be checked for accuracy, approved for propriety, and recorded before being paid. The system reduces the likelihood that an invoice will be mislaid or the discount lost, and it provides assurance that improper or unauthorized disbursements are not likely to be made.

Give the purposes or functions of each of the following procedures or techniques that may be included in an internal control structure, and explain how each has a purpose or function that is helpful in strengthening control:

a Fidelity bonding of employees

b Budgeting of capital expenditures

c Listing of mail remittances by the mail department when the mail is opened

d Maintaining a plant ledger for fixed assets

AICPA adapted

6-10 The Art Appreciation Society operates a museum for the benefit and enjoyment of the community. During hours when the museum is open to the public, two clerks who are positioned at the entrance collect a $5.00 admission fee from each nonmember patron. Members of the Art Appreciation Society are permitted to enter free of charge upon presentation of their membership cards.

At the end of each day, one of the clerks delivers the proceeds to the treasurer. The treasurer counts the cash in the presence of the clerk and places it in a safe. Each Friday afternoon the treasurer and one of the clerks deliver all cash held in the safe to the bank, and receive an authenticated deposit slip which provides the basis for the weekly entry in the cash receipts journal.

The Board of Directors of the Art Appreciation Society has identified a need to improve their control procedures for cash admission fees. The board has determined that the cost of installing turnstiles, sales booths, or otherwise altering the physical layout of the museum will greatly exceed any benefits which may be derived. However, the board has agreed that the sale of admission tickets must be an integral part of its improvement efforts.

Smith has been asked by the Board of Directors of the Art Appreciation Society to review the internal control structure for cash admission fees and provide suggestions for improvement.

Required: Indicate deficiencies in the existing procedures for cash admission fees, which Smith should identify, and recommend one improvement for each of the deficiencies identified.

Organize the answer in the following illustrative example:

Deficiency	Recommendation
1. There is no basis for establishing the documentation of the number of paying patrons.	1. Prenumbered admission tickets should be issued upon payment of the admission fee.

AICPA adapted

6-11 Properly designed and utilized forms facilitate adherence to prescribed internal control structure policies and procedures. One such form might be a multicopy purchase order, with one copy intended to be mailed to the vendor. The remaining copies would ordinarily be distributed to the stores, purchasing, receiving, and accounting departments.

The following purchase order is currently being used by National Industrial Corporation:

PURCHASE ORDER

SEND INVOICE ONLY TO:

297 HARDINGTEN DR., BX., NY 10461

TO _____   SHIP TO _____

_____   _____

_____   _____

DATE TO BE SHIPPED	SHIP VIA	DISC. TERMS	FREIGHT TERMS	ADV. ALLOWANCE	SPECIAL ALLOWANCE

QUANTITY	DESCRIPTION

PURCHASE CONDITIONS

1. Supplier will be responsible for extra freight cost on partial shipment, unless prior permission is obtained.

2. Please acknowledge this order.

3. Please notify us immediately if you are unable to complete order.

4. All items must be individually packed.

Required:

a In addition to the name of the company, what other necessary information would an auditor recommend be included in the illustrative purchase order?

b What primary internal control functions are served by the purchase order copies that are distributed to the stores, purchasing, receiving, and accounting departments?

AICPA

Separation of Duties

6-12 The Yazoo Company, a client of your firm, has come to you with the following problem: It has three clerical employees who must perform these functions:

1 Maintain general ledger
2 Maintain accounts payable ledger
3 Maintain accounts receivable ledger
4 Prepare checks for signature
5 Maintain disbursements journal
6 Issue credits on returns and allowances
7 Reconcile the bank account
8 Handle and deposit cash receipts

Assuming that there is no problem as to the ability of any of the employees, the company requests that you assign the above functions to the three employees in such a manner as to achieve the highest degree of internal control. It may be assumed that these employees will perform no other accounting functions than the ones listed and that any accounting functions not listed will be performed by persons other than these three employees.

   a State how you would distribute the above functions among the three employees. Assume that, with the exception of the nominal jobs of the bank reconciliation and the issuance of credits on returns and allowances, all functions require an equal amount of time.

   b List four possible unsatisfactory combinations of the above-listed functions.

AICPA adapted

6-13 Eagle Rock Corporation fabricates products, using very expensive components purchased from suppliers. Therefore, the company attempts to tightly control raw materials inventories through the use of the perpetual inventory records and employees who have sole responsibility for receipt and issuance of materials. Eagle Rock employs two people, Len Fels and Ben Gels, in the raw materials warehouse. Their duties are as follows:

Fels

1 Receives and counts incoming materials
2 Maintains perpetual inventory records in units and dollars
3 Issues materials to operating department supervisors

Gels

4 Keeps all inventory neat and orderly in the warehouse
5 Locates and assembles materials orders requested by operating departments
6 Assembles and prepares for return shipment to suppliers all defective or otherwise unusable materials

   a Criticize the assignment of duties to each man by listing the combinations of duties you believe should not have been assigned to the same man. Briefly explain why each combination is undesirable.

   b Assuming the list of six duties is complete, list the individual duty or duties you think should be reassigned to employees other than Fels and Gels. Briefly explain why you believe each duty you have listed should be reassigned.

AICPA adapted

6-14 Willow Paper Company engaged you to review its internal control structure. Willow does not prelist cash receipts before they are recorded, and it has other deficiencies in processing collections of trade receivables, the company's largest asset. In discussing the matter with the controller, you find the controller is chiefly interested in economy when assigning duties to the 15 office personnel. The controller feels the main considerations are that the work should be done by people who are most familiar with it, capable of doing it, and available when it has to be done.

The controller claims excellent control over trade receivables because receivables are pledged as security for a continually renewable bank loan and the bank sends out positive confirmation requests occasionally, based on a list of pledged receivables furnished by the company each week. You learn that the bank's internal auditor is satisfied if she gets an acceptable response on 70 percent of her requests.

a Explain how prelisting of cash receipts strengthens internal control over cash.

b Assume that an employee handles cash receipts from trade customers before they are recorded. List the duties which that employee should not do to withhold from him or her the opportunity to conceal embezzlement of cash receipts.

AICPA adapted

The Auditor's Consideration of the Internal Control Structure

6-15 The internal control structure includes the plan of organization and all of the coordinate methods and measures adopted within a business to safeguard its assets, check the accuracy and reliability of its accounting data, promote operational efficiency, and encourage adherence to prescribed managerial policies.

Required:

a What is the purpose of the auditor's consideration of the internal control structure?

b What are the objectives of obtaining an understanding of internal control structure?

c How is the auditor's understanding of the internal control structure documented?

d What is the purpose of tests of controls?

AICPA adapted

6-16 Bob Hines is employed by Marshall & Co., CPAs, and has been put in charge of the audit of a new client, the Family Clothing Store Ltd.

The Family Clothing Store Ltd., is owned by three men, Messrs. Smith, Jones, and Dobbs. Only one of the owners, Mr. Smith, is active in the business—the other two live and work in another city. Mr. Smith operated the business as a proprietorship until a few years ago, when he incorporated it and obtained additional capital for store improvements by selling to Dobbs and Jones 24 percent of his equity. In addition to Mr. Smith, the store employs three sales clerks and Miss Tears, the cashier-bookkeeper. Miss Tears has worked for Mr. Smith for many years.

Hines and the partner responsible for the Family Clothing Store Ltd. audit have agreed that one of the first things Hines should do when he starts work on the audit is to consider the internal control structure.

a Why would Hines bother to consider the internal control structure of this small company?

b What particular features of the internal control structure would Hines inquire into in the circumstances described above?

CICA adapted

6-17 When the auditor first obtained her understanding of the control procedures related to valuation for sales, she believed that performing tests of controls (to reduce the assessed level of control risk, to permit limiting substantive tests) would be the most efficient audit approach. The results of the completed tests of controls show that the control procedures were not consistently applied on Fridays (the head clerk's day off) or during the weeks that the head clerk was on vacation. The tests of controls have taken more time than planned because of the follow-up inquiry to determine the cause of the errors. The audit, which is on a fixed-fee basis, is over the budgeted amount of time.

a What is the effect on the auditor's assessment of control risk?

b What is the effect on the audit plan?

c How should the auditor proceed?

CASE

An important part of the audit of a company is the consideration of the company's internal control structure, in which the auditor identifies risks of potential misstatements that could affect the audit.

Assume that you are the auditor of X Ltd., which has annual sales of $5 million. One of the members of your audit staff has provided the list of internal control structure descriptions shown on page 230 and has noted the related deficiencies.

For each point considered by the audit staff member to be a deficiency:

1 Explain very briefly the significance of the deficiency, in terms of the materiality of misstatements that could result from it.

2 Describe the effect, if any, of the deficiency on your substantive procedures.

CICA adapted

Staff member's internal control descriptions	Staff member's notes as to believed deficiencies
"Because the company has no purchasing department, many employees make purchases. In general, employees make purchases applicable to their area of the company's operations, but it is not uncommon for employees also to make purchases of personal items through the company. A three-part purchase order form is supposed to be used whenever merchandise is ordered: one copy to be sent to the supplier, one to be sent to the shipping/receiving clerk, and one to be kept by the individual doing the ordering. When the merchandise arrives, the shipping/receiving clerk checks the merchandise and sends the packing slips and purchase order copies to the accounts payable clerk. If he or she has no purchase order for the merchandise, the shipping/receiving clerk ascertains by telephone who ordered the merchandise and attaches a photocopy of a form with this information on it to the packing slips.	1. No control over company's commitment to purchase goods. 2. No control over employees' personal purchasing. 3. Photocopied forms are not prenumbered.
"Inventories are stored at various locations in the plant, usually fairly handy to where they will be used. Because the company's sales and production activities have increased so much since last year, it has occasionally used public warehouses for its overflow inventory. A material requisition form is supposed to be completed whenever material is withdrawn from the raw materials inventory and put into production, but the night shift people often seem to neglect to follow this rule. The company does not have much money invested in shop supplies so there is no necessity to use requisition forms when supplies are consumed. Also, the company often has leftover supplies (purchased for special jobs but not consumed on those jobs) that can be used to some extent on other jobs. The shipping/receiving clerk keeps perpetual inventory records (quantities) for most inventory items, but 30 percent of the items are not included in the records. A physical inventory count is done to check the records whenever the clerk has time.	4. Little physical control over raw materials inventories. 5. No control over inventory of leftover supplies. 6. Shipping/receiving clerk keeps perpetual records and has access to inventories. 7. Incomplete perpetual records. 8. Casual checking of perpetual records.
"When the supplier's invoice arrives, the accounts payable clerk checks the additions and extensions on it, initials it, and staples the packing slip and purchase order or photocopied form to it. He or she enters the invoice in the accounts payable subsidiary account for the supplier, then sends the invoice to the manager of the department for which the employee ordering the goods works; the manager writes on the invoice the account number to which it is to be charged and then sends it to the cash disbursements department.	9. No control over managers' coding of invoices. 10. Apparent lack of price checking. 11. Managers do not specifically approve invoices for payment.
"The accounts payable clerk balances the accounts payable subsidiary ledger to the general ledger control account every month and keeps track of credits due to the company for purchases returned to suppliers. Occasionally the company pays some larger suppliers round amounts of money rather than paying according to the specific invoices as is its usual policy. When he or she has time, the accounts payable clerk attempts to reconcile suppliers' monthly statements to the subsidiary ledger accounts."	12. Accounts payable clerk balances ledger and reconciles suppliers' statements. 13. Irregular reconciliation of suppliers' statements.

CHAPTER

7

Planning Tests of Details of Transactions and Balances

CHAPTER OUTLINE

Learning Objectives

After studying this chapter you should be able to:

- Identify the decisions to be made in designing audit programs and the considerations that affect those decisions
- Explain how consideration of the nature of financial statement components and audit objectives, materiality, audit risk, and the efficiency of audit tests affect the planning of direct tests of balances
- Understand how the auditor's preliminary judgment on materiality for the financial statements is related to particular substantive tests
- Describe how the auditor assesses inherent risk and control risk in establishing the detection risk for a particular substantive test
- Explain how the double-entry accounting method affects the direction of testing to achieve efficiency
- Explain the uses of analytical procedures in planning audit programs
- Understand how tests of transaction classes are planned and coordinated with direct tests of balances and distinguish between the transaction approach and tests of transaction classes
- Explain why audit programs may need to be revised as the audit progresses and how client expectations affect audit programs
- Describe the factors that determine whether direct tests of balances can be made at an interim date
- Understand the auditor's approach to evaluating the reasonableness of an accounting estimate

Relevant Sections of Statements on Auditing Standards

AU 311 — Planning and Supervision
AU 312 — Audit Risk and Materiality in Conducting an Audit
AU 313 — Substantive Tests Prior to the Balance Sheet Date
AU 319 — Consideration of the Internal Control Structure in a Financial Statement Audit
AU 326 — Evidential Matter
AU 329 — Analytical Procedures
AU 342 — Auditing Accounting Estimates
AU 350 — Audit Sampling

This chapter explains the planning of detailed audit programs that begins after the auditor has obtained an understanding of the client and the internal control structure.

DESIGNING AUDIT PROGRAMS—AN INTRODUCTION

The designing of detailed audit programs for each component of the financial statements being audited completes the planning phase of the audit. The preceding steps in the audit, ending with the assessment of control risk, provide the basis for designing audit programs.

As explained in Chapters 5 and 6, the nature and extent of the preceding steps may vary, depending on the audit strategy the auditor has chosen. The nature and extent of the preceding steps are also influenced by whether the audit is an initial or continuing engagement. In an initial engagement, the planning phase is extensive and may consume more time than the remainder of the audit. In a continuing engagement, the planning phase is still extremely important, but may be less time-consuming because the auditor is updating existing information.

Decisions to Be Made

Written audit programs are specifically required by professional standards. According to SAS No. 22 (AU 311.05):

> In planning the audit, the auditor should consider the nature, extent, and timing of work to be performed and should prepare a written audit program (or a set of written audit programs).

As explained earlier, an *audit program* is a reasonably detailed description of the nature, timing, and extent of audit procedures to be applied to achieve the specific audit objectives developed for the components of financial statements being audited. Thus, the decisions the auditor needs to make concern the following aspects of the *scope* of audit procedures:

* *Nature*—the particular audit procedure to be applied and related matters
* *Timing*—when to apply the audit procedure selected
* *Extent*—how many items to which to apply the selected audit procedure

In ordinary language, these decisions might simply be called what, when, and how many. However, auditors prefer the technical terms of nature, timing, and extent because there are several aspects of the scope of audit procedures implicit in them.

Nature   Decisions about the nature of audit procedures usually include the particular type of procedure, the type of item to which the procedure is to be applied, and the direction of testing. For example, in designing an audit program for the property and equipment component of the balance sheet, one type of procedure the auditor may select is examining vendors' invoices and receiving reports for additions to the account. This decision includes the type of procedure (vouching); the type of item to which the procedure is applied (individual debits to the property and equipment account); and the direction of testing (from items recorded in the account to supporting documents).

Timing   Decisions about timing are largely decisions concerning when during the period covered by the financial statements or thereafter the selected procedures should be applied. However, timing decisions also include consideration of the coordination of related auditing procedures.

In deciding when to apply procedures, the primary consideration is usually whether to apply the selected procedure at an interim date or after year-end. For financial statement components such as property and equipment this decision is not complex. Since additions to property and equipment are made throughout the period, the auditor could vouch additions the company has made up to an interim testing date, and vouch additions made in the remaining period at year-end. Other accounts, such as accounts receivable, involve more complex timing decisions that are discussed later in this chapter. Property and equipment also do not pose many complexities in coordination of related procedures because the assets are usually relatively immobile and nonnegotiable. However, the auditor may need to coordinate the physical examination of readily negotiable assets such as cash and securities where there is a risk of substitution to cover misappropriation.

Extent   Decisions about extent are essentially decisions about *how many* items, and many auditors equate extent with sample size. Thus, it is worth emphasizing that *extent decisions and sample size decisions are not identical.*

A decision about sample size is, by definition, an extent decision. However, not all extent decisions are sample size decisions. In auditing, sampling has a technically defined meaning. According to SAS No. 39 (AU 350.01):

> Audit sampling is the application of an audit procedure to less than 100 percent of the items within an account balance or class of transactions for the purpose of evaluating some characteristics of the balance or class.

If audit sampling is involved, SAS No. 39 (AU 350) imposes several requirements of the planning, selection, and evaluation of sample items. These requirements are explained in Chapter 8. However, an auditor may decide to apply an audit procedure to less than all of the items in an account balance or transaction class without sampling. Essentially, sampling is not involved whenever the auditor does not extend the conclusion reached on items examined to the remaining unexamined items in the account balance or transaction class.

The auditor may, for example, analyze additions to property and equipment by the dollar amount of the additions as follows:

Number of additions	Dollar cutoff of individual additions	Total dollar amount
5	Over $10,000	$ 80,000
10	$5,000 to $10,000	68,000
60	Below $5,000	27,000
75		$175,000

The auditor may decide to vouch all additions over $5,000 and, thus, apply the audit procedure to less than 100 percent of the items (15 out of 75). However, if the auditor concludes that the dollar amount of the remaining items is sufficiently immaterial to the financial statements taken as a whole, the auditor's conclusion about the 15 additions examined need not be extended to the remaining items and sampling would not be involved.

Materiality is one of several considerations that influence the auditor's decisions about the nature, timing, and extent of auditing procedures.

Considerations in Deciding on Nature, Timing, and Extent

The considerations that influence the nature, timing, and extent of substantive tests of account balances and transaction classes are enumerated in SAS No. 31 (AU 326.11) as follows:

> In selecting particular substantive tests to achieve the audit objectives he has developed, an auditor considers, among other things, the risk of material misstatement of the financial statements, including the assessed levels of control risk, and the expected effectiveness and efficiency of such tests. His considerations include the nature and materiality of the items being tested, the kinds and competence of available evidential matter, and the nature of the audit objective to be achieved.

For reasons of convenience and logic these considerations are regrouped and reordered in this book as follows:

1 *Nature of financial statement component and audit objectives* (the nature of the item being tested, the kinds and competence of available evidential matter, and the nature of the audit objective to be achieved)
2 *Materiality* (the materiality of the item being tested)
3 *Audit risk* (the relative risk of material misstatement; the assessed level of control risk; the expected effectiveness of audit tests)
4 *Efficiency* (the expected efficiency of audit tests)

These considerations in designing audit programs are explained in later sections of this chapter. However, at this point it is useful to consider the relationship between the efficiency and effectiveness of audit tests.

Efficiency and Effectiveness of Audit Tests

The auditor cannot design audit programs without regard to considerations of time and cost. According to SAS No. 31 (AU 326.21):

> An auditor typically works within economic limits; his opinion to be economically useful, must be formed within a reasonable length of time and at reasonable cost.

This short passage in professional standards is intended to acknowledge several realities of practice. Competition among CPA firms exerts pressure on the fees charged for audits, and that fee pressure constrains the amount of time and effort that can be spent in accumulating evidential matter. Also, audited financial statements are often needed for some specific business purpose, such as issuing debt or stock, obtaining a loan, or meeting regulatory filing requirements. These needs often result in tight time schedules for completion of the audit. In practice, there is a continual tension between economics and professionalism. One of the functions of professional standards is to guide the auditor's judgment in resolving conflicts between the need for sufficient competent evidential matter and the time and cost required to obtain it.

The guiding principle for the auditor's consideration of time and cost is explained as follows in SAS No. 31 (Au 326.22):

> As a guiding rule, there should be a rational relationship between the cost of obtaining evidence and the usefulness of the information obtained. The matter of difficulty and expense involved in testing a particular item is not in itself a valid basis for omitting the test.

The guiding principle is obviously less than precise. Time and cost are valid considerations in selecting auditing procedures, but never alone provide justification for omitting particular procedures. The auditor's goal is to achieve a rational relationship between cost and usefulness, and this relationship is often expressed as obtaining *reasonable* assurance. This is one of the reasons that authoritative auditing literature indicates that audits do not provide absolute assurance and that the auditor is not an insurer or guarantor of the accuracy of financial statements.

The notion of balancing the cost and usefulness of evidence is captured in the concepts of the efficiency and effectiveness of audit tests. These terms are defined as follows:

- *Effectiveness* refers to the audit satisfaction that can be obtained from procedures, or, in effect, the persuasiveness of the evidential matter obtained by applying the procedures.
- *Efficiency* refers to the audit time and effort required to perform the procedures.

Effectiveness is the overriding consideration, but efficiency is an important consideration in choosing between procedures of similar effectiveness. For example, analytical procedures are usually less time-consuming and costly than tests of details. In examining sales commission expense, the auditor could vouch selected entries in the sales commission expense account or calculate the approximate expense by multiplying annual sales by the average commission rate. The two procedures would be similar in effectiveness, but the analytical procedure would be more efficient.

DIRECT TESTS OF BALANCES

Direct tests of balances are audit tests that substantiate the ending balance of a general ledger account. Thus, they are substantive tests that either provide reasonable assurance of the validity and propriety of the balance or identify monetary misstatement in it. A monetary misstatement may be caused by a variety of factors, but the effect on the financial statements will be to either overstate or understate the balance. In designing audit programs for account balances, the auditor is concerned with whether the balance is overstated or understated by a material amount.

Direct tests of balances are distinguished from tests of transaction classes. Designing programs for tests of transaction classes is explained in the next major section of this chapter. These tests are concerned with transaction classes, such as cash receipts, and may be substantive tests, tests of controls, or dual-purpose tests. Account balances and transactions are related, and the auditor needs to coordinate the audit programs for account balances and transaction classes.

Direct tests of balances are considered first because the auditor's ultimate objective is to express an opinion on financial statements which are made up of account balances. No matter what audit strategy is adopted, the auditor makes extensive use of direct tests of balances. In audits of the financial statements of small businesses, many auditors rely almost exclusively on direct tests of balances.

The following discussion of direct tests of balances is organized around the considerations that influence their nature, timing, and extent:

- Nature of financial statement component and audit objectives
- Materiality at the account balance level
- Audit risk at the account balance level
- Efficiency of audit tests

Nature of Financial Statement Component and Audit Objectives

A component of financial statements is simply a line item in the statements. Generally, it is more precise to refer to a component rather than an account balance because several general ledger accounts are usually combined into a line item in presenting financial statements. For example, a company may have general-purpose bank accounts in several locations, a payroll bank account, and several special-purpose accounts with a separate general ledger account for each. However, on the balance sheet the accounts will be combined in a single line item for cash. In this book, the term *account balance* is often used instead of financial statement component for convenience. Account balance should be understood to mean either an individual balance or a group of account balances in the general ledger combined for purposes of financial statement preparation.

The nature of the account balance and the related specific audit objectives the auditor has developed are important considerations in determining the nature, timing, and extent of audit procedures, especially the nature of procedures selected.

Specific Audit Objectives   The auditor develops specific audit objectives from the broad categories of financial statement assertions introduced in Chapter 4. The broad categories of assertions related to *balance sheet accounts* are as follows:

- *Existence.* Recorded assets and liabilities actually exist at the balance sheet date.
- *Completeness.* All items that should be included in account balances are included, and there are no undisclosed assets or liabilities.
- *Rights or obligations.* The company owns and has clear title to assets, and liabilities are obligations of the company.
- *Valuation.* Assets and liabilities are valued properly.
- *Presentation and disclosure.* Assets and liabilities are properly described and disclosed in the balance sheet.

Direct tests of balances are primarily audit tests of balance sheet accounts.

The auditor selects audit procedures to achieve each of the specific audit objectives for an account balance developed from the broad categories of assertions. The nature of the audit objective influences the nature of the procedure selected. The following examples illustrate the relationship:

- *Existence.* In designing substantive tests to achieve an objective related to the assertion of existence, the auditor selects from items contained in the account balance and obtains evidential matter that supports those items. The logical procedures to accomplish such objectives include physical examination, confirmation, and vouching. Note that these are tests for overstatement of the balance.
- *Completeness.* In designing substantive tests to achieve an objective related to the assertion of completeness, the auditor needs to identify evidential matter indicating items that should be included in the balance and investigate whether the items are included. A logical procedure to accomplish such objectives is tracing from documentation created when transactions originate, or other evidence of origination, to the account balance. In other words, the direction of the test is the opposite of that for objectives related to the existence assertion. Note that these are tests for understatement of the balance.
- *Rights and obligations.* In designing substantive tests to achieve an objective related to the assertion of rights or obligations, the auditor needs to obtain information on the terms of the agreement between the parties to the exchange transaction that created the right or obligation. Common procedures used to accomplish such objectives are inquiry and inspection of contracts, agreements, minutes, and similar documentation. Many of these procedures are called *general procedures* because they are done separately rather than in conjunction with other procedures directed to a specific account balance. For example, reading the minutes of meetings of the board of directors is a general procedure used to obtain evidential matter relevant to many account balances.
- *Valuation.* In designing substantive tests to achieve an audit objective related to the assertion of valuation, the auditor needs to consider the basis of presentation of the asset or liability under generally accepted accounting principles. If the basis is historical cost less accumulated depreciation of amortization, the likely procedure to accomplish the audit objective would be recomputation. If the basis is net realizable value, or a similar basis, the likely procedures are inquiry and analytical procedures to assess the reasonableness of management's estimation or inspection of external information on market prices. Naturally, omission of items (completeness) or inclusion of improper items (existence) would also affect valuation. However, because the cause of these types of misstatements is usually different, they are considered separately.
- *Presentation and disclosure.* In designing substantive tests to achieve an audit objective related to the assertion of presentation and disclosure, the auditor needs to consider the generally accepted accounting principles applicable to the classification, description, and disclosure of the item in the financial statements. Normally, the auditor does not need to apply any separate auditing procedures directed exclusively to

such objectives. The review of information obtained to achieve the other objectives is normally sufficient.

Nature of the Item and Available Evidential Matter   The nature of the item has an important influence on the auditor's selection of audit procedures. For example, the preceding discussion indicates that for audit objectives related to the existence assertion, likely audit procedures are physical examination, confirmation, and vouching. The item must have a physical existence and be present for the procedure of physical examination to be useful. An auditor can count cash or securities on hand, but must confirm a trade receivable with a customer or cash in a bank account.

Another aspect of the nature of the item is the size and volume of transactions during the period covered by the financial statements. If an account balance is affected by only a few large transactions, the auditor may design substantive tests directed to the individual transactions that increase or decrease the balance (assuming the beginning balance was substantiated last year) to substantiate the ending balance. For example, account balances for property and equipment, long-term debt, and stockholders' equity are often of this nature. However, if the account balance is affected by many relatively small transactions, the auditor would design substantive tests directed to selected items included in the ending balance. For example, trade accounts receivable and inventory are usually of this nature.

The available evidential matter also influences the selection of procedures to achieve audit objectives. For example, to confirm trade accounts receivable with individual customers, the auditor needs a detailed listing of the amount owed by each customer. The availability of evidential matter may influence the auditor's selection of procedures to achieve specific audit objectives. If a common audit procedure cannot be applied because the evidential matter is unavailable, an alternative procedure may be selected. However, the audit procedures selected must be adequate to achieve the specific audit objectives developed by the auditor.

Materiality at the Account Balance Level

As explained in Chapter 5, one of the general planning decisions the auditor makes is a preliminary judgment about the amount that will be considered material to the financial statements taken as a whole. This dollar amount of planning materiality is the auditor's estimate of the dividing line for a material misstatement of the financial statements. The auditor's overall objective is to reach a conclusion, with reasonable assurance, that the financial statements are not misstated by more than this amount. Thus, the auditor needs to plan the audit so that there is a relatively low risk of failing to detect monetary misstatements that in combination exceed this amount.

In designing detailed audit programs the auditor needs to relate the preliminary judgment to specific substantive tests. Naturally, the scope of audit procedures for a particular account balance will be influenced by the size of monetary misstatements that need to be detected to meet the auditor's overall objective.

Composition of Materiality at the Financial Statement Level   SAS No. 47 (AU 312.01) includes both errors and irregularities in the term "misstatement." The auditor's preliminary judgment about the amount to be considered material conceptually encompasses the total of known, likely, and potential undetected misstatement for the financial statements taken as a whole. These terms have the following meaning in auditing:

- *Known misstatement*—the amount of misstatement specifically identified by the auditor as a result of applying audit procedures to items examined. For example, an auditor vouches all additions to property and equipment that exceed $10,000 and detects monetary misstatements totaling $5,000. The $5,000 misstatement actually detected is known misstatement.
- *Likely misstatement*—the auditor's best estimate of the total misstatement in an account balance based on an extrapolation or projection of the misstatements actually detected. For example, assume that there are five additions to property and equipment that exceed $10,000 and 70 below that amount, and an auditor vouches 25 of those 70 and detects monetary misstatement totaling $1,000. The auditor might extrapolate misstatement for that portion of the account balance as $2,800 ($1,000 ÷ 25 × 70). In that case likely misstatement is $2,800 which includes the $1,000 of known misstatement in the 25 items selected from the 70.
- *Potential undetected misstatement*—the auditor's allowance for misstatement that remains undetected after applying audit procedures. For example, in the illustrations of known misstatement and likely misstatement presented above, the auditor estimates total known and likely misstatement for additions to property and equipment to be $7,800 ($5,000 + $2,800). However, the auditor has only vouched 30 of 75 additions so there is a potential undetected misstatement in total additions.

Thus, in planning detailed audit programs the auditor needs to make an allowance for potential undetected misstatement. Unless an allowance is made for potential undetected misstatement, the auditor will not have reasonable assurance that the total of known, likely, and potential undetected misstatement does not exceed a material amount. In the examples given above, the potential undetected misstatement arises because sampling was used. However, the allowance for undetected misstatement should encompass all causes of imprecision in applying audit procedures.

The auditor's preliminary judgment about the amount material to the financial statements taken as a whole includes known, likely, and potential undetected misstatement for all the account balances included in the financial statements. The first step in relating that preliminary judgment to substantive tests of individual account balances is to estimate the allowance for undetected misstatement for the financial statements taken as a whole.

Estimating the Allowance for Undetected Misstatement   If the auditor could be certain that the client would correct all known misstatements and that likely misstatement would be negligible, then the allowance for undetected misstatement could be nearly the same as the auditor's preliminary judgment about the amount material to the financial statements. In some engagements this may be the case, and the preliminary judgment and the allowance for undetected misstatement may be the same amount. How-ever, if the client will resist correcting known misstatements or if likely misstatement can reasonably be expected to be significant, the preliminary judgment needs to be reduced to estimate the allowance for undetected misstatement. The auditor will, in those cases, need to estimate the anticipated known misstatement that will not be corrected and the anticipated likely misstatement.

Initially, it might seem more appealing to simply correct all known and likely mis-statement, but that is usually a practical impossibility. The financial statements are the representations of management, and management rather than the auditor makes this deci-sion. As long as the combined effect of uncorrected known misstatement, likely mis-statement, and the allowance for undetected misstatement is less than the amount that would be material to the financial statements, the auditor can express an unqualified opinion.

Management usually considers the relative costs and benefits of correcting known mis-statements. For example, a known misstatement in depreciation expense may be con-sidered too costly or difficult to correct because depreciation expense has already been allocated among inventory items, selling expenses, and administrative expenses. Also, on matters involving judgment, such as accounting estimates and complex accounting principles, management may simply disagree with the auditor. Likely misstatement is typically not corrected because the sample sizes or other approximations used in extrap-olating it are considered an insufficient basis for adjusting the accounting records.

The auditor's estimate of anticipated uncorrected known misstatement is made for the financial statements taken as a whole. The estimate applies to all account balances or portions of account balances that the auditor plans to examine 100 percent. For exam-ple, for account balances affected by only a few large transactions, such as long-term debt, the auditor may plan to examine all the transactions. Whenever the auditor makes a 100 percent examination, all the misstatement detected is known misstatement.

The auditor's estimate of anticipated likely misstatement is also made for the finan-cial statements taken as a whole. This estimate applies to all account balances or por-tions of account balances that the auditor plans to examine by sampling. An additional cushion may need to be added to this estimate because the likely misstatement is an esti-mate rather than a precise amount.

The auditor's logical process for developing the allowance for undetected misstate-ment is summarized in Figure 7-1. The starting point in this process is making a pre-liminary judgment about the amount material to the financial statements taken as a whole as explained in Chapter 5. The residual after reducing this amount for the anticipated total known and likely misstatement is the allowance for undetected misstatement.

The allowance for undetected misstatement is based on estimates that the auditor makes using judgment and past experience with the client. Some auditors prefer to use a rule-of-thumb for determining the allowance for undetected misstatement. This is use-ful when the auditor has no experience with the client or prefers to avoid making the estimates. In practice, a range of 50 percent to 75 percent of the preliminary judgment about materiality has been used. For example, if the preliminary judgment is $100,000, the allowance for undetected misstatement could be anywhere from $50,000 to $75,000 depending on the individual auditor's judgment or CPA firm policy. The estimate of the

Materiality concept or component	How determined
Preliminary judgment about materiality for the financial statements	Developed by the auditor judgmentally or by using a rule-of-thumb such as 1 percent of the larger of total assets or total revenue (see Chapter 5)
Less estimate of total anticipated uncorrected known misstatement	Estimated by the auditor for all items to be examined 100 percent
Less estimate of total anticipated likely misstatement	Estimated by the auditor for all items to be examined by sampling
Equals allowance for undetected misstatement	A residual determined by the auditor based on the preceding judgments and estimates

FIGURE 7-1

The logical process for developing the auditor's allowance for undetected misstatement.

allowance for undetected misstatement made in planning needs to be reevaluated as the audit progresses.

Relating the Allowance for Undetected Misstatement to a Particular Substantive Test The allowance for undetected misstatement developed by the logical process explained above relates to the financial statements taken as whole.

Intuitively, it might seem reasonable to allocate the allowance among account balances in proportion to the ratio of the dollar amount of a particular account balance to the total dollar amount of account balances. However, this approach is both conceptually and practically unsound and would result in drastically overauditing the financial statements taken as a whole for several reasons.

First, the auditor is concerned with a net material overstatement or understatement of the financial statements. In other words, the concern is whether the combined effect of monetary misstatement materially distorts net assets or net income. Misstatements will not all be in the same direction—some will be overstatements, some will be understatements.

Second, the allowance for undetected misstatement is necessary because of the expected imprecision of auditing procedures. Some potential undetected misstatement will remain after auditing procedures are applied. However, some account balances can be examined to relatively tight tolerances at reasonable cost, and there is no reason to allow for potential undetected misstatement.

Finally, the imprecision that results from using sampling is not additive across account balances. The proper way of combining this imprecision depends on the sampling approach used. This subject is explained further in Chapter 8.

The relation of the allowance for undetected misstatement to particular substantive tests depends on the approach the auditor plans to use to substantiate the balance. Generally, a particular account balance can be placed in one of the following categories of approaches to the extent of tests of details:

1 *Tests of details of all items (100 percent).* The auditor plans to apply the substantive test to all the items comprising or changing the account balance because there are a relatively few large items.

2 *Tests of details of significant items.* The auditor plans to apply the substantive test to significant items only. For example, vouch all property additions above $5,000 and none below that amount because of the relative insignificance of the remaining amount.

3 *Tests of details of a sample of items.* The auditor plans to apply the substantive tests to a representative sample of items. Usually with this approach the auditor will first analyze an account balance into individually significant items and remaining items, and apply the substantive test to all significant items and to a sample of the remaining items.

4 *No tests of details of any items.* The auditor plans to rely exclusively on analytical procedures and does not plan to test the details of any of the items in certain account balances because of their relative insignificance.

All of these approaches involve materiality judgments. Many auditors relate the allowance for undetected misstatement to these materiality judgments by using a rule-of-thumb based on a sampling theory. The rationale behind this rule-of-thumb is explained in more detail in Chapter 8, but the mechanics are to divide the allowance for undetected misstatement by a number ranging from 3 to 6 to determine a cutoff amount for significant items. These numbers are based on the typical characteristics of accounting populations. Accounting populations tend to be highly skewed (relatively few large items and many medium to small items) and have relatively low error rates.

The allowance for undetected misstatement divided by 3 to 6 becomes the cutoff point for determining individually significant items. For example, if the allowance for undetected misstatement is $75,000, the cutoff point could be anywhere between $25,000 and $12,500. Generally, the cutoff point would be lowered from $25,000 as the importance of the substantive test increases or as the rate of misstatement expected increases. For example, if a substantive test was the only audit procedure being applied to achieve a specific audit objective then a cutoff closer to $12,500 would be used to identify individually significant items. All items above the cutoff amount in the account balance would be subjected to the audit procedure.

If all of the items in an account balance exceed the cutoff amount, the auditor would apply tests of details to all the items. If the remaining items are in total below the allowance for undetected misstatement, the auditor would apply tests of details to only the individually significant items. If remaining items exceed the allowance, the auditor would apply tests of details to a sample of the remaining items. Any account balances below the cutoff amount would be tested using analytical procedures only.

Alternatives in Establishing Materiality at the Account Balance Level   Not all auditors follow the approach described above of explicitly relating the allowance for undetected misstatement to substantive tests. Professional standards on materiality in auditing are described in SAS No. 47 (AU 312). According to SAS No. 47 (AU 312.18):

In determining the nature, timing, and extent of auditing procedures to be applied to a specific account balance . . . the auditor should design procedures to obtain reasonable assurance of detecting misstatements that he believes, based on his preliminary judgment about materiality, could be material, when aggregated with misstatements in other balances . . . , to the financial statements taken as a whole.

SAS No. 47 (AU 312) acknowledges that some auditors do this explicitly, but that other auditors take a more judgmental approach. Establishing an explicit relationship between the preliminary judgment about materiality and the amount used as material for an account balance is not a requirement of professional standards.

Professional standards establish the goal but do not mandate the specific steps an auditor should take to achieve that goal. At the end of the audit, the combined effect of uncorrected known misstatement, likely misstatement, and a reasonable allowance for undetected misstatement should not exceed the amount the auditor considers material to the financial statements taken as a whole. Some auditors use rules-of-thumb of the type described in this book to explicitly relate materiality to substantive tests at the account balance level. Other auditors establish materiality for this purpose judgmentally. However, all auditors attempt to achieve the same goal: a relatively low risk that the financial statements taken as a whole are misstated by a material amount.

Combined Consideration of Factors Affecting Scope   In focusing on the individual factors that affect decisions about the nature, timing, and extent of audit procedures, it is easy to lose sight of the fact that the auditor makes a combined consideration of these factors. The nature of the item and the audit objective, the materiality of the account balance, the assessment of audit risk, and efficiency considerations have a combined influence on scope decisions. For example, in considering the extent of tests of details, the auditor's decision to apply the test to all items, significant items, a sample of items, or no items in the account balance is not based solely on a materiality judgment. The auditor may conclude that a combination of tests of details of significant items and analytical procedures reduce the risk of misstatement to an acceptable level in a particular case. The considerations involved in making this type of decision are explained in the next section on the auditor's consideration of audit risk at the account balance level.

Audit Risk at the Account Balance Level

The concept of audit risk at the financial statement level is explained in Chapter 5. There is a direct relationship between the degree of audit risk and the degree of audit assurance. As explained earlier, absolute assurance is a practical impossibility and is economically undesirable. An audit is intended to provide reasonable assurance that the financial statements taken as a whole are not materially misstated. Audit risk is the complement of audit assurance. To obtain reasonable assurance the auditor needs to hold audit risk to a relatively low level. At the account balance level, according to SAS No. 47 (AU 312.19), this means that:

The auditor should seek to restrict audit risk at the individual balance or class level in such a way that will enable him, at the completion of his examination, to express an opinion on the financial statements taken as a whole at an appropriately low level of audit risk. Auditors use various approaches to accomplish that objective.

The audit risk the auditor seeks to restrict is the risk of a *material* misstatement remaining undetected after applying audit procedures. In other words, the auditor focuses on the risk of failing to detect monetary misstatement of precisely a material amount. The risk of failing to detect a smaller misstatement is greater, and the risk of failing to detect a larger misstatement is naturally less. Thus, the auditor's consideration of materiality and audit risk are really inseparable. Materiality relates to how precise auditing procedures need to be, and audit risk relates to the degree of certainty achieved by the procedures.

Components of Audit Risk   At the account balance level audit risk has the following components:

I The risk of material misstatement occurring in the accounting process:
   A *Inherent risk*—the susceptibility of an account balance to material misstatement given inherent and environmental characteristics, but without regard to internal control structure policies or procedures
   B *Control risk*—the risk that material misstatement in an account balance may occur and not be prevented or detected on a timely basis by the client's internal control structure policies or procedures
II *Detection risk*—the risk that an auditor's procedures will lead the auditor to conclude that material misstatement does not exist in an account balance when the account balance is actually materially misstated

The auditor's approach is to assess the level of inherent risk and control risk, and adjust detection risk accordingly, to restrict the combined risk (audit risk) for the account balance to a relatively low level. In other words, there is an inverse relationship between the combined degree of inherent risk and control risk and the detection risk established by the auditor.

In designing audit programs, the only way the auditor can control audit risk after performing procedures to assess control risk is to restrict detection risk. The degree of detection risk the auditor can accept for a particular substantive test is determined by assessing the degree of inherent risk and control risk that exists in the circumstances.

Methods of Assessing Inherent Risk and Control Risk   The auditor's objective in assessing inherent risk and control risk is to reach a conclusion on the likelihood of material misstatement existing in the account balance. The auditor's detailed audit program for the account balance will be modified in response to the auditor's assessment of the likelihood of material misstatement.

The methods of assessing control risk are explained in Chapter 6. For each account balance the auditor identifies the transaction classes that affect the balance and considers whether there is reasonable assurance that the specific control objectives for those transaction classes have been achieved. There is an inverse relationship between the degree of assurance that control objectives have been achieved and the degree of control risk. The specific audit procedures used are those described in Chapter 6 for understanding the internal control structure and tests of controls.

The information the auditor uses to assess inherent risk is obtained largely during general planning as described in Chapter 5. In assessing inherent risk at the account balance level, the auditor makes a focused consideration of the implications of the understanding of the client, its industry, its business, the nature of the account, and the transactions for the likelihood of material misstatement existing in a particular account balance.

Normally, the auditor will focus on factors such as the following:

- *Inherent characteristics*. The inherent nature of the account balance may influence the frequency and amount of misstatement expected. Examples of this influence are: complex calculations, such as lease capitalization, are more likely to be misstated than simple calculations, such as straight-line depreciation; cash is more susceptible to irregularities than an inventory of steel pellets; accounting estimates, such as a warranty reserve, are more likely to be misstated than routine factual data.
- *Environmental characteristics*. Some environmental characteristics relate to particular account balances and others relate to the financial statements taken as a whole, but also have implications for particular account balances. For example, if the client operates in an industry with rapid technological developments there is an increased risk of inventory obsolescence.
- *Prior-period misstatements*. The nature, cause, and amount of misstatements in particular account balances detected in prior periods' audits will influence the auditor's expectation of the likelihood of material misstatement in particular account balances.

The outcome of the auditor's assessment of inherent risk and assessed level of control risk is a judgment about the likelihood of material misstatement existing in the account balance for which a detailed audit program is being planned. Many auditors also use analytical procedures as an aid in making this judgment.

Analytical Procedures in Detailed Program Planning   The analytical procedures used as an aid in planning audit programs are more detailed than such procedures used in obtaining an understanding for the client. The auditor focuses on the detailed makeup of account balances and operating ratios related to specific account balances. For example, in obtaining an understanding of the client the auditor may have computed the gross profit ratio from the current annual financial statements and compared it to the ratio in prior years, the client's annual budget, and industry averages. In detailed program planning for inventory the auditor may make a gross profit analysis by product and location on a month-to-month basis.

The auditor uses analytical procedures in detailed program planning to quantify the relationships among accounts and the effects of changes in conditions and circumstances identified in general planning. For example, for trade accounts receivable the auditor may quantify in dollars and percentages the increase in amounts receivable by age and customer category and relate those increases to the understanding of credit and industry economic conditions identified in general planning.

The results of the detailed analytical procedures are then incorporated in the auditor's judgment about the likelihood of material misstatement existing in the account balance. The auditor may conclude that the likelihood of material misstatement is lower because the account balance is reasonable in light of the auditor's understanding or that the likelihood of material misstatement is greater because of unexplained significant fluctuations or the absence of such fluctuations when expected.

Methods of Establishing Detection Risk   The auditor's purpose in assessing inherent risk and control risk is to establish the degree of detection risk that can be accepted. As explained earlier, detection risk is the risk that an auditor's procedures will lead the auditor to conclude that material misstatement does not exist in an account balance when the account balance is actually materially misstated. This risk is inversely related to the effectiveness of audit procedures. The less detection risk that can be accepted, the more effective auditing procedures must be. Generally, the effectiveness of auditing procedures is related to the persuasiveness of the evidential matter obtained by applying the procedures. Evaluating the effectiveness of auditing procedures requires experienced professional judgment.

Combining the assessment of inherent risk and control risk to establish the acceptable detection risk can be accomplished by either qualitative or quantitative analysis. According to SAS No. 47 (AU 312.21):

> These components of audit risk may be assessed in quantitative terms such as percentages or in nonquantitative terms that range, for example, from a minimum to a maximum.

There are a variety of approaches to making a nonquantitative assessment. For example, either of the following approaches can be used:

- *Combined qualitative assessment.* The auditor considers the information obtained on inherent risk and control risk and the results of any detailed analytical procedures applied and makes a judgment that the likelihood of material misstatement in the account balance affected is either high, moderate, or low. If the likelihood of material misstatement is judged to be low, tests of details can be minimized. If the likelihood of material misstatement is high, tests of details should be extensive.
- *Separate qualitative assessment.* The auditor makes a separate qualitative assessment and reaches a conclusion that inherent risk is at a minimum, moderate, or maximum level and that control risk is at the minimum, moderate, or maximum level. These assessments are then combined along with the results of any detailed analytical procedures applied to make a judgment about the likelihood of material misstatement in the account balance affected.

These examples use three qualitative levels. In practice generally three or four levels are used.

Quantitative Estimation of Detection Risk   The estimation of detection risk as a specific percentage is necessary only when the auditor uses statistical sampling. The only component of audit risk that can be objectively quantified is the sampling risk associated

Risk component	Audit risk		Inherent risk		Control risk		Other procedures risk		Test of details risk
Formula symbol	AR	=	IR	×	CR	×	AP	×	TD
Concept	The combined risk of a material misstatement remaining in the account balance	=	The susceptibility of the account balance to material misstatement without regard to internal control structure policies and procedures	×	The risk that material misstatement may occur and not be prevented or detected by internal control structure policies and procedures	×	The risk that other relevant auditing procedures will fail to detect material misstatement in the account balance, for example, analytical procedures	×	The acceptable risk that the test of details being planned will fail to detect a material misstatement
Guidelines	Should be relatively low, for example, 5% or 10%		Assessed as*: Low 40% Moderate 60% Significant 80% Maximum 100%		Assessed as*: Low 40% Moderate 60% Significant 80% Maximum 100%		Assessed as*: Low 40% Moderate 60% Significant 80% Maximum 100%		Calculated on the basis of specified percentages for other risks

*The number of levels and the specific percentages associated with them are subjective probabilities determined by individual judgment or CPA firm policy.

FIGURE 7-2
Quantitative risk assessment model for estimation of detection risk for test of details being planned.

with statistical sampling as explained in Chapter 8. However, the quantitative audit risk model is explained in some detail here because it is a useful tool for visualizing the interaction of the components of audit risk.

Figure 7-2 summarizes the audit risk model. This summary is based on a quantitative model that appeared initially in SAS No. 39 (AU 350) on audit sampling, and that was expanded in SAS No. 47 (AU 312) on materiality and audit risk. Figure 7-3 is a graphic depiction of the audit risk model.

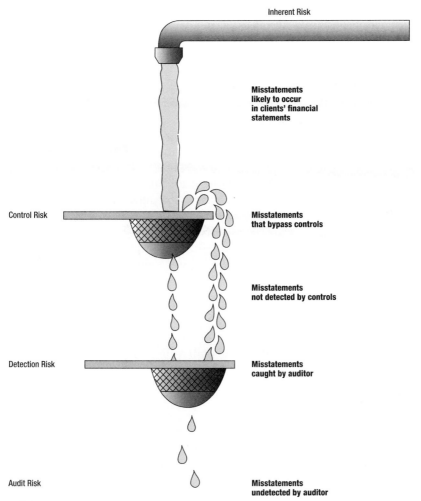

FIGURE 7-3
Graphic depiction of audit risk. *[Source: AICPA, Auditing Procedures Study, in "Audits of Small Businesses" (New York: AICPA, 1985), p. 44.]*

The underlying rationale of the model is that the combined risk of a material misstatement remaining undetected is a product of the independent component risks. This combined risk—the audit risk at the account balance level—should be relatively low. In quantitative terms, that would be 5 percent or 10 percent. In the examples used in this book 5 percent is used. The component risks and their corresponding formula symbols are as follows:

AR	=	IR	×	CR	×	AP	×	TD
(audit risk)		(inherent risk)		(control risk)		(other procedures risk)		(test of details detection risk)

The *other procedures risk* is the quantification of the detection risk for other audit procedures that are relevant to achieving the same audit objectives as the test of details being planned. It has the symbol AP because these other procedures frequently are analytical procedures.

To use the model the auditor has to quantify, as a percentage, the inherent, control, and other procedures risks. This is a subjective professional judgment. An approach often used in practice is to associate a percentage with a qualitative level of assessment. The maximum is obviously 100 percent. Specification of the percentage associated with the minimum is a critical professional judgment because it quantifies the lowest degree of risk, and implicitly the maximum degree of assurance, ever attributed to the component. For example, professional standards indicate that control risk cannot be assessed at so low a level that the auditor would not perform substantive tests for significant account balances or transaction classes. Often in practice the percentages associated with qualitative levels are established as a matter of CPA firm policy.

The interaction of the component risk is most easily explained by an example. Assume that an auditor has assessed the component risks as follows:

$$\text{Inherent risk (IR)} = 80\% \text{ (significant)}$$

$$\text{Control risk (CR)} = 60\% \text{ (moderate)}$$

$$\text{Other procedures risk (AP)} = 40\% \text{ (low)}$$

Then the model can be solved for the detection risk for the test of details being planned as follows:

$$TD = \frac{AR}{IR \times CR \times AP}$$

$$= \frac{0.05}{0.8 \times 0.6 \times 0.4}$$

$$= 26\%$$

This means that the auditor can accept a detection risk of 26 percent in the test of details being planned and still hold the audit risk for the account balance to 5 percent.

If the component risks are all assessed at the maximum, then the detection risk for the tests of details being planned would be estimated as follows:

$$TD = \frac{0.05}{1 \times 1 \times 1}$$

$$= 5\%$$

In this case, the test of details is the only procedure being relied on to detect material misstatement, and the acceptable risk is the same as the audit risk for the account balance.

If the component risks are all assessed at the minimum, the estimation of detection risk would be as follows:

$$TD = \frac{0.05}{0.4 \times 0.4 \times 0.4}$$

$$= 78\%$$

When the acceptable detection risk is high, the auditor might reconsider the need to perform any tests of details.

Controversy on Separate Assessment of Inherent Risk   In should be noted that the separate assessment of inherent risk at levels below the maximum is a controversial issue. The risk model in SAS No. 39 was initially presented with inherent risk assumed to be at the maximum. SAS No. 47 indicates that if inherent risk is assessed at less than the maximum the auditor should have an "appropriate basis" for the assessment.

Some auditors believe that the assessment of control risk is inevitably a joint assessment of inherent and control risks. Other auditors maintain that a separate assessment is feasible as long as matters that can affect both inherent risk and control risk, such as management's control consciousness, are not double counted. In this book, a separate assessment is explained because this approach is used by some auditors in practice and is particularly useful when control risk is assessed at the maximum level.

Efficiency of Audit Tests

The practice of modern auditing is heavily influenced by an emphasis on efficiency. This does not mean that auditors are willing to be less effective, but it does mean that auditors strive to follow the more efficient approach among various approaches of similar effectiveness. In everyday language this means auditors try to work smarter, not harder. Not all auditors do all the things explained here to achieve efficiency, but each of them has strong advocates.

Many of the approaches used to maximize efficiency are designed to make full use of the inherent properties of double-entry accounting systems. Students of accounting who are studying auditing are generally familiar with the mechanics of double-entry accounting but often fail to recognize its implications for auditing.

Auditing Implications of Double-Entry Accounting   *Transactions,* the original data of accounting, involve the exchange of consideration between two parties. Accountants enter the two equivalent halves of each exchange by recording the consideration received as a debit and the consideration given as a credit. From the auditor's perspective, this means that a test of one side of the transaction simultaneously tests the other side of the transaction. The choice of the side to test can be made on the basis of relative efficiency and effectiveness. Consider a credit sale transaction.

Dr. Trade Accounts Receivable	$400	
Cr. Sales		$400

If an auditor tests the debit side (trade accounts receivable) directly for overstatement, the auditor has simultaneously tested the credit side (sales) for overstatement. The debit side in this case is a balance sheet account balance, and the credit side is an income statement account balance. The transaction is, of course, one of the transaction classes—*credit sales.* Theoretically, the auditor could test either the transaction itself, the debit-side account balance, or the credit-side account balance. At this point relative efficiency and effectiveness are unclear, and other transaction classes in the sales cycle and the remainder of the accounting process need to be considered.

When the customer pays the amount owed, the journal entry will be:

Dr. Cash	$400	
Cr. Trade Accounts Receivable		$400

This transaction is of the transaction class *cash receipts,* and the account balances affected are both balance sheet accounts (cash and trade receivables). Notice, however, that testing the debit side (cash) for overstatement will simultaneously test the credit side (trade accounts receivable) for *understatement.* This means that testing one asset for overstatement simultaneously indirectly tests another asset for understatement.

The implications of these properties of double-entry accounting for auditing become clearer when planning of substantive tests for a particular account balance is considered. For example, at the year-end the activity in trade accounts receivable in general ledger form might be as follows:

Trade Accounts Receivable			
Beginning balance	$ 300,000	Cash receipts (reductions)	$900,000
Sales (additions)	$1,000,000		
Ending balance	$ 400,000		

The logic of testing one side of the transaction explained for individual transactions earlier also applies to the aggregate of transactions. It can usually be assumed that the auditor has substantiated the beginning balance in the prior period. One implication of double-entry accounting for auditing is that a direct test of trade accounts receivable for overstatement will simultaneously, indirectly test sales for overstatement and cash receipts for understatement. Conversely, directly testing sales for overstatement and cash receipts for understatement would indirectly test trade accounts receivable for overstatement.

These relationships are easier to contemplate when account balances are structured in activity format. Any asset, liability, or equity account balance may be viewed as consisting of four parts: beginning balance, total debits, total credits, and ending balance. Direct tests of the beginning and ending balances will indirectly test the total debits and credits. Also, direct tests of the beginning balance, total debits, and total credits will indirectly test the ending balance.

The trade accounts receivable example in activity format would be as follows:

Trade Accounts Receivable—Overstatement

Beginning balance	$ 300,000	(Tested last year)
Additions-debits (sales)	$1,000,000	(Tested indirectly for overstatement)
Reductions-credits (cash receipts)	$ (900,000)	(Tested indirectly for understatement)
Ending balance	$ 400,000	(Tested directly for overstatement)

This example indicates that the ending balance is tested directly. However, as explained earlier, the auditor has a choice. The total debits and credits could be tested directly to test the balance indirectly.

Generally, auditors prefer to directly test asset account balances for overstatement because that is usually more efficient and effective for the following reasons:

1 There are usually fewer items in the ending balance than the number of transactions that affect the balance. (For example, there would be fewer customers owing for uncollected sales than the number of sales transactions and cash collection transactions.)

2 There is usually more reliable evidential matter available to support ending balances in balance sheet accounts. (For example, confirmation of an amount owed from a customer is more reliable than inspection of the source documents supporting the debits and credits to trade accounts receivable.)

Remember, however, that the auditor is concerned with material misstatement and, thus, also must test for material understatement. Testing asset account balances directly for understatement is difficult because an independent record of unrecorded assets usually does not exist. However, the concept of direct and indirect testing also applies here.

For example, trade accounts receivable may be tested for understatement as follows:

Trade Accounts Receivable—Understatement		
Beginning balance	$ 300,000	(Tested last year)
Additions-debits (sales)	$1,000,000	(Tested directly for understatement)
Reductions-credits (cash receipts)	$ (900,000)	(Tested directly for overstatement or indirectly for overstatement by direct test of cash balance for overstatement)
Ending balance	$ 400,000	(Tested indirectly for understatement by above tests)

Thus, trade accounts receivable can be tested indirectly for understatement by tests of the transactions that affect the balance. Notice, however, that because of the preferability of directly testing asset account balances for overstatement, it would be more efficient and effective to indirectly test cash receipts for overstatement by testing the cash balance directly for overstatement.

The purpose of this rather detailed look at the properties of double-entry accounting is to provide background for the following discussions of coordination of the direction of testing and coordination of testing balances and transaction classes. However, to achieve the efficiency that this coordination provides, it is essential to recognize that an indirect test is equally effective as a direct test. Because of the properties of double-entry accounting it is possible to substantiate an ending account balance without necessarily substantiating any of the items comprising that ending balance.

Coordination of the Direction of Testing   The properties of double-entry accounting can be used to achieve efficiency by establishing a testing direction of primary concern for particular account balances. In other words, the auditor identifies the primary concern as overstatement or understatement. If the direction of testing is coordinated for all the account balances in the financial statements, each account balance needs to be tested directly only in one direction—for overstatement or for understatement.

By coordinating the direction of testing each account balance is simultaneously tested for both overstatement and understatement. For example, if all asset and expense balances are tested directly for overstatement and all liability, equity, and revenue balances are tested directly for understatement, then all account balances in the balance sheet and income statement will be tested, either directly or indirectly, for both overstatement and understatement.

Figure 7-4 presents the relationships for direction of testing for assets, liabilities, equities, revenues, and expense account balances. The first line of this table means that a direct test of an asset for overstatement will simultaneously indirectly test other assets for understatement, liabilities for overstatement, equity for overstatement, revenues for overstatement, and expenses for understatement.

Coordination of the direction of testing is a means of achieving *efficiency* in designing audit programs without sacrificing effectiveness. The testing direction chosen for the direct test for a particular account balance can be based on the availability of evidential

		Direct test		Simultaneous indirect test			
Account balance	Direction	Assets	Liabilities	Equity	Revenue	Expense
Assets	Overstatement (O)	U	O	O	O	U
Liabilities	Understatement (U)	U	O	O	O	U
Equity	Understatement (U)	U	O	O	O	U
Revenue	Understatement (U)	U	O	O	O	U
Expense	Overstatement (O)	U	O	O	O	U

The relationship between specific audit objectives and direction of testing is generally as follows:

- Existence   Specific audit objectives related to the existence assertion are tested by tests for overstatement.
- Completeness   Specific audit objectives related to the completeness assertion are tested by tests for understatement.
- Valuation   Specific audit objectives related to the valuation assertion are tested by both tests for overstatement and understatement.

Specific audit objectives related to the assertions of rights or obligations and presentation and disclosure are usually accomplished simultaneously by the above tests or by general procedures.

FIGURE 7-4

Relationships among account balances for coordination of the direction of testing. (Should be read across.)

matter and the time and cost of testing. Using this approach all account balances are tested for both material overstatement and material understatement. However, to achieve this, the approach needs to be coordinated for the entire audit. In this book, the following approach is used:

- Asset and expense account balances are tested directly for overstatement.
- Liability, equity, and revenue account balances are tested directly for understatement.

This approach has proven effective for the commercial company that sells goods or services on credit. The basic relationships presented in Figure 7-4, however, can be used to design other approaches for specialized industries or particular unusual circumstances.

Coordination of Testing of Balances and Transaction Classes   Another aspect of the auditing implications of double-entry accounting explained earlier is the relationship between account balances and transaction classes. This means that efficiency can be achieved by careful coordination of these types of tests, and that lack of attention to coordination will inevitably result in overauditing. Coordination of these types of tests is explained in the next major section.

Distinction between Transaction Classes and Transaction Approach   It is important to recognize the subtle distinction between testing transaction classes and the transaction approach to the direct test of a balance. This can be confusing because tests of transaction classes are often referred to simply as tests of transactions. As explained earlier, when an account balance during a period is affected by a relatively few large transactions, the auditor usually will design audit tests to substantiate the balance by testing the details of transactions that add to or reduce the beginning balance to result in the ending balance. This is referred to and understood by auditors to be a *direct test of the balance* by the *transaction approach.* It is in contrast to a direct test of the balance by the *balance approach* which means the items comprising the ending balance are substantiated. Generally, account balances with a low turnover, such as property and equipment, long-term debt, and equity accounts are susceptible to the transaction approach.

The distinction between the transaction approach to direct tests of balances and tests of transaction classes is essentially a distinction between a concern with specific isolated transactions versus a concern with the accounting process for an entire class of transactions. For example, in substantiating additions to property and equipment the auditor would examine supporting documentation for the transaction that resulted in the addition. If the addition was acquired for cash, the transaction would be part of the transaction class of cash disbursements. However, in testing the transaction class of cash disbursements, the auditor is concerned with the processing of cash disbursements through the accounting system. In testing the addition to property and equipment, the auditor is concerned with the validity and amount of the addition. The auditor's concern with the addition would not change if it was acquired by open credit (an account payable), a note payable, or long-term debt.

Analytical Procedures   Another means of increasing audit efficiency is to reduce or replace tests of details with analytical procedures. The rationale for considering analytical procedures as a means of obtaining evidential matter to achieve specific audit objectives is explained in SAS No. 56 (AU 329.02) as follows:

> A basic premise underlying the application of analytical procedures is that plausible relationships among data may reasonably be expected to exist and continue in the absence of known conditions to the contrary.

Professional standards, however, do not provide explicit guidance on how to apportion reliance on substantive tests between tests of details and analytical procedures. SAS No. 56 (AU 329.09) states:

> The auditor's reliance on substantive tests to achieve an audit objective related to a particular assertion may be derived from tests of details, from analytical procedures, or from a combination of both.

The general criteria for apportioning reliance between analytical procedures and tests of details concern the relative efficiency and effectiveness of audit tests.

The primary ways used by auditors to restrict tests of details in reliance on analytical procedures are explained earlier in the discussion of audit risk at the account balance level. Analytical procedures used to obtain an understanding of the client may influence the auditor's assessment of inherent risk. More detailed analytical procedures applied as part of audit program planning may influence the auditor's judgment about the likelihood of material misstatement in an account balance and the resulting judgment about the allowable detection risk for a test of details.

Analytical procedures that replace rather than restrict tests of details have to produce persuasive evidential matter that is essentially equivalent in persuasiveness to that produced by tests of details. Usually this type of test will take the form of a computation based on substantiated accounting data or reliable information from outside the accounting records that predicts the total of an account balance or a discrete portion of the account balance.

Figure 7-5 is an audit work paper that illustrates an analytical procedure to test the total of a type of revenue. Notice that the computation is based on operating records and

E/100	Clear Lake TV Cable Company		
	Test of TV Service Sales a/c # 100		L.W.
	Audit 12/31/x1		2/14/x8
Total number of subscribers 1/1/x1 per last year's work papers			31,010
Subscribers added during 19x1	6,200 V		
	x .5 Ø		3,100
Subscribers who cancelled service during 19x1	3,800 \		
	x .5 Ø		1,900
Total average # of Subscribers during year			38,210
yearly rate ($5/mo. x 12)		ⓧ	x $ 60
Total Estimated TV Service Sales			$2,292,600
Balance 12/31/x1, per books			2,291,900
Difference — Immaterial			100
			ⓣ
V — Per "new service order" file-orders signed by customers			
Ø — Assumed additions & cancellations occurred evenly throughout year			
\ — Per "service cancellation order" file orders signed by customers			
ⓧ — Per advertised rate schedule			
ⓣ — All computations checked—OK			

FIGURE 7-5
Overall analytical test for revenue.

data from outside the accounting system. The auditor in this case would have to have a reasonable basis for concluding that this information was reliable. This particular analytical procedure achieves all the specific audit objectives for the account balance.

An analytical procedure may also be used to achieve a single specific audit objective in some cases. For example, in designing audit procedures to test the specific audit objective related to completeness for sales, the auditor may place reliance on operating data about physical units. By reconciling units shipped to units billed the auditor may be able to substantiate the completeness of sales and trade accounts receivable.

An analytical procedure need not be based on data from outside the accounting system to produce persuasive evidential matter. For example, in designing audit procedures to test a specific audit objective related to the valuation assertion for manufacturing inventory, the auditor may use a reliable historical relationship between overhead and materials put into production to substantiate overhead. The auditor would calculate the overhead portion of inventory by multiplying the materials portion by the historical ratio between materials and overhead. In this case, the auditor would need to apply tests of details to materials, but no tests of details for the overhead portion might be necessary.

TESTS OF TRANSACTION CLASSES

Tests of transaction classes are concerned with the processing of particular classes of transactions through the accounting system. Generally, these tests are performed at an interim date and, regardless of whether performed at an interim date or at year-end, are performed before direct tests of balances. They are discussed at this point because they are usually *planned* at the same time as direct tests of balances. The coordinated program of tests of details of transaction classes and direct tests of balances is commonly referred to as the preliminary audit plan or approach.

Relation of Tests of Transaction Classes to Direct Tests of Balances

The basic relationships between transactions and account balances are discussed earlier in the review of the auditing implications of double-entry accounting. Tests of transactions classes are usually performed for major classes of transactions that are repetitive and large in volume. The major classes of transactions—sales, purchases, cash receipts, and cash disbursements—affect balance sheet accounts in the following manner:

Accounts receivable	Cash	Accounts payable
Beginning balance	Beginning balance	Beginning balance
Additions (sales)		Additions (expenditures)
Reductions (cash receipts) ⟵⟶	Additions (cash receipts)	
	Reductions (cash ⟵⟶ disbursements)	Reductions (cash disbursements)
Ending balance	Ending balance	Ending balance

In the abstract, if beginning balances were tested in the prior year, it would be possible to indirectly test the major transaction classes by direct tests of balances of these balance sheet accounts. There may be other sources of cash receipts and cash disbursements, but they would be substantiated by direct tests of balances of the balance sheet accounts affected. As explained earlier, direct tests of balances of balance sheet accounts are generally preferred because there are fewer items in the ending balance than the transactions that affect the balance, and there is generally more persuasive evidential matter available to support the ending balance.

Note also that the direct tests of balances of balance sheet accounts would indirectly test the income statement account balances (sales and expenditures). Taking one step back from this abstraction, it is obvious that even in a highly condensed income statement there would normally be more than one category of expenditures. This means some tests of recording accuracy as to account classification would be necessary. However, it would still be possible to plan an audit that consisted primarily of direct tests of balances of balance sheet accounts with selected tests of transaction classes for particular specific audit objectives.

This kind of audit—primary emphasis on direct tests of balances of balance sheet accounts—is, in fact, the approach typically used for small businesses. It is also the approach that has to be used when a larger company has material deficiencies in the processing of particular classes of transactions. This approach is called the *substantive approach* to an audit. Generally, it is the most efficient and effective approach to audit the financial statements of a small business. This approach can be especially efficient if the auditor can design effective analytical tests for those specific audit objectives, such as income statement account classification and those related to the completeness assertion, that are not achieved by direct tests of balances.

For a larger business, however, the substantive approach is often inefficient for the following reasons:

- The number of items in ending balances, while still fewer than the number of transactions that affect the balances, is relatively large.
- The accounting system for processing major classes of transactions is generally well designed and produces more reliable accounting data because management in a larger company has to rely more extensively on the accounting data to monitor and control the business.
- There are generally enough employees (needed because of the volume of transactions processed) that effective separation of duties can be achieved.

In these circumstances, the auditor is able to restrict the direct tests of balances that would otherwise be necessary by testing the processing of transaction classes.

Types of Tests of Transaction Classes

As explained earlier, tests of transaction classes may be tests of controls, substantive tests, or a combination test (referred to as a dual-purpose test).

Types of Tests of Controls   Also, as explained in Chapter 6, tests of controls are directed toward the following:

- Design of the internal control structure policies and procedures
- Operating effectiveness of those policies and procedures

Tests of controls directed toward operating effectiveness are usually classified by whether the control procedure being tested leaves a documentary trail. The types of control procedures that do not leave a documentary trail relate to separation of duties and restriction of physical access to assets (those related to the *safeguarding* control objective). These control procedures are tested by inquiry and observation as explained in Chapter 6. These tests and tests directed toward design of the procedures are not discussed further in this chapter.

Tests of controls that leave a documentary trail are usually classified in the following categories:

I Reperformance of completed accounting routines. Examples of such routines are:
   A Entering transactions in an initial record (e.g., prelist, log, or tape) and footing and crossfooting of such records
   B Posting from the initial record to intermediate records (e.g., journals) or the final records (e.g., journal voucher) and footing and crossfooting of such records
   C Posting from intermediate or final records to general ledger and footing of trial balance
   D Balancing routines, such as monthly bank reconciliations and trial balance of a subsidiary ledger and agreement of it to a control account
II Inspection of documents for indication of the performance of a checking routine or approval by stamps, initials, or signatures

These are often dual-purpose tests because the auditor inspects records or documents to see that the processing and related control procedure were performed and reperforms the routine or checks to see that it was performed effectively.

A test of transactions may be a purely substantive test if there are no internal control structure policies or procedures to be tested. For example, if the client's procedures provide for a second clerk to recompute sales invoices and initial or stamp them to indicate performance, then the auditor can inspect sales invoices to see whether they were checked to reperform the checking. However, if the client has no such policy or procedure, an auditor's recomputation of the invoice amount is purely a substantive test. Similarly, tests of footing and posting are purely substantive if the client has no procedures for recomputation and approval of these accounting processing routines to achieve the control objective.

Planning the Scope of Tests of Transaction Classes

Whether tests of transaction classes are dual-purpose tests or substantive tests, the auditor's underlying objective in making the tests is the same—to gain reasonable assurance of the reliability and accuracy of the processing of transactions of a particular class in order to restrict direct tests of balances. The considerations that affect the nature, timing, and extent of tests of transaction classes are explained in the following discussion.

Nature   As explained in Chapter 6, the specific control objectives for a transaction class provide a framework for designing tests of the transactions of that class. Based on the understanding of the internal control structure described in Chapter 6, the auditor identifies whether there are internal control structure policies or procedures to provide reasonable assurance of achieving those control objectives. If there are such policies or procedures prescribed, the auditor designs tests of their functioning (often dual-purpose tests). If there are no internal control structure procedures prescribed that provide reasonable assurance of achieving specific control objectives, the auditor designs substantive tests of details of transactions.

This planning process is best understood by considering a specific example. A specific control objective for sales transactions is that goods shipped (or services rendered) have been recorded. A test of controls would be to see that shipping documents are prenumbered, the numbers are accounted for, and the shipping documents are matched to sales invoices and approved sales orders. An auditor could alternatively apply substantive tests to see that this objective is achieved. The auditor would need to conduct his or her own test of the numerical sequence of shipping documents issued and select a sample of shipping documents and trace them to the related sales invoices.

The nature of procedures for tests of specific transaction classes is described in Chapter 10.

Timing   The considerations that influence the timing of tests are explained in SAS No. 55 (AU 319.55) as follows:

> When the auditor obtains evidential matter about the design or operation of internal control structure policies and procedures during an interim period, he should determine what additional evidential matter should be obtained for the remaining period. In making that determination, the auditor should consider the significance of the assertion involved, the specific internal control structure policies and procedures that were evaluated during the interim period, the degree to which the effective design and operation of those policies and procedures were evaluated, the results of the tests of controls used to make that evaluation, the length of the remaining period, and the evidential matter about design or operation that may result from the substantive tests performed in the remaining period.

This explanation is directed to tests of controls, but dual-purpose tests and substantive tests of transaction classes are also typically performed at an interim date.

The factors that influence whether tests of transaction classes are necessary for the remaining period (the period between the interim date and the balance sheet date) are as follows:

- *Results of the tests of the interim period.* If results indicate a lack of operating effectiveness of internal control structure policies and procedures, naturally control risk should be assessed at a high level, and substantive tests of transaction classes should be made for the remainder of the period. If expanded tests indicate the accounting data are not reliable, tests of transaction classes should not be relied on in determining the extent of direct tests of balances.

- *Response to inquiries concerning the remaining period.* The most important inquiries should be directed at determining whether there were any significant changes in control or accounting procedures during the remaining period.
- *Nature and amount of the transactions and balances involved.* If the transactions occurring between the completion of tests of transaction classes and the end of the year are atypical of the transactions for the year, this implies the need to test further. That is the case with a highly seasonal business or with a company that has several large or unusual transactions near the end of the year.
- *Evidence of compliance within the remaining period obtained from substantive tests.* Evidence obtained through such tests as the pricing of inventory or confirmation of accounts receivable indicate both the accuracy of total debits and credits to those accounts and the propriety of the ending balances. If these tests indicate satisfactory results, there is less need to test transaction classes in the remaining period. A review of the internal auditor's work papers if test results are satisfactory also reduces the need to test the remaining period.
- *Length of the remaining period.* When the time period between interim testing and the balance sheet date is relatively short, it is less important to test the remaining period.
- *Other matters the independent auditor considers relevant in the circumstances.* These include the auditor's assessment of inherent risk and the results of analytical procedures applied as an aid in program planning.

In practice, as stated earlier, the period covered by interim tests of transaction classes is commonly the first 9 months of the year, and there are 3 months in the remaining period. A remaining period of 1 month would be relatively short.

Extent   Tests of transaction classes that involve the inspection of documents for indication of the performance of a checking routine or approval by stamps, initials, or signatures, or those substantive tests that involve inspection of documents, are applied using audit sampling. Determination of the extent of tests of transaction classes using audit sampling is explained in Chapter 8.

Usually, reperformance of completed accounting routines is not considered to be audit sampling. Many reconciling and balancing routines are performed monthly. A common audit approach is to recompute one or a few such reconciliations or balancings and then see that the routine was performed in the other months. If the routine is performed much more frequently than monthly, the common approach is still to recompute only one or a few of the routines. However, a sample of routines is selected rather than all of them to see whether the routine was performed throughout the period.

The rationale for this approach is that merely inspecting a reconciliation or trial balance provides reasonable evidence that the routine was performed and that sloppy or improper performance will usually be apparent. Also, as a practical matter, completed accounting routines do not lend themselves to audit sampling, and the approach described is based on a consensus of audit practice.

DESIGNING AUDIT PROGRAMS—ADDITIONAL MATTERS

This section explains the following matters about designing programs that are either implicit in the matters explained so far or that require an understanding of the foregoing matters to comprehend:

- An audit program is only tentative and is subject to revision as the audit progresses.
- Client expectations may influence the scope of auditing procedures.
- Auditors usually rely on generalized materials and do not design audit programs from scratch on individual engagements.
- The performance of direct tests of balances at an interim date is permissible but requires an evaluation of incremental audit risks and costs.

Revision of Audit Program as Audit Progresses

Before the performance of tests of controls and substantive tests, the planned audit programs are tentative. A reflection on the matters explained in this chapter indicates why that is necessarily true. Direct tests of balances are planned on the basis of judgments and expectations that may have to be changed as audit procedures are performed and the results of those tests evaluated. Tests of transaction classes may indicate that the accounting data are unreliable and the planned audit approach may have to be modified and significantly more extensive direct tests of balances made. Direct test of balances results may indicate that uncorrected known misstatement and likely misstatement are much larger than anticipated. The allowance for undetected misstatement will have to be reduced and tests of details increased accordingly. Since audits are planned to emphasize efficiency, when auditing procedures are actually performed, expansion of the scope of planned procedures may be necessary.

Client Expectations

It is not unusual for audit programs to include audit procedures that are applied simply because a particular client expects them. For example, petty cash may be clearly immaterial to the balance sheet, but the auditor may count petty cash because a client has indicated that is a procedure the client wants performed to motivate the diligence of the custodian. In a particular industry, some procedures may be understood to be expected that are not essential to achieve specific audit objectives. For example, municipalities are very sensitive about even minor cash defalcations by government employees, and auditors typically perform more extensive cash procedures in such audits than would be considered necessary for a commercial business of comparable size. Generally, client expectations have a one-way effect on scope. An auditor may add procedures that are not strictly necessary to meet client expectations, but a client-imposed scope limitation generally requires the auditor to disclaim an opinion.

Generalized Materials

Students studying auditing often feel intimidated because after reading about how audit programs are designed, they still feel unprepared to actually design one on their own.

Do not worry. In practice, auditors almost universally rely on some form of generalized material as an aid in designing audit programs. This does not mean that practicing auditors rigidly follow standardized or "canned" audit programs. However, practicing auditors routinely refer to a variety of practice aids.

Standard programs are available for typical commercial companies and companies in many specialized industries. Generally, these programs require tailoring to the circumstances of the particular engagement at least to the extent of specifying the extent and timing of the procedures listed. Other standard programs provide basic procedures and additional procedures to be added for specific circumstances.

Another type of generalized material, especially favored by large CPA firms, is a source list of common audit procedures that can be used to achieve specific audit objectives. In designing audit programs using a source list, the auditor identifies specific audit objectives and then refers to a source list of procedures organized by type of audit objective.

The purpose of explaining, at some length, how audit programs are designed is to permit intelligent use of generalized materials.

Direct Tests of Balances at an Interim Date

Generally, the reason an auditor considers performing some direct tests of balances at an interim date is to meet a deadline for audited financial statements within a relatively short period after year-end. The deadline may result from things such as a planned offering of securities or industry custom. Usually, the direct tests of balances considered for interim performance are time-consuming procedures, such as confirmation of trade accounts receivable and observation of physical inventory taking. Normally, these are very important procedures to the auditor's ability to express an opinion on financial statements. This means that performing such tests at an interim date is a carefully considered program planning decision. Professional standards for this decision are specified in SAS No. 45 (AU 313), and this discussion is adapted from that source.

Before applying direct tests of balances to material asset or liability account balances at an interim date, the auditor should consider:

- The difficulty of controlling *incremental* audit risk
- The costs of substantive tests that will be necessary to cover the remaining period to provide appropriate audit assurance at the balance sheet date

The incremental audit risk is the increase in audit risk, as defined earlier, caused by applying the direct test of the balance at the interim date rather than at year-end. If the client is subject to rapidly changing business conditions or if there are circumstances that might predispose management to misstate the financial statements, the incremental audit risk will normally be considered unacceptable.

Considering the costs of substantive tests to cover the remaining period requires some knowledge of these procedures. These procedures are sometimes called roll-forward procedures. The auditor compares the details of the account balance at year-end to the details at the interim date. This analytical procedure identifies any amounts that appear unusual. In this context, unusual means anything different in nature or size than items examined at the interim date. Unusual amounts are investigated and, if warranted, additional tests of details are applied. Otherwise, the additional substantive tests may be limited to analytical procedures.

Unless the client has internal control structure policies and procedures that provide reasonable assurance of achieving relevant control objectives, interim testing may not be cost-effective. Essential internal control structure policies and procedures include those to achieve the *safeguarding* objective for assets. However, the auditor normally also has to be concerned with policies and procedures related to validity, completeness, and recording accuracy because the accounting records at year-end are compared with the information at the interim date as part of the roll-forward procedures.

AUDITING ACCOUNTING ESTIMATES

SAS No. 57 (AU 342) provides guidance on the planning and performance of audit procedures to substantiate estimates, such as net realizable values of inventory and accounts receivable.

SAS No. 57 makes clear that management is responsible for making the accounting estimates included in the financial statements, and the auditor is responsible for evaluating the reasonableness of accounting estimates made by management.

The auditor's objective when evaluating accounting estimates is to obtain sufficient competent evidential matter to provide reasonable assurance that (1) all accounting estimates that could be material to the financial statements have been developed, (2) those accounting estimates are reasonable in the circumstances, and (3) the accounting estimates are presented in conformity with applicable accounting principles and are properly disclosed.

The auditor's approach to evaluating the reasonableness of an accounting estimate is to obtain an understanding of how management developed the estimate and then use one or a combination of the following methods to substantiate the estimate:

- Review and test management's process
- Develop an independent expectation of the estimate
- Review subsequent events of transactions that affect the estimate

In other words, to evaluate the reasonableness of the client's estimate of the net realizable value of accounts receivable, the auditor might (1) test the client's aging of receivables and evaluate the reasonableness of the percentage of each age category reserved, (2) develop an independent estimate of uncollectible accounts, or (3) post subsequent cash collections to the aged receivables trial balance. Also, the auditor may use a combination of these methods.

CHAPTER 7 ASSIGNMENTS

OBJECTIVE QUESTIONS

7-1 For each one of the following statements indicate whether the statement is true or false.

T   F   a Decisions about the nature of auditing procedures to be applied are confined to selecting the particular type of procedure, such as confirmation or vouching.

T   F   b Decisions about the timing of auditing procedures include deciding when during the period to apply procedures and coordination of related procedures.

T   F   c Decisions about the extent of audit procedures are essentially sample size decisions.

T   F   d The time and cost of applying particular auditing procedures are not valid considerations under professional standards in making audit scope decisions.

T   F   e Audit procedures that might be selected to achieve audit objectives related to the existence assertion are physical examination, confirmation, and vouching.

T   F   f The auditor must estimate a single dollar amount that is material to the financial statements and allocate it proportionally to account balances in planning substantive tests of those balances.

T   F   g To control audit risk, the auditor restricts the level of inherent, control, and detection risks.

T   F   h The components of audit risk may be assessed qualitatively; estimation of a specific percentage for each component is not essential.

T   F   i It is possible to substantiate an ending account balance without necessarily substantiating any of the items comprising that ending balance.

T   F   j Analytical procedures may be used in place of tests of details of material amounts in the financial statements, providing the evidential matter produced is sufficiently persuasive.

T   F   k Tests of transaction classes are planned and performed before the planning and performance of direct tests of balances.

T   F   l Inspection of documents for indication of performance of a checking routine or approval are often an aspect of dual-purpose tests.

T   F   m Incremental audit risk is the increase in audit risk caused by applying the direct test of a balance at an interim date.

7-2 The following questions relate to various aspects of audit programs. Select the *best* response.

    a An audit program provides proof that:

      1 Sufficient competent evidential matter was obtained.

      2 The work was adequately planned.

      3 There was compliance with generally accepted standards of reporting.

      4 There was a proper consideration of internal control structure.

    b The procedures specifically outlined in an audit program are primarily designed to:

      1 Protect the auditor in the event of litigation

      2 Detect misstatements

      3 Test internal systems

      4 Gather evidence

    c Which of the following elements ultimately determines the specific auditing procedures that are necessary in the circumstances to afford a reasonable basis for an opinion?

      1 Auditor judgment

      2 Materiality

      3 Relative risk

      4 Reasonable assurance

AICPA adapted

7-3 The following questions relate to various aspects of selecting audit procedures. Select the *best* response.

    a The sequence of steps in gathering evidence as the basis of the auditor's opinion is:

    1 Substantive tests, understanding the internal control structure, and tests of controls

    2 Understanding the internal control structure, substantive tests, and tests of controls

    3 Understanding the internal controls structure, tests of controls, and substantive tests

    4 Tests of controls, understanding the internal control structure, and substantive tests

b Each of the following might, in itself, form a valid basis for an auditor to decide to omit a test *except* the:

    1 Relative risk involved

    2 Relationship between the cost of obtaining evidence and its usefulness

    3 Difficulty and expense involved in testing a particular item

    4 Assessed level of control risk

c An independent auditor has concluded that the client's records, procedures, and representations can be relied upon based on tests made during the year when internal control structure policies and procedures were found to be effective. The auditor should test the records, procedures, and representations again at year-end if:

    1 Inquiries and observations lead the auditor to believe that conditions have changed significantly.

    2 Comparisons of year-end balances with like balances at prior dates revealed significant fluctuations.

    3 Unusual transactions occurred subsequent to the completion of the interim audit work.

    4 Client records are in a condition that facilitate effective and efficient testing.

d An entity's financial statements were misstated over a period of years due to large amounts of revenue being recorded in journal entries that involved debits and credits to an illogical combination of accounts. The auditor could most likely have been alerted to this irregularity by:

    1 Scanning the general journal for unusual entries

    2 Performing a revenue cutoff test at year-end

    3 Tracing a sample of journal entries to the general ledger

    4 Examining documentary evidence of sales returns and allowances recorded after year-end

e The objective of tests of details of transactions performed as tests of controls is to:

    1 Detect material misstatements in the account balances of financial statements

    2 Evaluate whether an internal control structure policy or procedure operated effectively

    3 Determine the nature, timing, and extent of substantive tests for financial statement assertions

    4 Reduce control risk, inherent risk, and detection risk to an acceptably low level

f An auditor wishes to perform tests of controls on a client's cash disbursements procedures. If the control procedures leave *no* audit trail of documentary evidence, the auditor most likely will test the procedures by:

    1 Inquiry and analytical procedures

    2 Confirmation and observation

    3 Observation and inquiry

    4 Analytical procedures and confirmation

g An auditor selects a sample from the file of shipping documents to determine whether invoices were prepared. This test is performed to satisfy the audit objective of:

  1 Accuracy
  2 Completeness
  3 Control
  4 Existence

h To determine whether accounts payable are complete, an auditor performs a test to verify that all merchandise received is recorded. The population of documents for this consists of all:

  1 Vendor's invoices
  2 Purchase orders
  3 Receiving reports
  4 Canceled checks

AICPA adapted

DISCUSSION QUESTIONS

Discussion questions require the application of the concepts explained in the chapter to specific facts, issues, or problems. They are classified by the primary chapter topic to which they relate. However, responses should not be confined to the primary topics but should include all relevant implications.

Nature of Audit Procedures and Audit Objectives

7-4 The following list includes common auditing procedures. For each procedure: (1) describe the procedure; (2) identify the primary financial statement assertion, such as existence, for which the procedure might be used to achieve a related specific audit objective; and (3) give an example of the application of the procedure to a particular account balance.

  a Physical examination
  b Confirmation
  c Vouching
  d Tracing
  e Scanning
  f Inquiry
  g Analytical procedures

7-5 As explained in Chapter 4, evidential matter obtained through the auditor's personal knowledge is more reliable than evidential matter obtained from internal sources, such as the client's accounting records. Why do auditors not confine the procedures selected to those that are known to produce the most reliable evidential matter, such as physical examination?

7-6 The specific audit objectives for the inventory of a manufacturing company might include the following:

  1 Inventories included in the balance sheet physically exist.
  2 Inventory quantities include all products, materials, and supplies on hand.
  3 The entity has legal title or similar rights of ownership to inventories.
  4 Slow-moving, excess, defective, and obsolete items included in inventory are properly identified and valued.

Required:
a Identify the broad categories of financial statement assertions from which these specific audit objectives are derived.
b Identify one audit procedure that contributes to the achievement of all these specific audit objectives and explain how and to what extent it contributes to achievement of the objectives.
7-7 Important audit procedures for the balance accounts receivable usually include the following:

1 Confirm account balances with selected customers.
2 Inquire of management and read agreements and minutes for liens or pledges of accounts receivable.

Required:
a Identify the financial statement assertions and related specific audit objectives that each of these procedures contributes toward achieving.
b Identify the assertions and related audit objectives for accounts receivable to which these procedures do not contribute.
c What audit objectives might be achieved by the procedures identified in 2 above?

Materiality and Audit Risk at the Account Balance Level

7-8 The scope of audit procedures can be modified by varying the nature, timing, or extent of procedures selected. Explain how materiality at the account balance level may be a consideration that influences each of these aspects of the scope of audit procedures and illustrate your point by a specific example.
7-9 Listed below is the balance sheet portion of the 19X6 trial balance of Russ & Co. and additional information on some of the account balances. (Allowance accounts are ignored for convenience.) You are planning the audit of the 19X6 financial statements.

Trial Balance Information	
Cash	$10,000
Accounts receivable	36,000
Inventory	45,000
Property and equipment	90,000
Other assets	5,000
Accounts payable	31,000
Long-term debt	85,000
Owner's equity	70,000

Additional information:

1 Customer receivables range from balances of $100 to $3,000, and the 10 highest balances total $24,000. The next 15 largest balances total $10,000.
2 Inventory is composed of three product groups, and the average cost of items in each group ranges from $10 to $50.

3 Property and equipment had two additions this year of $10,000 and $5,000 and no retirements.

4 Accounts payable balances range from $500 to $3,000.

5 Long-term debt is a single loan from a venture capitalist with a lien on all assets and the owner of Russ & Co.'s personal guarantee.

6 Your CPA firm's guidance on financial statement materiality indicates that $2,000 would be material to Russ & Co.'s financial statements taken as a whole.

7 Since Russ & Co. is a small business that uses the accounting services department of your firm to prepare monthly and annual financial statements, you anticipate that the client will correct all misstatements you detect and only minor misstatements if any, are expected.

Required: Explain how you would use the financial statement materiality amount to plan the nature and extent of direct tests of balances of the balance sheet accounts in the 19X6 trial balance.

7-10 Winters & Allen is a mail-order seller of party supplies and novelty items. It sells to both businesses and individuals, but the accounting processing and controls are the same for all sales transactions. You have prepared the following analysis of the accounts receivable balance at year-end.

Number of accounts	Range of customer balances	Total
5	$50,000 to $150,000	$400,000
5	19,000 to 49,999	90,000
440	100 to 18,999	110,000
450		$600,000

Based on inquiry of the credit manager and discussions with corporate officers, you have determined that of the last category there are 15 accounts that are seriously past due and may be in dispute and 5 accounts with related parties. These 20 accounts total $10,000.

Required:

a Describe an efficient audit approach to determining the number of and specific accounts to confirm with customers.

b Your CPA firm's guidance on materiality indicates that $15,000 would be a material misstatement of the account receivable balance. How would the $15,000 amount be used in your determination of the extent of the confirmation procedure?

c If you decided not to use audit sampling to select any customer balances for confirmation, what additional information would you need about the composition of the account balance?

7-11 For the following account balances, what are some specific examples of items that might be considered individually significant because of their nature?

a Accounts receivable

b Inventory

c Property and equipment

d Accounts payable

7-12 Martin & Co., a CPA firm, has adopted the following specific percentages for the indicated qualitative levels of risk:

- Minimum 30 percent
- Moderate 50 percent
- Maximum 100 percent

Martin & Co. has also decided to use a 5 percent audit risk level for all audit engagements and not to make a separate assessment of inherent risk.

Required:

a A staff auditor of one of Martin & Co.'s audit engagements has assessed control risk as minimum and other procedures risk as moderate in planning confirmation of accounts receivable. What is the allowable detection risk for the confirmation procedure?

b If the staff auditor had assessed both control risk and other procedures risk as moderate, what would the allowable detection risk be for the confirmation procedure?

c What would the allowable detection risk be if the staff auditor had assessed the other component risks as minimum?

d The staff auditor wonders why the specific percentage associated with minimum risk is 30 percent. Why do you think Martin & Co. did not adopt risk levels of 5 percent or 10 percent for minimum risk?

7-13 Benis & Co., a CPA firm, has adopted the following specific percentages for the indicated qualitative levels of risk:

- Minimum 30 percent
- Moderate 50 percent
- Maximum 100 percent

Benis & Co.'s partners have decided to use audit risk levels of 5 percent to 10 percent, depending on the circumstances of the specific engagement. The partners have also decided to use a separate assessment of inherent risk.

Required:

a A staff auditor on one of Benis & Co.'s audit engagements is planning the confirmation of accounts receivable. Assume the staff auditor has assessed control risk and other procedures risk as moderate and inherent risk as maximum. What is the allowable detection risk for receivables confirmation to achieve an audit risk of 10 percent?

b If the staff auditor made the same decisions as in part a, but assessed inherent risk as moderate rather than maximum, what is the allowable detection risk?

c What basis would the staff auditor need for assessing inherent risk as moderate rather than maximum?

d What types of considerations would influence whether an audit risk of 5 percent or 10 percent was appropriate?

Audit Efficiency

7-14 Coordination of the direction of testing can increase the efficiency of audit tests. If an auditor has adopted the strategy of testing asset and expense account balances directly for overstatement and liability and revenue balances directly for understatement, how would planning the audit tests for accounts payable be structured?

a Using the activity format, indicate the direction of testing for the components of accounts payable.

b In general, how would an auditor test a liability balance, such as accounts payable, directly for understatement?

c How would the accounts payable ending balance be indirectly tested for overstatement?

7-15 Using the activity format for the balance sheet account *cash*, identify the indirect testing effects on the components of directly testing the ending balance for overstatement. Explain how the ending cash balance could be indirectly tested for understatement.

7-16 Your client is the Mission Mountain Shopping Center Inc., a shopping center with 30 store tenants. All leases with the store tenants provide for a fixed rent plus a percentage of sales, net of sales taxes, in excess of a fixed dollar amount computed on an annual basis. Each lease also provides that the landlord may engage a CPA to audit all records of the tenant for assurance that sales are being properly reported to the landlord.

You have been requested by your client to audit the records of the JaiLai Restaurant to determine that the sales, totaling $290,000 for the year ended December 31, 19X4, have been properly reported to the landlord. The restaurant and the shopping center entered into a 5-year lease on January 1, 19X4. The JaiLai Restaurant offers only table service. No liquor is served. During meal times there are four or five waitresses in attendance, who prepare handwritten prenumbered restaurant checks for the customers. Payment is made at a cash register, staffed by the proprietor, as the customer leaves. All sales are for cash. The proprietor also is the bookkeeper. Complete files are kept of restaurant checks and cash register tapes. A daily sales book and general ledger are also maintained.

List the auditing procedures that you would employ to test the annual sales of the JaiLai Restaurant. (Disregard vending machine sales and counter sales of chewing gum and candy, and concentrate on the overall checks that would be appropriate.)

AICPA adapted

7-17 Meals Inc. presents the following items in its balance sheet:

- Cash
- Accounts receivable
- Inventory
- Property
- Accounts payable
- Long-term debt
- Capital stock

Meals Inc. is a small business with two employees in its accounting department, and for that reason its internal control structure is considered deficient. In planning the audit of Meals Inc.'s annual financial statements, which account balances could you effectively test at an interim date and which balances would you want to test as of the balance sheet date?

Designing Audit Programs for Unusual Account Balances

7-18 In 19X1, Reid, who had been in the lumbering business for many years, incorporated his business as Reid Ltd. Reid became president of the company and Zilker, the chief accountant, was appointed treasurer.

Zilker continued to be responsible for the accounting and each year prepared financial statements and the company's tax returns. The company's accounts were never audited.

In late 19X8, however, the company applied for a bank loan and was informed that audited financial statements for the year ended December 31, 19X8, would have to be submitted.

Prior to the incorporation of his business, Reid had accumulated some timber-cutting rights, which were sold to the company upon incorporation. The company has since acquired further cutting rights. Zilker recorded all cutting rights at cost as a noncurrent asset and charged to expense each year a depletion allowance on the rights.

The December 31, 19X8, financial statements as prepared by Zilker include the following amounts with respect to the cutting rights:

Timber-cutting rights—at cost less accumulated depletion	$338,000
Depletion expense (shown under cost of sales)	$37,000

List the audit procedures the auditor might apply to substantiate the timber-cutting rights asset and depletion expense.

7-19 Your client, Zitzitz Inc., issues frequent buyers cards which are stamped at the time of the sale of merchandise. These cards are redeemable at Zitzitz when a card is filled. Thus, with each sale Zitzitz creates a liability. However, not all cards with stamps will ultimately be redeemed by customers. What should you, the auditor, do to satisfy yourself that the liability for redemption of frequent buyers cards carried on the books of Zitzitz is adequate?

7-20 Milenburg Inc., sells chemicals in large, costly returnable containers. Its procedures in accounting for the containers are as follows:

1 When containers are purchased, their cost is charged to "Inventory—containers on hand."

2 Containers are billed to customers at cost; full credit is allowed for all containers returned in usable condition. The containers remain the property of Milenburg Inc., at all times.

3 The cost of containers billed to customers is debited to "Accounts receivable—containers" and credited to "Liability for containers billed." At the same time, the cost of the containers billed is transferred to "Inventory—containers out" from "Inventory—containers on hand." Subsidiary ledgers are maintained for "Accounts receivable—containers" and "Inventory—containers out."

4 When containers are returned in usable condition, the entries in 3 are reversed.

5 A physical inventory of containers on hand is taken at the fiscal year-end.

6 As a partial control over containers in the hands of customers, sales representatives are asked to estimate periodically the number of containers held by each customer. These estimates are checked for reasonableness against the amount shown for the customer in the "Inventory—containers out" subsidiary ledger.

7 Physical shortages, unusable returned containers, and other inventory adjustments are charged or credited to "Containers expense—net." The corresponding adjustments to "Liability for containers billed" are also charged or credited to "Containers expense—net."

8 Containers kept by customers for more than 1 year are deemed unusable.

Wiley Norris had been the auditor of Milenburg Inc. for many years. He issued an unqualified opinion on the financial statements for the previous fiscal year. Two months before the current year-end, the company's accountant requested that he investigate a strange situation which had developed: The balance in the "Liability for containers billed" had been steadily increasing, to the point where it exceeded the *combined* balances in "Inventory—containers out" and "Inventory—containers on hand."

a What might have caused the situation described by the company's accountant?

b List the procedures Norris should employ to determine the nature and extent of the misstatement.

CICA adapted

CASE

Maxmilia J. Russell, CPA, has worked on the annual audits of Fleecydale Savings and Loan Association for 5 years. When Maxi was first assigned as the partner on the engagement, Fleecydale had experienced a problem with the loan servicer: The interest rates on loans to several important borrowers had been changed inappropriately, resulting in a loss of interest income. The borrowers affected by this problem included a real estate developer with 15 major loans totaling over $23 million, and the general partner in two shopping center developments who also happened to be on Fleecydale's board of directors. The problem was detected in the test of lending transactions. The sample size for the test had been increased based on a dip in interest income for commercial lending from that expected based on analytical procedures.

In the early years, Maxi's audit program in this area included the following procedures:

• Test the rate and terms used in income computations for all loans to related parties whose total loans exceed $300,000
• Test the rate and terms used in income computations for all loans to borrowers whose total borrowings exceed $7,000,000
• Test the rate and terms used in income computations for an extensive number of other loans
• Select a sample of income or loan fee adjustments to review for proper authorization and that the amount of the adjustment was accurately calculated and posted

In the past 2 years, the personnel in the loan servicing area were replaced and new procedures were implemented. The clerical accuracy of amounts billed are independently checked, including checking that the rate used is that approved by the loan committee. An independent officer approves all adjustments and credits, and changes to interest rates and terms on the lending master file require entry of the password assigned to that independent officer. The internal auditor selects a sample of such changes each quarter and reviews them for propriety. Maxi has reviewed the internal auditor's work papers and report for the year about to be audited and found that errors are now nearly nonexistent. This is consistent with the results of last year's testing performed by Maxi's audit team.

The loan portfolio has grown steadily over the past 5 years. Preliminary analytical procedures indicate that interest income appears reasonable, considering the growth in the loan portfolio and the rise in the average interest rate.

Maxi wants to change the audit program from last year's procedures. The extensive number of loans tested took considerable time. High audit hours result in a high audit fee, and the competition for Fleecydale's audit is brisk.

Required:

1 What is the specific audit objective of the audit procedures described in this case?
2 How have the changes in the past 2 years affected the components of audit risk?
3 What changes could be made to the nature, timing, and extent of audit procedures applied in this area?

CHAPTER

8

Audit Sampling

CHAPTER OUTLINE

Learning Objectives

After studying this chapter you should be able to:

- Define audit sampling and describe the requirements that apply to all audit samples—statistical and nonstatistical
- Describe the representative selection methods that should be used for audit sampling
- Identify the considerations that influence the planning, selection, and evaluation of audit samples for tests of transaction classes
- Understand the use of a statistical model and a formal nonstatistical approach for tests of transaction classes
- Describe the considerations that influence the planning, selection, and evaluation of audit samples for direct tests of balances
- Explain the use of a statistical model and a formal nonstatistical approach for direct tests of balances
- Understand how to establish tolerable misstatement for sampling applications for direct tests of balances

Relevant Section of Statements on Auditing Standards

AU 350 — Audit Sampling

An important aspect of designing audit programs is establishing the extent of audit tests. When audit sampling is involved, a critical aspect of the extent decision is estimating sample size. This chapter explains how to plan, select, and evaluate audit samples.

AN INTRODUCTION TO AUDIT SAMPLING

Some auditing procedures are susceptible to application by sampling, but many auditing procedures do not involve sampling. For example, inquiry, observation, analytical procedures, and general procedures, such as reading minutes and contracts, do not involve sampling. Also, as explained in Chapter 7, sampling is not involved when the auditor applies a procedure *only* to the significant items in an account balance or reviews a client's completed accounting routines.

Definition and Basic Features of Audit Sampling

Audit sampling, according to SAS No. 39 (AU 350.01), is defined as follows:

> Audit sampling is the application of an audit procedure to less then 100 percent of the items within an account balance or class of transactions for the purpose of evaluating some characteristic of the balance or class.

Several features of audit sampling are implicit in this definition. Two features of particular importance to understanding audit sampling are sampling risk and characteristic of interest.

Sampling Risk   As explained earlier, an auditor's objective is to obtain reasonable assurance, and that requires holding audit risk to a relatively low level. The risk component that is modified to control audit risk is detection risk. When an audit procedure is applied using sampling, detection risk arises from both uncertainties due to sampling and uncertainties due to factors other than sampling.

The cause of sampling risk is explained in SAS No. 39 (AU 350.10) as follows:

> Sampling risk arises from the possibility that, when [an audit test] is restricted to a sample, the auditor's conclusion may be different from the conclusions he would reach if the tests were applied in the same way to all items in the account balance or class of transactions.

In other words, if the auditor applied the audit procedure to every item instead of a sample, there would be no sampling risk.

Detection risk, however, can never be eliminated even if all items are examined. The nonsampling risk aspect of detection risk arises because of such things as the possibility that the auditor will fail to recognize misstatements included in examined items or apply a procedure that is not effective in achieving a specific objective. Generally, auditors plan to hold this nonsampling risk to a negligible level through adequate planning and supervision and adherence to appropriate quality control policies and procedures as described in Chapter 2.

Characteristic of Interest   The second half of the definition of audit sampling distinguishes sampling from other approaches to audit tests. The auditor examines a sample of items "for the purpose of evaluating some characteristic of the balance or class."

When the auditor uses sampling in direct tests of balances, the characteristic of interest is *monetary misstatement* in the balance. In other words, the auditor is concerned with the dollar amount of misstatement and specifically with whether monetary misstatement exceeds a material amount.

When the auditor uses sampling in tests of transaction classes, the characteristic of interest is usually a *deviation rate* for an internal control structure policy or procedure. In other words, the auditor is concerned with the rate of deviation from a prescribed policy or procedure and specifically with whether the deviation rate exceeds a rate the auditor has specified as acceptable.

Auditors using sampling sometimes refer to both monetary misstatements and deviations as sample misstatements. However, there is an important distinction between these two types of misstatements. A monetary misstatement indicates the misstatement of an account balance. A deviation does not necessarily indicate the presence of monetary misstatement. As the deviation rate increases, the risk of monetary misstatement increases. However, deviations from a prescribed internal control structure policy or procedure do not automatically result in monetary misstatement. For example, if the policy or proce-

dure is recomputation of a sales invoice by a second clerk, that clerk's failure to perform the procedure does not mean the invoice amount is wrong. The first clerk may have
computed the invoice correctly. Normally, the auditor considers the increased risk of
monetary misstatement associated with a particular deviation rate in assessing the control risk component of audit risk.

Nonstatistical versus Statistical Audit Sampling

When an auditor uses audit sampling, the same basic requirements apply whether the
approach to sampling is statistical or nonstatistical. SAS No. 39 (AU 350.02) states:

> There are two general approaches to audit sampling: nonstatistical and statistical. Both
> approaches require that the auditor use professional judgment in planning, performing, and
> evaluating a sample. . . . The guidance in this section applies equally to nonstatistical and
> statistical sampling.

Nonstatistical sampling was once called judgment sampling, but as the passage quoted
above states, both approaches require judgment and the imprecise term "judgment sampling" has been removed from the literature.

Basic Requirements of All Audit Samples   Whenever an auditor uses audit sampling (statistical or nonstatistical) the following basic requirements apply:

- *Planning*. In planning an audit sample the auditor should consider the relationship of
  the sample to the relevant specific audit objective or control objective and consider
  certain other factors that should influence sample size.
- *Selection*. Sample items should be selected in such a way that the sample can be
  expected to be *representative* of the population. Thus, all items in the population
  should have an opportunity to be selected. (The methods that meet this requirement
  for representative selection are explained later. The *population* is simply the account
  balance or transaction class, or the portion of the balance or class, from which the
  sample items are selected.)
- *Evaluation*. The auditor should *project* the results of the sample to the items from
  which the sample was selected and consider sampling risk. (The methods for pro-
  jecting sample results are explained later. The sample results would be monetary misstatement for a test of a balance and deviation rate for a test of a transaction class.)

As explained in later sections of this chapter, these basic requirements are necessarily
an integral part of statistical sampling. Their application to nonstatistical sampling is relatively new in auditing practice. The rationale of SAS No. 39 (AU 350) for imposing
these basic requirements on all audit samples is that there is an underlying logic for sampling that holds true whether the sampling approach is statistical or nonstatistical.

Distinguishing Features of Statistical Sampling   The essential features of *statistical* sampling are the following:

- The sample items should have a known probability of selection, that is, random selection.

- The sample results should be evaluated mathematically, that is, in accordance with probability theory.

Both of these essential features must be met for the sample to qualify as a statistical sample. For example, use of a random number generator to select sample items does not mean that statistical sampling is being used, unless the sample results are evaluated mathematically. Mathematical evaluation based on a nonrandom sample is not valid.

The mathematical evaluation that is the distinguishing feature of statistical sampling is quantification of sampling risk. One of the advantages of statistical sampling is that sampling risk can be objectively calculated as a percentage and controlled precisely by adjusting sample size. An auditor using nonstatistical sampling has to consider sampling risk and hold it to an acceptable level, but cannot quantify sampling risk precisely.

Distinction between Statistical and Nonstatistical Sampling   There is clearly a similarity between the basic requirements applicable to all audit samples, including nonstatistical samples, and the essential features of statistical sampling. The requirement for representative selection that applies to all audit samples is, at least in concept, the same as random selection. In practical application, however, some selection methods are considered to produce a representative sample that does not qualify as random selection, and that should not be used for statistical sampling. The requirement for projection of sample results that applies to all audit samples is a form of mathematical evaluation. However, there is a critical difference between statistical and nonstatistical sampling on this point. The chief conceptual difference between statistical and nonstatistical sampling is that the mathematical evaluation of a statistical sample includes quantification of sampling risk.

In the implementation of audit sampling, the conceptual similarity of statistical and nonstatistical sampling may not be readily apparent in practice. Statistical sampling has an inevitable degree of formality. For example, a formula is normally used to compute a sample size intended to restrict sampling risk to an acceptable level. Nonstatistical sampling plans have less formality and can take a variety of forms. For example, some nonstatistical plans have been designed to approximate the results of certain statistical plans and include use of a similar formula and steps. However, a nonstatistical sampling plan may use a sample size based entirely on the auditor's judgment.

Representative Selection Methods

SAS No. 39 (AU 350.24) specifies that sample items should be selected in such a way that the sample can be *expected* to be representative of the population. The auditor can never be certain that a sample is representative. Thus, the emphasis is on use of a proper selection method so that it is reasonable to expect the sample items to be representative. If this expectation were unreasonable, projection of sample results to the population would be invalid.

Representative Selection Methods for Both Statistical and Nonstatistical Sampling   SAS No. 39 (AU 350.24, footnote 4) enumerates the following selection methods that can be expected to produce representative samples: "random sampling, stratified random sampling, sampling with probability proportional to size, and systematic sampling (for example, every hundredth item) with one or more random starts." All of these are random selection methods and may be used for statistical or nonstatistical sampling. The primary features of these selection methods are as follows:

- *Random selection.* A simple random sample is a sample that is selected in such a way that every item in the population has an equal chance of being selected. This is accomplished by using a printed table of random numbers or computer software that generates random numbers. To use this selection method it is necessary to establish correspondence between the population and the random numbers. For example, if the auditor is selecting a sample of sales invoices, correspondence has to be established between the invoice numbers and the digits in the random number table, or the program should limit the numerical range of random numbers it generates.
- *Stratified random sampling.* Stratification is not a unique method of selection, but a means of improving the efficiency of sample design. When a population is highly variable, that is, has large variations between the amount of individual items and the average amount, sampling without stratification requires very large sample sizes. To stratify, the auditor groups the population into subpopulations, or strata, that are more similar in amount. The reduction in variability within each stratum results in a smaller overall sample size. Then one of the random selection methods is used to select sample items from each stratum. Generally, in auditing, stratification is based on the recorded amount of items in an account balance.
- *Sampling with probability proportional to size.* This method of sample selection emphasizes larger dollar items within an account balance. The name derives from the property of the selection method that the probability of an item being selected is directly proportional to its dollar amount. For example, a $1,000 item has twice the chance of being selected as a $500 item and 10 times the chance of a $100 item. Each individual dollar in the account balance has an equal chance of selection, but each physical unit does not. The other selection methods are based on physical units, but this selection method uses dollar units. This method is illustrated on pages 309 and 310 of this chapter.
- *Systematic sampling.* Using this selection method, the auditor counts through the population and selects items on the basis of a sampling interval. The interval is determined by dividing the number of physical items in the population by sample size. For example, if the auditor is selecting 100 items from a population of 1,000 items, the auditor selects every 10th item (1,000 ÷ 100). This method is easy to apply manually, but the auditor needs to exercise caution about the possibility of the population being arranged in an order that corresponds to the size of the sampling interval. If this correspondence exists, the sample will not be representative. One precaution that can be taken is to use several random starts.

With all of these selection methods, it is necessary to have a random start and, as explained above, with systematic selection several random starts are desirable. When statistical sampling is used, one of these methods, which are sometimes called random-based selection methods, should be used.

Representative Selection for Nonstatistical Sampling   Naturally, any of the random-based selection methods may also be used for nonstatistical sampling. However, there is a method that is considered to produce a representative sample that is not one of the random-based methods. It is called *haphazard selection* and is described in the Auditing Procedure Study of the AICPA, *Audit Sampling,* as follows:

> A *haphazard sample* consists of sampling units selected without any conscious bias, that is, without any special reason for including or omitting items from the sample. It does not consist of sampling units selected in a careless manner; rather it is selected in a manner that can be expected to be representative of the population.[1]

The key to haphazard selection is avoiding being biased by the nature, size, appearance, or location of items. For example, if the auditor is selecting invoices from a cabinet of drawers, the auditor should not select items only from the middle of the drawers because that would not give invoices in the front or back of the drawers a chance of selection.

Unacceptable Sample Selection Methods   Certain selection methods that have been used by auditors in the past are methods that cannot be expected to produce representative samples. This means these methods are not acceptable for statistical *or nonstatistical* audit sampling.

- *Block selection.* Using this selection method the auditor selects all items of a specified type processed on a particular day, week, or month. For example, the auditor might examine all cash disbursement transactions in the first week of June and the last week of December. The problem with this selection method is that the sampling unit is a period of time rather than an individual transaction. In the example given, the auditor has selected two units in a population of 52 units. If the blocks or time periods were selected randomly, the sample could be representative, but a valid sample size would normally be impractically large. For example, to have reasonable assurance the auditor might need to select 45 out of 52 weeks.
- *Judgmental selection.* Using this selection method the auditor selects large or unusual items from the population or uses some other judgmental criterion for selection. Obviously, this selection method has a conscious bias and cannot be considered a representative selection method.

Because these selection methods have been used rather extensively in practice, it is important to recognize that they are unacceptable selection methods even for nonstatistical sampling.

Judgmental Selection for Nonsampling Applications   The fact that judgmental selection is not appropriate for audit sampling does not mean that auditors should stop using judgment in selecting items to examine. The point is only that the items selected using judgmental criteria are not necessarily representative of the population, and conclusions based on items selected judgmentally should not be extended to the population.

---

[1]AICPA, Auditing Procedure Study, in *Audit Sampling* (New York: AICPA, 1994).

In establishing the *extent* of an audit test an auditor would normally first identify the large and unusual items and plan to examine all of them. If the remaining items are sampled, this approach usually allows smaller sample sizes. However, the large and unusual items are not being sampled. These items are being examined 100 percent. Audit sampling is being used only for the remaining items. SAS No. 39 (AU 350.21) explains the point as follows:

> When planning a sample for a substantive test of details, the auditor uses his judgment to determine which items, if any ... should be individually examined and which items, if any, should be subject to sampling. The auditor should examine those items for which, in his judgment, acceptance of some sampling risk is not justified. ... Any items that the auditor has decided to examine 100 percent are not part of the items subject to sampling.

Using this approach, after identifying large or unusual items—sometimes called individually significant items—the auditor may conclude that the dollar amount of remaining items is sufficiently immaterial that no tests of details need to be applied to them. In this case, use of audit sampling is not necessary.

AUDIT SAMPLING FOR TESTS OF TRANSACTION CLASSES

As explained above, some audit tests involve sampling and some audit tests (such as selection of individually significant items) do not. This section of the chapter applies to all tests of transactions that use audit sampling. It applies to both statistical samples and nonstatistical samples.

The types of tests of transaction classes for which audit sampling is useful are those that involve inspection of source documents and that are frequently dual-purpose tests as explained in Chapter 7.

Planning Samples for Tests of Transaction Classes

One of the basic requirements that applies to all audit samples concerns the matters that should be considered in planning the sample. SAS No. 39 (AU 350.31) describes these matters as follows:

- The relationship of the sample to the objective of the test of controls
- The maximum rate of deviations from the prescribed internal control structure policies and procedures that would support the auditor's planned assessed level of control risk
- The auditor's allowable risk of assessing control risk too low
- Characteristics of the population, that is, the items comprising the account balance or class of transactions of interest

In the following discussion, these considerations are identified by the following shorthand terms commonly used in SAS No. 39 (AU 350) and practice:

- Sample-objective relationship
- Tolerable rate
- Risk of assessing control risk too low
- Expected rate

Whether the auditor is using statistical or nonstatistical sampling, these considerations apply to planning the sample.

Sample-Objective Relationship   Considering the relationship between the sample and the objective of the test is probably the most difficult aspect of using audit sampling in tests of transaction classes. As with the other planning considerations, these difficulties are not created by sampling. However, use of audit sampling forces the auditor to be more specific, before testing, about matters that were always implicit in this type of test. The following steps are necessary in considering the relationship between the sample and the objective of the test:

- *Identify relevant control objectives and internal control structure policies and procedures.* The auditor needs to specify the control objectives and the internal control structure policies and procedures that achieve them, for a particular transaction class, that are relevant to restricting substantive tests of the related account balances. For example, for the trade accounts receivable account balance there are at least two relevant transaction classes—credit sales and cash receipts. For each transaction class, the auditor would need to identify the control objectives that if achieved would permit an assessed level of control risk at less than maximum. For example, for both credit sales and cash receipts, relevant control objectives would include those related to the validity, completeness, and recording accuracy of transaction processing. Normally, control objectives related to safeguarding and reconciliations are very important to permit reducing the assessed level of control risk, but are not usually tested by sampling. For example, tests of controls for separation of duties are made by inquiry and observation.
- *Identify population and sample unit.* In tests of transaction classes, identifying the population includes specifying the time period to be covered by the test. For example, the period covered may be the entire period under audit or, as explained in Chapter 7, a period up to an interim date. In tests of credit sales, for example, the auditor might identify the population as all credit sales transactions between January 1 and September 30. A sample unit is any of the individual items included in the population. In the example given above, a sample unit would be an individual sales invoice. The auditor also has to specify the physical representation of the population, sometimes called the *frame,* from which sample units will be selected. For example, the frame might be sales invoices recorded in the sales journal or sales invoices maintained in a file drawer. Also, the auditor needs to establish that the population is physically complete. Usually this is accomplished by footing or counting. For example, the auditor might establish that the dollar total of invoices in a filing cabinet agrees with the dollar total of sales posted to the general ledger. This step is very important because the auditor must establish correspondence between the sample frame and the population to validly project conclusions from the sample to the population. Natu-

rally, the appropriate population and sample unit are influenced by the objective of the test. For example, if the auditor is concerned with a control objective related to completeness, a shipping document rather than a sales invoice would be the appropriate sample unit.

• *Define characteristic of interest.* This step is explained in the remainder of this section.

Since several control objectives for a transaction class may be relevant to restricting a particular substantive test and several internal control structure policies or procedures may be relevant to achieving a control objective, a number of samples may be necessary.

Planning samples for tests of transaction classes usually includes both tests of controls and substantive tests. Since the control objectives for a transaction class provide the framework for designing both types of tests, this does not create any unusual problems in considering the relationship between the sample and the objective of the test. However, it does affect the one remaining step in considering this relationship—*defining the characteristic of interest.* SAS No. 39 (AU 350.33) describes this step as follows:

> When designing samples for tests of controls the auditor ordinarily should plan to evaluate operating effectiveness in terms of deviations from prescribed internal control structure policies or procedures, as to either the rate of such deviations or the monetary amount of the related transactions.

This is a relatively complex point and in practice several distinctly different approaches are used. The complexity arises in part from the fact that the underlying mathematics commonly used for evaluating tests of transaction classes uses a characteristic of interest that is a condition or an attribute. An attribute either exists or does not exist. For example, a control procedure has either been complied with or not complied with. However, a monetary misstatement may also be evaluated as a condition or an attribute. For example, a transaction is either affected by a monetary misstatement or not affected without regard to the dollar amount of the misstatement. Also, SAS No. 39 (AU 350.33), as quoted above, points out that the condition or attribute of deviation may be evaluated as a rate or in relation to the monetary amount of related transactions. This means that the deviation rate can be converted into a dollar amount of misstatement. For example, one method would be to multiply the sample mean (average dollar amount of sample items) by the sample deviation rate by the number of physical items in the population.

The complexity also arises in part because most tests of transaction classes that use sampling are dual-purpose tests (both a test of controls and a substantive test applied to the same sample items). For example, the auditor selects a sample of sales invoices, inspects them to see whether they are initialed to indicate recomputation (test of controls), and reperforms the computation (substantive test).

The obvious question is why not simply evaluate the sample as two separate tests: estimate a deviation rate for the test of controls and estimate monetary misstatement for the substantive test. The answer is that some auditors do approach it that way, but that other auditors believe that the distinction between the two types of tests is artificial. These auditors maintain that the overall objective in making these tests of transaction classes is to evaluate the validity, completeness, and recording accuracy of transaction processing. When the auditor detects either a deviation from a prescribed internal control structure policy or procedure or a monetary misstatement, that is an indication of a deficiency in the internal control structure and the primary implication is a lack of reasonable assurance that control objectives are being achieved.

In this book, sampling for tests of transaction classes is explained using the combined definition of a deviation (either noncompliance with a prescribed policy or procedure, or monetary misstatement) and samples are planned and evaluated using a rate. When deviations and monetary misstatements are evaluated separately, the sample size for the dual-purpose test should be the larger of the sample sizes necessary for the test of controls or substantive test.

Tolerable Rate   The maximum rate of deviation that would support the auditor's planned assessed level of control risk is the tolerable rate. In general, as the tolerable rate increases, sample size decreases. The number of assessed levels of control risk from maximum to minimum is a matter of professional judgment. In practice auditors have found that three or four levels work well. Having a few levels recognizes that the degree of effectiveness of policies and procedures can vary. For example, the auditor might decide to use four qualitative levels of assessment as follows:

- Minimum
- Moderate
- Significant
- Maximum

For "maximum," the auditor would omit the test of controls.

The next decision the auditor has to make is what tolerable rate to associate with the levels of control risk. The tolerable rate decreases as the level of control risk is reduced. As the tolerable rate increases, the risk of monetary misstatement in the related account balance also increases. This decision is a difficult professional judgment. There is no formula or rule-of-thumb to establish the appropriate tolerable rate.

The most likely process for making the decision is to start at one extreme. What rate of deviation would mean an assessment of control risk at the maximum level or what rate of deviation would permit a low assessed level?

In practice, auditors sometimes use rates as high as approximately 5 percent to 7 percent for a low assessed level of control risk and assess control risk at the maximum level when the rate exceeds 20 percent. Tolerable rates that large for a low level of control risk may at first seem relatively high. However, it must be remembered that a deviation does not mean that a monetary misstatement has resulted. In those circumstances in which lack of compliance with a prescribed internal control structure policy or procedure is certain to result in monetary misstatement, tolerable rates would need to be lowered. When both control deviations and monetary misstatements are evaluated as a rate, the auditor should switch to a monetary misstatement evaluation if sample results are predominantly monetary misstatements.

Figure 8-1 relates tolerable rates and planned assessed level of control risk to the risk model explained in Chapter 7. Control risk would need to be reduced to a specific percentage only when statistical sampling is being used for a direct test of a balance that

Control risk as a specific %	Qualitative level of control risk	Tolerable rate for deviations (approximate), %
40	Low	5 to 7
60	Moderate	10 to 12
80	Significant	20
100	Maximum	Omit test

FIGURE 8-1
Relationship between tolerable rate and planned assessed level of control risk.

is being restricted based on a low assessed level of control risk. However, the quantitative model makes the relationships easier to visualize.

Risk of Assessing Control Risk Too Low   The auditor's allowable risk of assessing control risk too low is the risk the auditor is willing to accept that the sample supports the auditor's planned level of control risk for a transaction class when the true deviation rate does not justify such a low assessed level. It is an aspect of sampling risk for tests of transaction classes.

The risk of assessing control risk too low should be established at a relatively low level because tests of a transaction class are the auditor's primary means of assessing whether prescribed internal control structure policies or procedures that leave a documentary trail are being complied with satisfactorily.

In general, a relatively low level is translated in quantitative terms to a 5 percent to 10 percent risk of assessing control risk too low. A common approach in practice is to fix the risk of assessing control risk too low at 10 percent. In general, as the allowable risk of assessing control risk too low increases, the necessary sample size decreases.

There is another aspect of sampling risk for tests of transaction classes—the risk of assessing control risk *too high.* This is the risk that the sample does not support the auditor's planned assessed level of control risk when the true deviation rate supports such a level. In practice, many sampling plans do not even attempt to control this aspect of sampling risk, and SAS No. 39 (AU 350) does not identify it as a consideration in planning samples. The reason is that the risk of assessing control risk too high relates to audit efficiency rather than effectiveness.

If the auditor unnecessarily increases the assessed level of control risk, the auditor ordinarily would increase the scope of substantive tests to compensate for the higher level. In these circumstances, the audit might be less efficient but would nevertheless be effective.

Expected Rate   The population characteristic that is relevant to the planning of a test of a transaction class is the *expected rate* of deviation from the policy or procedure being tested. Generally, the closer the expected rate is to the tolerable rate, the larger the sample size that will be necessary. However, when the expected rate is relatively high, the auditor ordinarily will not plan to assess control risk at less than the maximum level. Therefore, the auditor will not perform a test of controls (and will instead perform more substantive testing).

The effect of tolerable rate, risk of assessing control risk too low, and expected rate on sample size are considered in more detail in the sections on statistical and nonstatistical applications.

Selection of Samples for Tests of Transaction Classes

The representative selection methods discussed earlier are generally applicable to both tests of transaction classes and direct tests of balances. However, *stratification* is not usually applicable to tests of transaction classes. In auditing, stratification is normally based on the recorded amount of items included in an account balance. Usually, the same control and processing procedures apply to transactions in a class regardless of the dollar amount of the transactions. If a particular type of transaction in a class is subject to different processing or different control procedures, tests of these transaction types should be planned and evaluated separately. For example, if a company makes both retail and wholesale sales, and retail sales are subject to different processing steps and control procedures, samples of retail sales and wholesale sales should be designed separately.

Systematic selection is often useful for tests of transaction classes because it can be applied to a population that is not in a numbered sequence.

Evaluation of Sample Results of Tests of Transaction Classes

Audit procedures are applied to the items selected, and the deviation rate of the sample is determined. If the auditor cannot apply the planned procedure (or an effective alternative procedure) to the item, the item should be counted as a deviation in evaluating the sample. For example, assume the control procedure being tested is approval of a voucher based on examination of supporting documents. The auditor selects a voucher and sees that it is initialed indicating approval, but the supporting documents cannot be located. This item should be counted as a deviation. However, legitimately voided or unused documents are not deviations.

Considering Sampling Risk   The sample deviation rate is the auditor's best estimate of the population deviation rate. For example, the auditor selects a sample of 25 items, applies the planned audit procedure, and finds one deviation. The sample deviation rate is 4 percent, and the best estimate of the population deviation rate is also 4 percent. If the tolerable rate was established as 9 percent for the planned assessed level of control risk, the sample result might initially appear to support the level. However, the auditor needs to consider sampling risk. What is the risk that this result might be obtained even though the deviation rate in the population exceeds 9 percent? Actually, at the 10 percent risk of assessing control risk too low often used for tests of transaction classes, the population deviation rate could be nearly 16 percent because the sample size was so small, and the auditor should increase the planned assessed level of control risk. In other words, there is a 10 percent risk that the population deviation rate exceeds nearly 16 percent and 90 percent assurance that it is not more than nearly 16 percent. Obviously, this is a statistical evaluation and the computation method is explained in the next section. However, an auditor using a nonstatistical approach would need to judgmentally make the same consideration.

A judgmental evaluation of sample results can be difficult. For example, consider the following situations. The auditor selects a sample from a population of 4,000 invoices and applies audit procedures to test for operating effectiveness of prescribed control procedures. The tolerable rate has been established at 5 percent and the risk of assessing control risk too low at 5 percent. Identify whether sample A or sample B provides better support for the planned assessed level of control risk.[2]

Situation[2]	Sample	Sample size	Deviations found	Sample deviation rate, %
1	A	75	1	1.3
	B	200	4	2.0
2	A	100	1	1.0
	B	125	3	2.4

Actually for situation 1, sample B supports the planned level but sample A does not. For situation 2, sample A supports the planned level, but sample B does not. The reason is the sampling risk associated with the sample sizes and sample results.

Qualitative Analysis   The auditor's evaluation of sample results is not limited to quantitative analysis. A projection of sample results and consideration of sampling risk are required for all audit samples, but so is a qualitative evaluation. The auditor needs to consider the nature and cause of the deviations. As explained in SAS No. 39 (AU 350.42):

> In addition to the evaluation of the frequency of deviations from pertinent procedures, consideration should be given to the qualitative aspects of the deviations. These include (a) the nature and cause of the deviations, such as whether they are errors or irregularities or are due to misunderstanding of instructions or to carelessness, and (b) the possible relationship of the deviations to other phases of the audit.

If the analysis of deviations indicates that prescribed internal control structure policies or procedures have been intentionally circumvented, the auditor should consider the possibility of material fraud.

Practice Problems in Evaluation   Several common problems are encountered in evaluation of sample results of tests of transaction classes. One such problem occurs when the auditor is unable to apply the planned procedure because the item is not available or not applicable. The proper response differs depending on the cause of the problem. As mentioned earlier, if the planned procedure cannot be applied because

[2]Adapted from William R. Kinney, "Judgment Error in Evaluating Sample Results," *The CPA Journal,* March 1977, pp. 61–62.

appropriate supporting documents for a selected item cannot be located, there are usually no alternative procedures and the item should be counted as a deviation.

A similar type of problem may be caused by unused or legitimately voided documents. This can occur when the auditor is using the simple random selection method, and the document that corresponds to a random number included in the sample has not been used or has been legitimately voided. The proper response in this case is to decrease the sample size by one. Substituting another item, such as the one before or after the selected item, would bias the randomness of the sample.

A related problem is caused by imprecise identification of prescribed controls and deviation conditions. For example, in testing cash disbursements, the auditor may define a deviation as lack of a supporting purchase order and receiving report. However, some disbursements are for services, such as utilities, that are acquired without a purchase order being issued and that are received directly by user departments. In these circumstances, the lack of a purchase order or receiving report are not applicable. In this case, the cause of the problem is an improper deviation definition and the definition should be revised.

Revision of the deviation definition may also be appropriate in other circumstances. In general, a deviation is defined as a departure from *pertinent* control policies or procedures. SAS No. 39 (AU 350.00) explains the meaning of "pertinent" as follows:

> In this context, pertinent internal control structure policies or procedures are ones that, had they not been included in the design of the internal control structure, would have adversely affected the auditor's planned assessed level of control risk.

Another way of looking at the identification of pertinent control structure policies procedures is that they should be policies or procedures that are *necessary* for achievement of the specific control objectives the auditor believes are important for an assessment at less than the maximum level.

If the auditor has not exercised care in identifying pertinent policies or procedures, the sample results may indicate a deviation rate that exceeds the tolerable rate, but the policy or procedure tested may be unimportant to the auditor's planned assessment. In this case, the definition of a deviation should be revised.

Statistical Sampling for Tests of Transaction Classes

Audit sampling must meet the requirements of SAS No. 39 (AU 350), but statistical sampling is not required. However, statistical sampling allows the auditor to use the power of probability theory to calculate and precisely control sampling risk.

Selecting a Statistical Technique   Statistical sampling is a collection of techniques based on probability theory and not a single method. Use of statistical sampling in auditing, or any other field, requires selection of a statistical technique that fits the particular circumstances. A statistical technique can be thought of as a mathematical model. The way that variables in the model behave is governed by the internal laws of the model. To apply the model it is necessary to establish correspondence between the variables in the model and variables in the situation being dealt with.

For a statistical technique, the behavior of variables in the model is determined by the properties of the underlying sampling distribution. In statistics courses a number of sampling distributions, such as the normal (bell-shaped) distribution and the binomial distribution are usually studied. In this book the statistical technique explained uses the *Poisson distribution.* It is a continuous distribution that is not symmetric, and it is completely specified by a single parameter which, technically, is determined by the product of *n* (the number of trials) and *P* (the probability of occurrence for one trial).

This statistical technique has been chosen for the following reasons:

- It is the most widely used technique in statistical applications in practice.
- The same distribution can be used for both tests of transaction classes and direct tests of balances, so once the technique is learned for one type of audit test, application to the other type of test can be learned more quickly.
- The properties of the distribution are the same as many accounting populations (highly skewed and low deviation rates).
- Most of the calculations and formulas are simpler than other statistical techniques.

Relating the Statistical Model to Audit Sampling   The statistical model based on the Poisson distribution allows the computation of a maximum rate of occurrence at a specified level of risk, given a rate of occurrence in a sample of size *n*. In tests of transaction classes, an occurrence is a deviation from prescribed policies or procedures. Rather than introduce the traditional symbols for the statistical model and then equate them with the audit sampling terms, the formula for the maximum deviation rate is presented using audit sampling terms and simple letter symbols.

$$\begin{matrix} \text{Maximum} \\ \text{deviation rate} \\ \text{(MDR)} \end{matrix} = \frac{\begin{matrix}\text{risk factor for allowable} \\ \text{risk of assessing control risk too low (R)}\end{matrix}}{\text{sample size } (n)}$$

The risk factor that corresponds to the risk percentage specified for risk of assessing control risk too low is found in a table for the Poisson distribution. Figure 8-2 presents the portion of such a table that is usually relevant for tests of transaction classes.

The related formula for sample size is as follows:

$$\text{Sample size } (n) = \frac{\begin{matrix}\text{risk factor for allowable} \\ \text{risk of assessing control risk too low (R)}\end{matrix}}{\text{tolerable rate (TR)}}$$

Sample Size Estimation   To use the model to estimate sample size in planning a test of a transaction class, the auditor needs to specify the following:

- The tolerable rate
- The risk of assessing control risk too low
- The expected number of deviations

Number of occurrences	Risk of assessing control risk too low	
	5%	10%
0	3.0	2.4
1	4.8	3.9
2	6.3	5.4
3	7.8	6.7
4	9.2	8.0
5	10.6	9.3
6	11.9	10.6
7	13.2	11.8
8	14.5	13.0
9	16.0	14.3
10	17.0	15.5

FIGURE 8-2
Risk factor table. *[Adapted from "Audit Sampling: An Introduction" (New York: John Wiley & Sons, 1994), p. 61.]*

The last two specifications considered together determine the appropriate risk factor (R). Notice that these specifications are essentially the same as the planning considerations identified by SAS No. 39 (AU 350.38):

> To determine the number of items to be selected for a particular sample for a test of controls, the auditor should consider the tolerable rate of deviation from the control structure policies or procedures being tested, the likely rate of deviations, and the allowable risk of assessing control risk too low.

Use of the statistical model for sample size estimation can best be explained by example. Assume an auditor has specified a tolerable rate of 7 percent, a risk of assessing control risk too low of 10 percent, and expects to find at most 1 deviation. Then using the formula, a necessary sample size of 56 could be computed as follows:

$$n = \frac{R}{TR} = \frac{\text{risk factor}}{\text{tolerable rate}}$$

$$= \frac{3.9}{0.07}$$

$$= 56$$

Notice that 3.9 is the risk factor for 1 expected deviation at a 10 percent risk of assessing control risk too low, from the table in Figure 8-2.

Sample size can also be determined using tables such as those shown in Figures 8-3 and 8-4.

Evaluation of Sample Results   The formula presented earlier for the maximum deviation rate is used to evaluate sample results. Assume the auditor in the example

Expected population deviation rate, %	Tolerable rate										
	2%	3%	4%	5%	6%	7%	8%	9%	10%	15%	20%
0.00	114(0)	76(0)	57(0)	45(0)	38(0)	32(0)	28(0)	25(0)	22(0)	15(0)	11(0)
0.25	194(1)	129(1)	96(1)	77(1)	64(1)	55(1)	48(1)	42(1)	38(1)	25(1)	18(1)
0.50	194(1)	129(1)	96(1)	77(1)	64(1)	55(1)	48(1)	42(1)	38(1)	25(1)	18(1)
0.75	265(2)	129(1)	96(1)	77(1)	64(1)	55(1)	48(1)	42(1)	38(1)	25(1)	18(1)
1.00	*	176(2)	96(1)	77(1)	64(1)	55(1)	48(1)	42(1)	38(1)	25(1)	18(1)
1.25	*	221(3)	132(2)	77(1)	64(1)	55(1)	48(1)	42(1)	38(1)	25(1)	18(1)
1.50	*	*	132(2)	105(2)	64(1)	55(1)	48(1)	42(1)	38(1)	25(1)	18(1)
1.75	*	*	166(3)	105(2)	88(2)	55(1)	48(1)	42(1)	38(1)	25(1)	18(1)
2.00	*	*	198(4)	132(3)	88(2)	75(2)	48(1)	42(1)	38(1)	25(1)	18(1)
2.25	*	*	*	132(3)	88(2)	75(2)	65(2)	42(1)	38(1)	25(1)	18(1)
2.50	*	*	*	158(4)	110(3)	75(2)	65(2)	58(2)	38(1)	25(1)	18(1)
2.75	*	*	*	209(6)	132(4)	94(3)	65(2)	58(2)	52(2)	25(1)	18(1)
3.00	*	*	*	*	132(4)	94(3)	65(2)	58(2)	52(2)	25(1)	18(1)
3.25	*	*	*	*	153(5)	113(4)	82(3)	58(2)	52(2)	25(1)	18(1)
3.50	*	*	*	*	194(7)	113(4)	82(3)	73(3)	52(2)	25(1)	18(1)
3.75	*	*	*	*	*	131(5)	98(4)	73(3)	52(2)	25(1)	18(1)
4.00	*	*	*	*	*	149(6)	98(4)	73(3)	65(3)	25(1)	18(1)
5.00	*	*	*	*	*	*	160(8)	115(6)	78(4)	34(2)	18(1)
6.00	*	*	*	*	*	*	*	182(11)	116(7)	43(3)	25(2)
7.00	*	*	*	*	*	*	*	*	199(14)	52(4)	25(2)

Note: This table assumes a large population.
*Sample size is too large to be cost-effective for most audit applications.
Source: AICPA, Auditing Procedure Study, in *Audit Sampling* (New York: AICPA, 1994).

FIGURE 8-3
Determination of sample size: reliability, 90%
(Risk of assessing control risk too low, 10%)
(Allowable number of deviations in parentheses)

Expected population deviation rate, %	Tolerable rate										
	2%	3%	4%	5%	6%	7%	8%	9%	10%	15%	20%
0.00	149(0)	99(0)	74(0)	59(0)	49(0)	42(0)	36(0)	32(0)	29(0)	19(0)	14(0)
0.25	236(1)	157(1)	117(1)	93(1)	78(1)	66(1)	58(1)	51(1)	46(1)	30(1)	22(1)
0.50	*	157(1)	117(1)	93(1)	78(1)	66(1)	58(1)	51(1)	46(1)	30(1)	22(1)
0.75	*	208(2)	117(1)	93(1)	78(1)	66(1)	58(1)	51(1)	46(1)	30(1)	22(1)
1.00	*	*	156(2)	93(1)	78(1)	66(1)	58(1)	51(1)	46(1)	30(1)	22(1)
1.25	*	*	156(2)	124(2)	78(1)	66(1)	58(1)	51(1)	46(1)	30(1)	22(1)
1.50	*	*	192(3)	124(2)	103(2)	66(1)	58(1)	51(1)	46(1)	30(1)	22(1)
1.75	*	*	227(4)	153(3)	103(2)	88(2)	77(2)	51(1)	46(1)	30(1)	22(1)
2.00	*	*	*	181(4)	127(3)	88(2)	77(2)	68(2)	46(1)	30(1)	22(1)
2.25	*	*	*	208(5)	127(3)	88(2)	77(2)	68(2)	61(2)	30(1)	22(1)
2.50	*	*	*	*	150(4)	109(3)	77(2)	68(2)	61(2)	30(1)	22(1)
2.75	*	*	*	*	173(5)	109(3)	95(3)	68(2)	61(2)	30(1)	22(1)
3.00	*	*	*	*	195(6)	129(4)	95(3)	84(3)	61(2)	30(1)	22(1)
3.25	*	*	*	*	*	148(5)	112(4)	84(3)	61(2)	30(1)	22(1)
3.50	*	*	*	*	*	167(6)	112(4)	84(3)	76(3)	40(2)	22(1)
3.75	*	*	*	*	*	185(7)	129(5)	100(4)	76(3)	40(2)	22(1)
4.00	*	*	*	*	*	*	146(6)	100(4)	89(4)	40(2)	22(1)
5.00	*	*	*	*	*	*	*	158(8)	116(6)	40(2)	30(2)
6.00	*	*	*	*	*	*	*	*	179(11)	50(3)	30(2)
7.00	*	*	*	*	*	*	*	*	*	68(5)	37(3)

Note: This table assumes a large population.
*Sample size is too large to be cost-effective for most audit applications.
Source: AICPA, Auditing Procedure Study, in Audit Sampling (New York: AICPA, 1994).

FIGURE 8-4
Determination of sample size: reliability, 95%
(Risk of assessing control risk too low, 5%)
(Allowable number of deviations in parentheses)

applies the planned procedures to the 56 items and finds no deviations. The maximum deviation rate that could exist in the population at the specified risk level, given these sample results, can be determined as follows:

$$\text{MDR} = \frac{R}{n} = \frac{\text{risk factor}}{\text{sample size}}$$

$$= \frac{2.4}{56}$$

$$= 4.3\%$$

This means that there is 10 percent risk that the true deviation rate could be more than 4 percent and 90 percent assurance that it is no greater than 4 percent, given a sample of 56 with no deviations. Notice that the appropriate risk factor is 2.4 for a 10 percent risk of assessing control risk too low with 0 deviations. Since the tolerable rate was specified as 7 percent, the sample results indicate that the planned assessed level of control risk is appropriate.

If the auditor found 2 deviations in the sample of 56, the evaluation computation would be as follows:

$$\text{MDR} = \frac{R}{n} = \frac{\text{risk factor}}{\text{sample size}}$$

$$= \frac{5.4}{56}$$

$$= 9.6\%$$

Since the true deviation rate could be 10 percent, given a sample of 56 with 2 deviations with a 10 percent risk of assessing control risk too low and the tolerable rate is 7 percent, the auditor would conclude that the planned assessed level of control risk was not appropriate.

The maximum deviation rate can also be determined through use of tables such as those shown in Figures 8-5 and 8-6. The resulting rate is approximately the same.

Additional Features of the Statistical Model   This particular statistical model allows considerable flexibility in implementation. As a review of the illustrations for planning and evaluation indicates, whenever the number of deviations found exceeds the number expected, the maximum deviation rate will exceed the specified tolerable rate.

This means that the auditor may stop applying the planned procedures to selected items as soon as the expected number of deviations is exceeded. For example, if the first 2 items of the 56 selected are found to have deviations, there is no need to continue. However, this statistical model makes continuation convenient. For example, if after finding 2 deviations the auditor believes it is reasonable to expect no more deviations in additional items selected, a new sample size could be calculated as follows:

Sample size	Actual number of deviations found										
	0	1	2	3	4	5	6	7	8	9	10
20	10.9	18.1	*	*	*	*	*	*	*	*	*
25	8.8	14.7	19.9	*	*	*	*	*	*	*	*
30	7.4	12.4	16.8	*	*	*	*	*	*	*	*
35	6.4	10.7	14.5	18.1	*	*	*	*	*	*	*
40	5.6	9.4	12.8	16.0	19.0	*	*	*	*	*	*
45	5.0	8.4	11.4	14.3	17.0	19.7	*	*	*	*	*
50	4.6	7.6	10.3	12.9	15.4	17.8	*	*	*	*	*
55	4.1	6.9	9.4	11.8	14.1	16.3	18.4	*	*	*	*
60	3.8	6.4	8.7	10.8	12.9	15.0	16.9	18.9	*	*	*
70	3.3	5.5	7.5	9.3	11.1	12.9	14.6	16.3	17.9	19.6	*
80	2.9	4.8	6.6	8.2	9.8	11.3	12.8	14.3	15.8	17.2	18.6
90	2.6	4.3	5.9	7.3	8.7	10.1	11.5	12.8	14.1	15.4	16.6
100	2.3	3.9	5.3	6.6	7.9	9.1	10.3	11.5	12.7	13.9	15.0
120	2.0	3.3	4.4	5.5	6.6	7.6	8.7	9.7	10.7	11.6	12.6
160	1.5	2.5	3.3	4.2	5.0	5.8	6.5	7.3	8.0	8.8	9.5
200	1.2	2.0	2.7	3.4	4.0	4.6	5.3	5.9	6.5	7.1	7.6

Note: This table presents upper limits as percentages. This table assumes a large population.
*Over 20 percent.
Source: AICPA, Auditing Procedure Study, in *Audit Sampling* (New York: AICPA, 1994).

FIGURE 8-5

Evaluation of results: reliability, 90%
(Risk of assessing control risk too low, 10%)
Table presents achieved upper precision limit: percent rate of deviation

$$n = \frac{R}{TR} = \frac{\text{risk factor}}{\text{tolerable rate}}$$

$$= \frac{5.4}{0.07}$$

$$= 78$$

The auditor could expand the sample size to 78, and if no more deviations were found, the auditor could conclude that the maximum deviation rate did not exceed the tolerable rate.

Because of this feature of the statistical model it is sometimes called *stop-or-go sampling*. This feature of being able to incrementally expand sample size and continue testing is not possessed by other statistical models.

Other Statistical Models Other statistical models can be used for tests of transaction classes. These models, which are based on the binomial distribution, are generally called *acceptance sampling* and *discovery sampling*. Estimation of sample size with these models requires specification of

- Tolerable rate
- Risk of assessing control risk too low (and for certain acceptance sampling plans, risk of assessing control risk too high)

Sample size	Actual number of deviations found										
	0	1	2	3	4	5	6	7	8	9	10
25	11.3	17.6	*	*	*	*	*	*	*	*	*
30	9.5	14.9	19.6	*	*	*	*	*	*	*	*
35	8.3	12.9	17.0	*	*	*	*	*	*	*	*
40	7.3	11.4	15.0	18.3	*	*	*	*	*	*	*
45	6.5	10.2	13.4	16.4	19.2	*	*	*	*	*	*
50	5.9	9.2	12.1	14.8	17.4	19.9	*	*	*	*	*
55	5.4	8.4	11.1	13.5	15.9	18.2	*	*	*	*	*
60	4.9	7.7	10.2	12.5	14.7	16.8	18.8	*	*	*	*
65	4.6	7.1	9.4	11.5	13.6	15.5	17.4	19.3	*	*	*
70	4.2	6.6	8.8	10.8	12.6	14.5	16.3	18.0	19.7	*	*
75	4.0	6.2	8.2	10.1	11.8	13.6	15.2	16.9	18.5	20.0	*
80	3.7	5.8	7.7	9.5	11.1	12.7	14.3	15.9	17.4	18.9	*
90	3.3	5.2	6.9	8.4	9.9	11.4	12.8	14.2	15.5	16.8	18.2
100	3.0	4.7	6.2	7.6	9.0	10.3	11.5	12.8	14.0	15.2	16.4
125	2.4	3.8	5.0	6.1	7.2	8.3	9.3	10.3	11.3	12.3	13.2
150	2.0	3.2	4.2	5.1	6.0	6.9	7.8	8.6	9.5	10.3	11.1
200	1.5	2.4	3.2	3.9	4.6	5.2	5.9	6.5	7.2	7.8	8.4

Note: This table presents upper limits as percentages. This table assumes a large population.
*Over 20 percent.
Source: AICPA, Auditing Procedure Study, in *Audit Sampling* (New York: AICPA, 1994).

FIGURE 8-6
Evaluation of results: reliability, 95%
(Risk of assessing control risk too low, 5%)
Table presents achieved upper precision limit: percent rate of deviation

- Expected rate
- Population size

Because the Poisson distribution approximates the binomial distribution for large population sizes (approximately 1,000 or more), sample sizes and sample evaluation results are very similar. For relatively small populations, the binomial distribution produces more precise results and the Poisson distribution tends to be conservative (larger sample sizes and higher maximum deviation rates).

The formulas for the binomial distribution are much more complex so tables have been developed for computation of sample size and evaluation of results.

In a discovery sampling plan the expected rate is set at zero, and the auditor has assurance equal to 1 minus the risk of assessing control risk too low that at least 1 deviation will be found if the true deviation rate exceeds the tolerable rate. This type of plan minimizes the sample size necessary to evaluate whether a critical type of deviation exceeds the tolerable rate. The use of a zero expected rate to minimize sample size is also a feature of some formal nonstatistical sampling plans for tests of transaction classes.

Nonstatistical Sampling for Tests of Transaction Classes

The relationships among the sample size for a test of transaction classes and the considerations for planning the sample are as follows:

Tolerable rate. Sample size increases as the tolerable rate decreases. If the planned assessed level of control risk allows a higher tolerable rate, the sample size can be smaller.

Risk of assessing control risk too low. Sample size increases as the allowable risk of assessing control risk too low decreases. That is, to ensure low risk requires larger samples. If the auditor can accept a higher risk, the sample size can be smaller.

Expected rate. Sample size increases as the expected rate increases. Generally, as the expected rate approaches the tolerable rate, relatively large sample sizes are necessary.

The Informal Approach   An auditor could judgmentally estimate sample size by making a qualitative analysis of these planning considerations. The auditor could then judgmentally evaluate the sample results by considering the sample deviation rate and the sampling risk. That is one possible approach to nonstatistical sampling for tests of transaction classes.

Many auditors, however, are using a more formal approach. One of the reasons for not using the less formal approach explained above is that any randomly selected sample can be evaluated statistically and SAS No. 39 (AU 350) requires a representative selection method even for nonstatistical samples. This means that the sample results for a judgmentally established sample size can be evaluated with a quantification of sampling risk. For example, assume an auditor judgmentally establishes a sample size of 20, selects sample items randomly, applies the planned audit procedure to the selected items, and finds 1 deviation. What is the assessed level of operating effectiveness for the control procedure tested? A simple computation using the risk factor table in Figure 8-2 indicates that at a 10 percent risk of assessing control risk too low, the true deviation rate in the population could be as high as approximately 20 percent ($3.9 \div 20$). There is a 10 percent risk that it is higher. When sampling risk is considered, the sample results do not support an assessed level of control risk below "significant" using the table in Figure 8-1.

Would a judgmental consideration of sampling risk lead to the same conclusion? About the only acceptable justification for a conclusion not to change the planned assessed level would be that a qualitative analysis of the deviation indicated that it was not indicative of an important control deficiency. This could be true if the auditor's original definition of a deviation was poorly developed or if the deviation could be reliably established to be an isolated event with no chance of recurrence. However, this qualitative analysis of sample results would be equally valid for a statistical sample. Whether the sample is statistical or nonstatistical, a qualitative analysis of results is important.

A Formal Approach   Several CPA firms have adopted sampling plans for tests of transaction classes after making policy decisions on the following matters:

- How many qualitative levels of assessed control risk to use
- What tolerable rates would ordinarily permit those assessed levels of control risk (that is, the firm's version of Figure 8-1)
- Whether to use a fixed or variable risk of assessing control risk too low and if fixed, whether to use 5 percent or 10 percent
- How to incorporate differing circumstances for expected rates

Figure 8-7 presents a sample planning and evaluation table that a CPA firm might use based on the following policy decisions; four assessed levels of control risk (low, moderate, significant, and maximum); tolerable rates corresponding to those levels of low (7 percent), moderate (10 to 12 percent), significant (20 percent), and maximum (over 20 percent); a fixed 10 percent risk of assessing control risk too low.

An auditor using this table would consider the desired assessed level of control risk and the number of deviations expected. For example, if the auditor believed that the internal control structure would permit a low level of control risk, and expected no deviations, a sample size of 30 would be selected. If the planned audit procedure applied to selected items resulted in no deviations, an assessed level of low would be possible. If the sample of size 30 disclosed 1 deviation, the auditor would increase the assessed level of control risk to moderate. However, if the auditor believed that it was reasonable to expect no more deviations if sampling were continued, the auditor could expand the sample size to 50. If no more deviations were found, an assessed level of low would be possible. This flexibility is possible because the underlying sampling model is the Poisson distribution explained earlier. This approach is not appropriate with other attribute sampling models.

Several properties of the table should be noted. If the sample disclosed no deviations, a 30 sample size permits an assessed level of control risk of low and there is no point in using a larger sample size. This result is due to the subjective policy decision made about the relationship between tolerable rates and assessed levels of control risk. A sample of size 20 never permits more than a moderate level, and if more than 1 deviation is found results in assessment at maximum. This result is due to the policy decisions and the sampling risk associated with so small a sample. The table stops at a sample size of 60 even though the number of deviations and sample sizes could theoretically be increased indefinitely. Stopping at 60 is strictly a policy decision. At some point it makes more sense as a matter of both efficiency and effectiveness to assess control risk at significant or maximum and expand direct tests of balances. In other words, in some situations a substantive approach to the audit is better.

Number of deviations (planned or actual)	Sample size				
	20	30	40	50	60
0	Moderate	Low	Low	Low	Low
1	Significant	Moderate	Moderate	Low	Low
2	Maximum	Significant	Significant	Moderate	Moderate
3	Maximum	Maximum	Significant	Significant	Moderate
4	Maximum	Maximum	Significant	Significant	Significant
5	Maximum	Maximum	Maximum	Significant	Significant
6	Maximum	Maximum	Maximum	Maximum	Significant

FIGURE 8-7
Table for planning or evaluating tests of transaction classes using sampling. (The body of the table indicates the assessed level of control risk planned for conditions expected or found.)

This plan is called nonstatistical because approximations are used in the table for convenience. However, given the policy decisions, the sample sizes and evaluations are essentially the same as the statistical model presented earlier.

A formal plan of this nature has the following advantages over the alternative of supplying individual auditors with the formulas, a table of risk factors, and a calculator:

- The table is small and can be incorporated in a preprinted worksheet with space for related planning decisions and test results. Thus, it is convenient to use in the field.
- There is more assurance that auditors faced with the same circumstances will be using the same extent for tests.
- Extensive training in statistics is not necessary to implement the plan.
- Because the plan is simple and easy to use, there is more assurance that it will be followed with less chance of nonsampling error.

Except for these matters of implementation there is little difference between such a formal nonstatistical plan and a statistical plan. The reason for this is the relative simplicity of the mathematics of attribute sampling. In using sampling for direct tests of balances, additional complications result because the concern is with a monetary misstatement rather than a deviation rate.

AUDIT SAMPLING FOR DIRECT TESTS OF BALANCES

Audit sampling applies to direct tests of balances using either the balance approach or the transaction approach when the auditor intends to extend a conclusion based on testing a portion of the items to the balance. Generally, in the authoritative auditing literature these tests are referred to as substantive tests of details of account balances.

Planning Samples for Direct Tests of Balances

SAS No. 39 (AU 350.16) specifies that the following matters should be considered in planning the sample:

- The relationship of the sample to the relevant audit objective
- Preliminary judgments about materiality levels
- The auditor's allowable risk of incorrect acceptance
- Characteristics of the populations, that is, the items comprising the account balance ...

In the following discussion, these considerations are identified by shorthand terms commonly used in SAS No. 39 (AU 350) and practice:

- Sample-objective relationship
- Tolerable misstatement
- Risk of incorrect acceptance
- Expected misstatement, variability, and population size

Whether the auditor is using statistical or nonstatistical sampling, these considerations apply to planning the sample.

Sample-Objective Relationship The objectives that are relevant to direct tests of balances are the specific audit objectives for an account balance derived from the broad categories of assertions: existence, completeness, rights or obligations, valuation, and presentation and disclosure. Because of the characteristics of misstatements that can be detected by sampling, the *relevant audit objectives* are usually those related to *existence* or *valuation*. For example, by selecting from a list of items included in an account balance and applying audit procedures to them, the auditor could detect fictitious items, items incorrectly included in the balance (misclassifications), and misvalued items. However, the auditor could not detect items omitted from the balance (specific audit objectives related to the completeness assertion).

Generally, the other decisions in this step are similar to those for the comparable step in planning tests of transaction classes. The auditor should identify the population and sample unit; specify the physical representation (frame) of the population from which sample items will be selected; establish that the frame is physically complete and corresponds to the population (usually by footing). Naturally, the characteristic of interest is a monetary misstatement of the account balance.

An aspect of identifying the population that is unique to direct tests of balances is analysis of the account balance to *identify individually significant items.* An item could be individually significant because of its size or its nature. This type of analysis is illustrated for property and equipment in Chapter 7, based on the size of items. An item could be individually significant because of its nature for a variety of reasons. Essentially, anything that causes the auditor to believe that particular items in the account balance are subject to a greater risk of material misstatement could cause those items to be considered significant. For example, a gross profit analysis by product and location may indicate that certain inventory items are more likely to be misstated. The portion of the account balance remaining after identification of individually significant items is the population subject to sampling.

Tolerable Misstatement The tolerable misstatement for an account balance is, in effect, materiality at the account balance level. It is the maximum amount of monetary misstatement that can exist in an account balance that when combined with monetary misstatement in other account balances would not cause the financial statements taken as a whole to be materially misstated. As tolerable misstatement increases, the necessary sample size decreases.

Tolerable misstatement, as explained in Chapter 7, is related to the allowance for undetected misstatement for the financial statements taken as a whole. Because the nature of this relationship is more easily understood after certain statistical concepts are understood, the relationship is explained in a later section of this chapter.

Risk of Incorrect Acceptance The auditor's allowable risk of incorrect acceptance is the risk the auditor is willing to accept that the sample supports the conclusion that the recorded account balance is not materially misstated when it is materially misstated. It is an aspect of sampling risk for a direct test of a balance using audit sampling.

In planning the sample for a direct test of a balance, the risk of incorrect acceptance is the *detection risk* for the test. Thus, it is established using the risk model presented in Chapter 7 in the discussion of audit risk at the account balance level. The auditor assesses inherent risk and control risk and establishes detection risk at the level appropriate to hold audit risk for the account balance to a relatively low level.

In quantitative terms, a relatively low level of audit risk would be 5 percent or 10 percent. Notice, however, that audit risk and not detection risk needs to be held to this relatively low level. If the auditor concludes that the likelihood of material misstatement in the account balance is low, the detection risk for the direct test of a balance using audit sampling can be relatively high. As the allowable risk of incorrect acceptance increases, the necessary sample size decreases.

When the auditor uses statistical sampling for a direct test of a balance, the detection risk for the audit procedure using sampling (risk of incorrect acceptance) has to be specified as a percentage. The model for quantitative estimation of detection risk explained in Chapter 7 can be used for this purpose. For nonstatistical samples, the evaluation can be entirely qualitative. Methods for qualitative evaluation are explained in Chapter 7.

There is another aspect of sampling risk for direct tests of balances—the *risk of incorrect rejection*. This is the risk that the sample supports the conclusion that the account balance is materially misstated when it is not. This aspect of sampling risk is not specified as a consideration in planning samples because it relates to audit efficiency rather than effectiveness. If the auditor incorrectly concludes that an account balance is materially misstated, the auditor would ordinarily expand direct tests of balances and ultimately reach the appropriate conclusion.

Expected Misstatement, Variability, and Population Size   The characteristics of the population that are relevant to a direct test of a balance are expected misstatement, variability, and population size. Generally, as the size and frequency of expected misstatement increase or as the variability increases, or as population size increases, larger sample sizes are necessary. However, expected misstatement and variability have a much more significant influence on sample size than the size of the population. The auditor can reduce the effects of variability by using stratified random selection or the probability proportional to size selection method.

Selection of Samples for Direct Tests of Balances

The representative selection methods discussed earlier are generally appropriate for selection of samples for direct tests of balances. However, as mentioned above, some form of stratification may increase efficiency. SAS No. 39 (AU 350.22) explains the point as follows:

> The auditor may be able to reduce the required sample size by separating items subject to sampling into relatively homogeneous groups on the basis of some characteristic related to the specific audit objective. For example, common bases for such groupings are recorded or book value of the items. . . .

This advice applies to both statistical and nonstatistical audit samples.

Evaluation of Sample Results of Direct Tests of Balances

After the planned audit procedure has been applied to selected items, the auditor may have detected monetary misstatement. This monetary misstatement has to be projected to the population from which the sample was selected.

There are several ways to project monetary misstatement. For example, assume that an auditor has examined the support for additions to property and equipment and found a net monetary overstatement in the sample. The relevant information is as follows:

Amount of additions	$1,000,000
Number of additions	1,000
Sample size	60
Tolerable misstatement	$ 50,000
Sample misstatement	$ 2,000
Sample balance	$ 100,000

For simplicity, it is assumed that the auditor did not identify individually significant items or stratify the items so that the total dollar amount of additions and the population subject to sampling are the same. However, in practice these steps would usually be considered necessary. The sample balance is the dollar total of sample items.

The *difference method* of projection is an extrapolation of the average misstatement of the sample items. Projected misstatement by this method is $33,334 ($2,000 ÷ 60 × 1,000). The *ratio method* of projection is based on the ratio of the sample balance to the population balance or, in this case, 10 percent ($100,000 ÷ $1,000,000). The sample misstatement is divided by this ratio to estimate projected misstatement of $20,000 ($2,000 ÷ 0.10). Generally, the ratio method is appropriate. The difference method is appropriate only when the auditor expects that the amount of misstatement in a sample item will not be influenced by the size of the item, that is, the amount of misstatement will be constant.

The auditor next compares projected misstatement to tolerable misstatement and considers the sampling risk. In the example given, projected misstatement of $20,000 is less than tolerable misstatement of $50,000, but the auditor has to consider the risk that this result might be obtained from a sample of 60 out of 1,000 items even though the true monetary misstatement exceeds tolerable misstatement. This risk can be quantified for a statistical sample but must be evaluated judgmentally for a nonstatistical sample.

The auditor also needs to consider the qualitative aspects of sample misstatement. The auditor should consider the nature and cause of the misstatement and their implications for other phases of the audit. A misstatement in the application of a complex accounting principle has different implications than a potential irregularity.

Finally, the auditor needs to relate the sample evaluation to the results of other audit procedures relevant to the account balance and combine the results of all audit tests and evaluate the effect on the financial statements taken as a whole. The combination of results of all audit tests is considered in Chapter 12.

Nonstatistical Sampling for Direct Tests of Balances

Nonstatistical sampling for direct tests of balances can be applied formally or informally. The informal approach would be to judgmentally evaluate the planning considerations to estimate sample size and judgmentally consider the sampling risk in evaluating sample results. For example, the auditor knows that larger tolerable misstatement and allowable risk of incorrect acceptance permit smaller sample sizes. The auditor could judgmentally relate these considerations and combined with past experience establish a judgmental sample size. Also, the auditor knows that as projected misstatement approaches tolerable misstatement the sampling risk increases. The auditor could compute projected misstatement and judgmentally compare it to tolerable misstatement in considering sampling risk.

A more formal approach to nonstatistical sampling is to use a method that approximates a statistical model. The formal approach explained here uses the Poisson distribution explained earlier. The nonstatistical approximation is explained first because some of the computations for approximation are easier to understand than the comparable, but more precise, statistical computations.

Sample Size Estimation   Recall that the underlying statistical model estimates sample size by dividing the appropriate risk factor by the tolerable rate (R/TR). The same method can be used for a direct test of a balance by converting tolerable misstatement to a rate. If the population subject to sampling is designated as book value (BV), then the ratio of tolerable misstatement (TM) to book value (BV) is the tolerable rate. The formula as presented earlier then becomes

$$n = \frac{R}{TM/BV} = \frac{\text{risk factor}}{\text{tolerable misstatement} \div \text{book value}}$$

For convenience, this is usually presented as

$$n = \frac{BV \times R}{TM}$$

If the portion of the amount balance subject to sampling is $1,000,000 (BV), and the tolerable misstatement is $50,000 (TM), the risk of incorrect acceptance is 5 percent, and an appropriate risk factor (R) is identified in the table in Figure 8-2 as 3.0, then the sample size *(n)* can be estimated as follows:

$$n = \frac{\$1,000,000 \times 3}{\$50,000}$$

$$= 60$$

On this point, the approximation and the statistical model are identical. The same formula is used to estimate sample size.

Selecting the Risk Factor   The risk factors for the Poisson distribution are the same for tests of transaction classes or direct tests of balances. However, it is usually more efficient to construct a specialized table for direct tests of balances for several reasons.

One reason is that there are more complex considerations for establishing the risk of incorrect acceptance. The risk of assessing control risk too low needs to be relatively low because there are few relevant sources of information other than the results of the tests of transaction classes. However, the allowable risk of incorrect acceptance (detection risk for the audit procedure using sampling) is established by considering audit risk at the account balance level as explained in Chapter 7. Audit risk has to be relatively low, but the risk of incorrect acceptance may be higher if other components of audit risk, such as control risk, have been assessed as relatively low.

The method for making a quantitative estimate of detection risk, explained in Chapter 7, may be used to establish a specific percentage for the risk of incorrect acceptance. The relationship between risk factors and specific percentages of the risk of incorrect acceptance is as follows:

Risk of incorrect acceptance, %	Risk factor
5.0	3.0
7.5	2.6
10.0	2.3
12.5	2.1
15.0	1.9
20.0	1.6
25.0	1.4
30.0	1.2
40.0	0.9
50.0	0.7

The risk factors are taken from the Poisson distribution for the specified risk levels for zero expected misstatement. The consideration of expected misstatement is another reason for the additional complexity of selecting the appropriate risk factor. The statistical model incorporates the frequency of deviation, but a direct test of a balance is concerned with the dollar amount of misstatement. In the approach presented here expected misstatement is considered in establishing tolerable misstatement, as explained later, and the risk factors used to estimate sample size are those presented above for specified percentages of the risk of incorrect acceptance.

Figure 8-8 presents a table of risk factors for estimating sample size based on qualitative evaluations for the assessed level of control risk and other relevant audit procedures directed to the same specific audit objective as the audit procedure being planned using sampling. Notice that the assessed level of control risk can be directly related to the table for evaluating tests of transaction classes presented in Figure 8-7.

The table presented in Figure 8-8 is stated and can be used based entirely on qualitative evaluations. However, the table was prepared using the quantitative risk model and specified percentages in Figure 7-2 with inherent risk at the maximum. As explained in Chapter 7, a separate assessment of inherent risk is controversial. Inherent risk is assumed to be at the maximum here for convenience.

Assessed level of control risk	Reliance on other relevant audit procedures			
	None	Little	Moderate	Substantial
Maximum	3.0	3.0	2.6	2.1
Significant	3.0	2.6	2.3	1.9
Moderate	2.6	2.3	2.1	1.6
Low	2.1	1.9	1.6	1.2

FIGURE 8-8
Table for selecting appropriate risk factor based on the assessed level of control risk and other relevant auditing procedures.

Establishing the allowable risk of incorrect acceptance is a necessary step in both statistical and nonstatistical sampling. If an informal nonstatistical approach is used, no purpose is served by identifying a risk factor to correspond to a specified percentage for the risk of incorrect acceptance. However, the formal nonstatistical plan presented here and the statistical model are identical on this point—both require identification of the appropriate risk factor. The risk factor may also be used to determine the cutoff amount for individually significant items. The rule-of-thumb of dividing tolerable misstatement by 3 to determine a cutoff amount is based on the risk factor for a 5 percent detection risk.

Sample Selection   The appropriate selection method for the statistical model is the probability proportional to size (PPS) method discussed earlier. For the formal nonstatistical plan, this method may be approximated. The PPS method gives each item in the population a chance of being selected that is proportional to its dollar size. Essentially, this means that larger items are more likely to be selected. Auditors have traditionally emphasized this approach so it is intuitively appealing. The auditor can approximate this selection method simply by selecting more large items and fewer smaller items. However, when a population has many items, a good approximation is difficult to achieve.

PPS selection is often done using audit software. The time required to obtain the information about the client data file and set up the audit software application may sometimes exceed the effort to perform the selection manually. The auditor should select the most efficient method to select the sample. One nonstatistical approach to approximate PPS selection is to subdivide the population into a few groups of approximately equal dollar amount. Approximate subdivisions may be determined by (1) frequently subtotaling when footing the population, (2) footing without using some of the rightmost digits and frequently subtotaling, or (3) using page totals that may have already been accumulated and substantiated. For example, assume the auditor is trying to approximate PPS sampling in selection of property and equipment addition items from a detail listing:

Remaining population recorded amount: $1,000,000
Estimated sample size: 60 items

The auditor decides to subdivide the remaining population into three groups of items with an approximately equal recorded amount; therefore, each subdivision should approximately equal $334,000 ($1,000,000/3, rounded), and 20 items (60/3) should be selected from each subdivision. The auditor foots the remaining population, ignoring the four rightmost digits (XX.XX). The auditor subtotals the pages and determines the following subdivisions for the purpose of sample selection:

Pages 1–10: $311,000
Pages 11–35: $337,000
Pages 36–40: $352,000

The auditor selects sample items from each subdivision by scanning the subdivisions and selecting more large items than small items. The use of this type of approximation is a significant difference from the statistical model. The PPS selection method is illustrated later.

Sample Evaluation   Whether the auditor uses statistical or nonstatistical sampling for direct tests of balances, a projection of sample misstatement results to the population is necessary. The projection method explained here is based on the PPS sampling model and recognizes that larger items are selected more often than smaller items. Each misstatement is evaluated using the percentage of misstatement occurring—the so-called misstatement proportion.

The misstatement proportion is calculated by dividing the misstatement amount by the recorded amount. For example, if a $100 item (recorded amount) is misstated by $10 (audit value $90), the misstatement proportion is 10 percent. The projected misstatement is calculated by determining the sum of the misstatement proportions (SMP), multiplying by the dollar amount of the remaining population (BV), and dividing by the sample size as shown in the following formula:

$$\frac{\text{SMP} \times \text{BV}}{n}$$

For example, assume that in testing property and equipment additions, the auditor detects the following errors and computes the sum of misstatement proportions as shown in the following table:

SAMPLE ITEMS THAT CONTAIN MISSTATEMENTS

Recorded amount	Audited amount	Misstatement amount	Misstatement proportion
$10,530	$10,310	$ 220	0.02
5,740	4,018	1,722	0.30
3,114	3,425	(311)	(0.10)
			0.22

Using the formula explained above and the amounts for BV and *n* from the earlier example, the auditor calculates projected misstatement as follows:

$$\frac{0.22 \times \$1,000,000}{60} = \$3,667$$

Notice that by converting the dollar amount of sample misstatement to a proportion, the auditor is converting to a rate. In effect, the relation of the sum of misstatement proportions to sample size (SMP/n) is the auditor's best estimate of the rate of misstatement for the sample. Multiplying by the book value converts to the best estimate of monetary misstatement for the population. However, this computation does not consider the sampling risk. Using this approach to sample evaluation, the auditor can only consider sampling risk judgmentally. The statistical model allows a more precise projection of misstatement and quantifies the sampling risk.

Importance of Qualitative Evaluation   A qualitative evaluation of sample results is equally as important as quantitative evaluation whether the auditor is using a statistical or nonstatistical sampling approach. SAS No. 39 (AU 350.27) provides the following guidance related to the use of audit sampling in direct tests of balances:

> In addition to the evaluation of the frequency and amounts of monetary misstatements, consideration should be given to the qualitative aspects of the misstatements. These include (a) the nature and cause of misstatements, such as whether they are differences in principle or in application, are errors or irregularities, or are due to misunderstanding of instructions or carelessness, and (b) the possible relationship of the misstatements to other phases of the audit. The discovery of an irregularity ordinarily requires a broader consideration of possible implications than does the discovery of an error.

An important part of the auditor's qualitative evaluation is a consideration of whether the nature and cause of misstatements indicate that they are either isolated or systematic. An *isolated misstatement* is one caused by unusual circumstances that the auditor is convinced occurred only once. A *systematic misstatement* is one that would occur every time particular conditions occurred. A quantitative projection of either a systematic misstatement or an isolated misstatement would be incorrect. A projected misstatement based on an isolated misstatement would be overstated, and a projection of a systematic misstatement could be seriously understated.

For example, an auditor samples additions to property and finds two misstatements. One is for an addition constructed by the company and is caused by interest cost that should have been but was not capitalized. The auditor knows that all additions except this one were acquired from outside vendors. This isolated misstatement should not be projected. The other misstatement occurred because one of several clerks working on the property ledger did not understand that freight cost should be capitalized. This is a systematic misstatement, and all additions recorded by this clerk will be in error. The client should be asked to identify the additions recorded by the clerk and recompute acquisition cost.

Statistical Sampling for Direct Tests of Balances

Having considered the nonstatistical approximation of PPS sampling, it is possible to focus on those aspects of the statistical model that differ. These were identified in the earlier discussion as sample selection and sample evaluation.

Sample Selection   Using the PPS statistical model, the sample unit is individual dollar units rather than physical units. A population with $1,000,000 that contains 1,000 physical units is viewed as a population with 1,000,000 sample units—the individual dollars. When an individual dollar is selected, however, it is naturally attached to the other dollars associated with the physical unit, and the dollar selected drags the dollar amount of the item with it. In other words, the dollar unit identifies which physical unit the audit procedure is used to test.

In practice, the most commonly applied method of PPS selection is systematic sampling with a *dollar* interval. The dollar interval is determined by dividing the dollar amount of the population by sample size (BV ÷ n). To use this method the characteristic of interest—dollars—should be randomly distributed. This means items should not, for example, be listed in descending order from the largest dollar item to the smallest. In accounting populations, items are usually listed in chronological order, by item sequence number, or by some characteristic other than dollar size so this is not a problem.

To use systematic dollar-interval selection, the auditor needs to accumulate the cumulative dollar total of items in the population by item. A random start is established within the first interval to determine the first item selected, and the dollar interval is added to determine the next item. The random start plus two times the sampling interval determines the third item and so on through the population.

Figure 8-9 presents an example of the use of this PPS selection method. The invoice numbers and dollar amounts of the items would be listed in the client's accounting records. The cumulative total would have to be computed by the auditor. This would be accomplished by footing through the population either manually or with computer assistance.

The random start could be established by multiplying the dollar sampling interval by the serial number of a dollar bill with a decimal placed in front of it. In the example of Figure 8-9 the random start is the 14,068th dollar. This dollar is contained in item A1003 so that is the first item selected. The dollar sampling interval is added to the random start to determine the next item to be selected. The 30,735th dollar is contained in item A1005 so that is the next item selected. The selection process continues in this manner through the population. Notice that all items larger than the sampling interval are always selected.

Manual selection using the PPS method can be time-consuming if the population is large. However, computer software is often used to make the selection.

Because the PPS selection method makes the probability of an item's selection directly proportional to its size, items with a negative or a zero amount need to be treated as a separate population. For example, an accounts receivable trial balance might contain credit balances (overpayments or advances) and zero balances (paid-up accounts). These accounts would not have to be physically removed from the trial balance, but the auditor would need to skip them in calculating the cumulative total and use another method to select them if applying the planned audit procedure to zero or credit balances was necessary.

Sample Evaluation   The evaluation of sample results is the most complex aspect of PPS statistical sampling. The first important concept to understand is the so-called basic bound of monetary misstatement. The *basic bound* is the maximum monetary

Invoice no.	Amount of item	Cumulative total
A1001	$ 6,000	$ 6,000
A1002	1,000	7,000
A1003	15,000	22,000
A1004	5,000	27,000
A1005	12,000	39,000
A1006	10,000	49,000
A1007	9,000	58,000
A1008	17,000	75,000
A1009	11,000	86,000
A1010	8,000	94,000
A1011	7,000	111,000
•	•	•
•	•	•
•	•	•

Population size (BV)	$1,000,000
Sample size (n)	60
Sampling interval (SI)	
($1,000,000 ÷ 60)	$16,667
Random start (RS)	$14,068

ITEMS SELECTED

		Invoice no.	Amount
RS	$14,068	A1003	$15,000
RS + SI	30,735	A1005	12,000
RS + 2SI	47,402	A1006	10,000
RS + 3SI	64,609	A1008	17,000
RS + 4SI	80,736	A1009	11,000
RS + 5SI	97,403	A1011	7,000
•	•	•	•
•	•	•	•
•	•	•	•

FIGURE 8-9
Illustration of PPS selection using systematic sampling with a dollar interval.

misstatement that could exist in the population when no monetary misstatements are found in the sample. The ability to compute an upper limit on monetary misstatement when no misstatements are found in the sample is one of the advantages of this method.

Since the statistical model for the PPS method is the Poisson distribution, the computations are very similar to those explained earlier for tests of transaction classes. Recall that the maximum deviation rate is computed by dividing the appropriate risk factor by sample size (R/n). To compute the basic bound; the ratio of R to n is multiplied by the dollar amount of the population (BV). The formula is

$$\frac{R_0}{n} \times BV$$

The use of R_0 means the risk factor for zero misstatement at the specified risk percentage. For example, if the auditor took a sample of 60 from a population of $1,000,000 and found no monetary misstatements, the basic bound at a 5 percent risk of incorrect acceptance would be computed as follows:

$$\frac{3.0}{60} \times \$1,000,000 = \$50,000$$

The risk factor for zero error, 3.0, and other risk factors in the following discussion are from the table in Figure 8-2.

Notice that the basic bound will, other matters remaining the same, equal the tolerable misstatement used to estimate sample size. As explained earlier, the sample size formula is

$$n = \frac{BV \times R_0}{TM}$$

At a specified risk of incorrect acceptance of 5 percent:

$$n = \frac{\$1,000,000 \times 3.0}{\$50,000}$$

$$= 60$$

The tolerable misstatement and sample size are established in planning, but as demonstrated above, the basic bound computed in evaluation will equal the tolerable misstatement used to estimate sample size. Of course, if monetary misstatements are found and the initial sample size is expanded, the basic bound may also be changed.

The computation of the basic bound explained above is a conservative allowance for undetected misstatement in the population. It combines the upper limit on frequency of error (R_0/n) with an assumption that each item in error is completely misstated. In accounting populations that is seldom the case, but this conservative approach is generally used in practice because of lack of a reasonable basis for a less than complete misstatement.

When monetary misstatements are found in the sample, there is a reasonable basis for evaluating partial rather than complete misstatements. The misstatement proportions, as calculated in the example for sample evaluation using the formal nonstatistical plan, can be used. For example, if a $100 item is misstated by $10 (audit value $90), the misstatement proportion is 10 percent.

The misstatement proportion of each misstatement is used to compute *additions to the basic bound* for the effect of finding each misstatement. The incremental effect of each misstatement is computed by the difference between risk factors. $R_1 - R_0/n$ would be the incremental effect of finding one monetary misstatement and $R_2 - R_1/n$ would be the incremental effect of a second monetary misstatement. This incremental effect is then weighted by the misstatement proportion and multiplied by book value to compute the addition to the basic bound. An addition to the basic bound is made for each misstatement, and overstatements and understatements are computed separately. Also, misstatements need to be ranked in descending order.

The result of these computations will be a maximum monetary overstatement and a maximum monetary understatement that includes quantification of sampling risk. Figure 8-10 presents these computations for the three monetary misstatements used in the earlier example for nonstatistical sample evaluation.

Also illustrated in Figure 8-10 are computations for projected overstatement and projected understatement. These projected misstatements represent the auditor's best esti-

---

Overstatements

1st addition to basic bound

$$\frac{4.8 - 3.0}{60} \times \$1,000,000 \times 0.30 = \$\ 9,000$$

2nd addition to basic bound

$$\frac{6.3 - 4.8}{60} \times \$1,000,000 \times 0.02 = \$\quad 500$$
$$= \$\ 9,500$$

Understatements

$$\frac{4.8 - 3.0}{60} \times \$1,000,000 \times 0.10 = \$\ 3,000$$

Maximum overstatement

$50,000 + \$9,500 \qquad\qquad = \$59,500$

Maximum understatement

$50,000 + \$3,000 \qquad\qquad = \$53,000$

Projected overstatement

$$\frac{0.32}{60} \times \$1,000,000 \qquad\qquad = \$5,333$$

Projected understatement

$$\frac{0.10}{60} \times \$1,000,000 \qquad\qquad = \$1,667$$

Net maximum overstatement

$59,500 - \$1,667 \qquad\qquad = \$57,833$

Net maximum understatement

$53,000 - \$5,333 \qquad\qquad = \$47,667$

FIGURE 8-10
Computation for evaluation of sample misstatements using PPS statistical methods.

mate of misstatement. They are computed for both overstatements and understatements using the sum of misstatement proportions for misstatement of each type. The projected overstatement is deducted from the maximum understatement to determine net maximum understatement. The projected understatement is deducted from the maximum overstatement to determine net maximum overstatement. The purpose of these adjustments is to control for the risk of incorrect rejection. The auditor's evaluation of sample results is based on these net maximum amounts. The auditor has to decide whether to accept the account balance as not materially misstated or to reject it. However, the projected misstatement for the account balance needs to be combined with uncorrected known misstatement and projected misstatement from other account balances to consider the effect on the financial statements taken as a whole. This combined evaluation is explained in Chapter 12.

The auditor's basic criterion in deciding whether to accept or reject an account balance is whether the projected misstatement exceeds the expected misstatement considered in planning the sample. If the auditor rejects the account balance, the most effective approach is usually to expand the portion of the account balance examined 100 percent. The auditor would identify individually significant items and examine all of them. The remaining population would be sampled. Any monetary misstatement in items examined 100 percent is known misstatement, and the known misstatement can readily be corrected by the client.

In PPS statistical applications all items larger than the sampling interval are considered to be individually significant and are examined 100 percent. Monetary misstatement in these items is known misstatement and is not projected. For this reason the actual sample size may be smaller than the planned sample size. However, the remaining population sampled (BV) will also be smaller than the amount used in planning.

Also, the auditor's qualitative analysis of detected misstatement may influence the evaluation. The auditor always considers the nature and cause of detected misstatements. This analysis may allow the auditor to focus on a particular cause of misstatement and result in modification of projected misstatement. For example, if the auditor finds that all misstatement in additions to property and equipment occurred in only one division out of four in the company, the misstatement would be projected only for the portion of the population attributable to that division.

Establishing Tolerable Misstatement for Sampling Applications

As explained in Chapter 7, the auditor makes a preliminary judgment during general planning about the amount to be considered material to the financial statements taken as a whole. Based on estimates of the uncorrected known misstatement and projected misstatement that will exist after audit procedures are applied, the auditor reduces the preliminary judgment for these estimates to derive the allowance for potential undetected misstatement.

Relation of Allowance for Undetected Misstatement to Tolerable Misstatement

In sampling applications based on the Poisson distribution, the tolerable misstatement and the allowance for undetected misstatement for the financial statements taken as a whole may be equal. This relationship holds for PPS statistical sampling and nonstatistical approximations based on the PPS model.

This relationship is not intuitively apparent and requires some explanation. In the PPS model the sample unit is an individual dollar. The financial statements taken as a whole may be viewed as a collection of dollars and considered to be one population subject to sampling. Obviously, the allowance for undetected misstatement is the tolerable misstatement for the financial statements. It is the maximum amount of misstatement that could exist in the financial statements that when combined with uncorrected known misstatement and projected misstatement would not cause the financial statements to be materially misstated. The tolerable misstatement for the financial statements also applies to each of the sampling applications.

The sample size formula for the PPS model allocates the extent of audit tests among sampling applications, but the tolerable misstatement for all the sampling applications can be the same. This property of the PPS model is demonstrated in Figure 8-11. Conceptually, because the PPS model focuses on dollar units rather than physical units, the populations for sampling applications may be totaled to find one population of dollars. The combined sample size for this combined population can be determined using the

Sample size for individual sampling applications

Receivables

$$\frac{\$950,000 \times 3.0}{\$50,000} = 57$$

Inventory

$$\frac{\$1,220,000 \times 3.0}{\$50,000} = 73$$

Property and equipment

$$\frac{\$630,000 \times 3.0}{\$50,000} = \underline{38}$$

Total   168

Sample size for combined sampling applications

Receivables	$ 950,000
Inventory	1,220,000
Property and equipment	630,000
	$2,800,000

$$\frac{\$2,800,000 \times 3.0}{\$50,000} = \underline{168}$$

FIGURE 8-11
Comparison of individual and combined sample sizes using PPS sampling.

PPS formula. The example uses a tolerable misstatement of $50,000 and a risk of incorrect acceptance of 5 percent. Notice that when sample size is computed for each of the individual sampling applications using the same tolerable misstatement for each, the total of the individual sample sizes is the same as the combined sample size.

This nonadditive nature of tolerable misstatement may also be understood by considering an example unrelated to accounting populations. Assume that you are able to estimate the weight of each person in a room of 30 students to within 5 pounds for each student and that your weight estimates are unbiased (some are overestimates and some are underestimates). Would you expect the total of your estimates to equal the combined weight of the 30 students within 5 pounds or within 150 pounds (5 pounds for each of the 30 students)? You would expect your combined estimate to be off by closer to 5 pounds than 150 pounds. The same principle applies to tolerable misstatement for sampling applications.

Conceptually, all the sampling applications in an audit could be viewed as one population, but that is seldom done because the appropriate risk factor is usually different for each application. The auditor's assessment of the level of control risk and other relevant audit procedures will result in different allowable risks of incorrect acceptance for each application. However, the tolerable misstatement for all sampling applications using the PPS statistical model or nonstatistical approximations of it may by the same.

Estimates of Projected Misstatement for Sampling Applications   The use of the PPS statistical model adds one complicating feature to the development of an allowance for undetected misstatement and, thus, the tolerable misstatement for sampling applications. When sample misstatement is projected, the projected misstatement is itself an estimate, and there is a sampling risk attached to making the estimate. The PPS statistical evaluation method quantifies this sampling risk. This quantification can be seen by comparing related amounts in Figure 8-10. Notice that for the two overstatement errors the combined additions to the basic bound are $9,500, but the projected overstatement for the same two misstatements is only $5,333. The difference between these two amounts is the quantification of sampling risk of the projection. The statistical term for this is the *precision-widening gap.*

When projected misstatement is expected in PPS sampling applications, the auditor's preliminary judgment about materiality needs to be reduced for both the amount of projected misstatement and this precision-widening effect in establishing the allowance for undetected misstatement and, thus, tolerable misstatement. The following guideline has been developed for this purpose:

Projected misstatement as a percentage of adjusted materiality, %	Additional imprecision as a percentage of adjusted materiality, %
10	10
20	15
30	20
40	25
50	25

Adjusted materiality is the auditor's preliminary judgment about materiality reduced by anticipated, uncorrected known misstatement. As mentioned in Chapter 7, some auditors simply use 50 percent to 75 percent of the preliminary judgment as the tolerable misstatement instead of making these estimates.

Other Statistical Models

The PPS statistical model has a variety of other names that emphasize particular aspects of the model. It is called *DUS (dollar unit sampling)* or *MUS (monetary unit sampling)* because the sampling unit is a dollar or other monetary unit. It is called *CAV (combined attribute-variable)* sampling because the evaluation method combines attribute mathematics with conclusions about variables (monetary misstatement). It is also called *CMA (cumulative monetary amount)* sampling because the selection method requires computation of the cumulative amount of each population item.

The other statistical models that can be used in direct tests of balances differ in many respects from the PPS model. Generally, these models are referred to as classical statistical sampling methods because they all use the normal distribution and related mathematics. They are also called *variables sampling methods* because the characteristic of interest is a variable rather than an attribute, and *estimation sampling* because they are used to estimate the characteristic of interest. In auditing, the characteristic of interest is monetary misstatement, and the estimation sampling methods are used in a hypothesis testing format—does monetary misstatement in a recorded balance exceed a material amount? The appendix to this chapter describes estimation sampling using an audit hypothesis testing approach.

The primary classical statistical sampling methods used in auditing are mean-per-unit estimation, difference estimation, and ratio estimation. These are described in the appendix to this chapter. Some of the essential differences of these methods from the PPS model are as follows:

- Sample size is influenced by the standard deviation of the population (a measure of population variability). The standard deviation needs to be estimated to determine sample size. (Thus, sample size can be reduced by stratification to reduce the standard deviation within each subgroup.)
- Both the risk of incorrect acceptance and the risk of incorrect rejection are specified to estimate sample size.
- The tolerable misstatement for a sampling application cannot be equal to the allowance for undetected misstatement for the financial statements taken as a whole. The allowance for undetected misstatement needs to be allocated to sampling applications, but the relationship is still not additive. The sum of tolerable misstatements for sampling applications can exceed the allowance for undetected misstatement for the financial statements.

No matter what statistical model is used for direct tests of balances, the basic requirements are those established by SAS No. 39 (AU 350). The relationships among tolerable misstatement, risk of incorrect acceptance, expected misstatement, and variability and sample size remain the same. The auditor should consider these relationships in planning and evaluating the sample for all audit sampling applications.

APPENDIX: ESTIMATION SAMPLING—AN AUDIT HYPOTHESIS TESTING APPROACH

Accounting Estimation versus Audit Hypothesis Testing

Variables sampling can be used to develop an estimate of an amount. An accountant might use variables sampling to calculate an amount to be included in the financial statements [for example, a LIFO (last in, first out) inventory calculation]. In auditing, variables sampling can be used to test an amount in an account balance. The auditor uses sampling to create an estimate of the amount, and compares it to the amount recorded by the client. If the estimate is reasonably close to the recorded amount, the sampling procedure has provided audit evidence supporting the balance.

When sampling is used to develop the estimate to be recorded in the account balance, the accountant is using an *accounting estimation approach.* When the auditor compares sample results to the recorded amount to decide whether the recorded amount is materially misstated, the auditor is using an *audit hypothesis testing approach.* In using the audit hypothesis testing approach, the auditor needs to be concerned about both the *risk of incorrect rejection* and the *risk of incorrect acceptance.*

There are several estimation sampling techniques auditors use:

- Mean per unit (MPU) (unstratified and stratified)
- Difference estimation
- Ratio estimation

Mean-per-Unit Estimation

In the mean-per-unit technique, the auditor selects sample items from the population and determines the audited value of each item selected. The auditor calculates the average value (the *mean*) of the items and multiplies the average value by the number of items in the population. This type of estimate is called a *simple extension.* If the average value of the items is $30.75 and there are 1,000 items in the population, the estimated value is $30,750. The mean times the number of items is called the *point estimate.* The audit sample assures the auditor that the point estimate plus or minus the precision limit at a specified reliability percentage includes the true value of the population. For example, using this technique the auditor would be able to make a statement such as, "I am 95 percent confident that the range of $1,375,457 plus or minus $38,450 includes the actual value of the inventory."

When to Use Mean-per-Unit Estimation   Without stratification, the mean-per-unit technique requires relatively large sample sizes to reduce sampling risk to a reasonable level. Auditors would not use a technique that requires such large sample sizes if a more efficient alternative were available. Auditors tend to use this technique when, for example, there are recorded values equal to zero in the account balance that should be audited to see if they should equal zero (which would not be selected using PPS), or when the book value for each item in the population is not easily available. In such situations, the MPU audit sample can provide useful audit evidence.

Auditing especially large or unusual items separately, removing them from the sample population, helps reduce the needed sample size. Also stratifying the population into two or more subpopulations also tends to reduce the total number of sample items needed. A measure of the variability of the population, called the *standard deviation,* is used in calculating the sample size. A widely diverse population tends to have a large standard deviation. If the population is divided up into several smaller subpopulations *(strata)* containing similar items, each subpopulation of similar items will have a smaller standard deviation than that of the population taken as a whole. For example, if inventory consists of airplanes, airplane engines, and airplane engine parts, the standard deviation of the items in inventory as one population is large. The auditor would divide the population into four subpopulations: (1) whole airplanes; (2) airplane engines; (3) relatively expensive parts; and (4) nuts, bolts, screws, and other relatively inexpensive parts. The standard deviation of each of the four subpopulations is much smaller than the standard deviation of the one large population.

How to Do Mean-per-Unit Estimation   The chapter subsection on Planning Samples for Direct Tests of Balances applies to mean-per-unit estimation. First, the auditor defines the sample-objective relationship—the auditor is performing the sampling procedure to obtain evidence about the *audit hypothesis* that a recorded account balance is not materially misstated. There are differences in the sampling formulas used in using MPU for developing accounting estimates versus using MPU in audit hypothesis testing—in audit testing the auditor adjusts for the risk of incorrect acceptance as well as the risk of incorrect rejection.

The relevant audit objective is generally related to *existence* or *valuation.* The auditor defines the *population,* and determines the number of sampling units that make up the population size. This is important because population size is used in the calculation of sample size and in determining the estimate after sampling. Other factors also enter into the sample size calculation. These are the *confidence level,* the amount material to the account balance (the *precision),* and the estimated variability of the population (the *standard deviation).* The equation to calculate the sample size is the following:

$$n' = \left(\frac{U_R \cdot \text{SD} \cdot N}{A} \right)^2$$

where n' = the sample size
N = population size
U_R = the confidence level coefficient
SD = estimated standard deviation of the population
A = acceptable precision

The Confidence Level Coefficient (U_R)   The auditor decides what level of risk of incorrect rejection that he or she is willing to accept, as previously discussed in this chapter. The confidence level coefficient is based on this level of reliability the auditor selects.

The auditor finds the U_R coefficient for the equation from a table such as the following:

Risk of incorrect rejection	Reliability level	U_R coefficient
0.01	0.99	2.58
0.05	0.95	1.96
0.10	0.90	1.65

At 95 percent reliability, there is a 5 percent risk of incorrect rejection, and the U_R the auditor uses in the equation is 1.96.

Precision (A)   The precision is the plus-or-minus amount in the auditor's statement "I am 95 percent confident the range of $1,375,457 plus or minus $38,450 includes the actual value of inventory." The planned precision is calculated based on the following:

- *Tolerable misstatement.* This is the maximum degree of misstatement (either plus or minus) that the auditor will accept. It is the amount the auditor determines would be material to the account balance.
- *The risk of incorrect acceptance.* An explanation of how to establish the risk of incorrect acceptance *(detection risk)* was included in Chapter 7.
- *The risk of incorrect rejection determined in the previous paragraph.*

The auditor calculates the acceptable precision *(A)* using the following formula:

$$A = TM \times \text{adjustment factor}$$

where   TM $=$ tolerable misstatement (the amount material to the account balance)

Adjustment factor $=$ the sampling risk adjustment. It adjusts for the risk of incorrect acceptance at a specified level of risk of incorrect rejection (taken from Figure 8-12). It is based on the normal curve distribution theory.

If the auditor using the audit risk model has calculated an acceptable risk of incorrect acceptance of 1 percent and decided on an acceptable risk of incorrect rejection of 5 percent, the adjustment factor from Figure 8-12 to be used is .457.

Estimated Standard Deviation (SD)   The auditor needs to determine an estimate of the standard deviation. If the auditor performed a similar test in the previous year, last year's standard deviation could be used as an estimate. If the auditor does not have previous knowledge of the population standard deviation, a preliminary sample of approximately 30 items is taken to estimate the standard deviation of the population. The auditor performs the appropriate auditing procedures to determine an audited value for each presample item. The auditor then calculates the average of the presample audited values. The standard deviation is then calculated using the following formula:

Risk of incorrect acceptance, %	Risk of incorrect rejection		
	10%	5%	1%
1	.415	.457	.525
2.5	.457	.500	.568
5	.500	.543	.609
7.5	.534	.576	.641
10	.563	.605	.668
15	.613	.653	.712
20	.663	.700	.753
25	.708	.742	.791
30	.757	.787	.829
35	.809	.834	.868
40	.864	.883	.908
50	1.000	1.000	1.000

FIGURE 8-12
Tolerable misstatement adjustments.

$$ SD = \sqrt{\frac{\Sigma(x - \bar{x})^2}{n - 1}} = \sqrt{\frac{\text{the sum of the differences between presample audited values and the mean value, squared}}{\text{presample size} - 1}} $$

where SD = standard deviation

x = numeric value of the item

$\bar{x}$ = the presample mean (the sum of the numeric value of the presample items divided by the number of individual items included in the presample)

n = the number of items included in the presample

Calculating the Sample Size   The auditor has now defined or determined the following:

- The population and the number of units it contains
- The desired confidence level for the audit test
- The amount material to the account balance adjusted for the sampling risk (the planned acceptable precision)
- The estimated standard deviation of the population.

The auditor calculates the sample size using the following formula:

$$ n' = \left(\frac{U_R \cdot SD \cdot N}{A} \right)^2 $$

This results in a sample size on a "with replacement" basis. The auditor can reduce the sample size by performing the test on a "without replacement" basis. To adjust the sample size to a "without replacement" basis, the auditor performs the following calculation (called the *finite population correction factor*):

$$n = \frac{n'}{1 + (n'/N)}$$

Executing the MPU Estimation Sample Test The auditor uses random selection techniques to select n items, and performs the appropriate audit tests to determine an audited value for each. If a presample was taken to estimate the standard deviation, the first 30 items making up n are already done, and the auditor only has to randomly select as many as are needed to complete the calculated sample size n. (If n were less than 30, no more would be needed.)

The auditor then calculates the average of the sample's audited values, and calculates the standard deviation of the sample audited values.

The *planned acceptable precision* (the plus-or-minus amount that would be material to the account balance adjusted for sampling risk) was set during planning using the auditor's judgment. After the sample audit work has been performed, the auditor calculates the *achieved precision A'* using the following formula:

$$A' = U_R \cdot \frac{\text{SD}}{\sqrt{n}} \cdot N \sqrt{1 - (n/N)}$$

where A' = achieved precision
U_R = confidence level coefficient
SD = the standard deviation of the sample
n = the sample size
N = the population size

If the achieved precision (A') is less than or equal to the planned acceptable precision (A), the auditor completes the estimation calculation (described below) and decision interval.

The achieved precision is sometimes greater than the planned acceptable precision, that is, the plus-or-minus interval exceeds the amount the auditor considers material for the account balance. (This happens when the estimated standard deviation of the population used in planning the sample size turns out to have been lower than the actual standard deviation for the population.) In this case, the auditor can shorten the plus-or-minus interval to an acceptable precision. An adjustment that reduces the size of the interval makes it a tighter audit test, keeping the risk of incorrect acceptance low. The auditor performs a calculation to adjust the achieved precision to be equal to the acceptable risk of incorrect acceptance, using the following formula:

$$A'' = A' + \text{TM}\left(1 - \frac{A'}{A}\right)$$

where A'' = the new adjusted precision
A = the planned acceptable precision
A' = the achieved precision

The auditor calculates the mean x for the full sample:

$$\bar{x} = \frac{\Sigma x}{n} = \frac{\text{sum of each audited sample item}}{\text{sample size}}$$

The auditor calculates the estimated audited value (EAV) by multiplying mean of the audited values of the sample items by the number of items in the population, as follows:

$$\text{EAV} = x \cdot N$$

The auditor is then ready to compare the actual value of inventory to the range of $1,375,457 (the EAV) plus or minus $38,450 (the achieved or adjusted precision). If the book value of the inventory in this example is between $1,337,007 and $1,413,907, the audit test supports the conclusion that the book value is not materially misstated. If not, the client should investigate, determine the cause, and consider adjusting the book value. The auditor should also keep in mind that this situation could arise if there was something wrong with the MPU procedure as performed in the audit, such as selecting a sample that was not representative of the population (through failure to recognize a systematic pattern, etc.) or because the sample size was too small, for example, because of a faulty or outdated estimate of the standard deviation.

Stratified Mean-per-Unit Estimation

Stratifying the population into several subpopulations can substantially reduce the sample size, while maintaining sampling risk at an appropriate level. In practice, MPU estimation is usually performed with stratification for audit efficiency reasons.

The auditor first defines each strata or subpopulation, designating the high and low values for each. The auditor then performs the MPU estimation sampling procedures for each strata, calculating the sample size, standard deviation, and mean for each stratum. Then the results (achieved precision A', estimated audited value EAV) for the individual strata are calculated and combined to create an overall point estimate, plus or minus the overall precision. The overall point estimate is simply the sum of the individual strata point estimates. The overall achieved precision is combined with the following formula:

$$A' = U_R \sqrt{\sum \frac{N_i \ SD_i \ (N_i - n_i)}{n_i}}$$

Difference Estimation

In difference estimation, the auditor calculates the difference between the audited value and the book value of each item in the sample. The average of the differences is calculated and then multiplied by the number of items in the population to obtain an *estimated total projected difference*. The population value is then estimated as the total book value plus the total projected difference. The sample sizes when using this method tend to be much smaller than those using mean-per-unit estimation.

When to Use Difference Estimation   This technique is reliable only when many differences exist. Thus, the auditor should not use difference estimation unless relatively high difference rates are expected. For example, the technique would be useful when the client's inventory pricing methods yield small differences from the audited value for nearly every item. Stratification is sometimes used in difference estimation to increase its effectiveness.

How to Do Difference Estimation   The factors to determine the sample size are the same as those used in mean-per-unit estimation. The formula to calculate the sample size is also the same, only the standard deviation is of the *differences* rather than the standard deviation of the audited values. The sample size calculated turns out to be much smaller than that in MPU estimation because the estimated standard deviation of the differences between audited values and book values is smaller than the estimated standard deviation of the audited values themselves.

The sample items are selected using random selection techniques, and an audited value and book value determined for each item. The auditor calculates the difference between the two values. A positive difference indicates an overstatement and a negative difference indicates an understatement. The auditor computes the average difference by calculating the sum of the differences and dividing by the number of items in the sample. The auditor then calculates the standard deviation of the sample differences. The achieved precision is calculated using the same formula as discussed for mean-per-unit estimation (except that the standard deviation of the differences is used instead of the standard deviation of the audited values).

The auditor calculates the mean of the differences of all the sample items. The *estimated total projected difference* is the number of items in the population times the mean (average) difference.

The estimated audited value is the recorded book value plus the estimated total projected difference. The projected difference could be either positive (overstatement) or negative (understatement).

As for mean-per-unit estimation, the auditor calculates a range—the estimated audited value plus or minus the achieved precision (A'). If the range includes the book value, the audit test has supported the hypothesis that the account balance is not materially misstated. If the book value is outside the range, additional work to determine whether an adjustment is needed should be performed.

Ratio Estimation

Ratio estimation is very similar to difference estimation. For each item selected, the auditor determines an audited value and a book value. In ratio estimation, the sum of all of the book values of the sampled items is calculated, and the sum of all of the audited values of the sampled items is calculated. The auditor calculates a ratio by dividing the sum of the audited values by the sum of the sample book values. The ratio is multiplied by the recorded total book value for the account balance, to create the estimated audited value.

As in difference estimation, achieved precision is calculated (using the standard deviation of the individual ratios in the sample). The auditor calculates a range—the estimated audited value plus or minus the achieved precision—and determines whether the recorded book value falls within the range.

When to Use Ratio Estimation   The conditions for using ratio estimation are generally the same as those for using difference estimation. If the size of the misstatement is proportionate to the size of the book values in the population (that is, items with small book values have small differences from audited values, and larger items have larger differences), ratio estimation results in a smaller sample size than difference estimation. If the differences between audited and book values do not follow that pattern, difference estimation will result in a smaller sample size. Another consideration is that the standard deviation of the individual ratios needs to be calculated, which is cumbersome unless the audit test is computer-assisted.

CHAPTER 8 ASSIGNMENTS

OBJECTIVE QUESTIONS

8-1 For each one of the following statements indicate whether the statement is true or false.

T   F   a When the auditor's approach to substantiating an account balance is to apply an audit procedure to less than 100 percent of the items included in the balance, audit sampling is being used.

T   F   b If audit sampling is used to apply a substantive test, the detection risk for that test is caused, in part, by sampling risk.

T   F   c A characteristic of interest in an audit sample may be either monetary misstatement or deviations from prescribed internal control structure policies or procedures.

T   F   d If an auditor selects a sample by using a random number table, the auditor is using a statistical approach to audit sampling.

T   F   e According to SAS No. 39 (AU 350), an audit sample should be selected using a method that can be expected to produce a representative sample. This means it is inappropriate for auditors to use judgment in selecting items to examine.

T   F   f In planning an audit sample for a test of a transaction class, the auditor needs to specify the control objectives and the internal control structure policies and procedures that achieve them for that transaction class.

T   F   g In planning a test of controls using audit sampling, the auditor needs to consider the tolerable rate, risk of assessing control risk too high, and expected rate.

T   F   h If the auditor has estimated sample size judgmentally, the sampling risk associated with the sample results cannot be quantified even if the sample was selected randomly.

T   F   i In planning a direct test of a balance using audit sampling, the auditor must consider the relation between the specific audit objective and the sample. In such sampling applications, the audit objectives are usually those related to existence and valuation.

T F j As tolerable misstatement as a percentage of the account balance to be sampled increases, sample size increases.

T F k In planning a sample for a direct test of a balance, the risk of incorrect acceptance is the detection risk for that test.

T F l The sum of the tolerable misstatements used in individual sampling applications may exceed the allowance for undetected misstatement for the financial statements taken as a whole.

8-2 The following questions relate to general aspects of audit sampling. Select the *best* response.

  a Which of the following is an element of sampling risk?
1 Choosing an audit procedure that is inconsistent with the audit objective
2 Choosing a sample size that is too small to achieve the sampling objective
3 Failing to detect a deviation on a document that has been inspected by the auditor
4 Failing to perform audit procedures that are required by the sampling plan

  b Which of the following best illustrates the concept of sampling risk?
1 A randomly chosen sample may *not* be representative of the population as a whole on the characteristic of interest.
2 An auditor may select audit procedures that are *not* appropriate to achieve the specific objective.
3 An auditor may fail to recognize deviations in the documents examined for the chosen sample.
4 The documents related to the chosen sample may *not* be available for inspection.

  c In which of the following cases would the auditor be most likely to conclude that all of the items in an account under consideration should be examined rather than tested on a sample basis?

The measure of tolerable misstatement is	Misstatement frequency is expected to be
1 Large	Low
2 Small	High
3 Large	High
4 Small	Low

  d An advantage of using statistical sampling techniques is that such techniques:
1 Mathematically measure risk
2 Eliminate the need for judgmental decisions
3 Define the values of precision and reliability required to provide audit satisfaction
4 Have been established in the courts to be superior to judgmental sampling

  e The risk of incorrect acceptance and the likelihood of assessing control risk too low relate to the:
1 Effectiveness of the audit
2 Efficiency of the audit
3 Preliminary estimates of materiality levels
4 Allowable risk of tolerable misstatement

AICPA

8-3 The following questions relate to the selection of audit samples. Select the *best* response.

a Which of the following statistical selection techniques is *least* desirable for use by an auditor?

1 Systematic selection

2 Stratified selection

3 Block selection

4 Sequential selection

b If certain forms are *not* consecutively numbered:

1 Selection of a random sample probably is *not* possible.

2 Systematic sampling may be appropriate.

3 Stratified sampling should be used.

4 Random number tables can*not* be used.

c Which of the following sampling methods is most useful to auditors when performing a test of controls?

1 Stratified random sampling

2 Attribute sampling

3 Variables sampling

4 Unrestricted random sampling with replacement

d When performing a test of controls with respect to control over cash disbursements, a CPA may use a systematic sampling technique with a start at any randomly selected item. The biggest disadvantage of this type of sampling is that the items in the population:

1 Must be recorded in a systematic pattern before the sample can be drawn

2 May occur in a systematic pattern, thus destroying the sample randomness

3 May systematically occur more than once in the sample

4 Must be systematically replaced in the population after sampling

AICPA

8-4 The following questions relate to use of audit sampling for tests of transaction classes. Select the *best* response

a Given random selection, the same sample size, and the same tolerable rate for the testing of two unequal populations, the risk of assessing control risk too low for the smaller population is:

1 Higher than the risk of assessing control risk too low on the larger population

2 Lower than the risk of assessing control risk too low on the larger population

3 The same as the risk of assessing control risk too low on the larger population

4 Indeterminable relative to the risk of assessing control risk too low on the larger population

b The tolerable rate of deviations for a test of controls is generally:

1 Lower than the expected deviation rate in the related accounting records

2 Higher than the expected deviation rate in the related accounting records

3 Identical to the expected deviation rate in the related accounting records

4 Unrelated to the expected deviation rate in the related accounting records

c If the auditor is concerned that a population may contain exceptions, the determination of a sample size sufficient to include at *least* one such exception is a characteristic of:

1 Discovery sampling

2 Variables sampling

3 Random sampling

4 Dollar-unit sampling

d If all other factors specified in an attribute sampling plan remain constant, changing the tolerable rate from 6 percent to 10 percent, and changing the risk of assessing control risk too low from 3 percent to 7 percent would cause the required sample size to:

1 Increase

2 Remain the same

3 Decrease

4 Change by 4 percent

AICPA

8-5 The following questions relate to use of audit sampling for direct tests of balances. Select the *best* response.

  a A number of factors influences the sample size for a substantive test of details of an account balance. All other factors being equal, which of the following would lead to a larger sample size?

    1 Greater reliance on internal accounting controls

    2 Greater reliance on analytical procedures

    3 Smaller expected frequency of misstatements

    4 Smaller measure of tolerable misstatement

  b When planning a sample for a substantive test of details, an auditor should consider tolerable misstatement for the sample. This consideration should:

    1 Be related to the auditor's business risk

    2 Not be adjusted for qualitative factors

    3 Be related to preliminary judgments about materiality levels

    4 Not be changed during the audit process

  c Which of the following would be designed to estimate a numerical measurement of a population, such as a dollar value?

    1 Sampling for variables

    2 Sampling for attributes

    3 Discovery sampling

    4 Numerical sampling

AICPA

8-6 The following questions relate to use of estimation sampling using an audit hypothesis testing approach. Select the *best* response.

  a When using classical variables sampling for estimation, an auditor normally evaluates the sampling results by calculating the possible error in either direction. This statistical concept is known as:

    1 Precision

    2 Reliability

    3 Projected error

    4 Standard deviation

  b Stratified mean-per-unit sampling is a statistical technique that may be more efficient than unstratified MPU because it usually:

    1 May be applied to populations where many monetary misstatements are expected to occur

    2 Produces an estimate having a desired level of precision with a smaller sample size

    3 Increases the variability among items in a stratum by grouping sampling units with similar characteristics

    4 Yields a weighted sum of the strata standard deviations that is greater than the standard deviation of the population

  c An auditor is performing substantive tests of pricing and extensions of perpetual inventory balances consisting of a large number of items. Past experience indicates numerous pricing and extension errors. Which of the following statistical sampling approaches is most appropriate?

1 Unstratified mean per unit
2 Probability proportional to size
3 Stop or go
4 Ratio estimation

DISCUSSION QUESTIONS

Discussion questions require the application of the concepts explained in the chapter to specific facts, issues, or problems. They are classified by the primary chapter topic to which they relate. However, responses should not be confined to the primary topics but should include all relevant implications.

Audit Sampling—General

8-7 The Doran Dairy's principal activity is buying milk from dairy farmers, processing the milk, and delivering the milk to retail customers. You are engaged in auditing the retail accounts receivable of the company and determine the following:

1 The company has 50 retail routes; each route consists of 100 to 200 accounts, the number that can be serviced by a driver in a day.
2 The driver enters cash collections from a day's deliveries to each customer directly on a statement form in record books, of which one is maintained for each route. Mail remittances are posted in the route record books by office personnel. At the end of the month the statements are priced, extended, and footed. Photocopies of the statements are prepared and left in the customers' milk boxes with the next milk delivery.
3 The statements are reviewed by the office manager, who prepares a list for each route of accounts with 90-day balances or older. The list is used for intensive collection action.
4 The audit program used in prior audits for the selection of retail accounts receivable for confirmation stated: "Select two accounts from each route, one to be chosen by opening the route book at random and the other as the third item on each list of 90-day or older accounts."

Your review of the accounts receivable leads you to conclude that statistical sampling techniques may be applied to their examination.

a Give the reasons why the audit procedure previously used for selection of accounts receivable for confirmation (as given in No. 4 above) would not produce a valid statistical sample.
b What are the audit objectives or purposes in selecting 90-day accounts for confirmation? Can the application of statistical sampling techniques help in attaining these objectives or purposes? Discuss.
c Assume that the company has 10,000 accounts receivable and that your statistical sampling disclosed six monetary misstatements in a sample of 200 accounts. Is it reasonable to assume that 300 accounts in the entire population are misstated?

AICPA adapted

8-8 The following is a list of audit procedures that might be applied to sale transactions. Identify those procedures that would be applied using audit sampling.

a Scan the accounting records to identify large and unusual transactions.

b Observe the mailing of monthly statements to customers.

c Inspect sales invoices for indication of checking and recompute extensions and footings.

d Trace shipping documents to sales invoices and compare details (customer, description, quantity, and amount).

e Foot sales journals and trace to the general ledger.

8-9 The following is a list of audit procedures that might be applied to property and equipment. Identify those procedures that might be applied using audit sampling.

a Inquire about procedures followed to ensure that retirements are recorded.

b Review capital budgets for the period and compare to accounting records.

c Vouch additions by inspecting supporting documents.

d Tour the plant and note the existence and appearance of new equipment.

e Scan repair and maintenance expense and inspect supporting documents for large disbursements.

8-10 An auditor has analyzed additions to property and equipment for the year as follows:

Number of additions	Range	Dollar amount
5	Above $10,000	$ 90,000
20	1,000 to 9,999	60,000
25		$150,000

The auditor plans to substantiate all the additions above $10,000 and rely on analytical procedures for the remaining amount.

Required:

a Is this audit approach acceptable?

b Is there any detection risk associated with this approach?

c Is there any sampling risk associated with this approach?

8-11 An auditor is selecting shipping documents as part of testing sales transactions. There were 3,000 shipping documents issued during the period being tested and the auditor has judgmentally decided to select 60 documents. The auditor counts through the documents selecting every 50th one. The auditor uses a random start and during the selection process makes several additional random starts.

Required:

a Is audit sampling being used?

b Is the selection method a random-based method?

c Is statistical sampling being used?

d Why did the auditor use more than one random start?

Audit Sampling—Tests of Transaction Classes

8-12 The sample size for a test of a transaction class should be based on the auditor's consideration of the following:

1 Tolerable rate

2 Risk of assessing control risk too low

3 Expected rate

Required: For each of the considerations listed:

a Define the concept or term

b Identify whether the auditor's quantification of the consideration in a specific circumstance to determine sample size is based primarily on professional judgment, professional standards, or past experience with the client.

8-13 The questions below relate to estimating the sample size necessary for tests of transaction classes given the specified decisions for the considerations that affect sample size.

Situation	Risk of assessing control risk too low, %	Tolerable rate, %	Expected *number* of deviations
1	10	7	0
2	5	7	0
3	10	12	0
4	10	12	2
5	5	25	1
6	10	10	3

Required:

a For each of the situations 1 through 6 above, what is the initial sample size for the test of controls?

b Based on your understanding of the relationships among the factors above and sample size, explain the effect of changing each of the following while the others remain unchanged.

1 Risk of assessing control risk too low is increased.

2 Tolerable rate is decreased.

3 Number of deviations expected increases.

4 Population size increases.

8-14 For the sample sizes calculated in Problem 8-13 above, assume that application of the planned audit test to the items selected produced the following results:

Situation	Number of deviations found
1	0
2	1
3	1
4	2
5	3
6	1

Required:

a What is the maximum deviation rate for situations 1 to 6 at the specified risk of assessing control risk too low in Problem 8-13?

b For which situations does the maximum deviation rate not exceed the tolerable rate?

c Was it necessary to answer part a to be able to answer part b above?

8-15 Shoe & Shoe, a CPA firm, wants to adopt a sampling plan for tests of transaction classes based on the Poisson distribution, with the following specifications:

- A risk of assessing control risk too low fixed at 5 percent
- Tolerable rates corresponding to levels of control risk of:
  - Low 5%
  - Moderate 10%
  - Maximum (omit test)

Required:

a What is the minimum sample size that Shoe & Shoe should use for tests of transaction classes to permit assessment of the control risk at less than maximum?

b What is the maximum sample size that Shoe & Shoe should use for tests of transaction classes?

c Without regard to your answer to part b, assume that Shoe & Shoe specifies a maximum sample size of 120. Construct a sample planning and evaluation table for Shoe & Shoe to incorporate in a work paper that permits evaluations of samples that find up to 3 deviations.

8-16 Martin, a CPA, has selected a sample of 50 cash disbursement transactions and has found the following sample results:

- Two vouchers are not initialed to indicate that the supporting documents were inspected and the vendor's invoice recomputed before disbursement. However, Martin found that the supporting documents were all present, the details (quantity, price, etc.) of the documents were in agreement, and the vendor's invoice was correct.
- One voucher is initialed, but the supporting documents are not in agreement and the vendor's invoice is incorrect.
- One voucher does not have the supporting documents attached. However, Martin has communicated with the department that received the item, the purchasing department, and the vendor and determined that the transaction is appropriate and recorded correctly.
- One voucher has been spoiled and has been marked to prevent any use but has been retained.

Required:

a How many deviations has Martin detected? Explain why you believe each sample result is or is not a deviation.

b Without regard to your answer to part a, assume that Martin found 5 deviations. What is the maximum deviation rate that could exist in the population of cash disbursements sampled at a 10 percent risk of assessing control risk too low.

c Based on your answer to part b, what level of control risk could Martin assess on controls over cash disbursements?

8-17 Dennis, a CPA, has selected a sample of 50 sales transactions. The sample size was based on the CPA's judgment rather than statistically estimated but selected using a random number generator. However, Dennis, since planning the audit, has taken a continuing education course on audit sampling and has decided to evaluate all audit samples statistically. The first selected sales transaction examined disclosed a deviation.

Required:

a Is it acceptable for Dennis to statistically evaluate the results of a sample whose size was determined judgmentally?

b Without regard to your answer to part a, make a statistical evaluation of finding 1 deviation in a sample of 50 assuming that Dennis believes a 10 percent risk of assessing control risk too low and a tolerable rate of 5 percent are appropriate for assessing control risk at a low level.

c If the first transaction in a sample of 50 discloses a deviation, is it necessary to apply the planned procedures to the remaining items (assuming the same evaluation criteria as stated in part b)?

d Based on the evaluation criteria stated in part b, what alternatives or options does Dennis have if the first transaction in a sample of 50 disclosed a deviation?

Audit Sampling—Direct Tests of Balances

8-18 The sample size for a direct test of a balance should be based on the auditor's consideration of the following:

1 Tolerable misstatement
2 Risk of incorrect acceptance
3 Population characteristics

Required: For each of the considerations listed:

a Define the concept or term.

b Identify whether the auditor's quantification of the consideration to determine sample size in a specific circumstance is based primarily on professional judgment, professional standards, or past experience with the client.

8-19 PIC Inc. has prepared a trial balance of general ledger accounts from which the following information is extracted:

Accounts receivable	$ 100,000
Total assets	900,000
Total revenue	2,000,000
Pretax income	500,000

For convenience assume that all known misstatement will be corrected and expected misstatement will be negligible. Also, assume that in planning tests of details for accounts receivable you have decided that a 5 percent risk of incorrect acceptance is appropriate and that the receivable balance contains no individually significant items.

Required: What sample size would you use for confirmation of accounts receivable under each of the following circumstances:

a Planning materiality is to be 1 percent of total revenue.

b Planning materiality is to be 1 percent of total assets.

c Planning materiality is to be 10 percent of pretax income.

Which sample size is correct?

8-20 In planning an audit sample, one of the important considerations is the relationship between the sample and the objective of the test. How do these considerations differ for tests of transaction classes and direct tests of balances?

8-21 You are planning an audit sample for confirmation of accounts receivable. The aged trial balance of receivables after removal of individually significant items has a remaining population of $2,000,000.

Assume that you have concluded that a tolerable misstatement of $100,000 is appropriate in the circumstances and that you believe a moderate assessed level of control risk and moderate reliance on analytical procedures are appropriate.

Required:
a What sample size would you use for confirmation of accounts receivable?
b How would you decide the assessed level of control risk or other procedures risk such as analytical procedures?

8-22 You are examining additions to property and equipment for the year using the PPS statistical method. The remaining population recorded amount is $1,000,000, and you believe a tolerable misstatement of $25,000 is appropriate. You have concluded that a 10 percent risk of incorrect acceptance is appropriate.

Required:
a What sample size should you use?
b What dollar sampling interval should you use in sample selection?
c In determining the remaining population recorded amount, what dollar cutoff would have been a reasonable amount for identifying individually significant additions?

8-23 In examining additions to property and equipment for the year using the PPS statistical method you estimated a sample size of 40 additions. The remaining population recorded amount was $1,000,000, and you used a 5 percent risk of incorrect acceptance.

After vouching the additions you found errors in two items as follows:

Recorded amount	Audited amount
$5,000	$4,000
2,000	3,000

Required:
a What tolerable misstatement did you use in estimating sample size?
b What is the basic bound of monetary misstatement for your sample?
c What are the maximum understatement and maximum overstatement?
d What are the projected overstatement and projected understatement?
e What are the net maximum overstatement and the net maximum understatement?
f Would you accept or reject the account balance?

CHAPTER OUTLINE

Learning Objectives

After studying this chapter you should be able to:

- Recognize when reliance on the computer is necessary
- Distinguish among user controls and EDP controls, general controls and application controls, and manual controls and programmed controls
- Identify the application controls and general controls that may affect the auditor's assessment of control risk in a computerized system
- Explain how consideration of a client's computer affects general planning, the consideration of the internal control structure, and planning tests of details
- Describe some common computer-assisted audit techniques and the circumstances in which they might be used.

Relevant Section of Statements on Auditing Standards

AU 319 — Consideration of Internal Control Structure in a
Financial Statement Audit

As a result of advances in technology and corresponding decreases in cost, use of computers in business data processing is widespread. Many auditors find that most of their audit clients have at least some computerized accounting applications. This chapter explains the effect of computers on the audit of financial statements.

THE RELATION OF COMPUTERS TO AUDITING

Relation to Phases of the Audit

Consideration of the computer is an integral part of an audit of financial statements. Every chapter of this book has included discussion of computer-related topics and examples involving computerized systems. Why is the effect of computers on the audit the subject of a separate chapter of this book?

Prior chapters emphasize the auditor's objectives in each of the phases of the audit discussed. A thorough understanding of objectives is necessary before getting into the details of how to accomplish those objectives when a computer is involved. In a computerized system, objectives do not change, but there are often different methods of achieving them.

Because virtually all audit clients have both manual and computerized portions of their accounting systems, the emphasis in practice is for all auditors to be proficient at understanding the accounting system and internal control structure (both EDP and manual) and planning the audit to address both portions of the accounting systems. Computer audit specialists, as explained in Chapter 5, may still be used, but the determination of the need for their skills and the evaluation of their results and conclusions is the responsibility of the auditor who will issue the opinion on the financial statements. For example, the auditor may wish to reduce control risk below the maximum in an area because transaction input and processing is strictly controlled using a computerized access control/password facility. The actual audit procedures (to evaluate whether the access control facility has been effectively installed and implemented, and to obtain the information from computer records on *who* has access to *what*) may be outside the knowledge of the auditor. The computer audit specialist performs the procedures and reports his or her findings to the auditor (e.g., a conclusion that the facility is effectively implemented, with appropriate supporting audit documentation, and a list of who has access to the data and functions of audit interest).

The following list identifies the phases of the audit, as explained in this book, that are most affected by the computer and summarizes a part of SAS No. 48 that amends several sections of the authoritative literature:

- *Understanding the client and general planning* (Chapter 5). The auditor should consider the methods the entity uses to process accounting information in planning the audit because such methods influence the design of the accounting system and the nature of control structure policies and procedures. The extent to which the computer is used in significant accounting applications, as well as the complexity of that processing, may also influence the nature, timing, and extent of audit procedures [AU 311.09].
- *Understanding the accounting system and related control activities* (Chapter 6). The methods an entity uses to process significant accounting applications may influence the control procedures designed to achieve the internal control structure objectives. Those characteristics that distinguish computer processing from manual processing include the following:
  a *Transaction trails.* Some computer systems are designed so that a complete transaction (audit) trail might exist for only a short period of time or only in computer-readable form.
  b *Uniform processing of transactions.* Computer processing uniformly subjects like transactions to the same processing instructions.
  c *Segregation of functions.* Many control procedures once performed by separate individuals in manual systems may be concentrated.
  d *Potential for misstatements.* The potential for individuals to gain unauthorized access to data or alter data without visible evidence, as well as to gain access (direct or indirect) to assets, may be greater.
  e *Potential for increased management supervision.* Computer systems offer management a wide variety of analytical tools that may be used to review and supervise operations.
- *Planning tests of details of transactions and balances* (Chapter 7). The auditor's specific audit objectives do not change whether accounting data is processed manually or by computer. However, the methods of applying audit procedures to gather evidence may be influenced by the methods of data processing. The auditor can use either manual audit procedures, computer-assisted audit techniques, or a combination of both to obtain sufficient, competent evidential matter [AU 326.12].

In essence, the client's use of the computer in the accounting system and the auditor's use of the computer in auditing do not affect objectives but may affect the methods used to accomplish those objectives. Computerization of an accounting application does not change specific internal control structure objectives, but the control policies and procedures necessary to accomplish those objectives may be changed. Also, the specific audit objectives for the account balances or transaction classes involved in a computerized accounting application are the same, but the audit procedures necessary to accomplish them may be affected.

The effect of the computer on each of the phases of the audit identified above is explained later in this chapter. However, it is worth recognizing at this point that, when a client has significant computerized accounting applications, some reliance on the computer in the audit is usually necessary and the auditor normally needs to identify and test computer-related controls or test the results of computer processing.

Recognizing Reliance on the Computer

A computerized accounting application normally includes both manual and computer portions. The auditor needs to understand the path transactions take through both the manual and the computer portions of the accounting system.

Some aspects of the computerized portion of the system are obviously different than in a manual system. They are unique to computer processing and not difficult to identify. For example, some control procedures, such as edit checks, may be included in a computer program and no visible evidence of their execution may be available. If the auditor intends to assess control risk at below the maximum level based on such control procedures, testing the computer program may be necessary. However, it is often possible to substantiate directly computer-generated information or to test manual controls maintained by computer users instead of testing programmed control procedures.

The most common forms of reliance on the computer occur when a manual control procedure or an audit procedure are dependent on computer-generated information.

Manual Control Policies and Procedures Dependent on the Computer   In some cases, a manual control policy or procedure that is necessary to achieve a specific control objective is dependent on the results of computer processing. For example, in a computerized billing application the auditor is concerned with whether control procedures are adequate to provide reasonable assurance that products shipped are billed.

If the control procedure that achieves this objective involves a billing clerk reviewing a computer-generated report of missing shipping documents based on a numerical sequence test in a computer program, then the auditor must place some reliance on the computer in order to use the manual control procedure in the control risk assessment.

Audit Procedures Applied to Computer-Generated Information   In some cases, audit procedures applied to computer-generated information are dependent on the computer. No computer reliance is usually involved when the auditor makes a direct test of a balance at year-end. For example, if the auditor uses a computer-generated aged trial balance of accounts receivable as the frame for selecting customer accounts to confirm, reliance on the computer is not necessary. The audit procedure—confirmation—tests the validity and accuracy of the selected customer accounts. If the auditor manually foots the trial balance and compares it to the general ledger control account balance, the specific audit objectives achieved by confirmation are accomplished without reliance on computer processing.

However, if the auditor applies the confirmation procedure at an interim date, reliance on the computer is necessary if the auditor compares the computer-generated trial balance of receivables to a similar trial balance at year-end to decide whether the audit conclusion at the interim date can be extended to the balance sheet date. Also, if the auditor's analytical procedures to assess collectibility are applied to a computer-generated aged trial balance of receivables, the procedure is dependent on the validity, completeness, and accuracy of computer processing.

Auditor Use of the Computer

Another aspect of the relation of computers to auditing is the auditor's use of a computer to perform audit tests, which is sometimes referred to as using "computer-assisted audit techniques." For example, instead of manually selecting items from a printed trial balance, the auditor could use a computer program to select the items from a computer-readable file. Instead of manually preparing a trial balance spreadsheet, spreadsheet software on a microcomputer could be used.

Generally, whatever the auditor might do manually could conceivably be automated to some extent by using computer assistance. The decision to use manual procedures or computer assistance depends on the auditor's evaluation of the relative efficiency of the alternative approaches.

Some of the common methods of computer assistance used by auditors, including use of microcomputers (personal computers, or PCs), are explained later in this chapter.

THE INTERNAL CONTROL STRUCTURE AND COMPUTERIZED SYSTEMS

In considering the internal control structure that involves a computerized system, it is useful to distinguish between various categories of controls.

Control Classifications in Computerized Systems

Controls in computerized systems can be placed in two broad categories: user controls and EDP controls.

User Controls versus EDP Controls   User controls are those controls established and maintained by departments whose processing is performed by computer. Accounting students sometimes have difficulty understanding this distinction because the EDP (electronic data processing) department is often organizationally one of several accounting departments reporting to the controller. However, whether the EDP department is under the controller, reports to a Vice President of Information Systems, or has some other organizational location, it is important to identify data processing as a separate department or function from the user departments or groups.

The nature of user departments is probably easiest to understand if a specific situation is considered. For example, Figure 6-3 in Chapter 6 presents an organization chart for a medium-size manufacturing company. Referring specifically to Figure 6-3, all departments other than EDP are potential user departments. Traditional accounting functions, such as billing, accounts receivable, and cost accounting are user departments. Also, departments outside accounting, such as shipping, receiving, and stores may be user departments.

User departments are responsible for the validity, completeness, and accuracy of information outside the EDP department. This means that users are responsible for any errors that originate outside the EDP department.

User departments are also responsible for establishing and maintaining controls over the information for their application processed by computer. For example, a payroll department may determine gross payroll and the number of payroll checks to be prepared before processing and then compare the computer output received from the EDP department with those totals.

Thus, the distinction between user controls and EDP controls is based on the location where the controls are maintained. EDP controls are controls that are maintained in the location of the computer. EDP controls are also usually classified in two broad categories: general controls and application controls. User controls are always application controls.

General Controls versus Application Controls   *General controls* are those controls that relate to all or many computerized accounting applications. For example, controls over development and changes to application software would affect all accounting applications and would be included in the auditor's consideration of the control environment. *Application controls* relate to individual computerized accounting applications. For example, a programmed edit control for validating customers' account numbers and credit limits would affect only the computerized sales accounting application and would be considered in assessing control risk for assertions in that area. This example introduces another important distinction—that between programmed and manual controls.

Programmed versus Manual Controls   An EDP control may be either a programmed control procedure or a manual control procedure. A manual procedure is performed by personnel, and a programmed procedure is executed by computer software. When the computer rejects an invalid account number, a programmed control is in effect. When a data entry operator checks for the authorized signature or a document before keying in data, a manual control is in effect. When the computer generates a report of unusual transactions or conditions (e.g., payroll hours exceeding 50 for 1 week) for management review, that is a manual control that depends on a programmed control.

Application Controls

Application controls are often dependent on general controls. For example, a programmed EDP control, or a manual control procedure that depends on computer-generated information, may not be effective if control over development and changes to application software are ineffective. However, in the following discussion, application controls are presented first because application controls contribute to achievement of specific control objectives that the auditor considers in tests of transaction classes. The auditor assesses the effect of application controls on control risk to restrict the scope of direct tests of balances. As explained earlier, application controls may be user controls or EDP controls.

User Controls   Since user controls are performed by personnel in user departments, they are manual control procedures. The significance of this to the auditor is that these controls may be tested in the same manner as control procedures in a manual processing system. The auditor may test the functioning of user controls by inquiry, observation, and inspection of documents.

The types of user controls relevant to providing reasonable assurance of the validity, completeness, and accuracy of data processed by computer generally may be classified in the following categories:

1 Control totals
2 Review and reconciliation of data
3 Error correction and resubmission

Control totals may be used to detect errors in input or processing when information is batched before entry. Generally, there are three types of control totals:

1 *Financial totals.* These are the total of field amounts for all the records in a batch that are normally computed as a result of processing. For example, in a sales accounting system, financial totals would be total dollars received or total dollars billed.
2 *Hash totals.* Hash totals are the total of field amounts for all the records in a batch that are computed for control purposes only. For example, the total of customer numbers would be a hash total.
3 *Record totals.* Record totals are the total of the number of logical or physical records in a batch. For example, the total number of sales invoices or the total number of line items on invoices in a batch would be record totals.

If a user department establishes control totals before data entry and reconciles those totals to output returned from the EDP department, loss of data or changes in data that occur outside the user department can be detected. For this type of control procedure to be effective, the user department must maintain detailed documentation, reconcile output to input, and investigate discrepancies. The procedures are as follows: a batch number is assigned to identify a batch; the number of items in a batch are limited to facilitate reconciliation; control totals are recorded manually in a log maintained by the user and on a transmittal ticket that accompanies the batch; the control totals on output reports are reconciled to the input control totals; differences and their resolution are also documented.

Review and reconciliation of data by users is an important control procedure for computerized systems. Users should make a manual review of the data before its transmittal or entry. This helps to ensure the accuracy and completeness of data submitted for processing. Also, users should carefully review computer output received and reconcile it to input. In a computerized system, transactions may be automatically initiated or executed by application programs. Users should review a list of all computer-generated transactions for their applications. Review of file maintenance changes to master files is also important. For example, customer addresses or credit limits on the accounts receivable master file may be changed. Changes not authorized through user control procedures should be investigated. User review of these types of changes helps to ensure that they are authorized and accurate. Since users are more knowledgeable about the file data for their applications, user reviews of output for reasonableness are important.

Error correction and resubmission procedures are generally much more formal in computerized systems. Users are responsible for correction of errors that originate outside the EDP department. Procedures in user departments generally should include: a user's procedure manual with written error correction procedures, maintenance of a log for errors and resubmissions, and careful review and approval of resubmitted source documents before transmittal.

EDP Controls Every time that data are transferred from one media to another or are changed by processing, such as summarization or calculation, there is potential for error. For this reason, EDP application controls are usually classified as input, file, processing, and output controls. At each of these stages in a computerized system, errors may be introduced.

Input controls naturally differ for batch input versus on-line entry. Batch input goes through a data preparation step for conversion of manual source documents to computer-readable form. Batch data preparation is an off-line process and generally includes the following control procedures:

- *Control totals.* Control totals are computed as a byproduct of data preparation and compared to the total manually established by the user department. Also, as part of data preparation, a batch header record (computer-readable) including control totals, is often created and added to the input.
- *Key verification.* Key verification is simply a duplicate keying of data to detect errors by the key entry operator. A second operator rekeys the same set of source documents and differences from the first keying are identified and corrected. Since key verification is expensive, it is usually confined to critical data fields on source documents.
- *Key entry validation.* In computerized systems, data validation is a general term for tests to detect inaccurate or incomplete data. Key-to-tape or key-to-disk equipment has logic capabilities that permit data validation. Since these logic tests are essentially the same as computer input validation, they are explained later.

On-line entry controls include (1) batch controls in on-line entry with batch processing and (2) general controls to ensure that only authorized and valid transactions are entered into terminals. These controls over terminal entry are explained in the section on general controls.

After data preparation in batch input systems, the batch input is read on-line from tape or disk into primary storage. This step takes place under control of the CPU, and a variety of edit and data validation tests can be made using the logic capability of the CPU. The following edit and data validation tests are examples of programmed control procedures:

- *Check digit.* A check digit is used to validate record identification fields. For example, a check digit may be used for customer numbers, vendor numbers, or employee numbers. The check digit is calculated from the identification number and attached to that number when the number is originally assigned. The calculation is a numeric operation on the identification number. For example, simple calculation would be to add the numbers and divide by 10. If the number was 65946, the check digit would be 3 (6 + 5 + 9 + 4 + 6 = 30 ÷ 10), and the number assigned would be 659463. The application program would perform the numeric operation on the numbers preceding the check digit and compare the result to the check digit. The numeric operations used in computer applications are much more complex than this oversimplified illustration. For example, use of a check digit would detect common key entry errors such as transposition of a number, but the simplified example would not.

- *Limit or reasonableness test.* This type of logic test is used to determine whether a data amount falls within previously established limits. An amount that is outside the limit is identified for investigation. For example, in a weekly payroll application, employee time records with greater than 48 hours or less than 0 hours might be rejected or printed out for investigation. In a cash disbursement application, all disbursements over a specified amount, such as $10,000, might be printed out for investigation. This type of programmed control procedure helps compensate for the lack of human involvement in computer processing. Humans will notice when data do not make sense or are out of line; computers will not, unless specifically programmed to apply predefined criteria.

- *Field tests.* This type of logic test is based on the characteristics that data in particular fields should exhibit. For example, characters should be alphabetic or numeric; the field should have a specified size; the field should have a specified sign or in some cases, value.

- *Valid code test.* In this type of logic test a code field in a record is compared to a table of valid codes stored on-line. For example, a transaction code might be used in accounts receivable processing so that only transactions with certain codes, such as credit sales or cash collections, would be accepted to update the customers' master file.

The programmed control procedures listed above are only a few examples and not an exhaustive explanation of the programmed control procedures that are possible.

File controls are concerned with ensuring that the proper version of files are used in processing. For example, the current period's transaction file and the latest version of the master file should generally be used in processing. Control procedures in this area include *file label controls.* Internal file labels are computer-readable data that are actually part of the file to identify the file as to data and content. External file labels are attached to the outside of the file, such as a printed or handwritten adhesive label on a diskette or magnetic tape reel.

Processing controls are concerned with detecting errors in data and errors that occur in processing as a result of logic errors in application programs or systems software errors. Controls for data errors include programmed control procedures such as transaction code tests, checking the numerical sequence of records on a file, and comparing related fields in files. Controls to prevent or detect processing errors include programmed control procedures such as reasonableness or limit tests and use of redundant program calculations (double arithmetic). Also, control totals accumulated during processing are compared to input totals and prior computer run totals.

Output controls include manual control procedures that relate to the visual review of output by EDP personnel and users to ensure propriety and reasonableness and proper output handling to ensure distribution of output only to authorized users. Output controls also include programmed controls restricting access to display specified information (for example, payroll data) on a terminal or PC.

General Controls

General controls are those EDP controls that relate to all or many computerized accounting applications. A variety of controls fall into this broad category, but the general controls that are usually important to the planning and conduct of an audit of financial statements are as follows:

1 The plan of organization and operation of EDP (separation of incompatible functions or segregation of duties)
2 Control procedures to ensure that development, acquisition, and changes to programs are authorized, tested, and approved before being used for processing (control over programs)
3 Control procedures to ensure that access to data files is restricted to authorized users and programs (control over data)

Segregation of Duties   In a computerized accounting system the separation of duties related to EDP has the following aspects:

- Separation between EDP and user department functions
- Separation of incompatible functions within the EDP department

Separation of the EDP department from user department functions is important for the effectiveness of user controls. Ideally, of the functions of authorization, execution, recording, and accountability, the EDP department should be responsible for recording. However, in some systems, initiation or execution of transactions is an automatic step in an application program.

Normally, there will be an adequate segregation of duties if user departments independently exercise review and reconciliation controls over original input and resubmissions. User departments should independently reconcile manual documentation of input, such as control totals, with computer output. Also, errors should be returned for correction to the originating user department, and the user department should maintain an independent record (log) of corrections and resubmissions.

Within the EDP department, there will normally be the following positions or functions:

- *Manager of data processing*—the senior management position within the department responsible for supervising the data processing staff.
- *Systems analyst*—responsible for designing accounting systems, developing data processing projects in conjunction with user departments, and developing specifications for applications programmers
- *Applications programmer*—responsible for developing and testing new applications programs and changes to existing programs that meet the specifications established by the systems analyst
- *Systems programmer*—responsible for maintaining and adapting the operating system and other systems software
- *Computer operator*—responsible for the human intervention required to run application programs, such as mounting tapes onto tape drives
- *Data entry clerk*—responsible for keying information from manual source documents to computer-readable form
- *Data control clerk*—responsible for the handling and control of data within the EDP department, including comparing control totals to manually established or data preparation totals and correction of errors that originate in the EDP department
- *Librarian*—responsible for maintaining, and releasing for authorized use, files (magnetic tapes or disks) maintained off-line and written documentation of production programs (source code and related information)

Ideally, all these functions should be kept separate. An EDP department for a large mainframe computer installation might have 80 to 100 personnel in EDP. Except for the position of EDP manager, there would be a staff for every function and additional functions, such as a security officer for physical and software security. However, in smaller installations with fewer than six to eight personnel, some important functions have to be combined.

The critical separation of duties is that between operations and programming. These functions are incompatible and should not be combined because those who have knowledge of how the accounting systems and applications programs operate, including how to modify programs, should not be permitted the access to data files and production programs that accompany operations. Figure 9-1 presents the common EDP department functions separated between those positions with *knowledge* and those positions with *access* to data files or production programs.

In a small computer system (minicomputer or microcomputer) it is not unusual to find too few personnel to achieve an adequate separation of duties within EDP or between EDP and the user. The auditor, in such circumstances, would usually conclude that

Separate	Positions within EDP department
Knowledge (those with an understanding of systems and programs)	EDP manager
	Systems analysts
	Applications programmers
Access (those with access to the computer, production programs, and data files)	Computer operators
	Data entry clerks (no access to computer console, data control records, or programs)
	Data control clerks (no access to computer console)
	Librarian (no access to computer console)
	Systems programmers

FIGURE 9-1

Segregation of duties within EDP. (The position of systems programmer must have *access* to perform the function. Systems programmers should have no detailed knowledge of the company's accounting systems or application programs.)

general controls are seriously deficient, and reducing the assessment of control risk below the maximum level based on EDP controls would not be possible. However, the auditor might still be able to assess control risk below the maximum level based on user controls.

Control over Programs   Usually, controls over programs apply to all computerized accounting applications. The controls are concerned with whether development of new programs, acquisition of programs from software vendors, and changes to existing programs are adequately controlled. Adequate control includes authorization, testing, and approval before new or changed programs are placed into production (actually used in processing applications).

Ordinarily, control procedures for development, acquisition, or changes to programs are conceptually similar to other control procedures that leave a documentary trail, and they may be tested by inspection of documents for approval signatures. The essential features of control are *written procedures and documentation* for the following steps:

- *Initiation*—authorization for the EDP department to develop or acquire new programs or change existing programs. There should be written documentation, such as a program request form, that is formally approved by the relevant user department and EDP management.
- *Testing*—formal testing procedures that include the involvement of users, EDP management, and internal auditors. There should be an approved testing plan, and test data and results, indicating approval, should be retained.
- *Implementation*—formal approval by users and EDP management before a program is placed into production by EDP personnel independent of programming. Programmers should not have access to production programs so there should be separate test programs, and production programs should be protected from unauthorized access.

In many computerized systems, access to programs is protected by specialized systems software. For example, program library management software protects application programs that are stored on-line. This systems software also logs changes to programs and any attempts to obtain unauthorized access to programs. When this type of systems software is used, the auditor may be able to use management reports produced by the software to determine the date of the last change to each program.

Control over Data   Control procedures in user departments and EDP controls over input and processing help to ensure that processed data are authorized, valid, complete, and accurate. Control over access to data files is concerned with ensuring that data maintained on computer-readable files *remain* authorized, valid, complete, and accurate.

The control procedures that help ensure that access to data files is restricted to authorized users and programs are a mixture of physical devices, manual control procedures, and programmed control procedures. Physical security measures are necessary to ensure that only authorized personnel have access to the computer room. These measures include locks, badges, and passes for admittance. In a computerized system with on-line inquiry or entry capabilities, physical security measures for terminals, such as locks and a secure, supervised location, are also important. In a system where there is remote transmission from terminals to the CPU, physical security is more difficult to achieve and programmed procedures assume even greater significance.

For data files maintained off-line, a librarian function separate from programming and operations is important. The librarian function should release files only in accordance with established procedures for authorized use. Authorization should include both the individuals to whom files may be released and an authorized processing schedule. File label procedures, as discussed earlier, also help to ensure protection of data files from incorrect and unauthorized use.

In systems with on-line capabilities, access to on-line files is accomplished through terminals and a variety of programmed procedures are necessary, including, particularly, procedures accomplished by systems software. When terminals are located in user departments, the access to master files should be restricted to appropriate terminals. For example, terminals in the billing department should not have access to the accounts payable master file. This could be achieved by on-line storage of the identity of authorized terminals for each function using a master file and a systems comparison of the identity of the terminal requesting access to the designated authorized terminals for the requested file. It would also be necessary to restrict use of terminals to authorized users. For example, this could be achieved by systems software that requires users to enter an ID and a password to obtain access to particular data files and programs.

Also, in systems with on-line capabilities measures should be taken to restrict the access of those involved in the programming function to data files. Application programmers need to use files in testing programs, and provisions need to be made so that the files used in testing are copies or files of fictitious data rather than live data files. Also, systems software may be used to bypass programmed control procedures that restrict the access of application programs to data files. Thus, use of systems software should be controlled, and systems programmers' use of systems software should be monitored.

Systems security software packages are available that monitor access to data files and control unauthorized access. This type of software will either prevent or detect unauthorized access to data files. However, some systems software of this type, such as ACF2, may be operated in different modes at the client's choosing and only some modes prevent unauthorized access. Other modes will detect and produce a management report of unauthorized access to data files, and their effectiveness is dependent on manual investigation and follow-up of the reports.

In on-line systems where control over access to data files is dependent on systems software, the assistance of a computer audit specialist is usually essential. The computer audit specialist will assist in obtaining an understanding of the systems software dependent controls and in evaluating their effectiveness in restricting access to data files to authorized users and programs.

Other General Controls   There are a variety of other general controls, but usually they do not have an effect on the auditor's assessment of control risk. For example, some general controls are concerned with the ability to recover computer operations if various problems arise. These general controls relate to measures taken to back up hardware, software, and files and to ensure recovery when the computer installation or particular computer files or programs are damaged or destroyed. For example, the client should have a contingency plan to follow if computer processing is disrupted by a disaster such as a fire or a flood.

Backup procedures relate to the ability to reconstruct data files if the current version of the file is damaged by hardware or software error. For example, in a system with batch input and batch processing a tape file retention policy should be in effect to allow the reconstruction of master files. A tape retention policy often used is called the grandfather-father-son concept. As the name implies, it involves retaining three generations of a particular master file and the related transaction files. The current version of the master file is on the son file, and the two prior versions are the father and grandfather. In an on-line entry system, data file retention requires periodically dumping the entire contents of master files to tapes on a daily basis creating a transaction log tape of processed transactions.

Some CPA firms have adopted a policy of reviewing such general controls as a matter of client service even though there may be no effect on the scope of audit procedures. For the same reason, a review of general controls is often made even though the auditor does not plan to base any portion of the control risk assessment on EDP controls.

CONSIDERATION OF THE COMPUTER IN PLANNING THE AUDIT

The discussion in this chapter emphasizes matters that are unique to computerized systems. However, even when the extent of computer involvement in accounting applications is extensive, the computer is not the focus of the audit. The independent auditor audits financial statements, not computers. In a computerized system, financial statements are the product of a combination of manual accounting and control procedures, programmed accounting and control procedures, and manual and computer-readable data in transaction files and master files. The following discussion supplements the discussion in earlier chapters on the planning phases of the audit.

Understanding the Client and the Control Environment

During general planning the auditor obtains information on the client's computer installation as part of the consideration of the control environment. Generally, the auditor obtains information on the following matters:

- Type of computer equipment and its configuration, including input and processing modes used
- Types of systems software
- Organizational structure of computer processing activities, including the organizational location of the EDP department, number of personnel, and internal organization plan
- Number and nature of computerized accounting applications

This information allows the auditor to assess the size and complexity of the computerized portion of the accounting system and the extent of assistance of computer audit specialists that will be required.

Understanding the Accounting System

The auditor needs to obtain an understanding of the path that transactions take through both the manual and computerized portions of the accounting system, consider the anticipated computer-related controls that may contribute to a control risk assessment at less than the maximum level, and document and test controls contributing to the control risk assessment.

An efficient approach to understanding the accounting system is to start at the end rather than the beginning. The auditor identifies significant amounts in the financial statements being audited. The transactions that affect those amounts are traced back from the financial statements to their sources—the original source document prepared or data screen used when the data are captured by the accounting system. The auditor then identifies the processing points in that flow. These are the points at which transactions are initiated, recorded, calculated, summarized, or reported. Generally, misstatements can occur at any of these processing points, and these are the points at which control procedures are necessary.

As part of this step of obtaining an understanding of the accounting system, the auditor identifies the extent to which the computer is used in each significant accounting application. For significant computerized accounting applications, the auditor obtains the following type of information:

- The purpose of the application, including particularly the documents, reports, and updated master files generated by the application and the general ledger account balances affected by the application

- The source, volume, and form of input to the application, including particularly the user departments in which transactions originate or other computerized accounting applications that generate input for the application
- The master files affected by the application, including particularly the storage media, file maintenance process, and the size and organization of files
- The mode and frequency of processing
- The form of output of the application and the distribution of output

The auditor uses this information to obtain an understanding of the relationship between the manual and computerized portions of the accounting system for significant accounting applications and the nature and extent of computer involvement.

Understanding Control Activities

If there are significant computerized accounting applications, the auditor may need to obtain an understanding of the general controls. As mentioned earlier, many auditors as a matter of policy do a general controls review even when the auditor does not plan to assess control risk at below the maximum level because it is a client service opportunity. Usually the review is done by a computer audit specialist or an auditor with additional training in computerized systems.

The review is conducted by inquiry and observation of client EDP personnel and review of existing documentation, such as client manuals, prior years' work papers, and other information on the computer installation and computerized accounting applications. The auditor's objective is to decide whether there appears to be reasonable assurance that:

- There is an adequate separation of duties between EDP and users and within the EDP department.
- The development or acquisition of programs and changes to programs are authorized, tested, and approved before implementation.
- Access to data files is restricted to authorized users and programs.

The evaluation of whether there appears to be reasonable assurance can be complex. Absolute assurance is an unworkable goal, and most systems will have some deficiencies. For example, in an on-line entry system there may be strong controls over terminal and user access to data files, but some systems programmers may have access to systems software that can bypass those controls. The auditor needs to evaluate the seriousness of the deficiency in the circumstances.

After obtaining the understanding of general controls, the auditor concludes whether general controls appear to be effective. Whether including such controls as part of the basis to reduce the control risk assessment is necessary or desirable depends on the auditor's consideration of application controls. If the general controls are part of the basis for reducing the control risk assessment, it is necessary to test the control procedures.

Tests of general controls are, as mentioned earlier, conceptually similar to tests in a manual system.

- Inquiry and observation are used to test the separation of duties within EDP and between EDP and users.
- Physical access to the computer room, terminals, and data files are also tested by inquiry and observation.
- Inspection of documents by sampling can generally be used to test the operation of control procedures for authorization, testing, and approval of new programs or changes to existing programs. For example, a random sample of program request forms can be selected and inspected for indication of approval.
- If library management systems software is used, the reports produced by the software can be used to obtain a sample of new or changed programs, and these can be traced to program testing results and program request forms.

If reports generated by systems software are used, the assistance of a computer audit specialist is necessary to understand and evaluate the software. Also, the computer audit specialist can design various "beat-the-system" tests to test access-control software. For example, with client management's cooperation, a terminal can be used by the auditor to attempt to obtain unauthorized access to programs and data files. This will confirm the computer audit specialist's understanding of the implementation of the system software.

Planning Tests of Details of Transactions and Balances

The specific control objectives for tests of transaction classes and the specific audit objectives for direct tests of balances are not affected by computerization of accounting applications. In any of the following circumstances, the auditor plans tests of details of transactions and balances without use of any EDP controls as part of the basis for a reduced level of control risk:

- The client has no computerized significant accounting applications.
- Specific control objectives for transaction classes are not dependent on the results of computer processing.
- Serious deficiencies exist in general controls, and there are no compensating controls.

Tests of Transaction Classes   If there are significant computerized accounting applications and if achievement of specific control objectives for transaction classes in those applications is dependent on the results of computer processing, some consideration of the effectiveness of EDP controls in the control risk assessment is necessary. The EDP controls that are relevant for this purpose are the application controls for the application and the general controls relevant to the application. Tests for general controls were explained earlier.

The auditor may select among several approaches for testing EDP application controls. Applications software includes both programmed accounting procedures for the calculation and summarization of data and programmed control procedures. The programmed accounting procedures usually leave a documentary trail in the form of computer printouts of documents, lists, files, and reports. On the other hand, programmed control procedures usually leave no documentary trail unless transactions are rejected or flagged for review. For example, a programmed limit test in an accounting application will not result in a printed report unless transactions are input that exceed the established limits.

The auditor's basic choice in testing EDP application controls is between manual and computer-assisted testing:

- *Manual.* The auditor selects samples of transactions from the transaction classes processed by the accounting application and applies audit procedures to substantiate the validity, completeness, and accuracy of the data. The auditor also inspects the automated error reports produced by the application and investigates the nature and cause of the errors and the client's investigation and follow-up of errors, and manually tests user application controls.
- *Computer-assisted.* The auditor uses one of several possible approaches, explained in the next major section, to test the client's computer programs used in the accounting application.

In the abstract, either approach should meet the auditor's objectives because the manual and computer-assisted approaches are both dual-purpose tests. Computer-assisted testing of client programs should allow the auditor to reach a conclusion on whether both programmed accounting procedures and programmed control procedures are operating satisfactorily. However, auditors in practice are understandably reluctant to reach a conclusion on the validity, completeness, and accuracy of accounting data without ever actually testing the data. For this reason, the *manual approach* to testing transaction classes is often followed. This approach also has the advantage of familiarity to auditors and does not require specialized knowledge of computers.

Whether the auditor uses the manual or computer-assisted approach in testing EDP application controls, some consideration of the effectiveness of general controls is still usually necessary and these controls should be tested as explained earlier.

Direct Tests of Balances   When the auditor makes direct tests of balances at year-end, computer reliance is usually not necessary. If the scope of direct tests of balances is planned with anticipated reliance on computer-related control procedures or direct tests of balances are to be applied at an interim date, some consideration of the effectiveness of general controls is usually necessary.

When direct tests of balances are applied using computer-generated information, the auditor generally has a choice of approaches. The following alternatives might be considered:

- Directly test the computer-generated information at year-end. This approach involves no reliance on application controls or general controls in the control risk assessment but may not be the most efficient approach.
- Test the computer-generated information and general controls through an interim date and update the assessment of controls through year-end. In many cases, the updating can be accomplished through inquiry and observation.

- Test the computer-generated information at an interim date and use automated reports produced by systems software to determine that the application program has not changed since the interim date. This approach is useful when general controls have some deficiencies, but systems software is reliable.

Additional planning is necessary, as explained in the following section, if the auditor decides to use computer assistance in applying direct tests of balances to client files in computer-readable form.

COMPUTER-ASSISTED AUDIT TECHNIQUES

The use of computer assistance in an audit of financial statements generally falls into one of the following categories:

- Testing client programs
- Testing client files
- Use of a microcomputer as an audit tool

Figure 9-2 summarizes some common techniques for the first two categories. These categories generally involve use of the client's computer, but the third category is independent of the client's computer.

Broad category	Specific examples	Type of information
Testing client programs (a production program for an accounting application)	Program code review	A nonprocessing approach; source code of application software
	Controlled processing, reprocessing, or parallel processing	Actual client transaction data and master files
	Test data	Simulated transaction data and copies of master files
	Integrated test facility	Simulated transaction data and actual client master files
Testing client data files (a master file or transaction file)	Generalized audit software	Copies of client transaction files or master files
	Custom-designed programs	Copies of client transaction files or master files
	Utility programs	Copies of client transaction files or master files
	Regression analysis or other special-purpose programs	Copies of client transaction files or master files or auditor-prepared input

FIGURE 9-2
Examples of computer-assisted audit techniques using the client's computer.

Testing Client Programs

As explained earlier, client application programs include programmed accounting procedures for calculating and summarizing data and programmed control procedures for providing reasonable assurance that data are authorized, valid, complete, and accurate. If the auditor tests client programs, both aspects of programmed procedures are usually tested.

However, auditors generally prefer to take a manual approach to dual-purpose testing of transaction classes for significant computerized accounting applications. Following this approach, tests of general controls are necessary, but the auditor would not use computer assistance to test the client's application programs.

Computer-assisted audit techniques may need to be used in complex systems with real-time processing. Also, some CPA firms have relatively large contingents of computer audit specialists and may use computer-assisted techniques more frequently.

The following discussion explains some of the common types of computer-assisted audit techniques for testing client programs.

Test Data   The test data approach is explained first not because it is the most widely used, but because it conceptually depicts what the auditor is trying to accomplish by testing client programs.

Using this approach the auditor prepares *simulated* transaction data. These test transactions include both correct data to test processing and incorrect data to test control procedures in the client's application program. The auditor manually calculates what the processing results should be and compares them to the results produced by processing the test data with the client's application program. The auditor needs to ensure that the program tested is the production program used in actual processing and that the same program was used throughout the period covered by the control risk assessment. Generally, it is necessary to identify general controls and consider their effectiveness for that assurance.

The test data approach may be used in a system with on-line entry capability if the auditor obtains client permission to use a terminal to enter transactions.

Integrated Test Facility   An integrated test facility (ITF) is an adaptation of the test data approach. Dummy records are included in the client's files. For example, dummy customers might be included for an accounts receivable application. The auditor's simulated transactions are processed with the production program against the live files during regular processing. This approach overcomes several of the drawbacks of the test data approach, but the auditor must still assess general controls for reasonable assurance that the program tested is not changed during the period. However, it is essential to prevent dummy records from being summarized with live data when financial statements or other reports are prepared.

Processing Client Data   Both the test data approach and the ITF use *simulated* transactions. Another group of techniques for testing client programs uses actual client data to test processing and simulated data to test controls. These techniques are presented together because of this similarity, but the auditor might use only one of the techniques for a particular computerized accounting application.

- *Controlled processing.* The auditor establishes control over client input and independently calculates key processing results such as the ending balance of a control account. The auditor maintains control over the computer processing and output and compares the computer output to the auditor's calculated results.
- *Controlled reprocessing.* The auditor maintains control over the reprocessing of previously processed results using a version of the program the auditor has tested and compares the computer output of the original processing and reprocessing.
- *Parallel processing.* The auditor compares the results of the client's processing with results obtained by using the client's input and files and the auditor's own program. The auditor's program used for this purpose may be a custom-designed program or generalized audit software. Generally, the auditor's program will calculate key processing results rather than duplicate all of the client's processing.

These techniques are generally more useful for testing the processing accuracy of client programs than for testing programmed control procedures.

Nonprocessing Approaches   Some approaches to testing client programs are essentially *manual* procedures. However, they need to be used in conjunction with some computer-assisted techniques. Two examples are as follows:

- *Program code review.* The auditor reviews the client's programs documentation, including a narrative description and the source code. The auditor goes over the relevant code line by line and considers whether the processing steps and control procedures are properly coded and logically correct.
- *Review of job accounting data.* The auditor reviews the printed log produced as jobs are run and considers any excessive processing time, error conditions, or abnormal halts. (This technique does not test the client's program but has similar objectives.)

These techniques have several drawbacks. Reviewing program code requires extensive knowledge of programming, and the auditor still must use some other techniques to ensure that the source code reviewed corresponds to the object code of the production program used throughout the period. Reviewing job accounting information is time-consuming and difficult because the information is voluminous and may not be easy to interpret. Specialized software is available to assist the auditor in these tasks. There is also software to compare programs to determine whether they are identical. These techniques and the use of the specialized software require a computer audit specialist.

Testing Client Files

If client files are voluminous, it can be efficient to apply audit procedures to records in their computer-readable form. For example, a very large company may have master files with over 100,000 individual records in applications such as inventory and accounts receivable. In these circumstances, it may be more efficient for the auditor to use a computer program to automate application of auditing procedures. An auditor's computer program may be used with master files or transaction files so the audit procedures may be tests of details of transactions or balances. However, using an auditor's computer program to test a client's master files is more common. The following approaches might be used to automate auditing procedures.

Generalized Audit Software   The most widely used form of computer-assisted audit technique is *generalized audit software*. This technique involves a software package used to perform specific audit tasks, such as footing and comparing items, on a computer-readable file. A generalized program that can be used for many clients to perform several audit tasks is more efficient than programs specially written for particular clients and tasks. However, a generalized audit software package is not an all-purpose device that is usable for all clients with computers. The auditor's software must interact with the operating system of the client's computer. This means that a particular package is usually designed for a family of hardware using a particular operating system. Large CPA firms have developed their own packages, and some software vendors offer audit packages. In some cases, versions of these packages have been developed for different hardware and operating systems.

Since there are many audit software packages and they are not identical, this discussion describes the general features of this type of software. When generalized software is run, the first step is to read the client's file. The processing is performed on a copy of the client's file, and the client's data are not changed. The other two aspects of generalized audit software are as follows:

- *File formats.* Client file formats vary considerably. For example, the number, type, and size of fields in a record on an accounts receivable master file differ dramatically from client to client. One of the advantages of generalized audit software is its ability to deal with different file formats. The file format is defined by the auditor as part of the input specification. Some packages reformat the data in a standardized manner. The auditor must specify the file layout and the fields and their location in the file.
- *Processing instructions.* Generalized audit software is designed to perform several types of processing tasks. The package must provide some means for the auditor to instruct the package on the particular tasks to be performed. Several approaches are used. In many cases, the auditor fills out coding or specification sheets to identify the tasks. Another approach is for the auditor to write a simplified program in a specially designed macro-command language similar to COBOL.

Generalized audit software packages are usually designed to accomplish the following types of tasks:

- *Footing*—adding specified fields in a file, such as totaling invoice amounts on an accounts receivable open item file
- *Calculating*—performing extensions or other computations, such as extending inventory quantities time unit costs or recomputing interest charges

- *Selecting*—printing a list of items that conform to specified criteria or using a random-based selection method, such as identifying all customer balances over $5,000 and a random sample of balances below that amount
- *Comparing*—making a comparison of fields on a file, such as comparing the quantity of inventory items on hand with the quantity used or sold during the period and printing out items with excessive quantities on hand
- *Form printing*—printing forms, such as confirmation requests or work paper account analyses

To make effective use of generalized audit software, the auditor needs to plan carefully. Specific audit objectives remain the same whether audit procedures are applied manually or by using generalized audit software. The starting point in both cases is to develop specific audit objectives from financial statement assertions. However, in using generalized audit software, specification of objectives and criteria in advance of testing becomes extremely important. In applying procedures manually, for example, the auditor may notice other unusual items in selecting specified items from the accounting records. When generalized audit software is used, an item cannot be selected unless the auditor has specified the criteria for its selection completely in advance.

Custom-Designed Programs   If generalized audit software cannot be used on a particular client's computer, the auditor might consider having a program specially written to accomplish specific audit tasks. This can be expensive and time-consuming because the program can only be used for a single client.

Utility Programs   Software vendors and hardware vendors have developed software designed to accomplish common tasks, such as sorting. The auditor may be able to use a utility program to print the entire contents of a file or sort a file into a sequence useful for an audit task.

Special-Purpose Software   Some special-purpose software is available for performing common auditing or accounting tasks. For example, software is available for regression analysis or ratio computation for purposes of applying analytical procedures, consolidating or combining financial statements, and preparing corporate tax returns. Some of the programs may run on the client's computer, but much of this type of software is used on microcomputers.

Use of a Microcomputer as an Audit Tool

Another use of computers in auditing is the use of microcomputers for audit-related tasks. The micro may be a portable taken to the field or a larger micro used in the auditor's own office.

Spread Sheets   One of the primary advantages of micros is that they can be used effectively without learning to program. A variety of application software packages are available. An auditor may use an electronic spreadsheet or software specially designed for auditors. An electronic spreadsheet is an electronically stored and manipulated worksheet with many rows and columns that has the ability to handle predefined mathematical relationships among numbers in the rows and columns. Electronic spreadsheets can be used to create *templates* for common accounting or auditing-related calculations. A template is a model of relationships among specified components. The following are some of the types of applications for which an electronic spreadsheet with templates can be used:

- *Working trial balance.* The auditor keys in account titles and amounts to prepare an unadjusted trial balance. The spreadsheet will, based on the assumptions, instructions, and index of the template, prepare lead schedules and financial statements and recalculate the results based on entered adjusting entries.
- *Analytical procedures.* Using the same data entered for the trial balance, another template can be used to calculate specified ratios or percentage relationships among account balances.
- *Complex computations.* If the components of a calculation and the relationships among them can be specified, templates can be prepared for a variety of complex computations. For example, a template might be prepared to compute a corporate tax provision, including the deferred tax carry forward and analysis of taxes payable, based on pretax income and a list of items from the relevant tax return schedule.

Automating Work Papers   Essentially a microcomputer automates the auditor's work papers. In the past, microcomputers were not used extensively to apply tests of details to client files because any processing the microcomputer did was of data entered manually through the keyboard. However, downloading of data through modems and off-line conversion of client files to microdiskettes are overcoming this problem. Whether use of the microcomputer will be efficient on an audit is a function of the time consumed in entering data, the capability of the software purchased or developed, and the auditor's proficiency in using the micro.

The auditor's work paper file generally contains printed copies of the final working trial balance, spreadsheets, and calculation output reports. Each of these should indicate the preparer and reviewer, as for any other work paper. A copy of the information on diskette or other machine-readable media is also generally retained in the file.

Expert Systems   Some CPA firms use specialized microsoftware for *expert systems* (also called "artificial intelligence") to help in designing audit programs and to assist the auditor in analyzing internal control features of complex systems. For example, using an expert system internal control questionnaire for general controls, when the auditor enters the type of computer, the system asks which of the available operating systems is being used. The system then asks questions relevant only to that hardware and operating system. As each question is answered, the system narrows its questioning to the specific computer environment. For example, if the auditor responds that RACF is being used as access control software, the computer will ask a series of questions about the specific features of RACF that are relevant. Similarly, in designing audit programs, the auditor provides information about the specific audit areas, and the system suggests relevant audit procedures. Use of such automated tools is helpful to provide a wide range of relevant information to the auditor in the field, but must not be used as a substitute for auditor judgment.

A Terminology Note

The following terms are sometimes used to describe the effect of computers on auditing:

- *Auditing around the computer.* A term used to describe the approach of manually testing transaction data by reconciling hard copy computer output to input in the form of manual source documents.
- *Auditing through the computer.* A term used to describe the approach of testing the client's application programs using techniques such as test data.
- *Auditing with the computer.* A term used to describe the use of audit software to automate audit procedures, or other computer-assisted audit techniques.

The student should be familiar with these terms. Note, however, that even when the auditor takes the approach of manually testing transaction classes, the auditor must obtain an understanding of both the manual and computer portions of the accounting system and may need to identify and test general controls.

OTHER COMPUTER-RELATED CONSIDERATIONS

The following topics are explained briefly because they are relatively specialized considerations:

- Real-time processing systems
- Electronic data interchange
- Computer service centers
- Database management systems
- LANs and other networks

Real-Time Processing Systems

In a system with on-line entry *and* real-time processing, the master file may be updated when a transaction is entered into a terminal. This eliminates the use of batch control totals as a visual audit trail and as a device for maintaining the completeness and accuracy of data. The auditor may find it necessary to use advance computer-assisted audit techniques to test client programs in this type of system. However, it is desirable, from a control viewpoint, to create artificial batches and, in that case, the audit approach is as explained earlier in this chapter.

Electronic Data Interchange

Large companies are increasing their use of *electronic data interchange* (EDI) as a form of input and output. For example, a large carmaker requires its thousands of suppliers to accept orders for parts through electronically transmitted purchase orders. When the parts are shipped, the supplier transmits an invoice. This cuts down the number of data entry personnel required, mailing costs, and time to complete transactions.

EDI is simply a different medium for input and output. For example, the objectives of control over payment of invoices remain the same, but the timing and method of performing the control procedures may change when the supplier inputs the invoice to the company computer. Receiving reports of goods actually received by the company should be input and matched to the invoice data before payment is released, and the system should compare the payment terms and amounts with the originally transmitted purchase orders, and any changes (back-ordered items, substitutions) should be authorized.

Computer Service Centers

A client may have some or all computerized accounting applications processed at an outside service center, or bureau, rather than using its own computer. Even many companies with large computer installations prefer to have applications such as payroll processed outside. The usual approach in this circumstance is for the auditor to view the client as a user department and the service bureau as the EDP department. If there are adequate user controls, the auditor may apply manual procedures at the client's location without concern about the controls at the service bureau. If the user controls are inadequate, the auditor must be concerned with the controls at the service bureau. The most efficient approach is to obtain what is generally called a third-party review report from the service bureau's auditor on the design and operating effectiveness of the service bureau's controls. The considerations that apply to this type of report are explained in SAS No. 70 (AU 324), *Reports on the Processing of Transactions by Service Organizations.*

Database Management Systems

A database is a computer-readable file of records that is used by several accounting applications. For example, a file of suppliers or vendors might be used by purchase ordering, accounts payable, and inventory applications. In a file-based system, there is usually a separate file for each application even though essentially similar information is maintained on each file. In a database system, such a file would be shared by the applications.

The database approach requires a file indexing system with primary and secondary identifying key fields because different applications require different identifying keys. Because of the complexity of the file structure, special systems software called a *database management system (DBMS)* is necessary to handle programming and related tasks for managing the database. The person with overall responsibility for the data is the database administrator.

One effect on the audit associated with database management systems is that generalized audit software usually cannot be used to directly access files maintained by the database management system. Possible approaches are to dump the contents of the database to tape before using generalized audit software, to use the database software itself to retrieve data, or to develop special software as an interface between the generalized audit software and database management system.

Another effect on the audit of a database system is that the general controls necessary to ensure that access to data files is restricted to authorized users and programs are more complex because data files are shared by users and programs.

The client's use of a database management system may require the involvement of computer audit specialists in planning and conducting the audit.

LANs and Other Networks

In the past few years, many companies have moved accounting applications from mainframes to microcomputers (PCs) on local area networks (LANs). In most cases, internal control risk has risen significantly. Over the years, companies with critical mainframe applications developed effective security and control procedures. By distributing the processing to many microcomputers at many locations, many of the security and control procedures and techniques designed for the mainframe no longer work or apply, and often little has been put in place to replace the controls. *Viruses* (unauthorized programs causing mischief or significant damage) can spread from microcomputer to microcomputer quickly in a LAN environment. Complicating the design of the controls is the increasing trend to connect LANs with other LANs or even nationwide networks.

The operating system software that runs the LANs does not have the built-in control features that were eventually developed for mainframe and minicomputers. Software to add onto the LAN operating system to provide security and control features is being developed, but many have significant weaknesses. Encryption software slows down processing and some encryption packages have a tendency to cause networks to "crash." Utility software designed to troubleshoot LAN problems often permits users to discover others' IDs and passwords.

Security and control features for LANs and other networks will continue to improve. Originally, mainframe computers had few control features, but the industry responded to the demand for internal control over the applications processed. A similar process will result in improved control in LANs.

ADVANCED COMPUTER-ASSISTED TECHNIQUES

All of the computer-assisted audit techniques explained so far, with the exception of the integrated test facility technique, are used *after* computer processing. However, several more advanced audit techniques are used *concurrently* with processing. These techniques use live data, files, or programs and may be useful when computer reliance is necessary and when a visible audit trail is not available, such as in some real-time processing systems. These techniques produce evidence on current system performance and require extensive on-site audit supervision. For these reasons, they are used more frequently by internal auditors than by independent auditors.

Some examples of advanced computer-assisted audit techniques are as follows:

- *Systems control audit review file (SCARF).* This technique uses audit modules embedded in application programs to monitor transaction activity at designated points and select transactions for the auditor's review. The auditor provides criteria when the application program is developed so that the auditor's program module can be inserted at the point in processing logic where errors are most likely to occur and so that transactions selected meet the auditor's specifications.

- *Snapshot.* This technique involves transaction tagging (indicator added to data) at input and recording at selected points in the path of tagged transactions through the system. Tags may be assigned randomly or in accordance with specified criteria. When an application program encounters a tagged transaction, the transaction data, date and time of occurrence, the application program involved, and the point in the program at which generated, are written to an audit log. This provides the auditor with a picture, hence *snapshot,* of the data at particular points in processing. This approach provides the auditor with more detailed information than is provided by a technique such as SCARF and permits review of intermediate results during processing.
- *Audit hooks.* This technique provides "exit" points in application programs that allow the auditor to insert commands for special processing. For example, database management system might contain an audit hook that allows the auditor to insert additional coding to obtain independent control totals as a result of normal processing.

These techniques all permit the auditor to conduct testing during normal computer processing. However, they require advanced computer knowledge and training and have the inherent potential danger of causing modification of transaction data.

APPENDIX: BASIC CONCEPTS OF COMPUTER PROCESSING

Hardware

Every computerized system has two primary components that are unique to computers—hardware and software. The hardware component includes all the electronic equipment used in processing. Every computerized system needs hardware components to accomplish the functions of input, processing, storage, and output.

Types of Computers   Computers are commonly classified in three categories: mainframes, minicomputers, and microcomputers. Microcomputers are sometimes called "personal computers" or "PCs." Essentially, all computers perform identical internal functions; at the heart of every computer is a *central processing unit (CPU)* that performs arithmetic and logic (less than or greater than) operations on data. The CPU is the device that does the actual processing of data. In addition to the arithmetic-logic unit, the CPU has a control unit and a storage unit.

In some cases, there is a slight difference in terminology for hardware components among types of computers. For example, the CPU in a microcomputer is called a microprocessor. However, the differences among mainframes, minis, and micros are primarily matters of size and processing speed. Some distinguishing features among types of computers have auditing implications. These are explained at relevant points in the following discussion.

Input and Output Devices and Media   Input devices are simply machines for entering data to the CPU, and output devices are machines for the exit of data from the CPU. Some machines are used exclusively for input or exclusively for output, but some devices serve both functions. The primary types of input and output devices or media are as follows:

- *Key entry devices.* The data entry clerk enters the data on a typewriter-like keyboard. The data is then stored in the computer or on other media to await processing.
- *Magnetic tape.* This medium can be used for input, storage, and output. It is physically similar to the media used for home tape recorders or audio or video cassettes. Data on magnetic tape are input or output from the computer by a device called a tape drive. Special reading and writing heads on the drive transmit data to and from the computer.
- *Magnetic disk.* This medium can also be used for input, storage, and output. Physically, this medium is similar to several phonograph records stacked on top of each other with a small arm between each. The arms are equipped with reading and writing heads for transmission of data. The machine that holds the disks is called the disk drive.
- *Diskette.* Diskettes are a commonly used medium in microcomputer systems. They are similar to magnetic tape in that there are generally many diskettes that are used interchangeably with one disk drive.
- *Printer.* This device is used exclusively for output. It produces the "hard copy" that can be distributed to various users of computer-generated reports.
- *Terminal.* This hardware device permits interaction between the human and the computer. The physical characteristics of a terminal include a keyboard similar to a typewriter for input of commands or data and a visual screen or cathode-ray tube (CRT) similar to a television screen for displaying output.
- *Other media and devices.* CD-ROM is similar to compact disks (CDs) used in audio CD players for music or video CD players for movies. Scanners are devices to input text or pictures into a computer file. In auditing, a portion of a computer printout may be efficiently entered into a spreadsheet by use of a scanner.

Hardware Controls   Hardware controls are electronic features built into machines by the manufacturer to detect failure in an electronic or mechanical part of computer equipment. There is really no need for auditors to become involved in the specifics of hardware controls. These built-in controls are designed by the manufacturer and are not subject to modification by the purchaser. However, an auditor is usually concerned with the frequency of hardware-induced errors and the provisions made by the client for responding to machine errors.

Software

The other primary component of computerized systems is software. Computer software broadly refers to sets of instructions that control and direct computer hardware. Software can be classified in two broad categories—systems software and application software.

Systems Software   Systems software is a collective term for all programs (instructions to the computer) that coordinate and control the use of hardware or support the execution of application software. Some of the primary examples of systems software are as follows:

- *Operating system.* A set of internally stored instructions that control and coordinate the use of the CPU, including input, storage, processing, and output. Usually, the operating system (such as DOS) is supplied by the manufacturer of the hardware.
- *Compilers, assemblers, and interpreters.* This specialized software converts (translates) the instructions written in a programming language into a machine language. Each programming language, such as COBOL, uses a unique compiler or interpreter based on that language's structure. Assemblers perform the same function for programs written in assembly language—a programming language more similar to machine language. Compilers, assemblers, and interpreters are usually supplied by the manufacturer of hardware.
- *Utilities.* This software is designed to perform standard input/output tasks, such as sorting and merging of data.

Other systems software explained in this chapter are systems security software, program library management software, and database management systems.

Application Software   Application software, or programs, are the specific sets of instructions for performing specific data processing tasks such as order entry, billing, accounts receivable processing, or payroll processing.

Application programs are written in a programming, or *source,* language. The most common programming language used in business today is COBOL—a language specifically designed to meet the needs of business data processing, particularly the input and output of large amounts of data. Another programming language used in business applications is BASIC—a simple language that can be learned quickly and is used primarily in applications on small computer systems (minicomputers and microcomputers).

A program written in a source language must be translated by use of a compiler or interpreter into machine language. The machine language version of the application program is called the *object program.* It is the object program that is acted on by the control unit of the CPU to actually perform the processing of data.

Application software may be written by the purchaser of the hardware or supplied by a software vendor.

Data Processing and Storage

An important consideration for the auditor in general planning is the method the client uses to process accounting data and the complexity of that processing. A characteristic of computerized systems that has a significant influence on complexity is the mode of transaction input and processing. This section explains the input and processing modes the auditor may encounter and the underlying computer processing concepts necessary to understand them.

On-Line versus Off-Line   An important concept in understanding input and processing modes is the distinction between on-line and off-line. These terms are used to describe both the relationship of computer hardware to the CPU and the accessibility of data and programs to the CPU. *On-line* means that the hardware is in constant contact with the CPU or that data or programs are accessible to the CPU without human intervention. For example, terminals and disks are hardware that is generally on-line. In contracts, a tape or diskette is *off-line* because human action is necessary to place it on the drive before it is accessible to the CPU.

Data Storage   The storage of data in computerized systems has several complexities. The CPU of every computer has a storage unit that is called *main memory, internal memory, primary storage,* or *core memory.* Naturally, data stored in primary storage is on-line because it is always accessible within the CPU. However, primary storage has several drawbacks. First, it is temporary. If the computer is shut off or the power fails, the information in primary storage is lost. Second, it is limited in capacity even in large mainframe computers. Business data processing requires very large storage capacity and must make extensive use of secondary storage. (This type of storage is also called *auxiliary, external,* or *peripheral.*)

Secondary storage is usually maintained on magnetic tape or magnetic disk and may be on-line or off-line. Generally, magnetic tapes are kept off-line until needed for processing and magnetic disks are on-line. Another aspect of the accessibility to the CPU of data in secondary storage is whether access is sequential or direct.

Sequential versus Direct Access and Files   *Sequential access* simply means that the data is stored in sequence and the computer's access to the data is sequential. In other words, data stored at the beginning of the storage media must be passed before the computer can obtain access to data stored at the end. For example, magnetic tape is a sequential access storage media.

Direct, or random, *access* means that the computer's access to the data is not affected by location of the data on the media; all data on the storage media are equally accessible to the computer. For example, magnetic disks are direct access storage media.

Sequential and direct are also the terms for corresponding file organization methods. In a computerized system, a *file* is a group of records of a particular type. For example, the file containing all the balances of individual customer accounts is the accounts receivable *master file.* A *transaction file* is comprised of all the transactions of a particular type for a particular time period. For example, all credit-sales transactions on a particular day would be a transaction file. The individual records on a file are collections of *data fields.* For example, an individual customer record on the accounts receivable master file would contain separate fields for customer number, customer name, address, credit limit, account balance, and similar information.

Sequential file organization mean the records are arranged in sequence based on an identifying field such as the customer number. *Direct file organization* means the records are not stored in physical sequential order, but that the computer keeps track of a particular record's storage location by a type of indexing method.

Input and Processing Modes   Computerized accounting systems vary in the methods, or modes, of transaction input and processing. The primary categories of input and processing modes are as follows:

* *Batch input and processing.* Manually prepared source documents, such as payroll time cards or sales orders, are accumulated over a logical interval—daily, weekly, or monthly. An accumulated batch of documents is converted to computer-readable form off-line, and the input is validated to create a transaction file. Generally, the transaction file is sorted based on the identifying field in the master file and processed sequentially to update the master file.
* *On-line input with batch processing.* In this input and processing mode, transactions are entered individually at a terminal. A manual source document may be the basis for entry or entry may be immediate. Transactions are stored on-line and processed against the master file in batches at scheduled intervals. The most likely form of storage media for this input and processing mode is magnetic disk. On-line input with batch processing is likely to be used in applications that are facilitated by file inquiry capabilities. For example, in the entry of sales orders the on-line inquiry capability can be used to determine credit limits and product availability. This input and processing mode is subject to the most variation in practice. For example, a terminal may be used merely as a batch entry device to input accumulated manual source documents or individual transactions may be entered immediately. When transactions are entered immediately a manual record may or may not be prepared.
* *On-line input with real-time processing.* In this input and processing mode, transactions are entered individually by terminal, and the master file is updated at the time of entry. This is the most complex input and processing mode. Magnetic disks are the form of secondary storage in this type of system.

Batch input and processing is the least complex type of system and is usually easiest to audit because, as explained on pages 341 and 342, batching is conducive to an effective internal control structure. On-line input with batch processing may operate in a manner that is virtually equivalent to batch input and processing when terminals are used as batch entry devices. However, any system with on-line entry capability uses computer technology that makes auditing more complex. On-line input with real-time processing is the most complex type of system and usually requires the use of sophisticated computer-assisted audit techniques. On-line real-time systems, thus, often require use of computer audit specialists.

A particular audit client may use a mixture of input and processing modes. For example, payroll, because periodic processing is involved, may be a batch input and processing system, but the sales accounting system may be an on-line input with batch processing system. Also, there may be a mixture of manual and computer processing for a particular system. For example, a sales accounting system includes entry of sales orders, billing, and accounts receivable processing. All of these functions may be computerized in an integrated system, but it is also possible for only some of the functions to be computerized. For example, order entry and billing may be manual, but accounts receivable processing (updating the accounts receivable master file for invoices and cash collections) may be computerized.

CHAPTER 9 ASSIGNMENTS

OBJECTIVE QUESTIONS

9-1 For each one of the following statements indicate whether the statement is true or false.

T F a Use of a computer for significant accounting applications does not in any way change specific audit objectives or specific control objectives.

T F b When a client has significant computerized accounting applications, some reliance on the computer is usually necessary in the control risk assessment and the auditor must identify and test EDP controls.

T F c An auditor should obtain an understanding of the hardware controls in a client's computer equipment if there are significant computerized accounting applications.

T F d In a computerized system with on-line input capability, the audit trail is eliminated and the auditor is unable to manually trace a specific transaction through processing.

T F e An EDP control may be either a programmed control procedure or a manual control procedure.

T F f Financial totals are totals of field amounts for all the records in a batch that are computed for control purposes only.

T F g Within the EDP department the critical separation of duties is between those with knowledge of systems and programs and those with access to the computer, programs, and files.

T F h Some general controls, such as those related to backup and recovery or system and program documentation, usually have no bearing on the scope of audit procedures.

T F i General controls related to acquiring or changing programs normally can be tested by traditional manual audit procedures, such as inquiry, observation, and inspection of documents.

T F j When an auditor documents a computerized accounting system and related controls, it is important to include all the document and information flows of the particular system.

T F k Whether an auditor uses a manual or computer-assisted approach to testing EDP applications, testing of general controls is still usually necessary.

T F l Processing on microcomputers on LANs tends to be more secure than processing on a mainframe computer.

T F m A generalized audit software package is a multipurpose software package that an auditor may use for any clients with significant computerized accounting applications.

T F n A microcomputer is used more to automate work paper preparation than to automate audit procedures.

9-2 The following questions relate to basic computer processing concepts. Select the *best* response.

a The machine-language program that results when a symbolic-language program is translated is called a(n):

1 Processor program

2 Object program

3 Source program

4 Wired program

b Which of the following is *not* a characteristic of a batch-processed computer system?

   1 The collection of like transactions which are sorted and processed sequentially against a master file

   2 Keying of transactions, followed by machine processing

   3 The production of numerous printouts

   4 The posting of a transaction, as it occurs, to several files, without intermediate printouts

c When an on-line, real-time (OLRT) EDP system is in use, the internal control structure can be strengthened by:

   1 Providing for the separation of duties between keying and error listing operations

   2 Attaching plastic file protection rings to reels of magnetic tape before new data can be entered on the file

   3 Making a validity check of an identification number before a user can obtain access to the computer files

   4 Preparing batch totals to provide assurance that file updates are made for the entire input

AICPA

9-3 The following questions relate to the control risk assessment in computerized systems. Select the *best* response.

a In obtaining an understanding of a client's EDP controls, the auditor will encounter general controls and application controls. Which of the following is an application control?

   1 Dual read

   2 Hash total

   3 Systems flowchart

   4 Control over program changes

b To replace the human element of error detection associated with manual processing, a well-designed automated system will introduce:

   1 Dual circuitry

   2 Programmed limits

   3 Echo checks

   4 Read after write

c Which of the following computer documentation would an auditor most likely utilize in obtaining an understanding of the internal control structure?

   1 Systems flowcharts

   2 Record counts

   3 Program listings

   4 Record layouts

d An auditor would most likely be concerned with which of the following controls in a distributed data processing system?

   1 Hardware controls

   2 Systems documentation controls

   3 Access controls

   4 Disaster recovery controls

e The completeness of EDP-generated sales figures can be tested by comparing the number of items listed on the daily sales report with the number of items billed on the actual invoices. This process uses:

    1 Check digits

    2 Control totals

    3 Validity tests

    4 Process tracing data

f After obtaining an understanding of a client's EDP control, an auditor may decide not to perform tests of controls within the EDP portion of the client's system. Which of the following would *not* be a valid reason for choosing to omit tests of controls?

    1 The controls duplicate operative controls existing elsewhere in the system.

    2 There appear to be major deficiencies that would preclude reliance on the stated procedure.

    3 The time and dollar costs of testing controls exceed the time and dollar savings in substantive testing if the tests show the controls to be operative.

    4 The controls appear adequate enough to be relied upon in assessing level of control risk.

g If a control total were to be computed on each of the following data items, which would *best* be identified as a hash total for a payroll EDP application?

    1 Gross pay

    2 Hours worked

    3 Department number

    4 Number of employees

AICPA

9-4 The following questions relate to the use of computer-assisted audit techniques. Select the *best* response.

a Which of the following is true of generalized audit software packages?

    1 They can be used only in auditing on-line computer systems.

    2 They can be used on any computer without modification.

    3 They each have their own characteristics which the auditor must carefully consider before using in a given audit situation.

    4 They enable the auditor to perform all manual test procedures less expensively.

b Auditors often make use of computer programs that perform routine processing functions such as sorting and merging. These programs are made available by EDP companies and others and are specifically referred to as:

    1 Compiler programs

    2 Supervisory programs

    3 Utility programs

    4 User programs

c A primary advantage of using generalized audit packages in the audit of an advanced EDP system is that it enables the auditor to:

    1 Substantiate the accuracy of data through self-checking digits and hash totals

    2 Utilize the speed and accuracy of the computer

    3 Verify the performance of machine operations which leave visible evidence of occurrence

    4 Gather and store large quantities of supportive evidential matter in machine-readable form

d An auditor will use the EDP test data method in order to gain certain assurances with respect to the:

    1 Input data

    2 Machine capacity

3 Procedures contained within the program

4 Degree of keying accuracy

e Assume that an auditor estimates that 10,000 checks were issued during the accounting period. If an EDP application control which performs a limit check for each check request is to be subjected to the auditor's test data approach, the sample should include:

  1 Approximately 1,000 test items

  2 A number of test items determined by the auditor to be sufficient under the circumstances

  3 A number of test items determined by the auditor's reference to the appropriate sampling tables

  4 One transaction

f Which of the following statements is *not* true of the test data approach when testing a computerized accounting system?

  1 The test data need consist of only those valid and invalid conditions which interest the auditor.

  2 Only one transaction of each type need be tested.

  3 The test data must consist of all possible valid and invalid conditions.

  4 Test data are processed by the client's computer programs under the auditor's control.

g An auditor using audit software probably would be *least* interested in which of the following fields in a computerized perpetual inventory file?

  1 Economic order quantity

  2 Warehouse location

  3 Date of last purchase

  4 Quantity sold

h Which of the following computer-assisted auditing techniques allows fictitious and real transactions to be processed together without client operating personnel being aware of the testing process?

  1 Parallel simulation

  2 Generalized audit software programming

  3 Integrated test facility

  4 Test data approach

AICPA

DISCUSSION QUESTIONS

Discussion questions require the application of the concepts explained in the chapter to specific facts, issues, or problems. They are classified by the primary chapter topic to which they relate. However, responses should not be confined to the primary topics but should include all relevant implications.

Understanding the Internal Control Structure

9-5 Carl Applewhite has been the auditor for a number of years of Reardon Ltd., a large merchandising concern which carries over 50,000 different items is inventory. During the current fiscal year the company has completed the installation of a sophisticated computer system for inventory control.

The computer system utilizes magnetic disks which facilitate random-access processing. All pertinent data relating to individual items of inventory are carried on the magnetic disks.

The system is equipped with 15 remote inquiry terminals, distributed at various locations throughout the operations. Using these terminals, employees can inquire into the computer system by using a keyboard which forms part of the remote terminal. The answer is relayed back instantaneously on the same terminal. The inventory records on the disks are updated via the remote terminals as stock movements occur.

a Describe the effect of the new computer system on Applewhite's present audit approach, which was developed for use with the previous manual system.

b What steps would Applewhite take before developing new audit procedures for the computerized inventory control system?

CICA adapted

9-6 On page 371 is a flowchart that depicts the payroll processing function of Campbell Company. Write your own descriptions for each of the numbered blank symbols.

AICPA adapted

9-7 Carla Andress is the auditor of Alexis Company, Ltd., a large manufacturing company with several plants across Canada. The company has used EDP equipment since 19X3 to process most of its accounting information and presently has two mainframe computers at its head office.

In prior years, Alexis Company, Ltd. had never recorded accrued vacation pay in its accounts but instead had recognized the expense when vacations were taken by the employees. For the year ended December 31, 19X5, however, the company decided to set up the liability at that date of accrued vacation pay.

The company employs approximately 2,400 employees, each of whom belongs to one of four unions. Employees' entitlement to vacation pay is based on length of service (calculated from the month of employment) and varies according to the terms of each union contract.

Complete personnel information for all employees is maintained on a payroll master file which is updated daily. An "Employee Status Report" containing all master file details for specified employees is produced daily on a request basis.

A specially written computer program was used to determine the amount of accrued vacation pay. This program extracted the relevant data from the payroll master file as of December 31, 19X5, calculated the amount of accrued vacation pay for each employee, recorded the details on an output tape, and printed a summarized report showing only the grand total of the accrued vacation pay.

a How would an audit trail be provided to enable Andress to perform tests of the details of the accrued vacation pay? What practical difficulties may arise?

b Explain how Andress could use test data to test the computer program.

CICA adapted

9-8 You have been engaged by San Jacinto Savings and Loan Association to audit its financial statements for the year ended December 31, 19X6. The CPA who audited the financial statements at December 31, 19X5 rendered an unqualified opinion.

In January 19X6 the association converted from an on-line input, batch system to an OLRT computer system. Each teller in the association's main office and its seven branch offices has an on-line input-output terminal. Customers' mortgage payments and savings account deposits and withdrawals are recorded in the accounts by the

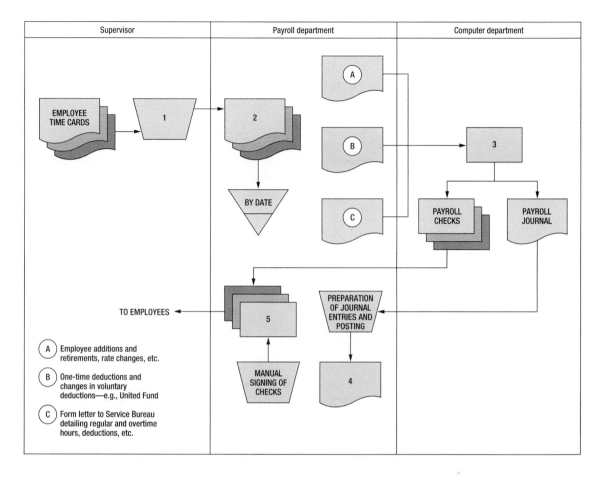

computer from data input by the teller at the time of the transaction. The teller keys the proper account by account number and enters the information on the terminal keyboard to record the transaction. The accounting department at the main office also has terminal input-output devices. The computer is housed at the main office.

You would expect the association to have certain controls in effect because an OLRT computer system is employed. List the controls which should be in effect solely because this system is employed, classifying them as:

a Those controls pertaining to input of information

b All other types of computer controls

AICPA adapted

9-9 When auditing in an environment with significant computerized accounting systems, the CPA must be aware of the different types of controls.

    a Define and give the purpose of each of the following program checks and controls:

       1 Record counts

       2 Limit check

       3 Reverse multiplication

       4 Sequence check

       5 Hash totals

b When magnetic tapes are used, the CPA has to be familiar with the method of processing. A common form of magnetic-tape-record retention employs the grandfather-father-son principle.

1 Define the grandfather-father-son principle.

2 Why are grandfather-father-son tapes usually stored at different locations?

AICPA

9-10 The independent auditor assesses the level of control risk to determine the extent to which various auditing procedures must be employed. A client who uses a computer should provide the CPA with a flowchart of the accounting system so the CPA can evaluate the control features in the system. On page 373 is a simplified flowchart, such as a client might provide. Unfortunately the client had only partially completed the flowchart when it was requested by you.

a Indicate the major weaknesses of this flowchart.

b Describe what each blank item in the flowchart indicates. When complete, your description should provide an explanation of the processing of the data involved.

AICPA adapted

9-11 The independent auditor must be aware of those control procedures that are commonly referred to as "general" controls and those that are commonly referred to as "application" controls. General controls relate to all EDP activities and application controls relate to specific accounting tasks.

Required:

a What are the general controls that should exist in EDP-based accounting systems?

b What are the purposes of each of the following categories of application controls?

1 Input controls

2 Processing controls

3 Output controls

9-12 Johnson, CPA, was engaged to audit the financial statements of Horizon Inc. Johnson found that Horizon lacked proper segregation of the programming and operating functions in the data processing department. As a result, Johnson intensified his procedures to understand the internal control structure surrounding the computer and concluded that the existing compensating controls provided reasonable assurance that the controls objectives were being met.

Required:

a In a properly functioning EDP environment, how is the separation of the programming and operating functions achieved?

b What are the compensating controls that Johnson most likely found? *Do not discuss hardware and application controls.*

Computer-Assisted Audit Techniques

9-13 What are the relative advantages and disadvantages of generalized audit software versus special programs written for a particular application?

9-14 A staff accountant has read several articles on the use of computers in auditing. She has read about test data and computer audit programs but does not fully understand what they are, when they are used in the audit, and what the distinction is between them with respect to audit purpose.

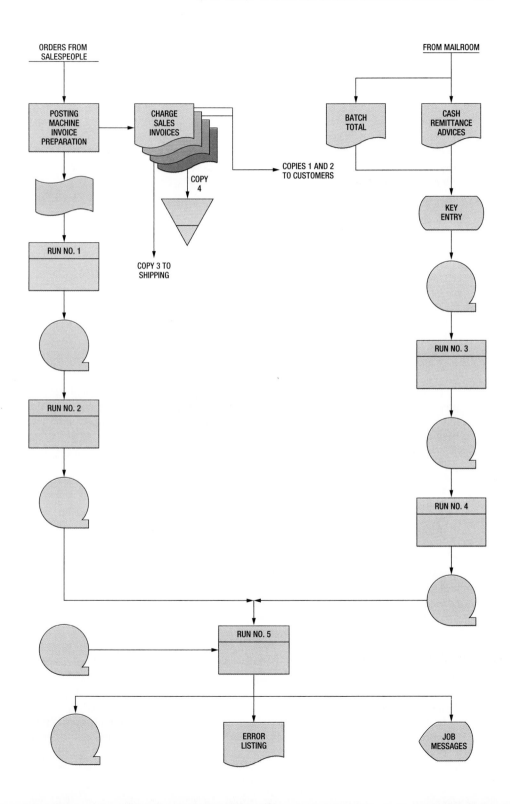

a How would you explain these matters?

b If neither test data or computer audit programs are used in the audit of a client with a computerized system, does this mean the client's computer has not affected the audit? Explain.

9-15 A CPA's client, Boos & Baumkirchner, Inc., is a medium-size manufacturer of products for the leisure-time activities market (camping equipment, scuba gear, bows and arrows, etc.). During the past year, a computer system was installed, and inventory records of finished goods and parts were converted to computer processing. The inventory master file is maintained on a disk. Each record of the file contains the following information:

> Item or part number
> Description
> Size
> Unit of measure code
> Quantity on hand
> Cost per unit
> Total value of inventory on hand at cost
> Date of last sale or usage
> Quantity used or sold this year
> Economic order quantity
> Code number of major vendor
> Code number of secondary vendor

In preparation for the year-end inventory the client has two identical sets of preprinted inventory count cards. One set is for the client's inventory counts and the other is for the CPA's use to make audit test counts. The following information has been keyed into the system:

> Item or part number
> Description
> Size
> Unit of measure code

In taking the year-end inventory, the client's personnel will write the actual counted quantity on the face of each card. When all counts are complete, the counted quantity will be keyed into the system. The counts will be processed against the disk file, and quantity-on-hand figures will be adjusted to reflect the actual count. A computer listing will be prepared to show any missing inventory count cards and all quantity adjustments of more than $100 in value. These items will be investigated by client personnel, and all required adjustments will be made. When adjustments have been completed, the final year-end balances will be computed and posted to the general ledger.

The CPA has available a general-purpose computer audit software package that will run on the client's computer.

Required:

a In general and without regard to the facts above, discuss the nature of general-purpose computer audit software packages and list the various types and uses of such packages.

b List and describe at least five ways a general-purpose computer audit software package can be used to assist in all aspects of the audit of the inventory of Boos & Baumkirchner, Inc. (For example, the package can be used to read the disk inventory master file and list items and parts with a high unit cost or total value. Such items can be included in the test counts to increase the dollar coverage of audit tests.)

AICPA adapted

9-16 Roger Peters, CPA, has audited the financial statements of the Solt Manufacturing Company for several years and is making preliminary plans for the audit for the year ended June 30, 19X2. During this audit Mr. Peters plans to use a set of generalized computer audit programs. Solt's EDP manager has agreed to prepare special tapes of data from company records for the CPA's use with the generalized programs.

The following information is applicable to Mr. Peters' audit of Solt's accounts payable and related procedures:

   I The formats of pertinent tapes are on page 376.
   II The following monthly runs are prepared:
      A Cash disbursements by check number
      B Outstanding payables
      C Purchase journals arranged (1) by account charged and (2) by vendor
   III Vouchers and supporting invoices, receiving reports, and purchase order copies are filed by vendor code. Purchase orders and checks are filed numerically.
   IV Company records are maintained on magnetic tapes. All tapes are stored in a restricted area within the computer room. A grandfather-father-son policy is followed for retaining and safeguarding tape files.

Required:
a Describe the controls that the CPA should maintain over:
   1 Preparing the special tape
   2 Processing the special tape with the generalized computer audit programs
b Prepare a schedule for the EDP manager outlining the data that should be included on the special tape for the CPA's examination of accounts payable and related procedures. This schedule should show the:
   1 Client tape from which the item should be extracted
   2 Name of the item of data

AICPA adapted

MASTER FILE VENDOR NAME

Vendor code | Rec'd Type | Space | Blank | Vendor name | Blank | Code 100

MASTER FILE VENDOR ADDRESS

Vendor code | Rec'd Type | Space | Blank | Address—Line 1 | Address—Line 2 | Address—Line 3 | Blank | Code 120

TRANSACTION FILE EXPENSE DETAIL

Vendor code | Rec'd Type | Voucher number / Blank | Batch | Voucher number | Voucher date | Vendor code | Invoice date | Due date | Invoice number | Purchase order number | Debit account | Prd Type | Product code | Blank | Amount | Quantity | Code 160

TRANSACTION FILE PAYMENT DETAIL

Vendor code | Rec'd Type | Voucher number / Blank | Batch | Voucher number | Voucher date | Vendor code | Invoice date | Due date | Invoice number | Purchase order number | Check number | Check date | Blank | Amount | Blank | Code 170

9-17 Below is a flowchart representing the process of using test data for auditing purposes. It is only partially labeled. Complete the flowchart by labeling each blank symbol.

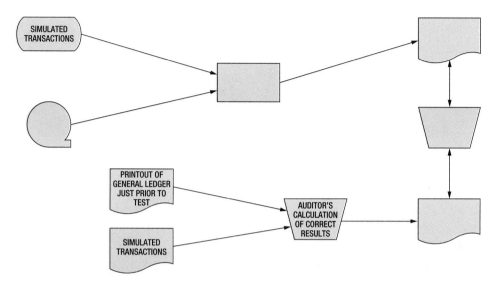

SIMULATED TRANSACTIONS

PRINTOUT OF GENERAL LEDGER JUST PRIOR TO TEST

SIMULATED TRANSACTIONS

AUDITOR'S CALCULATION OF CORRECT RESULTS

9-18 In the past, the records to be evaluated in an audit were printed reports, listings, documents, and written papers all of which are visible output. However, in computerized systems that employ daily updating of transaction files, output and files are frequently in machine-readable forms such as tapes or disks. Thus, they often present the auditor with an opportunity to use the computer in performing an audit.

Required:
Discuss how the computer can be used to aid the auditor in examining accounts receivable in such a computerized system.

CHAPTER

10

Tests of Transaction Classes and Related Balances

CHAPTER OUTLINE

Learning Objectives

After studying this chapter you should be able to:

- Describe the specific control objectives, common control procedures, and tests of transaction classes for the revenue, receivables, and receipts cycle
- Describe the specific control objectives, common control procedures, and tests of transaction classes for the expenditures, payables, and disbursements cycle
- Identify the account balances related to the revenue and expenditures cycles
- Explain the financial statement assertions, specific audit objectives, and audit procedures to achieve those objectives for accounts receivable, accounts payable, and cash

Relevant Sections of Statements on Auditing Standards

AU 326 — Evidential Matter
AU 330 — The Confirmation Process

This chapter explains tests of transaction classes for the central cycles or activities of most businesses—buying and selling—and the direct tests of balances for the account balances included in these cycles. The examples used assume the client has computerized systems for revenues, receivables, and receipts, and for expenditures, payables, and disbursements. Although some of the descriptive terms may differ, most businesses are engaged in acquiring goods or services from vendors or suppliers and providing goods or services to customers. These cycles are usually characterized by large volume (many relatively small transactions) and are repetitive and recurring in nature (transactions of a particular type are very similar and continuing). For these reasons, the audit approach in these areas often emphasizes tests of transaction classes with anticipated testing of control procedures as a basis to assess control risk at less than the maximum level. When tests of controls are not feasible or efficient, the scope of direct tests of balances for the related account balance has to be expanded.

REVENUES, RECEIVABLES, AND RECEIPTS

This section is concerned with the sales cycle of the type of company that accepts sales orders for shipment of merchandise to customers on credit. For this type of company the sale, delivery, and collection occur within a short time (a few weeks to a few months). The sales accounting system of such a company is relatively unaffected by whether the merchandise is acquired from others or produced by converting raw materials to a finished product. Thus, the discussion is applicable to most manufacturing companies and wholesale merchandise companies, and many retail companies. Some of the special considerations that apply to other industries or other types of sales transactions are discussed briefly at the end of the section.

One characteristic of this type of sales accounting system is that the audit problems tend to be those related to high-volume clerical processing rather than complex accounting principles issues. For example, revenue is typically recognized when merchandise is shipped and recording of sales and receivables is routine rather than involving complicated revenue recognition issues. Relatively large clerical staffs tend to be in the accounting and operating departments involved, and the intricate document flow among operating and accounting departments is confusing to beginning auditors.

Functions, Documents, Inputs, and Accounting Systems

Everyone usually has some personal experience as a customer on the other side of sales accounting systems. Consider all the details that need to be accomplished on the company's side of credit sales transactions. Customer orders are received, accepted, and translated into shipping and billing instructions. Merchandise is shipped, customers are billed, and cash, usually in the form of checks, is collected from customers. Formal procedures have to be established to accomplish these functions and responsibility for performing them needs to be assigned to departments or groups within the company.

An Overview of Functions, Documents, Inputs, and Accounting Systems   An *order entry function* is the starting point in the credit sales cycle. In this function, orders are received, accepted, and then translated into shipping and billing instructions. Order entry is an operating department and may or may not be integrated in the accounting system. The original order may be a written purchase order mailed in by a customer, or orders may be taken over the phone. The first document or input by the company will usually be a *sales order.* At this point a decision needs to be made of whether to accept the order. Specific approval of the *credit department* may be required, there may be a list of approved customers determined by the credit department, or credit limits may be established that are checked by order entry.

After an order is accepted, a *shipping order* is sent to shipping and a copy of the order is maintained in a pending file. The system generates an aged open order report. Usually, this report is used as a record of backlog and a routine review of this open order report helps to prevent loss of orders. Physical control of the forms used as shipping orders and physical inspection of shipments for a shipping document help to prevent unauthorized shipments.

The *shipping function* is an operating department that physically sends merchandise to customers. When shipments are made, the shipping department completes a *shipping notice.* Input of the shipping notice clears the open order file, and initiates processing to bill the customer. If a common carrier is used for shipments, the shipping notice is a copy of a *bill of lading* (the contract with the carrier). Common terminology in the auditing literature refers to any source document that serves the purpose of recording the event of shipment simply as a *shipping document.*

The *billing function* is usually the first department involved in the sequence that is an accounting department. The billing department is responsible for ensuring that a *sales invoice* is sent to bill the customer. Usually, a sales invoice is a multipart form whose original is mailed to the customer, and duplicate sales invoices are used to notify other departments. Conventionally, the term "duplicate" is often dropped in auditing literature and reference is made simply to sales invoices. At this point things can become very confusing for accounting students and in practice, because a sales invoice may have as many as six or more copies. Seldom is it necessary to trace or document the flow of all these copies.

The flow of primary concern to the auditor is the one that creates the *debit to accounts receivable.* Two other accounting department functions are normally involved in this flow—accounts receivable detail and general ledger. The individual sales invoices from billing processing are one of the inputs to accounts receivable processing. Sales invoices are used to update the accounts receivable subsidiary ledger and customer master file. The billing department also compares a total of bills prepared (control total of sales invoices) that is sent to the general ledger function to become the debit to the accounts receivable control account. The totals sent to the general ledger function should not go through·the accounts receivable function. If this separation is maintained, a reconciliation of the control account with the accounts receivable detail can be a key control in the auditor's control risk assessment.

Cash collection is the next step in the cycle, and several functions may be involved. The first step is *opening mail* and creating an initial record of cash received. This function may be performed by a receptionist or a separate mail room department, but the important consideration from a control viewpoint is that the function be separate from other functions involved in handling cash and keeping cash and accounts receivable detail records. The function responsible for opening the mail should create a *prelist of cash receipts,* which is simply a list of the amount received and from whom it was received, that usually is used strictly for control purposes. Mail receipts will usually be accompanied by a *remittance advice,* which is often a tearoff portion of the sales invoice that is returned by the customer.

The remittance advices and the cash (usually checks) are sent to the *cashier function.* The cashier restrictively endorses the checks to the payment of the company and prepares the bank deposit. The remittance advices are sent to the accounts receivable function and become the input for posting to the subsidiary ledger master file. The total of remittance advices is sent to the general ledger function to update the control amount in the general ledger.

Another arrangement that may be used when the volume of cash receipts is large is a *lockbox* system. With this type of system, customers send remittances to a post office box controlled by the company's bank. The bank credits the company's account directly for cash receipts and sends remittance advices or a report of receipts to the company. A lockbox system improves control effectiveness and the efficiency of cash management.

Accounting systems can differ substantially in the summarization steps that take place between the source document, such as a sales invoice or remittance advice, and the entries to the general ledger. Computer reports and files are generally titled as they were historically in manual systems—a *sales journal* for credit sales and a *cash receipts journal* for remittances. The systems usually have some form of printed report or computer-readable file that includes all daily activity. That is, all the transactions entered that day are recorded and retained for backup and recovery purposes. The auditor can generally use these *daily activity reports* or *sales journals.* However, in some systems only summary information is retained for more than a short time, and advance arrangements must be made if more detail is required by the auditor.

Adjustments and Cost of Sales Two complicating factors are omitted from the foregoing overview of credit sales and cash collections. In addition to the debits to accounts receivable for sales and credits for cash collections, adjustments (both debits and credits) are always necessary. These adjustments are for such things as credits for return of merchandise, allowances for defective merchandise, write-offs of bad debts, or cash discounts allowed, and debits for chargebacks for allowances or discounts taken by customers, but not allowed. Adjustments will also likely be made for clerical mistakes in processing.

From a control standpoint, these adjustments are of concern because they are less routine than sales and collections and require the exercise of some discretion in deciding whether that adjustment should be allowed. The usual approach is to use a specialized source document, a *credit memorandum* or *debit memorandum,* and to require the approval of responsible supervisory personnel before processing.

The other complication is the relation between sales and cost of sales. Ideally, there should be a direct correlation between the items of merchandise recorded as sales and the items recorded as cost of sales. In some accounting systems, the recording of sales and cost of sales are simultaneous, and copies of the shipping document are used as notification for both billing the customer and relieving the inventory of the quantity and cost of merchandise sold. In this chapter, the simplifying assumption is made that recording of cost of sales is not integrated with recording sales to reduce the complexities of sales accounting. However, the correlation between sales and cost of sales should always exist, and some weaknesses in sales accounting may cause the auditor to expand direct tests of balances of inventory.

Primary Control-Related Features

Specific control procedures are considered later in relation to specific control objectives and related tests of transaction classes. However, at this point it is worthwhile to summarize the primary control-related features of a sales accounting system.

Segregation of Duties As explained in the overview of sales accounting, the following departments or functions are involved in processing transactions and handling assets:

Operating	Accounting
Order entry	Billing
Credit extension	Accounts receivable detail
Opening mail	General ledger
Cashier	

Ideally, all of these functions should be independent. Combining them may result in an incompatible combination of functions because the perpetration and concealment of errors or irregularities is possible. However, separation of these functions is usually an integral part of the plan of organization. In other words, separation can usually be achieved as a byproduct of efficient specialization of tasks rather than as an overlay on existing processing and handling of assets. A small business, however, may have too few people in the accounting department to achieve an adequate separation of accounting functions.

Control over Source Documents and Inputs   The source documents created during processing, such as shipping documents, invoices, and credit memoranda, should be printed and prenumbered forms. If prenumbered forms are used, the sequence can be accounted for by personnel independent of processing to help ensure the completeness of processing. Missing or out-of-sequence numbers may indicate lost or improper transactions. Adequate physical safeguards are necessary for unused forms and files of forms used in processing.

Often copies of originals of prepared forms are maintained in the originating department. These files usually serve both control and operating purposes. The following are examples:

Department or function	Source document	File
Order entry	Customer order	Customer order file
	Accepted sales order or shipping order	Open order file
Shipping	Bill of lading or shipping document	Bill of lading file
Billing	Sales invoice	Sales invoice file
Opening mail	Prelist of cash receipts	Prelist file
Cashier	Deposit ticket	Bank records file

These files maintained in originating departments are technically not part of the accounting system. Even though billing is usually an accounting department, the initial entry in the accounting records is the debit to accounts receivable. However, the files are used for implementation of control procedures and are part of the internal control structure, and they are inspected when applying audit procedures for tests of transaction classes.

Input is often batched in the originating department and keyed into the system in a data entry department. Alternatively, the originating department may use on-line entry. In this case, access control for the entry function is important.

Checks, Approvals, and Reconciliations   The checks, approvals, and reconciliations that are added to processing are overlays for control purposes. Before each processing step an independent preprocessing approval could be required, each processing step could be checked for completeness and accuracy by a second person, and many reconciliations between separate but related records and files could be made. Supervisory review and approval at various points is also possible. The more independent checks, reviews, approvals, and reconciliations that are added, the greater the control.

Additional cost is associated with such controls and a balance must be achieved. The checks, reviews, approvals, and reconciliations that are common control procedures used to achieve specific control objectives are discussed later in relation to specific tests of transaction classes.

Account Balances and Transactions

The financial statement account balances involved in a sales accounting system are as follows:

Income statement	Balance sheet
Sales	Accounts receivable
Sales discounts	Cash
Sales returns and allowances	Allowance for bad debts
Bad debt expense	

The transactions that are recorded in a sales accounting system are generally as follows:

- Credit sales to customers
- Cash collections from customers
- Adjustments for return of merchandise, allowances for defective merchandise, write-offs of bad debts, and chargebacks for disallowed customer credits

Often the adjustments, except for chargebacks, are referred to collectively as "noncash credits to accounts receivable."

In addition, the sales cycle includes accounting estimates that are not exchange transactions but more in the nature of allocations of recorded amounts among accounting periods. Invariably, an estimate is necessary of customer accounts that will become uncollectible (bad debt expense and the allowance for bad debts). In some cases, liability under warranty arrangements has to be estimated (warranty expense and warranty reserve). Usually, sales returns and allowances are recorded in the period in which they occur, but if a material increase can be reasonably estimated, expected returns and allowances should be recorded in the period of sale by an accrual for unissued credits.

Notice that the initial step in processing credit sales—order entry—is not a transaction and is not entered in the accounting records.

Potential Misstatements

Generally, the types of misstatements that may occur in an accounting system may be classified in the following broad categories:

- Clerical mistakes (omissions, misclassifications, or miscalculations)
- Employee fraud
- Accounting principles misapplications
- Management fraud

Clerical Mistakes   At each of the steps in processing it is possible for transactions to be lost or for unauthorized or duplicate transactions to be inadvertently added. If computations, such as extensions or summarizations, are made in processing, they can be done incorrectly. One of the purposes of developing specific control objectives is to avoid having to catalog all the different processing errors that may be made. The control objectives should encompass all possible errors that would cause the objective not to be achieved. For example, a specific control objective related to completeness would encompass any errors that would cause a transaction to be omitted before entry in the accounting system.

Employee Fraud   Many inadvertent clerical mistakes can also be made intentionally to conceal employee fraud. For employee fraud to occur, the employee must have access to cash, or other negotiable assets, either by handling the asset, such as having access to cash receipts (including checks) or being an authorized check signer or being in a position to intercept signed checks. However, misappropriating the asset is only part of the problem. If the misappropriation is to be concealed to avoid detection, the accounting records must be brought into agreement with the physical asset. Concealment may take place before or after the misappropriation as long as it occurs before the accounting records are reconciled with the asset count.

One of the verities of concealment of misappropriation of assets in a double-entry accounting system is that credits achieve the concealment, but the problem is where to put the related debits. For example, if cash is misappropriated, a fraudulent entry can be made to bring the cash account into agreement with cash in the bank by crediting cash. However, the debit half of the fraudulent entry needs to be concealed in the accounting records. Accounts receivable is a possible storehouse for concealing debits because it has a normal debit balance, and there are often a large number of individual customer accounts. This is one of the reasons that audit procedures and control procedures emphasize ensuring the authenticity of recorded accounts receivable.

A type of employee fraud associated with accounts receivable is called *lapping*. An employee misappropriates cash received from a customer and covers the shortage the next day by using receipts from another customer. Continued concealment requires continually delaying the recording of credits to different customers' accounts so the receipts may be credited to accounts affected by the initial misappropriation. To perpetrate this fraud, an employee must have access to cash receipts *and* be able to make entries to the accounting records for both cash and accounts receivable detail.

Accounting Principles Misapplications   As mentioned previously, when sale, delivery, and collection occur within a relatively short period, complex revenue recognition issues do not arise. When a more extended period is required for sale (real estate), delivery (construction contracting), or collection (installment sales), the accounting principles for revenue recognition are more often misapplied.

On the other hand, accounting estimates almost invariably create a risk of misapplication of accounting principles. Accounts receivable should be stated at net realizable value. Failure to promptly identify and provide an adequate allowance for uncollectible accounts may arise from extending credit without control, poorly controlled billing practices, or insufficient management monitoring of the aging and collection follow-up. Even if these areas are well-controlled, unanticipated changes in economic conditions or customer mix may cause a misstatement of bad debt expense and the allowance. Other accounting estimates that may be misstated for similar reasons include unissued credits for sales returns and allowances or warranty reserves.

Management Fraud   A management motivated to inflate net income may engage in involved fictitious sales transactions. This risk is more likely to be an audit problem in industries where revenue results from a relatively few large transactions, such as real estate, or manufacturing expensive products to special order, such as defense contracting. The possibility of this type of fraud is the primary reason that auditors assess audit risk to identify circumstances that might predispose management to make material misrepresentations and apply audit procedures such as the following:

- Scanning the accounting records for large or unusual transactions, particularly those recorded late in the period
- Identifying related parties and considering whether material transactions may involve parties with an undisclosed relationship
- Making analytical tests to identify revenue or gross profit changes that are seriously disproportionate to changes in the level or volume of activity

Accounting estimates are also susceptible to management bias ranging from exaggerated optimism to outright misrepresentation. Generally, accounting estimates affect the presentation of sales and receivables at net realizable amounts, but in industries involving long-term contracts, accounting estimates, such as percentage of completion, may affect revenue recognition.

In industries with a relatively large number of small revenue transactions, the inherent risk of recording fictitious sales and receivables is reduced, but not eliminated. If management engages in this type of deception to achieve an increase in earnings, it is usually necessary to reduce the receivables in the next period by noncash credits, such as sales returns and allowances or write-off of accounts as uncollectible. However, the McKesson & Robbins fraud involved a more elaborate deception. Management had both fictitious receivables and fictitious purchases of merchandise recorded. The cash which was disbursed for fictitious purchases was recycled to record cash collections on the fictitious receivables. The fictitious receivables and inventory grew to a hefty amount (approximately $19 million), but the fraud occurred before confirmation of receivables directly with customers and observation of physical inventory taking became generally accepted audit procedures.

Tests of Transaction Classes for Sales

The exact nature and extent of tests of transaction classes are influenced by the specific control procedures and the auditor's consideration of the most efficient audit strategy. The auditor may on the basis of the understanding of the internal control structure, as described in Chapter 6, decide that it would be more efficient to apply more extensive direct tests of balances. In that case, tests of transactions for a particular class of transactions, such as sales, may be omitted. Direct tests of balances for accounts receivable and the relationship of those tests to tests of transaction classes are discussed in a later section. If the auditor plans to assess control risk at less than the maximum level for a particular transaction class, the auditor needs to identify specific control procedures that provide a basis for the risk assessment and perform tests of controls for those control procedures.

Identifying Specific Control Objectives and Procedures   A widely used approach to identifying control procedures that may provide a basis to assess control risk at less than maximum is to first develop specific control objectives for the transaction class using broad categories of objectives such as those introduced in Chapter 6. The broad categories of control objectives are as follows:

* Authorization and approval
* Validity
* Completeness
* Recording accuracy
* Safeguarding
* Reconciliation

Figure 10-1 presents specific control objectives for sales transactions for the type of company described in the overview of functions, documents, and accounting systems for the sales cycle. The broad category of safeguarding is not directly applicable to sales transactions because the related asset—accounts receivable—has no physical existence. However, because of the correlation between sales and cost of sales, a separation of functions among shipping, billing, and merchandise (inventory) storekeeping is important.

Common control procedures to achieve these specific control objectives are also presented in Figure 10-1. The presentation of common control procedures does not mean that all of these procedures are necessary in every circumstance to achieve the objective. Nor does it mean that other control procedures would not achieve the objective.

The auditor needs to consider whether the specific control procedures the client has adopted provide *reasonable assurance* of achieving the objective. The auditor's consideration of whether there is reasonable assurance may be influenced by the extent of supervision and the auditor's assessment of the control environment.

For example, consider the objective that "all merchandise shipped is billed." In a company with a strong control environment and good supervision of organizationally separate shipping and billing functions, an independent reconciliation of quantities shipped to quantities billed may be unnecessary for reasonable assurance of achieving the

General control objective	Specific control objective	Common control policies and procedures	Tests of transaction class
Authorization and approval	Merchandise shipped to customers does not exceed established credit limits or depart from established terms.	• Established policy of authorization of credit and terms • Approval of credit and terms independent of marketing and order entry	• Select a sample of sales transactions from the sales journal (daily activity report) and inspect supporting documents for indication of approval in accordance with established policy.
Validity	Recorded sales are for merchandise actually shipped to customers.	• Sales invoices prenumbered and sequence accounted for • Quantities shipped periodically reconciled to quantities billed independently of shipping and billing • Monthly statements mailed to customers	• Review the accounting for numerical sequence of sales invoices or test numerical sequence. • Select a sample of sales transactions from sales journal (daily activity report) and trace to shipping document file. • Inspect reconciliations of shipments to billings. • Observe mailing of monthly statements, examine customer correspondence file, and investigate noncash credits to accounts receivable.
Completeness	All merchandise shipped is billed.	• Shipping documents prenumbered and sequence accounted for • Quantities shipped periodically reconciled to quantities billed independently of shipping and billing • Open order file or backlog report reviewed independently of shipping and billing • Shipments checked for shipping documents	• Review the accounting for numerical sequence of shipping documents or test numerical sequence. • Inspect reconciliations of shipments to billings. • Select a sample of shipping documents and trace to sales invoices. • Inspect indication of supervisory review. • Observe checking of shipments or inspect selected shipments.

FIGURE 10-1

Control policies and procedures and audit tests for sales transactions.

General control objective	Specific control objective	Common control policies and procedures	Tests of transaction class
Recording accuracy	Billings have been recorded correctly as to account, amount, and period and summarized correctly.	• Sales invoices prenumbered and sequence accounted for	• Review the accounting for numerical sequence of sales invoices or test numerical sequence.
		• Approval of invoices independent of preparer including recomputation and comparison of details (quantity, price, terms) to supporting documents • Separation of functions among billing, shipping, accounts receivable detail, and general ledger	• Select a sample of transactions from the sales journal (daily activity report) and apply the following procedures to supporting sales invoice and shipping document: —Trace prices to approved list. —Recompute extensions and footings. —Compare details. —Consider account classification. —Trace posting to accounts receivable detail. • Inspect sales invoices selected for indication of approval.
		• Monthly statements mailed to customers • Supervisory review and approval of summarization and posting	• Review customer correspondence and complaint file. • Inspect indication of supervisory review and approval or observe. • Foot sales journal (daily activity report) and trace to general ledger.
Reconciliation	Accounts receivable detail is periodically reconciled with the general ledger.	• Independent reconciliation of accounts receivable detail to control account and accounts receivable posting to sales journal (daily activity report)	• Inspect reconciliations and consider explanations of reconciling items.
		• Periodic aging of accounts receivable including established collection procedures and approval of write-offs of uncollectible accounts	• Inspect agings and indications of collection follow-up and approval of write-offs.

FIGURE 10-1 *(concluded)*

objective. In another company, this type of reconciliation may be essential for reasonable assurance.

The auditor identifies control policies and procedures that would permit assessing control risk at less than the maximum level, if effectiveness can be shown to be satisfactory, when obtaining an understanding of the internal control structure as described in Chapter 6. The next step is to plan and conduct audit tests for the particular class of transactions reviewed.

Selecting Audit Procedures for Tests of Controls and Substantive Tests   Typical tests of transaction classes are presented in Figure 10-1. The arrangement of audit tests in Figure 10-1 is often referred to as a "design format for tests of transaction classes." In the planning phase the auditor plans tests using specific control objectives as a guide. Using this format helps to ensure that the auditor has not omitted consideration of the achievement of an important objective. However, the audit procedures selected need to be rearranged in the most logical sequence, and duplications need to be eliminated. Since some control procedures and some audit tests relate to more than one objective, in the design format some audit tests are unavoidably listed more than once. Sequence is also important because when the auditor selects a sample of documents it is efficient to apply all the planned procedures relevant to those documents at that point. The listing of the procedures to be performed in the order of performance is the preliminary audit program.

The most logical sequence for audit tests is affected by the nature of the test. The general categories of tests of transaction classes related to tests of controls and substantive tests are listed below with examples of such tests for sales transactions from Figure 10-1.

   I Inquiry and observation of segregation of duties and restricted access to assets, documents, records, and on-line functions (if applicable):
      A Observe and inquire concerning the separation of duties among:
         1 Order entry
         2 Shipping
         3 Billing
         4 Accounts receivable detail
         5 General ledger
      B Observe checking of shipments for shipping documents.
      C Observe mailing of monthly statements to customers and review customer correspondence and complaint file.
  II Inspection of completed accounting routines and reperformance of one or a few such routines:
      A Review the accounting for numerical sequence of shipping documents and sales invoices or test numerical sequence.
      B Inspect reconciliations of quantities shipped to quantities billed.
      C Inspect reconciliations of accounts receivable detail to control account and sales journal (daily activity report) to accounts receivable.

D Inspect periodic agings of accounts receivable.

E Inspect indication of supervisory review of footing and posting of sales journal (daily activity report) to general ledger and foot and trace a few postings.

III Inspection of documents for indication of the performance of a checking routine or approval and reperformance to establish effectiveness:

A Select a sample of shipping documents from the shipping document file and trace to sales invoices or sales journal (daily activity report).

B Select a sample of sales transactions from the sales journal (daily activity report), obtain the supporting documents, and:

1 Inspect sales order for approval of credit and terms.

2 Compare details (customer, descriptions, quantities, and prices) among sales order, shipping document, and sales invoice.

3 Trace prices on sales invoice to approved price list or other indication of approval.

4 Recompute extensions and footings on sales invoices.

5 Inspect sales invoices for indication of checking.

Note that if the direction of testing is coordinated for all account balances, as explained in Chapter 7, and sales transactions are tested directly only for understatement, the auditor would select only a sample of shipping documents. The shipping documents would be traced to the sales journal (daily activity report) and the procedures listed for the sample from the sales journal would be applied to the sales invoices and sales orders related to the selected shipping documents.

As explained in Chapter 7, tests of transaction classes are often made at an interim date and generally tests in all of the three categories would be conducted at that point. A logical approach would be to begin by doing a *walk-through of the processing of sales transactions* by starting in the order entry department with the receipt of a customer order, selecting one or a few orders, and walking those orders through the system to recording in accounts receivable detail and the general ledger. At that time the auditor could make the *inquiries and observations* necessary to evaluate segregation of duties and restricted access to assets, documents, records, and on-line functions.

The next logical step would be to *inspect completed accounting routines* and reperform one or two such routines. After that, the auditor would be ready to apply the planned tests involving *inspection of documents.* Any misunderstandings about the system would have been clarified and the auditor's knowledge of the segregation of duties and effectiveness of accounting routines would be considered to evaluate whether the planned nature and extent of inspection of documents still appeared appropriate.

The considerations that influence the nature and extent of inspection of source documents are explained in Chapters 7 and 8. These tests are applied using audit sampling and usually are dual-purpose tests. The sample of documents is inspected for indication of checking or approval and substantive matters, such as recomputing extensions and footings on invoices, are also tested. Using the type of sampling plan explained in Chapter 8, if the company appears to have control procedures that would achieve specific control objectives, the auditor might select a sample of 30 documents. If the company does not have control procedures that leave a documentary trail and the tests made by inspecting source documents are primarily tests of substantive matters, the sample size might be expanded to 60. The effect of the results of these tests on direct tests of balances is considered later in this chapter.

Tests of Transaction Classes for Cash Receipts

The specific control objectives for cash receipts and examples of common control policies and procedures and tests of transaction classes are summarized in Figure 10-2. In general, the concepts discussed for sales transactions for identifying control policies and procedures that achieve specific control objectives and selecting audit procedures for tests of controls and substantive tests also apply to cash receipts transactions. This discussion concentrates on matters that might be misunderstood without some explanation.

Generally, tests of cash receipts and tests of sales transactions are not combined. For example, a sample of sales invoices or shipping documents may be traced to accounts

General control objective	Specific control objective	Common control policies and procedures	Tests of transaction class
Authorization and approval	Cash discounts taken by customers are in accordance with established policy.	• Approval of remittance advices for discounts taken	• Select a sample of remittance advices and inspect for indication of approval and comparison to established policy.
Validity	Recorded cash receipts are for collection of receivables from customers.	• Cash receipts matched to specific sales invoices in posting accounts receivable detail	• Select a sample of remittance advices from file or cash receipts journal (daily activity report) and trace to accounts receivable detail.
Completeness	All cash receipts are recorded and deposited.	• Opening of mail and prelisting of cash receipts independently of cashier, accounts receivable detail, and general ledger	• Observe opening of mail and preparation of prelist.
		• Comparison of deposit slips, prelists, and posting from cash receipts journal (daily activity report) independently of cashier, accounts receivable detail, general ledger, and opening mail	• Select a sample of remittance advices or deposit slips and trace to deposits on bank statement and recorded cash receipts.
		• Prelist forms prenumbered and sequence accounted for	• Review the accounting for numerical sequence.
		• Monthly statements mailed to customers	• Observe mailing of monthly statements, examine customer correspondence and complaints, and investigate noncash credits to accounts receivable.

FIGURE 10-2
Control policies and procedures and audit tests for cash receipts transactions.

General control objective	Specific control objective	Common control policies and procedures	Tests of transaction class
Recording accuracy	Cash receipts have been recorded correctly as to account, amount, and period.	• Cash receipts matched to specific invoices in posting accounts receivable detail • Monthly statements mailed to customers • Supervisory review and approval of postings to general ledger	• Select a sample of remittance advices from the cash receipts journal and trace to accounts receivable detail. • Foot cash receipts journal (daily activity report) and trace to general ledger posting. • Inspect posting for indication of supervisory review and approval.
Safeguarding	Cash receipts on hand are protected and deposited promptly and intact.	• Cash handling (receipt and deposit) independent of accounting functions and authorized check signing • Restrictive endorsement on checks received • Policy of depositing cash receipts intact and daily	• Observe opening of mail and preparation of deposits and inquire about authorized check signers. • Inspect deposits for restrictive endorsement. • Inquire about policies and fidelity insurance.
Reconciliation	Recorded cash is periodically reconciled with bank accounts.	• All bank accounts are reconciled promptly with cash records independently of cash handling, accounts receivable detail, and general ledger	• Inspect client reconciliations and reperform one or a few reconciliations. • Consider reasonableness of reconciling items and explanations of such items.

FIGURE 10-2 *(concluded)*

receivable detail and a sample of remittance advices may be traced to accounts receivable detail. However, the sales invoices or shipping documents and the remittance advices are not necessarily for the same sales transactions. If the internal control structure is extremely deficient and there is a serious risk of employee fraud that could be material, the sales debits and the credits to those specific debits might be linked.

Notice also that some control procedures for sales transactions, such as sending monthly statements to customers, contribute to the achievement of specific control objectives for cash receipts. Tests of these control procedures are performed either in testing sales transactions or in testing cash receipts; they are not duplicated.

Tests of Adjustments to Accounts Receivable

The auditor's concern with adjustments, such as sales returns and allowances, depends on whether the adjustments are material. For example, if sales returns and allowances are immaterial, the auditor omits any tests for the transaction class. Generally, the control procedures and audit tests are the same in concept as those for sales and cash receipts. For example, sales returns and allowances would be controlled by prenumbered credit memoranda approved before issuance. The auditor would select a sample of credit memoranda and inspect the documents for approval and inspect the accounting for, or test, numerical sequence. Also, the auditor would be particularly concerned with the authorization and approval procedures for write-off of accounts as uncollectible. Usually, such accounts are transferred to a separate ledger and may be turned over to a collection agency.

Special Considerations

With minor variations, most of the control policies and procedures and audit tests for companies that accept sale orders for shipment of merchandise to customers on credit can be adapted to other circumstances. However, some of the special considerations that apply to particular types of sales transactions are explained below as illustrative examples:

- *Cash sales.* When merchandise is sold for cash rather than on credit, the primary control and audit problem is ensuring that all cash received is captured by the accounting system. Prenumbered sales slips or cash register tapes are used to establish control totals for individual sales personnel. More extensive observation by supervisory personnel is also extremely important.
- *Long-term contracts.* When revenue is generated by contracts that extend over one or more accounting periods, the audit emphasis is usually influenced by the concern with proper application of accounting principles. For example, construction contractors may recognize revenue by the percentage-of-completion method. Recognition of revenue is based on partial performance, and the accumulation of costs by contract affects the recognition of revenue. Thus, the controls over and testing of recorded expenses are important.
- *Real estate.* Sale of real estate is an excellent example of the type of sales transaction for which the primary audit concern is misstatement arising from misapplication of accounting principles—including both inadvertent and intentional departures. Several criteria must be met before a sales transaction is even recognized as occurring, and whether profit is recognized by the full accrual method or one of several delayed recognition methods also depends on several additional criteria.

EXPENDITURES, PAYABLES, AND DISBURSEMENTS

Conceptually, the expenditures cycle includes all exchange transactions in which assets or services used in operating the business are acquired for cash or on credit. However, because of the diversity of the "buying" activities of most companies, auditors often organize the audit approach by transaction type within the expenditures transaction class. This is one of several differences from the sales cycle.

Differences from the Sales Cycle

The differences between the normal audit approach to the expenditures cycle and the approach to the sales cycle are influenced by differences between the transaction types included within the cycle and matters related to audit efficiency.

Focus on Transaction Type Categories   The acquisition of assets and services, and payments for them, encompass many transaction types. For example, auditors often distinguish the following broad categories of transaction types and they are considered separately in this book:

- Payroll costs, including salaries, wages, and related benefits for production, service, selling, or administration
- Property and equipment
- Purchase of goods and services for inventory (production or merchandising)
- Income taxes
- Incurrence of selling and administrative expenses
- Miscellaneous expenses paid from petty cash

Control risk assessments for specific control procedures are made separately for these categories of transaction types. The central focus of the discussion of the expenditure cycle in this chapter is on purchases of goods and services for inventory. The acquisition and payment of selling and administrative expenses is very similar to purchases of goods and services for inventory and the minor variations in controls and audit tests for these expenditure transactions are explained in a later part of this section. Payroll is largely a stand-alone accounting application and some of the basic features of controls and audit tests for payroll are explained in a later part of this section. Also, explained briefly later are controls and audit tests for petty cash disbursements (an inconsequential area in most audits).

The acquisition of property and equipment and payments for income taxes are discussed in Chapter 11, because a substantive audit approach is normally used for these items.

Concurrent Testing of Disbursements and Acquisitions   Primarily for reasons of audit efficiency, the normal audit approach is to test concurrently the items acquired and the related cash disbursement. For example, the auditor would select a sample of cash disbursements for selling or administrative expense items and apply audit procedures to the canceled check and the documents supporting acquisition of the goods or services. In contrast, the audit tests in the sales cycle are normally applied separately to sales and cash receipts.

Increased Concern with Classification of Debits   Another distinguishing feature of transactions in the expenditure cycle compared to the sales cycle is the significantly greater number of account balances involved. For example, *administrative expenses* include office supplies, rent, officers' travel expenses, legal and audit fees, property taxes, and insurance. *Selling expenses* include advertising, commissions, travel and entertainment, and freight out. For a manufacturing company, *purchases of goods or services for inventory* include raw material purchases and overhead expenses, including supplies, utilities, repair and maintenance, and freight in.

The greater number of account balances causes an increased concern with the proper classification of the debit when a liability is incurred or a cash disbursement made. The auditor is concerned with proper classification in testing sales transactions also, but the relative risk of misclassification is much greater for the expenditure cycle. Sales accounting systems are generally designed to process credit sales to customers. The risk of another type of transaction, such as disposition of manufacturing equipment or marketable securities, being recorded as a sale in the ordinary course of business is usually relatively low. In contrast, the account classification of an expenditure is far more susceptible to error.

Differences between Accounts Payable and Accounts Receivable   In the sales cycle the balance sheet account of primary concern is accounts receivable, in the expenditure cycle it is accounts payable. Except for the obvious point that one is an asset and the other a liability, the account balances are in some respects similar. Accounts receivable represents uncollected sales invoices, accounts payable represents unpaid vendors' invoices. However, important differences from the perspectives of the client's management and the auditor have auditing implications.

Generally, accounts payable processing is influenced more by cash management concerns than is accounts receivable processing. A company can only encourage prompt collections, but, within limits, a company can control precisely the timing of disbursements. Often, an accounts payable processing system is designed primarily to facilitate timing the payment of individual vendor invoices on the most advantageous basis, such as realizing discounts, and there is less concern with the recording accuracy and completeness of the obligation to each vendor or in total.

From the auditor's perspective, the primary difference from accounts receivable is the focus on detecting understatement of accounts payable. Recall that if the direction of testing is coordinated for all account balances, as explained in Chapter 7, liabilities are tested directly for understatement. Even if the direction of testing is not coordinated, many auditors would still emphasize detection of understatement because of business risk considerations. These auditors argue that an overstatement of net assets caused by understating liabilities is far more likely to result in litigation than an understatement of net assets. Also, the inherent risk for accounts payable is one of understatement because of the emphasis on timing the payment of individual invoices, explained earlier, and the apparent improvement in financial position that can be achieved by omitting liabilities.

Functions, Documents, Inputs, and Accounting Systems

This discussion explains the functions, documents, inputs, and accounting systems for purchases of inventory items. In a manufacturing company, this includes raw materials and overhead expenses. In a merchandising company, this includes goods acquired for resale and related acquisition cost.

An Overview of Functions, Documents, Inputs, and Accounting Systems   A *purchase requisition* is the starting point for this category of transaction in the expenditure cycle. It is a formal request from an operating department for raw materials or merchandise, or goods or services used in production. For example, automatic reorder points may be established for various inventory items that trigger a manual or computerized request.

The purchase requisition is sent to the *purchasing department.* To the extent possible, it is desirable for acquisition of goods and services to be handled by a centralized purchasing function. This permits centralized review of requisitions for compliance with established policy and sound practices such as obtaining competitive bids. The purchasing department prepares a *purchase order* and sends it to the vendor of the goods or services. (Vendors are sometimes referred to simply as suppliers.) The order is processed through the vendor's sales accounting system and the result is shipment and billing, or delivery of service and billing.

Goods received are accepted by a *receiving department* or function. The receiving department inspects and counts the goods before determining whether to accept them. To evaluate whether the goods conform to the specifications ordered, the receiving department should have been sent a copy of the purchase order. The receiving department prepares a *receiving report* and forwards notification copies to the purchasing department and accounting.

Within the accounting department, the *accounts payable function* receives *vendors' invoices.* Services, such as utilities or insurance, are received directly by operating departments rather than through the receiving department. The usual approach is to send vendors' invoices for such services to responsible supervisors in operating departments, or company officers, who approve the invoices and acknowledge receipt of the service. Vendors' invoices are one of the inputs to accounts payable processing. Vendors' invoices are used to update the accounts payable subsidiary ledger and vendor master file. The system records and summarizes the day's invoices in a *purchases journal,* which is a daily activity report.

To help ensure that disbursements are made only for goods or services that are authorized and received, a specialized source document designed for control purposes is often used. This source document, called a *voucher,* is simply a cover sheet or large envelope for collecting the source documents that support disbursements. A type of expenditures accounting system, as explained later, is called a voucher system. However, vouchers may be used in several types of expenditures accounting systems. The account distribution (classification of debits) is normally indicated on the voucher.

The *cash disbursements function* assembles the supporting documents for disbursements (vendors' invoices, receiving reports, and purchase orders). This is called "putting together the voucher package."

Most companies take all reasonable precautions possible to prevent unauthorized disbursements. Using *prenumbered checks,* protecting unissued checks, and accounting for the numerical sequence of issued and unissued checks are important. This includes defacing and retaining voided checks. Segregation of duties is also extremely important. In this respect, a distinction should be made between preparing checks for signature and actually signing checks.

Personnel responsible for preparing checks for signature should not be in a position to initiate purchase requisitions or other requests for disbursement, or prepare receiving reports. Individuals with authority to sign checks should be separated from the accounting function of recording accounts payable and the general ledger. Usually a company officer or other responsible supervisory personnel are responsible for signing checks. For disbursements above a specified amount, a cosignature may be required. Many companies use a mechanical check signing machine because of the large volume of checks. The check signing machine or removable signature plates should be protected and under the control of *authorized check signers.*

The scheduling of payments to vendors and other creditors is an important part of cash management. The computer may generate a report for manual identification of items to be paid, or items may be selected by computer. The output of computer selection may be a report of the details necessary for manual review and approval, or may be checks ready for signature. Computer generation of signed checks is feasible but not desirable from the viewpoint of good control.

Authorized check signers should have evidence at the time of signing the check that disbursement is appropriate. The check signer should review the supporting documents (vendor's invoice, receiving report, and purchase order), inspect indication of prior checking and assembly of supporting documents, and indicate supervisory approval. Supporting documents should be canceled so they cannot be reused to support another disbursement. Often, the check number and date are written on the supporting documents for this purpose, but additional alteration is desirable. The original of the check should be mailed directly to the payee without being returned to personnel involved in processing disbursements.

The information for the individual checks is generally the basis for recording in the *cash disbursements journal.* The details from the cash disbursements journal are used to update the accounts payable subsidiary ledger, and totals are posted to the general ledger accounts (accounts payable control and cash). If a multicopy check is used, only the original is a signed negotiable instrument. A daily activity report of cash disbursements is usually generated as part of the updating of the vendor master file.

Voucher Systems and Other Variations   A voucher system is designed to improve control over disbursements by establishing a sequential prenumbered record of vendors' invoices and to improve efficiency by eliminating unessential recordkeeping and facilitating timing of disbursements. Difficulty in obtaining control over vendors' invoices results because some invoices are paid shortly after receipt, and it is possible to not record them until cash is disbursed. For example, utility bills are normally payable within a short period of receipt, and there is no receiving report for the service. The utility bill is sent to an operating department for approval and entered directly as a cash disbursement after the invoice is approved. Using this approach, the transaction does not enter the accounting system until cash is disbursed. Also, vendors' invoices are prenumbered for the vendor's system, and the sequence of vendor's invoices cannot be accounted for by the purchaser.

Using a voucher system, the traditional books of original entry and accounts payable detail records are changed as follows:

- A *voucher register* replaces the purchases journal and accounts payable subsidiary ledger.
- A *check register* replaces the cash disbursements journal.

The recordkeeping sequence is as follows. All vendors' invoices are assigned to a prenumbered source document, a voucher, on receipt. The voucher is input into the voucher register file and sorted by due date. Vouchers are approved for payment on the basis of supporting documents (vendor's invoice, receiving report, purchase order) collected in the voucher package. A check is prepared and recorded in the check register, and the voucher register is updated to indicate payment. Paid vouchers are marked and stored in a paid voucher file by voucher number.

Posting from the check register and voucher register to the general ledger is done at the end of the accounting period when financial statements are prepared. Usually, this is done monthly, less frequently in some small businesses. The distribution of the debits to expense and asset accounts is originally recorded in the voucher register and often also on the voucher. In summary form, the entry is:

Dr. (Expense or asset accounts)	$ (Total)
Cr. Cash	$ (Paid vouchers)
Accounts payable	$ (Unpaid vouchers)

Notice that the determination of the accounts payable liability is based on the preparation of a *schedule of unpaid vouchers*. There is no accounts payable subsidiary ledger with balances owed to each vendor. This makes it difficult to reconcile vendors' statements (monthly statements mailed to customers by vendors of the balance owed) with the company's records. However, within the company's accounting system there should be an independent reconciliation of the following:

1 Total of the schedule of unpaid vouchers
2 The accounts payable balance of the general ledger
3 Total of vouchers in the unpaid vouchers file

Another variation in expenditures systems is use of a *vendor invoice register file*. Vendors' invoices are assigned numbers as they are received and input into the invoice register file in numbered sequence. Some companies use an invoice register in place of a voucher register, others use it as a prevoucher register as an added measure of control over incoming invoices.

Adjustments and Inventory   Accounts payable processing has additional complicating factors that are similar to those for accounts receivable processing. In addition to the credits to accounts payable for purchases and debits for cash disbursements, there are adjustments for such things as return to vendors of goods that do not meet purchase order specifications. Controls and processing for those adjustments are similar to those for sales accounting. *Prenumbered debit memoranda* are used and supervisory approval is required before processing. Also, memoranda issued can be matched with shipping reports for goods returned and the corresponding credit memoranda from vendors.

In an expenditures system, the receiving reports for raw materials or merchandise are the input for updating inventory records. *Perpetual inventory records* are a running total of inventory items on hand, and they may be maintained in quantities only or in both quantities and dollars. Perpetual records in dollars are integrated with sales accounting systems. Audit and control considerations for inventory are discussed in Chapter 11. However, personnel responsible for *inventory storekeeping* should be separated from purchasing, receiving, and accounting.

Primary Control-Related Features

The primary control-related features of the expenditures cycle are concerned with seg-regation of duties; control over source documents; and checks, approvals, and reconcil-iations.

- *Segregation of duties.* The basic separations that should be incorporated in the plan of organization are among purchasing, receiving, storekeeping, access to cash (check signing), and accounting. Within the accounting department, responsibility for accounts payable detail should be separated from the general ledger function. In a voucher system, voucher preparation should be separated from voucher approval. Finally, any reconciliations should be made independently of the other functions.
- *Control over source documents.* The source documents used in accounts payable pro-cessing—purchase orders, receiving reports, vouchers, and checks—should be pre-numbered and the sequence should be accounted for. The periodic accounting for checks should include both used and unused checks, and a comparison should be made to recorded cash disbursements.
- *Checks, approvals, and reconciliations.* The more checks and approvals that are built in at each processing step, the more effective the control. In an expenditures system one very important check is the comparison of supporting documents (purchase order, receiving report, vendor's invoice) and recomputation of the vendor's invoice that should be made before approval for payment. Reconciliations are also important but vary with the type of accounting system.

Account Balances and Transactions

The account balances and the categories of transaction types for the expenditures cycle are enumerated in the discussion of differences from the sales cycle. In addition to the account balances discussed earlier, the expenditures cycle may also include prepaid expenses for advance disbursements for goods or services not yet received and accrued liabilities for goods or services received, but not yet billed by vendors.

Potential Misstatements

One goal of using the approach of developing specific control objectives as a basis for designing tests of transaction classes is to avoid the need for memorization of long lists of control procedures or misstatements that can occur. However, auditors should have an awareness of the following types of irregularities that may occur in the expenditures cycle:

- *Classic disbursements fraud.* The classic pattern for employee fraud in the disburse-ments area involves the preparation of fraudulent supporting documents that are used to obtain an authorized check. Because this type of fraud requires careful planning *before* commission, the deception involved is often elaborate. Some frauds of this type have included the opening of post office boxes and bank accounts in the names of fictitious companies. Clever frauds of this type may be virtually impossible for inter-nal auditors or independent auditors to detect as long as the perpetrator is not too greedy. If the discrepancy between goods or services received and goods or services paid for becomes too great, accountability tests may disclose the fraud. Also, this fraud is one of the reasons that auditors investigate unusual or unfamiliar names of vendors.

- *Kickbacks.* Personnel responsible for purchasing may enter into arrangements with vendors to receive kickbacks on goods or services purchased from them. Since collusion is involved, it could be argued that auditors have no responsibility to attempt to detect kickbacks. However, when competitive bidding practices are not followed, many auditors compare unit prices on items of the same type acquired from different vendors to consider the possibility of a kickback scheme.

- *Illegal acts.* The auditor's responsibility with respect to illegal acts is explained in Chapter 5. The most likely place in the audit for questionable transactions that may be indicative of bribery, illegal political contributions, or other illegal payments to come to the auditor's attention, is in the examination of disbursement transactions. The most likely transaction type is selling or administrative expense. For example, a sales commission may be a bribe to obtain business. As explained in Chapter 5, the auditor does not plan audit procedures specifically to detect illegal acts but remains aware of the possibility of such acts.

- *Unauthorized executive perks.* The personal use of business assets is inappropriate unless the use is authorized and appropriately considered as part of executive compensation. For public companies, SEC requirements apply to disclosure of management remuneration. For private companies, the auditor is still usually concerned with such practices because of tax return preparation responsibilities and tax liability implications.

- *Kiting.* The term "kiting" is used to describe the practice of inflating the cash balance by using the "float" period for concealment. Cash is transferred from one bank account to another and the cash receipt (deposit) is recorded in the period under audit, but recording the disbursement (withdrawal) is delayed until the following period. During the float period the money transferred will appear to be in both bank balances. This device may be used by an employee to conceal a cash shortage or by management to improve financial position.

Tests of Transaction Classes for Purchases for Inventory

Conceptually the approach to tests of transaction classes for purchases of goods or services for inventory is similar to tests of sales transactions. The auditor needs to consider whether the specific control procedures the client follows provide reasonable assurance of achieving the specific control objectives. After identifying specific control procedures as a basis for reducing the assessment of control risk, the auditor selects audit procedures to perform tests of controls and substantive tests.

The specific control objectives for purchases of goods or services for inventory and examples of common control procedures and tests of transaction classes are summarized in Figure 10-3. The arrangement and approach to listing audit procedures in Figure 10-3 is, as explained earlier, referred to as a design format. The auditor would need to eliminate duplications and reorder the procedures into a logical and efficient sequence.

General control objective	Specific control objective	Common control policies and procedures	Tests of transaction class
Authorization and approval	Goods or services for inventory are purchased only with the proper authorization.	• Established policy for approval by specified personnel of requisitions and purchase orders • Purchasing independent of receiving, stores, and accounts payable	• Select a sample of purchases for inventory and inspect for indication of approval of purchase orders. • Observe and inquire about purchasing.
Validity	Recorded purchases for inventory are for goods or services authorized and received.	• Goods received counted, inspected, and compared to purchase order before acceptance • Services received acknowledged in writing • Prenumbered receiving reports with sequence accounted for issued by receiving department independent of stores and accounts payable • Comparison of purchase order, receiving report, and vendor's invoice and recomputation of vendor's invoice before recording liability	• Select a sample of vouchers and inspect for existence of supporting documents, agreement of details, clerical accuracy of vendor's invoice, indication of approval. • Review the accounting for numerical sequence of purchase orders and receiving reports or test numerical sequence. • Observe and inquire about receiving procedures.
Completeness	All goods or services for inventory received are recorded.	• Vendors' invoices numbered using an invoice register or prenumbered vouchers and the sequence accounted for • Vendors' invoices matched to receiving reports and unmatched items investigated	• Review the accounting for numerical sequence by inspecting the invoice register or voucher register. • Review reports of unmatched items and inquire about disposition. • Select a sample of receiving reports and trace to purchases journal or voucher register.

FIGURE 10-3
Control policies and procedures and audit tests for purchases for inventory transactions.

As explained earlier, the transaction tests for the expenditures cycle combine the tests of the asset or expense acquired and the tests of the related cash disbursement. This means that the canceled check and the supporting documents for the purchase, such as the vendor's invoice, receiving report, and purchase order, are examined concurrently. Thus, the preliminary audit program for purchases of goods or services for inventory would include the audit procedures applied to cash disbursement source documents in Figure 10-4.

General control objective	Specific control objective	Common control policies and procedures	Tests of transaction class
Recording accuracy	Purchases of goods or services for inventory are recorded correctly as to account, amount, and period and summarized correctly.	• Established procedures for review of voucher and account distribution (expense classification) before recording and for review of summarization and posting	• For the sample of vouchers selected (see validity), review for correct classification and accounting period and indication of review and approval. • Foot voucher register file and trace to general ledger and inspect supervisory review and approval of summarization and posting • Or, foot purchases journal and trace to accounts payable subsidiary ledger and inspect supervisory review and approval of summarization and posting.
Reconciliation	Accounts payable detail is periodically reconciled with the general ledger and vendors' statements.	• Periodic reconciliation of: —Accounts payable subsidiary ledger to general ledger control —Unpaid voucher file with general ledger —Vendors' statements to supporting vendors' invoices	• Inspect reconciliation and reperform one or a few reconciliations.

FIGURE 10-3 *(concluded)*

Tests of Transaction Classes for Cash Disbursements

The specific control objectives for cash disbursements and examples of common control policies and procedures and tests of transaction classes are summarized in Figure 10-4. For those tests that involve inspection of documents, audit sampling would be used. This means that the sample size for canceled checks to be selected would need to be adequate for each of the transaction types within the expenditures cycle to support each control risk assessment. For example, assume the auditor was using the audit sampling approach explained in Chapter 8 and concluded that a sample of 30 transactions was necessary. If the auditor planned to assess control risk at less than maximum for purchases of goods or services for inventory, purchases of goods and services for selling and administration, and payroll, then a sample of 90 canceled checks would need to be selected with 30 for each type of expenditure transaction.

General control objective	Specific control objective	Common control policies and procedures	Tests of transaction class
Authorization and approval	Cash disbursements are not made unless goods and services are authorized and received.	• Checks printed or prepared only when receipt of goods or services and approval are documented (e.g., supporting documents compared, recomputed, and voucher approved) • Checks signed only after reviewing supporting documentation and prior approval	• Select a sample of canceled checks and inspect supporting documentation for indication of checking, review, and approvals and reperform checking.
Validity	Recorded cash disbursements are for goods or services authorized and received.	• Check signing independent of initiating or approving purchases, check preparation, and accounting functions • Cosignature required for disbursements above a specified amount and advance signing prohibited • Supporting documentation canceled and referenced to check number	• Observe and inquire about check preparation and signing. • For the sample of canceled checks (see authorization and approval) inspect supporting documents for cancelation, check number, and endorsement.
Completeness	All cash disbursements are recorded.	• Checks prenumbered and the sequence accounted for • Unissued checks protected and the sequence accounted for • Voided checks defaced and retained • Canceled checks compared to cash disbursement records (The above control procedures usually are done as part of the bank reconciliation.) • Check signing machines and signature plates protected	• Observe and inquire about preparation of bank reconciliation and reperform one or a few, including numerical sequence testing and tracing canceled checks to cash disbursement records. • Observe and inquire about check signing, including protective measures for unissued checks and check signing devices.

FIGURE 10-4
Control policies and procedures and audit tests for cash disbursements transactions.

General control objective	Specific control objective	Common control policies and procedures	Tests of transaction class
Recording accuracy	Cash disbursements are recorded correctly as to account, amount, and period.	• Check signer reviews account distribution (expense classification) • Canceled checks compared to cash disbursement • Bank transfers (both deposit and withdrawal side) reviewed for recording in proper period • Summarization and posting of cash disbursement records reviewed and approved	• For the sample of canceled checks (see authorization and approval) compare check number, amount, payee, and date with cash disbursement record. • Consider whether canceled checks cleared the bank within a reasonable period of recording and were treated properly in bank reconciliation. • Foot the cash disbursements journal or check register and trace to general ledger and bank statement.
Safeguarding	Access to cash is restricted to authorized personnel.	• Signed checks mailed directly to payee • Unissued checks protected and periodically accounted for • Custody and use of check signing machine or removable signature plates restricted to authorized check signers	• Observe and inquire about check signing and mailing and protection of unissued checks.
Reconciliation	Recorded cash is periodically reconciled with bank accounts.	• Bank accounts reconciled with cash records independently of check signing and accounting functions • Reconciliation includes: —Accounting for all issued and unissued checks (both manual checks and computer stock checks) —Comparison of canceled checks to disbursement records —Review of bank transfers (both deposit and withdrawal side) for recording in proper period	• Inspect bank reconciliations and reperform one or a few.

FIGURE 10-4 *(concluded)*

Variations for Other Types of Expenditure Transactions

The following discussion explains the primary variations in the nature of control policies and procedures and audit tests for some other categories of types of expenditure transactions:

- *Selling and administrative expense.* The processing and related control policies and procedures for selling and administrative expense are very similar to those for purchases for inventory. The primary difference is a greater emphasis on budgetary control of selling and administrative expenses. Review and approval of budgets and obtaining satisfactory explanation of variances are important. For some expenses, such as travel and entertainment, a well-defined expense reimbursement policy is important. The auditor needs to understand the business purpose of selling and administrative expense transactions examined and review supporting documentation, such as expense reports. A comparison of budgets and level of activity in prior periods to actual expenses, budgets, and level of activity in the current period is an important audit procedure.
- *Payroll.* Important control procedures for payroll include segregation of the following duties:

  - Approval of hiring and firing and pay rates (personnel or senior management)
  - Approval of time worked (supervisor)
  - Payroll preparation
  - Payroll distribution
  - Custody of unclaimed paychecks

  The primary misstatements that may occur are a padded payroll (fictitious employees) and misappropriation of unclaimed paychecks. Generally, employees can be relied on to detect errors of understatement. Audit procedures in the payroll area are similar to those for other expenditures, but the terms for source documents differ. For example, there may be time cards instead of vendors' invoices. The auditor is concerned with assessing the validity and accuracy of pay rates and time worked. Personnel should be separated from other payroll-related functions and payroll data can be compared to personnel records. On the disbursement side, an important control is comparison of net payroll with payroll checks issued. Observation of payroll distribution, once a common audit procedure, is now used only when there is a serious risk of fictitious employees on the payroll. Because effective analytical procedures are often possible for payroll, the auditor may sometimes omit tests of details in this area. Also, when a company constructs or refurbishes assets for its own use, the auditor should consider the risk that the cost of the work of production employees has been improperly capitalized.
- *Petty cash disbursements.* The expenses paid out of cash on hand are usually so insignificant that the auditor applies no tests. However, the primary control procedure is an *imprest fund.* The total of cash on hand and the documentation of expenses paid out of the fund should always equal a preestablished control total. When the fund is reimbursed, someone other than the custodian counts the cash and documents. If audit

procedures are applied, the auditor would count the fund *in the custodian's presence* and examine the supporting documents for disbursements out of the fund for propriety and reasonableness.

RELATED DIRECT TESTS OF BALANCES

This section explains the direct tests of balances for the primary balance sheet accounts associated with the selling and expenditure cycles—accounts receivable, accounts payable, and cash. The other primary balance sheet account affected by the transactions in these cycles—inventory—is discussed in Chapter 11.

As explained earlier, *direct tests of balances focus on balance sheet accounts.* Account balances in the income statement are not ignored. However, substantiation of income statement balances is often viewed more as a byproduct of direct tests of balance sheet accounts. For example, direct tests of accounts receivable include audit procedures to evaluate the allowance for bad debts. The related income statement balance, bad debt expense, is the increase in the allowance and is substantiated as a byproduct of testing the allowance. However, analytical procedures used as direct tests of balances are usually applied concurrently to income statement and balance sheet account balances.

Accounts Receivable

The essential features of direct tests of balances for accounts receivable are emphasis on specific audit objectives related to *existence* and *valuation* achieved primarily by *confirmation* directly with customers and *review of the aged trial balance* of accounts receivable. As explained in more detail later, the aged trial balance is the basic work paper schedule in the receivables area because of audit efficiency considerations.

Assertions, Objectives, and Procedures   As explained in Chapter 7, the preliminary audit program for an account balance is prepared by developing specific audit objectives from the broad categories of financial statement assertions and selecting audit procedures to achieve those objectives.

Figure 10-5 summarizes the financial statement assertions, specific audit objectives, and the common audit procedures traditionally used to achieve the objectives for accounts receivable and related account balances. It cannot be overemphasized that these examples, and the others presented in this book, are not, unless otherwise noted, required procedures. The critical point is always whether the specific procedures applied achieve the audit objectives.

In a sense, the specific audit objectives presented in Figure 10-5 are also examples. The broad categories of financial statement assertions are an invariable element, but the only important consideration is that the specific audit objectives cover all the assertions. In this book, a specific audit objective is developed for each assertion to visually demonstrate completeness of coverage and facilitate study of the relationship of assertions, objectives, and procedures. However, auditors in practice may develop more objectives than assertions by subdividing assertions or may develop fewer objectives by combining assertions. For example, some auditors develop a separate specific objective for cut-

Broad category of financial statement assertion	Specific audit objective	Common audit procedures to achieve objective
Existence	Accounts receivable are authentic obligations owed by customers at the balance sheet date.	Confirmation Cutoff
Completeness	Accounts receivable include all amounts owed by customers at the balance sheet date.	Analytical procedures Cutoff (tests of sales transactions)
Rights or obligations	Accounts receivable are owed to the company and not pledged or subject to other claims.	General procedures Inquiry and scanning
Valuation	Accounts receivable are presented at the net realizable amount.	Review of aged trial balance Analytical procedures
Presentation and disclosure	Accounts receivable are properly described and classified in the balance sheet and related disclosures are adequate.	General procedures Inquiry and scanning

FIGURE 10-5
Assertions, objectives, and procedures for accounts receivable.

off (recording of items in the proper accounting period), because it is an aspect of both existence and completeness. An example of a combined objective is as follows:

Accounts receivable represent all (completeness) authentic amounts due from customers (existence) that are owned by the company (rights) at the balance sheet date (cutoff).

The common audit procedures listed in Figure 10-5 are the *primary* procedures traditionally used to achieve the related specific audit objective. These audit procedures are defined generally in Chapter 4 and some are explained further in earlier chapters. As applied in the accounts receivable area, the procedures have the following features:

- *Confirmation.* Requests are mailed directly to selected customers asking them to "confirm" an amount owed at a date specified in the request. Since this procedure is so central, it is explained further in a separate section.
- *Cutoff.* This audit procedure is designed to determine that all significant transactions of the current period are recorded and no significant transactions of the next period are recorded as of a specified date. For accounts receivable, cutoff tests are concerned with *shipments* and *cash collections*. The auditor would identify the number of the last prenumbered shipping document and the last prenumbered sales invoice for the period and determine that lower numbers are recorded in the current period and higher numbers in the next period. If documents are not prenumbered or the sequence is not accounted for, the auditor would examine all sales transactions above a specified cutoff amount within a few days before and after the end of the period to test proper cutoff. Cash collection cutoff is tested by identifying the last cash receipt recorded in the period and comparing the date to the date of deposit in the bank. The "as of" date for cutoff tests for receivables should be the same as that used for confirmation.

- *Analytical procedures.* Analytical procedures in the accounts receivable area include comparison of amounts and ratios for relationships among sales and receivables, allowance accounts and sales, and cost of sales and sales. Comparisons would be made to prior periods, budgets, and information on unit quantities (units shipped to units billed). The type of analytical test that provides the most persuasive evidence for objectives related to completeness is a predictive test of sales based on reliable data. The exact nature of the test depends on the circumstances. For example, for a membership organization, revenue from members' dues can be predicted, based on reliable data on the number of members and the dues schedule.
- *Tests of sales transactions.* The transaction test that is relevant to completeness of receivables is tracing from shipping documents to sales invoices. If the auditor's preliminary audit program includes this procedure in tests of transaction classes, the results of the test also bear on the completeness of receivables. If the audit approach does not include tests of controls related to completeness of sales transactions, the auditor has to consider the need for transaction testing as part of direct tests of the receivable balance because the primary procedure—confirmation—is directed to existence. Analytical tests of sales and receivables combined with consideration of the results of audit procedures applied to inventory are often sufficient. (Note that unrecorded sales should result in inventory shrinkage.)
- *General procedures.* As explained in Chapter 7, general procedures are procedures that are usually applied separately rather than in relation to specific balances, such as reading minutes and contracts. However, the results of general procedures are considered in relation to the balances affected. For receivables, the relevant information would concern the existence of pledging, factoring, or other liens on receivables.
- *Inquiry and scanning.* Scanning includes visually reviewing accounting records and financial statements in relation to the knowledge obtained from applying other audit procedures. Inquiries relevant to accounts receivable would include the existence of nonstandard sales terms (consignment sales or other right of return) and related-party transactions.
- *Review of aged trial balance.* An aged trial balance of receivables lists all customer balances as of a specified date and for each customer shows the total balance and the components of the balance by age category, such as 30 days or below, 31 to 60 days, 61 to 90 days, and over 90 days. A periodic aging is used by a company's financial management to monitor collectibility and for related cash management concerns. The auditor reviews the aged trial balance as of the balance sheet date with the credit manager as part of the evaluation of the reasonableness of the allowance for bad debts. Since the aged trial balance is usually a client-prepared schedule, the auditor needs to test clerical accuracy by footing and tracing. The extent of the testing of the aged trial balance depends on the validity, completeness, and recording accuracy of processing sales and cash receipts.

Confirmation Procedures   SAS No. 67 (AU 330.04) explains what *confirmation* is:

Confirmation is the process of obtaining and evaluating a direct communication from a third party in response to a request for information about a particular item affecting financial statement assertions.

Direct confirmation of accounts receivable by mail with customers has the distinction of being one of the only two auditing procedures described as *generally accepted auditing procedures.* The other is observation of physical inventory taking. According to SAS No. 67 (AU 330.34):

> Confirmation of accounts receivable is a generally accepted auditing procedure. . . . It is generally presumed that evidence obtained from third parties will provide the auditor with higher-quality audit evidence than is typically available from within the entity.

SAS No. 67 (AU 330.34) goes on to explain:

> . . . there is a presumption that the auditor will request the confirmation of accounts receivable during an audit unless one of the following is true:
>
> - Accounts receivable are immaterial to the financial statements.
> - The use of confirmations would be ineffective.
> - The auditor's combined assessed level of inherent and control risk is low, and the assessed level, in conjunction with the evidence expected to be provided by analytical procedures or other substantive tests of details, is sufficient to reduce audit risk to an acceptably low level. . . .

The SAS explicitly states that an auditor who has not requested confirmations in the examination of accounts receivable should document how he or she overcame this presumption. In other words, if the auditor does not confirm receivables, there better be a good reason.

In developing an audit program for accounts receivable the *nature* of the procedure has for all practical purposes been removed from the auditor's judgment. However, the *timing and extent* of the procedure are within the auditor's judgment. The considerations that affect timing and extent are explained later in relation to materiality and audit risk. The other matter within the auditor's judgment is the "*method of requesting the confirmation.*"

Generally, there are two alternatives in the method of requesting confirmation—positive and negative:

- *Positive form.* The positive form asks the customer to respond whether or not the customer agrees with the information on the amount owed in the request. The receipt of a response from the customer provides evidence of the authenticity of the receivable and, if the customer agrees, evidence of the accuracy of the amount. It provides no positive evidence of collectibility but may detect a disputed amount which indicates doubtful collectibility. Some auditors request recipients of the confirmation to provide the auditor with the balance or invoice amounts owed. Because the auditor leaves the amount blank, this form of positive confirmation is called a *blank form.*
- *Negative form.* The negative form of request asks the customer to respond only if there is disagreement with the information given. Generally, the negative form is considered to provide less reliable evidence and the number of confirmations sent should be greater than the number of positive requests that would be sent in similar circumstances. If the number of confirmations returned as undeliverable is more than expected, the auditor would suspect the possibility of fictitious receivables.

Figure 10-6 illustrates a positive form, Figure 10-7 illustrates a negative form. Generally, auditors have found that response is improved when the request accompanies a regular monthly statement to the customer. Note that the request comes from the client and the auditor should exercise the precautions described in Chapter 3 for *maintaining control over confirmations.*

SAS No. 67 (AU 330.20) states that negative confirmations may be used only when:

1 The combined assessed level of inherent and control risk is low.
2 A large number of small balances is involved.
3 The auditor believes the confirmation recipients will consider the requests.

The confirmation process has to be started soon enough during the audit to allow adequate time to mail initial requests, send second and third requests if necessary, and analyze responses.

When planning the accounts receivable confirmations, the auditor should consider the following:

- *Prior experience.* The auditor should consider prior experience with the client or similar clients, especially when there have been poor response rates or other indications that confirmations are ineffective. Is enough information provided to help the recipient respond? Is the confirmation being directed to the wrong person?
- *The nature of the information being confirmed.* Should invoices or balances be confirmed? For example, if most of the customers' accounting systems track individual invoices rather than balances, sending a balance confirmation will be ineffective.

  Have there been unusual transactions such as large sales at or near year-end? The auditor might design the confirmation to request information to identify "bill and hold" transactions where merchandise is billed to customers before delivery.

  Is there a moderate or high risk of oral agreements, such as liberal rights of return of merchandise? If so, the confirmation should request information on the terms of agreements.
- *Respondent.* Care should be taken to direct the confirmations to the individuals knowledgeable about the transactions or arrangements.

The auditor's *analysis of responses* is essentially a consideration of whether disagreements noted by customers indicate merely discrepancies caused by timing, such as those caused by mailing time for cash receipts or shipping time for shipments, or actual clerical errors or disputed amounts. This can be one of the most time-consuming and tedious parts of procedures for accounts receivable. The auditor does not want to project monetary misstatement for timing discrepancies or isolated errors so the qualitative analysis of confirmation responses is extremely important.

Second or third requests may be sent if the initial positive request does not result in a response. The reasons for this are that the lack of response may be an indication of fictitious receivables and that possibility must be pursued, and because the alternative procedures to confirmation are usually more costly and time-consuming.

[Client's Letterhead]

_____
[Date]

_____
_____
_____
[Customer's Name and Address]

Our auditors, __[Name]_____ , are making an
annual audit of our financial statements. Please confirm the balance due at __[Date]_____ ,
which is shown on our records and the enclosed statement as $_____ .

Please indicate in the space below whether this is in agreement with your records. If there are
differences, please provide any information that will assist our auditors in reconciling the
difference.

Please sign and date your response and mail your reply directly to __[Auditor's Name and Address]__
_____ ,
in the enclosed return envelope. PLEASE DO NOT MAIL PAYMENTS ON YOUR ACCOUNT
TO THE AUDITORS.

Very truly yours,

_____
[Officer's Signature and Title]

_____
[Client's Name]

To: _____
    [Auditor's Name]

The balance due __[Client's Name]_____ of $_____
as of __[Date]_____ is correct with the following exceptions (if any):
_____
_____
_____

Signature: _____
Title: _____
Date: _____

FIGURE 10-6
Format of positive accounts receivable confirmation request with itemized statement
enclosed.

[Client's Letterhead]

[Date]

_____

[Customer's Name and Address]

Our auditors are making an annual audit of our financial statements. Our records show an amount of $ _____ due from you as of _____[Date]_____ If the amount is *not* correct, please report any differences directly to our auditors, _____[Auditor's Name and Address]_____ , _____using the space below and the enclosed return envelope. NO REPLY IS NECESSARY IF THIS AMOUNT AGREES WITH YOUR RECORDS. PLEASE DO NOT MAIL PAYMENTS ON ACCOUNT TO OUR AUDITORS.

Very truly yours,

_____

[Officer's Signature and Title]

_____

[Company Name]

Differences Noted (If Any)

The balance due _____[Client's Name]_____ of $ _____ at _____[Date]_____ does not agree with our records because: (No reply is necessary if your records agree.)

Date: _____ By: _____

[Individual or Company]

FIGURE 10-7
Format of negative accounts receivable confirmation request.

Alternative Procedures to Confirmation   SAS No. 67 (AU 330.31) observes that if a response is not received to positive requests the situation requires the auditor to "apply alternative procedures to the nonresponses to obtain the evidence necessary to reduce audit risk to an acceptably low level." These procedures may include examination of evidence of subsequent cash receipts, cash remittance advices, sales and shipping documents, and other records. The alternative procedures are essentially the same vouching, tracing, and recomputing of source documents involved in tests of transaction classes. However, instead of a representative sample of source documents, the auditor applies procedures to the specific documents for nonresponding accounts.

Generally, subsequent cash receipts are considered to be a superior form of evidence because sales and shipping documents originate in the client's system and substantiating subsequent collection simultaneously achieves the audit objectives related to existence and valuation. The intensiveness of the alternative procedures depends on the effectiveness of the internal control structure. If controls over the validity and recording accuracy of cash receipts are good, the auditor may trace credits to a nonresponding account back to the cash receipts journal. If those controls are deficient, the auditor would trace to the remittance advice. If controls were extremely deficient, the auditor might believe it necessary to maintain audit control of actual cash receipts.

SAS No. 67 (AU 330) recognizes that it is not always necessary to perform alternative procedures on all nonresponses. They could be treated as misstatements, if doing so does not change the auditor's decision about whether the financial statements are materially misstated. However, the auditor needs to consider the qualitative characteristics of the nonresponses. Is there a systematic characteristic, such as tending to be the year-end transactions?

Materiality   In the accounts receivable area, materiality is used primarily to identify individually significant customer accounts, all of which are confirmed, and to estimate the sample size for confirmation of customer accounts selected from the remaining recorded amount. If accounts receivable are immaterial in total, confirmation would not be necessary.

Examples of customer accounts that might be identified as individually significant are as follows:

- Large dollar balances (The cutoff amount or what is "large" might be tolerable misstatement divided by 3, as explained in Chapters 7 and 8.)
- Significantly past due balances
- Accounts with unusual names
- Related-party balances
- Credit balances

Often the remaining recorded amount after identifying individually significant items exceeds tolerable misstatement, and audit sampling is necessary. In fact, confirmation of accounts receivable is one of the most frequent audit sampling applications among direct tests of balances.

Audit Risk   The timing and extent of confirmation and the extensiveness of collectibility tests are influenced significantly by consideration of audit risk. The inherent risk factors considered would include the nature of products, nature of distribution methods, complexity of billing, and economic developments. The control risk evaluation focuses on specific control objectives. Generally, those specific objectives of the greatest significance for confirmation include validity and recording accuracy for sales transactions and validity and recording accuracy for cash receipts. Deficiencies in control procedures to achieve those objectives would influence confirmation procedures as follows:

- *Nature*—positive form of confirmation rather than negative form
- *Timing*—confirm at the balance sheet date rather than at an interim date
- *Extent*—lower the dollar cutoff amount for individually significant amounts and lower the allowable risk of incorrect acceptance for the portion of the balance sampled

The extensiveness of procedures to test collectibility is influenced by environmental considerations such as changes in national or industrial economic conditions and whether the specific control objective for authorization and approval of credit limits and terms for sales transactions was achieved.

Audit Efficiency   Many efficiencies in the accounts receivable area can be achieved by organizing the documentation of audit procedures around the schedule for the *aged trial balance of accounts receivable.* If receivables are confirmed at year-end, subsequent cash receipts can be posted to the aged trial balance to reduce the number and amount of accounts to which other audit procedures need to be applied.

Customer accounts can be selected from the aged trial balance for confirmation. By footing the trial balance and comparing the total to the general ledger and financial statements, the auditor simultaneously establishes the physical completeness of the population being sampled and an aspect of the clerical accuracy of the trial balance.

Accounts Payable

The essential features of direct tests of balances for accounts payable are emphasis on the specific audit objective related to *completeness* achieved primarily by a procedure referred to as an *out-of-period liability test,* or a search for unrecorded accounts payable, and analytical tests of related expense account balances.

Assertions, Objectives, and Procedures   The financial statement assertions, specific audit objectives, and the common audit procedures traditionally used to achieve the objectives for accounts payable and related accounts are summarized in Figure 10-8. As applied in the accounts payable area, these procedures have the following features:

- *Confirmation.* Use of confirmation procedures for accounts payable balances is not as widely accepted as confirmation of accounts receivable. Confirmation is generally considered relevant to achieving specific audit objectives related to existence and to some extent valuation. Some auditors confirm accounts payable balances when control objectives related to validity and recording accuracy have serious deficiencies. Other auditors believe confirmation of accounts payable can be an efficient and effective procedure for achieving specific audit objectives related to existence and completeness. Confirmation requests are sent to vendors with whom the company has done a relatively large volume of business during the period. The auditor is concerned with what should be recorded rather than what is recorded so the emphasis is placed on selecting vendors who are *likely* to have large balances. Thus, the accounts payable balances selected include zero and small recorded balances. The normal form of confirmation request for payables is positive and asks the vendor to state the balance due

Broad category of financial statement assertion	Specific audit objective	Common audit procedures to achieve objective
Existence	Accounts payable and accrued liabilities are valid obligations to vendors at the balance sheet date.	Confirmation Vouching
Completeness	Accounts payable and accrued liabilities include all obligations owed to vendors at the balance sheet date.	Out-of-period liability search General procedures
Rights or obligations	Accounts payable and accrued liabilities are obligations owed by the company.	Analytical procedures General procedures
Valuation	Accounts payable and accrued liabilities are presented at the appropriate amount.	Recomputation Analytical procedures
Presentation and disclosure	Accounts payable and accrued liabilities are properly described and classified in the balance sheet and related disclosures are adequate.	Inquiry and scanning General procedures

FIGURE 10-8
Assertions, objectives, and procedures for accounts payable.

from the client (a so-called blind request). The auditor's analysis of responses is similar to that for confirmation of receivables. A distinction must be made between discrepancies caused by disbursements and shipments in transit and those caused by clerical errors, disputes, and unrecorded invoices.

- *Vouching.* Some auditors regard vouching recorded payables balances to vendors' statements as equivalent in reliability to confirmation because the evidential matter originates outside the client's accounting system. Vouching can be very effective when recorded accounts payable are reconciled to monthly statements received from vendors. However, if the client's system does not include maintenance of an accounts payable subsidiary ledger or vendor master file, such a reconciliation is time-consuming and difficult.
- *Out-of-period liability search.* This procedure is essentially a cutoff test to see that vendors' invoices, receiving reports, and cash disbursements are recorded in the proper period, but the emphasis is on identifying obligations that should have been recorded at the balance sheet date. It directly tests the accounts payable balance for understatement and, because it is the central procedure in the accounts payable area, it is explained further in a separate section.
- *General procedures.* The out-of-period liability search focuses on detecting unrecorded accounts payable or accrued liabilities for goods or services received at the balance sheet date. However, other unrecorded liabilities may arise from matters such as commitments under contracts, unasserted claims, or other loss contingencies.

The auditor normally relies on general procedures, such as reading minutes, contracts, loan agreements, leases, and correspondence from government agencies to detect unrecorded liabilities for which no indication exists in the accounting records or source documents. For example, reading minutes of meetings of the board of directors may detect an unrecorded dividend payable.

- *Analytical procedures.* Comparison of expenses, budgets, and level of activity in the current period with similar information of prior periods can provide evidential matter for recorded expense and liability balances. In some cases, an analytical test can substantiate the total expense and related accrued liability. For example, sales commission expense and accrued commissions payable can usually be reliably estimated based on recorded sales and knowledge of the terms for commissions.
- *Recomputation.* Some accrued liabilities, such as accrued property taxes, can be substantiated by examining disbursements in the subsequent period and calculating the portion attributable to the prior period under audit. In general, recomputation is used for accruals and deferrals that are recurring adjustments in closing the accounting records.
- *Inquiry and scanning.* The auditor uses inquiry and scanning in conjunction with other general procedures to identify matters relevant to the description, classification, and related disclosure of liabilities in the balance sheet. For example, inquiry and scanning may identify *related-party payables* or losses under sales or purchase commitments.

Out-of-Period Liability Search   This procedure is also sometimes called "the search for unrecorded liabilities" or "the review of subsequent disbursements." This audit procedure is invariably included in audit programs for direct tests of the accounts payable balance. Control procedures for specific control objectives on completeness, recording accuracy, and reconciliation for purchases and cash disbursement transactions influence the extent of the procedure but not usually the nature or timing.

The potential for unrecorded liabilities arises from both errors and irregularities. Errors result because of practical problems in closing the accounting records. Invariably some goods or services received before the end of the period do not become known and recorded until the next period. Controls over vendors' invoices and receiving reports, matching of these source documents, and investigation of unmatched items can minimize this problem. The auditor's objective is to obtain reasonable assurance that material liabilities have not been omitted.

Intentional omission of liabilities that exist at the balance sheet date does not change the auditor's objective. In fact, the same audit procedures should detect material omissions whether they are inadvertent or intentional. Goods or services received will ultimately have to be paid for in the next period to avoid disputes with vendors, loss of credit lines, or litigation with creditors.

The auditor selects from cash disbursements recorded in the subsequent period and traces to the schedule of accounts payable at the balance sheet date those disbursements that pertain to the period under audit. Those not included in the schedule are unrecorded liabilities. The proper period for recording the liability is determined by examining supporting documents—vendors' invoices and receiving reports. Before applying this procedure, the auditor would determine the last receiving report, last voucher, and last check of the current period by reference to the prenumbered numerical sequence for those documents.

The auditor also reviews and selects from unmatched receiving reports and vendors' invoices at the balance sheet date and vendors' invoices received in the subsequent period to detect liabilities that should have been recognized at the balance sheet date.

Any vendors' invoices representing unrecorded liabilities at the balance sheet date that are not received or paid before the auditor applies these procedures would not be detected. Thus, effectiveness is improved by doing the out-of-period search relatively late in field work. Confirmation of accounts payable balances is not subject to this disadvantage and can be an important complement to the out-of-period liability search particularly when the audit is scheduled for completion relatively close to year-end.

Materiality   In the out-of-period liability search, materiality is used primarily to establish the cutoff point for items to be selected. In other words, the auditor will select all cash disbursements, vendors' invoices, or receiving reports from the relevant period or files that exceed a cutoff amount related to tolerable misstatement. Since all items above the cutoff amount are selected, audit sampling is not being used.

An effective approach is to establish the cutoff amount by dividing tolerable misstatement by a number between 3 and 6. The cutoff amount is reduced in response to the auditor's assessment of inherent risk and control risk. If the auditor assesses inherent risk or control risk as high, tolerable misstatement will be divided by 6 to establish the cutoff amount.

Audit Risk   The inherent risk factors the auditor would consider include the number of principal vendors, vendor billing practices, the clients' purchasing methods, and the principal types of goods or services purchased. Also, environmental considerations such as management's control consciousness and the existence of factors that would predispose management to make material misrepresentations would be particularly important.

Control risk considerations would generally focus on achievement of specific control objectives related to completeness and reconciliation. Considerations that would be particularly important in determining the extent of the out-of-period liability search would be the following:

- The effectiveness of the client's review and investigation of unmatched prenumbered purchase orders and receiving reports at the end of the period
- The effectiveness of the client's reconciliation of vendors' statements with accounts payable balances
- The effectiveness of the client's monthly reconciliation of the schedule of accounts payable with the general ledger accounts payable balance

Audit Efficiency   Some audit efficiencies are possible in the accounts payable area. For example, because selection of vendors for confirmation is based on volume of purchases rather than the amount of the recorded balance, the confirmation requests can be sent before the accounts payable trial balance is prepared or tested. Also, sending the confirmation requests on or around the balance sheet date allows the vendor to respond through the normal billing process. However, the primary efficiency consideration is coordinating the out-of-period liability search and confirmation of payable balances to avoid duplication of audit procedures to achieve specific audit objectives related to completeness and valuation.

Cash

The essential feature of direct tests of the cash balance is to substantiate the client's bank reconciliations to achieve specific audit objectives related to *existence, completeness,* and *valuation.* Most cash receipts and cash disbursements pass through the client's bank accounts, and most of the cash balance at year-end is in the client's bank accounts. Thus, most of the direct tests of the cash balance make use of information obtained directly from banks. Usually, cash on hand is clearly immaterial and not counted. However, in industries that involve substantial amounts of cash on hand, such as banks or casinos, a cash count may be an important and time-consuming procedure.

Assertions, Objectives, and Procedures   The financial statement assertions, specific audit objectives, and the common audit procedures traditionally used to achieve the objectives for cash balances are summarized in Figure 10-9. The primary procedures are:

- Confirmation of balances and related information for all general bank accounts
- Tests of the client's bank reconciliations including use of cutoff bank statements

Broad category of financial statement assertion	Specific audit objective	Common audit procedures to achieve objective
Existence	Cash in the balance sheet exists at the balance sheet date.	Confirmation Tests of bank reconciliations
Completeness	Cash in the balance sheet includes all cash items at the balance sheet date and a proper cutoff of receipts and disbursements.	Tests of bank reconciliations
Rights or obligations	Cash in the balance sheet is owned by the company and not restricted or committed.	Confirmation General procedures
Valuation	Cash in the balance sheet is stated at the correct amount.	Tests of bank reconciliations
Presentation and disclosure	Cash balances are properly described and classified in the balance sheet and related disclosures are adequate.	General procedures Inquiry and scanning

FIGURE 10-9
Assertions, objectives, and procedures for cash balances.

General procedures and inquiry and scanning are concerned with identifying restrictions on cash or cash commitments arising from such things as escrow accounts or compensating balance arrangements. Generally, valuation of cash is not a significant concern unless the company engages in foreign currency transactions. Ownership of cash is generally established by the procedures used to achieve objectives related to existence, completeness, and valuation.

Relation of Tests of Transaction Classes   There is a relationship between transactions in the selling and expenditures cycles and the cash balance. Some errors that ultimately affect cash can only be detected in tests of sales transactions and purchase transactions. For example, not billing a customer, billing at the wrong amount, paying a vendor's invoice twice, or paying for goods or services not received will not be detected by cash balance procedures. However, errors confined to cash receipts and cash disbursements may be detected in tests of cash transactions or by cash balance procedures. For example, omission of a check from recorded cash disbursements or inclusion of cash received after year-end in cash receipts of the current period might be detected by examining cash transactions or testing bank reconciliations.

The specific control objectives that relate most directly to the extensiveness of cash balance procedures are those concerned with completeness, safeguarding, and reconciliation for cash receipts and cash disbursements. If control procedures to achieve these objectives are lacking or have serious weaknesses, cash balance procedures will be much more extensive. The extended procedures for cash balances are as follows:

- *Proof of cash*—tests of a multicolumn bank reconciliation designed to substantiate balances and cash receipts and disbursements
- *Bank transfer schedule*—a listing matching deposits and withdrawals designed to detect kiting

These extended procedures are explained further, following the explanation of the more common procedures of confirmation and tests of client's bank reconciliations.

Confirmation of Bank Balances   Common practice is for the auditor to confirm the year-end cash balance by direct correspondence with all banks with which the client has had accounts during the period. Figure 10-10 presents the standard form typically used for requesting confirmation of cash balances. Banks are mailed the original and a duplicate. One copy is completed, signed, and returned directly to the auditor, the other is retained by the bank.

Note that the form does not request information on such matters as guarantees and other contingent liabilities. In addition, the form does not provide for requesting a cutoff bank statement or information on compensating balance arrangements or securities held in safekeeping by the bank. A separate request letter covering such matters is sent to the relevant banks. Figure 10-11 presents an example of a separate request letter.

The bank's response is invalid if it is not signed and dated. If an item is left blank instead of being filled in or marked "none," the auditor should request clarification from the bank officer who signed the confirmation.

CUSTOMER NAME

We have provided to our accountants the following information as of

the close of business on _____ , 19_____ , regarding our deposit and loan balances. Please confirm the accuracy

Financial [of the information, noting any exceptions to the information provided.
Institution's] If the balances have been left blank, please complete this form by
Name and furnishing the balance in the appropriate space below.* Although we
Address do not request nor expect you to conduct a comprehensive, detailed
search of your records, if during the process of completing this confirmation additional information about other deposit and loan accounts
[ ] we may have with you comes to your attention, please include such
information below. Please use the enclosed envelope to return the
form directly to our accountants.

1. At the close of business on the date listed above, our records indicated the following deposit balance(s):

ACCOUNT NAME	ACCOUNT NO.	INTEREST RATE	BALANCE*

2. We were directly liable to the financial institution for loans at the close of business on the date listed above as follows:

ACCOUNT No./ DESCRIPTION	BALANCE*	DATE DUE	INTEREST RATE	DATE THROUGH WHICH INTEREST IS PAID	DESCRIPTION OF COLLATERAL

_____
(Customer's Authorized Signature)

_____
(Date)

The information presented above by the customer is in agreement with our records. Although we have not conducted a comprehensive, detailed search of our records, no other deposit or loan accounts have come to our attention except as noted below.

_____
(Financial Institution Authorized Signature)

_____
(Date)

_____
(Title)

EXCEPTIONS AND/OR COMMENTS

Please return this form directly to our accountants:

[ ]

* Ordinarily, balances are intentionally left blank if they are not available at the time the form is prepared.

[ ]

FIGURE 10-10
Standard form to confirm account balance information with financial institutions.

[Client's Letterhead]

[Date]

[Financial Institution Official's Name and Address]

In connection with an audit of the financial statements of [Company Name] as of [Date] and for the [Period] then ended, we have advised our independent auditors that as of the close of business on [Date] there (were) (were not) compensating balance arrangements as described in our agreement dated [Date of Agreement]. Although we do not request nor expect you to conduct a comprehensive, detailed search of your records, if during the process of completing this confirmation additional information about other compensating balance arrangements between ourselves and your financial institution comes to your attention, please include such information below.

Withdrawal by [Company Name] of the compensating balance (was) (was not) legally restricted at [Balance Sheet Date]. The terms of the compensating balance arrangements at [Balance Sheet Date] were as follows:

[Describe terms]

In determining compliance with compensating balance arrangements, the Company uses a factor for uncollected funds of [Number] (business) (calendar) days.

(The following changes were made) (There were no changes made) in the compensating balance arrangements during the [Period] and subsequently through the date of this letter.

[Describe any changes in the compensating balance agreements]

The Company (was) (was not) in compliance with the compensating balance arrangements during the [Period] and subsequently through the date of this letter.

There were (no) (the following) sanctions applied or imminent by the financial institution because of noncompliance with compensating balance arrangements.

[Describe any applied or imminent sanctions by the financial institution]

During the [Period] and subsequently through the date of this letter (no) (the following) compensating balances were maintained by the Company at the financial institution on behalf of an affiliate, director, officer, or any other third party, and (no) (the following) third party maintained compensating balances at the financial institution on behalf of the Company.

[List any such compensating balances]

Please confirm whether the above information is in agreement with your records. If it is not, please provide our auditors with any information you may have that will assist them in reconciling the difference.

FIGURE 10-11
Confirmation of compensating balances.

After signing and dating your reply, please mail it directly to [Audit Firm's Name and Address] in the enclosed envelope.

Very truly yours,

[Client's Signature and Title]

To: [Audit Firm's Name]

The above information regarding compensating balances agrees with the records of this financial institution. Although we have not conducted a comprehensive, detailed search of our records, no information about other compensating balance arrangements came to our attention. [Note exceptions below or in an attached letter.]

_____

_____

_____

_____ _____ .

Name of Financial Institution:_____

Signature:_____

Title:_____

Date:_____

FIGURE 10-11 *(concluded)*

Tests of Client-Bank Reconciliations   The essential objective of testing client reconciliations is to substantiate that the balance confirmed with the bank agrees with the client's cash accounting records. Differences will be caused by deposits in transit, outstanding checks, and other reconciling items. The auditor's objective is to obtain reasonable assurance that reconciling items are authentic, complete, and treated accurately. As part of achieving this objective, the auditor usually obtains a cutoff bank statement.

A *cutoff bank statement* is a partial period bank statement, including canceled checks, deposit tickets, and other related documents, that is mailed by the bank directly to the auditor. Normally, it would be for a period ending approximately 1 or 2 weeks after year-end. Alternatives to using a cutoff bank statement include having the bank mail the regular monthly statement for the subsequent month directly to the auditor or "proving" the subsequent month's bank statement by recomputing all amounts in the statement and examining returned items for alteration.

The extensiveness of testing the client's reconciliations will vary depending on the assessed level of control risk. Recall that the auditor may plan for three or four assessment levels, such as low, moderate, significant, or maximum. For example, if the auditor plans to assess control risk as low, the procedures for a client's reconciliation might be as follows:

1 Compare amounts on the reconciliation with totals in the bank statement, general ledger, and cash receipts and cash disbursements records, including a comparison of the beginning balance per bank to the amount confirmed by the bank.
2 Test the clerical accuracy of the reconciliation.
3 Compare canceled checks returned with the cutoff bank statement to the list of outstanding checks on the reconciliation.
4 Compare deposits in transit on the reconciliation with deposits appearing in the cutoff bank statement and consider whether the time lag between the end of the period and recording by the bank is reasonable.
5 Vouch other reconciling items in the reconciliation to supporting documents.
6 Consider the need for investigation of outstanding checks or other reconciling items that have not cleared. (Large or unusual items would always be investigated.)

When a low assessed level of control risk is appropriate, this testing might be done at an interim date and year-end procedures might be confined to scanning the client reconciliations and comparing balances per bank to bank confirmations. A moderate assessed level might result in applying the procedures listed above at year-end and some additional procedures described below.

If the assessed level of control risk is significant or maximum, the auditor would extend the procedures in testing the client's reconciliation by examining the individual details of reconciling items. The individual supporting documents would be examined and traced to the cash accounting records. For example, canceled checks returned with the cutoff bank statement would be examined for the proper payee, signature, and endorsement. Outstanding checks that did not clear would be traced to cash disbursement records, and old or unusual items would be thoroughly investigated and resolved.

Extended Cash Procedures   When control risk is assessed at the maximum level because of deficiencies in the internal control structure, there is usually a serious risk of fraud, and a proof of cash for a substantial portion of the period is necessary. This is not a common procedure because most clients tend to maintain at least moderately effective controls over cash.

A *proof of cash* is a four-column bank reconciliation that is used to summarize and schedule the examination of cash records for a given period. The outside columns reconcile the balances per bank at the beginning and end of the period to the balances per books. The two middle columns reconcile the cash receipts and cash disbursements per bank with those amounts per books for the period. The period covered may be anywhere from 1 month to 12 months. However, if a proof of cash is really necessary, it should be done for a substantial portion of the period, such as 6 to 9 months.

Figure 10-12 presents the format for a proof of cash. The illustration is highly simplified to permit the relationships among the reconciling items to be easily understood. It should be recognized that this is a "no frills" illustration. There are no complicated

	Balance at beginning of period	Cash receipts	Cash disbursements	Balance at end of period
Per bank statement	$30,000	$300,000	$290,000	$40,000
Deposits in transit				
Beginning	2,000	(2,000)		
End		1,000		1,000
Oustanding checks				
Beginning	(4,000)		(4,000)	
End			3,000	(3,000)
Per books	$28,000	$299,000	$289,000	$38,000

FIGURE 10-12
Illustrative format for a proof of cash.

reconciling items, and the bank totals reconcile with the book totals. If the beginning and ending balances reconcile, but the receipts and disbursements do not, then there are unrecorded items and probably a concealed misappropriation of cash.

In format, the four-column reconciliation is not significantly more difficult to prepare than a single column reconciliation. In fact, it is generally more useful to the auditor if the client uses the four-column format for regular monthly reconciliations.

The increased time and cost of using the proof of cash as an audit test are caused by the application of audit procedures to the detailed items in the reconciliation. In addition to footing and cross-footing the columns, the auditor would apply the types of procedures described earlier for significant or maximum assessed levels of control risk, but there would be more individual items examined because a substantial portion of the period rather than 1 month would be covered by the reconciliation.

Preparation and review of a *bank transfer schedule* is the other extended cash balance procedure. Such a schedule is used when there is a serious risk of kiting because cash controls have deficiencies and there are many bank accounts and many bank transfers. When there are few bank accounts and few transfers, the auditor may scan the bank statements and cash records to determine whether deposits and withdrawals between bank accounts are recorded in the same and the correct period. A bank transfer schedule lists all transfers and the dates of recording on the books and bank statements.

As explained earlier, the use of a bank transfer schedule or proof of cash is generally considered necessary only when there is a serious risk of material fraud.

CHAPTER 10 ASSIGNMENTS
OBJECTIVE QUESTIONS

10-1 For each one of the following statements indicate whether the statement is true or false.

T F   **a** It is usually important to trace and document the flow of all copies of sales invoices created when a customer is billed.

T F b A test of whether the specific control objective for sales transactions related to completeness is achieved is to select a sample of sales invoices and trace to shipping documents.

T F c A prelist of cash receipts is a document that is used to help ensure that all cash receipts are recorded and deposited.

T F d In performing tests of transaction classes the normal audit approach is to test purchases and cash disbursements concurrently and to test sales and cash collections concurrently.

T F e A voucher is a specialized source document that helps to ensure that disbursements are made only for goods or services authorized and received.

T F f In a voucher system an important control procedure to achieve the specific control objective related to reconciliation is to periodically reconcile the accounts payable subsidiary ledger to the general ledger control account.

T F g According to SAS No. 67 (AU 330), confirmation of accounts receivable is a generally accepted audit procedure and use of the positive form of request is preferable when there are a large number of small customer balances.

T F h One essential feature of direct tests of balances for accounts payable is emphasis on the specific audit objective of *existence* achieved primarily by *confirmation* of accounts payable balances with vendors.

T F i The normal form of accounts payable confirmation request is positive and blind, that is, it asks the vendor to respond and state the balance due from the client.

T F j An auditor normally confirms the cash balance by direct correspondence by use of a standardized form with all banks where the client has had accounts during the period.

T F k A four-column proof of cash is a schedule used for examination of cash records for a given period and is a step usually included in audit programs for cash balances.

10-2 The following questions relate to the revenue, receivables, receipts cycle. Select the *best* response.

   a At which point in an ordinary sales transaction of a wholesaling business would a lack of specific authorization be of *least* concern to the auditor in the conduct of an audit?
   1 Granting of credit
   2 Shipment of goods
   3 Determination of discounts
   4 Selling of goods for cash

   b For an effective internal control structure, the billing function should be performed by the:
   1 Accounting department
   2 Sales department
   3 Shipping department
   4 Credit and collection department

   c When a customer fails to include a remittance advice with a payment, it is a common practice for the person opening the mail to prepare one. Consequently, mail should be opened by which of the following four company employees?
   1 Credit manager
   2 Receptionist
   3 Sales manager
   4 Accounts receivable clerk

d Which of the following sets of duties would ordinarily be considered basically incompatible in terms of an effective internal control structure?

1 Preparation of monthly statements to customers and maintenance of the accounts receivable subsidiary ledger

2 Posting to the general ledger and approval of additions and terminations relating to the payroll

3 Custody of unmailed signed checks and maintenance of expense subsidiary ledgers

4 Collection of receipts on account and maintaining accounts receivable records

e Which of the following might be detected by an auditor's cutoff review and examination of sales journal entries for several days prior to and subsequent to the balance sheet date?

1 Lapping year-end accounts receivable

2 Inflating sales for the year

3 Kiting bank balances

4 Misappropriating merchandise

f Tracing copies of sales invoices to shipping documents will provide evidence that all:

1 Shipments to customers were recorded as receivables.

2 Billed sales were shipped.

3 Debits to the subsidiary accounts receivable ledger are for sales shipped.

4 Shipments to customers were billed.

g Tracing bills of lading to sales invoices provides evidence that:

1 Shipments to customers were invoiced.

2 Shipments to customers were recorded as sales.

3 Recorded sales were shipped.

4 Invoiced sales were shipped.

h During the review of a small business client's internal accounting control system, the auditor discovered that the accounts receivable clerk approves credit memos and has access to cash. Which of the following controls would be most effective in offsetting this weakness?

1 The owner reviews errors in billings to customers and postings to the subsidiary ledger.

2 The controller receives the monthly bank statement directly and reconciles the checking accounts.

3 The owner reviews credit memos after they are recorded.

4 The controller reconciles the total of the detail accounts receivable accounts to the amount shown in the ledger.

i An auditor's purpose in reviewing credit ratings of customers with delinquent accounts receivable most likely is to obtain evidence concerning management's assertions about:

1 Presentation and disclosure

2 Existence or occurrence

3 Rights and obligations

4 Valuation or allocation

AICPA

10-3 The following questions relate to the expenditures, payables, disbursements cycle. Select the *best* response.

a Which of the following is a primary function of the purchasing department?

    1 Authorizing the acquisition of goods
    2 Ensuring the acquisition of goods of a specified quality
    3 Verifying the propriety of goods acquired
    4 Reducing expenditures for goods acquired

b Propex Corporation uses a voucher register and does *not* record invoices in a subsidiary ledger. Propex will probably benefit most from the additional cost of maintaining an accounts payable subsidiary ledger if:
    1 There are usually invoices in an unmatched invoice file.
    2 Vendors' requests for confirmation of receivables often go unanswered for several months until paid invoices can be reviewed.
    3 Partial payments to vendors are continuously made in the ordinary course of business.
    4 It is difficult to reconcile vendors' monthly statements.

c Which of the following is a procedure that would prevent a paid disbursement voucher from being presented for payment a second time?
    1 Vouchers should be prepared by individuals who are responsible for signing disbursement checks.
    2 Disbursement vouchers should be approved by at least two responsible management officials.
    3 The date on a disbursement voucher should be within a few days of the date the voucher is presented for payment.
    4 The official signing the check should compare the check with the voucher and should deface the voucher documents.

d When an auditor selects a sample of items from the vouchers payable register for the last month of the period under audit and traces these items to underlying documents, the auditor is gathering evidence primarily in support of the assertion that:
    1 Recorded obligations were paid.
    2 Incurred obligations were recorded in the correct period.
    3 Recorded obligations were valid.
    4 Cash disbursements were recorded as incurred obligations.

e Which of the following would detect an understatement of a purchase discount?
    1 Test footings and cross-footings of purchases and disbursement records
    2 Compare purchase invoice terms with disbursement records and checks
    3 Compare approved purchase orders to receiving reports
    4 Test the receipt of items ordered and invoiced

f Which of the following control procedures is *not* usually performed in the vouchers payable department?
    1 Determining the mathematical accuracy of the vendor's invoice
    2 Having an authorized person approve the voucher
    3 Controlling the mailing of the check and remittance advice
    4 Matching the receiving report with the purchase order

g Which of the following is the most effective control procedure to detect vouchers that were prepared for the payment of goods that were *not* received?
    1 Count goods upon receipt in storeroom
    2 Match purchase order, receiving report, and vendor's invoice for each voucher in accounts payable department
    3 Compare goods received with goods requisitioned in receiving department
    4 Verify vouchers for accuracy and approval in internal audit department

h Internal accounting control is strengthened when the quantity of merchandise ordered is omitted from the copy of the purchase order sent to the:

1 Department that initiated the requisition

2 Receiving department

3 Purchasing agent

4 Accounts payable department

i Effective internal control procedures over the payroll function may include:

1 Reconciliation of totals on job time tickets with job reports by employees responsible for those specific jobs

2 Verification of agreement of job time tickets with employee clock card hours by a payroll department employee

3 Preparation of payroll transaction journal entries by an employee who reports to the supervisor of the personnel department

4 Custody of rate authorization records by the supervisor of the payroll department

j Which of the following departments should have the responsibility for authorizing payroll rate changes?

1 Personnel

2 Payroll

3 Treasurer

4 Timekeeping

10-4 The following questions relate to direct tests of balances for accounts receivable, accounts payable, and cash. Select the *best* response.

a Which of the following is the best argument against the use of negative accounts receivable confirmations?

1 The cost-per-response is excessively high.

2 There is *no* way of knowing if the intended recipients received them.

3 Recipients are likely to feel that in reality the confirmation is a subtle request for payment.

4 The inference drawn from receiving no reply may *not* be correct.

b Customers having substantial year-end past due balances fail to reply after second request forms have been mailed directly to them. Which of the following is the most appropriate audit procedure?

1 Examine shipping documents

2 Review collections during the year being audited

3 Intensify the procedures to test the effectiveness of the internal control structure elements with respect to receivables

4 Increase the balance in the accounts receivable allowance (contra) account

c In determining the adequacy of the allowance for uncollectible accounts, the *least* reliance should be placed upon which of the following?

1 The credit manager's opinion

2 An aging schedule of past due accounts

3 Collection experience of the client's collection agency

4 Ratios calculated showing the past relationship of the valuation allowance to net credit sales

d For effective internal accounting control, employees maintaining the accounts receivable subsidiary ledger should *not* also approve:

1 Employee overtime wages

2 Credit granted to customers

    3 Write-offs of customer accounts

    4 Cash disbursements

e When there are a large number of relatively small account balances, negative confirmation of accounts receivable is feasible if internal accounting control is:

    1 Strong, and the individuals receiving the confirmation requests are unlikely to give them adequate consideration

    2 Weak, and the individuals receiving the confirmation requests are likely to give them adequate consideration

    3 Weak, and the individuals receiving the confirmation requests are unlikely to give them adequate consideration

    4 Strong, and the individuals receiving the confirmation requests are likely to give them adequate consideration

f Which of the following procedures relating to the examination of accounts payable could the auditor delegate entirely to the client's employees?

    1 Test footings in the accounts payable ledger

    2 Reconcile unpaid invoices to vendors' statements

    3 Prepare a schedule of accounts payable

    4 Mail confirmation for selected account balances

g Which of the following is the *most* efficient audit procedure for the detection of unrecorded liabilities at the balance sheet date?

    1 Confirm large accounts payable balances at the balance sheet date

    2 Compare cash disbursements in the subsequent period with the accounts payable trial balance at year-end

    3 Examine purchase orders issued for several days prior to the close of the year

    4 Obtain an attorney's letter from the client's attorney

h Auditor confirmation of accounts payable balances at the balance sheet date may by *unnecessary* because:

    1 This is a duplication of cutoff tests.

    2 Accounts payable balances at the balance sheet date may *not* be paid before the audit is completed.

    3 Correspondence with the audit client's attorney will reveal all legal action by vendors for nonpayment.

    4 There is likely to be other reliable external evidence available to support the balances.

i Which of the following cash transfers results in a misstatement of cash at December 31, 19X7?

		BANK TRANSFER SCHEDULE		
	Disbursement		Receipt	
Transfer	Recorded in books	Paid by bank	Recorded in books	Receive by ban
1	12/31/X7	1/4/X8	12/31/X7	12/31/X
2	1/4/X8	1/5/X8	12/31/X7	1/4/X8
3	12/31/X7	1/5/X8	12/31/X7	1/4/X8
4	1/4/X8	1/11/X8	1/4/X8	1/4/X8

Questions j and k are based on the following:

Miles Company
Bank Transfer Schedule
December 31, 19X8

Check number	Bank accounts		Amount	Date disbursed per		Date deposited per	
	From	To		Books	Bank	Books	Bank
2020	1st Natl.	Suburban	$32,000	12/31	1/5 ◆	12/31	1/3 ▲
2021	1st Natl.	Capital	21,000	12/31	1/4 ◆	12/31	1/3 ▲
3217	2nd State	Suburban	6,700	1/3	1/5	1/3	1/6
0659	Midtown	Suburban	5,500	12/30	1/5 ◆	12/30	1/3 ▲

j The tick mark ◆ most likely indicates that the amount was traced to the:
  1 December cash disbursements journal
  2 Outstanding checklist of the applicable bank reconciliation
  3 January cash disbursements journal
  4 Year-end bank confirmations
k The tick mark ▲ most likely indicates that the amount was traced to the:
  1 Deposits in transit of the applicable bank reconciliation
  2 December cash receipts journal
  3 January cash receipts journal
  4 Year-end bank confirmations

AICPA

DISCUSSION QUESTIONS

Discussion questions require the application of the concepts explained in the chapter to specific facts, issues, or problems. They are classified by the primary chapter topic to which they relate. However, responses should not be confined to the primary topics but should include all relevant implications.

Revenues, Receivables, Receipts

10-5 During the year, Strang Corporation began to encounter cash flow difficulties, and a cursory review by management revealed receivable collection problems. Strang's management engaged Stanley, CPA, to perform a special investigation. Stanley studied the billing and collection cycle and noted the following:

The accounting department employs one bookkeeper who receives and opens all incoming mail. This bookkeeper is also responsible for depositing receipts, filing remittance advices on a daily basis, recording receipts in the cash receipts journal, and posting receipts in the individual customer accounts and the general ledger accounts. There are no cash sales. The bookkeeper prepares and controls the mailing of monthly statements to customers.

The concentration of duties and the receivable collection problems caused Stanley to suspect that a systematic defalcation of customers' payments through a delayed posting of remittances (lapping of accounts receivable) is present. Stanley was surprised to find that no customers complained about receiving erroneous monthly statements.

Required: Identify the procedures which Stanley should perform to determine whether lapping exists. *Do not discuss deficiencies in the internal control structure.*

AICPA

10-6 After determining that computer general controls are valid, Hastings is reviewing the sales system of Rosco Corporation in order to determine how a computerized audit program may be used to assist in performing tests of Rosco's sales records.

Rosco sells crude oil from one central location. All orders are received by mail and indicate the preassigned customer identification number, desired quantity, proposed delivery date, method of payment, and shipping terms. Since price fluctuates daily, orders do not indicate a price. Price sheets are printed daily and details are stored in a permanent disk file. The details of orders are also maintained in a permanent disk file.

Each morning the shipping clerk receives a computer printout which indicates details of customers' orders to be shipped that day. After the orders have been shipped, the shipping details are input in the computer which simultaneously updates the sales journal, perpetual inventory records, accounts receivable, and sales accounts.

The details of all transactions, as well as daily updates, are maintained on disks which are available for use by Hastings in the performance of the audit.

Required:

a How may a computerized audit program be used by Hastings to perform substantive tests of Rosco's sales records in their machine-readable form? *Do not discuss accounts receivable and inventory.*

b After having performed these tests with the assistance of the computer, what other auditing procedures should Hastings perform in order to complete the examination of Rosco's sales records?

AICPA

10-7 Prepare a single flowchart of the order receiving, shipping, billing, and collection functions of the following small company.

The customer billing and collection functions of the Pigskin Company, a small football manufacturer, are handled by a receptionist, an accounts receivable clerk, and a cashier who also serves as a secretary. The company's footballs are sold to retail stores.

The following describes all the procedures performed by the employees of Pigskin pertaining to customer orders and billings, shipments to customers, and collections:

I All orders are received by mail which is opened by the receptionist who gives the customers' purchase orders to the accounts receivable clerk. Fifteen to 20 orders are received each day. The accounts receivable clerk prepares a four-copy sales invoice form which is distributed as follows:

A Copy No. 1 is the customer billing copy and is held by the accounts receivable clerk until notice of shipment is received.

B Copy No. 2 is the accounts receivable department copy and is held for posting of the accounts receivable records until notice of shipment is received.

C Copy No. 3 is sent to the shipping department.

D Copy No. 4 is sent to the warehouse as authority for release of the goods to the shipping department.

II After the football order has been moved from the warehouse to the shipping department, the shipping department prepares the bill of lading and labels the carton. Sales invoice copy No. 3 is inserted in the carton as a packing slip. After the trucking company has picked up the shipment, the customer's copy of the bill of lading is returned to the accounts receivable clerk. The Pigskin Co.'s copy of the bill of lading is filed by the shipping department.

III When the customer's copy of the bill of lading is received by the accounts receivable clerk, the clerk mails copy No. 1 and the copy of the bill of lading to the customer.

IV The individual accounts receivable records are posted by the accounts receivable clerk using a microcomputer whereby the sales journal is prepared automatically. Postings are made from copy No. 2 which is then filed in numerical order. Monthly the general ledger clerk summarizes the sales journal for posting to the general ledger accounts.

V After preparing a list of checks received, the receptionist turns over all mail receipts and related correspondence to the accounts receivable clerk. The accounts receivable clerk posts the accounts receivable records on the microcomputer which perpares a cash receipts journal. Monthly the general ledger clerk summarizes the cash receipts journal for posting to the general ledger accounts. The accounts receivable clerk then files the remittance advices, endorses the checks, and gives them to the cashier who prepares the daily deposit slip. No currency is received in the mail, and no footballs are sold over the counter at the factory.

10-8 The customer billing and collection functions of the Trinity Company, a small paint manufacturer, are attended to by a receptionist, an accounts receivable clerk, and a cashier who also serves as a secretary. (A general ledger clerk is also employed.) The company's paint products are sold to wholesalers and retail stores.

The following describes all the procedures performed by the employees of Trinity pertaining to customer billings and collections:

I The mail is opened by the receptionist, who gives the customers' purchase orders to the accounts receivable clerk. Fifteen to 20 orders are received each day. Under instructions to expedite the shipment of orders, the accounts receivable clerk at once prepares a five-copy sales invoice form, which is distributed as follows:

    A Copy No. 1 is the customer billing copy and is held by the accounts receivable clerk until notice of shipment is received.

    B Copy No. 2 is the accounts receivable department copy and is held for ultimate posting of the accounts receivable records.

    C Copies No. 3 and No. 4 are sent to the shipping department.

    D Copy No. 5 is sent to the storeroom as authority for release of the goods to the shipping department.

II After the paint ordered has been moved from the storeroom to the shipping department, the shipping department prepares the bills of lading and labels the cartons. Sales invoice copy No. 4 is inserted in a carton as a packing slip. After the trucker has picked up the shipment, the customer's copy of the bill of lading and copy No. 3, on which are noted any undershipments, are returned to the accounts receivable clerk. The company does not "back order" in the event of undershipments; customers are expected to reorder the merchandise. Trinity's copy of the bill of lading is filed by the shipping department.

III When copy No. 3 and the customer's copy of the bill of lading are received by the accounts receivable clerk, copies No. 1 and No. 2 are completed by numbering them and inserting quantities shipped, unit prices, extensions, discounts, and totals. The accounts receivable clerk then mails copy No. 1 and a copy of the bill of lading to the customer. Copies No. 2 and No. 3 are stapled together.

IV The individual accounts receivable records are posted by the accounts receivable clerk on a microcomputer whereby the sales register is generated. Postings are made from copy No. 2, which is then filed, along with staple-attached copy No. 3, in numerical order. Monthly the general ledger clerk summarizes the sales register for posting to the general ledger accounts.

V Since Trinity is short of cash, the deposit of receipts is also expedited. The receptionist turns over all mail receipts and related correspondence to the accounts receivable clerk, who examines the checks and determines that the accompanying vouchers or correspondence contains enough detail to permit posting of the accounts. The accounts receivable clerk then endorses the checks and gives them to the cashier, who prepares the daily deposit. No currency is received in the mail, and no paint is sold over the counter at the factory.

VI The accounts receivable clerk uses the vouchers or correspondence that accompanied the checks to post the accounts receivable records. The microcomputer generates a cash receipts register. Monthly the general ledger clerk summarizes the cash receipts register for posting to the general ledger accounts. The accounts receivable clerk also corresponds with customers about unauthorized deductions for discounts, freight or advertising allowances, returns, and so forth, and prepares the appropriate credit memos. Disputed items of large amount are turned over to the sales manager for settlement. Each month the accounts receivable clerk runs a trial balance of the open accounts receivable and compares the resultant total with the general ledger control accounts for accounts receivable.

Discuss the deficiencies in the internal control structure for Trinity's procedures related to customer billings and remittances and the accounting for these transactions. In your discussion in addition to identifying the deficiencies, explain what could happen as a result of each deficiency.

AICPA adapted

10-9 You are engaged in your first audit of the Pesky Pest Control Company for the year ended December 31, 19X6. The company began doing business in January 19X6 and provides pest control services for industrial enterprises. Additional information is as follows:

1 The office staff consists of a bookkeeper, a typist, and the president, T. Licitra. In addition, the company employs 20 service representatives on an hourly basis who are assigned to individual territories to make both monthly and emergency visits to customers' premises. The service representatives submit weekly time reports, which include the customer's name and the time devoted to each customer. Time charges for emergency visits are shown separately from regular monthly visits on the reports.

2 Customers are required to sign annual contracts which are prenumbered and prepared in duplicate. The original is filed in numerical order by contract anniversary date and the copy is given to the customer. The contract entitles the customer to pest control services once each month. Emergency visits are billed separately.

3 Fees for monthly services are payable in advance—quarterly, semiannually, or annually—and recorded on the books as "income from services" when the cash is received. All payments are by checks received by mail.

4 Prenumbered invoices for contract renewals are prepared in triplicate from information in the contract file. The original invoice is sent to the customer 20 days prior to the due date of payment, the duplicate copy is filed chronologically by due date, and the triplicate copy is filed alphabetically by customer. If payment is not received by 15 days after the due date, a cancellation notice is sent to the customer, and a copy of the notice is attached to the customer's contract. The bookkeeper notifies the service representatives of all contract cancellations and reinstatements and requires written acknowledgment of receipt of such notices. Licitra approves all cancellations and reinstatements of contracts.

5 Prenumbered invoices for emergency services are prepared weekly from information shown on the service representative's time reports. The customer is billed at 200 percent of the service representative's hourly rate. These invoices, prepared in triplicate and distributed as shown above, are recorded on the books as "income from services" at the billing date. Payment is due 30 days after the invoice date.

6 All remittances are received by the typist, who prepares a daily list of collections and stamps a restrictive endorsement on the checks. A copy of the list is forwarded with the checks to the bookkeeper, who posts the date and amount of each check received on the copies of the invoice in both the alphabetical and the chronological files. After posting, the copy of the invoice is transferred from the chronological file to the daily cash receipts binder, which serves as a subsidiary record for the cash receipts book. The bookkeeper totals the amounts of all remittances received, posts this total to the cash receipts book, and attaches the daily remittance tapes to the paid invoices in the daily cash receipts binder.

7 The bookkeeper prepares a daily bank deposit slip and compares the total with the total amount shown on the daily remittance tapes. All remittances are deposited in the bank the day they are received. (Cash receipts from sources other than services need not be considered.)

8 Financial statements are prepared on the accrual basis.

List the audit procedures you would employ in the examination of the income from services account for 19X6.

AICPA adapted

Expenditures, Payables, Disbursements

10-10 To improve the current financial position as stated in the year-end balance sheet, a great many checks were written to vendors and entered in the check register about December 27. This action reduced accounts payable to a small amount. The checks, however, were not mailed to the payees but held in the treasurer's desk until the following month.

a Would this situation be of concern to the auditor? Briefly explain.

b How might the auditor discover this situation?

AICPA adapted

10-11 The diagram on pages 436–437 illustrates a manual system for executing purchases and cash disbursements transactions.

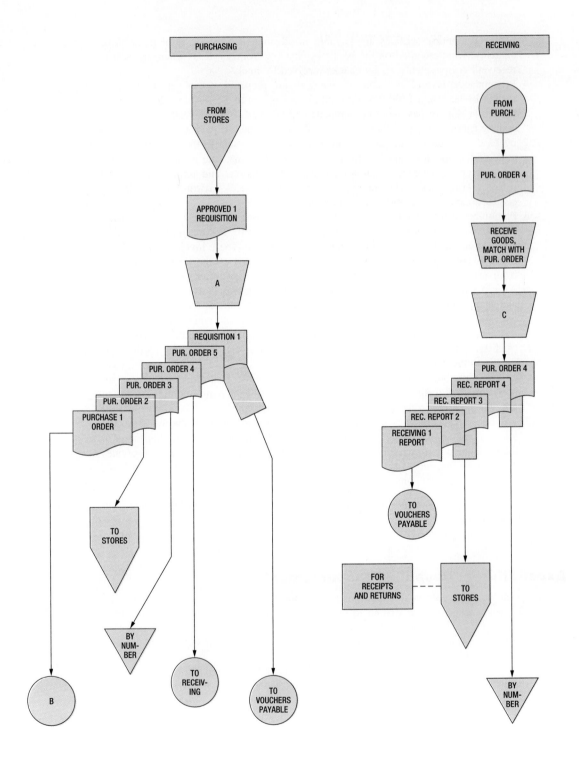

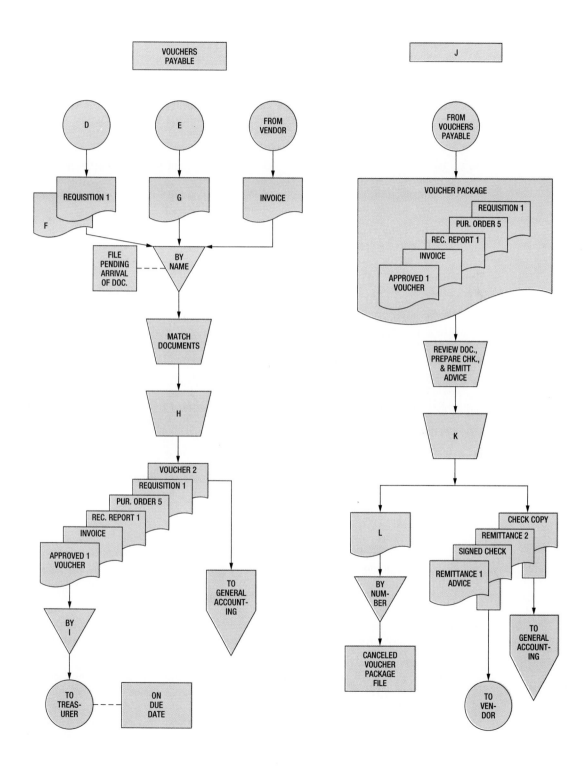

Required: Indicate what each of the letters (A) through (L) represents. Do not discuss adequacies or inadequacies in the internal control structure.

AICPA

10-12 Dunbar Camera manufacturing is a manufacturer of high-priced precision motion picture cameras in which the specifications of component parts are vital to the manufacturing process. Dunbar buys valuable camera lenses and large quantities of sheetmetal and screws. Screws and lenses are ordered by Dunbar and are billed by the vendors on a unit basis. Sheetmetal is ordered by Dunbar and is billed by the vendors on the basis of weight. The receiving clerk is responsible for documenting the quality and quantity of merchandise received.

In obtaining an understanding of the internal control structure, the auditor determined that the following procedures are being followed:

Receiving report

1 Properly approved purchase orders, which are prenumbered, are filed numerically. The copy sent to the receiving clerk is an exact duplicate of the copy sent to the vendor. Receipts of merchandise are recorded on the duplicate copy by the receiving clerk.

Sheetmetal

2 The company receives sheetmetal by railroad. The railroad independently weighs the sheetmetal and reports the weight and date of receipt on a bill of lading (waybill), which accompanies all deliveries. The receiving clerk only checks the weight on the waybill to the purchase order.

Screws

3 The receiving clerk opens cartons containing screws, then inspects and weighs the contents. The weight is converted to number of units by means of conversion charts. The receiving clerk then checks the computed quantity to the purchase order.

Camera lenses

4 Each camera lens is delivered in a separate corrugated carton. Cartons are counted as they are received by the receiving clerk and the number of cartons are checked to purchase orders.

Required:

a Explain why the control procedures as they apply individually to receiving reports and the receipt of sheetmetal, screws, and camera lenses are adequate or inadequate. *Do not discuss recommendations for improvements.*

b What financial statement distortions may arise because of the inadequacies in Dunbar's internal control structure and how may they occur?

AICPA

10-13 A CPA's audit work papers contain a narrative description of a segment of the Croyden Factory payroll system and an accompanying flowchart (pp. 440–441) as follows:

Narrative

The control procedures element of the internal control structure with respect to the personnel department is well-functioning and is *not* included in the accompanying flowchart.

At the beginning of each work week, payroll clerk No. 1 reviews the payroll department files to determine the employment status of factory employees and then prepares time cards and distributes them as each individual arrives at work. This payroll clerk, who is also responsible for custody of the signature stamp machine, verifies the identity of each payee before delivering signed checks to the supervisor.

At the end of each work week, the supervisor distributes payroll checks for the preceding work week. Concurrent with this activity, the supervisor reviews the current week's employee time cards, notes the regular and overtime hours worked on a summary form, and initials the aforementioned time cards. The supervisor then delivers all time cards and unclaimed payroll checks to payroll clerk No. 2.

Required:
a Based upon the narrative and accompanying flowchart, what are the deficiencies in the internal control structure?
b Based upon the narrative and accompanying flowchart, what inquiries should be made with respect to clarifying the existence of *possible additional deficiencies* in the internal control structure?

Note: Do not discuss the control procedures of the personnel department.

Accounts Receivable

10-14 The Bimbo Appliance Company, a manufacturer of minor electrical appliances, deals exclusively with 20 distributors situated at focal points throughout the country. At December 31, the balance sheet date, receivables from these distributors aggregated $875,000. Total current assets were $1,300,000.

With respect to receivables, the auditor followed the procedures outlined below in the course of the annual audit of financial statements:

1 Obtained an understanding of the internal control structure. It was exceptionally effective.
2 Tied detail with control account at year-end.
3 Aged accounts. None were overdue.
4 Examined detailed sales and collection transactions for the months of February, July, and November.
5 Received positive confirmations of year-end balances.

Criticize the completeness or incompleteness of the above program, giving reasons for your recommendations concerning the addition or omission of any procedures.

AICPA adapted

10-15 You are auditing the Lamp Corporation. Accounts receivable represent a significant proportion of the total assets of the company. At the beginning of the audit you mailed out positive confirmations on a test basis. Included in your tests were confirmations requested from several United States government departments; the confirmation requests for these accounts were returned, along with the following notation:

Your confirmation letter is returned herewith without action inasmuch as the type of information requested therein cannot be compiled by the office with sufficient accuracy to be of any value.

Your test also included customers whose accounts payable systems were either decentralized or a voucher system which made it impossible or impractical to give the requested information. These customers either informed you of their inability to comply with the request or did not reply.

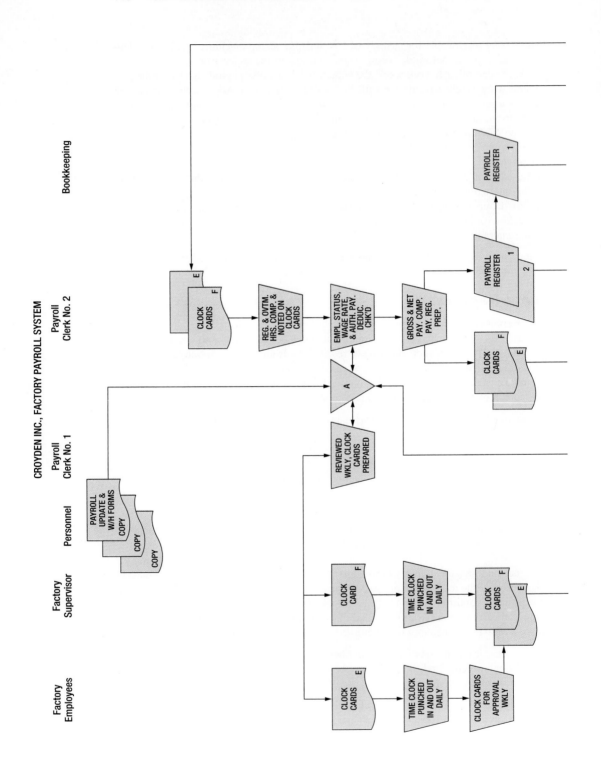

CROYDEN INC., FACTORY PAYROLL SYSTEM

Factory Employees | Factory Supervisor | Personnel | Payroll Clerk No. 1 | Payroll Clerk No. 2 | Bookkeeping

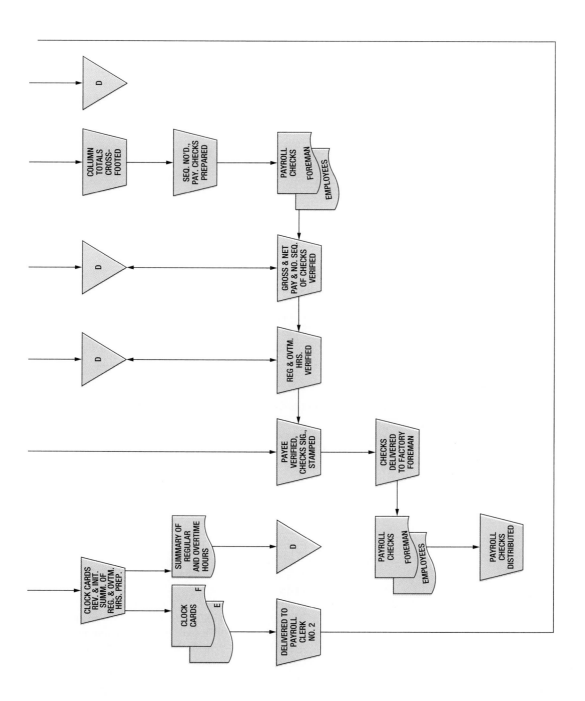

a Assuming the number and amount of responses to confirmation requests are unsatisfactory, what additional auditing procedures would you apply?

b If satisfaction is obtained by these procedures, what effect, if any, would your difficulties with the examination of receivables have on your report?

AICPA adapted

10-16 The assets of Capital Western Wear Shop at May 31, 19X7, are listed below:

Assets	Amount
Cash	$ 60,000
Accounts receivable (net)	190,000
Merchandise inventory	460,000
Equipment (net)	105,000
Total	$815,000

During the course of your annual audit of the company's financial statements, the owner will not permit circularization of the accounts receivable because the customers would resent it.

a State the conditions, if any, under which you would render an unqualified opinion on the financial statements.

b Describe generally the major audit procedures you would use to audit the accounts receivable to satisfy yourself as to their validity, considering the imposed limitation.

AICPA adapted

10-17 You have been assigned to the first audit of the accounts of the Holland Company for the year ending March 31, 19X8. The accounts receivable were confirmed December 31, 19X7, and at that date the receivables consisted of approximately 200 accounts with balances totaling $956,750. Seventy-five of these accounts, with balances totaling $650,725, were selected for confirmation. All but 20 of the confirmation requests have been returned; 30 were signed without comments, 14 had minor differences which have been cleared satisfactorily, while 11 confirmations had the following comments:

1 "We are sorry but we cannot answer your request for confirmation of our account as we use an accounts payable voucher system."

2 "The balance of $1,050 was paid on December 23, 19X7."

3 "The above balance of $7,750 was paid on January 5, 19X8."

4 "The above balance has been paid."

5 "We do not owe you anything at December 31, 19X7, as the goods, represented by your invoice dated December 30, 19X7, number 25,050, in the amount of $11,550, were received on January 5, 19X8, on f.o.b. destination terms."

6 "An advance payment of $2,500 made by us in November 19X7 should cover the two invoices totaling $1,350 shown on the statement attached."

7 "We never received these goods."

8 "We are contesting the propriety of this $12,525 charge. We think the charge is excessive."

9 "Amount okay. As the goods have been shipped to us on consignment we will remit payment upon selling the goods."

10 "The $10,000 representing a deposit under a lease, will be applied against the rent due to us during 19X9, the last year of the lease."

11 "Your credit dated December 5, 19X7, in the amount of $440 cancels the above balance."

What steps would you take to clear satisfactorily each of the above 11 comments?

AICPA adapted

10-18 Concho Corporation uses a perpetual inventory system and has already adjusted inventory to actual. In testing sales cutoff as 12/31/X4, you find the following situation. Prepare any necessary adjusting journal entries. (Concho sells all goods f.o.b. the Concho plant.)

Sales inv. no.	Amount	Dates entered in sales journal	Date shipped	Cost of sales
9781	430	12/31/X4	12/27/X4	$ 300
9782	700	12/31/X4	12/31/X4	390
9783	1,080	12/31/X4	1/2/X5	580
9784	1,400	12/31/X4	12/28/X4	810
9785	650	12/31/X4	12/30/X4	300
9786	1,010	1/2/X5	12/30/X4	500
9787	1,100	1/2/X5	1/7/X5	630
9788	320	1/2/X5	1/2/X5	170
9789	590	1/2/X5	12/31/X4	275
9790	1,500	1/2/X5	1/3/X5	1,100

Accounts Payable

10-19 You were in the final stages of your audit of the financial statements of Pakonite Corporation for the year ended December 31, 19X7, when you were consulted by the corporation's president, who believes there is no point to your examining the 19X8 voucher register and testing data in support of 19X8 entries. The president stated that (1) bills pertaining to 19X7 which were received too late to be included in the December voucher register were recorded as of the year-end by the corporation by journal entry, (2) the internal auditor made tests after the year-end, and (3) the internal auditor would furnish you with a letter certifying that there were no unrecorded liabilities.

a Should a CPA's test for unrecorded liabilities be affected by the fact that the client made a journal entry to record 19X7 bills which were received late? Explain.

b Should a CPA's test for unrecorded liabilities be affected by the fact that a letter is obtained in which a responsible management official certifies that to the official's best knowledge all liabilities have been recorded? Explain.

c Should a CPA's test for unrecorded liabilities be eliminated or reduced because of the internal audit tests? Explain.

d Assume that the corporation, which handled some government contracts, had no internal auditor but that an auditor for a federal agency spent 3 weeks auditing the records and was just completing the work at this time. How would the CPA's unrecorded liability test be affected by the work of the auditor for a federal agency?

e What sources in addition to the 19X8 voucher register should the CPA consider to locate possible unrecorded liabilities?

AICPA adapted

10-20 Compare the confirmation of accounts receivable with the confirmation of accounts payable under the following headings:

a Generally accepted auditing procedures (Justify the differences revealed by your comparison.)

b Form of confirmation requests

c Selection of accounts to be confirmed

AICPA

10-21 Taylor, CPA, is engaged in the audit of Rex Wholesaling for the year ended December 31, 19X2. Taylor obtained an understanding of the internal control structure relating to the purchasing, receiving, trade accounts payable, and cash disbursement cycles and has decided not to proceed with any tests of controls. Based upon analytical procedures, Taylor believes that the trade accounts payable balance on the balance sheet as of December 31, 19X2, may be understated.

Taylor requested and obtained a client-prepared trade accounts payable schedule listing the total amount owed to each vendor.

Required: What additional substantive audit procedures should Taylor apply in examining the trade accounts payable?

AICPA

Cash

10-22 The following client-prepared bank reconciliation is being examined by Kautz, CPA, during an audit of the financial statements of Cynthia Company:

Cynthia Company
BANK RECONCILIATION
VILLAGE BANK ACCOUNT 2
December 31, 19X2

Balance per bank (a)		$18,375.91
Deposits in transit (b)		
12/30	$1,471.10	
12/31	2,840.69	4,311.79
Subtotal		22,687.70
Outstanding checks (c)		
837	6,000.00	
1941	671.80	
1966	320.00	
1984	1,855.42	
1985	3,621.22	
1987	2,576.89	
1991	4,420.88	(19,466.21)
Subtotal		3,221.49
NSF check returned 12/29 (d)		200.00
Bank charges		5.50
Error check No. 1932		148.10
Customer note collected by the bank ($2,750 plus $275 interest) (e)		(3,025.00)
Balance per books (f)		$ 550.09

Required: Indicate one or more audit procedures that should be performed by Kautz in gathering evidence in support of each of the items **(a)** through **(f)** above.

AICPA

CASE

Sioux Valley Rural Electric Power Cooperative issues books of sight drafts to the supervisors of its 10 field crews. The supervisors use the drafts to pay the expenses of the field crews when they are on line duty requiring overnight stays.

The drafts are prenumbered and, as is clearly printed on the drafts, are limited to expenditures of $300 or less. The supervisors prepare the drafts in duplicate and send the duplicates, accompanied by the expense reports substantiating the drafts, to the general office.

The draft duplicates are accumulated at the general office, and a voucher is prepared when there are two or three draft duplicates on hand. The voucher is the authority for issuing a company check for deposit in an imprest fund of $5,000 maintained at a local bank to meet the drafts as they are presented for payment. The cooperative maintains a separate general ledger account for the imprest fund.

The audit of the voucher register and cash disbursements disclosed the following information pertaining to sight drafts and the reimbursement of the imprest fund:

I Voucher No. 10524, dated 12/31/X4, paid by check No. 10524, dated 12/31/X4, for the following drafts:

Draft no.	Date	Crew no.	Explanation	Amount
6001	12/24/X4	3	Expenses, 12/22–24	$160
2372	12/28/X4	6	Expenses, 12/26–28	310
5304	12/30/X4	7	Cash advance to supervisor	260
			Voucher total	$730

II Voucher No. 10531, dated 12/31/X4, paid by check No. 10531, dated 1/3/X5, for the following drafts:

Draft no.	Date	Crew no.	Explanation	Amount
4060	12/29/X4	1	Expenses, 12/27–29	$150
1816	1/3/X5	4	Expenses, 1/1–3	560
			Voucher total	$710

III Voucher No. 23, dated 1/8/X5, paid by check No. 23, dated 1/8/X5, for the following drafts:

Draft no.	Date	Crew no.	Explanation	Amount
1000	12/31/X4	9	Expenses, 12/28–31	$270
2918	1/3/X5	10	Expenses, 12/28–31	190
4061	1/7/X5	1	Expenses, 1/4–6	210
			Voucher total	$670

IV All the above vouchers were charged to travel expense.

V Examination of the imprest fund's bank statement for December, the January cut-off bank statement, and accompanying drafts presented for payment disclosed the following information:

A Reimbursement check No. 10524 was not credited on the December bank statement.

B The bank honored draft No. 2372 at the established maximum authorized amount.

C Original 19X4 drafts drawn by supervisors but not presented to the client's bank for payment by 12/31/X4 totaled $1,600. This total included all 19X4 drafts itemized above except No. 4060 and No. 2372, which were deducted by the bank in December.

D December bank service charges listed on the December bank statement but not recorded by the client amounted to $80.

E The balance per the bank statement at December 31, 19X4, was $5,650.

a Prepare the auditor's adjusting journal entry to correct the books at December 31, 19X4. (The books have not been closed.) A supporting work paper analyzing the required adjustments should be prepared in good form.

b Prepare a reconciliation of the balance per bank statement and the financial statement figure for the imprest cash account. The first figure in your reconciliation should be the balance per bank statement.

AICPA adapted

CHAPTER OUTLINE

Learning Objectives

After studying this chapter you should be able to:

- Explain the specific audit objectives and the common audit procedures traditionally used to achieve those objectives for:
  —Inventories
  —Property and equipment
  —Investments
  —Intangible assets
  —Long-term obligations
  —Owners' equity
  —The income statement
  —Income taxes
- Describe the auditor's responsibilities for the various circumstances that may arise for the observation of a client's physical inventory
- Understand the audit approach typically used for account balances such as property and equipment, long-term obligations, and owners' equity
- Identify several different audit approaches that may be used for account balances included in the income statement
- Explain how the auditor's approach to income taxes differs from many other audit areas

Relevant Sections of Statements on Auditing Standards

AU 331 — Inventories
AU 332 — Long-Term Investments

This chapter explains the direct tests of balances for the primary financial statement components not discussed in Chapter 10. The broad categories covered are as follows:

- Inventories
- Long-term assets and obligations and owners' equity
- The income statement and income taxes

For the account balances included in the first two categories, the audit approach tends to be largely substantive. Although the internal control structure is not ignored, audit emphasis is focused on substantiating the account balances.

INVENTORIES

Inventories consist of goods to be sold, or used in production of salable goods, in the ordinary course of business. Usually, if inventory is material at all, it is very material and one of the most complex areas of the audit. The form of inventory varies depending on the nature of the business. A manufacturer has inventories of raw materials, work in process, and finished goods. A retailer or wholesaler has goods acquired for resale. This discussion is generalized to apply to both types of inventory and significant differences are identified at relevant points. Some types of service industries, such as hospitals or repair services, also have supplies that are inventoriable, and the audit approach is generally similar if the inventories are material.

Differences from the Sales and Expenditures Cycles

The inventory area of the audit is sometimes referred to as the production or conversion cycle, and there is a relationship between inventory and the sales and expenditures cycles. For example, for a manufacturer, the sales cycle includes the shipment of finished goods and the expenditures cycle includes the acquisition of raw materials, direct labor (payroll), and overhead expenses. However, the inventory area is different in nature for reasons explained in the following discussion.

Nature and Frequency of Accountability Tests   Recall that for the sales and expenditures cycles, accountability tests are usually important control procedures as a basis for the auditor's assessment of control risk. For example, the accounts receivable subsidiary ledger is reconciled to the general ledger control account, prelists of cash receipts are reconciled to deposits and accounting postings, and cash in bank accounts is reconciled to cash accounting records. Also, outside parties may provide information that acts as a type of accountability test. Monthly statements are mailed to customers and complaints are independently resolved; vendors' statements may be reconciled with accounts payable balances.

The accountability tests in the sales and expenditures cycles are usually performed at least monthly, and some are more frequent. Almost invariably, these accountability tests are control procedures that are important to achieving specific control objectives that permit the auditor's reduction of the assessed level of control risk.

In the inventory area, an accountability test is also made, and it is probably the single most important control procedure in that area. It is the client's taking of a *physical inventory.* Inventory items are counted, priced, and compared to accounting records. However, this accountability test usually only occurs annually and it is essentially a stand-alone procedure—its effectiveness depends on procedures that are only applied when the inventory is counted.

In practice, usually two types of inventory-taking approaches are distinguished—a *wall-to-wall count* means that operating activity largely stops and a complete count is made at one time. A *cycle count* means that periodic counts of selected inventory items are made during the year, with all items counted at least once each year. Thus, with a cycle count the counts occur during the year, but the *entire* inventory is usually counted only once each year.

The central focus of the auditor's procedures in the inventory area is on the client's physical inventory, and the audit procedures are regarded as a direct test of the inventory balance. Technically, the procedures are dual-purpose tests, because the auditor is concerned with both accuracy and effectiveness of the control procedures over the client's counting and pricing.

Importance of Accounting Principles   For the types of companies with material inventories, the audit problems associated with the sales and expenditures cycles tend to be those related to high-volume clerical processing rather than complex accounting principles issues. Accounting principles cannot totally be ignored. For example, the auditor has to be concerned with classification and recording in the proper period. However, in the inventory area there may be both a large number of items and complex matters of accounting principle.

Generally, the auditor is concerned with application of accounting principles in the following respects:

- Assignment of costs to inventory in accordance with an acceptable accounting method, such as first-in, first-out (FIFO) or last-in, first-out (LIFO), or average cost, and the consistency of the accounting method and the methods of application
- Identification and proper accounting treatment of obsolete, slow-moving, excess, or defective inventory items
- Reduction of inventory items to replacement cost or net realizable value (lower of cost or market)

The assignment of costs to inventory can involve many complexities. A manufacturer may use a *standard cost* system, and the auditor must be concerned with whether the adjustments to standard cost result in a reasonable approximation of actual cost. A retailer may use the *retail inventory method,* and the auditor must be concerned with whether the adjustment of inventory at selling price approximates actual cost or net realizable value if lower. For a manufacturer the allocation of overhead expenses involves several considerations. For example, if a *direct costing* method is used, only variable overhead expenses are assigned to inventory; this method is not in accordance with generally accepted accounting principles or the IRS code and regulations. Also, no matter what accounting method is used by a manufacturer, the auditor must be concerned with conformity with the IRS code and regulations for the proper inclusion of expenses in overhead. Finally, the LIFO inventory method involves accounting problems, such as valuation reserves for reduction to "market" and liquidation of LIFO layers, and issues of conformity with the IRS code and regulations.

The client's costing, or pricing, of the quantities determined by counting inventory usually occurs sometime later to allow for investigation of differences. Generally, this step, referred to as the "pricing and summarization," is considered to be part of the client's physical inventory. When a wall-to-wall count is made, the pricing and summarization is based on that count. When a cycle count is made, the pricing and summarization must be based on perpetual inventory records.

Perpetual inventory records are a running record of the items in inventory. This means that receipts and withdrawals of inventory are recorded concurrently with the movement of the physical units. Perpetual inventory records may be maintained in quantities only or in both quantities and prices. The prices may be actual or standard cost. Perpetual inventory records are essential for cycle counting but may also be used when there is a wall-to-wall count.

Materiality and Method of Allocation   In accounting, the process of apportioning costs incurred between expenses of the current period and assets that benefit future periods is broadly referred to as *allocation.* The general accounting records accumulate the totals of costs incurred for inventory, such as purchases and payrolls. Source documents provide a record of units purchased (receiving reports) and units sold (shipping reports), or, as in a perpetual inventory system, a separate record of units may be maintained.

At the end of the accounting period, the costs incurred for inventory during the period must be allocated between units sold and units on hand. This is the function of the cost accounting system. The term *cost accounting system* is usually applied to manufacturers. However, even a merchandiser who acquires goods for resale will often need a system for assigning costs of acquiring and storing goods, such as freight and warehousing, to inventory. Inventory costs are seldom confined to the vendor's invoice price.

Cost accounting systems vary greatly in complexity and sophistication. A job order or a process cost system may concurrently track the internal usage and movement of inventory units and costs, and be integrated with the general accounting system. On the other hand, the system may consist simply of spreadsheets based on general accounting records and unit records that are prepared periodically or only annually.

Whether the costing approach is sophisticated or rudimentary, the resulting allocation between the current period and future periods usually has a significantly material effect on income. Cost of sales will often be 60 percent or more of sales, the largest expense in the income statement. Also, inventory is usually material to the balance sheet and a very material component of current assets. Thus, the misstatement of the allocation between cost of sales and inventory can cause a material misstatement of the operating results and financial position.

The substantiation of both cost of sales and ending inventory is usually dependent on direct tests of the ending inventory balance combined with tests of transaction classes for the expenditures cycle or direct tests of balances of accounts related to that cycle. In a continuing engagement, beginning inventory has been substantiated in the prior period. The amount of cost of sales is, in effect, a residual of the following activity analysis:

> Beginning inventory
> Plus expenditures for goods and services for inventory
> Less ending inventory
> _____
> Cost of sales

It is usually tested indirectly by tests of inventory and expenditures.

The significance of ending inventory to the determination of net income combined with the high volume of activity and accounting complexities often creates a high *risk of material misstatement*. The inventory area is particularly susceptible to intentional misstatements designed to manipulate net income, and it is important for the auditor to maintain *professional skepticism*. If the auditor's procedures detect discrepancies between accounting records and supporting documentation or other corroborating information, the auditor should consider the possibility of material misrepresentations by management.

Assertions, Objectives, and Procedures

The essential features of direct tests of balances for inventories are emphasis on specific audit objectives related to *existence* and *valuation* achieved primarily by *observation of physical inventory* and *tests of pricing and summarization*. The financial statement assertions, specific audit objectives, and the common audit procedures to achieve the objectives are summarized in Figure 11-1. As applied in the inventory area, these procedures have the following features:

- *Observation of physical inventory.* This term is used to describe the combination of observation, inquiry, and physical examination (test counts) that provides the base for achieving several specific audit objectives for inventory. It is explained further in a separate section.
- *Analytical procedures.* Analytical procedures in the inventory area include computation of ratios for inventory turnover and detailed gross margin (by product type or code and location) and comparison to prior periods. For a manufacturer, computation of the ratio of overhead to materials and labor, and comparison to prior periods may be an important substantive test. If a standard cost system is used, a study of variance reports and consideration of the reasonableness of explanations for variances are

Financial statement assertion	Specific audit objective	Common audit procedures to achieve objective
Existence	Inventories included in the balance sheet physically exist and represent items held for sale in the ordinary course of business.	• Observation of physical inventory • Analytical procedures
Completeness	Inventory quantities include all items on hand or in transit. Inventory listings are accurately compiled and properly included in the inventory accounts.	• Observation of physical inventory • Cutoff • Analytical procedures • Tests of pricing and summarization
Rights or obligations	The company has legal title or ownership rights to inventory items, and inventories exclude items billed to customers or owned by others.	• Observation of physical inventory • General procedures • Cutoff
Valuation	Inventories are properly stated with respect to: • Cost determined by an acceptable method consistently applied. • Slow-moving, excess, defective, and obsolete items identified. • Reduced to replacement cost or net realizable value if lower than cost.	• Tests of pricing and summarization • Analytical procedures • Observation of physical inventory • Inquiry and scanning
Presentation and disclosure	Inventories are properly described and classified in the balance sheet and related disclosures are adequate.	• Inquiry and scanning • General procedures

FIGURE 11-1

Assertions, objectives, and procedures for inventory.

usually important. Sales forecasts and analyses and marketing plans and reports may provide information relevant to the net realizable value of inventory. In general, analytical tests usually receive more emphasis in the inventory area than in many other audit areas.

- *Cutoff.* This procedure is directed to the control over shipping and receiving activities at the physical inventory date. Usually, the auditor identifies the numbers of the last prenumbered shipping and receiving documents at the time of the observation of physical inventory. These numbers are used for cutoff tests for accounts receivable and accounts payable recording. The document numbers are also used to determine whether the related inventory items were properly included or excluded from the physical inventory, and, if perpetual records are maintained, the inventory record. The inclusion or exclusion of inventory items in transit should ideally be based on passage of title as determined by f.o.b. terms (destination or shipping point). However, unless the difference would be material, purchases are often recorded when received and sales when shipped.
- *Tests of pricing and summarization.* This term is used to describe the combination of vouching, tracing, and recomputation procedures used to test the client's pricing and summarization of inventory counts. It is explained further in a separate section.
- *General procedures.* The general procedures relevant to inventory include reading minutes, debt instruments, and agreements for indications of liens or pledging of inventory, unrealized losses on purchase commitments, or inventories held on consignment.
- *Inquiry and scanning.* The important inquiries for inventory include discussion with management concerning obsolete, excess, or slow-moving inventory and the same matters as described above for general procedures. Scanning includes reviewing perpetual records or other records or reports of inventory usage and movement to identify obsolete, excess, or slow-moving items.

Observation of the Physical Inventory

As mentioned in Chapter 10, observation of the client's physical inventory is one of two auditing procedures that are officially called "generally accepted auditing procedures." The following list highlights points that are often misunderstood about observation of physical inventory:

1 The client's taking of the physical inventory is a control procedure, but it is a stand-alone activity and its effectiveness is not dependent on control over processing transactions.

2 The procedures the auditor uses are a *combination* of observation, inquiry, and physical examination (making test counts of client counts).

3 The auditor's goal is to obtain reasonable assurance that the client's methods of counting inventory result in an accurate count. The auditor makes test counts as an aid in making this assessment and not to directly substantiate inventory quantities by counting.

4 There are no satisfactory alternative procedures to making or observing some counts of items in inventory for the *ending* inventory.

Since inventory observation and receivables confirmation are both generally accepted auditing procedures, there is an understandable, but unfortunate, tendency for students studying auditing to equate the procedures. However, there are distinct differences in the auditor's approach and methods.

In confirming receivables the auditor is attempting to directly substantiate the receivable balance by communication with customers, and audit sampling is often used. In making test counts the auditor is attempting to assess the care and accuracy of client counts, and audit sampling is usually not applicable. Monetary misstatements detected by confirmation may be projected to assess whether the receivable balance is misstated. When an unacceptably high rate of inventory counting errors is apparent, the auditor would usually insist on recounts.

The auditor's responsibilities for various circumstances that may arise concerning the client's physical inventory are summarized in Figure 11-2. The figure is adapted from SAS No. 1 (AU 331). It identifies one of the most significant differences between confirmation of receivables and observation of physical inventory: If the auditor is unable to confirm receivables, there is usually satisfactory alternative evidential matter available from examining the accounting records and underlying source documents. However, in the inventory area, tests of the accounting records alone are not considered to be a satisfactory alternative for substantiating ending inventory. It is always necessary for the auditor to make, or observe, some counts as a basis for assessing the accuracy of the client's physical inventory.

For example, the auditor may not be engaged until after the client's physical inventory. A satisfactory alternative procedure would be for the auditor to make test counts at a later date and by examining the documentation of inventory receipts, issues, movements, and shipments work back to the quantities on hand at the count date and make comparisons to the client's counts. This means the client must either maintain good perpetual records, or other sufficient documentation of inventory movements to permit the equivalent of perpetual records to be prepared, for the period between the count date and the auditor's test counts. The auditor would also review the client's documentation retained of counts and counting methods.

The desirable features of client procedures for taking a physical inventory include the following:

- A written plan of instructions for inventory counting
- Arrangement of inventory items to facilitate counting
- Numerical control of inventory tags or count sheets and accounting for all used and unused tags or sheets
- Personnel on inventory count teams who are independent of inventory storekeeping
- Supervision of counting by internal auditors or supervisory personnel who recount on a test basis

The auditor's procedures usually include becoming familiar with the instructions for counting, making a tour of the storage area, observing the diligence and demeanor of

Inventory-taking method or circumstance	Independent auditor's responsibility
Wall-to-wall count (Inventories are determined solely by means of physical count at or near balance sheet date.)	Ordinarily necessary for the auditor to: • Be present at time of the count. • By observation, test counts, and inquiry be satisfied about: —Effectiveness of inventory-taking methods. —Reliance to be placed on client's representations on quantities and physical condition. (AU 331.09)
Cycle counts (Well-kept perpetual records are checked by periodic comparison with physical counts.)	The auditor's observation procedures usually can be performed either during or after the end of the period under audit. (AU 331.10)
Statistical estimation (Inventories are determined by statistical sample rather than annual physical count of each item.)	The auditor should: • Be satisfied the client's methods are sufficiently reliable to produce results substantially the same as those that would be obtained by an annual count of all items. • Be present to observe enough counts to be satisfied about the effectiveness of counting procedures. • Be satisfied the sampling plan is reasonable, statistically valid, properly applied, and produced reasonable results. (AU 331.11)
Unobserved count—current year (The auditor was not present at the client's count of ending inventories or was otherwise unable to apply necessary procedures at the time of the count.)	The auditor should: • Make, or observe, some physical counts of the inventory. • Apply appropriate tests of intervening transactions. • Review records of client counts and counting methods. (Tests of the accounting records alone are not sufficient.) (AU 331.12)
Unobserved count—prior year (The auditor did not observe the inventory taking of prior periods—beginning inventory.)	Provided the auditor is satisfied about current inventory, the auditor may become satisfied about prior inventories by: • Tests of prior transactions (accounting records). • Review of the records of prior counts. • Gross profit tests. (AU 331.13)

FIGURE 11-2
Observation of physical inventory—auditor's responsibilities.

client count teams, and making test counts of some of the inventory items. Also, the auditor makes inquiries concerning the existence of obsolete, excess, or slow-moving items and the client's procedures for identifying such items. The auditor also observes the condition of inventory items for obvious signs of age or unsalability.

Some additional features of cycle counts and retail inventory counts are as follows:

- *Cycle counts.* Since the client counts are made periodically, the auditor's observation may be made either during or after the period under audit. To assess the effectiveness of cycle counting procedures, the auditor would need to review the client's formal schedule of counts, and the assignments of personnel to make the counts, in order to plan the observation and test counts and consider the continuity of functioning of the counting procedure.

- *Retail inventory counts.* A retail inventory count is usually made by specialists who take a nondescriptive inventory that accumulates the prices and quantities of items. Tags are not used and count sheets are typed later. The auditor's planning for the count usually includes reviewing a map of the stores and identifying the sections for test counts. The pace of counting is very rapid so the auditor usually has to test count a section ahead of the count team and then observe the count team's count of the section and be alert for discrepancies. The auditor's objectives and procedures are not generally affected by whether the specialists are an outside service or employees.

Tests of Pricing and Summarization

The auditor's tests of pricing and summarization are a combination of vouching, tracing, and recomputation to test the following aspects of the client's procedures:

- Summarization of quantities from the count tags or sheets to the inventory listing
- Application of prices to the quantities in the listings
- Computation of the extensions and footings of the listings
- Identification of obsolete, excess, or slow-moving items and reduction of their prices to replacement cost or net realizable value

The auditor's procedures for testing the summarization of quantities are designed to provide reasonable assurance that all items counted are included in the listing and that no items have been inappropriately added to the listing.

Thus, the auditor is concerned with both existence and completeness. The auditor reviews the listing to see that only tags or sheets used for the client's counts are included and compares selected items on the listing to the auditor's record of the auditor's test counts and to the client's tags or sheets.

The auditor tests the application of prices by vouching items to vendors' invoices and to cost accounting records. This aspect of audit procedures for inventory is most similar to audit procedures for the sales and expenditures cycles and related account balances. Audit sampling may be used, and the extent of testing may be restricted when control risk for purchases and cost accounting is less than maximum.

The extent of testing for obsolete, excess, or slow-moving items depends on the care and thoroughness of the client's own review for such items. If the company has adopted specific criteria, such as a reduction for all items over a year's supply and all items that have not been sold or used within 6 months, the auditor evaluates the reasonableness of the criteria and tests the client's application. The auditor also may vouch unit prices to vendor invoices, open purchase orders, current vendor price lists, or published prices, and review records of internal usage and movement of inventory.

Materiality

The auditor uses materiality in the inventory area primarily as a means of identifying individually significant inventory items. The auditor would regard items as individually significant because of their dollar size by using a cutoff amount determined as a fraction of tolerable misstatement. The auditor would usually include these items in the items test-counted. However, the number of test counts to make is generally not a sample size decision. It is influenced more by considerations such as the number of count teams involved, whether the physical arrangement of items facilitates observation and accurate counting, and the extent of the client's planning, supervision, and testing of the counts.

The auditor usually makes more test counts than would be necessary to use in testing the client's pricing and summarization. Normally, the auditor makes a record only of the test counts to be used in price tests. As explained earlier, the tests of the client's pricing and summarization may use audit sampling. The test counts used in price testing would be selected using the "haphazard" method, and the sampling approach would be nonstatistical.

To decide whether sampling is necessary, the auditor first identifies items to be regarded as individually significant because of their size or nature. For price tests, the items considered individually significant would include the following:

- Large extended dollar amounts (cutoff amounts would be determined as a fraction of tolerable misstatement)
- Raw material items included in many finished goods (the quantity of raw material on hand may be small, but it may account for a large portion of the cost of most finished goods)
- Items with significantly different quantities than prior periods
- Items with quantities greater than the amount that can reasonably be expected to be sold or used within a year

All of the individually significant items would be tested. If the remaining amount is material, a sample of these items would be tested.

Audit Risk

The extensiveness of the auditor's coverage of the client's physical inventory is based largely on the review of the client's plans and arrangements, and past experience. Extensiveness of coverage is generally a matter of the number of audit staff assigned and the time spent. If the client counts have produced large adjustments to inventory records in the past, more extensive coverage would be necessary. If the inventory records are integrated with sales accounting, coverage of the physical inventory would be heavier if tests of sales transactions detected deficiencies in controls over sales recording accuracy and completeness. For example, deficiencies in controls that help ensure that all shipments are billed would be expected to result in inventory shortages.

Consideration of audit risk is also a very important factor in deciding whether the observation of physical inventory can be made at an interim date. The specific control objectives that are relevant to this consideration include those for recording accuracy for purchases, sales, and cost accounting and safeguarding controls over inventory. Important safeguarding and related controls for inventory include the following:

- Storage responsibilities for inventory assigned to specified storekeepers independent of receiving, shipping, and inventory counting and recordkeeping

- Storage areas secured against unauthorized admission by protective measures such as guards, alarm systems, fences or locked areas, and admission by identification badge or pass
- Bonding of personnel with access to valuable and moveable items
- Inspection of all materials leaving the premises for authorized shipping documents
- Use of prenumbered documents, with the sequence accounted for independently, for receiving, materials requisitions, production orders, and shipping

The auditor needs reasonable assurance that the relevant control procedures continue to function in the intervening period between the date of the observation and the balance sheet date. This means the auditor has to test the control procedures related to safeguarding around the balance sheet date. If controls over recording accuracy for purchases, sales, and cost accounting are functioning satisfactorily at an interim date, the auditor's understanding of these control procedures may also be updated by inquiry and observation. If there are deficiencies in these controls but safeguarding procedures are adequate, the auditor may be able to test transactions during the intervening period to extend the auditor's conclusion based on the interim observation to the balance sheet date. If there are serious deficiencies in safeguarding controls or if the auditor believes there is a serious risk of management misrepresentations, then the observation of the physical inventory must be performed at or near the balance sheet date.

Additional Considerations

Two broad categories of circumstances fall outside the auditor's normal approach to inventories—inventories in the possession or control of an outside custodian and unusual or difficult inventories.

Outside Custodian   Inventories may be in the hands of a public warehouse or other outside custodian or on consignment. Ordinarily, the auditor would obtain direct confirmation in writing from the custodian. However, if such inventories are a significant portion of total assets or current assets, the auditor would have to apply additional procedures. The auditor in those circumstances, according to SAS No. 1 (AU 331.14) should apply one or more of the following procedures:

1 Review and test the client's procedures for investigating the custodian and evaluating the custodian's performance
2 Obtain an independent accountant's report on the custodian's controls over goods in custody
3 Observe the custodian's physical inventory
4 If warehouse receipts have been pledged as collateral, confirm pertinent details with lenders

The first two procedures are concerned with obtaining evidence of the trustworthiness and diligence of the custodian. If the custodian can be relied on, then confirmation from the custodian is reliable evidential matter. In some cases, the auditor may need to observe the custodian's physical inventory. The last procedure would be applied in addition to one of the first three when pledging is significant.

Unusual Inventories   Some inventories fall in the category of unusual or difficult inventories for which it is apparent that the normal observation of physical inventory is not "practicable or reasonable." For example, inventories of logs in a river, grain in a silo, coal or raw material for cement in piles, and chemicals in a vat are generally recognized as difficult to count. In these circumstances, the auditor's objectives do not change, but unusual means may be necessary to achieve them.

The primary consideration is the method used by the client for the annual physical inventory. For example, specialized methods such as photographic studies or engineering studies may be used. The auditor's responsibility is essentially the same as for the more conventional physical inventory. The auditor must be satisfied about the effectiveness of the client's inventory-taking methods and the extent of reliance that can be placed on the client's representations on quantities and physical condition.

LONG-TERM ASSETS AND OBLIGATIONS AND OWNERS' EQUITY

The audit approach to account balances in this broad category is generally similar. The account balances are usually affected by a relatively few large transactions, and amounts from prior periods have continuing significance; that is, the account does not turn over frequently. Thus, the approach to the direct tests of balances for account balances in this broad category is to directly test the transactions that affected the account during the period to indirectly substantiate the ending balance. The related revenue and expense accounts are normally examined in conjunction with the balance-sheet accounts. For example, depreciation expense is tested in conjunction with property and equipment. Also, these account balances are generally more susceptible to material misstatement caused by misapplication of generally accepted accounting principles.

Property and Equipment

Property and equipment generally includes land, buildings, and manufacturing equipment. It may also include office equipment, furniture, and fixtures, and, even when these assets are classified separately, the audit approach is generally the same as for property and equipment.

The essential features of direct tests of balances for property and equipment are emphasis on specific audit objectives related to *existence, ownership,* and *valuation* achieved primarily by *substantiating additions* and *identifying retirements* during the period and analytically testing or recomputing related expense and allowance accounts.

Assertions, Objectives, and Procedures   The financial statement assertions, specific audit objectives, and the common audit procedures traditionally used to achieve the objectives for property and equipment and related account balances are summarized in Figure 11-3. As applied in the property and equipment area, these procedures have the following features:

- *Vouching.* This procedure consists of inspecting the supporting documentation for additions and retirements during the period. For example, the auditor examines the

Financial statement assertion	Specific audit objective	Common audit procedures to achieve objective
Existence	Property and equipment included in the balance sheet physically exists. Additions include only the capitalizable cost of assets purchased, constructed, or leased and retirements are removed.	Vouching Physical examination Analytical procedures
Completeness	Property and equipment includes all capitalizable costs and capitalizable costs are not expensed.	Vouching Inquiry and scanning Physical examination
Rights or obligations	The company has legal title or equivalent ownership rights to property and equipment included in the balance sheet and the related lease obligation of capitalized leased assets is recognized.	General procedures Inquiry and scanning Recomputation
Valuation	Property and equipment is stated at cost and allowances for depreciation or depletion are computed on the basis of acceptable and consistent methods.	Recomputation Analytical procedures
Presentation and disclosure	Property and equipment is properly described and classified in the balance sheet and related disclosures are adequate.	General procedures Inquiry and scanning

FIGURE 11-3
Assertions, objectives, and procedures for property and equipment.

vendor's invoice, canceled check, and receiving report for equipment additions and considers the appropriateness of capitalization in light of company policy and generally accepted accounting principles.

- *Physical examination.* The auditor obtains firsthand knowledge of additions and retirements by touring the plant. Often the tour of the plant is coordinated with the observation of physical inventory. The auditor notes whether new additions are recorded in the accounting records and whether items in the accounting records can be located in the plant.
- *Analytical procedures.* Several analytical procedures may be useful for detecting misclassified additions, unrecorded retirements, and miscalculation of depreciation expense. The auditor compares property and equipment balances with amounts of prior years and budgets, current additions to capital budget, and depreciation expense to prior years and budgets. Also, the auditor computes the ratio of depreciation expense and accumulated depreciation to equipment balances in the current and prior periods. The auditor also relates changes in property and equipment balances to

expected related changes in insurance expense, property taxes, and repairs and maintenance expense.

- *Inquiry and scanning.* The auditor makes inquiries of operating management and personnel concerning actual additions and retirements and concerning decisions, such as adding or discontinuing a product or line of business, that would affect additions and retirements. The auditor also scans the accounting records for miscellaneous revenue resulting from sale of retired equipment.
- *Recomputation.* The auditor recomputes depreciation expense and considers whether depreciation is calculated in accordance with an acceptable accounting method consistently applied. Consistency of application includes adherence to company policy on the portion of depreciation attributable to years of addition and retirement. Usually, the auditor does not need to make a detailed recomputation when depreciable assets are voluminous. Depreciable assets may be grouped in categories with similar lives and the same depreciation method, and the calculation may be made on an overall basis. Technically, this is an analytical procedure.
- *General procedures.* The general procedures relevant to property and equipment include reading minutes, inspecting debt agreements, and inquiry of management to identify significant changes in the composition of property and equipment and related liens and mortgages requiring disclosure.

The discussion of procedures above refers to property and equipment, depreciation expense, and the allowance for depreciation. However, the discussion is also generally applicable to natural resources, such as oil and gas, and leasehold improvements and the related depletion or amortization.

Substantiation of Additions   The auditor uses a combination of vouching (inspecting supporting documentation), physical examination (touring the plant during inventory observation), and analytical procedures to substantiate additions to property and equipment. The vouching includes both additions recorded in property and equipment accounts and items recorded in the repair and maintenance expense account. In reviewing the charges to *repair and maintenance expense,* the auditor is concerned with the specific audit objective related to *completeness* for property and equipment. Repair and maintenance expense may contain costs that should be capitalized rather than expensed. The appropriateness of the accounting treatment of the item as capitalized or expensed depends on both conformity with generally accepted accounting principles and adherence to company policy.

Identifying Retirements   In achieving the specific audit objective related to existence for property and equipment, the auditor is concerned with detecting significant unrecorded retirements. Generally, the auditor uses a combination of vouching, physical examination, and analytical procedures to identify unrecorded retirements.

In vouching additions the auditor notes whether the item is new or a replacement and traces the replacements to the recording of a retirement. During the tour of the plant, the auditor notes whether or not significant recorded items are in the plant. A study of relationships among related accounts, such as property insurance, property taxes, and miscellaneous revenue may also disclose unrecorded retirements. For example, sale of retired equipment as scrap may be recorded as miscellaneous income. Also, the auditor's knowledge of the business may be an important factor in identifying unrecorded retirements. For example, the auditor's knowledge of the discontinuance of a particular product combined with knowledge that certain equipment is used exclusively for making that product would lead the auditor to expect to see a recorded retirement or reclassification for that equipment.

Materiality   The usual approach to substantiating additions is to vouch all those above a specified cutoff dollar amount. This cutoff amount is established as a fraction of tolerable misstatement. For example, if tolerable misstatement is $20,000, the auditor might vouch all additions above $4,000. The cutoff amount is established judgmentally by dividing tolerable misstatement by a number between 3 and 6 based on the consideration of audit risk; in the example, 5 was used, indicating relatively high inherent and control risk.

Audit Risk   In the property and equipment area, account balances are relatively more susceptible to misstatement caused by misapplication of accounting principles. The accounting principles for the proper costs to include in acquisition cost and the proper accounting treatment of extraordinary repairs, improvements, and similar matters are relatively complex. Also, the FASB accounting standards related to capitalization of leased assets (Current Text L10) and capitalization of interest costs during construction of assets (Current Text I67) are particularly complex.

The auditor's assessment of control risk would also be influenced by the results of tests of transaction classes for the expenditures cycle. The auditor might incorporate this assessment into the direct tests of balances for property and equipment by adjusting the cutoff amount for additions to be vouched. The cutoff amount would be tolerable misstatement divided by 3 if control risk were at a low level, by 6 if the assessed level was high. Other factors the auditor would consider in assessing the likelihood of material misstatement in property and equipment include whether the client's procedures include the following measures to reduce control risk:

- Use of capital budgeting for acquisition of property and equipment with careful monitoring and follow-up
- Detailed property and equipment ledgers maintained and periodically reconciled to general ledger control accounts
- Identification tags in prenumbered order fixed to new property and equipment and issued tags reconciled to detailed property and equipment ledger
- Formal policy for capitalization/expense decisions, partial depreciation, and procedures for reporting of retirements established and incorporated in procedures manuals

Normally, companies do not make an annual physical inspection of property and equipment comparable to a physical inventory. However, such inspections may be made over a longer period, such as every 3 to 5 years, on a cycle basis. The auditor would not insist on observing a physical inspection of property and equipment unless there were very serious deficiencies in controls. In some industries, such as state and local government, accounting records on property and equipment may be limited and control procedures relatively ineffective, and the audit procedures for property and equipment must be more extensive to express an unqualified opinion. Also, when a company capitalizes a significant portion of production costs as machinery and equipment, much more extensive testing is usually appropriate.

Investments and Intangible Assets

The audit approach and the audit problems for investments and for intangibles are similar to those for property and equipment. The auditor focuses on directly testing the transactions that affect the balances during the period and consideration of conformity with generally accepted accounting principles is very important. However, investments in the ending balance are normally substantiated directly.

Investments   The form of investments can vary considerably. The investments may be in debt or equity securities; the securities may be marketable or nonmarketable; the companies whose securities are held may be affiliated or nonaffiliated. Also, the investment may be a loan or advance rather than a security. This discussion focuses on long-term investments. However, the primary distinction between long-term investments and investments classified as current assets is management's intention and ability to hold the investment for longer than 1 year. Thus, the discussion is generally applicable to most investments.

The financial statement assertions, specific audit objectives, and the common audit procedures traditionally used to achieve the objectives for investments are summarized in Figure 11-4.

The essential features of direct tests of balances for long-term investments are emphasis on specific audit objectives related to *existence* and *ownership,* achieved primarily by physical examination or confirmation and vouching, and on specific audit objectives related to *valuation* by a combination of recomputation, vouching and tracing, or other specialized procedures.

If the investment has a physical existence and is in the client's possession, such as stock certificates in a safety deposit box, physical examination is appropriate. If the investment has no physical existence, such as a loan or advance, or is held in safekeeping by an independent custodian, then confirmation is the appropriate procedure.

The difficult accounting and auditing issues in the long-term investment area usually relate to specific audit objectives concerned with *valuation.* Generally, the relevant auditing procedures are determined largely by the method of valuation that is appropriate under generally accepted accounting principles.

FASB Statement No. 115, "Accounting for Certain Investments in Debt and Equity Securities," provides guidance on valuation and presentation of investments in securities. Whether investments in securities are carried at cost or at market depends on the nature and classification of the securities. Cost is substantiated by vouching the acquisition price in the accounting records, and market price is substantiated by comparison to publication of market quotations of security prices. The reference to published market prices is commonly called a "Wall Street Journal" test.

Financial statement assertion	Specific audit objective	Common audit procedures to achieve objective
Existence	Investments in securities (stock, bonds, notes) physically exist and loans and advances exist.	Physical examination Confirmation
Completeness	Investments are all included in the balance sheet.	General procedures
Rights or obligations	The company owns or has ownership rights to all investments included in the balance sheet.	Vouching Physical examination Confirmation
Valuation	Investments are valued properly with respect to: • Other than temporary impairment of cost is recognized for investments at cost. • Marketable securities are reduced to market price if lower than cost. • Debt securities are properly classified as for trading, investment, or held for sale. • Equity investments are adjusted to recognize proportionate share of income or loss.	Recomputation, vouching, and tracing Inspection of market quotations or financial statements
Presentation and disclosure	Investments are properly described and classified in the balance sheet and related disclosures are adequate.	General procedures Inquiry and scanning

FIGURE 11-4
Assertions, objectives, and procedures for investments.

The direct tests of balances for investments also include tests of the related investment income and gains or losses in investment transactions. "Wall Street Journal" tests are also used to substantiate dividend and interest income on investments and the trading price at the time of purchase or sale of securities.

If APB Opinion No. 18 (Current Text I82), "The Equity Method of Accounting for Investment in Common Stock," applies, then the carrying amount of the investment and related income and losses are based on the financial statements of the investee. Generally, *audited* financial statements of the investee are considered sufficient competent evidential matter for this purpose. In contrast, *unaudited* financial statements of the investee are considered competent evidential matter but are not by themselves sufficient evidential matter. According to SAS No. 1 (AU 332.05):

> By application of auditing procedures to the financial statements of the investee, the auditor obtains evidential matter as to the equity in underlying net assets and results of operations of the investee. The auditor for the investor may use the investee's auditor for this purpose. The materiality of the investment in relation to the financial statements of the investor is a factor which should be considered in determining the extent and nature of such procedures.

Note that the auditor is not required to audit the investee's financial statements. The auditor may apply auditing procedures to selected items or portions of items in the investee's statements.

Intangible Assets   A variety of items falls in this asset category. Intangibles include patents, copyrights, organizational costs, franchise fees, and goodwill acquired in a business combination.

The essential features of direct tests of balances for intangibles are emphasis on specific audit objectives related to *existence* and *valuation* achieved primarily by vouching, inspection of legal documents, and recomputation or analytical procedures. The primary risk of misstatement arises from misapplication of generally accepted accounting principles.

The accounting issues generally relate to whether a cost may properly be deferred and the appropriate amortization period. For example, research and development costs generally must be charged as expenses in the period incurred. However, some costs, such as startup costs or preopening costs, are not dealt with specifically in authoritative accounting pronouncements, and the appropriateness of the deferral depends on the specific circumstances. In some cases, the useful life of an intangible may be determinable by reference to a law or contract. However, for goodwill, the basic guideline is that amortization should be by the straight-line method over a period not to exceed 40 years unless there is evidence of a loss of value.

Long-Term Obligations

Generally, long-term obligations include loans, bonds, and notes payable due after 1 year from the balance sheet date. The current portions of long-term obligations are classified as current liabilities but are examined in conjunction with long-term obligations. Also, interest expense and related account balances are examined in conjunction with long-term obligations.

Assertions, Objectives, and Procedures   The financial statement assertions, specific audit objectives, and the common audit procedures that are traditionally used to achieve those objectives for long-term obligations are summarized in Figure 11-5. As applied in the long-term obligations area, these procedures have the following features:

- *Confirmation.* Normally, the auditor confirms the balance and related details, such as interest rate and terms, directly with all significant debtholders. The form of confirmation is similar to that for accounts payable. In some cases, a trustee keeps the detailed records of debtholders and makes interest payments to them. In those circumstances, the confirmation request is sent to the trustee. The standard bank confirmation form can be used for banks that are holders of debt. However, the standard confirmation form confirms only direct loans. Details of compensating balances, lines of credit, and contingent liabilities should be separately confirmed with the bank. Care should be given to achieve the specific audit objectives related to completeness as well as those related to existence.

Financial statement assertion	Specific audit objective	Common audit procedures to achieve objective
Existence	Debt and similar obligations in the balance sheet exist at the balance sheet date.	Confirmation General procedures
Completeness	The balance sheet includes all debt and similar obligations incurred at the balance sheet date.	General procedures Confirmation Analytical procedures
Rights or obligations	Debt and similar obligations are legal, or specific and definite, obligations of the company.	General procedures Inquiry
Valuation	Debt and similar obligations are presented at the proper amounts and include the effect of related discounts or premiums.	Recomputation, vouching, and tracing
Presentation and disclosure	Debt and similar obligations are properly described and classified and related disclosures are adequate.	General procedures Inquiry

FIGURE 11-5
Assertions, objectives, and procedures for long-term obligations.

- *General procedures.* In the long-term obligation area, general procedures contribute more directly to the achievement of audit objectives than is often the case in other areas. The most important general procedures are reading minutes of meetings of the board of directors and reading debt agreements. The auditor is concerned with ascertaining that all obligations are authorized by the board of directors. Debt agreements are extremely important because violation of the terms may result in automatic acceleration of the due date. This would materially affect financial position when the debt is reclassified as current and might affect the company's ability to meet obligations on a timely basis. The auditor will request the client's management to obtain a waiver by the debtholder of *any* violations. Debt agreements often contain provisions requiring maintenance of specified working capital and debt-to-equity ratios and restrictions on payment of dividends or other financing activities. Also, the debt may be secured by liens on company assets.
- *Analytical procedures.* Analytical procedures in the long-term obligations area include comparison of balances with the prior period and comparison of new debt proceeds and principal repayments with cash flow projections. Also, the auditor considers the reasonableness of the company's average cost of capital (interest expense divided by the average of the beginning and ending debt balances). An unreasonably high average cost of capital might indicate unrecorded debt.
- *Inquiry.* The classification of debt as short-term or long-term may depend on the intent and ability of management to refinance obligations. The auditor substantiates ability by examining evidence of actual refinancing in the subsequent period or a noncancelable financing agreement. However, inquiries of management to corroborate intent are also made. Also, some obligations, such as pension obligations and obligations that

arise when a decision is made to dispose of a segment of a business, are recognized under generally accepted accounting principles before a liability is legally incurred. Inquiries of management concerning such obligations are important.

- *Recomputation, vouching, and tracing.* The auditor tests interest expense by recomputing the amount based on the outstanding balance, interest rate, and fraction of the year outstanding. Interest payments are vouched to canceled checks and the proceeds of new issues are traced to cash receipts records. The volume of debt transactions is generally low and all items are tested. If volume is high, an analytical procedure may be used, or audit software may be used to reperform all the computations.

Materiality and Audit Risk   In the long-term obligations area, consideration of materiality is not usually a significant factor in the nature, timing, and extent of tests. There are a few large transactions or items and all of them are material.

Audit risk considerations of importance are the establishment and adherence to a clear policy that all long-term obligations must be authorized by the board of directors and the formal assignment of responsibility for monitoring compliance with the requirements and restrictions of debt agreements.

Accounting principles for long-term obligations are voluminous and complex, so more audit emphasis in this area is placed on the specific audit objective related to *presentation and disclosure.*

Owners' Equity

The equity accounts differ depending on the form of organization. However, the presentation of partnership and proprietorship capital are relatively simple. Presentation of a single amount properly described is sufficient even though more detail is often disclosed in practice. This discussion focuses on stockholders' equity of a corporation.

The specific audit objectives and common audit procedures for stockholders' equity are substantially the same as for long-term obligations, so a separate figure summarizing them is not presented. The primary differences for particular procedures are as follows:

- *Confirmation.* Many corporations use the services of independent registrars and transfer agents to maintain detailed stockholder records. In that case confirmation requests are sent to those agents. If a corporation keeps its own stock records, the auditor would examine the stock certificate book rather than send confirmations to stockholders. The auditor's chief concern when the company keeps stockholder records is with the specific audit objective related to completeness. The auditor examines the stock certificate book and observes company procedures to ensure that all issued shares are recorded and that all authorized and unissued shares are safeguarded.
- *General procedures.* In addition to reading the minutes of meetings of the board of directors and stockholders, the auditor would read the articles of incorporation. The description of stock, par value, and number of shares authorized as presented in the financial statements should correspond to the information in the articles of incorporation. Authorization of dividends should be in the minutes of board meetings.

- *Recomputation, vouching, and tracing.* The auditor's procedures for cash dividends are similar to those for interest payments.

Additional audit procedures are necessary when there are treasury stock transactions, stock options, sale of stock rights or warrants, and stock dividends or stock splits.

THE INCOME STATEMENT AND INCOME TAXES

This section discusses the separate, but related, topics of examining the income statement and examining the provision for income taxes and related balances. The common feature of these areas is their interdependence with all other areas of the audit.

The Income Statement

As explained in Chapter 7, direct tests of balances generally focus on balance sheet accounts. In all of the explanations of assertions, objectives, and procedures for financial statement areas in prior discussions, the specific audit objectives are stated for balance-sheet accounts. This section explains the relation between specific audit objectives for income statement account balances and those for balance-sheet accounts.

Assertions and Objectives   The financial statement assertions presented in Chapter 4 are broadly worded to cover both balance-sheet and income statement accounts. In Chapter 7, these assertions are stated to apply specifically to balance-sheet accounts. The broad categories of financial statement assertions stated with the focus on income statements accounts are as follows:

- *Occurrence.* Reported revenues and expenses actually occurred during the period covered by the income statement.
- *Completeness.* All revenue and expense transactions that occurred in the period covered by the income statement are included.
- *Rights and obligations.* Reported revenues and expenses represent transactions to which the company was actually a party.
- *Allocation.* Revenues and expenses are measured properly.
- *Presentation and disclosure.* Revenues and expenses are properly described and classified in the income statement and related disclosures are adequate.

As explained in Chapter 7, in a double-entry accounting system, testing one side of a transaction automatically tests the other side. This means that an audit procedure that achieves an audit objective for one side of a transaction should achieve a comparable audit objective for the other side.

Sales and Receivables—An Example   The relationship among specific audit objectives for related account balances can be demonstrated by an example from the sales cycle. The financial statement assertion of "existence or occurrence" would be translated into the specific audit objectives as follows:

Financial statement assertion	Specific audit objectives	
	Balance sheet	Income statement
Existence or occurrence	Accounts receivable are authentic obligations owed by customers at the balance sheet date.	
		Reported sales to customers actually occurred during the period covered by the income statement.

Audit procedures applied to achieve the specific audit objective related to existence for accounts receivable should also achieve the specific audit objective related to occurrence for sales. Recall from Chapter 7 that directly testing the accounts receivable balance for overstatement (existence) simultaneously indirectly tests the total debits to accounts receivable (sales) for overstatement (occurrence).

The audit procedures used to achieve audit objectives for balance-sheet and income statement account balances in the sales cycle are often a combination of tests of transaction classes for sales and cash receipts transactions and direct tests of balances for accounts receivable as explained in Chapter 10.

Another way of considering the relationships is to use the activity analysis format introduced in Chapter 7. The activity analysis of accounts receivable can be rearranged as follows:

> Ending balance of accounts receivable
> + Cash receipts from customers during the period
> − Beginning balance of accounts receivable
> _____
> Sales to customers during the period

Audit tests of the other components of accounts receivable also simultaneously test sales.

There are similar relationships for the other financial statement assertions. For example, the financial statement assertion of "valuation or allocation" involves the increase of a valuation allowance—a balance-sheet account—and the corresponding expense allocated to the accounting period. The following example illustrates the relationships for the sales cycle:

Financial statement assertion	Specific audit objectives	
	Balance sheet	Income statement
Valuation or allocation	Accounts receivable are presented at the net realizable amount.	
		Bad debt expense represents the portion of sales made during the period that are reasonably expected to be uncollectible.

Direct tests of balances of accounts receivable for the specific audit objective related to valuation (reduction of receivables to net realizable value) are concerned with the adequacy of the allowance for bad debts. The related income statement balance, bad debt expense, is the increase in the allowance for the period and is tested simultaneously with tests of the allowance account.

Audit Procedures for Income Statement Accounts   The account balances in the income statement are generally tested by one of the following categories of audit approach:

- *Substantiation indirectly by simultaneous tests.* This category includes those income statement account balances that are simultaneously tested indirectly by direct tests of balances of related balance-sheet accounts. The primary income statement account balances that usually fall in this category are sales, cost of sales, and many expenses.
- *Substantiation directly in conjunction with balance-sheet accounts.* Some income statement account balances are subjected to direct tests of balances in conjunction with tests of related balance-sheet accounts. Examples of these account balances, with the related balance-sheet accounts shown parenthetically, are as follows:
  - Depreciation expense (property and equipment)
  - Amortization expense (intangible assets)
  - Investment income (investments)
  - Interest expense (long-term obligations)
- *Substantiation directly by analytical procedures.* The auditor usually applies several analytical tests to income statement account balances as additional overall tests of reasonableness or to provide necessary assurances on appropriate classification or completeness. Income statement account balances are compared with amounts of prior periods and budgets. Also, the relationship for amounts that are expected to follow a predictable pattern are considered. For example, a relationship should exist between the amount of sales, accounts receivable, and bad debt expense. When there are significant fluctuations from logical or historical relationships, the auditor should obtain explanations and consider their reasonableness. Analytical procedures may be particularly important for considering the appropriate classification of expenses.
- *Substantiation by separate direct tests.* Some income statement account balances are usually substantiated by separate direct tests of balances. Generally, these account balances fall into two broad categories—individually significant transactions or events, and account balances of intrinsic interest.

Individually Significant Transactions or Events   Some income statement items that enter into the determination of net income are individually significant, and the auditor applies separate direct tests of balances to the items. Generally the following items fall into that category:

- *Discontinued operations.* The results of discontinued operations and any related gain or loss are reported separately from continuing operations. Usually, the amount is very material, and complex accounting issues are involved in the recognition of gain or loss.

- *Extraordinary items.* An item is extraordinary if it is both unusual and infrequent. Extraordinary items are reported separately from income from continuing operations. Also, an item that is unusual or infrequent, but not both, may be reported as a separate component of income from continuing operations. Although the income statement classification differs, the audit interest is essentially the same as for extraordinary items.
- *Accounting changes.* The cumulative effect of changing to a new accounting principle is also reported separately from income from continuing operations. As explained in Chapter 13, the auditor needs to obtain evidence to evaluate management's justification for the change, the accounting effect and treatment of the change, and the acceptability of the new accounting principle.

All of these items generally involve reasonably complex accounting issues. The auditor uses recomputation to test the proper application of generally accepted accounting principles, but audit procedures are also usually necessary to substantiate the underlying transaction or event. In specific circumstances, other transactions or events, such as a sale of real estate, may be individually significant and would be tested directly.

Account Balances of Intrinsic Interest   Some account balances are analyzed and the details of items in the balance are vouched to supporting documents, because there is some interest in the account balance that is out of proportion to the effect of the balance on net income. For example, *travel and entertainment expense* and *officers' salaries* often fall in this category because of the income tax implications of these items. Another common example is *legal fees.* As explained in Chapter 12, the auditor is concerned with identifying all lawyers consulted by the client's management during the period. An analysis of the legal fees account is a good source for identifying the lawyers consulted.

Income Taxes

This section discusses the auditor's examination of a corporate client's provision for income taxes and other related account balances. The tax-related auditing issues of proprietorships, partnerships, S corporations, and not-for-profit organizations are not considered; these organizations are generally exempt from income tax, and the auditor's concern is primarily with maintenance and adequate disclosure of the relevant exempt status. Corporations file the Form 1120 U.S. Corporation Income Tax Return for federal income taxes; state and local income taxes generally follow the same pattern as federal taxation; and this discussion applies generally to federal, state, and local taxes on corporate income.

Differences from Other Audit Areas   Auditors frequently accept tax return preparation responsibilities for audit clients. Tax laws and regulations can be extremely complex, and many clients expect the CPA engaged to audit the financial statements to provide assistance in tax return preparation. Although this practice is normal, it is not universal and the matter should be covered explicitly in an engagement letter when the responsibility is assumed. Many CPA firms routinely complete some form of tax savings checklist on audit engagements as an additional client service whether or not responsibility has been assumed for return preparation.

Tax compliance is a specialized field in accounting, and CPA firm policies differ on the relative responsibilities of auditors and tax specialists. Some firms expect the auditor to prepare the tax return or make the initial review of a client-prepared return and have the auditor's work reviewed by a tax specialist. Other firms reverse the process and a tax specialist does the initial work.

Income tax for the period is dependent on the reported assets, liabilities, expenses, and revenues of the period, and the auditor needs to coordinate the work in all other areas of the audit with the audit procedures for income taxes. For example, if the income tax area is examined before some other area is completed, any audit adjustments in the other area have to be posted to income tax–related amounts and the conclusion for income taxes may have to be reconsidered. The extent of audit procedures in other areas also may be influenced by tax return preparation responsibilities. For example, the auditor may recompute depreciation expense rather than analytically testing it; the analytical procedure might be considered sufficiently persuasive to achieve audit objectives but not precise enough for tax return preparation.

Finally, the generally accepted accounting principles for income taxes are among the most complex in accounting. Many clients who have no difficulty with routine accruals and deferrals rely on the auditor for the computation of the provision for income taxes and related account balances. The accounting complexities include interperiod tax allocation, investment tax credits, net operating loss carryforwards, and several special areas. FASB Statement No. 109, "Accounting for Income Taxes," prescribes the liability method which is a balance-sheet approach to accounting for income taxes.

Assertions, Objectives, and Procedures   In contrast to many other audit areas, the emphasis in the income tax area is on direct tests of an income statement balance—provision for income taxes. Balance-sheet accounts for taxes payable or refundable and deferred debits and credits are tested in conjunction.

The essential features of direct tests of balances for incomes taxes are audit procedures directed to the tax return (compliance with tax laws and regulations) for achievement of specific audit objectives related to *existence or occurrence, completeness,* and *rights or obligations* and audit procedures directed to the proper application of accounting principles for achievement of specific audit objectives related to *valuation and allocation* and *presentation and disclosure.*

Generally, the auditor obtains reasonable assurance about occurrence (revenues or expenses are not overstated) and completeness (revenues or expenses are not understated) from audit procedures applied in other areas of the audit. In the income tax area, the concern is with whether items are taxable or deductible under the relevant tax laws and regulations. Once reasonable assurance has been obtained on tax compliance, the auditor's accounting knowledge is applied to evaluate conformity with the complex accounting principles applicable to income taxes.

The financial statement assertions, specific audit objectives, and the common audit procedures traditionally used to achieve the objectives for income taxes are summarized in Figure 11-6. As applied in the income tax area, these procedures have the following features:

Financial statement assertion	Specific audit objectives	Common audit procedures to achieve objective
Occurrence and existence	Taxable revenues and deductible expenses included in the tax return are in accordance with tax laws and regulations and were actually realized or incurred by the company during the period; the income taxes estimated to be currently payable and the related liability are adequate but not excessive.	Inquiry and scanning General procedures Tracing and vouching Recomputation
Completeness	All taxable revenues realized and deductible expenses incurred during the period are included in taxable income.	General procedures Tracing and vouching
Rights or obligations	Tax returns have been filed and estimated payments made on a timely basis, and other inquiries or assessments of taxing authorities have been responded to appropriately.	General procedures Inquiry and scanning
Allocation and valuation	The provision for income taxes in the income statement and income taxes payable and related deferred tax liabilities or assets in the balance sheet are properly stated in accordance with accounting principles of tax allocation.	Recomputation Inquiry and scanning
Presentation and disclosure	Income tax–related amounts are properly described and classified in the financial statements and related disclosures are adequate.	Inquiry and scanning

FIGURE 11-6
Assertions, objectives, and procedures for income taxes.

- *Inquiry and scanning.* The auditor inquires of appropriate client personnel about applicable tax jurisdictions, filing requirements, and procedures followed to help ensure compliance with applicable tax laws and regulations. The auditor scans prior years' tax returns and inquires about the status of IRS or other taxing authority examinations. Of particular importance is the auditor's discussion with appropriate personnel of the tax treatment of items that may be challenged by taxing authorities because the client's position is known to be contrary to the views of taxing authorities or because the law or regulations are known to be uncertain. As discussed in Chapter 5, violations of the Internal Revenue Code and other tax laws are considered illegal acts that have a direct and material effect on financial statement amounts.

Therefore, the auditor's responsibility is to design the audit procedures to detect such misstatements that are material to the financial statements.

- *General procedures.* In addition to reviewing prior years' tax returns, the auditor reviews correspondence with taxing authorities. In general, the auditor applies the knowledge of the business obtained in other audit areas to the matters of interest described for inquiry and scanning procedures.
- *Tracing and vouching.* The auditor analyzes the taxes payable account and vouches and traces to or from supporting documents for tax payments, estimated taxes, or refunds during the period.
- *Recomputation.* The audit procedure of recomputation is used to reconcile taxable income and pretax accounting income, calculate the effect of permanent and temporary differences, and calculate the components of the provision for income taxes, including taxes currently payable, the tax effect of temporary differences, and tax effects of operating losses, and the related change in balance-sheet accounts for taxes payable and deferred tax liabilities or assets. A deferred tax liability or asset is recognized for the estimated tax effects of temporary differences between assets and liabilities and their tax basis. A valuation allowance must be recognized to reduce a deferred tax asset if it is more likely than not that some portion of it will not be realized.

The consideration of the specific audit objective on presentation and disclosure related to income taxes usually does not require any audit procedures in addition to those necessary to achieve other audit objectives. However, the requirements on description, classification, and disclosure are complex and necessitate careful review of the information obtained and a thorough knowledge of relevant accounting principles.

Additional Complexities   A variety of additional complexities can arise in the income tax area. The following complexities are discussed briefly:

- Tax cushions
- IRS access to work papers

A *tax cushion* is essentially a difference between taxes owed as determined on the tax return and taxes ultimately payable after assessments by taxing authorities and tax litigation. The balance-sheet liability should be adequate for taxes ultimately payable for matters that have occurred by the balance sheet date.

At least a modest cushion is normally necessary because the tax return is often filed after field work is completed. Thus, taxes payable may be judgmentally increased over the amount estimated to be payable to allow for miscellaneous matters that come to the client's attention after the audited financial statements are issued in the interest of conservatism. However, the auditor must also be concerned that this cushion is not excessive.

The controversy concerning tax cushions arises from the treatment of disputable items that may be challenged by the taxing authority and disallowed. As a tax preparer, a CPA may resolve doubt in the client's favor. As an auditor, a CPA's concern is with conformity with generally accepted accounting principles.

FASB Statement No. 5 (Current Text C59) on loss contingencies requires accrual when it is probable a loss has been incurred and the amount of the loss can be estimated. In tax matters, this means a tax cushion for disputable items should be recorded to increase an actual or deferred tax liability only when the auditor believes it is probable the client's tax positions will trigger an examination, the examining agent will challenge the positions, the positions will be disallowed, and the amount of the disallowance can be reasonably estimated. Many auditors believe that signing the return as preparer in these circumstances is incompatible because allowing the client to take the positions is no longer a matter of resolving "doubt" in the client's favor. As mentioned earlier, for a deferred tax asset, the criterion for recognizing a valuation allowance is "more likely than not" rather than "probable."

IRS access to audit work papers became an issue because of tax cushions. The type of work papers in contention are generally referred to as *tax accrual work papers*. An auditor uses a tax accrual work paper to identify a client's disputable tax positions and estimate the tax liability in light of those positions. A tax accrual work paper is a "road map" for an IRS agent, and clients and auditors have strongly protested IRS access to such work papers. In the cases that have been litigated on this issue, the auditors have not been acting as tax return preparers. The appropriateness of IRS access to work papers supporting the tax return has never been seriously questioned. However, auditors unsuccessfully attempted to retain the confidentiality of tax accrual work papers. In spite of the impediments the position creates for candor in auditor-client communications and for adequate work paper documentation of important audit conclusions, the current legal position is that the IRS can obtain access to an auditor's tax accrual work papers.[1]

CHAPTER 11 ASSIGNMENTS

OBJECTIVE QUESTIONS

11-1 For each one of the following statements indicate whether the statement is true or false.

T F **a** The extent of the auditor's observation of the client's physical inventory is significantly influenced by controls over processing transactions during the period.

T F **b** The auditor's observation of the physical inventory means essentially that the auditor tests the client's inventory records by counting a sample of inventory items and comparing the counts to the records.

T F **c** The audit procedure of physical examination (test counts) in the inventory area is essentially equivalent to the procedure of confirmation in the accounts receivable areas.

T F **d** The auditor's approach to property and equipment is comparable to inventory; the auditor selects items included in the ending balance and substantiates those items by physical examination and vouching.

[1]*United States v. Arthur Young & Co. et al.,* U.S. Sup. Ct., no. 82-687 (March 21, 1984).

T F e The auditor's procedures relevant to property and equipment include reading minutes and inspecting debt agreements.

T F f The auditor may need to apply audit procedures to the financial statements of an entity other than the client to achieve some specific audit objectives for investments.

T F g Normally, the auditor sends blind confirmation requests to all significant debtholders.

T F h In the long-term debt area, general procedures, such as reading minutes, are relatively less important than in other audit areas.

T F i Audit procedures applied to achieve the specific audit objective related to existence for a balance-sheet account may also achieve a specific audit objective related to occurrence for a related income statement account.

T F j The nature of audit procedures for income taxes is generally unaffected by whether the client is a corporation, proprietorship, or partnership.

T F k The auditor's approach to income taxes is essentially substantive; the auditor makes direct tests of balances of balance-sheet accounts, and the related income statement amounts are substantiated as a byproduct.

11-2 The following questions relate to audit procedures for inventories. Select the *best* response.

a For several years a client's physical inventory count has been lower than what was shown on the books at the time of the count so that downward adjustments to the inventory account were required. Contributing to the inventory problem could be deficiencies in the internal control structure that led to the failure to record some:

1 Purchases returned to vendors

2 Sales returns received

3 Sales discounts allowed

4 Cash purchases

b An auditor has accounted for a sequence of inventory tags and is now going to trace information on a representative number of tags to the physical inventory sheets. The purpose of this procedure is to obtain assurance that:

1 The final inventory is valued at cost.

2 All inventory represented by an inventory tag is listed on the inventory sheets.

3 All inventory represented by an inventory tag is bona fide.

4 Inventory sheets do *not* include untagged inventory items.

c When an auditor tests a client's cost accounting system, the auditor's tests are *primarily* designed to determine that:

1 Quantities on hand have been computed based on acceptable cost accounting techniques that reasonably approximate actual quantities on hand.

2 Physical inventories are in substantial agreement with book inventories.

3 The system is in accordance with generally accepted accounting principles and is functioning as planned.

4 Costs have been properly assigned to finished goods, work in process, and costs of good sold.

d An inventory turnover analysis is useful to the auditor because it may detect:

1 Inadequacies in inventory pricing

2 Methods of avoiding cyclical holding costs

3 The optimum automatic reorder points

4 The existence of obsolete merchandise

e When an outside specialist has assumed full responsibility for taking the client's physical inventory, reliance on the specialist's report is acceptable if:

    1 The auditor is satisfied through application of appropriate procedures as to the reputation and competence of the specialist.

    2 Circumstances made it impracticable or impossible for the auditor either to do the work personally or observe the work done by the inventory firm.

    3 The auditor conducted the same audit test and procedures as would have been applicable if the client employees took the physical inventory.

    4 The auditor's report contains a reference to the assumption of full responsibility.

f A client maintains perpetual inventory records in both quantities and dollars. If the assessed level of control risk is high, an auditor would probably:

    1 Insist that the client perform physical counts of inventory items several times during the year

    2 Apply gross profit tests to ascertain the reasonableness of the physical counts

    3 Increase the extent of tests of controls of the inventory cycle

    4 Request the client to schedule the physical inventory count at the end of the year

g When auditing merchandise inventory at year-end, the auditor performs a purchase cutoff test to obtain evidence that:

    1 All goods purchased before year-end are received before the physical inventory count.

    2 No goods held on consignment for customers are included in the inventory balance.

    3 No goods observed during the physical count are pledged or sold.

    4 All goods owned at year-end are included in the inventory balance.

h An auditor generally tests physical security controls over inventory by:

    1 Test counts and cutoff procedures

    2 Examination and reconciliation

    3 Inspection and recomputation

    4 Inquiry and observation

i Which of the following internal control procedures most likely addresses the completeness assertion for inventory?

    1 Work in process account is periodically reconciled with subsidiary records.

    2 Employees responsible for custody of finished goods do *not* perform the receiving function.

    3 Receiving reports are prenumbered and periodically reconciled.

    4 There is a separation of duties between payroll department and inventory accounting personnel.

AICPA

11-3 The following questions relate to audit procedures for investments. Select the *best* response.

a The auditor should insist that a representative of the client be present during physical examination of securities in order to:

    1 Lend authority to the auditor's directives

    2 Detect forged securities

    3 Coordinate the return of all securities to proper locations

    4 Acknowledge the receipt of securities returned

b Which of the following is *not* one of the auditor's primary objectives in an examination of marketable securities?

    1 To determine whether securities are authentic

    2 To determine whether securities are the property of the client

    3 To determine whether securities actually exist

    4 To determine whether securities are properly classified on the balance sheet

c Which of the following is the most effective audit procedure for verification of dividends earned on investments in marketable equity securities?

    1 Tracing deposit of dividend checks to the cash receipts book

    2 Reconciling amounts received with published dividend records

    3 Comparing the amounts received with preceding year dividends received

    4 Recomputing selected extensions and footings of dividend schedules and comparing totals to the general ledger

d To establish the existence and ownership of a long-term investment in the common stock of a publicly traded company, an auditor ordinarily performs a security count or:

    1 Relies on the client's internal control structure if the auditor has reasonable assurance that the control procedures are being applied as prescribed

    2 Confirms the number of shares owned that are held by an independent custodian

    3 Determines the market price per share at the balance sheet date from published quotations

    4 Confirms the number of shares owned with the issuing company

e An auditor would most likely verify the interest earned on bond investments by:

    1 Vouching the receipt and deposit of interest checks

    2 Confirming the bond interest rate with the issuer of the bonds

    3 Recomputing the interest earned on the basis of face amount, interest rate, and period held

    4 Testing the internal controls over cash receipts

f A company has additional temporary funds to invest. The board of directors decided to purchase marketable securities and assigned the future purchase and sale decisions to a responsible financial executive. The best person(s) to make periodic reviews of the investment activity should be:

    1 The investment committee of the board of directors

    2 The treasurer

    3 The corporate controller

    4 The chief operating officer

AICPA

11-4 The following questions relate to audit procedures for property and equipment. Select the *best* response.

  a In the examination of property, plant, and equipment, the auditor tries to determine all of the following *except* the:

    1 Effectiveness of the internal control structure

    2 Extent of property abandoned during the year

    3 Adequacy of replacement funds

    4 Reasonableness of the depreciation

  b In violation of company policy, Lowell Company erroneously capitalized the cost of painting its warehouse. The auditor examining Lowell's financial statements would most likely detect this when:

    1 Discussing the capitalization policies with Lowell's controller

    2 Examining maintenance expense accounts

3 Observing, during the physical inventory observation, that the warehouse had been painted

4 Examining the construction work orders supporting items capitalized during the year

c Which of the following auditing procedures would be *least* likely to lead the auditor to find unrecorded fixed asset disposals?

1 Examination of insurance policies

2 Review of repairs and maintenance expense

3 Review of property tax files

4 Scanning of invoices for fixed asset additions

d Which of the following is the *best* evidence of real estate ownership at the balance sheet date?

1 Title insurance policy

2 Original deed held in the client's safe

3 Paid real estate tax bills

4 Closing statement

e The controller of Excello Manufacturing wants to use ratio analysis to identify the possible existence of idle equipment or the possibility that equipment has been disposed of without having been written off. Which of the following ratios would best accomplish this objective?

1 Depreciation expense/book value of manufacturing equipment

2 Accumulated depreciation/book value of manufacturing equipment

3 Repairs and maintenance cost/direct labor costs

4 Gross manufacturing equipment cost/units produced

f A weakness in internal accounting control over recording retirements of equipment may cause the auditor to:

1 Inspect certain items of equipment in the plant and trace those items to the accounting records

2 Review the subsidiary ledger to ascertain whether depreciation was taken on each item of equipment during the year

3 Trace additions to the "other assets" account to search for equipment that is still on hand but no longer being used

4 Select certain items of equipment from the accounting records and locate them in the plant

g An auditor analyzes repairs and maintenance accounts primarily to obtain evidence in support of the audit assertion that all:

1 Noncapitalizable expenditures for repairs and maintenance have been properly charged to expense.

2 Expenditures for property and equipment have *not* been charged to expense.

3 Noncapitalizable expenditures for repairs and maintenance have been recorded in the proper period.

4 Expenditures for property and equipment have been recorded in the proper period.

AICPA

11-5 The following questions relate to audit procedures for long-term obligations and stockholders' equity.

a An auditor's program to examine long-term debt should include steps that require:

1 Examining bond trust indentures

2 Inspecting the accounts payable subsidiary ledger

3 Investigating credits to the bond interest income account
4 Verifying the existence of the bondholders

b When a client company does *not* maintain its own stock records, the auditor should obtain written confirmation from the transfer agent and registrar concerning:
1 Restrictions on the payment of dividends
2 The number of shares issued and outstanding
3 Guarantees of preferred stock liquidation value
4 The number of shares subject to agreements to repurchase

c The auditor can *best* verify a client's bond sinking fund transactions and year-end balance by:
1 Confirmation with the bond trustee
2 Confirmation with individual holders of retired bonds
3 Recomputation of interest expense, interest payable, and amortization of bond discount or premium
4 Examination and count of the bonds retired during the year

d The primary reason for preparing a reconciliation between interest-bearing obligations outstanding during the year and interest expense presented in the financial statements is to:
1 Assess control risk for securities
2 Determine the validity of prepaid interest expense
3 Ascertain the reasonableness of imputed interest
4 Detect unrecorded liabilities

e During the year under audit, a company has completed a private placement of a substantial amount of bonds. Which of the following is the *most* important step in the auditor's program for the examination of bonds payable?
1 Confirming the amount issued with the bond trustee
2 Tracing the cash received from the issue to the accounting records
3 Examining the bond records maintained by the transfer agent
4 Recomputing the annual interest cost and the effective yield

f All corporate capital stock transactions should ultimately be traced to the:
1 Minutes of the board of directors
2 Cash receipts journal
3 Cash disbursements journal
4 Numbered stock certificates

g An auditor would be *least* likely to use confirmations in connection with the examination of:
1 Inventories
2 Long-term debt
3 Property, plant, and equipment
4 Stockholders' equity

AICPA

DISCUSSION QUESTIONS

Discussion questions require the application of the concepts explained in the chapter to specific facts, issues, or problems. They are classified by the primary topic to which they relate. However, responses should not be confined to primary topics but should include all relevant implications.

Inventories

11-6 During the month of April, you are engaged to audit the balance sheet of a new client as of March 31. The client manufactures steel castings and forgings. A physical count of all inventories is made at the end of each quarter of the fiscal year, and the company adjusts its inventory book amounts to reflect the physical counts. As you were not engaged at the time of the physical inventory on March 31, you request that the company make another physical inventory count at the end of April in order that you may observe and make test counts. The client agrees, and another inventory is taken on April 30 which you witness.

Inventories of raw materials, work in process, and finished goods totaled $125,000 at March 31. Total current assets amounted to $188,000, total current liabilities were $186,000, and total assets were $450,000.

The company maintains perpetual inventory records of raw materials and supplies, but has no job cost system or perpetual records of work in process or finished goods. Production records are kept in the plant showing the tons of castings poured each day, and sales records reflect the tons of castings and forgings sold daily to various customers of the company.

a What audit procedures would you use to satisfy yourself as to the *quantities* on hand at balance sheet date?

b Assuming that the results of your tests of inventories are satisfactory, would you issue an audit report unqualified as to opinion and scope of the audit, in view of the fact that you were not on hand to observe inventories at March 31? Give reasons for your answer. (Limit your discussion to a consideration of the inventory problem.)

AICPA

11-7 Your client, the Bambi Corporation, manufacturers baby carriages as its only product. The corporation maintains perpetual inventory records in quantities and values and also takes a complete physical inventory each October 31. You observed the physical inventory at October 31, 19X0 and were satisfied with the procedures followed. From your test counts you are satisfied that the client's counts were substantially accurate.

There were differences between the client's count and the perpetual records for about 75 percent of the items. Before adjusting the inventory records for the larger differences, of which there were about 25, the records were checked and the items were recounted. Typical examples of adjustments for the larger differences are as follows:

	Perpetual record before adjustment	Perpetual record after adjustment
Black paint (in gallons)	662	647
Cotter pins (in dozens)	2,260	2,160
Hub caps	8,592	8,703
Assembled wheels	6,901	6,883

Bambi made no further physical tests of inventories during 19X0. For its year-end closing at December 31, 19X0, the corporation used inventory quantities shown by the perpetual inventory records.

Prepare in outline form an audit program setting out the essential procedures to be followed in your audit of inventories as of December 31, 19X0. Do not include procedures unless you believe them to be essential under the conditions as stated.

AICPA adapted

11-8 Rocks Ltd. quarries limestone, crushes it to standard commercial size, stockpiles it, and eventually ships it to customers by rail. Production is measured by the number of quarry truckloads fed to the stone crushing equipment, and each truck is considered to carry 20 tons. The railroad weighs every carload, and most of the customers weigh the stone again when delivered by the railroad.

Every month-end the inventory is determined by the company engineer, who takes into consideration the geometric shapes and dimensions of the stockpiles. A predetermined compaction factor is applied to the volume in the stockpiles to convert it to weight of stone.

Rocks Ltd.'s records for the last 4 months of the year show the following information in tons of limestone:

	Per production records				Physical closing inventory
	Opening inventory	Production	Shipments	Closing inventory	
September	4,520	780	(760)	4,540	4,560
October	4,540	800	(750)	4,590	4,450
November	4,590	740	(760)	4,570	4,160
December	4,570	620	(790)	4,400	3,840

A. Carl, the company's auditor, is asked to determine the causes for the year-end inventory shortage. What audit procedures should Carl's investigation follow, and what areas would Carl explore to account for the differences?

CICA adapted

11-9 On January 10, 19X8, you were engaged to audit the financial statements of Caten Equipment Corporation for the year ended December 31, 19X7. Caten has sold trucks and truck parts and accessories for many years but has never had an audit. The company maintains good perpetual records for all inventories and takes a complete inventory each December 31.

The parts inventory account includes the $2,500 cost of obsolete parts. Caten's executives acknowledge that these parts have been worthless for several years, but they have continued to carry the cost as an asset. The amount of $2,500 is material in relation to net income and year-end inventories but not material in relation to total assets or capital at December 31, 19X7.

a List the procedures you would add to your inventory audit program for new trucks because you did not observe the physical inventory taken by the corporation as of December 31, 19X7.

b Should the $2,500 of obsolete parts be carried in inventory as an asset? Discuss.

c Assume your alternative auditing procedures satisfy you as to the corporation's December 31, 19X7 inventory but that you were unable to apply these alternative procedures to the December 31, 19X6 inventory. Discuss (ignoring the obsolete parts) the effect this would have on your auditor's report in (1) the scope paragraph and (2) the opinion paragraph.

AICPA adapted

11-10 A processor of frozen foods carries an inventory of finished products consisting of 50 different types of items valued at approximately $2,000,000. About $750,000 of this value represents stock produced by the company and billed to customers prior to the audit date. This stock is being held for the customers at a monthly rental charge until they request shipment and is not separate from the company's inventory.

The company maintains separate perpetual ledgers at the plant office for both stock owned and stock being held for customers. The cost department also maintains a perpetual record of stock owned. The above perpetual records reflect quantities only.

The company does not take a complete physical inventory at any time during the year, since the temperature in the cold storage facilities is too low to allow one to spend more than 15 minutes inside at a time. It is not considered practical to move items outside or to defreeze the cold storage facilities for the purpose of taking a physical inventory. Because of these circumstances, it is impractical to test count quantities to the extent of completely counting specific items. The company considers as its inventory valuation at year-end the aggregate of the quantities reflected by the perpetual record of stock owned, maintained at the plant office, priced at the lower of cost or market.

a What are the two principal problems facing the auditor in the audit of the inventory? Discuss briefly.

b Outline the audit steps that you would take to enable you to render an unqualified opinion with respect to the inventory. (You may omit consideration of tests of unit prices and clerical accuracy.)

AICPA

11-11 The Jumbolith Press Company is engaged in the manufacture of large-size presses under specific contracts and in accordance with customers' specifications. Customers are required to advance 25 percent of the contract price. Jumbolith records sales on a shipment basis and accumulates costs by job orders. The normal profit margin over the past few years has been approximately 5 percent of sales, after providing for selling and administration expenses of about 10 percent of sales. Inventory is valued at the lower of cost or market.

Among the jobs you are reviewing in the course of your annual audit of Jumbolith's December 31 financial statements is No. 2357, calling for delivery of a three-color press at a firm contract price of $50,000. Costs accumulated for the job at the year-end aggregated $30,250. The company's engineers estimated that the job was approximately 55 percent complete at that time. Your audit procedures have been as follows:

1 Examined all contracts, noting pertinent provisions
2 Observed physical inventory of jobs in process and reconciled details to job order accounts
3 Tested input of labor, material, and overhead charges into the various jobs to determine that such charges were authentic and had been posted correctly
4 Confirmed customers' advances at year-end
5 Balanced work in process job ledger with control account

With respect to job No. 2357:

a State what additional audit procedures, if any, you would follow, and explain the purpose of the procedures.

b Indicate the manner in which and at what amount you would include job No. 2357 in the balance sheet.

AICPA adapted

11-12 On May 15, 19X2, you are engaged to make an audit of Boro Corporation, whose records you have not previously audited. Your client is a retail coal dealer with a fiscal year ending May 31. Perpetual inventory records are in use, and sales are accumulated as to both dollar amount and tonnage for each type of coal sold. A part of the coal on hand at May 31, 19X2 is stored in loading bins, while the remainder is piled in the open or contained in railroad cars.

a List audit procedures to be followed in the tests of inventories at May 31, 19X2.

b Assuming that no audit had been made at May 31, 19X1, suggest procedures to test the cost of goods sold figure.

AICPA adapted

11-13 In auditing a company engaged in wholesaling goods, you find that a very substantial part of the inventory of merchandise is on consignment to customers in other cities and at independent warehouses in other cities. State the procedures you would follow in your tests of the inventory on consignment and in warehouses.

AICPA

11-14 Monola uses a perpetual inventory system and has taken a physical inventory on December 31, 19X4. The inventory account has been adjusted to the actual figure per the count. In testing purchases cutoff you find the situation depicted below. Prepare any necessary adjusting entries. (Monola consistently records purchases upon receipt regardless of f.o.b. terms.)

Purchase order no.	Amount	Date entered in purchase journal	Date received
14777	310	12/31/X4	1/3/X5
13997	475	12/31/X4	12/19/X4
15001	1,100	12/31/X4	12/31/X4
14886	4,300	1/2/X5	12/31/X4
3793	6,200	1/2/X5	11/10/X4
11001	1,400	1/2/X5	1/3/X5

11-15 You have been engaged by the management of Alden to review its internal control structure for the purchase, receipt, storage, and issue of raw materials. You have prepared the following comments which describe Alden's procedures.

Raw materials, which consist mainly of high-cost electronic components, are kept in a locked storeroom. Storeroom personnel include a supervisor and four clerks. All are well-trained, competent, and adequately bonded. Raw materials are removed from the storeroom only upon written or oral authorization of one of the production supervisors.

There are no perpetual inventory records; hence, the storeroom clerks do not keep records of goods received or issued. To compensate for the lack of perpetual records, a physical inventory count is taken monthly by the storeroom clerks who are well-supervised. Appropriate procedures are followed in making the inventory count.

After the physical count, the storeroom supervisor matches quantities counted against a predetermined reorder level. If the count for a given part is below the reorder level, the supervisor enters the part number on a materials requisition list and sends this list to the accounts payable clerk. The accounts payable clerk prepares a purchase order for a predetermined reorder quantity for each part and mails the purchase order to the vendor from whom the part was last purchased.

When ordered materials arrive at Alden, they are received by the storeroom clerks. The clerks count the merchandise and agree the counts to the shipper's bill of lading. All vendors' bills of lading are initialed, dated, and filed in the storeroom to serve as receiving reports.

Describe the deficiencies in the internal control structure and recommend improvements of Alden's procedures for the purchase, receipt, storage, and issue of raw materials.

AICPA

11-16 Concho Corporation uses a perpetual inventory system and has already adjusted inventory to actual. In testing sales cutoff at 12/31/X4, you find the following situation. Prepare any necesary adjusting journal entries. (Concho sells all goods f.o.b. the Concho plant.)

Sales inv. no.	Amount	Date entered in sales journal	Date shipped	Cost of sales
9781	430	12/31/X4	12/27/X4	$ 300
9782	700	12/31/X4	12/31/X4	390
9783	1,080	12/31/X4	1/2/X5	580
9784	1,400	12/31/X4	12/28/X4	810
9785	650	12/31/X4	12/30/X4	300
9786	1,010	1/2/X5	12/30/X4	500
9787	1,100	1/2/X5	1/7/X5	630
9788	320	1/2/X5	1/2/X5	170
9789	590	1/2/X5	12/31/X4	275
9790	1,500	1/2/X5	1/3/X5	1,100

11-17 Your client, a distiller of alcohol, suggests that it is not necessary for you to observe the taking of physical inventories at his plants. The client points out that the Treasury Department's Alcohol Tax Unit checks regularly on the inventories of raw materials, work in process, finished product, and revenue stamps. Procedures followed by the Tax Unit's agents include auditing of production, sales, and other reports and the taking of physical inventories at unannounced intervals. Your client maintains perpetual inventory records.

Assuming that you agree to the client's suggested restriction of the scope of your audit, answer the following two questions. (In each case, your answer should include a discussion of the specific effects of this restriction on your standard report.)

a Your review of such of the records of the tax audits as are available and your appraisal of the procedures employed in such audits convince you that the client's record of inventory quantities can be relied upon. Would you be justified in accepting the work of a governmental agency in lieu of your own observation and in consequently giving an unqualified opinion? Discuss.

b Your review of the tax audit record and procedures does not satisfy you that you would be justified in relying solely on those quantities. What effects would your omission of observation procedures have on your standard report? Discuss.

AICPA

11-18 Decker, CPA, is performing an audit of the financial statements of Allright Wholesale Sales for the year ended December 31, 19X0. Allright has been in business for many years and has never had its financial statements audited. Decker has gained satisfaction with respect to the ending inventory and is considering alternative audit procedures to gain satisfaction with respect to management's representations concerning the beginning inventory which was not observed.

Allright sells only one product (bottled microbrewery brand "X" beer), and maintains perpetual inventory records. In addition, Allright takes physical inventory counts monthly. Decker has already confirmed purchases with the manufacturer and has decided to concentrate on evaluating the reliability of perpetual inventory records and performing analytical procedures to the extent that prior years' unaudited records will enable such procedures to be performed.

Required: What are the audit tests, including analytical procedures, which Decker should apply in evaluating the reliability of perpetual inventory records and gaining satisfaction with respect to the January 1, 19X0 inventory?

AICPA

Investments and Intangibles

11-19 Kent, CPA, who is engaged in the audit of the financial statements of Bass Corporation for the year ended December 31, 19X2, is about to commence an audit of the noncurrent investment securities. Bass's records indicate that the company owns various bearer bonds, as well as 25 percent of the outstanding common stock of Commercial Industrial. Kent is satisfied with evidence that supports the presumption of significant influence over Commercial Industrial. The various securities are at two locations, as follows:

- Recently acquired securities are in the company's safe in the custody of the treasurer.
- All other securities are in the company's bank safe deposit box.

All of the securities in Bass's portfolio are actively traded in a broad market.

Required:
a Assuming that the internal control structure for securities is effective, what are the objectives of the examination of these noncurrent investment securities?
b What audit procedures should be undertaken by Kent with respect to examination of Bass's noncurrent investment securities?

AICPA

11-20 The schedule on page 487 was prepared by the controller of World Manufacturing for use by the independent auditors during their audit of World's year-end financial statements. All procedures performed by the audit assistant were noted at the bottom

World Manufacturing, Inc.
Marketable Securities
Year Ended December 31, 19X1*

Description of security			Serial No.	Face value of bonds	Gen. ledger 1/1	Purch. in 19X1	Sold in 19X1	Cost	Gen. ledger 12/31	12/31 market	Dividends and interest		
Corp. Bonds	%	Yr. Due									Pay date(s)	Amt. rec.	Accruals 12/31
A	6	Y1	21-7	10000	9400a				9400	9100	1/15 7/15	300**b, d** 300**b, d**	275
D	4	X3	73-0	30000	27500a				27500	26220	12/1	1200**b, d**	100
G	9	Y8	16-4	5000	4000a				4000	5080	8/1	450**b, d**	188
Rc	5	X5	08-2	70000	66000a		5700**b**	66000					
Sc	10	Y9	07-4	100000		100000**e**			100000	101250	7/1	5000**b, d**	5000
					106900	100000	5700	66000	140900	141650		7250	5563
					a, f	**f**	**f**	**f**	**f, g**	**f**		**f**	**f**
Stocks													
P 1,000 shs. Common			1044		7500a				7500	7600	3/1 6/1 9/1 12/1	750**b, d** 750**b, d** 750**b, d** 750**b, d**	
U 50 shs. Common			8530		9700a				9700	9800	2/1 8/1	800**b, d** 800**b, d**	250
					17200				17200	17400		4600	667
					a, f				**f, g**	**f**		**f**	917
													f

*The year Y1 is 10 years after X1.
Legends and comments relative to above:
a = Beginning balances agreed to 19X0 work papers
b = Traced to cash receipts
c = Minutes examined (purchase and sales approved by the board of directors)
d = Agreed to 1099
e = Confirmed by tracing to broker's advice
f = Totals footed
g = Agreed to general ledger

"legend" section, and it was properly initialed, dated, and indexed, and then submitted to a senior member of the audit staff for review. The internal control structure is considered to be effective.

Required:

a What information that is essential to the audit of marketable securities is missing from this schedule?

b What are the essential audit procedures that were not noted as having been performed by the audit assistant?

AICPA

11-21 You are in charge of the audit of the financial statements of the Tomed Corporation for the year ended December 31, 19X4. The corporation has had the policy of investing its surplus funds in marketable securities. Its stock and bond certificates are kept in a safe deposit box in a local bank. Only the president and the treasurer of the corporation have access to the box.

You were unable to obtain access to the safe deposit box on December 31 because neither the president nor the treasurer was available. Arrangements were made for your assistant to accompany the treasurer to the bank on January 11 to examine the securities. Your assistant has never examined securities that were being kept in a safe deposit box and requires instructions. Your assistant should be able to inspect all securities on hand in an hour.

a List the instructions that you would give to your assistant regarding the examination of the stock and bond certificates kept in the safe deposit box. Include in your instructions the details of the securities to be examined and the reasons for examining these details.

b Upon returning from the bank, your assistant reported that the treasurer had entered the box on January 4. The treasurer stated that an old photograph of the corporation's original building had been removed. The photograph was loaned to the local chamber of commerce for display purposes. List the additional audit procedures that are required because of the treasurer's action.

AICPA adapted

11-22 During your first audit of the financial statement of the Luh Corporation, you find the following accounts and balances among the various other items in the trial balance:

1 Claim for refund—federal income taxes	$124,000
2 Investment of stock in XYZ Company (5,000 shares of 100,000 shares issued and outstanding, organized 5 years ago)	500,000
3 Treasury stock—at cost	110,000

Assuming that each of these three accounts is material in relation to the total assets of the company, select any two of them and state for each:

a The audit procedures you would apply to each of them.

b How you would present each of the two selected in part a in the balance sheet to accompany your standard audit report. (Assume that you were able to satisfy yourself as to their carrying value.)

AICPA adapted

11-23 You are engaged in the audit of the accounts and records of an investment company. You find that during the year the company has purchased from a bank the mortgage notes of several individuals. Some of the notes were purchased at face value, some at premium, and others at a small discount. The notes call for equal monthly payments to cover interest and principal. By agreement, each mortgagor makes additional fixed monthly payments to cover property taxes and insurance. The seller of the mortgage notes continues to service them, remitting monthly to your clients the payments received on account of principal and interest and retaining the payments for taxes and insurance in escrow until the tax bills and insurance bills are received for payment.

a State the documents which should be on hand in support of your client's investment.

b Outline the steps you would take in the audit of the transactions, covering both principal and income features.

AICPA

11-24 During your audit of the financial statements of the Dolomite Corporation for the year ended December 31, 19X1, you determine that the company's surplus funds have been temporarily invested in securities. The company's books are maintained on the accrual basis. A transcript of the investments account is shown below.

The Dolomite Corporation
Worksheet to Adjust the Investments Account
December 31, 19X1

Date			Account per books		
19X1			**Fol**	**Debit**	**Credit**
Jan.	3	Purchased 100 shares, Cal Motors	CD	$ 4,500	
	5	Purchased 100 shares, Micro Electronics	CD	500	
Mar.	1	Purchased $6,000 City of San Luis bonds	CD	6,060	
	31	Cash dividend, Cal Motors	CR		$ 50
Apr.	5	Sold 100 shares, Cal Motors	CR		4,800
	6	Purchased 100 shares, Hud Investment	CD	2,300	
	6	Purchased 100 shares, Valley Utility	CD	2,400	
May	1	Received 100 stock rights, Valley Utility	J	100	
July	2	Purchased 10 shares, Valley Utility	CD	130	
	15	Purchased 50 shares, Lox Laboratories	CD	1,900	
	18	Purchased 20 shares, Dolomite Corporation	CD	3,000	
Aug.	15	Sold 10 shares, Dolomite Corporation	CR		1,550
Sept.	1	Interest, City of San Luis bonds	CR		90
	1	Purchased $10,000 U.S. Treasury bonds	CD	10,067	
Dec.	8	Received 2 shares, Lox Laboratories	J	80	
	8	Cash dividend, Lox Laboratories	CR		20
	15	Cash dividend, Hud Investment	CR		90
	31	Interest, U.S. Treasury bonds	CR		200
	31	Cash dividend, Valley Utility	J	120	
				$31,157	$ 6,800
					24,357
				$31,157	$31,157

The following information and data were developed from your audit procedures:

1 The City of San Luis bonds were purchased as a new issue. No accrued interest was purchased.

2 The 100 Valley Utility rights were recorded at the May 1 quoted price on the stock exchange. (The credit of the journal entry was to miscellaneous income.) The stock was quoted at $19 per share ex-rights on May 1. For each five rights held, one share of Valley Utility stock could be purchased at $13 per share. The company exercised rights to buy 10 shares on July 2, when the market price was $16 per share. The rights expired on August 15.

3 The Dolomite Corporation purchased 20 shares of its own stock from the estate of a deceased stockholder. The stock has a par value of $100 and was originally issued for $115 per share. Of the 20 shares 10 were sold to an officer of the company for $155 per share.

4 In August Micro Electronics was reorganized. The original issue of stock was eliminated. New common stock was issued to bondholders and other creditors.

5 The purchase price of the U.S. Treasury bonds included accrued interest of $67.

6 During December Lox Laboratories declared a 5 percent stock dividend. In lieu of fractional shares cash was distributed based on the current market price of $40 per share. (The credit of the journal entry was to miscellaneous income.)

7 The Hud Investment Co. letter accompanying its annual dividend check gave the following composition of the dividend:

$0.80	Derived from income from investments
0.10	Return of stockholders' capital
$0.90	Total dividend

8 On December 15 Valley Utility declared a cash dividend of $1 per share payable on January 15, 19X2, to stockholders of record of December 29, 19X1. (The credit of the journal entry was to miscellaneous income.)

9 The securities are kept in a safe deposit box. You examined the securities on January 8, 19X2, after determining from the bank's records that the last entry to the box was on December 8. All securities were examined and properly accounted for.

Prepare a worksheet showing the adjustments to arrive at the corrected balance in the investments account at December 31, 19X1, and other adjustments or reclassifications arising from your audit of the account. Your worksheet should include the names of other accounts affected by the adjustments or reclassifications. (Formal journal entries are not required.) The books have not been closed.

11-25 C. A. Mellon has been appointed auditor of Mamolite Inc. and its subsidiary companies for the year ended May 31, 19X4, replacing another CPA who had retired. No information is available from the former auditor.

The company's consolidated balance sheet as at May 31, 19X4 contained the following account, amounting to about 8 percent of the net assets:

Investment in unconsolidated subsidiary (see *Note*), $612,478.

Note
The company acquired 57 percent of the common shares of Bastrop Corporation on July 1, 19X1, for $500,000. The investment is carried at cost plus equity in undistributed earnings since acquisition.

What procedures should the auditor carry out in order to form an opinion on the above item?

CICA adapted

11-26 For several years you have made the annual audit for the Winsford Company. This company is *not* a dealer in securities. A list of presently held securities is kept, but an investment register is not maintained. During the audit, the following worksheet was prepared:

Column no.	Column heading
1	Description of security (name, maturity, rate, etc.)
	Balance at beginning of year
2	Face value or number of shares
3	Cost or book value
	Additions during period
4	Date
5	Face value or number of shares
6	Cost
	Deductions during period
7	Date
8	Face value or number of shares
9	Cost or book value
10	Proceeds on disposals (net)
11	Profit or (loss) on disposals
	Balance at end of year
12	Face value or number of shares
13	Cost or book value
14	Market value
	Interest and dividends
15	Accrued at beginning of year
16	Purchased
17	Earned
18	Received
19	Accrued at end of year

Draw a line down the middle of a lined sheet of paper.

a On the left of the line, state the specific source(s) of information to be entered in each column and, where required, how the data of previous columns are combined.

b On the right of the line, state the principal way(s) that such information would be tested.

AICPA adapted

Property and Equipment

11-27 Big Bend Iron Corporation operates a small iron castings shop. As a part of the audit, you have been assigned the task of testing depreciation expense on equipment in this shop. The shop manager gives you the schedule of equipment shown at the top of page 492. Big Bend depreciates equipment at the rate of 10 percent per year. The company records a half year's depreciation in the year of purchase and sale of equipment.

Analyze the depreciation expense and prepare any necessary adjusting journal entries.

EQUIPMENT—CASTINGS SHOP

	Asset			
Description	Balance, 1/1/X1	Additions	Retirements	Balance, 12/31/X1
Milling machinery	$17,000	$3,000	. . .	$20,000
Casting equipment	24,387	2,000	$4,000	22,387
Polishing equipment	12,000	. . .	. . .	12,000

	Accumulated depreciation			
Description	Balance, 1/1/X1	Depreciation	Retirements	Balance, 12/31/X1
Milling machinery	$ 3,550	$1,850	. . .	$ 5,400
Casting equipment	7,830	234	$800	7,264
Polishing equipment	12,000	1,200	. . .	13,200

11-28 You have been engaged to make an audit of the financial records of a new client, the Ana Manufacturing Corporation, for its fiscal year ended December 31, 19X5. Among the fixed assets group are the accounts *land and buildings,* with a balance of $1,007,000 and *accumulated depreciation, land and buildings,* with a balance of $301,000.

The president informs you that:

The land and factory were donated by Central City to Ana on January 1, 19X2. This property had been purchased by Central City in November 19X1 for $1,000,000. Ana will get title to the donated property on January 1, 19X8, provided the average weekly payroll numbers a minimum of 200 each calendar year after 19X2. The corporation intends to meet these provisions.

List the procedures you would follow in auditing these accounts.

AICPA adapted

11-29 Gasco owns and operates gas wells which are accounted for in three classifications:

1 *Producing*—for wells currently producing, there are engineers' estimates of the gas reserves. Each well is depleted on the basis of the gas produced as compared to its total reserve.

2 *Suspended*—although engineers' estimates indicate that these wells have considerable reserves of gas, they will not be operated until such time as additional production is required.

3 *Abandoned*—these wells either never produced commercially useful quantities of gas or the gas reserves have been used up.

The properties on which the wells are located are leased from the owners at a specified annual rental, and payments are made until the well is abandoned. In addition, royalty payments are made at a specified rate, based on every 1,000 cubic feet of gas extracted from each well.

The wells are recorded on the books at cost (including engineers' fees, materials and equipment purchased, labor, etc.), depleted only while producing, and written off when abandoned.

What procedures should the auditor follow to substantiate that all wells owned by the company are properly recorded, classified, and valued? What supporting evidence would the auditor examine in this connection?

CICA adapted

11-30 In your audit of the financial statements of Scotia Corporation at December 31, 19X1, you observe the contents of certain accounts and other pertinent information as follows:

		Building			
Date	Explanation	LF	Debit	Credit	Balance
12/31/X0	Balance	X	$100,000		$100,000
7/1/X1	New boiler	CD	16,480	$1,480	115,000
9/1/X1	Insurance recovery	CR		2,000	113,000

		Allowance for depreciation—building			
Date	Explanation	LF	Debit	Credit	Balance
12/31/X0	Balance–15 years 4% of $100,000	X		$60,000	$ 60,000
12/31/X1	Annual depreciation	GJ		4,440	64,440

You learn that on June 15 the company's old high-pressure boiler exploded. Damage to the building was insignificant, but the boiler was replaced by a more efficient oil-burning boiler. The company received $2,000 as an insurance adjustment under terms of its policy for damage to the boiler.

The disbursement voucher charged to the building account on July 1, 19X1 is shown below:

TO: Zick Heating Company	
List price—new oil-burning boiler (including fuel oil tank and 5,000 gallons fuel oil)	$16,000
Sales tax—3% of $16,000	480
Total	16,480
Less: Allowance for old coal-burning boiler in building— to be moved at the expense of the Zick Heating Company	1,480
Total price	$15,000

In vouching the expenditure, you determine that the terms included a 2 percent cash discount, which was properly computed and taken. The sales tax is not subject to discount.

Your audit discloses that a voucher for $1,000 was paid to Tourmaline Company, on July 2, 19X1, and charged to the repair expense account. The voucher is adequately supported and is marked "installation costs for new oil-burning boiler."

The company's fuel oil supplier advises the fuel oil had a market price of 16 cents per gallon on July 1 and 18 cents per gallon on December 31. The fuel oil inventory at December 31 was 2,000 gallons.

A review of subsidiary property records discloses that the replaced coal-burning boiler was installed when the building was constructed and was recorded at a cost of $10,000. According to the manufacturers of the new boiler, it should be serviceable for 15 years.

In computing depreciation for retirements, Scotia Corporation consistently treats a fraction of a month as a full month.

Prepare the adjusting journal entries that you would suggest for entry on Scotia's books. The books have not been closed. Support your entries with computations in good form.

AICPA adapted

11-31 While auditing an urban bus company in a city of 50,000 population, you encounter the following situation:

1 You have checked an authorization for the purchase of five engines to replace the engines in five buses.

2 The cost of the old engines was removed from property and that of the new engines properly capitalized. The work was done in the company garage.

3 You find no credits for salvage or for the sale of any scrap metal at any time during the year. You have been in the garage and did not see the old engines.

4 The accountant, who is also treasurer and office manager, is an authorized check signer and has access to all cash receipts. Upon inquiry the accountant does not recall the sale of the old engines or of any scrap metal.

Assuming that the engines were sold as scrap, outline all steps which this fact would cause you to take in connection with your audit. Give consideration to steps beyond those related directly to this one item.

AICPA

Long-Term Obligations and Owners' Equity

11-32 Andrews, CPA, has been engaged to audit the financial statements of Broadwall Corporation for the year ended December 31, 19X1. During the year, Broadwall obtained a long-term loan from a local bank pursuant to a financing agreement which provided that:

1 The loan was to be secured by the company's inventory and accounts receivable.

2 The company was to maintain a debt-to-equity ratio not to exceed two to one.

3 The company was not to pay dividends without permission from the bank.

4 The monthly installment payments were to commence July 1, 19X1.

In addition, during the year the company also borrowed, on a short-term basis, from the president of the company, including substantial amounts just prior to the year-end.

Required:

a For purposes of Andrews' audit of the financial statements of Broadwall, what procedures should Andrews employ in examining the described loans? *Do not discuss internal control structure.*

b What are the financial statement disclosures that Andrews should expect to find with respect to the loans from the president?

AICPA

11-33 During the audit of Pecos Land and Cattle Company for the year 19X1 you discover the following general ledger accounts. Prepare any necessary adjusting journal entries.

| | Notes payable | | | |
| | | Acct. 304 | | |
Date	Description	Dr.	Cr.	Bal.
1/1/X1	Balance	. . .	. . .	-0-
1/3/X1	Wilson State Bank, 6% due 1/3/X3	. . .	10,000	10,000
3/1/X1	Alpine Nat'l. Bank, 6% due 6/1/X1	. . .	50,000	60,000
4/15/X1	Hondo Inc., 5% due 10/15/X1	. . .	10,000	70,000
6/1/X1	Alpine Nat'l. Bank	50,000	. . .	20,000
7/1/X1	Cattleman's Nat'l. Bank, 5% due 7/1/X2	. . .	70,000	90,000
10/15/X1	Hondo Inc.	10,000	. . .	80,000
11/1/X1	Paso Nat'l. Bank, 6% due 5/1/X2	. . .	100,000	180,000

| | Interest expense | | | |
| | | Acct. 644 | | |
Date	Description	Dr.	Cr.	Bal.
1/3/X1	Wilson State Bank	1,200	. . .	1,200
6/1/X1	Alpine Nat'l. Bank	750	. . .	1,950
10/15/X1	Hondo Inc.	250	. . .	2,200
12/31/X1	Accrual	375	. . .	2,575

11-34 Bunn is a Canadian manufacturing company, with a June 30 fiscal year-end. Until recently, the company had financed its operations with equity capital, supplemented by bank loans and other current indebtedness.

On August 31, 19X4, the company issued $10 million of 20-year 7 1/2 percent first mortgage sinking fund bonds, secured by a specific charge against certain company properties. The bonds were distributed to the public through a group of investment dealers for a fee equaling 2 percent of the par value of the issue. The bonds were sold to the public at 99.

The trust company agreed to act as trustee under the bond indenture and was also appointed transfer agent and interest-paying agent. The company paid fees totaling $25,000 for legal, audit, printing, and other costs in connection with the issue.

The company's auditor of long standing retired in March 19X5; Brown was then appointed auditor. Brown has reviewed the company's accounting system and control procedures but has not yet performed any further audit procedures.

What audit procedures should Brown perform in order to form an opinion on the bond indebtedness and interest expense shown in the June 30, 19X5, financial statements?

CICA adapted

11-35 The following covenants are extracted from the indenture of a bond issue. The indenture provides that failure to comply with its terms in any respect automatically advances the due date of the loan to the date of noncompliance (the regular date is 20 years hence). Give any audit steps or reporting requirements you feel should be taken or recognized in connection with each of the following:

1 The debtor company shall endeavor to maintain a working capital ratio of 2 to 1 at all times, and, in any fiscal year following a failure to maintain said ratio, the company shall restrict compensation of officers to a total of $200,000. Officers for this purpose shall include chairman of the board of directors, president, all vice-presidents, secretary, and treasurer.

2 The debtor company shall keep all property which is security for this debt insured against loss by fire to the extent of 100 percent of its actual value. Policies of insurance comprising this protection shall be filed with the trustee.

3 The debtor company shall pay all taxes legally assessed against property which is security for this debt within the time provided by law for payment without penalty, and shall deposit receipted tax bills or equally acceptable evidence of payment of same with the trustee.

4 A sinking fund shall be deposited with the trustee by semiannual payments of $300,000, from which the trustee shall, at his discretion, purchase bonds of this issue.

AICPA adapted

The Income Statement and Income Taxes

11-36 You are meeting with executives of Comal Cosmetics Corporation to arrange your firm's engagement to audit the corporation's financial statements for the year ended December 31, 19X8. One executive suggested that the audit work be divided among three audit staff members so one person would examine asset accounts, a second would examine liability accounts, and the third would examine income and expense accounts. to minimize audit time, avoid duplication of staff effort, and curtail interference with company operations.

a To what extent should a CPA follow the client's suggestions for the conduct of the audit?

b List and discuss the reasons why audit work should not be assigned solely according to asset, liability, and income and expense categories.

AICPA adapted

11-37 Ancira is a mail-order house that sells a single product which it produces in its completely automated plant. The only major expenses of the company are depreciation on plant and equipment and advertising. The advertising done by Ancira is all placed in magazines with national circulations.

a List the audit procedures the CPA should use to test:

1 Advertising expense
2 Depreciation

b Can the auditor ignore all other income statement items? Explain.

11-38 Bowen has been the auditor of Talltale Corporation for many years. The company's financial statements at December 31, 19X9, include the following amounts:

On the balance sheet, under "current liabilities":	
Income and other taxes payable	$ 563,800
On the balance sheet, as a separate item under "liabilities":	
Deferred tax liability	$2,479,400
On the income statement, following "income before income taxes":	
Income taxes—current	$1,033,300
—deferred	117,100
	$1,150,400

Indicate the audit procedures required to test each of the amounts shown above.

CICA adapted

Learning Objectives

After studying this chapter you should be able to:

- Explain the significance of the audit report date and the general nature of audit procedures applied near the completion of the engagement
- Define subsequent events of audit interest and describe the audit procedures applied specifically to identify such events
- Describe the nature and purpose of written representations obtained from the client's management and legal counsel
- Explain the purpose and steps involved in reviewing work papers and financial statements, including the summarization and evaluation of audit results, and performance of analytical procedures in an overall review
- Understand the auditor's responsibilities in consideration of the client's ability to continue as a going concern
- Identify the significant activities that may occur after the audit concerning maintaining the quality of practice, subsequent discovery of facts, and subsequent discovery of departures from auditing standards

Relevant Sections of Statements on Auditing Standards

AU 331 — Planning and Supervision

AU 312 — Audit Risk and Materiality in Conducting an Audit

AU 329 — Analytical Procedures

AU 333 — Client Representations

AU 337 — Inquiry of a Client's Lawyer Concerning Litigation, Claims, and Assessments

AU 341 — The Auditor's Consideration of an Entity's Ability to Continue as a Going Concern

AU 390 — Consideration of Omitted Procedures after the Report Date

AU 530 — Dating of the Independent Auditor's Report

AU 560 — Subsequent Events

AU 561 — Subsequent Discovery of Facts Existing at the Date of the Auditor's Report

This chapter explains the *general procedures* applied near the completion of field work and the review and evaluation procedures that are necessary before issuing an audit report on financial statements. Usually, the nature, timing, and extent of general procedures are influenced less by the client's circumstances than the audit procedures applied to specific account balances and transaction classes. For this reason, authoritative professional standards are relatively specific on the nature, timing, and extent of general procedures required near the completion of field work. The matters covered by the authoritative pronouncements relevant to general procedures covered in this chapter are as follows:

- SAS No. 1 (AU 560), "Subsequent Events," defines the types of subsequent events the auditor must evaluate and specifies the procedures that should be used to determine the occurrence of such events.
- SAS No. 12 (AU 337), "Inquiry of a Client's Lawyer Concerning Litigation, Claims, and Assessments," identifies the procedures to search for contingencies and establishes requirements for obtaining information from a client's lawyers.
- SAS No. 19 (AU 333), "Client Representations," requires that the auditor obtain certain written representations from management.
- SAS No. 22 (AU 311), "Planning and Supervision," establishes broad requirements for review of the work of assistants.
- SAS No. 47 (AU 312), "Audit Risk and Materiality in Conducting an Audit," establishes requirements on the evaluation of audit findings, including the analysis and aggregation of misstatements.
- SAS No. 56 (AU 329), "Analytical Procedures," establishes a requirement for the use of analytical procedures in the overall review stage of all audits, as well as in the planning stage.
- SAS No. 59 (AU 341), "The Auditor's Consideration of an Entity's Ability to Continue as a Going Concern," describes the auditor's responsibility for evaluating whether there is substantial doubt about the client's ability to continue as a going concern for a reasonable time period.

NATURE OF COMPLETION AND REVIEW PROCEDURES

Almost every audit engagement has a deadline for issuance of the audit report. For example, some engagements have a deadline for release of audited financial statements because of SEC filing requirements or securities offerings. Other engagements have a self-imposed deadline based on the audit plan, but there is usually some pressure for release of audited data. Thus, audit procedures need to be completed in time to allow for adequate review and evaluation of work papers and the financial statements before the opinion is signed.

Date of the Audit Report

The audit report should generally be dated as of the completion of field work. The date is important because it fixes the auditor's responsibility for knowledge of important events that should be reflected in the financial statements. The auditor cannot be responsible for knowledge of events that occur after field work is completed and the audit report signed.

When the auditor completes all significant audit procedures and leaves the client's premises, field work is completed. Usually, this will be the date of the final conference with the client's management to agree on the form and content of the financial statements. Before this conference the auditor must decide whether any material adjustments to the financial statements are necessary and whether the results of audit tests support an opinion on the financial statements.

The overall timing of an audit engagement is discussed in Chapter 5. The basic time segments are identified as follows:

- *Financial statement period*—the time period from the beginning of the period covered by the financial statements to the balance sheet date
- *Subsequent period*—the period from the balance sheet date to the date of completion of field work (This later date becomes the date of the audit report.)
- *Report preparation period*—the period from the date field work is completed, and the report signed and dated, to the date of issuance of the financial statements

Normally, a period of 2 to 3 weeks elapses from the date of the audit report to the date of delivery. This period is necessary for report typing, collation, and reproduction. The auditor has no responsibility to keep informed of events that occur during the report preparation period. However, management's responsibility for considering subsequent events extends to the date of issuance. Since management has firsthand knowledge of events in this period, management should inform the auditor of significant, relevant events that may occur.

Audit Procedures after Year-End

The audit procedures after the balance sheet date include a variety of activities. Many audit procedures may be performed after year-end as a normal part of direct tests of balances. Examples of such procedures are inspection of documents supporting transactions in the subsequent period to determine that proper cutoffs have been made and to test the valuation of assets. For example, the collectibility of receivables may be evaluated by reviewing cash collections after the balance sheet date. The search for unrecorded liabilities is another example of procedures applied to subsequent transactions.

If direct tests of balances, such as observation of the physical inventory are made at an interim date, the auditor must consider whether audit conclusions can be extended from that date to the date of the financial statements. The auditor will scan the activity in the account for large or unusual transactions, investigate significant intervening transactions, inquire about other changes that might affect the balance, and apply analytical procedures. These are sometimes called "roll-forward procedures."

Work papers are considered account by account to assure completion of the audit program, dispose of remaining exceptions and unusual matters, summarize the results of audit tests for evaluation, and in general prepare the work papers for the inspection of audit supervisors. Also, the auditor evaluates the results of the audit procedures, considering whether there is substantial doubt about the client's ability to continue as a going concern. This is discussed later in this chapter.

A review is made of the period after that covered by direct tests of balances to identify events which may need to be reflected in the financial statements. This review, called the subsequent events review, is explained in the next section. As part of the review, documentation is obtained of the representations of the client's management and legal counsel.

A final review and evaluation of the financial statements and work papers is made and a closing conference is held with the client's management before issuance of the audit report.

SUBSEQUENT EVENTS AND RELATED REVIEW PROCEDURES

Some specific audit procedures are necessary to provide reasonable assurance that the auditor is aware of significant events that occur after the date of the financial statements but before the date of the audit report. The length of the subsequent period will depend on the practical requirements of each engagement. It may be a period of a few weeks if there is a tight deadline for audited statements or it may be a few months if there are problems in closing the accounting records.

Subsequent Events Review

The audit procedures that are usually part of the subsequent events review are specified in SAS No. 1 (AU 560.12). They are summarized as follows:

1 Read all available significant information bearing on financial matters subsequent to year-end, such as interim financial statements and minutes of meetings of stockholders, directors, and appropriate committees.
2 Inquire of officers and financial executives about the existence of unusual adjustments, changes in significant components of financial statements, such as working capital, and other significant financial events.
3 Obtain formal letters of representation from client officers concerning the completeness and accuracy of financial matters, and from legal counsel concerning litigation, claims, and assessments.

In addition, the auditor may need to make further substantive tests to dispose of any questions or unusual matters disclosed by the review procedures.

Subsequent Events of Audit Interest

Two types of subsequent events may materially affect the financial statements and thus require consideration by management and evaluation by the auditor. One type of event requires adjustment of the financial statements, but the other requires disclosure only. The distinction between the two rests on both their nature and timing.

The first type of event that requires adjustment, according to SAS No. 1 (AU 560.03):

> ... consists of those events that provide additional evidence with respect to conditions that existed at the date of the balance sheet and affect the estimates inherent in the process of preparing financial statements. All information that becomes available prior to the issuance of the financial statements should be used by management in its evaluation of the conditions on which estimates were based. The financial statements should be adjusted for any changes in estimates resulting from the use of such evidence.

Note that the event must both affect an inherent estimate and relate to an existing condition. Thus, the auditor may need to investigate the circumstances of an event to determine whether it relates to a condition that existed at the balance sheet date. For example, estimation of uncollectible receivables is an inherent estimate, but a subsequent loss on an uncollectible account does not automatically lead to adjustment. According to SAS No. 1 (AU 560.04):

> . . . a loss on an uncollectible trade account receivable as a result of a customer's deteriorating financial condition leading to bankruptcy subsequent to the balance-sheet date would be indicative of conditions existing at the balance-sheet date, thereby calling for adjustment of the financial statements before their issuance. On the other hand, a similar loss resulting from a customer's major casualty such as a fire or flood subsequent to the balance-sheet date would not be indicative of conditions existing at the balance-sheet date and adjustment of the financial statements would not be appropriate. The settlement of litigation for an amount different from the liability recorded in the accounts would require adjustment of the financial statements if the events, such as personal injury or patent infringement, that gave rise to the litigation had taken place prior to the balance-sheet date.

If a subsequent event does not relate to a condition that existed at the balance sheet date, adjustment is not appropriate, but disclosure may be required. According to SAS No. 1 (AU 560.05):

> The second type consists of those events that provide evidence with respect to conditions that did not exist at the date of the balance sheet being reported on but arose subsequent to that date. These events should not result in adjustment of the financial statements.[1] Some of these events, however, may be of such a nature that disclosure of them is required to keep the financial statements from being misleading. Occasionally such an event may be so significant that disclosure can best be made by supplementing the historical financial statements with pro forma financial data giving effect to the event as if it had occurred on the date of the balance sheet. It may be desirable to present pro forma statements, usually a balance sheet only, in columnar form on the face of the historical statements.

For example, events that usually require disclosure, but that should not result in adjustment include:

1 Sale of bonds or capital stock
2 Purchase of a business
3 Loss of plant or inventories as a result of fire or flood

Sometimes an event that affects an inherent estimate may occur, but the auditor may not be able to determine whether it relates to a condition that existed at the balance sheet date. SAS No. 1 (AU 560.07) gives the following "nudge" toward adjustment:

> Subsequent events affecting the realization of assets such as receivables and inventories or the settlement of estimated liabilities ordinarily will require adjustment of the financial statements because such events typically represent the culmination of conditions that existed over a relatively long period of time. Subsequent events such as changes in the quoted market prices of securities ordinarily should not result in adjustment of the financial statements because such changes typically reflect a concurrent evaluation of new conditions.

---

[1]This paragraph is not intended to preclude giving effect in the balance sheet, with appropriate disclosure, to stock dividends or stock splits or reverse splits consummated after the balance sheet date but before issuance of the financial statements.

Figure 12-1 summarizes the types of subsequent events and the criteria for their treatment.

Subsequent Events and the Report Date

Ordinarily, the auditor has no responsibility to keep informed of subsequent events after the date of the report. However, a subsequent event may occur in the period between the date of the audit report and the time of issuance of the report. If the auditor becomes aware of the event, the auditor must consider whether it requires adjustment or disclosure and how the event should be covered in the audit report. This may occur before the original issuance or before reissuance. The auditor's alternatives for such events are:

1 *Dual date.* The event is covered in the audit report by including a new date applicable only to the subsequent event. For example, the date might read "February 25, 19X9, except as to the information in Note X for which the date is March 10, 19X9."

Category of subsequent event	Criteria for treatment of event	Example of events in subsequent period
Adjust (The auditor should propose an adjustment to the accounting records as of the balance sheet date.)	• Condition giving rise to the event existed at the balance sheet date. • Event affects an estimate inherent in the accounting process.	• A receivable becomes uncollectible because a customer goes bankrupt as a result of a gradually deteriorating financial condition. • Existing litigation settled unfavorably. • Legitimate claims under product warranties for goods sold during the period increase dramatically and unexpectedly.
Disclose (The auditor should insist on appropriate note disclosure or in some cases, a supplementary pro forma financial statement.)	• Condition giving rise to the event and the event are both after the balance sheet date. • Disclosure of the event is necessary to keep the financial statements from being misleading.	• A receivable becomes uncollectible because of a customer's bankruptcy caused by an uninsured fire in the subsequent period. • Bonds or capital stock are issued. • A significant subsidiary is disposed of or acquired. • An earthquake demolishes the company's main factory.

FIGURE 12-1
Subsequent events of audit interest.

2 *Extension of review.* The report is redated and review procedures are extended to the date of the event.

3 *Unaudited note.* The event is not covered by the audit report and the note is clearly labeled as unaudited information subsequent to the date of the audit report. (This option is available only for reissuance.)

The most common practice is dual dating. Generally, auditors are reluctant to use the new date and extend review procedures. Because of the auditor's significant responsibilities, the risks caused by the limited nature of review procedures often make redating unacceptable. If the additional time is relatively short, extension of review procedures may be acceptable. However, for events that require adjustment, dual dating is not feasible.

Reissuance of the Audit Report

An audit report may be reissued in any of the following circumstances:

- A client requests the auditor to furnish additional copies of a previously issued report.
- A client requests an auditor to permit inclusion of a previously issued audit report in a filing with the SEC or other regulatory agency.
- A successor auditor requests an auditor to permit the inclusion of the financial statements reported on by the auditor and the audit report in a comparative presentation with financial statements reported on by the successor.

In the first case, the auditor has no responsibility to make any further investigation or inquiry about events after the original report date. However, if the auditor is aware of material subsequent events, the events should be disclosed and, usually, the note disclosing the event will be marked "unaudited" and the original report date will be used.

In the case of filings, the auditor's responsibilities differ depending on the nature of the filing. In an annual SEC filing under the 1934 Act or any filing with another agency, the responsibility is as described above. In a filing of a registration statement under the 1933 Act, the auditor's responsibility for knowledge of subsequent events extends to the effective date of the registration statement and the review is extended.

In the case of inclusion of the audit report in a document containing financial statements examined by a successor auditor, the auditor should take the following steps before permitting inclusion:

- Read the financial statements of the current period.
- Compare the prior-period financial statements reported on with the financial statements for the same period to be reported on for comparative purposes.
- Obtain a letter of representation from the successor auditor that the successor is not aware of matters that materially affect the current form or manner of presentation of the financial statements of the prior period or any subsequent events that might make the predecessor's report inappropriate.

The auditor is never required to permit reissuance in any of the cases identified above. An auditor may decide to withhold permission because of considerations of business risk.

REPRESENTATION LETTERS

As part of the subsequent events review, the auditor obtains two types of formal representation letters—one from the client's management and one from its legal counsel. Normally, the letters should be dated as of the completion of field work. Since the inquiries documented in the letters may result in new information that will require investigation, the usual practice is to prepare the letters in draft form for review and discussion before the completion of field work. The formal letters are then signed and delivered at the audit report date or within a short period before the report date.

Legal Representation Letters

Litigation, claims, and assessments are contingencies that may require recognition of a loss or a gain, or disclosure in the financial statements. FASB Statement No. 5 (Current Text C59) specifies the criteria for recording and disclosing contingencies, including litigation, claims, and assessments. The auditor is concerned with obtaining evidence of the existence, completeness, valuation, and presentation of contingencies. Such matters may be disclosed by several general procedures usually performed during the audit, such as reading minutes of meetings of stockholders or directors and reading contracts and correspondence. However, the most direct search for legal contingencies involves a series of related inquiries of management and the client's legal counsel that are documented in a representation letter from legal counsel and in related written representations by the client's management.

In general, the auditor obtains information on the existence of litigation, claims, and assessments from management and attempts to substantiate the completeness of this information through legal counsel's representations. Since the auditor is not qualified to make legal judgments, the auditor also attempts to obtain evidence of the valuation of legal matters by inquiring as to the lawyer's opinion on their potential outcome.

However, in this exchange of information, lawyers are concerned with maintaining the attorney-client privilege and avoiding any admissions that might prejudice a client's position in litigation. Auditors maintain that the client in meeting financial reporting obligations has a duty to make adequate disclosure of contingencies, including litigation, claims, and assessments, and needs sound advice on such matters from legal counsel. Further, the auditor in meeting the obligation to obtain sufficient competent evidential matter to support an opinion on the client's financial statements needs reliable evidence of the client's litigation and related matters.

The resolution of these conflicting interests has resulted in an involved process that attempts to distinguish: (1) the existence of litigation, (2) the existence of potential unasserted claims, and (3) evaluation of the outcome of identified litigation and claims.

Inquiry of Management   The process starts with inquiry of management to determine the policies and procedures it uses to identify and evaluate legal matters and to obtain a description and evaluation of such matters. According to SAS No. 12 (AU 337.05) the auditor should:

obtain from management a description and evaluation of litigation, claims, and assessments that existed at the date of the balance sheet being reported on, and during the period from the balance sheet date to the date the information is furnished, including an identification of those matters referred to legal counsel, and obtain assurances from management, ordinarily in writing, that they have disclosed all such matters required to be disclosed by Statement of Financial Accounting Standards No. 5.

Inquiry of Legal Counsel   The next step is to request the client's management to send a letter of inquiry to those lawyers with whom it consulted concerning litigation, claims, and assessments. The legal inquiry letter ordinarily lists management's description and evaluation of *pending or threatened* litigation, claims, and assessments and requests the lawyer to state whether the list is complete and comment on any matters on which the lawyer has a different view from management. However, the letter may ask the lawyer to list and describe these matters.

The inquiry letter also includes a separate list of management's description and evaluation of *unasserted* claims and assessments, if any, that FASB Statement No. 5 (Current Text C59) requires be disclosed. Usually, management simply states there are none.

The auditor is interested in unasserted claims that management considers to be probable of assertion and that, if asserted, would have at least a reasonable possibility of an unfavorable outcome. For example, the crash of an airliner will predictably result in claims against the airline. The lawyer is asked to comment on differences of view with management about items on the list but not on the completeness of the list, because of concerns about the privileged status of the information. Instead, the auditor's assurance on completeness is obtained from a process based on notice to the lawyer and reliance on the lawyer's ethical obligations.

Notice to the lawyer involves an understanding stated in the inquiry letter and related client representations. The inquiry letter, according to SAS No. 12 (AU 337.09) should include:

> a statement by the client that the client understands that, whenever, in the course of performing legal services for the client with respect to a matter recognized to involve an unasserted possible claim or assessment that may call for financial statement disclosure, the lawyer has formed a professional conclusion that the client should disclose or consider disclosure concerning such possible claim or assessment, the lawyer, as a matter of professional responsibility to the client, will so advise the client and will consult with the client concerning the question of such disclosure and the applicable requirements of Statement of Financial Accounting Standards No. 5.

The lawyer is also asked in the inquiry letter to confirm this understanding as correct. In doing so, the lawyer affirms a professional responsibility to advise the client of unasserted claims that should be disclosed.

The notice to the lawyer is completed by obtaining assurance from management on the completeness of its lists of unasserted claims and informing the lawyer that management has given this assurance. According to SAS No. 12 (AU 337.05) the auditor should:

> obtain assurance from management, ordinarily in writing, that they have disclosed all unasserted claims that the lawyer has advised them are probable of assertion and must be

disclosed in accordance with Statement of Financial Accounting Standards No. 5. Also, the auditor, with the client's permission, should inform the lawyer that the client has given the auditor this assurance. This client representation may be communicated by the client in the inquiry letter or by the auditor in a separate letter.

Thus, the auditor obtains the lawyer's acknowledgment of a duty to inform the client of its disclosure obligations for unasserted claims and notifies the lawyer of those claims, if any, that management proposes to disclose. Presumably, if management is not meeting its disclosure obligations, the lawyer either will persuade management to make appropriate disclosure or will resign. The lawyer's resignation would put the auditor on notice of the possibility of inadequate disclosure. An illustrative audit inquiry letter to legal counsel is shown in Figure 12-2.

Lawyer's Response   The lawyer's response to such an inquiry is the legal representation letter. The response can be long and complex and requires careful evaluation by the auditor. SAS No. 12 (AU 337) is a comprehensive document of over 30 pages, and over half those pages contain a reprint of the American Bar Association's statement of policy on lawyers' responses to auditors' requests for information.

The lawyer's response may be appropriately limited to matters to which the lawyer has given substantive attention in the form of legal consultation or representation and to matters that are material if an understanding has been reached with the auditor on the limits of materiality. Also, a lawyer is often unable to form a judgment on the outcome of litigation, and the auditor must conclude that an uncertainty exists. However, if a lawyer *refuses* to furnish the information requested, there is a limitation on the scope of the audit sufficient to preclude an unqualified opinion.

Client Representation Letters

Obtaining written representations from client management was a customary auditing procedure that became a requirement of professional standards when SAS No. 19, "Client Representations," was issued. An auditor must obtain written representations from management. SAS No. 19 (AU 333.01) states:

> This section establishes a requirement that the independent auditor obtain written representations from management as part of an audit performed in accordance with generally accepted auditing standards. . . .

Purpose of Client Representation Letter   Obtaining a representation letter from the client's management serves two primary purposes. First, the inquiry procedure is formalized by putting in writing the replies to inquiries made by the auditor during the audit. For example, in the examination of inventory the auditor will ask a great many questions concerning such things as pricing methods and the existence of consigned merchandise. The representation letter is a record which is placed in the work papers to indicate that such questions have been answered. Second, the responsibility for the financial statements is clarified to management, and the client is reminded that the primary responsibility for the correctness of the statements remains with the client. In some cases, the

(Client's Letterhead)

February 18, 19X9

Black & Bag, Attorneys
16 Main Street
Houston, Texas

Gentlemen:

Our independent auditors, Johnson & Hinsey, CPAs (1217 Avenue of the Americas, New York, New York) are making an audit of our financial statements for the year ended December 31, 19X8. We have prepared and furnished to them a description and evaluation of certain contingencies, including those attached, involving matters with respect to which you have been engaged and to which you have devoted substantive attention on our behalf in the form of legal consultation or representation. These contingencies are regarded by us as material for this purpose. Your response should include matters that existed at December 31, 19X8, and during the period from that date to the date of your response.

Please furnish to our auditors such explanation, if any, that you consider necessary to supplement the attached list of pending or threatened litigation, including an explanation of those matters as to which your views may differ from those stated and an identification of the omission of any pending or threatened litigation, claims, and assessments or a statement that the list of such matters is complete.

We have informed our auditors that there are no unasserted possible claims that you have advised are probable of assertion and must be disclosed in accordance with Statement of Financial Accounting Standards No. 5 in our financial statements for the year ended December 31, 19X8.

We understand that whenever, in the course of performing legal services for us with respect to a matter recognized to involve an unasserted possible claim or assessment that may call for financial statement disclosure, if you have formed a professional conclusion that we should disclose or consider disclosure concerning such a possible claim or assessment, as a matter of professional responsibility to us, you will so advise us and will consult with us concerning the question of such disclosure and the applicable requirements of Statement of Financial Accounting Standards No. 5. Please specifically confirm to our auditors that our understanding is correct.

Please specifically identify the nature of and reasons for any limitation on your response.

Your very truly
Billings Corporation

E. M. Silver, President

FIGURE 12-2
Illustration of a letter of audit inquiry to legal counsel.

client's management is aware of important matters such as contingent liabilities but does not realize the importance of disclosing them in the financial statements. The representation letter draws attention to such items and avoids misunderstandings.

These written representations do not relieve the auditor from gathering adequate evidence about the items covered. Management representations complement other audit procedures but are not a substitute for them.

Although representation letters are signed by the client's management, they are normally prepared by the auditor and then submitted for signing. The letters may cover specific subjects like inventories and liabilities, or they may be comprehensive, covering nearly all items in the financial statements. A comprehensive letter is normally signed by a top executive officer and a top financial officer of the client. When separate letters are obtained for specific items, the company official responsible for the particular item is asked to sign. An example of a comprehensive representation letter is shown in Figure 12-3 (see pages 512-513).

Normal Content of a Representation Letter   According to SAS No. 19 (AU 333) on client representations, the auditor should ordinarily obtain written representations from the client on the following matters:

   I Management's acknowledgement of responsibility for the financial statements and assurance of the availability and completeness of information furnished to the auditor, such as:
      A Accounting records and related data, including the absence of unrecorded transactions and similar irregularities
      B Minutes of meetings of stockholders and directors
   II Assurance of the completeness of particular types of data to which auditing procedures are applied, such as information on:
      A Subsequent events
      B Related-party transactions
      C Irregularities involving management or employees
      D Noncompliance with contractual agreements, financial reporting practices required by regulatory agencies, and other laws or regulations that should be considered for disclosure
      E Liabilities, contingencies, and unasserted claims or assessments that should be accrued or disclosed
   III Information on matters that affect the valuation or presentation of specific financial statement items, such as:
      A Plans or intentions that may affect the valuation or classification of assets or liabilities
      B Compensating balance arrangements
      C Losses from sales or purchase commitments
      D Reduction of inventories to net realizable value
      E Satisfactory title to assets, liens on assets, and assets pledged as collateral
      F Asset repurchase agreements
      G Capital stock option, warrant, and conversion agreements

Importance of Obtaining Client Representations   The importance of obtaining a client's representations is emphasized by the fact that inability to obtain appropriate written representations prevents an auditor from expressing an unqualified opinion. According to SAS No. 19 (AU 333.11):

Management's refusal to furnish written representations constitutes a limitation on the scope of the audit sufficient to preclude an unqualified opinion.

Some clients mistakenly believe that the auditor is shirking responsibility by insisting on the representations ordinarily included in a client representation letter. However, the auditor is only seeking assurance that the client has not withheld important information. The purpose of the letter has to be tactfully explained without implying that the auditor suspects management is dishonest. If the auditor has serious cause to doubt management's integrity, merely obtaining a letter cannot cure the problem.

REVIEW OF WORK PAPERS AND FINANCIAL STATEMENTS

There is a continuous review of work papers and evaluation of the results of audit tests as the audit progresses. Planning and supervision should continue throughout the engagement. As each major step in the audit is completed, the auditor's understanding of the support for the financial statements grows, and modifications are made of audit procedures as the results of audit tests either confirm or call into question the auditor's earlier understanding. The reviews of work papers and financial statements made at the end of the engagement are a final check to help ensure that all significant matters and problems have been identified, considered, and satisfactorily resolved. Although one phase of the final review blends into the next, for purposes of discussion it can be divided into (1) summarization and evaluation of audit results, (2) evaluation of going concern status, (3) financial statement review, and (4) administrative completion of work papers. Evaluation of the client's ability to continue as a going concern for a reasonable time period is part of summarization and evaluation of audit results. It is discussed under a separate heading because of its importance.

Summarization and Evaluation of Audit Results

As the audit tests for each item in the financial statements are completed, the staff auditor doing the work will sign off completion of steps in the audit program, identify monetary misstatements in the financial statements, and propose adjustments to the financial statements. This work will be reviewed by the audit senior.

Monetary misstatements are misstatements that cause a distortion of the financial statements. The distortion may be a misstatement of net income or net assets or an error in classification. *Classification misstatements* are misstatements of components of the financial statements, such as current assets or income before extraordinary items, with no misstatement of net amounts. Monetary misstatements may result from mistakes in processing transactions, such as mistakes in quantities, prices, or computations, mistakes in the selection or application of accounting principles, and mistakes in facts or judgments about accounting estimates. Monetary misstatements may be accidental, a matter of differences of opinion, or deliberate misrepresentations.

The cause of misstatements must be considered and the implications determined for earlier decisions about the reliability of accounting records and internal control structure and the extent of audit tests. An important part of the review is an evaluation of whether audit procedures were adequate in light of the results of audit tests. This evaluation is usually made by the senior and reviewed by the manager.

(Client's Letterhead)

February 18, 19X9

Johnson & Hinsey, CPAs
1217 Avenue of the Americas
New York, New York

Gentlemen:

In connection with your audit of the financial statements for the year ended December 31, 19X8, for the purpose of expressing an opinion as to whether the financial statements present fairly the financial position, results of operations, and cash flows of Billings Corporation in conformity with generally accepted accounting principles, we confirm, to the best of our knowledge and belief, the following representations made to you during your audit.

1. We are responsible for the fair presentation in the financial statements of financial position, results of operations, and cash flows in conformity with generally accepted accounting principles.

2. We have made available to you all:
   a. Financial records and related data.
   b. Minutes of the meetings of stockholders, directors, and committees of directors, or summaries of actions of recent meetings for which minutes have not yet been prepared.

3. There have been no:
   a. Irregularities involving management or employees who have significant roles in the internal control structure.
   b. Irregularities involving other employees that could have a material effect on the financial statements.
   c. Communications from regulatory agencies concerning noncompliance with, or deficiencies in, financial reporting practices that could have a material effect on the financial statements.

4. We have no plans or intentions that may materially affect the carrying value or classification of assets and liabilities.

5. The following have been properly recorded or disclosed in the financial statements:
   a. Related-party transactions and related amounts receivable or payable, including sales, purchases, loans, transfers, leasing arrangements, and guarantees.
   b. Capital stock repurchase options or agreements or capital stock reserved for options, warrants, conversions, or other requirements.
   c. Arrangements with financial institutions involving compensating balances or other arrangements involving restrictions on cash balances and line-of-credit or similar agreements.
   d. Agreements to repurchase assets previously sold.

6. There are no:
   a. Violations or possible violations of laws or regulations whose effects should be considered for disclosure in the financial statements or as a basis for recording a loss contingency.
   b. Other material liabilities or gain or loss contingencies that are required to be accrued or disclosed by Statement of Financial Accounting Standards No. 5.

FIGURE 12-3
Illustration of a client representation letter.

7. There are no unasserted claims or assessments that our lawyer has advised us are probable of assertion and must be disclosed in accordance with Statement of Financial Accounting Standards No. 5.

8. There are no material transactions that have not been properly recorded in the accounting records underlying the financial statements.

9. Provision, when material, has been made to reduce excess or obsolete inventories to their estimated net realizable value.

10. The company has satisfactory title to all owned assets, and there are no liens or encumbrances on such assets nor has any asset been pledged.

11. Provision has been made for any material loss to be sustained in the fulfillment of, or from inability to fulfill, any sales commitments.

12. Provision has been made for any material loss to be sustained as a result of purchase commitments for inventory quantities in excess of normal requirements or at prices in excess of the prevailing market prices.

13. We have complied with all aspects of contractual agreements that would have a material effect on the financial statements in the event of noncompliance.

14. No events have occurred subsequent to the balance sheet date that would require adjustment to, or disclosure in, the financial statements.

_____
E. M. Silver, President

_____
T. Aranoff, Controller

FIGURE 12-3 *(concluded)*

Summarization of Monetary Misstatements Usually, the only practical way to consider whether the financial statements are materially misstated at the conclusion of the audit is to use a worksheet that determines the combined effect of *uncorrected* misstatement on important totals or subtotals in the financial statements.

As explained in Chapter 7, the broad categories of misstatement that need to be combined and compared with the amount considered material to the financial statements taken as a whole are as follows:

- *Known misstatement*—the amount of misstatement specifically identified by the auditor as a result of applying audit procedures to items examined
- *Likely misstatement*—the auditor's best estimate of misstatement based on an extrapolation or projection of misstatements detected in sampling applications
- *Allowance for undetected misstatement*—the auditor's allowance for potential misstatement that remains undetected after applying audit procedures

Known and likely misstatement would be determined for each account balance included in the financial statements. The allowance for undetected misstatement, as explained in Chapters 7 and 8, applies to the financial statements taken as a whole.

The known and likely misstatement component of audit results includes the following matters that are considered by the auditor:

- *Items examined 100 percent.* For audit procedures applied without using audit sampling, any misstatement detected is known misstatement. For example, the auditor examines all additions to property and equipment over $5,000 and detects a net overstatement of $10,000. The $10,000 is known misstatement and the amount is combined with other misstatement.
- *Accounting estimates.* Differences between any estimated amounts in the financial statements that the auditor considers unreasonable and the closest reasonable estimate are considered to be misstatements. For example, the client estimates that $10,000 of accounts receivable will be uncollectible. The auditor believes a reasonable estimate would be between $12,000 and $15,000. The difference between the client's estimate and the closest reasonable estimate is $2,000, and this amount is combined with other misstatement.
- *Prior-period misstatement.* Uncorrected prior-period misstatements that affect the current period's financial statements should be combined with other misstatement. This may be a difficult judgment because the accounting treatment of prior-period misstatements can be unclear. Essentially the auditor needs to be concerned about misstatements that are not self-reversing that may accumulate to a material amount in the balance sheet and self-reversing misstatements that combine with current misstatements to increase misstatement. For example, an overstatement of the ending inventory combined with an understatement of the beginning inventory will both overstate current income. Separately each misstatement may be immaterial, but the combined effect may be a material misstatement.

The auditor's aggregation of misstatement should include known misstatements that are immaterial when considered separately for individual account balances. Only when the combined effect of misstatements is considered can the auditor evaluate whether the financial statements taken as a whole are materially misstated. However, in practice, auditors often identify an amount for trivial misstatements, say $25, and misstatements less than that amount are not accumulated as the audit progresses.

Evaluation of Monetary Misstatements   As explained in Chapter 7, the consideration of materiality in planning is for practical reasons *quantitative*. The auditor's responsibility in evaluating audit findings at the conclusion of the engagement is explained in SAS No. 47 (AU 312.27) as follows:

In evaluating whether the financial statements are presented fairly, in all material respects, in conformity with generally accepted accounting principles, the auditor should aggregate misstatements that the entity has not corrected in a way that enables him to consider whether, in relation to individual amounts, subtotals, or totals in the financial statements, they materially misstate the financial statements taken as a whole. Qualitative considerations also influence an auditor in reaching a conclusion as to whether misstatements are material.

Thus, in evaluating whether the financial statements taken as whole may be materially misstated, the auditor considers both quantitative and *qualitative* factors.

- A small misstatement that affects working capital might be material if correcting it caused noncompliance with a requirement of a debt agreement.
- An illegal payment of an otherwise immaterial amount could be material if it could lead to a material contingent liability.
- Inadequate disclosure of some matters, such as related-party transactions or violation of statutes or regulatory requirements, might be considered material even though the amounts involved were quantitatively immaterial.

Whether a matter is qualitatively material is always very dependent on the circumstances, so these examples are not matters that are invariably material.

A Work Paper Example   SAS No. 47 (AU 312) does not specify a work paper approach for combining misstatements. Any approach that determines the combined effect on important financial statement totals and subtotals is appropriate.

One possible approach is to use two worksheets (as illustrated in Figure 12-4) for aggregating misstatements and considering further misstatement that could remain undetected. *Worksheet A* is used to summarize the results of sampling applications. *Worksheet B* is used to combine the net result of sampling applications with the results of audit tests that do not use sampling.

Possible columns for both worksheets are (1) description, (2) assets, (3) liabilities, (4) equity, and (5) earnings. These worksheets, of course, could be expanded to include more columns for other subtotals in the financial statements.

Worksheet A summarizes (1) projected misstatement, (2) the basic allowance for undetected misstatement, and (3) additional imprecision (explained in Chapter 8). Worksheet B summarizes (1) misstatements in items examined on a 100 percent basis, (2) misstatements in accounting estimates, (3) the total from worksheet A, and (4) the reversal for misstatements that are corrected by the client.

On worksheet A all projected misstatements in populations sampled are posted in a journal-entry format that would be required to correct the projected misstatement. Each column is subtotaled. The basic allowance for undetected misstatement (tolerable misstatement) used in determining sample sizes is listed in each column once, with the same sign as the total of projected misstatements. Also, the additional imprecision is added by calculating the increase in imprecision caused by detecting misstatements, as explained in Chapter 8.

Worksheet A is totaled and the total is transferred to worksheet B, where the auditor has also posted amounts in journal-entry format to correct misstatements in items

Worksheet A
EZS Company
12/31/X4
Debit (Credit)

Description	Assets	Liabilities	Equity	Earnings
a Debit cost of goods sold				$6,112
Credit inventory	$ (6,112)			
	(6,112)	–0–	–0–	6,112
b Basic allowance	(75,000)	$75,000	$75,000	75,000
c Additional imprecision	(11,250)			11,250
	$(92,362)	$75,000	$75,000	$92,362

Notes:
  a This entry corrects a projected inventory overstatement.
  b The basic allowance was used in determining sample sizes.
  c The additional imprecision was calculated by multiplying 0.15 by 75,000. The 0.15 factor was obtained from the table in Chapter 8. To use that table, the auditor calculates the percentage of projected misstatement to the basic allowance ($6,112/$75,000 = 0.08). Tracing down the left column to the next greater percentage of projected misstatement to the basic allowance, the auditor finds 0.20. Tracing across the table, the auditor obtains the corresponding factor of 0.15.

FIGURE 12-4

Illustration of a work paper format for summarizing and evaluating misstatements. [*Adapted from W. Wade Gafford and D. R. Carmichael, "Materiality, Audit Risk and Sampling: A Nuts-and-Bolts Approach (Part Two)," The Journal of Accountancy, November 1984, pp. 125–138.*]

examined 100 percent and misstatements in accounting estimates. The reversal of adjustments recorded by the client are also posted to the worksheet. Worksheet B is totaled in each column and compared to an appropriate amount for each column that the auditor considers material to that column. Because the auditor will plan the engagement for the smallest materiality level, some column totals may be significantly less than materiality for that column and some totals may approach or exceed materiality. If any column total exceeds materiality for that column by more than a small amount (say, 10 percent), the auditor should determine the most effective method of resolving the problem. The auditor may:

- Persuade the client to correct more of the known misstatements in the financial statements so that they may be deducted from the total on the worksheet
- Perform additional procedures to reduce the basic allowance for undetected misstatement
- Ask the client to record projected misstatement for those applications for which the auditor has been able to obtain a good understanding of the cause of misstatements (If the cause of misstatement seems to be random, however, the projected misstatement should not be used for adjustment purposes unless sample size is significantly increased—say two to three times normal.)
- Identify specific sampling applications with relatively large projected misstatement and ask the client to reprocess the items and select a new sample, or subdivide the

Worksheet B
EZS Company
12/31/X4
Debit (Credit)

Description	Assets	Liabilities	Equity	Earnings
a Misstatements discovered				
Debit cost of goods sold				$ 10,000
Credit allowance for inventory obsolescence	$(10,000)			
Debit cost of goods sold				30,000
Credit allowance for bad debts	(30,000)			
b Reversal of above adjustments recorded by client				
Debit allowance for bad debts	30,000			
Credit cost of goods sold				(30,000)
Subtotal	(10,000)	–0–	–0–	10,000
Worksheet A total	(92,362)	75,000	75,000	92,362
	$(102,362)	$75,000	$75,000	$102,362
c Materiality judgment	$ 175,000	$175,000	$250,000	$115,000

Notes:
a Correcting entries for misstatements discovered in accounting estimates and items examined on a 100% basis are recorded here.
b Correcting entries have been reversed for those adjustments that were recorded by the client.
c The auditor has decided that the judgment about materiality for evaluation has not changed from the planning judgment. The initial judgment of $115,000 is the smallest materiality level and that materiality amount relates to earnings. The auditor has decided that $175,000 reflects the judgment about materiality in relation to assets or liabilities, which is moderately greater than materiality for earnings. The auditor has also decided that materiality for equity (principally considered the threshold for recording prior-period adjustments) is $250,000. This reflects an amount that is significantly greater than materiality for earnings or assets or liabilities. The auditor believes this appropriately reflects a large threshold before requiring prior-period adjustments to be recorded. It does not reflect how the auditor may judge prior-period adjustments that affect earnings of a prior presented period.

FIGURE 12-4 *(concluded)*

population based on a qualitative evaluation of the items most likely to be misstated and examine all such items

If the auditor believes the financial statements are materially misstated after evaluation of audit results, the auditor cannot express an unqualified opinion. When this occurs, a conference is held with the client before the auditor reaches a final conclusion.

The auditor will attempt to persuade the client's management of the need for adjustment, and management will usually attempt to have adjustments waived as immaterial. Management may be able to supply information or raise points the auditor has not considered. However, if the auditor believes that financial statements are misstated by a material amount, the auditor will not issue an unqualified opinion. Such modifications of the audit report are considered in Chapter 13.

Evaluation of Going Concern Status

The auditor's responsibilities for evaluating whether there is substantial doubt about the client's ability to continue as a going concern for a reasonable period were discussed in Chapter 5's discussion of general planning. The auditor is not required to design audit procedures with the sole purpose of evaluating going concern status. Statement on Auditing Standards No. 59 (AU 341) requires that the auditor consider going concern status by evaluating the results of audit procedures designed and performed for other audit objectives.

The auditor makes an overall evaluation of going concern status near the end of the audit because his or her subsequent events review, inquiry of legal counsel, and analytical procedures and final reviews of work papers and financial statements are procedures that may provide evidence of going concern problems. SAS No. 59 (AU 341.06) lists examples of conditions the auditor should consider in the evaluation:

- *Negative trends*—for example, recurring operating losses, working capital deficiencies, negative cash flows from operating activities, and adverse key financial ratios
- *Other indications of possible financial difficulties*—for example, default on loan or similar agreements, arrearages in dividends, denial of usual trade credit from suppliers, restructuring of debt, noncompliance with statutory capital requirements, need to seek new sources or methods of financing or to dispose of substantial assets
- *Internal matters*—for example, work stoppages or other labor difficulties, substantial dependence on the success of a particular project, uneconomic long-term commitments, need to significantly revise operations
- *External matters*—for example, legal proceedings, legislation, or similar matters that might jeopardize an entity's ability to operate; loss of a key franchise, license, or patent; loss of a principal customer or supplier; uninsured or underinsured catastrophe such as a drought, earthquake, or flood

If the auditor believes there is substantial doubt about the client's ability to continue as a going concern for a reasonable period of time (not to exceed 1 year after the balance sheet date), the auditor should set up a meeting with client management. The auditor should inquire about management's plans for dealing with the adverse conditions and events, including such matters as:

- Plans to dispose of assets
- Restrictions on disposal of assets, such as covenants limiting such transactions in loan or similar agreements or encumbrances against assets
- Apparent marketability of assets that management plans to sell

- Possible direct or indirect effects of disposal of assets
- Plans to borrow money or restructure debt
- Availability of debt financing, including existing or committed credit arrangements, such as lines of credit or arrangements for factoring receivables or sale-leaseback of assets
- Existing or committed arrangements to restructure or subordinate debt or to guarantee loans to the entity
- Possible effects on management's borrowing plans of existing restrictions on additional borrowing or the sufficiency of available collateral
- Plans to reduce or delay expenditures
- Apparent feasibility of plans to reduce overhead or administrative expenditures, to postpone maintenance or research and development projects, or to lease rather than purchase assets
- Possible direct or indirect effects of reduced or delayed expenditures
- Plans to increase ownership equity
- Apparent feasibility of plans to increase ownership equity, including existing or committed arrangements to raise additional capital
- Existing or committed arrangements to reduce current dividend requirements or to accelerate cash distributions from affiliates or other investors

The auditor considers the adequacy of the support for the plans and decides whether the plans will mitigate the adverse effect for a reasonable period of time. If the auditor continues to believe that substantial doubt remains about the client's going concern status, the auditor considers the adequacy of disclosure and the effect on the audit report. When there is substantial doubt, the auditor needs to add a fourth explanatory paragraph to the standard report. These reporting issues are discussed in Chapter 13.

Financial Statement Review and Analytical Procedures

The final review of the financial statements and the final review of the work papers are closely related, and some parts are done simultaneously. For example, when the work paper for an item in the financial statements is completed, the related financial statement presentation and disclosure are usually considered. Information for the notes to financial statements is usually tested along with related amounts in the financial statements. For example, the note disclosing inventory components will be considered as part of direct tests of inventory balances.

Some CPA firms follow the practice of requiring the staff auditor to include the financial statement presentation and related note in the work paper completed for a financial statement item and to express an opinion on the presentation and disclosure. However, a separate schedule is usually prepared to collect financial statement disclosures for review.

Preparation of the financial statements and the related disclosures is technically the client's responsibility. Usually, the financial statements are the result of continuous consultation between the client and the auditor. The auditor's advice and assistance are sought because the auditor is an expert in accounting matters. For example, the auditor usually assists in wording notes to financial statements or drafts the notes.

The extent of the auditor's involvement depends on the size and competence of the client's accounting staff. For smaller clients, the auditor may provide substantial assistance. However, the decisions necessary to prepare financial statements are the client's responsibility. The auditor needs to be sure that the client has made informed judgments about the selection and application of accounting principles when the auditor is involved in financial statement preparation. The auditor's role is to make an objective appraisal of management's judgments, not to replace management's judgment.

During the final review of the financial statements and notes, the auditor considers whether there are any unusual or unexpected balances or relationships and the adequacy of the evidence gathered in response to them. If the unusual or unexpected balances were not noted before the final review, or if the auditor believes the evidence gathered about the previously noted unusual items is not sufficient, additional audit work may be needed. For example, if sales declined substantially while inventory increased, the auditor would consider whether or not sufficient evidence had been gathered to conclude that inventory was not materially overstated.

SAS No. 56 (AU 329) requires the use of analytical procedures in this stage of the audit, but leaves the selection of those procedures to the auditor's judgment. No specific ratios or comparisons are required.

The final review of the financial statements also includes a review of a draft of the audit report that will accompany the statements.

Administrative Completion of Work Papers

The primary purpose of the review of work papers is to assure that the audit of the financial statements is complete and adequately documented. Documentation is important because the quality of the audit may be challenged in litigation or peer review, and the work papers will be used in planning future audits.

A review can be complex and difficult, and CPA firms attempt to assist reviewers by preparing review forms and checklists to assure completeness and to document the review procedures. An excerpt from a financial reporting checklist is shown in Figure 12-5.

As the work papers on the engagement are reviewed, the reviewers systematically file and index them and determine which work papers may be discarded so that the work paper file does not include review notes or open items that were resolved. A separate, permanent work paper file is maintained of material of continuing interest, such as excerpts of important contracts.

The manager on the engagement usually has supervisory responsibility for the review. The partner makes an independent review and may seek the consultation of specialists for particularly complex or sensitive problems. Many CPA firms have some form of additional independent review by someone not associated with the engagement, but the nature and extent of it vary. A second partner may make the review, or there may be a separate review department with no direct client responsibilities. The review may be confined

II. FINANCIAL STATEMENT PRESENTATION

A. GENERAL	YES	NO	N/A
1. Is a description of all significant accounting policies of the reporting entity included with the financial statements?	☐	☐	☐
2. Do the financial statements or auditor's report clearly indicate the nature of the organization reported upon? If the entity is a trust, association, partnership, proprietorship, or nonprofit corporation, this should be described in a note or on the face of the statements.	☐	☐	☐
3. Do notes for proprietorship or partnership statements indicate that the statements only include items relating to the business of the proprietorship or partnership?	☐	☐	☐
4. Is the exact legal name of the reporting entity used?	☐	☐	☐
5. Have events subsequent to the balance sheet date been considered as to their effect on the financial statements or auditor's report?	☐	☐	☐

FIGURE 12-5
Excerpts from a financial reporting checklist.

to the financial statements and the audit report or it may be a "cold look" at the entire audit.

AFTER THE AUDIT

After the completion of the audit and review of work papers, several administrative and technical details remain. There may be special reports to be prepared and SEC forms or tax returns to be filed. Also, the time spent on the audit must be summarized, variances from budget analyzed, and bills for fees prepared. Then planning will begin for the next year's audit.

Some additional activities that may take place after the audit and that are important for an understanding of the auditor's responsibilities are described in the following discussion.

Maintaining Quality of Audit Practice

The policies and procedures that CPA firms may adopt to maintain the quality of practice are discussed in Chapter 2. One of the elements of quality control identified is inspection to assure that other quality controls are being observed in practice. An important aspect of inspection is a form of self-audit. Teams of auditors are organized to inspect practices in other offices of multioffice firms. These teams review the work papers, financial statements, and audit reports in selected engagements.

A related practice is inspection reviews by teams from outside a CPA firm. As explained in Chapter 2, the AICPA and state societies have developed peer review programs, and the SEC has required peer reviews in consent decrees obtained in injunction actions. Peer reviews can be made by a specially assembled team of CPAs or by another CPA firm. In 1988, the AICPA membership adopted a requirement for mandatory quality review of members in public practice.

Subsequent Discovery of Facts

The auditor may, after the audit, become aware of facts that existed at the date of the audit report and that might have affected the report had the auditor been aware of those facts. The subsequent discovery of facts that existed at the report date should be distinguished from events that occur after the audit report has been issued. Generally, the auditor has no responsibility to keep informed of subsequent events after the issuance of the audit report. However, there is a responsibility if the auditor becomes aware of a fact that existed at the date of the report. The auditor must first investigate the information to determine whether it is reliable. According to SAS No. 1 (AU 561.05-.06):

> When the subsequently discovered information is found both to be reliable and to have existed at the date of the auditor's report, the auditor should take action in accordance with the procedures set out in subsequent paragraphs if the nature and effect of the matter are such that (a) his report would have been affected if the information had been known to him at the date of his report and had not been reflected in the financial statements and (b) he believes there are persons currently relying or likely to rely on the financial statements who would attach importance to the information. With respect to (b), consideration should be given, among other things, to the time elapsed since the financial statements were issued.
>
> When the auditor has concluded, after considering (a) and (b), that action should be taken to prevent future reliance on his report, he should advise his client to make appropriate disclosure of the newly discovered facts and their impact on the financial statements to persons who are known to be currently relying or who are likely to rely on the financial statements and the related auditor's report. When the client undertakes to make appropriate disclosure, the method used and the disclosure made will depend on the circumstances.

If the client refuses to make the necessary disclosures, the auditor should notify the board of directors that in the absence of disclosure by the client the auditor will take steps to prevent future reliance on the report.

Subsequent Discovery of Omitted Procedures

If the auditor subsequently discovers that important audit procedures were omitted in an audit of financial statements, then SAS No. 46 (AU 390) applies. In contrast, SAS No. 1 (AU 561) provides guidance when the auditor becomes aware, subsequent to the date of the report on the audited financial statements, that facts may have existed at that date which might have affected the report had the auditor been aware of them. The "facts" relate to the financial statements and whether those financial statements are presented fairly in conformity with generally accepted accounting principles.

SAS No. 46 (AU 390) applies to the possible omission of auditing procedures. However, when omitted auditing procedures are applied, the auditor may become aware that facts may have existed at the date of the auditor's report and might have affected the report had the auditor been aware of those facts. In that situation, AU 561 becomes relevant. If the auditor decides that a situation involving an omitted procedure exists, he or she should determine if the omitted procedure currently affects the auditor's ability to support the previously expressed opinion.

The auditor should promptly attempt to apply the omitted procedure or alternative procedures that would provide a satisfactory basis for the original opinion on the financial statements if he or she:

1 Decides that the omitted procedure impairs his or her present ability to support the previously expressed opinion
2 Believes that there are persons currently relying or likely to rely on the financial statements and the related auditor's report

If the auditor is unable to apply the omitted procedure or appropriate alternative procedures, the auditor should consult his or her attorney to determine the proper action concerning the auditor's responsibility to:

1 The client
2 Regulatory authorities having jurisdiction over the client
3 Persons relying or likely to rely on the auditor's report

The issuance of SAS No. 46 (AU 390) is an indirect result of the development of peer review and quality control standards. An auditor is not required to carry out retrospective review of work once a report has been issued on audited financial statements. Work papers are reviewed, however, in connection with peer reviews and in-house inspections. These reviews may reveal the omission of necessary auditing procedures.

The initial stimulus for SAS No. 46 (AU 390) resulted from peer reviews of members of the AICPA Division for Firms and the oversight program on peer reviews of the Public Oversight Board (POB). The Division for Firms and the POB are described in Chapter 2. The POB informed the institute of its concern that when reviewers concluded that an audit had not been conducted in accordance with generally accepted auditing standards, auditors had no guidance on the appropriate action in these circumstances. The POB recommended that the proper standard-setting body issue guidance on what a CPA firm should be expected to do.

CHAPTER 12 ASSIGNMENTS

OBJECTIVE QUESTIONS

12-1 For each of the following statements indicate whether the statement is true or false.

T   F   **a**   The auditor cannot be responsible for knowledge of events that occur after the date of the financial statements.

T   F   **b**   All information that becomes available before the financial statements are issued should be used by management with respect to the measurement and presentation of accounting estimates.

T   F   **c**   A loss on an uncollectible trade account receivable caused by a customer's bankruptcy during the subsequent period sometimes must be adjusted for and sometimes must be disclosed but not adjusted for.

T   F   **d**   Stock dividends and stock splits consummated after the balance sheet date but before issuance of the financial statements may, with appropriate disclosure, be given effect in the balance sheet.

T   F   **e**   A lawyer's response to a request for information on litigation, claims, and assessments may appropriately be limited to comments on the list of litigation furnished by the client.

T   F   **f**   A lawyer's response to a request for information on litigation, claims, and assessments may appropriately be limited to matters to which the lawyer has devoted substantive attention in the form of legal consultation or representation.

T   F   **g**   A client representation letter is a document prepared and signed by the client's management that repeats all important representations made to the auditor during the course of the audit.

T   F   **h**   As long as the client's management furnishes legitimate reasons for not signing a representation letter, such a letter is not necessary because it complements rather than replaces other audit procedures.

T   F   **i**   As long as the combined effect of all the misstatements detected by the auditor that remain uncorrected is less than an amount material to the financial statements taken as a whole, an unqualified opinion may be expressed.

T   F   **j**   If work papers are reviewed by partners and staff assigned to an engagement, an independent review by someone not associated with the engagement is not required by generally accepted audit standards.

T   F   **k**   Once audited financial statements are issued, the auditor has no responsibilities in connection with subsequent events that materially affect those statements.

12-2 The following questions relate to the auditor's responsibility with respect to subsequent events. Select the *best* response.

a   "Subsequent events" for reporting purposes are defined as events which occur subsequent to the:

1   Balance sheet date

2   Date of the auditor's report

3   Balance sheet date but prior to the date of the auditor's report

4   Date of the auditor's report and concern contingencies which are not reflected in the financial statements

b   Which event that occurred after the end of the fiscal year under audit but prior to issuance of the auditor's report would *not* require disclosure in the financial statements?

1 Sale of a bond or capital stock issue

2 Loss of plant or inventories as a result of fire or flood

3 A major drop in the quoted market price of the stock of the corporation

4 Settlement of litigation when the event giving rise to the claim took place after the balance sheet date

c With respect to issuance of an audit report which is dual dated for a subsequent event occurring after the completion of field work but before issuance of the auditor's report, the auditor's responsibility for events occurring subsequent to the completion of field work is:

1 Extended to include all events occurring until the date of the last subsequent event referred to

2 Limited to the specific event referred to

3 Limited to all events occurring through the date of issuance of the report

4 Extended to include all events occurring through the date of submission of the report to the client

d A client acquired 25 percent of its outstanding capital stock after year-end and prior to completion of the auditor's field work. The auditor should:

1 Advise management to adjust the balance sheet to reflect the acquisition

2 Issue pro forma financial statements giving effect to the acquisition as if it had occurred at year-end

3 Advise management to disclose the acquisition in the notes to the financial statements

4 Disclose the acquisition in the opinion paragraph of the auditor's report

AICPA

12-3 The following questions relate to the auditor's responsibility with respect to litigation, claims, and assessments. Select the *best* response.

a When auditing contingent liabilities, which of the following procedures would be *least* effective?

1 Reading the minutes of the board of directors

2 Reviewing the bank confirmation letter

3 Examining customer confirmation replies

4 Examining invoices for professional services

b The letter of audit inquiry addressed to the client's legal counsel will *not* ordinarily be:

1 Sent to a lawyer who was engaged by the audit client during the year and soon thereafter resigned the engagement

2 A source of corroboration of the information originally obtained from management concerning litigation, claims, and assessments

3 Limited to references concerning only pending or threatened litigation with respect to which the lawyer has been engaged

4 Needed during the audit of clients whose securities are *not* registered with the SEC

c An attorney is responding to an independent auditor as a result of the audit client's letter of inquiry. The attorney may appropriately limit the response to:

1 Asserted claims and litigation

2 Matters to which the attorney has given substantive attention in the form of legal consultation or representation

    3 Asserted, overtly threatened, or pending claims and litigation

    4 Items which have an extremely high probability of being resolved to the client's detriment

  d When obtaining evidence regarding litigation against a client the CPA would be *least* interested in determining:

    1 An estimate of when the matter will be resolved

    2 The period in which the underlying cause of the litigation occurred

    3 The probability of an unfavorable outcome

    4 An estimate of the potential loss

AICPA

12-4 The following questions relate the auditor's responsibility for obtaining written representations from the client's management. Select the *best* response.

  a A representation letter issued by a client:

    1 Is essential for the preparation of the audit program

    2 Is a substitute for testing

    3 Does *not* reduce the auditor's responsibility

    4 Reduces the auditor's responsibility only to the extent that it is relied upon

  b Which of the following statements ordinarily is included among the written client representations obtained by the auditor?

    1 Management acknowledges that there are *no* material weaknesses in the internal control structure.

    2 Sufficient evidential matter has been made available to permit the issuance of an unqualified opinion.

    3 Compensating balances and other arrangements involving restrictions on cash balances have been disclosed.

    4 Management acknowledges responsibility for illegal actions committed by employees.

  c When considering the use of management's written representations as audit evidence about the completeness assertion, an auditor should understand that such representations:

    1 Complement, but do *not* replace, substantive tests designed to support the assertion

    2 Constitute sufficient evidence to support the assertion when considered in combination with a low control risk assessment

    3 Are *not* part of the evidential matter considered to support the assertion

    4 Replace results of analytical procedures as evidence to support the assertion

  d Ajax is an affiliate of the audit client and is audited by another firm of auditors. Which of the following is *most* likely to be used by the auditor to obtain assurance that all guarantees of the affiliate's indebtedness have been detected?

    1 Send the standard bank confirmation request to all of the client's lender banks

    2 Review client minutes and obtain a representation letter

    3 Examine supporting documents for all entries in intercompany accounts

    4 Obtain written confirmation of indebtedness from the auditor of the affiliate

  e If management refuses to furnish certain written representations that the auditor believes are essential, which of the following is appropriate?

    1 The auditor can rely on oral evidence relating to the matter as a basis for an unqualified opinion.

    2 The client's refusal does *not* constitute a scope limitation that may lead to a modification of the opinion.

3 This may have an effect on the auditor's ability to rely on other representations of management.

4 The auditor should issue an adverse opinion because of management's refusal.

AICPA

12-5 The following questions relate to subsequent discovery of facts and subsequent discovery of omitted procedures. Select the *best* response.

a Soon after Boyd's audit report was issued, Boyd learned of certain related-party transactions that occurred during the year under audit. These transactions were not disclosed in the notes to the financial statements. Boyd should:

1 Plan to audit the transactions during the next engagement

2 Recall all copies of the audited financial statements

3 Determine whether the lack of disclosure would affect the auditor's report

4 Ask the client to disclose the transactions in subsequent interim statements

b Six months after issuing an unqualified opinion on audited financial statements, an auditor discovered that the engagement personnel failed to confirm several of the client's material accounts receivable balances. The auditor should first:

1 Request the permission of the client to undertake the confirmation of accounts receivable

2 Perform alternative procedures to provide a satisfactory basis for the unqualified opinion

3 Assess the importance of the omitted procedures to the auditor's ability to support the previously expressed opinion

4 Inquire whether there are persons currently relying, or likely to rely, on the unqualified opinion

c An auditor concludes that an audit procedure considered necessary at the time of the examination had been omitted. The auditor should assess the importance of the omitted procedure to the ability to support the previously expressed opinion. Which of the following would be *least* helpful in making that assessment?

1 A discussion with the client about whether there are persons relying on the auditor's report

2 A reevaluation of the overall scope of the examination

3 A discussion of the circumstances with engagement personnel

4 A review of the other audit procedures that were applied that might compensate for the one omitted

d Ajax Company's auditor concludes that the omission of an audit procedure considered necessary at the time of the prior examination impairs the auditor's present ability to support the previously expressed unqualified opinion. If the auditor believes there are stockholders currently relying on the opinion, the auditor should promptly:

1 Notify the stockholders currently relying on the previously expressed unqualified opinion that they should *not* rely on it

2 Advise management to disclose this development in its next interim report to the stockholders

3 Advise management to revise the financial statements with full disclosure of the auditor's inability to support the unqualified opinion

4 Undertake to apply the omitted procedure or alternate procedures that would provide a satisfactory basis for the opinion

AICPA

DISCUSSION QUESTIONS

Discussion questions require the application of the concepts explained in the chapter to specific facts, issues, or problems. They are classified by the primary topic to which they relate. However, responses should not be confined to the primary topics but should include all relevant implications.

Subsequent Events

12-6 Windek, CPA, is nearing the completion of an audit of the financial statements of Jubilee for the year ended 12/31/X0. Windek is currently concerned with ascertaining the occurrence of subsequent events that may require adjustment or disclosure essential to a fair presentation in conformity with generally accepted accounting principles.

Required:
a Briefly explain what is meant by the phrase "subsequent events."
b How do those subsequent events which require financial statement adjustment differ from those that require financial statement disclosure?
c What procedures should be performed in order to ascertain the occurrence of subsequent events?

AICPA

12-7 Substantive tests of balances include tests of transactions and events recorded after the balance sheet date. For the following accounts, explain the nature and purpose of procedures involving transactions or events after the balance sheet date:
a Cash in the bank
b Accounts receivable
c Merchandise inventory
d Accounts payable

12-8 You are making an annual audit for the purpose of rendering an opinion on financial statements for use in an annual report to stockholders. Answer the following questions concerning events subsequent to the date of the financial statements:
a What auditing procedures should normally be followed in order to obtain knowledge of subsequent events?
b What is the period with which the auditor is normally concerned with regard to post-balance-sheet events?
c Give five different examples of events or transactions which might occur in the subsequent period.
d What is the auditor's general responsibility, if any, for reporting such events or transactions?

12-9 In your report, how would you deal with each of the examples you listed in part c above? You are in the process of "winding up" the field work on Charleston Stove Corporation, a company engaged in the manufacture and sale of kerosene space-heating stoves. The company had total assets at the balance sheet date of December 31, 19X9, of $4 million and a net profit for the year then ended (after deducting federal and state income tax provisions) of $285,000. The principal records of the company are a general ledger, cash receipts record, voucher register, sales register, check register, and general journal. Financial statements are prepared monthly. Your field work will be completed on February 20, and you plan to deliver the report and statements to the client by March 12.

a Prepare a brief statement as to the purpose and period to be covered in a postaudit review of material transactions.

b Outline the postaudit review program which you would follow to determine what transactions involving material amounts, if any, have occurred since the balance sheet date.

AICPA adapted

12-10 The following events occurred in different cases, but in each instance the event happened after the close of the fiscal year under audit, but before all representatives of the auditor had left the office of the client. State in each case what notice, if any, you would take in your report on the fiscal year; the closing date in each instance is December 31, 19X8.

a Merchandise handled by the company had been traded in the open markets in which it procures its supplies at $1.40 on December 31, 19X8. This price had prevailed for 2 weeks, following an official market report that predicted vastly enlarged supplies; however, no purchases were made at $1.40. The price throughout the preceding year had been about $2, which is the level experienced over several years. On January 18, 19X9, the price returned to $2, following public disclosure of an error in the official calculations of the prior December, correction of which destroyed the expectations of excessive supplies. Inventory at December 31, 19X8, was on a cost-or-market basis.

b On February 1, 19X9, the board of directors adopted a resolution accepting the offer of an investment banker to guarantee the marketing of $100 million of preferred stock.

c On January 22, 19X9, one of the three major plants of the client burned, with a loss of $50 million which was covered to the extent of $40 million insurance.

d The client in this case is an investment company of the open-end type. During the early part of 19X9 a wholly new management came into control. By February 20, 19X9, the new management had sold 90 percent of the investments carried at December 31, 19X8 and had purchased others of a substantially more speculative character.

e This company has a wholly owned but not consolidated subsidiary producing oil in a foreign country. A serious rebellion began in that country on January 18 and continued beyond the completion of your audit work. The press in this country has carried extensive coverage of the progress of the fighting.

AICPA

12-11 Assume that a CPA is expressing an opinion on Azalea Company's financial statements for the year ended September 30, 19X3, that the CPA completed field work on October 21, 19X3, and that the CPA now is preparing the opinion to accompany the financial statements. In each item a "subsequent event" is described. This event either was disclosed to the CPA in connection with the review of subsequent events or after the completion of field work. You are to indicate in each case the required financial statement disclosure of this event. Each of the six cases is independent of the other five and is to be considered separately.

a A large account receivable from Taylor Industries (material to financial statement presentation) was considered fully collectible at September 30, 19X3. Taylor suffered a plant explosion on October 25, 19X3. Since Taylor was uninsured, it is unlikely that the account will be paid.

b The tax court ruled in favor of the company on October 25, 19X3. Litigation involved deductions claimed on the 19X1 and 19X2 tax returns. Azalea had provided in accrued taxes payable for the full amount of the potential disallowances. The IRS will not appeal the tax court's ruling.

c Based on a directors' resolution on October 5, 19X3, Azalea's common stock was split 3-for-1 on October 10, 19X3. Azalea's earnings per share have been computed based upon common shares outstanding at September 30, 19X3.

d Azalea's manufacturing division, whose assets constituted 75 percent of Azalea's total assets at September 30, 19X3, was sold on November 1, 19X3. The new owner assumed the bonded indebtedness associated with this property.

e On October 15, 19X3, a major investment adviser issued a pessimistic report on Azalea's long-term prospects. The market price for Azalea's common stock subsequently declined by 50 percent.

f At its October 5, 19X3, meeting, Azalea's Board of Directors voted to double the advertising budget for the coming year and authorized a change in advertising agencies.

Legal Representation Letters

12-12 During an audit engagement, Harper, CPA, has satisfactorily completed an examination of accounts payable and other liabilities and now plans to determine whether there are any loss contingencies arising from litigation, claims, or assessments.

Required:

What are the audit procedures that Harper should follow with respect to the existence of loss contingencies arising from litigation, claims, and assessments? Do not discuss reporting requirements.

AICPA

12-13 In an audit of the Cotula Corporation as at December 31, 19X4, you have learned that the following situation exists. No entry in respect thereto has been made in the accounting records. What entry would you recommend, and what disclosure, if any, would you make of this situation in the financial statements for December 31, 19X4?

During the year 19X4, Cotula was named as defendant in a suit for damages by the Bixby Company for breach of contract. An adverse decision to Cotula was rendered and Bixby was awarded $40,000 damages. At the time of the audit, the case was under appeal to a higher court.

AICPA adapted

12-14 Legal expenses are normally not a material item in the financial statements. Nevertheless, auditors typically examine legal expenses in detail. Why?

12-15 In response to your client's request for a legal representation letter, the attorney has furnished the following opinion with respect to litigation brought against the client:

It is our opinion, based on the limited facts of which we are presently apprised, that the plaintiff's claims are without substantial merit. This opinion is based solely on the complaint, preliminary discussions with management of and attorneys for the corporation and a review of limited documentary materials. The opinion expressed in this letter is subject to amendment or qualification based on additional facts which might be developed or on amended pleadings.

The litigation involves a claim for damages that would be material with respect to your client's financial position if the plaintiff prevails.

a Evaluate the adequacy of the attorney's response as a matter of audit evidence on the litigation.

b What impact will the existence of the litigation have on your audit report?

12-16 Your client is involved in litigation involving a claim for damages that would be material with respect to its financial position if the plaintiff prevails. In response to your client's request for a legal representation letter the attorney has furnished the following opinion: "Based on the facts known to us, after a full investigation, it is our opinion that no liability will be established against the company in these suits."

a Evaluate the adequacy of the attorney's response as a matter of audit evidence on the litigation.

b What impact will the existence of the litigation have on your audit report?

c Should you refer to the attorney's opinion in your audit report?

12-17 In the course of auditing the financial statements of the Lowe Company for the year ended December 31, 19X2, you request that your client's attorney furnish a legal representation letter. The attorney's letter includes information on unbilled legal fees and comments on specific litigation identified in the client's request. However, with respect to other "claims, lawsuits in process, threatened or pending litigation" of which the attorney has knowledge, the attorney has responded: "This firm does not disclose information privileged under the attorney/client privilege, but if such information were disclosed, it would be material."

Explain the impact that this response will have on your audit report and write the audit report appropriate in the circumstances.

12-18 One of your clients in an attempt to control the expenses for legal fees has engaged a house counsel—an attorney deriving substantially all income from the company. The client is convinced of the competence of the house counsel, and you tend to agree. In response to your request for a legal representation letter the client indicates that the response this year will come from the house counsel. Is the house counsel's response acceptable to you?

Client Representation Letters

12-19 During the audit of the annual financial statements of Amis Manufacturing, the company's president, R. Alderman, and Luddy, the auditor, reviewed matters that were supposed to be included in a written representation letter. Upon receipt of the following client representation letter, Luddy contacted Alderman to state that it was incomplete.

To E. K. Luddy, CPA

In connection with your audit of the balance sheet of Amis Manufacturing as of December 31, 19X2, and the related statements of income, retained earnings, and cash flows for the year then ended, for the purpose of expressing an opinion as to whether the financial statements present fairly, in all material respects, the financial position, results of operations, and cash flows of Amis Manufacturing in conformity with generally accepted accounting principles, we confirm, to the best of our knowledge and belief, the following representations made to you during your audit. There were no

- Plans or intentions that may materially affect the carrying value or classification of assets and liabilities
- Communications from regulatory agencies concerning noncompliance with, or deficiencies in, financial reporting practices
- Agreements to repurchase assets previously sold
- Violations or possible violations of laws or regulations whose effects should be considered for disclosure in the financial statements or as a basis for recording a loss contingency
- Unasserted claims or assessments that our lawyer has advised are probable of assertion and must be disclosed in accordance with Statement of Financial Accounting Standards No. 5
- Capital stock repurchase options or agreements or capital stock reserved for options, warrants, conversions, or other requirements
- Compensating balance or other arrangements involving restrictions on cash balances

R. Alderman, President
Amis Manufacturing Inc.
March 14, 19X3

Required:
Identify the other matters that Alderman's representation letter should specifically confirm.

AICPA

12-20 As is customary in completing your audit, you request the client to furnish you with a comprehensive representation letter. Your client, J. Hawler, who operates the business as a sole proprietor, reads the representations you are requesting him to make and refuses to furnish the letter. Hawler stated the position as follows:

You are asking me to tell you all kinds of things that I hired you to figure out. For example, you are asking me to say that "the financial statements have been prepared in conformity with generally accepted accounting principles on a basis consistent with that of the preceding year." I paid you to make an audit and you should know whether or not that's true yourself.

a What explanation would you give Hawler of the need for a client representation letter?

b What would be the impact on your audit report if Hawler did not accept your explanation and continued to refuse to furnish the letter?

12-21 You are considering obtaining written representations from the client concerning the financial statements and matters pertinent to them.

a What are the reasons for obtaining written representations from the client?

b What reliance may the auditor place upon written representations from (1) the client, (2) independent experts, and (3) debtors?

12-22 a What are the objectives of the client's representation letters?

b Who should prepare and sign the client's representation letters?

c When should the client's representation letters be obtained?

d Why should the client's representation letters be prepared for each audit?

12-23 Since the management of a company is responsible for its financial statements and the auditor is responsible only for the report, management may choose the form of presentation and the degree of disclosure which does not lead to the most informative financial statements. One proposal is that management's duties be limited to the adoption and maintenance of an adequate accounting system while the independent auditor assumes the greater responsibility for preparing and reporting on the financial statements. These would then present an objective and impartial report on the performance of management.

Comment on this proposal.

CICA

Review of Work Papers and Summarization and Evaluation of Audit Results

12-24 You are the senior accountant in the audit of the Great Midwest Grain Corporation, whose business primarily involves the purchase, storage, and sale of grain products. The corporation owns several elevators located along navigable water routes and transports its grain by barge and rail. Your assistant submitted the following analysis for your review.

Great Midwest Grain Corporation
Advances Paid on Barges
under Construction—A/C 210
December 31, 19X6

Advances made	
1/15/X6—Ck. 3463—RiverKing Barge Construction Co.	$100,000[1]
4/13/X6—Ck. 4129—RiverKing Barge Construction Co.	25,000[1]
6/19/X6—Ck. 5396—RiverKing Barge Construction Co.	63,000[1]
Total payments	$188,000
Deduct cash received 9/1/X6 from Ling Life Ins. Co.	188,000[2]
Balance per general ledger—12/31/X6	$ –0–

[1]Examined approved check request and canceled check and traced to cash disbursements record.
[2]Traced to cash receipts book and to duplicate deposit ticket.

---

a In what respects is the analysis incomplete for report purposes? (Do not include any discussion of specific auditing procedures.)

b What different types of contractual arrangements may be inferred from your assistant's analysis?

c What additional auditing procedures would you suggest that your assistant perform before you accept the work paper as being complete?

AICPA adapted

12-25 If misstatements of relatively small amounts are found in an audit test, can the auditor ignore such misstatements without further work on the basis that the misstatements are immaterial relevant to the financial statements?

AICPA adapted

12-26 Your audit discloses a lawsuit pending against your client, Neece Corporation, on a patent owned by Neece, which the client's attorney is hopeful of winning. The patent is 70 percent amortized and the book value of the patent is $1,500. Neece's total net assets are $700,000. However, this patent is the major income-producing asset of the company. Would you mention this contingency in your audit report? If so, how?

12-27 A Ltd., a manufacturing company with total assets of about $7 million and 500,000 shares outstanding, is situated just outside a medium-size Canadian city. In early 19X9, the local newspaper published a series of articles charging that A Ltd. was polluting a river that runs through the city and that the company had irresponsibly paid annual dividends instead of providing funds for the restoration of the environment. CA has been A Ltd.'s external auditor for several years. Suppose that neither the newspaper nor the court has found out that the company is polluting the river. Discuss the extent of CA's responsibility in connection with disclosing to shareholders and society in general that the company is polluting the river. Your discussion may include any changes in CA's responsibility that you believe may, or should, be made in the future.

CICA adapted

Subsequent Discovery and Related Matters

12-28 You are the senior on an audit engagement. One of the staff accountants asks you why the public accounting firm for which you both work has established a report review department since the staff accountant believes the audit work on an engagement is always adequately reviewed by those assigned to the engagement. Explain.

CASE

On February 24, 19X9, you completed field work for the audit of the financial statements of Goldman Enterprises for the year ended December 31, 19X8. Goldman Enterprises is headed by P. B. Goldman, an aggressive, young entrepreneur who in January 19X8 replaced his father as chief executive officer by pressuring the board of directors to demand the senior Goldman's resignation. P. B. Goldman immediately announced plans to expand the organization through an intensive program of modernization and acquisitions.

P. B. Goldman hired M. Foxmire as financial vice president and gave Foxmire primary responsibility for negotiating acquisitions and a special assignment to streamline the accounting system. Foxmire was hired in midyear and quickly revamped the billing, collection, and payment routines and then began traveling extensively to identify potential acquisition candidates.

You have had a final conference with the client. The financial statements and audit report for Goldman Enterprises are being typed, collated, and reproduced in your report department when, on February 28, 19X9, you are surprised to read in the financial section of the local newspaper a feature story on Goldman Enterprises. Several matters arouse your interest.

Goldman Enterprises has settled litigation with the senior Mr. Goldman. He had charged various improprieties in his ejection from the company and sought a much larger amount than he had been given in severance pay and consultant's fees. The financial statements as of December 31, 19X8, disclose the litigation and contained an allowance for separation compensation of $50,000. The settlement agreement awards the senior Mr. Goldman $300,000, an amount material to the financial statements.

A call to P. B. Goldman confirms the terms of the settlement. P. B. Goldman explains he had some misgivings about the treatment of his father and persuaded the board to authorize the new agreement. P. B. Goldman agrees to send over the written agreement and the minutes of the emergency board meeting at which it was approved on February 26, 19X9.

The story also reports the purchase on February 26, 19X9, of Silverson, a business that manufactures a product similar to Goldman Enterprises' largest line, but with mail-order distribution to consumers. Goldman Enterprises sells to retailers and distributes through various common carriers. Silverson Inc. has manufacturing facilities approximately the same in size as Goldman Enterprises.

In your phone conversation, P. B. Goldman is enthusiastic about the acquisition and explains that production capacity has been doubled and significant new channels of distribution are available. P. B. Goldman is glad you called because you are to undertake an acquisition investigation of Silverson. The board approved the purchase at the February 26, 19X9, meeting, but the purchase price will be determined by an agreed-upon formula based on amounts in Silverson's audited financial statements. The audit will not be completed until around the end of March, but unaudited financial statements are available now.

You suggest delaying your own audit report until the acquisition investigation is completed. However, Goldman excitedly explains that audited financial statements are needed to obtain a significant loan by the first week in March. You agree to issue your audit report by March 2, 19X9.

At the end of March, you are at Goldman Enterprises to explain your report on the acquisition investigation. You stop in the cafeteria for a quick breakfast before your appearance at the board meeting. As you are eating and reviewing your report, you overhear two maintenance men talking at the next table: "That Foxmire really messed things up. Last night, I was cleaning up an old storage room and found twelve cartons of invoices nobody knew about. The assistant controller said there must be at least $600,000 in last year's expenses that weren't recorded." Suddenly, you are not very hungry.

a How should the events approved at the February 26, 19X9, board meeting be reflected in the financial statements and covered in your audit report, assuming that the report is issued by March 2, 19X9? Explain the reasons for your choice of coverage.

b   What are your responsibilities with respect to the information overheard in the cafeteria? Explain how you should proceed.

c   How would you evaluate your understanding of this client?

d   What audit procedures should have spared you from being surprised when reading the financial papers and losing your appetite at breakfast?

CHAPTER

13

The Auditor's Report

CHAPTER OUTLINE

Learning Objectives

After studying this chapter you should be able to:

- Identify the possible reasons for departure from a standard report and describe the types of audit reports other than a standard report
- Define qualified opinions, adverse opinions, and disclaimers of opinion and describe the circumstances in which the auditor would issue each type of report
- Explain the circumstances in which an auditor might add explanatory language to the standard report without expressing a qualified opinion
- Describe the auditor's responsibility in reporting on comparative financial statements
- Understand the auditor's responsibility with respect to other information in an annual report containing audited financial statements
- Describe communications other than an audit report between the auditor and stockholders, audit committees, boards of directors, and management, including communication of internal control structure related matters and other required communications

Relevant Sections of Statements on Auditing Standards

AU 325 — Communication of Internal Control Structure Related Matters Noted in an Audit

AU 341 — An Entity's Ability to Continue as a Going Concern

AU 380 — Communication with Audit Committees

AU 411 — The Meaning of "Present Fairly in Conformity with GAAP"

AU 420 — Consistency of Application of GAAP

AU 431 — Adequacy of Disclosure in Financial Statements

AU 508 — Reports on Audited Financial Statements

AU 543 — Part of Audit Performed by Other Independent Auditors

AU 550 — Other Information in Documents Containing Audited Financial Statements

An audit report formally communicates the auditor's conclusion on the presentation of financial statements and concisely states the basis for that conclusion. This chapter explains how the auditor decides the type of report that is appropriate and the various modifications of the standard report that may be appropriate in particular circumstances. This chapter also describes the auditor's communications with corporate clients, including communications with audit committees, stockholders, the board of directors, and senior management.

In general, the auditing standards on reporting are far more specific and detailed than those that relate to obtaining evidential matter. A substantial portion of the authoritative auditing literature deals with audit reports on financial statements and auditor's communications. The following pronouncements, however, are the primary ones:

- SAS No. 58 (AU 509), "Reports on Audited Financial Statements," specifies the meaning, form, and content of the different types of audit reports and the circumstances when each should be issued.
- SAS No. 61 (AU 380), "Communication with Audit Committees" establishes requirements for the auditor to communicate certain matters to those who have responsibility for oversight of the client's financial reporting process.
- SAS No. 60 (AU 325), "Communication of Internal Control Structure Related Matters Noted in an Audit," provides guidance on identifying and reporting conditions that the auditor observed regarding the client's internal control structure.

AUDITOR'S REPORTING OBLIGATION

The auditor's standard report is explained in Chapter 1. The standard report is an unqualified opinion which states that the financial statements present fairly, in all material respects, the financial position, results of operations, and cash flows in conformity with generally accepted accounting principles. The conclusion may be expressed only when the independent auditor has formed such an opinion on the basis of an audit made in accordance with generally accepted auditing standards.

The auditor's objective is to be able to express an unqualified opinion on the financial statements. Anything less than an unqualified opinion is usually considered undesirable by the client's management and is not as useful to users of the financial statements. Generally, the SEC will not accept a filing containing audited financial statements on which the auditor has been unable to express an unqualified opinion because of a departure from generally accepted accounting principles or generally accepted auditing standards.

Thus, auditors usually attempt to persuade clients to improve financial reporting practices, improve the condition of accounting records and control procedures, or permit as extensive an audit as is necessary to allow the expression of an unqualified opinion. Nevertheless, the auditor's obligation in reporting is to express as precisely as possible the auditor's conclusion on the presentation of the financial statements and the basis for this conclusion. This may require a departure from the standard unqualified opinion.

Four generally accepted auditing standards discussed in Chapter 1 are concerned with reporting. The reporting standards are repeated here for convenience [SAS No. 1 (AU 150.02)].

1 The report shall state whether the financial statements are presented in accordance with generally accepted accounting principles.
2 The report shall identify those circumstances in which such principles have not been consistently observed in the current period in relation to the preceding period.
3 Informative disclosures in the financial statements are to be regarded as reasonably adequate unless otherwise stated in the report.
4 The report shall either contain an expression of opinion regarding the financial statements, taken as a whole, or an assertion to the effect that an opinion cannot be expressed. When an overall opinion cannot be expressed, the reasons therefor should be stated. In all cases where an auditor's name is associated with financial statements,

the report should contain a clear-cut indication of the character of the auditor's work, if any, and the degree of responsibility the auditor is taking.

The most pervasive and detailed standard is the fourth standard of reporting. The objective of this standard is to enable users of financial statements to determine the extent to which the statements reported on by the auditor may be relied on. The fourth reporting standard requires that when the auditor is *associated* with financial statements, the report should contain both "a clear-cut indication of the character of the auditor's work" and "the degree of responsibility the auditor is taking."

Departures from a Standard Report

There are two ways that an audit report may vary from the standard report. The first is to depart from an unqualified opinion. There are a few types of such reports that may be appropriate, depending on the circumstances. The second way is to add explanatory language to the standard report, retaining the unqualified opinion.

Reasons for a Departure from an Unqualified Opinion   There are two basic reasons that the auditor may be unable to express an unqualified opinion:

1 *Scope limitation.* The scope of the audit may be significantly limited, so that the auditor is unable to apply audit procedures considered necessary or to obtain essential evidence.
2 *GAAP departure.* The financial statements may contain a departure from generally accepted accounting principles that has a material effect.

Types of Audit Reports Other than a Standard Report   The type of audit report is determined by the auditor's reason for not issuing a standard report. There are four basic types of audit reports other than a standard report with an unqualified opinion:

1 *Explanatory language added to the auditor's standard report.* The auditor adds an explanatory paragraph to the report in certain circumstances. It does not affect the auditor's unqualified opinion. The circumstances that require inclusion of such explanatory language are described later in the chapter.
2 *Disclaimer of opinion.* The auditor reports that an opinion is being disclaimed when the auditor has not been able to obtain sufficient evidence to form an opinion on the financial statements taken as a whole because of some limitation on the scope of the audit.
3 *Adverse opinion.* The auditor reports that the financial statements are not fairly presented in conformity with generally accepted accounting principles when the auditor has sufficient evidence to conclude that the financial statements taken as whole are misleading.
4 *Qualified opinion.* The auditor qualifies an opinion for either of the two reasons that cause a departure from an unqualified opinion—a scope limitation or a departure from generally accepted accounting principles.

A qualified opinion identifies some specific item in the financial statements and removes that item from the auditor's positive expression of an opinion on the financial statements.

With the exception of that item, the financial statements present fairly, in all material respects, the financial position, results of operations, and cash flows in conformity with generally accepted accounting principles.

Whenever the auditor is expressing less than an unqualified opinion the auditor must disclose in the report all the substantive reasons for doing so. For example, when the scope of the audit has been restricted, the auditor may disclaim an opinion. However, if the auditor is aware of a material departure from generally accepted accounting principles, the report must also disclose that departure. The report will still be a disclaimer, but it will also contain a reservation concerning the presentation of the financial statements.

The auditor must explain the reasons for not expressing an unqualified opinion in an explanatory paragraph of the report. The explanatory paragraph is important because it alerts the user of financial statements to a matter that should be considered in using the statements. For example, according to SAS No. 58 (AU 508.52), the explanatory paragraph(s) of a qualified opinion should:

> disclose the principal effects of the subject matter of the qualification on financial position, results of operations, and cash flows, if practicable. If the effects are not reasonably determinable, the report should so state. If such disclosures are made in a note to the financial statements, the explanatory paragraph(s) may be shortened by referring to it.

However, matters relating to the scope of the audit should be covered entirely in the auditor's report.

Qualified Opinions versus Other Types of Reports   Whenever a qualified opinion is expressed, the item to which the qualification relates is considered by the auditor to have a material effect on the financial statements. However, a departure from generally accepted accounting principles may result in a qualified opinion or adverse opinion, and a scope limitation may result in a qualified opinion or a disclaimer of opinion. Generally, the choice between a qualification and the more extreme types of reports depends on the seriousness and extensiveness of the deficiency.

Among other matters, the auditor would consider the following points:

1 *Ability to isolate the deficiency.* If the auditor can readily identify the item that is deficient, quantify the effect on the financial statements, and explain the nature of the deficiency in understandable terms, a qualified opinion is probably sufficient.
2 *Usefulness of financial statements.* If the effect of the deficiency is so large and involves so many items that a user would have great difficulty in making a meaningful analysis of the financial statements, a qualified opinion is probably not sufficient modification.
3 *Extent of disagreement with client.* If a client's management cannot reasonably correct the deficiency, or if the item represents an honest difference of opinion, a qualified opinion is more likely.

For example, if the client imposes a significant restriction on the scope of the audit, the auditor generally should disclaim an opinion on the financial statements. Figure 13-1 summarizes the types of audit reports and causes of other than a standard report.

Reporting variations or circumstances	Cause of modification is a material			
	Scope limitation	GAAP departure	Inconsistency	Uncertainty
Qualifying language	Except for*	Except for	Not applicable	Not applicable
Explanatory paragraph required?	Yes	Yes	Yes	Yes
Reference to additional information in a note to financial statements permitted?	No	Yes	Yes	Yes
Type of report when cause is pervasively material	Disclaimer	Adverse	Unqualified	Unqualified†

*Generally, a client-imposed scope limitation should cause the auditor to disclaim an opinion.
†An uncertainty is a matter expected to be resolved in the *future*. If a question arises for which sufficient evidence exists or did exist in the past, but management does not provide the evidence, the auditor considers whether a scope limitation would be more appropriate in the circumstances.

FIGURE 13-1
Summary of causes and types of audit reports other than a standard report.

Financial Statements and Periods Covered

The fourth standard of reporting requires that the auditor's report "shall either contain an expression of opinion regarding the financial statements, taken as a whole, or an assertion to the effect that an opinion cannot be expressed."

Comparative Financial Statements   SAS No. 58 (AU 508) as it relates to reporting on comparative financial statements, explains that the reference to "taken as a whole" applies to both the financial statements of the current period and those of past periods that are presented on a comparative basis. Thus, the standard report usually covers comparative balance sheets, income statements, and statements of cash flows for two fiscal periods.

The auditor's report should bear the date of completion of the most recent audit. However, the auditor makes separate audits of each period. When the auditor has audited the financial statements of the current period and the immediate past period or periods, the auditor updates and reexpresses the report on financial statements of the past period. Accounting to SAS No. 58 (AU 508.75):

During his audit of the current-period financial statements, the auditor should be alert for circumstances or events that affect the prior-period financial statements presented . . . or the adequacy of informative disclosures concerning those statements. . . . In updating his report on the prior-period financial statements, the auditor should consider the effects of any such circumstances or events coming to his attention.

An auditor who has audited the financial statements of the current period and the immediate past period or periods is called the *continuing auditor*. An updated report of a continuing auditor should be distinguished from a reissued audit report described in Chapter 12. A continuing auditor's standard report on comparative financial statements for two fiscal periods might be presented as follows:

Independent Auditor's Report

We have audited the accompanying balance sheets of X Company as of December 31, 19X2 and 19X1, and the related statements of income, retained earnings, and cash flows for the years then ended. These financial statements are the responsibility of the Company's management. Our responsibility is to express an opinion on these financial statements based on our audits.

We conducted our audits in accordance with generally accepted auditing standards. Those standards require that we plan and perform the audit to obtain reasonable assurance about whether the financial statements are free of material misstatement. An audit includes examining, on a test basis, evidence supporting the amounts and disclosures in the financial statements. An audit also includes assessing the accounting principles used and significant estimates made by management, as well as evaluating the overall financial statement presentation. We believe that our audits provide a reasonable basis for our opinion.

In our opinion, the financial statements referred to above present fairly, in all material respects, the financial position of X Company as of [at] December 31, 19X2 and 19X1, and the results of its operations and its cash flows for the years then ended in conformity with generally accepted accounting principles.

(Signature)

(Date)

If circumstances that affect the prior-period financial statements come to a continuing auditor's attention, the updated report may differ from the report in the prior period. Reports with a different updated opinion are explained later in this chapter.

If the auditor who is associated with comparative financial statements is not a continuing auditor, but the financial statements of the prior period were audited by a predecessor auditor, two equally acceptable alternatives are possible:

1 The report of the predecessor auditor may be reissued as described in Chapter 12, and the successor may report on only the current financial statements.

2 The successor auditor may expand the scope paragraph of the audit report to describe the predecessor's association with the prior-period statements and express an opinion only on the current-period financial statements.

A successor auditor's report when the report of a predecessor is not reissued might be worded as follows:

Independent Auditor's Report

We have audited the balance sheet of ABC Company as of December 31, 19X2, and the related statements of income, retained earnings, and cash flows for the year then ended. These financial statements are the responsibility of the Company's management. Our responsibility is to express an opinion on these financial statements based on our audits. *The financial statements of ABC Company as of December 31, 19X1, were audited by other auditors whose report dated March 31, 19X2, expressed an unqualified opinion on those statements.* [Emphasis added.]

[Same second paragraph as the standard report]

In our opinion, the 19X2 financial statements referred to above present fairly, in all material respects, the financial position of ABC Company as of December 31, 19X2, and the results of its operations and its cash flows for the year ended in conformity with generally accepted accounting principles.

(Signature)

(Date)

If the predecessor auditor's report was other than the standard report, an example of the wording that might be included in the successor's report is as follows:

. . . were audited by other auditors whose report dated March 1, 19X2, on those statements included an explanatory paragraph that described the litigation discussed in Note X to the financial statements.

Individual Financial Statements   The first paragraph of the auditor's report should specifically identify the financial statements audited. For example, the exact titles and dates of the client's financial statements should be used. Ordinarily, the document the auditor submits to the client will include the basic financial statements for two fiscal periods, the notes which are an integral part of statements, and the audit report bound in one cover. However, publicly owned corporations usually include this information along with additional financial and operating data in a public document, such as an annual report to stockholders. When other data are presented, it is particularly important to clearly identify the audited data.

The reference in the fourth reporting standard to "the financial statements taken as a whole" applies equally to a complete set of financial statements and to an individual financial statement, such as a balance sheet. The auditor may express an unqualified opinion on one of the financial statements and express a qualified or adverse opinion or disclaim an opinion on another if the circumstances call for this treatment.

Also, the scope of the audit may be limited to an individual financial statement. SAS No. 58 (AU 508.47) explains that:

The auditor may be asked to report on one basic financial statement and not on the others. For example, he may be asked to report on the balance sheet and not on the statements of income, retained earnings, or cash flows.

If the scope of the audit is limited to an individual financial statement and only that statement is presented, the auditor may identify that statement in the first paragraph and express an unqualified opinion on the statement audited. According to SAS No. 58 (AU 508.47) a report on an individual financial statement should be distinguished from an ordinary scope limitation:

> These engagements do not involve scope limitations if the auditor's access to information underlying the basic financial statements is not limited and if he applies all the procedures he considered necessary in the circumstances; rather, such engagements involve limited reporting objectives.

An example of an auditor's report on one basic financial statement follows:

Independent Auditor's Report

We have audited the accompanying balance sheet of X Company as of December 31, 19XX. This financial statement is the responsibility of the Company's management. Our responsibility is to express an opinion on this financial statement based on our audit.

We conducted our audit in accordance with generally accepted auditing standards. Those standards require that we plan and perform the audit to obtain reasonable assurance about whether the balance sheet is free of material misstatement. An audit includes examining, on a test basis, evidence supporting the amounts and disclosures in the balance sheet. An audit also includes assessing the accounting principles used and significant estimates made by management, as well as evaluating the overall balance-sheet presentation. We believe that our audit of the balance sheet provides a reasonable basis for our opinion.

In our opinion, the balance sheet referred to above presents fairly, in all material respects, the financial position of X Company as of December 31, 19XX, in conformity with generally accepted accounting principles.

(Signature)

(Date)

QUALIFICATIONS, DISCLAIMERS, AND ADVERSE OPINIONS

The form of audit reports for less than an unqualified opinion have been standardized to the extent possible. Limiting the language of qualifying phrases promotes understanding among users of the meaning and significance of such phrases.

Limitations on the Scope of the Audit

If the scope of the audit is restricted, an auditing deficiency exists. A scope limitation requires either a qualified opinion or a disclaimer of opinion. An auditor can express an unqualified opinion only if the audit has been conducted in accordance with generally accepted auditing standards. Restrictions on the scope of the audit—whether imposed by the client or by circumstances such as the timing of work, the inability to obtain sufficient competent evidential matter, or an inadequacy in the accounting records—may require the auditor to express a qualified opinion or to disclaim an opinion.

Qualified Opinion   The distinction between a qualified opinion and a disclaimer of opinion due to a scope limitation is based on the auditor's assessment of the importance of the omitted procedure(s) to the ability to form an opinion on the financial statements audited. This assessment will be affected by the nature and magnitude of the potential effects of the matter(s) in question and by their significance to the financial statements. If the potential effects relate to many financial statement items, this significance is likely to be greater than if only a limited number of items is involved.

For example, if the auditor is unable to obtain sufficient competent evidential matter concerning an investment in a foreign company, the pertinent portions of a qualified opinion might read as follows:

Independent Auditor's Report

[Same first paragraph as the standard report]

Except as discussed in the following paragraph, we conducted our audits in accordance with generally accepted auditing standards. Those standards require that we plan and perform the audit to obtain reasonable assurance about whether the financial statements are free of material misstatement. An audit includes examining, on a test basis, evidence supporting the amounts and disclosures in the financial statements. An audit also includes assessing the accounting principles used and significant estimates made by management, as well as evaluating the overall financial statement presentation. We believe that our audits provide a reasonable basis for our opinion.

We were unable to obtain audited financial statements supporting the Company's investment in a foreign affiliate stated at $_____ and $_____ at December 31, 19X2 and 19X1, respectively, or its equity in earnings of that affiliate of $_____ and $_____, which is included in net income for the years then ended as described in Note X to the financial statements; nor were we able to satisfy ourselves as to the carrying value of the investment in the foreign affiliate or the equity in its earnings by other auditing procedures.

In our opinion, except for the effects of such adjustments, if any, as might have been determined to be necessary had we been able to examine evidence regarding the foreign affiliate investment and earnings, the financial statements referred to in the first paragraph above present fairly, in all material respects, the financial position of X Company as of December 31, 19X2 and 19X1, and the results of its operations and its cash flows for the years then ended in conformity with generally accepted accounting principles.

(Signature)

(Date)

The most common restrictions on the scope of the audit apply to the observation of physical inventory taking or the confirmation of receivables by direct communication with customers. Circumstances such as the timing of the auditor's work may make it impracticable or impossible for the auditor to accomplish these procedures. For example, the auditor may be engaged after the physical inventory. If the auditor is able to satisfy himself or herself as to inventories or accounts receivable by applying alternative procedures, there is no significant limitation on scope, and reference in the report to the omission of the procedures or to the use of alternative procedures is not required. However, to satisfy himself or herself on ending inventory quantities the auditor must always observe or make some physical counts. If satisfaction has been obtained on ending inventory, tests of accounting records and analytical procedures may be sufficient for beginning inventory.

Disclaimer of Opinion   Restrictions on the application of audit procedures to important elements of the financial statements require the auditor to decide whether sufficient competent evidential matter has been examined to permit an unqualified or qualified opinion, or whether the auditor should disclaim an opinion. When restrictions on important procedures are imposed by the client, the auditor generally should disclaim an opinion on the financial statements. The following report illustrates such a limitation:

Independent Auditor's Report

We were engaged to audit the accompanying balance sheets of X Company as of December 31, 19X2 and 19X1, and the related statements of income, retained earnings, and cash flows for the years then ended. These financial statements are the responsibility of the Company's management.

[Second paragraph of standard report should be omitted.]

The Company did not make a count of its physical inventory in 19X2 or 19X1, stated in the accompanying financial statements at $_____ as of December 31, 19X2, and at $_____ as of December 31, 19X1. Further, evidence supporting the cost of property and equipment acquired prior to December 31, 19X1, is no longer available. The Company's records do not permit the application of other auditing procedures to inventories or property and equipment.

Since the Company did not take physical inventories and we were not able to apply other auditing procedures to satisfy ourselves as to inventory quantities and the cost of property and equipment, the scope of our work was not sufficient to enable us to express, and we do not express, an opinion on these financial statements.

(Signature)

(Date)

Disclaimers are more frequent in limited audits of smaller, closely held businesses and in initial audits. A disclaimer of opinion is also required when financial statements are prepared without audit or when the auditor is not independent. The requirements applicable to these types of engagements are explained in Chapter 14.

Departures from Generally Accepted Accounting Principles

When financial statements are materially affected by a departure from generally accepted accounting principles, the auditor should express a qualified or an adverse opinion. Whether the effects of a departure from generally accepted accounting principles are sufficiently material to require either a qualified or an adverse opinion depends in part on the dollar magnitude of the effects. However, materiality judgments involve qualitative as well as quantitative matters. Materiality does not depend entirely on relative size. The significance of an item to a particular company, such as inventories to a manufacturing company, and the effects on the amounts and presentation of other financial statement items are factors to be considered.

Qualified Opinion   When the auditor believes that an item in the financial statements is stated on a basis that materially departs from generally accepted accounting principles, the auditor should express a qualified opinion. The following extract illustrates a qualification of this type:

Independent Auditor's Report

[Same first and second paragraphs as the standard report]

The Company has excluded, from property and debt in the accompanying balance sheets, certain lease obligations that, in our opinion, should be capitalized in order to conform with generally accepted accounting principles. If these lease obligations were capitalized, property would be increased by $_____ and $_____, long-term debt by $_____ and $_____, and retained earnings by $_____ and $_____, as of December 31, 19X2 and 19X1, respectively. Additionally, net income would be increased (decreased) by $_____ and $_____ and earnings per share would be increased (decreased) by $_____ and $_____, respectively, for the years then ended.

In our opinion, except for the effects of not capitalizing certain lease obligations as discussed in the preceding paragraph, the financial statements referred to above present fairly, in all material respects, the financial position of X Company as of December 31, 19X2 and 19X1, and the results of its operations and its cash flows for the years then ended in conformity with generally accepted accounting principles.

(Signature)

(Date)

If the facts are disclosed in a note to the financial statements, the explanatory paragraph can be shortened by referring to the note, for example:

As more fully described in Note X to the financial statements, the Company has excluded certain lease obligations from property and debt in the accompanying balance sheets. In our opinion, generally accepted accounting principles require that such obligations be included in the balance sheets.

Generally accepted accounting principles include adequate disclosure. When the client does not disclose essential information in the financial statements, the independent auditor ordinarily should provide it in the audit report and should express a qualified or adverse opinion. The following is an example of a qualified opinion for inadequate disclosure:

Independent Auditor's Report

[Same first and second paragraphs as the standard report]

The Company's financial statements do not disclose [describe the nature of the omitted disclosures]. In our opinion, disclosure of this information is required by generally accepted accounting principles.

In our opinion, except for the omission of the information discussed in the preceding paragraph, the financial statements referred to above present fairly, in all material respects, the financial position of X Company as of December 31, 19XX, and the results of its operations and its cash flows for the year then ended in conformity with generally accepted accounting principles.

(Signature)

(Date)

Adverse Opinion   An adverse opinion states that financial statements do not present fairly the financial position, results of operations, or cash flows in conformity with generally accepted accounting principles. Such an opinion is required if the effect of a departure is sufficiently material and so pervasive that, in the auditor's judgment, the statements are not presented fairly in conformity with generally accepted accounting principles.

When an adverse opinion is issued, the opinion paragraph normally includes a direct reference to the paragraph that explains the basis for the adverse opinion. For example:

Independent Auditor's Report

[Same first and second paragraphs as the standard report]

As discussed in Note X to the financial statements, the Company carries its property, plant, and equipment accounts at appraisal values, and provides depreciation on the basis of such values. Further, the Company does not provide for income taxes with respect to differences between financial income and taxable income arising because of the use, for income tax purposes, of the installment method of reporting gross profit from certain types of sales. Generally accepted accounting principles require that property, plant, and equipment be stated at an amount not in excess of cost, reduced by depreciation based on such amount, and that deferred income taxes be provided.

Because of the departures from generally accepted accounting principles identified above, as of December 31, 19X2 and 19X1, inventories have been increased $_____ and $_____ by inclusion in manufacturing overhead of depreciation in excess of that based on cost; property, plant, and equipment, less accumulated depreciation, is carried at $_____ and $_____ in excess of an amount based on the cost to the Company; deferred income taxes of $_____ and $_____ have not been recorded; resulting in an increase of $_____ and $_____ in retained earnings and in appraisal surplus of $_____ and $_____, respectively. For the years ended December 31, 19X2 and 19X1, cost of goods sold has been increased $_____ and $_____, respectively, because of the effects of the depreciation accounting referred to above and deferred income taxes of $_____ and $_____ have not been provided, resulting in an increase in net income of $_____ and $_____, respectively.

In our opinion because of the effects of the matters discussed in the preceding paragraphs, the financial statements referred to above do not present fairly, in conformity with generally accepted accounting principles, the financial position of X Company as of December 31, 19X2 and 19X1, or the results of its operations or its cash flows for the years then ended.

(Signature)

(Date)

Adverse opinions are rare in practice. Ordinarily, the implications of an audit report that financial statements are, in effect, misleading create unacceptable legal risks for a company. However, regulated companies may be required by statute to follow accounting practices that depart from generally accepted accounting principles. In addition, some small or closely held businesses insist on presenting assets at appraisal value. In both circumstances, the auditor usually must express a qualified or adverse opinion.

EXPLANATORY LANGUAGE ADDED TO THE STANDARD REPORT

Certain circumstances require the auditor to add explanatory language to the standard report. The report remains an unqualified opinion. SAS No. 58 (AU 508.11) includes the following in its list of certain circumstances:

a. The auditor's opinion is based in part on the report of another auditor.

b. To prevent the financial statements from being misleading because of unusual circumstances, the financial statements contain a departure from an accounting principle promulgated by a body designated by the AICPA Council to establish such principles.

c. The financial statements are affected by uncertainties concerning future events, the outcome of which is not susceptible of reasonable estimation at the date of the auditor's report.

d. There is substantial doubt about the entity's ability to continue as a going concern.

e. There has been a material change between periods in accounting principles or in the method of their application.

f. Certain circumstances relating to reports on comparative financial statements exist.

g. Selected quarterly financial data required by SEC Regulation S-K has been omitted or has not been reviewed.

h. Supplementary information required by the Financial Accounting Standards Board (FASB) or the Governmental Accounting Standards Board (GASB) has been omitted, the presentation of such information departs materially from FASB or GASB guidelines, the auditor is unable to complete prescribed procedures with respect to such information, or the auditor is unable to remove substantial doubts about whether the supplementary information conforms to FASB or GASB guidelines.

i. Other information in a document containing audited financial statements is materially inconsistent with information appearing in the financial statements.

In addition, the auditor may add an explanatory paragraph to emphasize a matter regarding the financial statements.

Opinion Based in Part on the Report of Another Auditor

Sometimes it may be necessary for part of the audit of the financial statements on which an auditor is reporting to be made by another independent auditor. This circumstance may have a variety of causes. The client's operations may be spread over a wide geographical area including foreign locations. Companies having different auditors may combine by merger or acquisition. The auditor of an investor company may be different than the auditor of an investee company when an investment is accounted for by the equity method. In all these cases, an auditor finds it necessary to use the work of another auditor.

Reporting with Reference When a part of the audit has been made by other independent auditors, the unqualified opinion of the auditor reporting on the combined financial statements might read as follows:

Independent Auditor's Report

We have audited the consolidated balance sheets of ABC Company as of December 31, 19X2 and 19X1, and the related consolidated statements of income, retained earnings, and cash flows for the years then ended. These financial statements are the responsibility of the Company's management. Our responsibility is to express an opinion on these financial statements based on our audits. We did not audit the financial statements of B Company, a wholly owned subsidiary, which statements reflect total assets of $_____ and $_____ as of December 31, 19X2 and 19X1, respectively, and total revenues of $_____ and $_____ for the years then ended. Those statements were audited by other auditors whose report has been furnished to us, and our opinion, insofar as it relates to the amounts included for B Company, is based solely on the report of the other auditors.

We conducted our audits in accordance with generally accepted auditing standards. Those standards require that we plan and perform the audit to obtain reasonable assurance about whether the financial statements are free of material misstatement. An audit includes examining, on a test basis, evidence supporting the amounts and disclosures in the financial statements. An audit also includes assessing the accounting principles used and significant estimates made by management, as well as evaluating the overall financial statement presentation. We believe that our audits and the report of other auditors provide a reasonable basis for our opinion.

In our opinion, based on our audits and the report of other auditors, the consolidated financial statements referred to above present fairly, in all material respects, the financial position of ABC Company as of December 31, 19X2 and 19X1, and the results of its operations and its cash flows for the years then ended in conformity with generally accepted accounting principles.

(Signature)

(Date)

This modification of the opinion paragraph is the only officially sanctioned one that can be made without qualifying the opinion. The purpose of the modification is to indicate *divided responsibility* for the consolidated financial statements. The auditor of the parent company is dividing responsibility for the consolidated statements with the auditor of the subsidiary. To make the significance of the division of responsibility clear, the report complies with SAS No. 1 (AU 543.07) which requires that reference to other auditors be made "in both the introductory, scope and opinion paragraphs," and that the reference "disclose the magnitude of the portion of the financial statements audited by the other auditor."

Decisions concerning Reference   The auditor using the work of another independent auditor must decide (1) whether enough work has been done to serve as principle auditor, (2) whether to make reference to the other auditor in the report, and (3) how much work is needed to coordinate the audit with that of the other auditor, assuming the auditor is satisfied concerning the professional reputation and independence of the other auditor.

If significant parts of the audit have been performed by other auditors, a question is raised about the appropriateness of one auditor reporting on the consolidated statements. SAS No. 1 (AU 543.02) indicates that the auditor should consider the following factors in deciding whether to serve as principal auditor:

> . . . the materiality of the portion of the financial statements he has audited in comparison with the portion audited by other auditors, the extent of his knowledge of the overall financial statements, and the importance of the components he audited in relation to the enterprise as a whole.

If the principal auditor is willing to assume the responsibility for the work of the other auditor as if the auditor had performed it, then the auditor should not make reference to the other auditor in the report. An auditor probably would be willing to accept that responsibility only if he or she exercised a good deal of control over the work of the other auditor.

Whether or not reference is made to the work of the other auditor, the principal auditor should carry out inquiries as to the professional reputation and independence of the other auditor. Also, the auditor should coordinate activities with those of the other auditor to achieve a proper review of matters affecting the combined financial statements. For example, information on related parties or intercompany eliminations may be obtained from the other auditor.

Departure from a Promulgated Accounting Principle

Rule 203 of the AICPA Code of Professional Conduct states:

> A member shall not (1) express an opinion or state affirmatively that the financial statements or other financial data of any entity are presented in conformity with generally accepted accounting principles or (2) state that he or she is not aware of any material modifications that should be made to such statements or data in order for them to be in conformity with generally accepted accounting principles, if such statements or data contain any departure from an accounting principle promulgated by bodies designated by Council to establish such principles that has a material effect on the statements or data taken as a whole. If, however, the statements or data contain such a departure and the member can demonstrate that due to unusual circumstances the financial statements or data would otherwise have been misleading, the member can comply with the rule by describing the departure, its approximate effects, if practicable, and the reasons why compliance with the principle would result in a misleading statement.

SAS No. 69 (AU 411) further explains the application of Rule 203 in defining the meaning of the use of "present fairly in conformity with generally accepted accounting principles" in the audit report. Rule 203 and SAS No. 69 (AU 411) imply that application of accounting principles specified in authoritative pronouncements usually results in financial statements that are not misleading. Nevertheless, Rule 203 provides for the possibility that literal application of accounting principles specified in authoritative pronouncements might, in unusual circumstances, result in misleading financial statements.

When the unusual circumstances contemplated by Rule 203 exist and the statements thus depart from an authoritative pronouncement because following the pronouncement would result in misleading financial statements, the auditor's report should present in a separate paragraph or paragraphs the information required by Rule 203, including a description of the departure, its approximate effects, if practicable, and the reasons why the departure is necessary to make the financial statements not misleading. However, unless reasons other than the departure modify the opinion, the auditor should in these circumstances express an unqualified opinion with respect to conformity with generally accepted accounting principles. The accounting principle that departs from authoritative pronouncements is a generally accepted accounting principle because it is required in the unusual circumstances to make the statements not misleading. When the unusual circumstances contemplated by Rule 203 exist and the statements do not depart from the applicable authoritative pronouncement, the auditor should qualify the opinion or express an adverse opinion.

The explanatory paragraph for a departure might read as follows:

Independent Auditor's Report

[Same first and second paragraphs as the standard report]

As explained in Note X to the financial statements, the Company has changed its method of recording revenues from the recognition of revenue at the time of sale to the recognition of revenue over the membership term and has applied this change retroactively in its financial statements. Accounting Principles Board [APB] Opinion No. 20, "Accounting Changes," provides that such a change be made by including, as an element of net earnings during the year of change, the cumulative effect of the change on prior years. Had APB Opinion No. 20 been followed literally, the cumulative effect of the accounting change would have been included as a change in the 19X2 income statement. Because of the magnitude and pervasiveness of this change, we believe a literal application of APB Opinion No. 20 would result in a misleading presentation, and that the change should therefore be made on a retroactive basis. Accordingly, the accompanying consolidated financial statements for 19X1 have been restated.

In our opinion, the financial statements referred to above present fairly, in all material respects, the consolidated financial position of ABC Corporation and consolidated subsidiaries as of December 31, 19X2 and 19X1, and the consolidated results of their operations and their cash flows for the years then ended in conformity with generally accepted accounting principles.

(Signature)

(Date)

Uncertainties

When uncertainty exists with respect to a future event that could have a material effect on financial position or results of operations, SAS No. 58 (AU 508) requires the auditor to consider whether an explanatory paragraph needs to be added to the report. In preparing financial statements, management must estimate the outcome of future events. Estimates are made, for example, of the useful lives of depreciable assets, the collectibility of accounts receivable, the net realizable value of inventory items, and the amount of liability for product warranty. By considering various types of evidence, including the historical experience of the company and its relevance in estimating the effects of future events, the auditor ordinarily is able to obtain sufficient competent evidential matter on the propriety of management's estimates. If the auditor disagrees with management's estimates, the auditor should express a qualified or adverse opinion because of a departure from generally accepted accounting principles.

However, the outcome of some matters that may affect the financial statements or the related disclosures is not susceptible to reasonable estimation. When such uncertainties exist, it cannot be determined whether the financial statements should be adjusted and, if they should, in what amount. Examples are the outcome of a major contract or the likelihood that a material amount will become collectible or payable because of income tax or other litigation.

The pertinent portion of a report containing an explanatory paragraph because of an uncertainty might read as follows:

Independent Auditor's Report

[Same three paragraphs as the standard report]

As discussed in Note X to the financial statements, the Company is a defendant in a lawsuit alleging infringement of certain patent rights and claiming royalties and punitive damages. The Company has filed a counteraction, and preliminary hearings and discovery proceedings on both actions are in progress. The ultimate outcome of the litigation cannot presently be determined. Accordingly no provision for any liability that may result upon adjudication has been made in the accompanying financial statements.

Decisions concerning Uncertainties   If it is probable that the uncertainty will result in a material loss, but a reasonable estimate of the loss cannot be made, the auditor adds an explanatory paragraph to the standard report. If there is only a remote likelihood of material loss, no explanatory paragraph is added. If the likelihood is in between probable and remote that a material loss will occur, the auditor decides whether to add the explanatory paragraph by considering how large a material loss it might be and whether the likelihood is closer to "remote" or closer to "probable."

Uncertainties are different from scope limitations or departures from generally accepted accounting principles. Evidential matter that would resolve the uncertainty is neither available nor reasonably attainable by the application of auditing procedures. Nor does the auditor disagree with management's presentation of the financial statements. Thus, the opinion remains unqualified.

Uncertainties versus Scope Limitations   Uncertainties are matters that are expected to be resolved in the *future*. Currently, sufficient evidence does not exist to support an estimation of the outcome of the future events. If sufficient evidence exists or existed in the past but is not available to the auditor, the matter should not be addressed by including the explanatory paragraph for uncertainties. A qualified opinion or disclaimer because of a scope limitation would be more appropriate.

Uncertainties versus GAAP Departures   Uncertainties should be adequately disclosed and presented in accordance with GAAP. SFAS No. 5, "Accounting for Contingencies," provides guidance on GAAP for some, but not all, kinds of uncertainties. If the uncertainty is not disclosed in accordance with GAAP and the effect is material, a qualified or adverse opinion is appropriate.

Going Concern Uncertainties

Uncertainties also include doubt about a company's ability to continue operating because of complex, related problems, such as recurring operating losses, working capital shortages, inability to obtain financing, and failure to comply with the terms of loan agreements. These are so-called going concern uncertainties.

The auditor's responsibilities for considering whether conditions and events indicate that substantial doubt exists that the company will continue as a going concern, and for evaluating management's plans to deal with the adverse effects of the conditions and events are discussed in Chapters 5 and 12. "Substantial doubt" exists when the auditor does not believe liquidation is *probable,* but also cannot conclude that liquidation is *remote*.

If the auditor concludes that there is substantial doubt about the client's ability to continue as a going concern for a reasonable period (not to exceed 1 year from the date of the financial statements), an explanatory paragraph should be added to the standard report, for example:

Independent Auditor's Report

[Same three paragraphs as the standard report]

The accompanying financial statements have been prepared assuming that the Company will continue as a going concern. As discussed in Note X to the financial statements, the Company has suffered recurring losses from operations and has a net capital deficiency that raise substantial doubt about its ability to continue as a going concern. Management's plans in regard to these matters are also described in Note X. The financial statements do not include any adjustments that might result from the outcome of this uncertainty.

The explanatory paragraph for these circumstances must include the words "substantial doubt" and "going concern."

Inconsistent Application of Accounting Principles

When there is a change in accounting principles that has a material effect on the comparability of financial statements, the auditor should add an explanatory paragraph to the report that identifies the change and refers to the note in the financial statements that discusses the change. SAS No. 58 (AU 508.34) discusses appropriate report language for an inconsistency in the application of generally accepted accounting principles. The general subject of accounting changes, including changes in accounting principles, is covered in APB Opinion No. 20 (Current Text A06). That opinion indicates that some accounting changes should be reported by restating financial statements of prior years, but other accounting changes should be reported by recognizing the effect of the changes in current and future years. The following is an example of an appropriate explanatory paragraph:

> As discussed in Note X to the financial statements, the Company changed its method of computing depreciation in 19X2.

Figure 13-2 summarizes the effect of accounting changes and other changes on the standard report language.

Reporting on Other Aspects of Accounting Changes   When a company makes a change in an accounting principle, the auditor must be concerned with several aspects of the change in addition to its impact on consistency. According to SAS No. 58 (AU 508.59):

> The auditor should evaluate a change in accounting principle to satisfy himself that (a) the newly adopted accounting principle is a generally accepted accounting principle, (b) the method of accounting for the effect of the change is in conformity with generally accepted accounting principles, and (c) management's justification for the change is reasonable.

Effect on audit report	Type of accounting change or other change	Accounting treatment of change
Add explanatory paragraph (Both addition of an explanatory paragraph and financial statement disclosure are necessary.)	• Change in accounting principle	Cumulative effect adjustment or restatement
	• Change in reporting entity	Restatement
	• Correction of an error in principle	Prior-period adjustment
	• Change in principle inseparable from change in estimate	Current or prospective
No explanatory paragraph required (Disclosure of the matter in financial statements may be necessary.)	• Change in accounting estimate	Current or prospective
	• Error correction not involving principle	Prior-period adjustment
	• Change in classification	Restatement
	• Substantially different transactions or events	No adjustment necessary
	• Changes expected to have a material future effect	No adjustment necessary

FIGURE 13-2
The effect of types of accounting changes and other changes on the standard report language. [See APB Opinion No. 20 (Current Text A06) for explanation of accounting treatment.]

If a change in accounting principle does not meet these conditions, the auditor should qualify the opinion or express an adverse opinion as to the fair presentation of the financial statements in conformity with generally accepted accounting principles.

Comparative Financial Statements—Updated Reports

A continuing auditor's consideration of the effect on prior-period financial statements of matters that come to the auditor's attention during the current audit may cause the auditor to change the current report on the prior-period statements. For example, the method of accounting for an item that caused a qualification in the prior period may be changed and the item restated in the current period.

Whenever the auditor's updated report differs from the report issued the prior period, the auditor should include an explanatory paragraph in the current report on comparative statements that explains the change. The following example illustrates the requirements the explanatory paragraph should meet:

Independent Auditor's Report

[Same first and second paragraphs as the standard report]

In our report dated March 1, 19X2, we expressed an opinion that the 19X1 financial statements did not fairly present financial position, results of operations, and cash flows in conformity with generally accepted accounting principles because of two departures from such principles: (1) The Company carried its property, plant, and equipment at appraisal values, and provided for depreciation on the basis of such values, and (2) the Company did not provide for deferred income taxes with respect to differences between income for financial reporting purposes and taxable income. As described in Note X, the Company has changed its method of accounting for these items and restated its 19X1 financial statements to conform with generally accepted accounting principles. Accordingly, our present opinion on the 19X1 financial statements, as presented herein, is different from that expressed in our previous report.

In our opinion, the financial statements referred to above present fairly, in all material respects, the financial position of X Company as of December 31, 19X2 and 19X1, and the results of its operations and its cash flows for the years then ended in conformity with generally accepted accounting principles.

(Signature)

(Date)

Information outside the Basic Financial Statements

The auditor is required to add explanatory language to the standard report in certain circumstances related to information outside the basic annual financial statements. The auditor reads other information in the document containing the audited financial statements.

If the auditor concludes that the other information in the annual report document is materially inconsistent with information in the financial statements, one of his or her alternatives is to add an explanatory paragraph describing the inconsistency. This situation is discussed further in the next section, Auditor-Client Communications.

Another situation in which the auditor is required to add explanatory language to the report involves the supplementary information required by the FASB and GASB. The auditor applies certain limited procedures (e.g., inquiry of management and comparison to the audited financial statements) to the required supplementary information. The supplementary information is not considered audited. However, if the required information is omitted, the presentation departs materially from FASB or GASB requirements, or the auditor is unable to perform the limited procedures or to remove substantial doubt about whether the supplementary information conforms to the FASB or GASB guidelines, then the auditor would add an explanatory paragraph to the report.

Also, in certain circumstances, SEC Regulation S-K requires presentation of quarterly financial data in the annual financial statement. If that data were omitted or were not reviewed by the auditor, the auditor would add explanatory language to the report.

Emphasis of a Matter

The auditor may wish to emphasize a matter regarding the financial statements but still express an unqualified opinion. For example, the auditor may wish to point out that the entity is a component of a larger business enterprise or that it engages in transactions with related parties; or the auditor may wish to call attention to an unusually important subsequent event or to a matter affecting the comparability of the financial statements with those of the preceding period. Such explanatory information ordinarily is presented in a separate explanatory paragraph of the auditor's report.

Old Reporting Terms

At one time the standard report was called the short-form report to distinguish it from a long-form report—a report containing details of accounting records and audit scope, and sometimes analytical comments, in addition to the basic statements. Long-form reports are no longer as common, and the phrase "short-form" was dropped from the official literature in 1974.

At the same time "piecemeal" opinions were prohibited. A piecemeal opinion was a disclaimer or adverse opinion with the addition of a positive opinion on specific and identified financial statement items. Piecemeal opinions were prohibited because of the risk of overshadowing or contradicting a disclaimer or adverse opinion.

Many years ago the audit report was called a "certificate." At that time the standard report's opinion paragraph was introduced by the phrase "we hereby certify." This language was dropped, because it implied too much exactitude, and replaced by the current "in our opinion." This change was made over 50 years ago, but some people still refer to the audit report as a "certificate" and to the audit as a "certified audit." Outmoded terms often linger several years after an official change, but the longevity of "certificate" is a record.

Before the issuance of SAS No. 58 in 1988, a material uncertainty required the auditor to issue a report with a so-called "subject to" qualification. The report had a qualified opinion with the words "subject to" in place of "except for." After years of controversy, the "subject to" qualification has been eliminated, but knowledge of the term remains valuable to understand past reports, audit literature, and clients who may make reference to the old kind of report.

Another term that is not used in official literature is "clean" opinion. A clean opinion is an unqualified opinion. Auditors also sometimes refer to a "clean audit," meaning an audit that is trouble-free because client records are well maintained, control structure is good, and there are no unusual problems in the presentation of financial statements. Although unofficial, "clean" opinions and "clean audits" are still common phrases today.

AUDITOR-CLIENT COMMUNICATIONS

The relationship between auditor and client has many dimensions. One factor that has a significant effect on the relationship is the form in which the client is organized—corporation, partnership, or proprietorship. This section focuses on the corporate client whose stock is publicly traded.

Communicating with Stockholders

The most important communication between a corporation and its stockholders is the annual report. Normally, the financial statements included in the annual report are comparative balance sheets, income statements, and statements of cash flows. Beyond the inclusion of audited financial statements, the form and content of annual reports vary substantially. Some companies issue elaborate reports with pictures of physical facilities and personnel, graphs and charts of operating data, and supplemental financial information. Other companies may send stockholders only the basic financial statements with a covering letter. Regardless of the form or content of the annual report, the auditor's opinion on the financial statements included in the report is the principal means of communication between the auditor and stockholders.

Other Information in an Annual Report   Most annual reports include financial data that are not part of the basic comparative financial statements. For example, there are historical financial summaries of 5 or 10 years' operating results, highlights of key figures from the financial statements, and analyses of financial data in the president's letter. Much of this other information in an annual report is based on the audited financial statements.

According to SAS No. 8 (AU 550.04):

> Other information in a document may be relevant to an audit performed by an independent auditor or to the continuing propriety of his or her report.

Thus, the auditor should (1) read the entire annual report and (2) consider whether the *other information* is consistent with the audited financial statements. The auditor has no responsibility to apply audit procedures to the other information to corroborate it, but the auditor has a responsibility to read it and compare it with audited data.

Since much of the other information is derived from or related closely to the financial statements, the auditor should have a basis for recognizing material inconsistencies. For example, the president's letter might describe an increase in net income but omit the fact that net income for the current year includes a material extraordinary gain, or the financial highlights section may include cash flow per share which the SEC (ASR No. 142) believes may be misleading to investors and which is not permitted by SFAS No. 95, "Statement of Cash Flows."

If the auditor concludes that there is a material inconsistency and the problem is caused by the other information, the auditor should ask the client to revise it. If the client will not, the auditor should consider actions such as:

1 Revising the audit report to include an explanatory paragraph describing the material inconsistency
2 Withholding the use of the audit report in the annual report
3 Withdrawing from the engagement

The appropriate action will depend on the significance of the inconsistency. For example, the auditor might add an explanatory paragraph such as the following to the standard report:

> Revenues and net income for 19X8, as stated in the president's letter on page 2, have not been restated to give effect to the acquisition, in June 19X9, of ABC Co. in a transaction accounted for as a pooling of interests. Restated revenues and net income for 19X8, as reported in the statement of income referred to in the preceding paragraphs of this report, were $_____ and $_____, respectively.

Note that the auditor's opinion would be unqualified, because the deficiency is not in the audited financial statements.

Stockholders' Meetings Auditors in the United States do not have a legal right to attend meetings of stockholders, but many companies invite their auditors to attend. The auditors are then available to answer questions from stockholders about the audit, accounting policies followed by the company, or the company's accounting system. In addition, press coverage of financial disasters frequently raises questions from stockholders concerning the possibility of similar events befalling their company. Often the auditor can comment on the possibility of these events. Finally, attendance by auditors at annual stockholders' meetings seems desirable to demonstrate the auditor's role as an independent third party reviewing management's representations to company stockholders. The SEC, in an attempt to encourage auditor attendance at annual meetings, requires disclosure in the proxy statement of whether the auditor is expected to be present and available for questions.

Communicating with the Board of Directors

Normally, the authority to select the independent auditor is one of the powers of the board of directors, Thus, communications between the board and the independent auditor are more frequent and more extensive than with stockholders. In the United States, auditors do not have the right to attend meetings of the board of directors, but they may be invited to attend to discuss accounting or auditing matters. Sometimes the auditor may request to be present at a meeting of the board.

Many matters that might be discussed with the board of directors—such as the accounting system, internal control structure, and financial statement presentation—are the primary responsibility of the company's executive officers. Therefore, discretion is required in deciding what matters should be reported to the board. Discussion with the board is essential for matters that cannot be satisfactorily resolved with the executive officers. Unnecessary conflict with the executive officers usually can be avoided by allowing them to make a preliminary review of matters to be presented to the board, but the auditor cannot subordinate professional judgment concerning what matters should be reported directly to the board.

Communicating with Audit Committees

Usually, the board of directors of a publicly owned corporation will appoint an audit committee to serve as a channel of communication with the auditors. Appointment of an audit committee consisting primarily of "outside" directors has been endorsed by the New York Stock Exchange (NYSE), the SEC, and the AICPA. At the SEC's request, the NYSE amended its listing agreement to require that all listed companies have an audit committee made up of outside directors. In 1992, the American Stock Exchange began requiring listed companies to have an audit committee with a majority of the members being independent directors. NASDAQ-listed companies must also have such an audit committee.

Several Statements on Auditing Standards require certain communications to be made to the audit committee or, in organizations that do not have an audit committee, to individuals with an equivalent level of authority and responsibility. For example, the communication might be made to the board of directors, the board of trustees, or the owner of an owner-managed business. SAS No. 53 and SAS No. 54 require that irregularities or illegal acts, unless clearly inconsequential, be reported to the audit committee or the equivalent. However, irregularities and illegal acts involving senior management are not inconsequential and must always be reported. The same sort of communication requirement applies to reportable conditions in internal control structure.

Internal Control Structure Related Matters   SAS No. 60 (AU 325) requires that reportable conditions in internal control structure observed in an audit should be communicated to the audit committee or the equivalent.

SAS No. 60 (AU 325.02) defines a reportable condition as follows:

> . . . matters coming to the auditor's attention that, in his judgment, should be communicated to the audit committee because they represent significant deficiencies in the design

or operation of the internal control structure, which could adversely affect the organization's ability to record, process, summarize, and report financial data consistent with the assertions of management in the financial statements.

The reportable condition may involve any of the five components of internal control: the control environment, risk assessment, information and communication, control activities, or monitoring activities. In deciding whether a matter is a reportable condition, the auditor considers factors such as the size of the company and its ownership characteristics, the organizational structure, and the complexity and diversity of company activities. For example, an internal control structure deficiency that is a reportable condition for a large sophisticated financial institution may not be a reportable condition for a small manufacturing concern.

The auditor is not required to search for reportable conditions, but if he or she becomes aware of a reportable condition in obtaining an understanding of the internal control structure or in performing audit procedures, the condition should be communicated.

SAS No. 60 (AU 325) permits the communication to be oral or written, although it expresses a preference for the latter. An oral communication needs to be documented in the work papers. SAS No. 60 (AU 325) requires that any report issued on reportable conditions should meet the following requirements:

- Indicate that the purpose of the audit was to report on the financial statements and not to express assurance on the internal control structure
- Include the definition of reportable conditions
- Include a restriction on distribution that limits it to the use of management, the audit committee, and others within the organization

The communication is not required before issuance of the audit report. However, because timely communication may be important, the auditor may choose to communicate during the course of the audit.

The following example illustrates wording to satisfy the requirements:

In planning and performing our audit of the financial statements of the ABC Corporation for the year ended December 31, 19XX, we considered its internal control structure in order to determine our auditing procedures for the purpose of expressing our opinion on the financial statements and not to provide assurance on the internal control structure. However, we noted certain matters involving the internal control structure and its operation that we consider to be reportable conditions under standards established by the American Institute of Certified Public Accountants. Reportable conditions involve matters coming to our attention relating to significant deficiencies in the design or operation of the internal control structure that, in our judgment, could adversely affect the organization's ability to record, process, summarize, and report financial data consistent with assertions of management in the financial statements.

[Include paragraphs to describe the reportable conditions noted.]

This report is intended solely for the information and use of the audit committee (board of directors, board of trustees, or owners in owner-managed enterprises), management, and others within the organization (or specified regulatory agency or other specified third party).

Material Weaknesses   A very significant reportable condition may be a *material weakness*. SAS No. 60 (AU 325.15) defines a material weakness as:

> a reportable condition in which the design or operation of one or more of the internal control structure elements does not reduce to a relatively low level the risk that errors or irregularities in amounts that would be material in relation to the financial statements being audited may occur and not be detected within a timely period by employees in the normal course of performing their assigned functions.

Management or members of audit committees sometimes request the auditor to separately identify material weaknesses, or to state that the reportable conditions identified are not material weaknesses. If the auditor wishes to communicate that there are no material weaknesses among the reportable conditions identified, paragraphs like the following would be included in the report:

[Include the first paragraph of the previous example report.]

[Include paragraphs to describe reportable conditions noted.]

A material weakness is a reportable condition in which the design or operation of one or more of the internal control structure elements does not reduce to a relatively low level the risk that errors or irregularities in amounts that would be material in relation to the financial statements being audited may occur and not be detected within a timely period by employees in the normal course of performing their assigned functions.

Our consideration of the internal control structure would not necessarily disclose all matters in the internal control structure that might be reportable conditions and, accordingly, would not necessarily disclose all reportable conditions that are also considered to be material weaknesses as defined above. However, none of the reportable conditions described above is believed to be a material weakness.

[Include the final paragraph of the previous example report.]

The auditor should not issue a report stating that no reportable conditions were noted during the audit, because such a report might be misinterpreted.

Other Audit Committee Communications   SAS No. 61 (AU 380) deals with communications with audit committees. However, the communications covered by SAS No. 61 (AU 380) are required only for a public company or a company that has a formally designated audit committee or another group formally designated with responsibility for oversight of the financial reporting process. In this respect, the requirements of SAS No. 61 (AU 380) differ from those related to communication of irregularities, illegal acts, and reportable conditions which are required in all audits.

SAS No. 61 (AU 380) is designed to enhance communications between the auditor and the audit committee and to ensure that the audit committee is informed concerning matters significant to the financial reporting process.

The auditor should ensure that those with oversight responsibility know about the following matters:

- The auditor's responsibility:
  - Responsibility in an audit and the nature of assurance provided
  - Responsibility for other information in documents containing audited financial statements
- The financial statements:
  - Initial selection and changes in significant accounting policies or their application
  - Process management uses in formulating sensitive accounting estimates and the basis for the auditor's conclusion about reasonableness
  - Any audit adjustments, whether recorded or nor, that could have a significant effect
- Auditor-management relationships:
  - Any disagreements with management about matters significant to the financial statements or audit report, whether satisfactorily resolved or not
  - The auditor's view of significant matters on which management has consulted other accountants
  - Major issues discussed with management prior to retention of the auditor or continuation of the engagement
  - Serious difficulties encountered with management in completing the audit

Communications between the auditor and the audit committee may be oral or written. Oral communications should be documented in the work papers. A written communication should include a restriction on use, such as "prepared solely for the Company's audit committee and management." The communications are not ordinarily required before the audit report date, but more timely communication may be necessary. The auditor's responsibility is to see that the audit committee is informed about the matters. For example, management may communicate certain of the matters as long as the auditor is satisfied that the audit committee has been informed. Finally, not all of the matters need be communicated at the same time or in the same way. For example, the auditor's responsibilities in an audit may be covered in the engagement letter, selection of accounting principles in a separate written report, and other matters orally in a meeting.

Communicating with Management

Most of the communication between an auditor and a client is with the company's executive officers. Contacts between the auditor and management are more extensive, more frequent, and more informal than those with stockholders, audit committees, and boards of directors.

The Management Letter   The principal written communication between the auditor and management is the *management letter* that normally is issued annually at the conclusion of every audit engagement. This letter summarizes the auditor's recommendations for improvement in internal control structure.

The management letter is intended to be a private communication between the auditor and management. However, some parties, such as bankers, request copies of the management letter. In addition, SAS No. 60 (AU 325) requires that the auditor communicate to the audit committee the reportable conditions related to the internal control structure that came to his or her attention during the audit.

The management letter is the auditor's way of communicating matters that, in his or her judgment, are not significant enough to be reportable conditions. The auditor decides to communicate the matters for management's benefit, if he or she believes the comments would be helpful. Because the audit committee is also interested in the management letter, the report of "reportable conditions" and the management letter are often combined. Auditors generally indicate which of the comments relate to reportable conditions and which do not.

Client management sometimes asks the auditor to look into matters while doing the audit work. The client may wish to check into a particular area they believe could improve, or determine the cause of a problem or inefficiency, or may otherwise specify procedures for the auditor that would not otherwise be done in the audit.

Reporting on internal control structure is discussed further in Chapter 14.

Conferences with Management The most critical communication between the auditor and management concerns the form and content of the financial statements. The financial statements are management's representations, but, if the accounting principles or disclosures proposed by management differ materially from those which the auditor believes are appropriate, either an alternative presentation must be agreed on or the auditor will be unable to express an unqualified opinion.

If the auditor can convince management that a particular presentation is superior, management may be persuaded to change the financial statements. The auditor can attempt to demonstrate that the presentation proposed by management might be considered misleading or that it clearly departs from authoritative pronouncements or substantially favored practice. In some cases, management may be unfamiliar with accounting or auditing requirements of the accounting profession, the stock exchanges, or the SEC.

Sometimes questions concerning the appropriate application of generally accepted accounting principles or the adequacy of informative disclosures fall in a "gray" area. In this case, extensive discussion with management is usually necessary. Resolution of differences will depend on the attitudes and personalities of management and the auditor and the working relationship that has developed between them. The outcome may be a change in the financial statements, qualification of the auditor's opinion, or loss of the client.

CHAPTER 13 ASSIGNMENTS

OBJECTIVE QUESTIONS

13-1 For each of the following statements indicate whether the statement is true or false.

T F **a** The objective of the fourth standard of reporting is to enable users of financial statements to determine the extent to which financial statements reported on by an auditor may be relied on.

T F **b** The auditor will express an adverse opinion when the auditor has been prevented by management from obtaining sufficient competent evidential matter.

T F c The auditor need not explain the reason for a qualified opinion, provided the qualifying phrase refers to a note to the financial statements that explains the matter fully.

T F d The auditor may express an unqualified opinion on a balance sheet, but express a qualified opinion on the income statement for the period ended on the balance sheet date.

T F e When a client imposes restrictions on the scope of an audit, the auditor's decision about the type of report to issue depends entirely on the materiality of the financial statement items to which restriction relates.

T F f When a client does not disclose essential information in financial statements, the auditor ordinarily should provide the information in the audit report and express a qualified or adverse opinion.

T F g When the auditor disagrees with management concerning the outcome of a future event, the auditor may express an unqualified opinion.

T F h When part of the audit has been made by other independent auditors, but the auditor intends to express an unqualified opinion, the division of responsibility must be clearly disclosed in an explanatory paragraph.

T F i Rule 203 permits a departure from generally accepted accounting principles when following the correct accounting principle would result in misleading financial statements.

T F j When an annual report contains materially inconsistent "other information," the auditor would express an unqualified opinion on the financial statements even if the material inconsistency is not removed.

13-2 The following questions relate to circumstances resulting in departure from the auditor's standard report. Select the *best* response.

  a Which of the following will *not* result in modification of the auditor's report due to a scope limitation?
    1 Restrictions imposed by the client
    2 Reliance placed on the report of another auditor
    3 Inability to obtain sufficient competent evidential matter
    4 Inadequacy in the accounting records

  b A lawyer limits a response concerning a litigated claim because the lawyer is unable to determine the likelihood of an unfavorable outcome. Which type of opinion should the auditor express if the litigation is adequately disclosed and the range of potential loss is material in relation to the client's financial statements considered as a whole?
    1 Adverse
    2 Unqualified with explanatory language
    3 Qualified
    4 Unqualified

  c When restrictions that significantly limit the scope of the audit are imposed by the client, the auditor generally should issue which of the following opinions?
    1 Qualified
    2 Disclaimer
    3 Adverse
    4 Unqualified

  d Higgins Corporation is required to but does not wish to prepare and issue a statement of cash flows along with its other financial statements. In these circumstances, the independent auditor's report on the Higgins financial statements should include a(n):

    1 Unqualified opinion with a statement of cash flows prepared by the auditor included as part of the auditor's report

    2 Qualified opinion with an explanatory paragraph explaining that the company declined to present the required statement

    3 Adverse opinion stating that the financial statements, taken as whole, are *not* fairly presented because of the omission of the required statement

    4 Disclaimer of opinion with a separate explanatory paragraph stating why the company declined to present the required statement

e An auditor is confronted with an exception considered sufficiently material as to warrant some deviation from the standard unqualified auditor's report. If the exception relates to a departure from generally accepted accounting principles, the auditor must decide between expressing a(n):

    1 Qualified opinion and an unqualified opinion

    2 Adverse opinion and a qualified opinion

    3 Adverse opinion and a disclaimer of opinion

    4 Disclaimer of opinion and a qualified opinion

f A limitation on the scope of an auditor's examination sufficient to preclude an unqualified opinion will usually result when management:

    1 Presents financial statements that are prepared in accordance with the cash receipts and disbursements basis of accounting

    2 States that the financial statements are *not* intended to be presented in conformity with generally accepted accounting principles

    3 Does *not* make the minutes of the board of directors' meetings available to the auditor

    4 Asks the auditor to report on the balance sheet and *not* on the other basic financial statements

g In which of the following situations would an auditor ordinarily issue an unqualified audit opinion without an explanatory paragraph?

    1 The auditor wishes to emphasize that the entity had significant related-party transactions.

    2 The auditor decides to make reference to the report of another auditor as a basis, in part, for the auditor's opinion.

    3 The entity issues financial statements that present financial position and results of operations, but omits the statement of cash flows.

    4 The auditor has substantial doubt about the entity's ability to continue as a going concern, but the circumstances are fully disclosed in the financial statements.

h It is *not* appropriate to refer a reader of an auditor's report to a financial statement footnote for details concerning:

    1 Subsequent events

    2 The pro forma effects of a business combination

    3 Sale of a discontinued operation

    4 The results of confirmation of receivables

i An auditor concludes that there is a material inconsistency in the other information in an annual report to shareholders containing audited financial statements. If the auditor concludes that the financial statements do *not* require revision, but the client refuses to revise or eliminate the material inconsistency, the auditor may do the following:

    1 Issue an "except for" qualified opinion after discussing the matter with the client's board of directors

    2 Consider the matter closed since the other information is *not* in the audited financial statements

    3 Disclaim an opinion on the financial statements after explaining the material inconsistency in a separate explanatory paragraph

    4 Revise the auditor's report to include a separate explanatory paragraph describing the material inconsistency

  j If an auditor is satisfied that there is only a remote likelihood of a loss resulting from the resolution of a matter involving an uncertainty, the auditor should express a(n):

    1 Unqualified opinion

    2 Unqualified opinion with a separate explanatory paragraph

    3 Qualified opinion or disclaimer of opinion, depending upon the materiality of the loss

    4 Qualified opinion or disclaimer of opinion, depending on whether the uncertainty is adequately disclosed

AICPA

13-3 The following questions relate to circumstances resulting in departure from the auditor's standard report. Select the *best* response.

  a The management of Stanley Corporation has decided *not* to account for a material transaction in accordance with the provisions of a recent statement of the FASB. They have set forth their reasons in note "B" to the financial statements which clearly demonstrates that due to unusual circumstances the financial statements would otherwise have been misleading. The auditor's report will probably contain a(n):

    1 Consistency explanatory paragraph and a reference to note "B"

    2 Unqualified opinion and an explanatory paragraph

    3 Adverse opinion and an explanatory paragraph

    4 Qualified opinion and an explanatory paragraph

  b An auditor includes an explanatory paragraph in an otherwise unqualified report in order to emphasize that the entity being reported upon is a subsidiary of another business enterprise. The inclusion of this paragraph:

    1 Is appropriate and would *not* negate the unqualified opinion

    2 Is considered a qualification of the report

    3 Is a violation of generally accepted reporting standards if this information is disclosed in footnotes to the financial statements

    4 Necessitates a revision of the opinion paragraph to include the phrase "with the foregoing explanation"

  c Under which of the following set of circumstances might an auditor disclaim an opinion?

    1 The financial statements contain a departure from generally accepted accounting principles, the effect of which is material.

    2 The principal auditor decides to make reference to the report of another auditor who audited a subsidiary.

    3 There has been a material change between periods in the method of the application of accounting principles.

    4 There are significant uncertainties affecting the financial statements.

  d An auditor concludes that there is substantial doubt about an entity's ability to continue as a going concern for a reasonable period of time. If the entity's disclosures concerning this matter are adequate, the audit report may include a(n):

	Disclaimer of opinion	"Except for" qualified opinion
1	Yes	Yes
2	No	No
3	No	Yes
4	Yes	No

e An auditor should disclose the substantive reasons for expressing an adverse opinion in an explanatory paragraph:

1 Preceding the scope paragraph

2 Preceding the opinion paragraph

3 Following the opinion paragraph

4 Within the notes to the financial statements

f An auditor may *not* issue a qualified opinion when:

1 A scope limitation prevents the auditor from completing an important audit procedure.

2 The auditor's report refers to the work of a specialist.

3 An accounting principle at variance with generally accepted accounting principles is used.

4 The auditor lacks independence with respect to the audited entity.

g An auditor was unable to obtain audited financial statements or other evidence supporting an entity's investment in a foreign subsidiary. Between which of the following opinions should the entity's auditor choose?

1 Adverse and unqualified with an explanatory paragraph added

2 Disclaimer and unqualified with an explanatory paragraph added

3 Qualified and adverse

4 Qualified and disclaimer

AICPA

13-4 The following questions relate to the auditor's responsibility for reporting on inconsistency of application of accounting principles. Select the *best* response.

a Raider uses the last-in, first-out method of valuation for half of its inventory and the first-in, first-out method of valuation for the other half of its inventory. Assuming the auditor is satisfied in all other respects, under these circumstances the auditor will issue a(n):

1 Opinion qualified due to inconsistency

2 Unqualified opinion with an explanatory paragraph

3 Qualified or adverse opinion depending upon materiality

4 Unqualified opinion.

b Which one of the following would require a consistency explanatory paragraph in the auditor's report?

1 Changing the salvage value of an asset

2 Changing the presentation of prepaid insurance from inclusion in "other assets" to disclosing it as a separate line item

3 Division of the consolidated subsidiary into two subsidiaries which are both consolidated

4 Changing from consolidating a wholly owned subsidiary to carrying it on the equity basis

 c Which of the following should have a consistency explanatory paragraph in the auditor's report, whether or *not* the item is fully disclosed in the financial statements?

  1 A change in accounting estimate

  2 A change from an unacceptable accounting principle to a generally accepted one

  3 Correction of an error *not* involving a change in accounting principle

  4 A change in classification

 d If a client makes a change in accounting principle that is inseparable from the effect of a change in estimate, this material event should be accounted for as a change in:

  1 Estimate and the auditor would include a consistency explanatory paragraph

  2 Principle and the auditor would include a consistency explanatory paragraph

  3 Estimate and the auditor would *not* modify the report

  4 Principle and the auditor would *not* modify the report

 e A company has changed its method of inventory valuation from an unacceptable one to one in conformity with generally accepted accounting principles. The auditor's report on the financial statements of the year of the change should include:

  1 No reference to consistency

  2 A reference to a prior-period adjustment

  3 An additional paragraph explaining the change

  4 A justification for making the change and the impact of the change on reported net income

 f When there is a significant change in accounting principle, an auditor's report should refer to the lack of consistency in:

  1 The scope paragraph

  2 An explanatory paragraph between the second paragraph and the opinion paragraph

  3 The opinion paragraph

  4 An explanatory paragraph following the opinion paragraph

 g When management does *not* provide reasonable justification that a change in accounting principle is preferable and it presents comparative financial statements, the auditor should express a qualified opinion:

  1 Only in the year of the accounting principle change

  2 Each year that the financial statements initially reflecting the change are presented

  3 Each year until management changes back to the accounting principle formerly used

  4 Only if the change is to an accounting principle that is *not* generally accepted

                    AICPA

13-5 The following questions relate to the auditor's responsibility when associated with comparative financial statements. Select the *best* response.

 a When financial statements of a prior period are presented on a comparative basis with financial statements of the current period, the continuing auditor is responsible for:

  1 Expressing dual-dated opinions

  2 Updating the report on the previous financial statements only if there has *not* been a change in the opinion

  3 Updating the report on the previous financial statements only if the previous report was qualified and the reasons for the qualification no longer exist

  4 Updating the report on the previous financial statements regardless of the opinion previously issued

b An auditor's report on comparative financial statements should be dated as of the date of the:

1 Issuance of the report

2 Completion of the auditor's recent field work

3 Latest financial statements being reported on

4 Last subsequent event disclosed in the statements

c Comparative financial statements include the financial statements of a prior period which were audited by a predecessor auditor, whose report is *not* presented. If the predecessor auditor's report was qualified, the successor auditor must:

1 Express an opinion on the current year statements alone and make *no* reference to the prior-year statements

2 Disclose the reasons for any qualification included in the predecessor auditor's opinion

3 Obtain written approval from the predecessor auditor to include the prior year's financial statements

4 Issue a standard comparative report indicating the division of responsibility

d An auditor has previously expressed a qualified opinion on the financial statements of a prior period because of a departure from generally accepted accounting principles. The prior-period financial statements are restated in the current period to conform with generally accepted accounting principles. The auditor's updated report on the prior-period financial statements should:

1 Express an unqualified opinion concerning the restated financial statements

2 Be accompanied by the original auditor's report on the prior period

3 Bear the same date as the original auditor's report on the prior period

4 Qualify the opinion concerning the restated financial statements because of a change in accounting principle

e The predecessor auditor, who is satisfied after properly communicating with the successor auditor, has reissued a report because the audit client desires comparative financial statements. The predecessor auditor's report should make:

1 Reference to the report of the successor auditor only in the scope paragraph

2 Reference to the work of the successor auditor in the scope and opinion paragraphs

3 Reference to both the work and the report of the successor auditor only in the opinion paragraph

4 No reference to the report or the work of the successor auditor

AICPA

DISCUSSION QUESTIONS

Discussion questions require the application of the concepts explained in the chapter to specific facts, issues, or problems. They are classified by the primary topic to which they relate. However, responses should not be confined to primary topics but should include all relevant implications.

The Auditor's Reporting Obligation—General

13-6 J. O. Cole, a sole proprietor, operates a trucking business. Cole also has assets and liabilities in connection with other activities. You are retained to audit the accounts of the J. O. C. Truck Lines and to prepare a report to be used to obtain credit, but you are not to audit Cole's other business affairs. You find that the accounts of Truck Lines are in proper order, but you are concerned about the fact that Cole has other business operations and that he will have to pay income tax as an individual on the income of Truck Lines. No provision for this personal tax liability appears in the accounts of the Truck Lines.

a Give a brief discussion of the problem of reporting presented by this engagement.

b Assuming that a standard report is to be used, draft the report for J. O. C. Truck Lines.

AICPA adapted

13-7 A client, without consulting its CPA, has changed its accounting so that it is not in accordance with generally accepted accounting principles. During the regular audit engagement the CPA discovers that the statements based on the accounts are so grossly misleading that they might be considered fraudulent.

a Discuss the specific action to be taken by the CPA.

b In this situation what obligation does the CPA have to outsiders if he or she is replaced? Discuss briefly.

c In this situation what obligation does the CPA have to a new auditor if he or she is replaced? Discuss briefly.

AICPA

13-8 The client of a CPA is a partnership. The drawings of the managing partner are considerably in excess of the partner's pro rata share of earnings. Other partners are not aware of the excess drawings because financial statements and tax returns are submitted to them without details of individual partners' balances or withdrawals. No salaries are paid to the partners.

a Discuss the specific action to be taken by the CPA.

b In this situation what obligation does the CPA have to the other partners? Discuss briefly.

c In this situation what obligation does the CPA have to outsiders? Discuss briefly.

d What agreements might be found in the contract between the partners that make action by the CPA unnecessary?

AICPA

Consistency

13-9 Included with financial statements of the Bowie Manufacturing Company is a typical standard report. Based on this opinion, could you properly conclude that the company is applying generally accepted accounting principles on the same basis as it did 10 year ago? If not, why is such consistency not required by CPAs?

13-10 You are engaged in your second annual audit of the financial statements of the Nittany Corporation, a medium-size manufacturing company with 25 stockholders that manufactures optical instruments. During the audit the following matter comes to your attention:

The president's salary has been increased substantially over the prior year by action of the board of directors. The present salary is much greater than salaries paid to presidents of companies of comparable size and is clearly excessive. You determine that the method of computing the president's salary was changed for the year under audit. In prior years the president's salary was consistently based on sales. In the latest year, however, the salary was based on net income before taxes. The

Nittany Corporation is in a cyclical industry and would have had an extremely profitable year except that the increase in the president's salary syphoned off much of the income that would have accrued to the stockholders. The president is a substantial stockholder.

a Discuss your responsibility for disclosing this situation.
b Discuss the effect, if any, that the situation has upon your audit report as to:
   1 The conformity of the financial statements with generally accepted accounting principles
   2 The consistency of the application of accounting principles

AICPA adapted

Modification of the Auditor's Standard Report

13-11 The financial statements for the Old Salt Shipbuilding Company, prepared for the year ended June 30, 19X9, contain the following note:

> It is the Company's consistent accounting practice to recognize profit and loss from shipyard operations on the completed contract basis, except that estimated losses on uncompleted contracts are provided for when ascertainable. A substantial loss was incurred on completion during the current year of a contract for the construction of two patrol escort vessels for the United States Navy. Shipyard costs and expenses for the previous year included a provision for such loss in the net amount of $350,000 (representing the $630,000 loss estimated at that time, less $280,000 of federal income taxes expected to be recovered under carryback provisions of the Internal Revenue Code), and the remainder of the loss is included in the operating results for the current year. The financial statements for the previous year have been restated for purposes of comparability to include $630,000 in shipyard costs and expenses and to show $280,000 as an estimated tax refund.
>
> The loss on this contract may be reduced by indeterminable amounts which may be collected as a result of claims which have not been negotiated with the Navy.

Prepare the auditor's report to accompany the statements, assuming that the auditor has complied with generally accepted auditing standards and has no questions on any matters except those covered in the note.

13-12 You have assigned your assistant to the audit of the Bell Sales Company's fire insurance policies. All routine audit procedures with regard to the fire insurance register have been completed (i.e., vouching, footing, examination of canceled checks, computation of insurance expense and repayment, tracing of expense charges to appropriate expense accounts, etc.).

After reviewing your assistant's work papers, you concur in the conclusion that the insurance coverage against loss by fire is inadequate and that, if loss occurs, the company may have insufficient assets to liquidate its debts. After a discussion with you, management refuses to increase the amount of insurance coverage.

a What mention will you make of this condition and contingency in your standard report? Why?
b What effect will this condition and contingency have upon your opinion? Give reasons for your position.

AICPA adapted

13-13 Lerna Corporation (whose fiscal year will end December 31, 19X8) informs you on December 18, 19X8, that it has a serious shortage of working capital because of heavy operating losses incurred since October 1, 19X8. Application has been made to a bank for a loan, and the bank's loan officer has requested financial statements.

Indicate the type of report you would render under each of the following independent sets of circumstances. Give the reasons for your decision.

a Lerna asks that you save time by auditing the financial statements prepared by Lerna's chief accountant as of September 20, 19X8. The scope of your audit would not be limited by Lerna in any way.

b Lerna asks that you conduct an audit as of December 15, 19X8. The scope of your audit would not be limited by Lerna in any way.

c Lerna asks that you conduct an audit as of December 15, 19X8, and render a report by January 16. To save time and reduce the cost of the audit, it is requested that your audit not include circularization of accounts receivable or observation of the taking of inventory.

d Lerna asks that you prepare financial statements as of December 15, 19X8, from the books and records of the company without audit. The statements are to be submitted on plain paper without your name being associated in any way with them. The reason for your preparing the statements is your familiarity with proper form for financial statements.

AICPA adapted

13-14 You have been approached by promoters to give an opinion on the financial statements to be included in the prospectus of a proposed corporation to be named U-Park Corporation.

U-Park will own and operate a downtown parking garage and plans to purchase parking lots. The promoters now own and operate a parking garage which they acquired 3 months ago for $100,000. At the time of acquisition an independent expert appraiser placed a value of $300,000 on the property. There has been no change in the values of downtown properties in recent months. The property is currently mortgaged for $50,000.

The new corporation will have an authorized capital of 50,000 shares with a par value of $10 per share. The promoters will receive 25,000 shares of stock in exchange for the parking garage, which U-Park will acquire subject to the existing mortgage of $50,000. There will be a public offering on the remaining of 25,000 shares at $9 per share. The public sale will not be subject to SEC approval because the sale will be restricted to the residents of one state.

It is the intention of the promoters to have the prospectus balance sheet show a value of $300,000 for the parking garage and a net worth of $250,000.

Would it be proper to allow your name to be used in connection with this proposed balance sheet if full disclosure is made in a note to the balance sheet? Discuss fully.

AICPA adapted

13-15 The processing operations of Gaylord Company, your client, require a basic raw material, colgum, which is imported and refined by domestic suppliers. Colgum is combined with other raw materials of the same general category to produce the finished product. Gaylord Co. has been disturbed by the unreliability of the supply because of the international situation and labor troubles of the suppliers, and it has stockpiled a large supply of colgum to assure continued operations. This supply of colgum is a substantial portion of Gaylord's inventory, and you determine that it is a 3-year supply. Colgum is a staple commodity widely used in manufacturing operations. Gaylord has consistently applied the "lower of cost or market" rule to the valuation of its total inventory. The year-end market price of colgum is less than Gaylord's cost.

a What effect, if any, would this excess supply have upon the financial statements and your report? Discuss briefly.

b What effect, if any, would this excess supply have upon the application of the rule of "cost or market, whichever is lower" to the valuation of individual items as against category totals in the total inventory? Discuss briefly.

AICPA

13-16 You are engaged as the auditor for an employee's profitsharing pension trust which has been in existence for a number of years. Each qualified employee has an equity in the trust which the employee is entitled to receive when he or she leaves the company. The membership of participating employees changes each year because additional employees qualify while others are retired. The amount of equity received varies with length of service from zero for the first 5 years up to 100 percent with 10 years of service. The trust agreement does not state how the fund's assets should be valued.

The trust's assets consist of the following:

	Cost, $	Market, $
Cash	50,000	50,000
Rental properties (building)	100,000	250,000
Stocks	1,000,000	1,250,000
Bonds	500,000	400,000

a You are requested to give the trustees your recommendations for the valuation of the trust's assets in audited financial statements and the reasons for your recommendations.

b Would your opinion be a standard report, or would you vary it, and if so, how?

c The trustees inform you that the trust has entered into a 10-year lease on the rental property. The trust is to receive annual rents of $21,000 for 10 years, and the lessee has the option to purchase the building for $125,000 at the end of the lease. The lessee has installed an expensive air-conditioning system and has expended substantial sums for remodeling and modernization. The trustees would like your recommendations for valuing the building in the accounts this year and in the future, and your suggestions for the proper accounting entries to record the yearly $21,000 payments.

d What disclosure, if any, of the lease should be made in the financial statements?

AICPA

13-17 The Landa Manufacturing Company was incorporated and began business on January 1, 19X3. It has been successful and now requires a bank loan for additional working capital to finance expansion. The bank has requested an audited statement for the year ended December 31, 19X6. The company has not had an audit made in prior years. You have been retained to audit the financial statements.

The following is the condensed balance sheet as of November 30, 19X6:

Cash	$ 20,000	Current liabilities	$200,000
Accounts receivable	30,000	Mortgage	300,000
Inventory	300,000	Capital stock: 3,000	
Plant machinery and equipment	500,000	shares no par value	300,000
Other assets	50,000	Retained earnings	100,000
	$900,000		$900,000

Your audit disclosed the following facts:

1 The company started a job cost system in 19X6. Prior to that time no unit costs are available. The inventory includes 100 units of certain finished goods, manufactured prior to January 1, 19X6, estimated to cost $50,000, and component parts for an additional 100 units estimated to cost $25,000 in labor, material, and overhead. Sales during 19X6 were 20 units at $850 each. Management informs you that they overestimated the market for these items but that eventually they will recover the cost by sale of the units. However, your investigation discloses that this particular unit has been superseded by a more efficient model, and there is reason to question the optimism of management regarding the salability of the units on hand. The inventory value was estimated, since no cost records were maintained. You made tests in an effort to establish the validity of the cost estimates, but were unable to do so. The balance of the inventory consists of items manufactured or acquired during 19X6. Application of generally accepted auditing procedures established that this portion of the inventory is properly priced at the lower of cost or market on the first-in, first-out method.

2 On June 26, 19X6, the board of directors granted options to certain officers and employees for the purchase of 500 shares of unissued capital stock at $100 per share. The options may be exercised at any time prior to December 31, 19X8. No stock has been issued under these options.

a Do any of these matters require disclosure in the financial statements or explanation in the auditor's report? Give reasons for your conclusion in each case.

b If disclosure or explanation is required, prepare a note or paragraph for use in your audit report.

AICPA adapted

13-18 Prior to the current year, CA had been the auditor of all the company's subsidiaries. However, during the current year, the company had acquired five new subsidiary companies whose accounts will be included in the consolidated financial statements of the company and will be audited by different chartered accountants. The board of directors had recommended that these auditors be retained for the current year and resolutions to this effect had been passed at the shareholder's meetings. CA has decided not to enter into an agency relationship with these auditors.

Since the arrangements made for the audits of the new subsidiary companies may present some problems to CA in expressing an opinion on the consolidated financial statements of the company, the board has asked CA to explain the additional procedures necessary in order to rely on the work of the other auditors.

The board also informed CA that the accounting practice followed by two of the newly acquired subsidiaries with respect to intangible assets and inventory valuation were not consistent with the practices of the parent company and its other subsidiaries.

The parent company has instructed these two subsidiaries to change their accounting methods for these particular items to conform to the standard practices followed by the parent company and its other subsidiaries.

The board asked CA to consider the implications of these changes and their possible effects on the financial statements and auditor's reports of both the new subsidiaries and the parent company.

CA agreed to present at the next meeting comments on the points raised by the board.

Indicate CA's response to the questions raised by the board of directors with respect to the audit of subsidiary companies, outlining:

a The additional procedures which CA would consider necessary in order to rely on the work of the other auditors.

b The implications of the changes in accounting practices and their possible effects on the financial statements and auditors' reports of both the new subsidiaries and the parent company.

CICA

13-19 The consolidated profit of Y Ltd. and its subsidiaries for the year ended December 31, 19X6, is $490,000. During the audit of X Ltd., one of the subsidiaries, CA notices that there is $5,000 of intercompany profit in the inventory. The new profit of X Ltd. for the year ended December 31, 19X6, is $25,000. There was no adjustment on any of the organization's financial statements for this profit, and management refuses to allow any change in the statements.

Indicate the disclosures, with reasons, CA would make in the report on:

a X Ltd.

b Y Ltd. and its subsidiaries

CICA

13-20 You are finishing your audit of the financial statements of Pecan Corporation for the year ended September 30, 19X4. The corporation's report to stockholders, which will include your standard report, will contain the consolidated financial statements of Pecan and its substantial subsidiary, Oak Corporation. This is your third annual audit of Pecan, and you find that the following changes from the prior year have occurred:

1 Oak, which is located in another state, was acquired as a subsidiary during 19X4. Another independent auditor, who was engaged by the client, rendered an unqualified opinion on Oak financial statements for the year ended September 30, 19X4. While you are willing to use the report for the purpose of expressing your opinion on the consolidated statements, you are unwilling to assume responsibility for the performance of the work which served as the basis for the opinion.

You have reviewed the accounting procedures employed by the client to prepare the consolidated statements and approve of them. The corporation has appended to its financial statements a footnote that explains adequately the time of acquisition and the method of consolidation.

2 In accordance with your suggestion, on October 1, 19X3, for the 19X4 fiscal year Pecan had begun the procedure of estimating its total social security taxes expense for the calendar year and then allocating the total to monthly costs and expenses on the basis of the proportion of total estimated annual payroll actually earned each month. In prior years this tax expense was charged to costs and expenses in the same months that the related taxable wages were paid. The unallocated social security taxes expense on taxable wages earned through September 30, 19X4, amounted to $20,000 before consideration of income tax effect. (The income tax rate is 50 percent.) Oak uses the same method of accounting for social security taxes as Pecan adopted.

3 For 19X4 Pecan changed its policy of taking a complete physical inventory at September 30 to taking physical inventories of half the inventory on July 31, the other half on August 31. You were consulted on this change and approved it. Your observation of the two physical inventories and your other procedures produced no exceptions as to quantities.

4 A new customer of Pecan is a retail chain store company whose accounting system makes it unable to confirm the $56,000 balance of its account. You examined related remittances by this customer totaling $50,000 in post-balance sheet date audit procedures and satisfied yourself regarding the balance by examination of shipping documents, with the exception that there is a $200 charge in dispute, which you considered immaterial. The $56,000 is net of a credit memorandum of $150.

5 Your post-balance sheet date audit procedures disclosed that Pecan Corp. is considering shutting down, on December 31, 19X4, a division that has been a marginal operation. Because of the possible effect on stockholder and employee relations, management prefers not to make a disclosure of its consideration of the proposed shutdown in the annual report, which will probably be mailed to stockholders on November 15.

6 A number of substantial claims and lawsuits, which were given widespread publicity, were filed in 19X4 against Pecan for damages alleged to have resulted from the use of certain products sold in 19X3. The line of products was discontinued early in 19X4. The corporation's attorney is unable to predict the outcome of these claims and lawsuits. The management of the corporation believes that losses, if any, incurred in excess of the product liability insurance coverage would not have a material effect upon the company's financial position.

The scope of your audit of Pecan was not limited by the client in any way. No other items of importance were uncovered by your audit.

a Prepare the additional notes that you would suggest that the client should append to the financial statements.

b For each of the listed changes that you think does not require disclosure, justify your belief.

c Assuming that the client adopts your recommended notes, prepare the auditor's report.

AICPA adapted

13-21 Track Corporation acquired a large tract of land in a small town approximately 10 miles from Phoenix City. The company executed a firm contract on November 15, 19X8, for the construction of a 1-mile race track, together with related facilities. The track and facilities were completed December 15, 19X9. On December 31, 19X9, a 6 percent installment note of $100,000 was issued, along with other consideration, in settlement of the construction contract. Installments of $50,000 fall due on December 31 of each of the next 2 years. The company planned to pay the notes from cash received from operations and from sale of additional capital stock.

The company adopted the double-declining-balance method of computing depreciation. No depreciation was taken in 19X9 because all racing equipment was received in December after the completion of the track and facilities.

The land on which the racing circuit was constructed was acquired at various dates for a total of $43,000, and its approximate market value on December 31, 19X9, is $60,000.

Through the sale of tickets to spectators, parking fees, concession income, and income from betting, the company officials anticipated that approximately $175,000 would be taken in during the typical year's racing season. Cash expenses for a racing season were estimated at $123,000.

You have made an audit of the financial statements of Track as of December 31, 19X9. The balance sheet as of that date and statement of operations follow:

Track Corporation
Balance Sheet
December 31, 19X9

Assets

Cash		$ 14,500
Accounts receivable		1,000
Prepaid expenses		7,500
Property (at cost):		
Land	$ 43,000	
Grading and track improvements	68,200	
Grandstand	100,000	
Buildings	60,000	
Racing equipment	40,000	311,200
Organization costs		300
Total assets		$334,500

Liabilities and Stockholders' Equity

Accounts payable	$ 22,000
Installment note payable—6%	100,000
Stockholders' equity:	
Capital stock, par value $1 per share, authorized	
20,000 shares, issued and outstanding 47,800 shares	47,800
Capital in excess of par, representing amounts paid in	
over par value of capital stock	174,700
Retained earnings (deficit)	(10,000)
Total liabilities and stockholders' equity	$334,500

Track Corporation
Statement of Operations
For the Period from Inception,
December 1, 19X6, to December 31, 19X9

Income:	
Profit on sales of land	$ 5,000
Other	100
	$ 5,100
General and administrative expenses	15,100
Net loss for the period	($10,000)

On January 15, 19X0, state legislation which declared betting to be illegal was enacted and was signed by the governor. A discussion with management on January 17 about the effect of the legislation revealed it is now estimated that revenue will be reduced to approximately $48,000 and cash expenses will be reduced to one-third the original estimate.

Prepare the following:

a The explanatory notes to accompany the balance sheet.

b The most comprehensive auditor's *opinion* covering the balance sheet. The *scope* paragraph and *explanatory* paragraph, if any, should be *omitted* and the opinion dated February 1, 19X0.

c If the report is in any way qualified as to opinion, give an *explanation* of your reasons for the qualification.

AICPA adapted

13-22 You have performed an audit, in conformity with generally accepted auditing standards, of the financial statements of the Aurora Manufacturing Corporation for the year ended December 31, 19X7. These statements, together with those for 19X6 in comparative form (the Statement of Cash Flows has been omitted to save space) are presented on page 582.

This is your first audit of the company and you satisfied yourself regarding the opening inventory and the consistency of the application of accounting principles. Your work papers contain the following notes:

1 In the prior year, 19X6, the company changed its method of costing inventories from the average-cost method to the LIFO method. The average-cost method had been used consistently in prior years. The information shown in the middle of page 583 was developed.

2 A new highway will be constructed through the general area in which the company's building is located. The exact route of the highway will not be established for 6 months, and highway officials refuse to disclose their current plans other than that the building might be in the path of the highway. The officers' estimate of the value of the land and building is the amount for which they expect to sell the property to the highway department. Because of the indefinite location of the highway, there have been no recent sales of property in the general area, and real estate appraisers are not in agreement on the value of the property.

The Aurora Manufacturing Corporation
Balance Sheet
December 31, 19X7 and 19X6

	19X7	19X6	Increase (decrease)
Assets			
Current assets:			
Cash	$ 36,000	$ 20,000	$16,000
Accounts receivable (net of allowance for bad debts of $3,000 and $2,500)	78,000	60,000	18,000
Inventories	149,000	122,000	27,000
Prepaid expenses	3,200	4,000	(800)
Total	$266,200	$206,000	$60,200
Fixed assets (at cost):			
Land (officers' estimate of current value—$50,000)	$ 20,000	$ 20,000	
Building (net of accumulated depreciation of $8,000 and $6,000)	42,000	44,000	(2,000)
(officers' estimate of current value—$75,000)			
Machinery and equipment (net of accumulated depreciation of $24,000 and $18,000)	79,000	85,000	(6,000)
Total	$141,000	$149,000	$ (8,000)
Other assets:			
Goodwill	$ 30,000	$ 30,000	
Total	$437,200	$385,000	$52,200
Liabilities and Stockholders' Equity			
Current liabilities	$ 48,200	$ 35,000	$13,200
Accrued liabilities	39,000	15,000	24,000
Total	$ 87,200	$ 50,000	$37,200
Stockholders' equity			
Capital stock, $100 par value, 3,000 shares authorized and outstanding	$300,000	$300,000	
Capital contributed in excess of par value	65,000	65,000	
Deficit	(15,000)	(30,000)	15,000
Total	$350,000	$335,000	$15,000
Total	$437,200	$385,000	$52,200

The Aurora Manufacturing Corporation
Statement of Income and Retained Earnings
For the Years Ended December 31, 19X7 and 19X6

	19X7	19X6	Increase (decrease)
Sales	$980,000	$920,000	$60,000
Cost of sales	720,000	685,000	35,000
Gross profit	$260,000	$235,000	$25,000
Selling and administrative expenses	235,000	220,000	15,000
Profit from operations	$ 25,000	$ 15,000	$10,000
Other income and (deductions), net	$ (10,000)	$ (5,000)	(5,000)
Net income	$ 15,000	$ 10,000	$ 5,000
Deficit, January 1	(30,000)	(40,000)	10,000
Deficit, December 31	$ (15,000)	$ (30,000)	$15,000

	Calendar year		
	19X5	19X6	19X7
Ending inventories by LIFO method	. . .	$122,000	$149,000
Ending inventories by average-cost method	$141,000	$158,000	$173,000
Net income (loss) for period under average-cost method (estimated for 19X6 and 19X7)	$ (5,000)	$ 46,000	$ 39,000

3 The intangible asset is the total cost of the company's institutional advertising campaign that took place in 19X2 when the company began doing business. The officers believe that the company is continuing to benefit from the goodwill developed by the campaign, and they intend to write off the asset when it becomes reasonably evident that it is worthless.

4 An analysis of the deficit follows:

19X2 loss	$(55,000)
19X3 income	5,000
19X4 income	15,000
19X5 loss	(5,000)
19X6 income	10,000
19X7 income	15,000
Total	$(15,000)

No entries have been posted to the deficit account other than the above results of operations, which are in agreement with the income tax returns. The tax returns have not been examined. Management has decided that reporting the value of the carryforward loss in the balance sheet would not be conservative. Management prefers not to change the financial statements in any way but will consider adding notes. The income tax rate that has been in effect is 50 percent.

a Prepare the notes that you would suggest for the financial statements.

b Assuming that the suggested notes that will be adopted and that a statement of cash flows will be appropriately presented, prepare your audit report for the current year financial statements. Include in your report any comments that you consider necessary. If your report is in any way modified or qualified as to opinion, give a full explanation in your report.

AICPA adapted

Communications with Clients

13-23 In the review of the preliminary draft of the 19X6 annual report, CA notices that the president states in a message to shareholders that "the financial statements show an increase in operating profits of 120 percent." CA checks this and finds that "operating profits" have increased by only 50 percent, whereas "net profit" increased by 120 percent. The difference was due to profit on disposal of marketable securities.

Indicate the action CA should take, with reasons.

CICA

13-24 In a press release the XS Company stated that its consolidated profit for the first quarter ended March 31, 19X7, was $754,000. Although CA had nothing to do with the preparation of this figure, CA knows that it does not include a loss of $150,000 on the winding up of an unsuccessful division of the company.

Indicate the position CA should take, with reasons.

CICA

13-25 The shares of S Ltd., a manufacturing company, have recently been listed on a Canadian stock exchange. In anticipation of preparing the first quarterly interim report to shareholders (see Statement of Income, page 585), the comptroller has asked CA, the shareholders' auditor, for certain advice.

How should CA answer each of the following questions raised by the comptroller?

a The company plans to distribute a brief interim report containing a summary report by the president and the attached condensed statement of income. What other information should be reported in the interim financial statements?

b Since the company has no perpetual records and physical stocktaking can be carried out only at the fiscal year-end, how should the amount of cost of goods sold for the quarter be determined?

c Should an extraordinary item be prorated over a full year so as not to distort the results of the interim period in which it occurs?

d How should income taxes be reported if there is a profit in the first quarter and an anticipated loss in the second quarter?

CICA

S Ltd.
Interim Comparative Condensed Statements of Income
For the three months ended June 30

	19X2	19X1
Gross revenue from operations (including investment income)	$6,094,805	$5,375,700
Deduct:		
Cost of merchandise sold and all expenses, except for the undernoted items	$3,706,921	$3,074,693
Debenture interest	9,353	14,549
Directors' fees	1,750	2,350
Provision for depreciation	650,745	523,686
	$4,368,769	$3,615,278
Income before the following	$1,726,036	$1,760,422
Income taxes	826,036	880,211
Income before extraordinary item	$ 900,000	$ 880,211
Extraordinary item	100,000	
Net income	$ 800,000	$ 880,211
Number of common shares outstanding	400,000	400,000
Earnings per common share	$2.00	$2.20

Notes to interim financial statement:

1. The interim statement for 19X2 is unaudited.
2. An actual physical inventory was not taken on June 30, 19X2, nor on June 30, 19X1.

CASE

The Trevor Corporation commenced doing business on January 1, 19X1. It produces one product, which is sold to a single customer, Redford Corporation. R. Redford is president of both corporations and owns all of the outstanding stock except for a few qualifying shares.

You have been the CPA for Redford for some years and accepted the engagement of auditing the Trevor financial statements that appear on page 586.

Management cooperated in every respect during the audit. You did not confirm the account receivable. All other generally accepted auditing procedures were followed, and no items of importance were revealed by the audit except the following:

1 The selling and administrative expenses included R. Redford's salary of $35,000.
2 The client had made a $1,000 write down to adjust the finished goods inventory to the lower of average cost or market.
3 Land, building, machinery, and equipment are recorded at current market values determined as of January 1, 19X1, by a qualified appraiser. R. Redford purchased the assets from Redford Corporation at net book value and contributed them as part of the investment in Trevor. The net book values on the records of Redford were:

Land	$10,000
Building	25,000
Machinery and equipment	10,000
	$45,000

4 Depreciation was computed on the straight-line method.

5 The mortgage payable is the balance due on a 10-year, 5 percent $48,000 mortgage payable to the First National Bank in equal annual installments. The mortgage is secured by the company's fixed assets and is guaranteed by Redford.

6 The company customarily contracts for raw materials on a quarterly basis. An audit of post-balance-sheet events revealed that the quarterly raw material contract for the first quarter of 19X2 calls for a price increase of 10 percent.

7 The sales prices to Redford Corp. were approximately 25 percent above competitive prices.

8 Inventory and liability representation letters were signed by Redford. (Disregard the income tax problems arising from the intercorporate relationship and the control by a single stockholder.)

a State briefly the adjustments you would suggest that the client make to the financial statements. Formal journal entries are not required.

b Prepare the notes that you would suggest for the financial statements.

c Assuming that the client adopts your suggested adjustments and notes and that a statement of cash flows is also appropriately presented, prepare the auditor's report. The first two paragraphs should be omitted. If your report is in any way modified or qualified, give your reasons.

AICPA adapted

Trevor Corporation
Statement of Operations
For Year Ended December 31, 19X1

Sales	$150,000
Cost of sales	75,000
Gross profit	$ 75,000
Selling and administrative expenses	55,000
Net profit before taxes	$ 20,000
Provision for federal income taxes	6,000
Net profit	$ 14,000

Trevor Corporation
Balance Sheet
December 31, 19X1

Assets

Current assets:			
Cash		$ 8,000	
Account receivable		15,000	
Inventory		16,000	
Total current assets			$ 39,000
Fixed assets:			
Land		$20,000	
Building	$50,000		
Allowance for depreciation	2,000	48,000	
Machinery and equipment	$20,000		
Allowance for depreciation	2,000	18,000	
Total fixed assets			86,000
Total assets			$125,000

Liabilities and Stockholders' Equity

Current liabilities:		
Accounts payable	$11,800	
Liability for federal income taxes	6,000	
Total current liabilities		$ 17,800
Long-term liabilities:		
Mortgage payable		43,200
Stockholders' equity:		
Capital stock, authorized and issued,		
100 shares at $100 par value	$10,000	
Retained earnings	54,000	
Total stockholders' equity		64,000
Total liabilities and stockholders' equity		$125,000

CHAPTER

14

Attestation Services, Unaudited Financial Statements, and Specialized Reporting

CHAPTER OUTLINE

Learning Objectives

After studying this chapter you should be able to:

- Understand attestation services and the standards that apply to them
- Describe the form of report and related responsibilities of an accountant who compiles or reviews the financial statements of a nonpublic company
- Explain the responsibilities of an accountant who reviews the interim financial information or who is associated with other unaudited financial statements of a public company
- Understand the appropriate report forms and related responsibilities for the following types of specialized reporting circumstances:
  —Letters for underwriters
  —Special reports
  —Reports on accompanying information
  —Reports on prospective financial information
  —Reports on internal control structure
  —Reports on pro forma information
  —Reports on compliance with requirements of specified laws, regulations, rules, contracts, or grants

Relevant Sections of Statements on Auditing Standards

AU 504 — Association with Financial Statements
AU 551 — Reporting on Information in Auditor-Submitted Documents
AU 622 — Special Reports Applying Agreed-Upon Procedures to Specified Elements, Accounts, or Items of a Financial Statement
AU 623 — Special Reports
AU 634 — Letters for Underwriters
AU 711 — Filings under Federal Securities Statutes
AU 722 — Interim Financial Information
AU 801 — Compliance Auditing Applicable to Governmental Entities

Relevant Sections of Statements on Standards for Attestation Engagements

AT 100 — Attestation Standards
AT 200 — Financial Forecasts and Projections
AT 300 — Reporting on Pro Forma Financial Information
AT 400 — Reporting on an Entity's Internal Control Structure
AT 500 — Compliance Attestation

This chapter explains the types of reports that may be issued when a CPA has not made an audit of financial statements in accordance with generally accepted auditing standards. This chapter also explains a variety of specialized reporting circumstances that require the issuance of different types of reports.

CPAs are often engaged to provide services other than audits. For example, a CPA may be asked to prepare financial statements, provide assurance about a financial forecast, or provide an opinion on the internal control structure. This chapter discusses nonaudit services and reports that are commonly provided by CPAs.

In some cases, the CPA is asked to prepare financial statements using only the CPA's expertise in accounting and financial matters. This service is called a *compilation engagement*. In other cases, the CPA is asked to perform procedures to assess representations in a document and express a conclusion about their reliability. When a CPA expresses such a conclusion, the service performed is called an *attestation service*. Attestation services may involve financial forecasts and projections, pro forma financial information, internal control structure, compliance with laws or contracts, or other information.

ATTESTATION AND COMPILATION SERVICES

Statements on Standards for Attestation Engagements (SSAEs) are the professional standards that apply to attestation services. The standards apply to CPAs and to others working for a CPA firm, such as management consultants. SSAE No. 1 (AT 100.01) defines an attestation engagement as:

> one in which a practitioner is engaged to issue or does issue a written communication that expresses a conclusion about the reliability of a written assertion that is the responsibility of another party.

An assertion is "any declaration or set of related declarations taken as a whole, by a party responsible for it." An audit is one kind of attestation engagement. Throughout this book we have discussed the financial statement assertions. Management is the party responsible for the assertions. The auditor provides a written report (the audit opinion) that expresses a conclusion about the reliability of the assertions (financial statements in accordance with GAAP).

Other common types of attestation engagements include those to provide reports on:

- Financial forecasts or projections
- Pro forma financial information
- Internal control structure
- Compliance with statutory, regulatory, and contractual requirements
- Investment performance statistics
- Descriptions of computer software

Statements on Standards for Attestation Engagements do not supersede or override the applicability of other existing standards for engagements, even though they are attestation engagements. Where standards exist for the particular attestation engagement, the practitioner should follow them. For example, the practitioner should follow the guidance in Statements on Auditing Standards when performing an audit, and should follow

Statements on Standards for Accountants' Services on Prospective Financial Information for examinations of financial forecasts. When specific standards do not exist and the engagement is for an attestation service, the attestation standards should be followed.

Types of Engagements

SSAE No. 1 (AT 100) defines types of attestation engagements based on levels of assurance that the practitioner can give in the written report:

- *Examination*—an engagement designed to provide a high level of assurance on whether an assertion is presented in conformity with established or stated criteria against which it was measured. An examination includes performance of procedures sufficient to limit the risk of issuing the wrong conclusion to an appropriately low level. An audit is an examination attestation engagement.
- *Review*—an engagement designed to provide only a moderate level of assurance. The procedures the practitioner performs to assess the reliability of the assertions are not as extensive as they would be in an examination. The procedures generally consist of inquiry and analytical procedures.
- *Agreed-upon procedures*—an engagement designed to meet the particular needs of parties who agreed upon procedures to be applied or criteria to be used that is restricted to those parties.

The fourth commonly performed type of engagement is a *compilation*. It is not an attestation service because the practitioner does not express any conclusion about the assertions and explicitly disclaims any level of assurance. However, some minimal procedures should be performed whenever the practitioner is associated with financial statements or other assertions.

In a report for an examination, the practitioner provides *positive assurance,* i.e., makes a direct statement that the assertion is presented in conformity with established or stated criteria against which it was measured. In a report for a review, the practitioner provides *negative assurance,* i.e., states that nothing came to his or her attention that caused him or her to believe that the assertions were not presented in conformity with the established or stated criteria.

Negative assurance on financial statements was once a common method of reporting when the auditor was unable to express an opinion. However, it is now generally prohibited, except for specifically defined circumstances, because it might mislead the average user of financial statements about the degree of reliance to be placed on the data. The message of a disclaimer of opinion is that the auditor does not have a sufficient basis for forming a meaningful conclusion on the financial statement presentation. That message should not be tempered by a mitigating assurance of the absence of knowledge. Some auditors note that the less a CPA knows about financial statements or data the easier it is to say "nothing came to our attention. . . ."

Negative assurance is permitted by the attestation standards when the scope of the CPA's work is clearly understood.

Figure 14-1 summarizes the types of engagements.

Type of engagement	Level of assurance	Conclusion expressed	Nature and extent of procedures
Examination	Reasonable	Positive assurance	Sufficient to reduce assertion risk to appropriately low level
Review	Moderate	Negative assurance	Ordinarily limited to inquiries and analytical procedures
Compilation	None	Disclaimer	Minimal
Agreed-upon procedures	As agreed	Summary of findings, negative assurance, or both, as agreed	As agreed

FIGURE 14-1
Types of attestation and compilation engagements.

Attestation Standards

The attestation standards are similar to the auditing standards. They deal with the need for technical competence, independence in mental attitude, due professional care, adequate planning and supervision, sufficient evidence, and appropriate reporting. However, the scope, as described in SSAE No. 1 (AT 100), of the attestation standards is much broader. The eleven attestation standards include the following:

General Standards

1 The engagement shall be performed by a practitioner or practitioners having adequate technical training and proficiency in the attest function.
2 The engagement shall be performed by a practitioner or practitioners having adequate knowledge in the subject matter of the assertion.
3 The practitioner shall perform an engagement only if he or she has reason to believe that the following two conditions exist:
   • The assertion is capable of evaluation against reasonable criteria that either have been established by a recognized body or are stated in the presentation of the assertion in a sufficiently clear and comprehensive manner for a knowledgeable reader to be able to understand them.
   • The assertion is capable of reasonably consistent estimation or measurement using such criteria.
4 In all matters relating to the engagement, an independence in mental attitude shall be maintained by the practitioner or practitioners.
5 Due professional care shall be exercised in the performance of the engagement.

Standards of Field Work

1 The work shall be adequately planned and assistants, if any, shall be properly supervised.
2 Sufficient evidence shall be obtained to provide a reasonable basis for the conclusion that is expressed in the report.

Standards of Reporting

1 The report shall identify the assertion being reported on and state the character of the engagement.

2 The report shall state the practitioner's conclusion about whether the assertion is presented in conformity with the established or stated criteria against which it was measured.

3 The report shall state all of the practitioner's significant reservations about the engagement and the presentation of the assertion.

4 The report on an engagement to evaluate an assertion that has been prepared in conformity with agreed-upon criteria or on an engagement to apply agreed-upon procedures should contain a statement limiting its use to the parties who have agreed upon such criteria or procedures.

UNAUDITED FINANCIAL STATEMENTS

A substantial portion of the practice of many CPAs is the preparation of unaudited financial statements. Not all companies need or want audited statements. Closely held corporations, small noncorporate businesses, and individuals may not be required to have audits and may not feel an audit can be economically justified. Nevertheless, these companies may need the services of a CPA to prepare or assist in the preparation of financial statements and tax returns. This service requires application of accounting, tax, and business knowledge in the construction of financial information, not the substantiation process of auditing.

The services provided and types of reports issued on unaudited financial statements differ depending on whether the services are provided to a public or nonpublic company. For this purpose, a *nonpublic company* is defined as any company (or other entity) other than the following:

1 One whose securities trade in a public market either on a stock exchange or in the over-the-counter market, including securities quoted only locally or regionally

2 One that makes a filing with a regulatory agency in preparation for the sale of any class of its securities in a public market

3 A subsidiary, corporate joint venture, or other entity controlled by a type of entity described in 1 or 2 above

Compilation or Review of Financial Statements for Nonpublic Companies

An accountant cannot be associated with the unaudited financial statements of a nonpublic company unless the accountant has reviewed or compiled those financial statements. Technically, the term "associated" is confined to those services covered by Statements on Auditing Standards (SAS). A compilation or review of the financial statements of a nonpublic company is covered by Statements on Standards for Accounting or Review Services (SSARS) issued by the AICPA's Accounting and Review Services Committee. However, the "reporting obligation" of an accountant providing accounting or review services to a nonpublic company is essentially the same as that imposed by the Statements on Auditing Standards (AU 504) which defines association as explained in a following section of this chapter.

The services of compilation and review are defined in SSARS No. 1 (AR 100.04) as follows:

- *Compilation.* Presenting in the form of financial statements information that is the representation of management (owners) without undertaking to express any assurance on the statements.
- *Review.* Performing inquiry and analytical procedures that provide the accountant with a reasonable basis for expressing limited assurance that there are no material modifications that should be made to the statements in order for them to be in conformity with generally accepted principles. . . .

In other words, the accountant expresses no assurance on compiled financial statements, but limited assurance is expressed on reviewed financial statements. A compilation is strictly an accounting service, but a review combines an accounting service with expression of limited assurance that may be relied on by third parties. These services are generally provided to small businesses (corporations, partnerships, or proprietorships) and to individuals who do not need or want the level of assurance provided by audited financial statements.

Both a compilation and a review service involve the performance of some procedures and issuance of a standard report as specified by SSARS. An accountant engaged to compile or review financial statements must establish an understanding with the company on the services to be performed. The understanding should include the following matters:

1 A description of the services to be performed
2 A description of the report the accountant expects to render
3 An understanding that the engagement cannot be relied on to disclose errors, irregularities, or illegal acts
4 An understanding that the accountant will inform the company of any matters specified in 3 above that come to the accountant's attention

SSARS No. 1 (AR 100.08) says that this understanding should be "preferably in writing," but an engagement letter is not specifically required. However, the importance of an engagement letter was illustrated in the case of *1136 Tenants' Corporation v. Max Rothenberg & Company*. The managing agent of an apartment cooperative reported certain bills as paid in monthly statements to the tenants when, in fact, the bills were not paid. The plaintiff contended that the CPA firm should have detected the unpaid bills. The CPA firm countered that it had been engaged to perform bookkeeping services and to prepare unaudited statements solely from information furnished by the managing agent. The agreement between the CPA firm and the cooperative was oral, and the CPA firm failed to prove to the court's satisfaction that they had not been engaged to perform an audit.

Compilation of Financial Statements   The procedures for a compilation are limited because no assurance is intended to be provided. The following three basic requirements should be met before reporting on a compilation of financial statements:

I *Knowledge base.* The accountant should possess sufficient knowledge or understanding of the following matters:

   A The accounting principles or practices of the industry in which the company
operates

   B The nature of the company's business transactions

   C The form of its accounting records

   D The stated qualifications of its accounting personnel

   E The accounting basis on which the financial statements are to be presented

   F The form and content of the financial statements

   G Whether other accounting services, such as assistance in closing the accounting records, will be necessary

II *Reading statements.* Before issuing a report, the accountant should read the compiled financial statements and consider whether they appear to be appropriate in
form and free from obvious material errors.

III *Deficient information.* If the accountant becomes aware that information supplied
by the company is incorrect, incomplete, or otherwise unsatisfactory for the purpose of compiling financial statements, the accountant should obtain additional or
revised information.

Put less formally: The accountant should know enough about the business and the proper
accounting for it to be able to prepare financial statements; the accountant should investigate further if supporting information supplied by the company has apparent defects;
the accountant should not issue a standard compilation report if the financial statements
obviously are improperly presented.

The *accountant's standard report on a compilation* is worded as follows:

I (we) have compiled the accompanying balance sheet of XYZ Company as of December 31,
19XX, and the related statements of income, retained earnings, and cash flows for the year
then ended, in accordance with Statements on Standards for Accounting and Review Services
issued by the American Institute of Certified Public Accountants.

A compilation is limited to presenting in the form of financial statements information that is the
representation of management (owners). I (we) have not audited or reviewed the accompanying financial statements and, accordingly, do not express an opinion or any other form of
assurance on them.

(Signature)

(Date)

The essential features of this report are as follows:

1 A statement that a compilation has been performed in accordance with SSARS, the
AICPA standards (The standards are largely the three basic requirements enumerated
earlier.)

2 A statement that a compilation is limited to presenting in financial statement form information represented by management (owners)

3 A statement that the financial statements have not been audited or reviewed

Additional matters that apply to reporting are as follows:

- *Date.* The report is dated as of the completion of the compilation.
- *Addressee.* Addressing the report is not covered by SSARS, but presumably it would be the same as specified by SASs—the company, the board of directors, or stockholders, and for noncorporate entities as the circumstances dictate.
- *Reference.* A reference is required on each page of the financial statements to the accountant's report, such as "See Accountant's Compilation Report."
- *No procedures description.* Any procedures that the accountant performed should *not* be described in the accountant's report.

The stipulation on not describing procedures is considered necessary because a reader of compiled financial statements might attribute more assurance than is warranted to the accountant's report if procedures were described. For example, an accountant compiling financial statements obviously establishes the clerical accuracy of the statements by footing. However, if that procedure was described in the report, an uninformed reader might assume it meant more than that the arithmetic was correct.

The following situations may result in modified compilation reports:

- *GAAP departures.* If the accountant becomes aware of a departure from generally accepted accounting principles that is material to compiled financial statements, the accountant should disclose the nature of the departure in an additional paragraph of the report.
- *Omission of substantially all disclosures.* Omission of disclosures is also a GAAP departure. However, SSARS permit the omission of *substantially all* disclosures in compiled financial statements if the accountant's report contains an additional "caveat" paragraph describing management's election to omit the disclosures and warning that a user's conclusions might be influenced by the omitted information.
- *Accountant not independent.* An accountant who compiles financial statements is not required to be independent. However, when the accountant is not independent, the compilation report must be modified by adding the sentence "I am (we are) not independent with respect to the company" as the last paragraph of the report.

Note that a compilation report is not modified for the following matters that would cause modification of the language of a standard audit report:

- Scope restriction
- Uncertainty
- Inconsistent application of GAAP

If the scope of a compilation is restricted, the accountant should not issue a report. For example, if the accountant believes the allowance for uncollectible accounts is unreasonable based on a knowledge of the business and reading the financial statements, and management cannot provide information to support its estimate, the accountant should not report. If there was a significant uncertainty or a material change in accounting principle, the accountant would be concerned that the matter was adequately disclosed, but no report modification would be made.

Review of Financial Statements   The procedures for a review are more extensive than for a compilation because a review report provides limited assurance. The following basic requirements should be met before reporting on a review of financial statements:

I *Knowledge base.* The accountant should possess sufficient knowledge or understanding of the following matters:
   A The accounting principles and practices of the industry in which the company operates
   B The company's business, including its organization, operating characteristics, and the nature of its assets, liabilities, revenues, and expenses
II *Inquiries.* The accountant should make inquiries concerning:
   A The company's accounting principles and practices and the methods followed in applying them
   B The company's procedures for recording, classifying, and summarizing transactions, and accumulating information for disclosure
   C Actions taken at meetings of stockholders, board of directors, and board committees that may affect the financial statements
III *Analytical procedures.* The accountant should apply analytical procedures designed to identify relationships and individual items that appear to be unusual.
IV *Reading statements.* The accountant should read the financial statements to consider, on the basis of information coming to the accountant's attention, whether the financial statements appear to conform with generally accepted accounting principles.
V *Inquiries of senior financial management.* The accountant should make inquiries of persons responsible for financial and accounting matters concerning the following:
   A Whether the financial statements have been prepared in conformity with generally accepted accounting principles consistently applied
   B Changes in the company's accounting principles and practices or business activities
   C Matters about which questions arose in applying other procedures
   D Subsequent events that might materially affect the financial statements
VI *Management representation letter.* The accountant is required to obtain a representation letter from management. The chief executive officer and the chief financial officer should normally sign the letter.
VII *Deficient information.* If the accountant becomes aware that information coming to the accountant's attention is incomplete, incorrect, or otherwise unsatisfactory, the accountant should perform the additional procedures deemed necessary to achieve limited assurance that there are no material modifications that should be made to the financial statements.

A review (and, of course, a compilation) do not contemplate the following matters that are a normal feature of an audit of financial statements:

- Obtaining an understanding of the internal control structure
- Tests of accounting records
- Tests to obtain corroborating evidential matter to substantiate responses to inquiries or other matters
- Certain other procedures ordinarily performed in an audit, such as obtaining *written* representations from the client's legal counsel

However, an accountant reviewing financial statements should document the specific inquiries made and analytical procedures performed in work papers.

The accountant's standard report on a review of financial statements is worded as follows:

> I (we) have reviewed the accompanying balance sheet of XYZ Company as of December 31, 19XX, and the related statements of income, retained earnings, and cash flows for the year then ended, in accordance with Statements on Standards for Accounting and Review Services issued by the American Institute of Certified Public Accountants. All information included in these financial statements is the representation of the management (owners) of XYZ Company.
>
> A review consists principally of inquiries of company personnel and analytical procedures applied to financial data. It is substantially less in scope than an audit in accordance with generally accepted auditing standards, the objective of which is the expression of an opinion regarding the financial statements taken as a whole. Accordingly, I (we) do not express such an opinion.
>
> Based on my (our) review, I am (we are) not aware of any material modifications that should be made to the accompanying financial statements in order for them to be in conformity with generally accepted accounting principles.
>
> (Signature)
>
> (Date)

The essential features of this report are as follows:

1 A statement that a review has been performed in accordance with SSARS, the AICPA standards
2 A statement that all information included in the financial statements is the representation of management (owners)
3 A brief description of a review as consisting principally of inquiries and analytical procedures
4 A warning that a review is substantially less in scope than an audit
5 An expression of limited assurance that the accountant is not aware of any material modifications that should be made to the financial statements

Thus, a review report has several features that have no counterpart in a compilation report. The most notable feature is the expression of limited, or negative, assurance on the financial statements. Another feature is the brief description of what procedures are applied in a review. An accountant may not describe the *specific* procedures performed in a review or a compilation, but the stylized description in the standard review report is considered informative. Because a review report contains this description of scope and provides some assurance, the warning that a review is more limited in scope than an audit is considered necessary to avoid undue reliance by users of reviewed financial statements. The dating, addressing, and financial statement referencing to the accountant's report are essentially the same for a compilation or a review.

If the accountant becomes aware of a *departure from generally accepted accounting principles,* the accountant should modify the review report by adding a paragraph describing the departure. In an audit report, the effect on the financial statements of a departure should be disclosed in the report if "reasonably determinable." In a compilation or review report, the accountant has to include the effects in the report only if the effects have been determined by management or are known as a result of the accountant's procedures. There is no equivalent of an adverse opinion for a compilation or review. If the accountant believes that modification of the report in a compilation or a review is not adequate to indicate the deficiencies in the financial statements, the accountant should not issue a report and should withdraw from the engagement.

There are *no modifications of a review report for uncertainties, inconsistent application of accounting principles, or scope restrictions.* If the scope of a review is restricted, the accountant may be able to issue a compilation report. However, the accountant should consider whether the scope restriction on the review also impairs the accountant's ability to issue a compilation report. For example, if the accountant's analytical procedures cause the accountant to believe the allowance for uncollectible accounts is understated and management cannot provide adequate support for the estimate, neither a review report nor a compilation report can be issued.

An accountant who has been engaged to audit the financial statements of a nonpublic company may encounter scope limitations that preclude an unqualified or qualified opinion. In that case, the client may want to change the engagement from an audit to a review or compilation.

A *change in engagement* from an audit to a compilation or review is permissible, but the accountant has to consider carefully whether the circumstances that caused the audit scope limitation also impair the ability to complete a compilation or review. For example, if an auditor has significant nonresponses to confirmation requests and the client does not want to incur the added cost of alternative procedures, a change in the engagement cannot cure the problem. There is an indication that accounts receivable may be materially incorrect, and a satisfactory resolution of the potential misstatement is essential in a compilation, review, or audit.

When the client has prohibited correspondence with the company's legal counsel, however, an accountant is ordinarily *precluded* by SSARS No. 1 (AR 100.47) from permitting a change from an audit to a review or compilation. When management (owners) of an audit client refuse to sign a client representation letter, a review engagement is precluded because a representation letter is also required for a review. SSAE No. 7 (AT 100.47) points out that in such circumstances, issuance of a compilation report would also ordinarily be precluded.

Notice that in the foregoing discussion, a CPA performing a compilation or review is referred to as an *accountant,* and a CPA performing an audit is referred to as an *auditor*. The terminology is no accident. In the authoritative literature, the terms "auditor" and "audit" are confined to the service of auditing financial information in accordance with generally accepted auditing standards. When some other service is involved, the CPA is described as an accountant or a practitioner.

Review of Interim Financial Information of a Public Company

A compilation or a review of the financial statements of a nonpublic company may be performed under SSARS for *annual or interim financial statements*.[1]

An accountant may also provide a review service to a public company, but the service is confined to *interim* information, and the information reviewed may be financial information or financial statements. The standards that apply in this situation are in SAS No. 71 (AU 722), rather than SSARS. Generally, financial information differs from financial statements in the degree of condensation and extent of disclosure. For example, the presentation of operating results might include sales or gross revenue, provision for income taxes, net income, and significant components of net income, such as extraordinary items, rather than a complete income statement.

Framework and Scope of a Review of Interim Information   A review of the interim information of a public company is made in the framework of an annual audit of complete financial statements and is conducted and reported on in accordance with SAS No. 71 (AU 722). A public company whose securities are listed on a stock exchange is required to have its annual financial statements audited and is required to release interim financial information quarterly. Quarterly information also has to be filed on Form 10-Q with the SEC. However, a review of interim information by an independent accountant is not required except for certain large public companies whose securities are widely traded.[2]

If an accountant is engaged to review interim information, the scope of the review is influenced by the fact that the company has a recurring annual audit. The primary differences in the scope of a review of interim information under SAS No. 71 (AU 722) and the scope of a review of financial statements under SSARS are that a review of interim information includes the following:

- Inquiries are made concerning significant changes in internal control structure including particularly the accounting system to prepare interim information.

---

[1] When a public company does not have its annual financial statements audited, an accountant is permitted to review the annual or interim financial statements under SSARS.

[2] When a nonpublic company includes interim financial information in a note to the audited financial statements, SAS No. 71 (AU 722) applies.

- The accountant reads the minutes of directors' and stockholders' meetings instead of inquiring about actions taken at the meetings.
- The accountant's knowledge base includes an understanding of the client's accounting and financial reporting practices based on knowledge of the client's practices in preparing annual financial statements.

If the accountant reviewing interim information has not audited the client's financial statements for one or more annual periods, the accountant must acquire sufficient knowledge to have an equivalent understanding of the client's accounting and financial reporting practices and its internal control structure.

If the accountant believes the client's internal control structure appears to have deficiencies that do not permit the preparation of interim information in conformity with generally accepted accounting principles, the accountant should do the following:

1 Consider whether the deficiencies represent a restriction on the scope of the engagement sufficient to preclude completion of a review.
2 Advise senior management and the audit committee of the circumstances.

Standard Review Report for Interim Information The accountant's standard report on the review of interim financial information of a public company is worded as follows:

Independent Accountant's Report

We have reviewed the accompanying [describe the statements or information reviewed] of ABC Company and consolidated subsidiaries as of September 30, 19X1, and for the three-month and nine-month periods then ended. These financial statements (information) are (is) the responsibility of the company's management.

We conducted our review in accordance with standards established by the American Institute of Certified Public Accountants. A review of interim financial information consists principally of applying analytical procedures to financial data and making inquiries of persons responsible for financial and accounting matters. It is substantially less in scope than an audit conducted in accordance with generally accepted auditing standards, the objective of which is the expression of an opinion regarding the financial statements taken as a whole. Accordingly, we do not express such an opinion.

Based on our review, we are not aware of any material modifications that should be made to the accompanying financial statements (information) for them (it) to be in conformity with generally accepted accounting principles.

(Signature)

(Date)

The essential features of this report are as follows:

1 A statement that the review was made in accordance with AICPA standards
2 An identification of the interim information reviewed

3 A brief description of the procedures for a review of interim information
4 A warning that a review is substantially less in scope than an audit
5 A conclusion on whether the accountant is aware of any material modification that should be made to the interim information

Thus, the report is substantially the same as a report on a review for a nonpublic company. The primary difference is that "standards established" by the AICPA replace the reference to SSARS and the wording is organized in a slightly different manner.

Report Modifications and Other Responsibilities If the accountant becomes aware that the interim information is materially affected by a departure from generally accepted accounting principles, including inadequate disclosure, the accountant should modify the review report. The modification is made by adding an explanatory paragraph to the report immediately before the concluding paragraph describing the departure and, if practicable, the effects on the interim information. If the departure involves inadequate disclosure, the accountant should include the information in the report. However, the disclosure requirements for interim information are considerably less extensive than those necessary for annual financial statements. Several of the additional requirements that pertain to a review for a nonpublic company are also relevant to a review of interim information. For example, each page of the financial information should be marked "unaudited." However, a reference to the accountant's report is not necessary.

If interim information is included in a note to annual audited financial statements, the note should be labeled unaudited, but the review report does not have to be included, and the review does not have to be mentioned in the audit report. However, if interim information is included in a note that is not marked "unaudited" and the auditor has not reviewed interim information that accompanies audited annual statements, the accountant should expand the audit report to describe the status of the interim information. Also, SAS No. 71 (AU 722) specifies additional responsibilities that apply when interim information is included in SEC filings.

Other Unaudited Financial Statements of Public Companies

An accountant may be associated with a public company's statements that the accountant has not audited or reviewed. The term *association* is technically defined in Statements on Auditing Standards (AU 504.03) as follows:

> An accountant is associated with financial statements when he has consented to the use of his name in a report, document, or written communication containing the statements. Also, when an accountant submits to his client and others financial statements that he has prepared or assisted in preparing, he is deemed to be associated even though the accountant does not append his name to the statements.

The type of report that should be issued on the unaudited statements of a public company is a very brief disclaimer worded as follows:

The accompanying balance sheet of X Company as of December 31, 19X1, and the related statements of income, retained earnings, and cash flows for the year then ended were not audited by us and, accordingly, we do not express an opinion on them.

(Signature)

(Date)

In comparable circumstances, a nonpublic company would receive a compilation report and many analogous requirements apply. Each page of the financial statements should be marked "unaudited," and the accountant should modify the report to disclose any departures from generally accepted accounting principles that come to the accountant's attention.

A similar type of report is issued when an accountant who is not independent is associated with the financial statements of a public company. In those circumstances, the report would be worded as follows:

We are not independent with respect to XYZ Company, and the accompanying balance sheet as of December 31, 19X1, and the related statements of income, retained earnings, and cash flows for the year then ended were not audited by us and, accordingly, we do not express an opinion on them.

(Signature)

(Date)

This type of report should be issued no matter what the extent of procedures performed by the accountant. Actually, it would be a highly unusual situation for this type of report to be issued. However, the report illustrates an important conceptual point. When an accountant is not independent, any procedures that might be performed would not be in accordance with generally accepted auditing standards, because the accountant would have departed from the second general standard of independence.

One interesting note of historical importance is that until late 1978 when SSARS No. 1 (AR 100) was issued, the brief type of disclaimer described above for public companies was also applicable to unaudited financial statements of nonpublic companies. The authoritative guidance on accounting and review services was developed because of the dissatisfaction of many accountants who specialized in that type of service with guidance that described their function entirely in terms of what it was *not*—not an audit.

SPECIALIZED REPORTING CIRCUMSTANCES

Some reports are designed to meet the needs of special parties or to recognize special characteristics of the data examined.

Letters for Underwriters

Underwriters are investment bankers who market corporate securities. The distribution of corporate securities to the public is regulated by the SEC, and the investment banking house that has agreed to underwrite a corporation's public offering assumes certain risks and responsibilities. The underwriter must conduct a diligent investigation of the issuer of securities to preserve its reputation and to satisfy SEC regulations. This investigation includes a study of the issuer's financial statements, management, and properties.

An underwriter usually requests a letter from the independent auditor to assist it in its investigation. The letter covers financial statements and related matters included in the registration statement and prospectus.

The letter to the underwriter is called a *comfort letter,* sometimes a "cold" comfort letter because of the limited nature of the assurances given by the auditor. The comfort letter deals with the independence of the auditor; the compliance as to form of financial data with SEC regulations; subsequent material changes in financial statement items since the date of the latest audited statements; tables, statistics, and similar financial data; and unaudited financial statements for the period after the latest audited statements and the earlier corresponding interim period.

The auditor applies procedures to the unaudited statement and data as requested by the underwriter. The auditor does not assume responsibility for the underwriter's due diligence in investigation of unaudited financial statements and data. SAS No. 72 (AU 634) covers the preparation of comfort letters. It explains that the underwriter is responsible for specifying the procedures to be applied to unaudited financial statements and related data. However, the auditor does give the underwriter *negative assurance* that the procedures have not disclosed material misstatement of the unaudited statements. For example, the auditor might add a sentence such as the following to report on unaudited statements: "However, nothing came to our attention to cause us to believe that any material modifications should be made to the unaudited condensed financial statements. . . ."

Special Reports

Several reports to special parties or on specialized data are called special reports because the applicable reporting requirements are specified in SAS No. 62 (AU 623), which is titled "Special Reports." Thus, the term *special reports* is defined by the coverage of SAS No. 62 (AU 623). It includes reports on (1) financial statements intended to conform to an accounting basis other than generally accepted accounting principles (other comprehensive basis of accounting); (2) specified accounts, elements, or items of a financial statement; (3) compliance with contractual or regulatory requirements; (4) financial presentations to comply with contractual or regulatory requirements; and (5) financial data in prescribed forms or schedules.

Other Comprehensive Bases of Accounting (OCBOA)   Some financial statements are not intended to present financial position, results of operations, and cash flows in conformity with generally accepted accounting principles. If the financial statements are represented on a generally recognized basis, which SAS No. 62 (AU 623) defines as a comprehensive basis, then the auditor can report on the conformity of the statements with that basis and need not express a qualified or adverse opinion because of the departure from generally accepted accounting principles. SAS No. 62 (AU 623) specifies the following other comprehensive bases of accounting:

1 Financial reporting rules of a government regulatory agency when the statements are for the sole purpose of filing with the agency
2 The basis used in filing an income tax return
3 The cash receipts and disbursement basis, including accepted modifications such as recording depreciation
4 A definite set of criteria having substantial support that is applied to all material items, such as the price-level basis of accounting

The following report on cash basis statements illustrates the essential reporting requirements.

Independent Auditor's Report

We have audited the accompanying statements of assets and liabilities arising from cash transactions of XYZ Company as of December 31, 19X2 and 19X1, and the related statements of revenue collected and expenses paid for the years then ended. These financial statements are the responsibility of the Company's management. Our responsibility is to express an opinion on these financial statements based on our audits.

We conducted our audits in accordance with generally accepted auditing standards. Those standards require that we plan and perform the audit to obtain reasonable assurance about whether the financial statements are free of material misstatement. An audit includes examining, on a test basis, evidence supporting the amounts and disclosures in the financial statements. An audit also includes assessing the accounting principles used and significant estimates made by management, as well as evaluating the overall financial statement presentation. We believe that our audits provide a reasonable basis for our opinion.

As described in Note X. these financial statements were prepared on the basis of cash receipts and disbursements, which is a comprehensive basis of accounting other than generally accepted accounting principles.

In our opinion, the financial statements referred to above present fairly, in all material respects, the assets and liabilities arising from cash transactions of XYZ Company as of December 31, 19X2 and 19X1, and its revenue collected and expenses paid during the years then ended, on the basis of accounting described in Note X.

(Signature)

(Date)

Note that the basis of accounting is described, and the auditor's opinion is expressed on conformity with the described basis.

An accounting basis other than GAAP may be used because it is more convenient, and use of the financial statements outside the company is limited. For example, a small business might use the tax basis to avoid the difficulty and cost of preparing GAAP-basis financial statements in addition to records that must be maintained for tax reporting.

Specified Elements, Accounts, or Items   The auditor may be requested to report on some specific aspect of a financial statement or on specific financial data rather than on financial statements taken as a whole. For example, the auditor may be asked to report on royalties or profit participation based on an agreement that specifies computation of these items in relation to sales or production. A report on the adequacy of a provision for income taxes is another example.

In reporting on specified elements, accounts, or items, the auditor should clearly explain the extent and nature of procedures applied, the basis on which the matter is presented or determined, and the degree of responsibility being assumed, such as expressing an opinion or describing more limited findings.

Compliance with Contracts or Regulations   Companies may be required by contracts such as bond indentures or loan agreements, or by regulatory agencies to furnish reports by auditors on their compliance. Normally, the auditor furnishes a compliance report in connection with an audit of a company's financial statements. The auditor usually satisfies the request by giving negative assurance on the company's compliance with applicable requirements related to financial statements. The report may be given separately or in an additional paragraph of the standard report. For example, a debt covenant may require maintenance of a specified current ratio or maintenance of a specified level of insurance on secured property. The auditor reports that in the audit of financial statements nothing came to the auditor's attention that caused the auditor to believe the company was not in compliance.

Contractual or Regulatory Requirements   When a contract or regulatory provision specifies a special-purpose financial presentation that is not GAAP, or not an OCBOA, or an incomplete presentation, the auditor's report should contain a paragraph explaining the basis, and stating that it is not intended to be a complete presentation.

Prescribed Forms or Schedules   Printed forms or schedules may prescribe wording of an auditor's report or presentation of financial data that does not conform to generally accepted standards. For example, the prescribed report may state the auditor "certifies the accuracy of the data" or that the auditor made a "detailed examination of the records." Usually, the auditor must reword the form or leave it blank and attach a separate report to comply with professional standards.

Reports on Accompanying Information

The auditor is sometimes associated with financial statements in a document prepared for a special purpose that contains additional data and schedules to supplement the basic financial statements. For example, a questionnaire has been designed for finance companies by Robert Morris Associates, a bank credit grantors' association. The questionnaire contains substantial additional financial data and is signed by the auditor.

Supplemental data may also be included in a document prepared and submitted by the auditor at the client's request. For example, the client may find it useful to have schedules of the detailed items supporting the amounts presented in the basic financial statements, such as a schedule of investments or operating expenses.

Client-Prepared versus Auditor-Submitted Documents   The auditor's reporting responsibility in auditor-submitted documents is explained in SAS No. 29 (AU 551), "Reporting on Information Accompanying the Basic Financial Statements in Auditor-Submitted Documents." The key to understanding the auditor's responsibilities is the distinction between a client-prepared document and an auditor-submitted document.

If the document is client-prepared, there is a presumption that the auditor has audit responsibility only for the information identified explicitly in the audit report. A common example of a client-prepared document is the glossy-covered annual report typically released by a public company. In that type of document, the first paragraph of the audit report explicitly identifies the financial information on which the auditor is reporting. The auditor assumes no explicit responsibility for other information included in the document. However, certain implicit responsibilities are explained in Chapter 12.

This presumption changes for documents the auditor prepares and submits to the client or others. An auditor-submitted document is usually a bound report prepared by the auditor with a distinctive format and with a cover page that carries the logo or identifying letterhead of the CPA firm. Since the document obviously comes from the auditor, there is a need for the auditor to state explicitly the degree of responsibility assumed for all the information in the document. The responsibility for the basic financial statements is explained in the standard report. However, the auditor must add a report on the accompanying information to clarify the extent of responsibility assumed for it.

Nature of Responsibility for Accompanying Information   Note that the additional responsibility imposed by SAS No. 29 (AU 551) is a *reporting* responsibility; an expansion of audit scope is not required. If the audit procedures applied to form an opinion on the basic financial statements are not sufficient to provide the auditor with a basis for expressing some assurance on the accompanying information, the auditor may disclaim an opinion on that portion of the accompanying information.

The nature of the assurance that the auditor may provide on the accompanying information is whether the information is *fairly stated in all material respects in relation to the financial statements taken as a whole.* In other words, the audited basic financial statements (balance sheet, income statement, statement of retained earnings, statement of cash flows, and required disclosures) provide the framework for the assurance expressed. The materiality level used is the one that applies to the financial statements taken as a whole rather than what might be material to the accompanying information.

Report Form   The auditor's report on accompanying information may be added to the standard report or appear as a separate report immediately preceding the accompanying information. The report might be worded as follows:

> Our audit was conducted for the purpose of forming an opinion on the basic financial statements taken as a whole. The (identify accompanying information) is presented for purposes of additional analysis and is not a required part of the basic financial statements. Such information has been subjected to the auditing procedures applied in the audit of the basic financial statements and, in our opinion, is fairly stated in all material respects in relation to the basic financial statements taken as a whole.
>
> (Signature)
>
> (Date)

The essential features of this type of report are as follows:

1 A statement that the audit has been conducted for the *purpose of forming an opinion on the basic financial statements* taken as a whole
2 An *identification of the accompanying information* by descriptive title or page number
3 A statement that the accompanying information is *presented for purposes of additional analysis* and is not a required part of the basic financial statements
4 A conclusion on whether the accompanying information is fairly stated in all material respects in relation to the basic financial statements taken as a whole

This report wording would have to be modified if the auditor disclaimed an opinion on all or part of the accompanying information. If the auditor's report on the basic statements is other than an unqualified opinion, the effect on the accompanying information would have to be explained.

This type of report may also include an expanded description of the scope of the auditor's procedures. In that case, it is extremely important to maintain a clear distinction between the accompanying information which is management's representation and the auditor's representations in describing the examination.

Forecasts and Projections

The CPA's procedures and reporting standards for compilation or attestation services in connection with financial forecasts and projections are provided by the AICPA's "Statement on Standards for Accountant's Services on Prospective Financial Information." The statement includes the following definitions:

- *Financial forecast.* These are prospective financial statements that present, to the best of the responsible party's knowledge and belief, an entity's expected financial position, results of operations, and cash flows. A financial forecast is based on the responsible party's assumptions reflecting conditions it expects to exist and the course of action it expects to take. A financial forecast may be expressed in specific monetary amounts as a single point estimate of forecasted results or as a range, where the responsible party selects key assumptions to form a range within which it reasonably expects, to the best of its knowledge and belief, the item or items subject to the assumptions to actually fall.

- *Financial projection.* These are prospective financial statements that present, to the best of the responsible party's knowledge and belief, given one or more hypothetical assumptions, an entity's expected financial position, results of operations, and cash flows. A financial projection is sometimes prepared to present one or more hypothetical courses of action for evaluation, as in response to a question such as "What would happen if . . . ?" A financial projection is based on the responsible party's assumptions reflecting conditions it expects would exist and the course of action it expects would be taken, given one or more hypothetical assumptions. A projection, like a forecast, may contain a range.

A forecast is a company's best estimate of what will actually occur in the future. A projection is the company's estimate of what will occur if a specified hypothetical course of action is taken. The hypothetical assumption is not necessarily expected to occur.

Many large companies have prepared forecasts or projections for many years as an essential management tool. The standards in the Statement are not applicable when the accountant is simply assisting management with prospective information for their own internal use only. Many companies have provided forecasts or projections to selected security analysts or commented on the accuracy of forecasts made by analysts. The SEC allows forecasts in filings and has considered encouraging financial forecasts to make them available on a more equitable basis. However, the involvement of independent accountants with forecasts and projections has occurred largely outside the SEC's jurisdiction.

Many financing and investing transactions are not regulated under the federal securities laws. Private placements of securities, long-term loans by lending institutions, and revenue bonds issued by municipal authorities, such as airports, hospitals, and toll bridges, are examples of financing activities not so regulated. The financial data used in these activities have normally included forecasts as a central element. The forecasts are often reported on by an independent CPA.

Types of Services   An accountant associated with forecasts or projections that may reasonably be expected to be used by a third party may provide:

- *Compilation services*—assembling or assisting in assembling prospective financial statements
- *Examination services*—evaluating the preparation and presentation of the prospective financial statements and the support underlying the assumptions and reporting on the prospective financial statements
- *Applying agreed-upon procedures*—performing an engagement to apply procedures established by agreement and distributing a report limited to specified users

The Statement indicates that the accountant associated with prospective financial information should either examine, compile, or perform agreed-upon procedures. Note that review services are not included in the types of permissible services. Since a forecast is based primarily on assumptions rather than historical exchange transactions, the procedures for the highest level of service—an examination—consist principally of inquiry and analytical procedures. Thus, there is no intermediate level of service between an examination and compilation.

The Statement provides minimum presentation guidelines for prospective financial information. A *reasonably objective basis* is required for the prospective information, and guidance is provided on how to determine that a reasonably objective basis exists. For example, it would usually be difficult to establish that a reasonably objective basis exists if a forecast extends beyond 3 to 5 years. If the prospective financial information does not meet the minimum guidelines or is a partial presentation, the Statement does not apply. Also, the accountant is prohibited from compiling, examining, or applying agreed-upon procedures to prospective financial statements that omit a summary of significant assumptions. The assumptions are vital to the understanding of a financial forecast.

The standards attempt to avoid confusion between *projections* presenting the results of a course of action that may or may not occur, and a *forecast* presenting the expected future results. The Statement prohibits an accountant from consenting to the use of his or her name in conjunction with a financial projection if the projection is to be used by persons not negotiating directly with the responsible party unless the projection is used to supplement a forecast.

Reports   The Statement provides examples of a variety of reports on prospective financial information, addressing both forecasts and projections and including compilation reports, and qualified and adverse reports for an examination engagement. The following is an example of the accountant's standard report on an examination of a forecast:

We have examined the accompanying forecasted balance sheet, statements of income, retained earnings, and cash flows of XYZ Company as of December 31, 19XX, and for the year then ending. Our examination was made in accordance with standards for an examination of a forecast established by the American Institute of Certified Public Accountants and, accordingly, included such procedures as we considered necessary to evaluate both the assumptions used by management and the preparation and presentation of the forecast.

In our opinion, the accompanying forecast is presented in conformity with guidelines for presentation of a forecast established by the American Institute of Certified Public Accountants, and the underlying assumptions provide a reasonable basis for management's forecast. However, there will usually be differences between the forecasted and actual results, because events and circumstances frequently do not occur as expected, and those differences may be material. We have no responsibility to update this report for events and circumstances occurring after the date of this report.

(Signature)

(Date)

Internal Control Structure

An accountant may be engaged to report on a company's assertions regarding their internal control structure over financial reporting. The accountant may perform either of two levels of services:

- To examine and report on management's assertion about the effectiveness of an entity's internal control structure over financial reporting
- To apply agreed-upon procedures relating to the effectiveness of the internal control structure

Review engagements are prohibited.

There are four different ways management may present their assertions. The management assertions may be about:

- The design and operating effectiveness of an entity's internal control structure over financial reporting
- The design and operating effectiveness of a segment of the entity's internal control structure
- Only the suitability of the design of the entity's internal control structure (No assertion is made about the operating effectiveness.)
- The design and operating effectiveness of an entity's internal control structure based on criteria established by a regulatory agency

The accountant may accept the engagement to report on the internal control structure only if management (1) *accepts responsibility* for the effectiveness of the internal control structure and (2) provides a *written assertion* (3) which is based on *reasonable criteria* that can be supported (4) by *sufficient, competent evidential matter*. Identification of suitable criteria is a key aspect for engagement acceptance. One commonly used set of criteria was established in a report issued by the Committee of Sponsoring Organizations of the Treadway Commission (COSO), entitled *Internal Control—Integrated Framework*. Other criteria commonly used include standards established by regulatory agencies.

The auditor's standard examination report on the internal control structure over financial reporting is as follows:

Independent Accountant's Report

We have examined management's assertion [that W Company maintained an effective internal control structure over financial reporting as of December 31, 19XX] included in the accompanying management report ["W Company in 19XX"].

Our examination was made in accordance with standards established by the American Institute of Certified Public Accountants and, accordingly, included obtaining an understanding of the internal control structure over financial reporting, testing, and evaluating the design and operating effectiveness of the internal control structure. and such other procedures as we considered necessary in the circumstances. We believe that our examination provides a reasonable basis for our opinion.

Because of inherent limitations in any internal control structure, errors or irregularities may occur and not be detected. Also, projections of any evaluation of the internal control structure over financial reporting to future periods are subject to the risk that the internal control structure may become inadequate because of changes in conditions, or that the degree of compliance with the policies or procedures may deteriorate.

In our opinion, management's assertion [that W Company maintained an effective internal control structure of financial reporting as of December 31, 19XX] is fairly stated, in all material respects, based upon [criteria established in *Internal Control—Integrated Framework* issued by the Committee of Sponsoring Organizations of the Treadway Commission (COSO)].

(Signature)

(Date)

Note that the report identifies management's assertion (in an accompanying management report). The report states that the examination was made in accordance with standards established by the AICPA, and provides a standardized description of the examination. The report includes a warning about the inherent limitations in any internal control structure. The opinion states that management's assertion is itself fairly stated, in all material respects, based upon the identified criteria used.

The accountant's standard report is modified to restrict distribution of the report to management and the board of directors when management's assertions are presented only in a representation letter to the accountant instead of in an accompanying report.

The accountant's standard report is also modified when a material weakness exists. If management discloses the material weakness in its assertion, the accountant's opinion states "except for the effect of the material weakness described in its report, management's assertion . . . is fairly stated. . . ." If management disagrees with the accountant about the material weakness, the report should have an additional explanatory paragraph defining what a material weakness is and describing the particular material weakness discovered in the examination and its effect on achievement of the objectives of the control criteria. In this case the opinion paragraph states: "because of the effect of the material weakness described above on the achievement of the objectives of the control criteria, management's assertion . . . is not fairly stated. . . ."

The accountant's report on the internal control structure may also be modified for a scope limitation (qualification or disclaimer), or for an opinion based in part on the report of another practitioner.

Pro Forma Financial Information

Pro forma financial information shows what the effects on historical financial information might have been had a transaction or event occurred at an earlier date. Pro forma information is commonly used to show the effects of business combinations, proposed sales of securities and the applications of proceeds, changes in capitalization, and disposition of a significant portion of a business.

When a CPA is engaged to examine or review pro forma financial information, the general and field work standards for attestation engagements apply. Specific performance and reporting standards for such engagements are presented in a Statement on Standards for Attestation Engagements, "Reporting on Pro Forma Financial Information." The SSAE (AT 300.16) gives the following example report:

> We have examined the pro forma adjustments reflecting the transaction [or event] described in Note 1 and the application of those adjustments to the historical amounts in [the assembly of] the accompanying pro forma condensed balance sheet of X Company as of December 31, 19X1, and the pro forma condensed statement of income for the year then ended. The historical condensed financial statements are derived from the historical financial statements of X Company, which were audited by us, and of Y Company, which were audited by other accountants, appearing elsewhere herein [or incorporated by reference]. Such pro forma adjustments are based upon management's assumptions described in Note 2. Our examination was made in accordance with standards established by the American Institute of Certified Public Accountants and, accordingly, included such procedures as we considered necessary in the circumstances.
>
> The objective of this pro forma financial information is to show what the significant effects on the historical financial information might have been had the transaction [or event] occurred at an earlier date. However, the pro forma condensed financial statements are not necessarily indicative of the results of operations or related effects on financial position that would have been attained had the above-mentioned transaction [or event] actually occurred earlier.
>
> [Additional paragraph(s) may be added to emphasize certain matters relating to the attest engagement.]
>
> In our opinion, management's assumptions provide a reasonable basis for presenting the significant effects directly attributable to the above-mentioned transaction [or event] described in Note 1, the related pro forma adjustments give appropriate effect to those assumptions, and the pro forma column reflects the proper application of those adjustments to the historical financial statement amounts in the pro forma condensed balance sheet as of December 31, 19X1, and the pro forma condensed statement of income for the year then ended.
>
> (Signature)
>
> (Date)

Compliance Attestation

An accountant may report on management's assertions about compliance with laws, regulations, rules, contracts, or grants (the *specified requirements*). The accountant may also be engaged to report on the effectiveness of a company's internal control structure over compliance with those specified requirements. The accountant may be engaged to perform an examination or to perform agreed-upon procedures. A review is prohibited.

The standards that apply depend on the circumstances. In general, SSAE No. 3 (AT 500) applies. However, SAS No. 68 (AU 801) applies instead to engagements for which the objective is to report in accordance with the General Accounting Office's *Government Auditing Standards,* the Single Audit Act of 1984, the Office of Management and Budget's *Audits of State and Local Governments,* or *Audits of Institutions of Higher Education and Other Nonprofit Institutions* for institutions that receive government financial assistance.

Under SSAE No. 3 (AT 500), to accept the compliance attestation engagement, the accountant must obtain written representations from management including management's assertion about the entity's compliance with the specified requirements. In addition, reasonable criteria must have been established by a recognized body or stated in management's assertion.

The accountant's standard examination report on compliance with specified requirements is as follows:

Independent Accountant's Report

[Introductory paragraph]

We have examined management's assertion about [name of entity]'s compliance with [list specified compliance requirements] during the [period] ended [date] included in the accompanying [title of management report]. Management is responsible for [name of entity]'s compliance with those requirements. Our responsibility is to express an opinion on management's assertion about the Company's compliance based on our examination.

[Scope paragraph]

Our examination was made in accordance with standards established by the American Institute of Certified Public Accountants and, accordingly, included examining, on a test basis, evidence about [name of entity]'s compliance with those requirements and performing such other procedures as we considered necessary in the circumstances. We believe that our examination provides a reasonable basis for our opinion. Our examination does not provide a legal determination on [name of entity]'s compliance with specified requirements.

[Opinion paragraph]

In our opinion, management's assertion [identify management's assertion—for example, that Z Company complied with the aforementioned requirements for the year ended December 31, 19X1] is fairly stated, in all material respects.

(Signature)

(Date)

The accountant should modify the standard report if:

- There is a material noncompliance with specified requirements.
- There is a matter involving a material uncertainty that may affect the determination of compliance with specified requirements.

- There is a restriction on the scope of the engagement.
- The accountant decides to refer to the report of another accountant as the basis, in part, for the report.

CHAPTER 14 ASSIGNMENTS

OBJECTIVE QUESTIONS

14-1 For each of the following statements indicate whether the statement is true or false.

T F **a** The procedures for a compilation of financial statements include inquiries concerning a company's accounting principles and practices and the methods followed in applying them.

T F **b** An accountant's review report would not be modified for a significant uncertainty or an inconsistent application of accounting principles that materially affect the financial statements.

T F **c** The scope of a review of interim financial information is not influenced by the knowledge that might be obtained in an audit of the company's annual financial statements.

T F **d** An accountant does not become associated with the financial statements of a public company unless the accountant's name is appended to the statements.

T F **e** The auditor determines the extent of procedures to be applied in an engagement to issue a comfort letter to an underwriter based on what is necessary in the circumstances to express negative assurance.

T F **f** Even though cash-basis financial statements are not in conformity with generally accepted accounting principles, an auditor need not express a qualified or adverse opinion on such statements.

T F **g** If an auditor is requested to report on only the current asset section of the balance sheet, the auditor should disclaim an opinion because of the scope limitation.

T F **h** The auditor is obliged to report on all of the information in an auditor-submitted document.

T F **i** A public accountant may not be associated with a presentation of a company's operating results for a future accounting period.

T F **j** When the auditor reports on financial statements, the auditor is giving an opinion on management's assertions presented in those statements. When an accountant reports on the internal control structure, however, the accountant is presenting his or her own assertions about the effectiveness of the design of the internal control structure.

T F **k** The criteria for the accountant's evaluation of compliance with laws, regulations, contracts, or grants are specified in the attestation standards established by the AICPA.

14-2 The following questions relate to a public accountant's responsibilities for unaudited financial statements. Select the *best* response.

    a In performing a compilation of financial statements of a nonpublic entity, the accountant decides that modification of the standard report is not adequate to indicate deficiencies in the financial statements taken as a whole, and the client is not willing to correct the deficiencies. The accountant should therefore:

      1 Perform a review of the financial statements

    2 Issue a special report
    3 Withdraw from the engagement
    4 Express an adverse audit opinion
b Which of the following procedures is *not* included in an SSARS review engagement of a nonpublic entity?
    1 Inquiries of management
    2 Inquiries regarding events subsequent to the balance sheet date
    3 Any procedures designed to identify relationships among data that appear to be unusual
    4 An assessment of control risk
c Which of the following would *not* be included in a CPA's report based upon an SSARS review of the financial statements of a nonpublic entity?
    1 A statement that the review was in accordance with generally accepted auditing standards
    2 A statement that all information included in the financial statements are the representations of management
    3 A statement describing the principal procedures performed
    4 A statement describing the CPA's conclusions based upon the results of the review
d A modification of the CPA's report on a review of the interim financial statements of a publicly held company would be necessitated by which of the following?
    1 An uncertainty
    2 Lack of consistency
    3 Reference to another accountant
    4 Inadequate disclosure
e A CPA who is associated with the financial statements of a public entity, but has *not* audited or reviewed such statements, should:
    1 Insist that they be audited or reviewed before publication
    2 Read them to determine whether there are obvious material misstatements
    3 State these facts in the accompanying notes to the financial statements
    4 Issue a compilation report
f Prior to commencing the compilation of financial statements of a nonpublic entity, the accountant should:
    1 Perform analytical procedures sufficient to determine whether fluctuations among account balances appear reasonable
    2 Complete the control risk assessment
    3 Verify that the financial information supplied by the entity agrees with the books of original entry
    4 Acquire a knowledge of any specialized accounting principles and practices used in the entity's industry
g When providing limited assurance that the financial statements of a nonpublic entity require no material modifications to be in accordance with generally accepted accounting principles, the accountant should:
    1 Perform a control risk assessment
    2 Test the accounting records that identify inconsistencies with the prior year's financial statements
    3 Understand the accounting principles of the industry in which the entity operates
    4 Develop audit programs to determine whether the entity's financial statements are fairly presented

h Inquiry and analytical procedures ordinarily performed during a review of a nonpublic entity's financial statements include:

1 Inquiries concerning actions taken at meetings of the stockholders and the board of directors

2 Analytical procedures designed to test the accounting records by obtaining corroborating evidential matter

3 Inquiries designed to identify reportable conditions in the internal control structure

4 Analytical procedures designed to test management's assertions regarding continued existence

i An accountant who reviews the financial statements of a nonpublic entity should issue a report stating that a review:

1 Is substantially less in scope than an audit

2 Provides negative assurance that the internal control structure is functioning as designed

3 Provides only limited assurance that the financial statements are fairly presented

4 Is substantially more in scope than a compilation

j During a review of the financial statements of a nonpublic entity, an accountant becomes aware of a lack of adequate disclosure that is material to the financial statements. If management refuses to correct the financial statement presentations, the accountant should:

1 Issue an adverse opinion

2 Issue an "except for" qualified opinion

3 Disclose this departure from generally accepted accounting principles in a separate paragraph of the report

4 Express only limited assurance on the financial statement presentations

k Baker, CPA, was engaged to review the financial statements of Hall Company, a nonpublic entity. Evidence came to Baker's attention that indicated substantial doubt as to Hall's ability to continue as a going concern. The principal conditions and events that caused the substantial doubt have been fully disclosed in the notes to Hall's financial statements. Which of the following statements best describes Baker's reporting responsibility concerning this matter?

1 Baker is *not* required to modify the accountant's review report.

2 Baker is *not* permitted to modify the accountant's review report.

3 Baker should issue an accountant's compilation report instead of a review report.

4 Baker should express a qualified opinion in the accountant's review report.

AICPA

14-3 The following questions relate to specialized reporting circumstances. Select the *best* response.

a When reporting on financial statements prepared on a comprehensive basis of accounting other than generally accepted accounting principles, the independent auditor should include in the report a paragraph that:

1 States that the financial statements are *not* intended to be in conformity with generally accepted accounting principles

2 Justifies the comprehensive basis of accounting being used

3 Refers to the authoritative pronouncements that explain the comprehensive basis of accounting being used

4 States the financial statements are *not* intended to have been audited in accordance with generally accepted auditing standards

b The term "special reports" may include all of the following, *except* reports on financial statements:

1 Of an organization that has limited the scope of the audit

2 Prepared for limited purposes such as a report that relates to only certain aspects of financial statements

3 Of a not-for-profit organization which follows accounting practices differing in some respects from those followed by business enterprises organized for profit

4 Prepared in accordance with historical cost/constant dollar accounting.

c Whenever special reports, filed on a printed form designed by authorities, call upon the independent auditor to make an assertion that the auditor believes is *not* justified, the auditor should:

1 Reword the form or attach a separate report

2 Submit a short form with explanations

3 Submit the form with questionable items clearly omitted

4 Withdraw from the engagement

d A financial forecast is an estimate of financial position, results of operations, and cash flows that, to the best of management's knowledge, is:

1 At the midpoint of a given precision range

2 At the low point of a given precision range

3 Conservative

4 Most probable

e A CPA's understanding of the internal control structure in an audit:

1 Is generally more limited than that made in connection with an engagement to express an opinion on the internal control structure

2 Is generally more extensive than that made in connection with an engagement to express an opinion on the internal control structure

3 Will generally be identical to that made in connection with an engagement to express an opinion on the internal control structure

4 Will generally result in the CPA expressing an opinion on the internal control structure

f When an auditor is requested to express an opinion on the rental and royalty income of an entity, the auditor may:

1 Not accept the engagement because to do so would be tantamount to agreeing to issue a piecemeal opinion

2 Not accept the engagement unless also engaged to audit the full financial statements of the entity

3 Accept the engagement provided the auditor's opinion is expressed in a special report

4 Accept the engagement only if distribution of the auditor's report is limited to the entity's management

g The accountant's examination report on an entity's internal control structure over financial reporting should state that:

1 The examination was conducted in accordance with generally accepted auditing standards.

2 The establishment and maintenance of the system of internal accounting control are the responsibilities of management.

3 The projections of any evaluation of the internal control structure over financial reporting to future periods are subject to the risk that the internal control structure may become inadequate.

4 The client's management has provided assurance that the expected benefits of the internal accounting control procedures are in excess of their related costs.

h An auditor's consideration of the internal control structure and resulting control risk assessment made in connection with the annual audit is generally *not* sufficient to report on an entity's internal control structure because:

1 The evaluation of material weaknesses is subjective enough that an auditor should not report on the internal control structure alone.

2 Management may change the internal control structure policies and procedures to correct weaknesses.

3 The audit approach limits testing of the internal control structure to areas where control risk is reduced below maximum, and the audit testing may not be sufficient to report on the internal control structure based on specified criteria.

4 Internal control structure specialists rather than general auditors should perform the examination.

i When an accountant examines a financial forecast that fails to disclose several significant assumptions used to prepare the forecast, the accountant should describe the assumptions in the accountant's report and issue a(n):

1 "Except for" qualified opinion

2 "Subject to" qualified opinion

3 Unqualified opinion with a separate explanatory paragraph

4 Adverse opinion

j The objective of a review of interim financial information is to provide an accountant with a basis for reporting whether:

1 The financial statements are presented fairly in accordance with generally accepted accounting principles.

2 A reasonable basis exists for expressing an updated opinion regarding the financial statements that were previously audited.

3 Material modifications should be made to conform with generally accepted accounting principles.

4 The financial statements are presented fairly in accordance with standards of interim reporting.

k Which of the following professional services would be considered an attest engagement?

1 A management consulting engagement to provide EDP advice to a client

2 An engagement to report on compliance with statutory requirements

3 An income tax engagement to prepare federal and state tax returns

4 The compilation of financial statements from a client's accounting records

l When third-party use of prospective financial statements is expected, an accountant may *not* accept an engagement to:

1 Perform a review

2 Perform a compilation

3 Perform an examination

4 Apply agreed-upon procedures

m Which of the following is the authoritative body designated to promulgate attestation standards?

1 Auditing Standards Board

2 Governmental Accounting Standards Board

3 Financial Accounting Standards Board

4 General Accounting Office

n An auditor's report would be designated a special report when it is issued in connection with:

1 Interim financial information of a publicly held company that is subject to a limited review

2 Compliance with aspects of regulatory requirements related to audited financial statements

3 Application of accounting principles to specified transactions

4 Limited use prospective financial statements such as a financial projection

o An auditor who conducts an examination in accordance with generally accepted auditing standards and concludes that the financial statements are fairly presented in accordance with a comprehensive basis of accounting other than generally accepted accounting principles, such as the cash basis of accounting, should issue a:

1 Special report

2 Disclaimer of opinion

3 Review report

4 Qualified opinion

p Performing inquiry and analytical procedures is the primary basis for an accountant to issue a:

1 Report on compliance with requirements governing major federal assistance programs in accordance with the Single Audit Act

2 Review report on prospective financial statements that present an entity's expected financial position, given one or more hypothetical assumptions

3 Consulting service report prepared at the request of a client's audit committee

4 Review report on comparative financial statements for a nonpublic entity in its second year of operations

DISCUSSION QUESTIONS

Discussion questions require the application of the concepts explained in the chapter to specific facts, issues, or problems. They are classified by the primary topic to which they relate. However, responses should not be confined to the primary topics but should include all relevant implications.

Unaudited Financial Statements

14-4 You have been asked to prepare unaudited financial statements for the Marek Company for the year ended December 31, 19X5. Marek does not want the notes to financial statements to disclose that the company is involved in litigation on a question of patent infringement. Potential damages that might have to be paid by the company exceed its net worth. Since you are not expressing an opinion on the financial statements, Marek does not believe you should be concerned with the adequacy of disclosure.

a How would you respond to Marek?

b Write the CPA's report on the financial statements that you would issue if the matter is not disclosed.

14-5 You have prepared tax returns for the Hicks & Hocks Corporation for several years. Hicks called you and requested 50 additional copies of the return this year. You have never prepared audited or unaudited financial statements for the company.

a How would you respond to Hicks' request?

b Is it appropriate to meet the request simply by furnishing extra copies of the return?

14-6 W. E. Jolson, CPA, has issued the following report on the Bambino Lumber Company's balance sheet;

> I have audited the balance sheet of Bambino Lumber Co. for the period ended December 31, 19X1. Due to the urgency of the need for my statements my audit was not made in accordance with generally accepted auditing standards.
>
> The accompanying balance sheet fairly presents the book values of the assets of Bambino Lumber Co. as of June 30, 19X1. However, the balance sheet is not certified in conformity, on a consistent basis, with generally accepted accounting principles.

List and discuss the deficiencies in the CPA's report.

14-7 The following report was prepared by M. Salvemini, CPA, to accompany unaudited financial statements:

> We have prepared the statement of net worth, dated November 30, 19X1, that is attached hereto. This statement was prepared from the books and records of account as maintained in your office. At your request, our audit included verification that current asset and current liabilities were accurately stated. Each asset is stated at cost, and profit increment in the work in progress is not included as an asset.
>
> Since our audit did not include as many audit procedures as would be required in a complete certified audit, certification of the statement as a whole is withheld.

List and discuss the deficiencies in the CPA's report.

14-8 Assume that you prepared Moore Corporation's federal income tax return. Shortly thereafter Moore came to your office and requested that you prepare financial statements for the corporation solely from the data on the federal income tax return you prepared. The statements are to be submitted to a creditor. Discuss the ethical implications of your preparing the financial statements on:

a Your stationery

b Plain paper

AICPA adapted

Special Reports

14-9 R. Gilsdorf, CPA, has prepared the following report on the cash basis financial statements of the ABC Company.

> I have audited the balance sheet and income statement of ABC Company as of December 31, 19X9, and for the year then ended. My audit was made in accordance with generally accepted auditing standards and, accordingly, included such tests of the accounting records as I considered necessary in the circumstances.
>
> In my opinion, the above-mentioned financial statements present fairly, in all material respects, ABC Company's financial position and results of operations consistent with the cash basis of accounting.

Explain the deficiencies in this special report.

14-10 May & Day CPAs are engaged by XYZ Company to audit the records of gross sales of ABC Stores Corporation. ABC Stores leases space in a shopping center owned by XYZ Company that is located in Water Island, New York. The annual rental, according to the lease agreement, is based on a percentage of gross sales as defined in the agreement dated March 5, 19X8. Prepare the report that May & Day should issue on the gross sales for the year ended December 31, 19X9, to be used in computing the rental. The extent of audit procedures to be applied is not restricted in any way, and the lease agreement guarantees XYZ Company full access to the accounting records of ABC Stores.

14-11 The American National Bank has prepared an application form for long-term loans that must be prepared and signed by an independent CPA. The one-page form contains blanks for filling in financial statement amounts, and the line to be signed by the CPA is under the following sentence: "I certify the above to be true and correct." How would you complete the form if you were requested to do so by an audit client?

14-12 The Kohler Company, your client, is considering the acquisition of the Krunt Corporation. The assets of Krunt are composed primarily of receivables and inventory. Kohler is having its engineers evaluate Krunt's inventory, and they would like you to examine and report on the receivables.

a May you accept the engagement?

b What auditing standards would be applicable to the engagement?

c If you accept the engagement, how would you write your report?

14-13 Day, a small manufacturing company, has appointed you to audit and issue an opinion for the 19X9 calendar year. In January 19X9 the nine shareholders (all individuals) elected to be taxed as a small business corporation for 19X9 and later years under certain sections of the IRS Code.

In brief, these sections provide that where an election is made, the shareholders include in their own income for tax purposes the current taxable income of the corporation, both the part which is distributed and that which is not.

In the course of your 19X9 audit, you did not uncover any item which would preclude your issuing an unqualified report. As a result of the election to have the federal income tax on the corporate income paid directly by its stockholders, the following questions are raised:

a Should note disclosure be made of the election by the corporation shareholders? Explain.

b What information should be given to each stockholder at year-end to facilitate the preparation of the tax return? Explain.

c Explain the type of auditor's report you would issue under these circumstances.

AICPA adapted

CHAPTER OUTLINE

Learning Objectives

After studying this chapter you should be able to:

* Define operational auditing and explain how it is similar to and different than an audit of financial statements
* Identify the characteristics of operational auditing with respect to the auditor's qualifications, purpose of the engagement, engagement arrangements, methods of conducting the engagement, and report form and content
* Explain the similarities and differences of operational audit engagements conducted by independent CPAs, governmental auditors, and internal auditors
* Outline the basic steps in the conduct of an operational audit engagement
* Describe how an operational auditor develops and uses performance criteria
* Understand some examples of operational audit engagements performed by an independent CPA, a governmental auditor, or an internal auditor

Auditing, as explained in Chapter 1 (Auditing Concepts Committee, "Report of the Committee on Basic Auditing Concepts," *The Accounting Review,* Vol. 47, Supp. 1972, p. 18), may be defined broadly as follows:

> A systematic process of objectively obtaining and evaluating evidence regarding assertions about economic actions and events to ascertain the degree of correspondence between those assertions and established criteria and communicating the results to interested users.

The term "auditing" has a precise meaning only when used with a limiting modifier. "Financial" auditing is the main focus of this book. The modifier "operational" is used to identify a distinct type of auditing that is concerned primarily with identifying opportunities for greater efficiency and economy or for improved effectiveness in carrying out an organization's operations.

FRAMEWORK OF OPERATIONAL AUDITING

Operational auditing involves a study of the operating, managerial, or administrative performance of selected aspects of an activity of an organization. Operational audits may be performed by internal auditors, governmental auditors, or independent public accountants. Operational auditing and financial auditing differ in several ways, but one distinguishing feature of operational auditing is that the direct benefits of the audit flow almost entirely to the entity being audited or, if different, the party who engaged the auditor. Third-party reliance on operational audit reports is not a common feature of operational audits.

Operational Auditing Defined

What is an operational audit? One definition that captures the essential aspects of operational auditing is as follows[1]:

A systematic review of an organization's activities, or of a stipulated segment of them, in relation to specified objectives for the purpose of:

1 Assessing performance
2 Identifying opportunities for improvement, or
3 Developing recommendations for improvement or further action

Comparison to General Definition   How well does operational auditing fit the general, abstract definition of auditing? A detailed comparison of the general definition and the specific definition highlights some important features of an operational audit.

- The systematic process of objectively obtaining and evaluating evidence is a "systematic review." This means there is an orderly and planned observation and analysis of operations, but it is more in the nature of a study than an examination in accordance with specified professional standards for the competence and sufficiency of evidence.
- Assertions about economic actions and events may be included in the scope of an operational audit, but the scope is usually more comprehensive. The systematic review is made of the *activities* concerned with planning, executing, and controlling operations. Also, the activities may be for the operation of an entire organization but are more commonly restricted to the activities of a segment of the organization. The segment may be a division or department, or it may be a function such as data processing, production, distribution, or purchasing.
- The degree of correspondence with established criteria is an important feature of operational audits because the systematic review is made "in relation to specified objectives." Criteria for judging performance are essential in conducting an operational audit. However, the operational auditor often has to take the broadly specified objectives of an organization or segment and define those objectives much more precisely. In some cases, the development of appropriate performance standards may be an additional separate engagement.
- Communicating the results of the audit in a formal report is a feature of operational audits, but the format and content of the report vary widely with the circumstances of the engagement. An operational audit report generally describes the objectives, scope, and approach of the engagement and presents specific findings and recommendations. The report identifies areas and ways for improvement of operations rather than expressing an opinion on the overall effectiveness of operations.

Thus, operational auditing fits within the general definition of auditing. However, its focus is the actual activities of an organization or segment, rather than representations

[1]Adapted from AICPA, *Operational Audit Engagements* (New York: AICPA, 1982), p. 2.

about those activities, and the established criteria for evaluating those activities are often developed, or at least specified in more detail, by the operational auditor.

Administrative versus Accounting Controls   Internal auditing and governmental auditing literature refer to *administrative controls* and *accounting controls*. These concepts were originally defined in a now superseded Statement on Auditing Standards, but the terms remain useful concepts and are commonly used. The definitions distinguish between types of control procedures based on the objectives to be achieved by the controls. The definitions are:

> *Administrative control* includes, but is not limited to, the plan of organization and the procedures and records that are concerned with the decision processes leading to management's authorization of transactions . . . and is the starting point for establishing accounting control over transactions.
>
>   *Accounting control* comprises the plan of organization and procedures and records that are concerned with the safeguarding of assets and the reliability of financial records and consequently are designed to provide reasonable assurance that:
>
> 1 Transactions are executed in accordance with management's general or specific authorization.
> 2 Transactions are recorded as necessary (1) to permit preparation of financial statements in conformity with generally accepted accounting principles or any other criteria applicable to such statements and (2) to maintain accountability for assets.
> 3 Access to assets is permitted only in accordance with management's authorization.
> 4 The recorded accountability for assets is compared with the existing assets at reasonable intervals and appropriate action is taken with respect to any difference.

Administrative control procedures tend to be outside the scope of the audit of financial statements. Achievement of administrative control objectives makes the company more efficient, effective, or profitable. However, achievement of administrative control objectives does not reduce the level of control risk in the financial auditor's audit risk model; achievement of accounting control objectives does.

Operational auditing has a different focus. Operational audit objectives include efficiency and profitability. Accordingly, administrative controls are a key part of operational audit consideration.

Comparison to Financial Auditing   What are the similarities and differences between an operational audit and an audit of financial statements? Since this book focuses primarily on financial auditing, it is both convenient and important to carefully distinguish between operational and financial auditing. For this purpose, the following categories are used:

- Auditor's qualifications
- Purpose of the engagement
- Arrangements for the engagement
- Form and content of the report

Operational Auditor's Qualifications

As mentioned earlier, operational audits may be performed by internal auditors, governmental auditors, and independent public accountants. Each of these groups has some requirements for entry to practice. Independent public accountants are licensed by state agencies as certified public accountants. Internal auditors may voluntarily take an examination administered by the Institute of Internal Auditors (IIA) to earn the designation certified internal auditor. Governmental auditors do not have a comparable license or designation but become expert in their field largely through on-the-job training and experience. However, operational auditing is unregulated, and there is no license or designation that may be earned to qualify as an operational auditor. The essential requirement is that the organization or party engaging the auditor considers the auditor qualified to undertake the engagement.

Knowledge and Skills   Generally, CPAs, internal auditors, and governmental auditors possess insight into business or government operations, knowledge of auditing procedures, and an appreciation of the relationship between financial and operating controls. In addition, an operational auditor must have sufficient expertise to perform the necessary fact-finding and evaluation of the specific operations to be reviewed. Often the expertise needed requires knowledge and skills outside the fields of accounting and auditing. In these cases, an expert in the relevant field has to be included on the audit team.

CPA firms consider operational audits to be consulting service engagements. Many CPA firms employ consulting services specialists who possess the necessary knowledge and skills required to review specialized operations, for example, engineers, actuaries, system analysts, and so on. The U.S. General Accounting Office (GAO) has staff members from engineering, atomic energy, mathematics, actuarial sciences, economics, and other fields as well as from accounting.[2]

Standards   The AICPA's Statement on Standards for Consulting Services No. 1 (CS 100.05) categorizes operational audits as *advisory services,* for which the general standards for consulting services apply. The general standards of the profession under Rule 201 of the AICPA Code of Professional Conduct require:

- *Professional competence.* Undertake only those professional services that the member or the member's firm can reasonably expect to be completed with professional competence.
- *Due professional care.* Exercise due professional care in the performance of professional services.
- *Planning and supervision.* Adequately plan and supervise the performance of professional services.
- *Sufficient relevant data.* Obtain sufficient relevant data to afford a reasonable basis for conclusions or recommendations in relation to any professional services performed.

---

[2]Leo Herbert, "An Historical Perspective of Government Auditing—with Special Reference to the U.S. General Accounting Office," *Auditing Symposium V,* University of Kansas, Lawrence, May 1980.

Statement on Standards for Consulting Services No. 1 (CS 100.07) promulgates three additional general standards for all consulting services:

- *Client interest.* Serve the client interest by seeking to accomplish the objectives established by the understanding with the client while maintaining integrity and objectivity.
- *Understanding with client.* Establish with the client a written or oral understanding about the responsibilities of the parties and the nature, scope, and limitations of services to be performed, and modify the understanding if circumstances require a significant change during the engagement.
- *Communication with client.* Inform the client of (1) conflicts of interest that may occur pursuant to interpretations of Rule 102 of the Code of Professional Conduct [ET section 102.03], (2) significant reservations concerning the scope or benefits of the engagement, and (3) significant engagement findings or events.

These additional general standards are enforceable under Rule 202 of the AICPA Code of Professional Conduct.

The General Accounting Office's *Government Auditing Standards (1994 Revision)* categorizes operational audits as *performance audits* and promulgates general standards addressing the auditor's qualifications, independence, due professional care, and quality control.[3] The field work standards address planning, supervision, compliance with laws and regulations, management controls, and evidence. The GAO's reporting standards for performance audits address the form of report, timeliness, report contents, report presentation, and report distribution.

The Institute of Internal Auditors also provides similar guidance for its members.

Independence   In the operational auditing field, the independence of the auditor is more a matter of possessing integrity and objectivity, and the requirements are not as stringent as the ethical rule on independence that applies to audits of financial statements by an independent CPA.

As mentioned earlier, a CPA firm views an operational audit engagement as a type of consulting service. The AICPA consulting standards (CS 100.07) require *integrity* and *objectivity* rather than *independence*. The Code of Professional Conduct (ET 54.02) distinguishes between *objectivity* and *independence:*

> Objectivity is a state of mind, a quality that lends value to a member's services. It is a distinguishing feature of the profession. The principle of objectivity imposes the obligation to be impartial, intellectually honest, and free of conflicts of interest. Independence precludes relationships that may appear to impair a member's objectivity rendering attestation services.

However, the AICPA consulting standards (CS 100.07) do not prohibit the CPA from performing consulting services when he or she has a conflict of interest. The standards simply require that the CPA communicate the conflict of interest to the client. An exam-

---

[3]U.S. General Accounting Office, *Government Auditing Standards (1994 Revision)* (Washington, DC: U.S. GAO, 1994).

ple of a conflict of interest that could arise in an operational audit is when the CPA makes a recommendation for improvement that involves purchasing a product or service from the CPA or from an entity with which the CPA has a significant relationship.

The GAO standards (Government Auditing Standards 3.11) require the auditor to be "free from personal and external impairments to independence, should be organizationally independent, and should maintain an independent attitude and appearance." Generally, governmental auditors are considered organizationally independent if they are auditing a level or branch of government other than the one to which they are assigned, for example, a state auditor auditing a program of a municipality within the state; if they are elected to office; or if they are appointed by and report to a legislative body of government.

Internal auditors cannot be disassociated from their employing organization but still seek an organizational status that will protect the internal audit function from impairment of integrity and objectivity. The independence of internal auditors is enhanced if they are administratively responsible to a top-level executive in the organization and have, at least, a reporting responsibility to the board of directors. In this way, internal auditors can be free from the control or influence of the managers whose activities are being audited.

Purpose of the Operational Audit Engagement

Operational audits usually are directed to a combination of the three purposes identified in the definition of operational auditing of (1) assessing performance, (2) identifying opportunities for improvement, and (3) developing recommendations for improvement or further action. These purposes have been explained as follows:

- *Assess performance.* Any operational audit involves an assessment of the reviewed organization's performance. To assess performance is to compare the manner in which an organization is conducting activities (1) to objectives established by management or the engaging party, such as organizational policies, standards, and goals, and (2) to other appropriate measurement criteria.
- *Identify opportunities for improvement.* Increased economy, efficiency, or effectiveness are the broad categories under which most improvements are classified. The practitioner may identify specific opportunities for improvements by analyzing interviews with individuals (within or outside of the organization), observing operations, reviewing past and current reports, studying transactions, making comparisons with industry standards, exercising professional judgment based on experience, or other appropriate means.
- *Develop recommendations for improvement or further action.* The nature and extent of recommendations developed in the course of operational audits vary considerably. In many cases, the practitioner may be able to make specific recommendations. In other cases, further study, not within the scope of the engagement, may be required, and the practitioner may simply cite reasons why further study of a specific area may be appropriate.[4]

[4]AICPA, *Operational Audit Engagements* (New York: AICPA, 1982), p. 3.

In a particular operational audit engagement, one of these purposes may take precedence over the others.

The purposes of an operational audit contrast rather dramatically with the purpose of an audit of financial statements made to express an opinion on whether the statements fairly present financial position, results of operations, and cash flows in conformity with generally accepted accounting principles.

The criteria for judging the representations in financial statements—generally accepted accounting principles—are codified in authoritative accounting pronouncements. These authoritative pronouncements are not the sole source of accounting principles that have general acceptance. A body of convention, rules, and procedures has also developed from common usage in practice. Operational auditing is very different in this respect. The operational auditor needs "specified objectives" that perform essentially the same role as generally accepted accounting principles. However, the specified objectives are often unique to the program or activity being reviewed, and the detailed development of specified objectives is often part of the operational auditor's assignment.

Arrangements for the Operational Audit Engagement

How does the operational auditor get an engagement to conduct an operational audit? The answer to this question has some important differences for internal auditors, governmental auditors, and independent CPAs and also some important differences from an audit of financial statements.

Internal auditors undertake operational audit engagements on their own initiative and in response to special requests of top management or the audit committee of the board of directors. An effective internal audit department usually takes the initiative in identifying departments or programs that would benefit from an operational audit. Also, top management or the audit committee may request a special review of a department or function to determine whether a new or existing program is achieving established goals or whether resources are being used economically and efficiently.

Internal auditors also have continuing assignments to examine financial and operating information for reliability, to determine compliance with company policies and procedures, and to test controls over the safeguarding of assets. Operational auditing must be coordinated with these other duties. A common practice is to extend this financial-related auditing in selected departments on some systematic basis over a few years. For example, internal auditors may test control procedures in the EDP department on a continuing basis. Every 3 years this work might be extended to make an operational review of whether the EDP department is operating efficiently, economically, and effectively. Any inefficiencies or possibilities for improvement recognized by the auditor would be communicated to management whether the auditor's focus was financial or operational.

Governmental auditors also undertake operational audits on their own initiative or in response to a request from a legislative body. A governmental auditor may initiate an operational audit by recognizing the importance of a new program or activity. Also, a legislative body may request an operational audit to see whether a program is achieving the results or benefits envisioned when it was established.

The GAO, as mentioned in Chapter 1, is an independent agency in the legislative branch of the federal government that acts as the external auditor of other federal departments and agencies. Any member of Congress may request the GAO to conduct an operational audit of a government program or activity.

An independent CPA normally undertakes an operational audit only in response to a specific request. The request may come from the audit committee or board of directors of a financial audit client but also may originate from an organization that is not a client. In the government area, the process is very formalized. A government agency that desires an operational audit by an independent CPA issues a request for proposal (RFP). An independent CPA who responds to the RFP is effectively bidding for the operational audit engagement in competition with other respondents.

Since operational audits are far more varied and less structured than financial audits, it is extremely important that there be an understanding of the purpose of the engagement and the anticipated benefits between auditor and client. Many CPAs regard obtaining a formal engagement agreement in an operational audit assignment as even more important than obtaining an engagement letter in an audit of financial statements.

An important difference between financial audits and operational audits is that by their nature operational audit engagements are not continuing engagements. There is no guarantee that an assignment to audit financial statements will continue. Financial audits are normally separate annual engagements. However, the normal expectation is that the same CPA firm will conduct the audit for several years. This arrangement is more efficient for the client and the CPA firm. An operational audit engagement, in contrast, usually arises from a special need, has unique characteristics, and normally carries no implication of a continuing assignment.

Methods of Conducting the Operational Audit Engagement

The systematic review made in conducting the operational audit is a process of fact-finding and analysis that makes use of many of the procedures that are used in an audit of financial statements. The procedures used in an operational audit include inquiry, observation, inspection of documents, and analytical procedures.

Inquiry is used extensively as a means of gathering information; good interviewing skills are essential to an operational auditor. Operational auditors find that the comments, impressions, and suggestions of organizational personnel provide important clues to inefficiencies and opportunities for improvement.

Observation of operations is a matter of seeing what is actually being done in the activity under review. The operational auditor needs to consider whether it is being done efficiently and effectively or whether some approach would achieve the same objectives at less cost or more effectively.

An important difference between an operational audit and a financial audit is the amount of evidence that is necessary to corroborate the information obtained from interviews and observations. In an audit of financial statements, the auditor's judgments on the sufficiency and competence of evidence are guided by generally accepted auditing standards and the criterion of reasonable assurance necessary to express an opinion on financial statements.

In this respect an operational audit is very different. There is no comparable body of literature to generally accepted auditing standards and their interpretation in statements on auditing standards. An operational auditor must have sufficient support for the specific findings and recommendations made. However, findings and recommendations can vary widely from engagement to engagement.

The GAO's standards for performance audits (Government Auditing Standards 6.46) contain the following guidance:

> Sufficient, competent and relevant evidence is to be obtained to afford a reasonable basis for the auditor's judgments and conclusions. A record of the auditor's work should be retained in the form of working papers. Working papers should contain sufficient information to enable an experienced auditor having no previous connection with the audit to ascertain from them the evidence that supports the auditors' significant conclusions and judgments.

In wording, this standard seems very similar to the third standard of field work of the generally accepted auditing standards. The key distinction is that in an operational audit "the auditor's judgments and conclusions" are specialized to the circumstances of the particular operational audit engagement. In an audit of financial statements the conclusion the auditor must reach to issue an unqualified opinion is specified by professional standards.

Form and Content of the Operational Audit Report

The purpose of an operational audit report is to convey an understanding of the facts and the rationale for the auditor's conclusions. An operational audit report usually describes the objectives, scope, and approach of the engagement and the specific findings and recommendations.

- *Objectives, scope, and approach.* A summary of the agreed-upon objectives and scope provides the reader with a framework for considering the findings and recommendations. A description of any limitations on the engagement imposed by the engaging party should be included. A general description of the procedures (interviewing, flowcharting, and so on) is often useful. This section might include a discussion of the rationale for selecting particular procedures and a description of the origin and application of the measurement criteria. A reminder that an operational audit report generally focuses on weaknesses and areas for improvement, rather than on the many strengths of the organization, may be appropriate.
- *Specific findings.* The nature, number, and detail of recommendations involve the exercise of professional judgment based on the purpose and scope of the engagement and the information gathered and conclusions reached during the course of the review. Recommendations are not always limited to matters that can be determined objectively. The report may include recommendations for further study of areas that were not subjected to a sufficiently detailed review or of areas where appropriate recommendations were not developed due to the constraints of the engagement. Generally, a recommendation for further study is supported by an explanation of why it would

be beneficial. It may be appropriate to state that the report's findings and conclusions are based on the organization's operations during a specified period.[5]

Although an operational audit report issued by an independent CPA to a business client normally covers the matters specified above, there is no standardized format for an operational audit report. Any arrangement that seems suitable in the circumstances may be used.

The GAO standards contain five standards that apply to reports on performance audits, including a rather detailed prescription of report content. These standards are as follows:

I *FORM.* Auditors should prepare written audit reports communicating the results of each audit.

II *TIMELINESS.* Auditors should appropriately issue the reports to make the information available for timely use by management, legislative officials, and other interested parties.

III *REPORT CONTENTS*

    A *Objectives, scope, and methodology.* Auditors should report the audit objectives and the audit scope and methodology.

    B *Audit results.* Auditors should report significant audit findings, and where applicable, auditors' conclusions.

    C *Recommendations.* Auditors should report recommendations for actions to correct problem areas and to improve operations.

    D *Statement on auditing standards.* Auditors should report that the audit was made in accordance with generally accepted government auditing standards.

    E *Compliance with laws and regulations.* Auditors should report all significant instances of noncompliance and all significant instances of abuse that were found during or in connection with the audit. In some circumstances, auditors should report illegal acts directly to parties external to the audited entity.

    F *Management controls.* Auditors should report the scope of their work on management controls and any significant weaknesses found during the audit.

    G *Views of responsible officials.* Auditors should report the views of responsible officials of the audited program concerning auditors' findings, conclusions, and recommendations, as well as corrections planned.

    H *Noteworthy accomplishments.* Auditors should report noteworthy accomplishments, particularly when management improvements in one area may be applicable elsewhere.

    I *Issues needing further study.* Auditors should refer significant issues needing further audit work to the auditors responsible for planning future audit work.

    J *Privileged and confidential information.* If certain information is prohibited from general disclosure, auditors should report the nature of the information omitted and the requirement that makes the omission necessary.

IV *REPORT PRESENTATION.* The report should be complete, accurate, objective, convincing, and as clear and concise as the subject permits.

---

[5]AICPA, *Operational Audit Engagements* (New York: AICPA, 1982), pp. 14–15.

V *REPORT DISTRIBUTION.* Written audit reports are to be submitted by the audit organization to the appropriate officials of the auditee and to the appropriate officials of the organizations requiring or arranging for the audits, including external funding organizations, unless legal restrictions prevent it. Copies of the reports should also be sent to other officials who have legal oversight authority or who may be responsible for acting on audit findings and recommendations and to others authorized to receive such reports. Unless restricted by law or regulation, copies should be made available for public inspection.[6]

The GAO reporting standards apply to a report on the operational audit of a government entity by a government auditor or an independent CPA. The GAO standards provide useful guidance on the content of an operational audit report.

Operational audit reports issued by internal auditors have no prescribed format and the content varies widely. Generally, they include a description of the scope of the operational review and present specific findings and recommendations as clearly and concisely as possible.

The key distinguishing feature between an operational audit report and a report on an audit of financial statements is that the operational audit report normally does not contain an overall opinion on the results of the operational audit engagement. It comments on specific findings. The financial auditor's standard report must express an opinion on the financial statements taken as a whole or state that such an opinion cannot be expressed. The reason for this distinction is the absence of overall measurement criteria comparable to generally accepted accounting principles in the operational audit.

CONDUCT OF AN OPERATIONAL AUDIT

The approach to be followed in conducting an operational audit is similar in concept to a financial audit. The following five broad steps would be performed for almost any type of audit:

1 A preliminary survey of the activity being reviewed is made to obtain necessary background information.

2 The basic charter or assignment of responsibility for the activity being reviewed is studied to ascertain the authorized purposes and related authorities of the activity and restrictions or limitations, if any, and performance criteria are developed.

3 Pertinent parts of the management policies to control activities under review are studied. This includes testing the effectiveness of specific administrative control procedures and exploring the problem areas or weaknesses encountered.

4 Specific conclusions are developed based on corroboration of information obtained in the above steps.

5 Reports on the results of the work are prepared and submitted to those responsible for receiving or acting on the auditor's findings and recommendations.[7]

---

[6]U.S. General Accounting Office, *Government Auditing Standards (1994 Revision)* (Washington, DC: U.S. GAO, 1994).

[7]This description of the conduct of an operational audit engagement is adapted from Ellsworth H. Morse, Jr., "Performance and Operational Auditing," *The Journal of Accountancy,* June 1971. pp. 41–46.

Preliminary Survey

During the preliminary survey information is obtained on how an activity is supposed to function and on how control procedures are supposed to work. Key features are identified that appear to be difficult to control or to be susceptible to abuse.

In a purchasing function, for example, the following steps may be the key points:

- Decisions made on quantities and of materials to be purchased
- Steps followed in obtaining best prices
- Methods for determining whether correct quantities and quality are received

If the operational auditor concludes that these steps are the most critical to good performance, the testing work would be concentrated on them.

The purpose of the preliminary survey is to identify problem areas. Procedures that are used in making the preliminary survey include inquiry (interviewing), observation, and inspection of internal reports.

Interviewing   The operational auditor can usually obtain valuable information on problem areas warranting attention through discussions with responsible officials in the organization and employees concerned with the operations being reviewed. The success in obtaining useful information is largely dependent on the auditor's reputation for independent and constructive inquiry and the auditor's interviewing skill. Usually, open-ended and noncritical questioning is the most productive approach. For example, the auditor should ask "How do you know whether the quantities and quality ordered are received?" not "Why do you not use prenumbered receiving reports?"

Observation   Physical observation of an organization's activities and facilities can be a useful way of identifying possible inefficiencies or problems. Examples are excess accumulations of equipment or material, idle or little-used equipment, employee idleness, rejections of product by inspectors, extensive rework operations, or disposal of useful materials or equipment.

Inspection of Internal Reports   The operational auditor's inspection of internal reports that management regularly uses to obtain information on the progress or status of operations can be valuable sources of information on possible problem areas. Internal audit reports can also be valuable. Of particular interest to the operational auditor are those reports with specific findings that management has not acted on. The operational auditor should inquire into the reasons for inaction. These circumstances could highlight weaknesses in the management system and related administrative controls.

Walk-Throughs   Another technique used in financial audits that is useful in an operational audit is the so-called walk-through of transactions. This is a way to obtain working knowledge of the efficiency of procedures by following several transactions pertaining to the operations under review completely from beginning to end. A walk-through of this type will provide the operational auditor with valuable information on the way the organization's activities are conducted, on the usefulness of prescribed procedures, on the capabilities of personnel involved, and on weaknesses in procedures or practices.

Review of Charter and Development of Performance Criteria

The operational auditor needs to review the basic charter, grant of authority, or assignment of responsibility of the activity under review and identify, or develop, pertinent performance criteria.

Review of Charter   The operational auditor needs to identify the stated purposes or objectives of the activity under review. This is usually accomplished by inspecting policy statements, procedure manuals, established performance standards, applicable laws and regulations, and similar pertinent data. For a government agency or program, it may be necessary to review the legislative history leading up to the creation of the agency or program.

Development of Performance Criteria   The first step in developing performance criteria is usually to identify how the organization's management determines whether prescribed policies and procedures are being followed, whether they are effective, and whether they are being applied in an efficient and economical manner. This gives a perspective from the manager's viewpoint. Also, if management has developed, as part of its control system, techniques for evaluating performance against predetermined criteria, the operational auditor should inquire to see whether he or she can apply them. However, the techniques should not be used blindly. The operational auditor has to be satisfied that they are logical and valid as a basis for judging performance. If specific measures of internal performance are not available, the operational auditor must then develop methods of evaluation using all available pertinent facts and factors, in arriving at supportable findings and recommendations.

Instead of trying to measure performance against precise criteria, it may be more productive to focus on whether waste is occurring or whether there is a less costly or more effective way to conduct the operations.

An AICPA publication on operational audits provides the following advice on the development of performance criteria:

> Whenever possible, the practitioner should measure the activities under study against objective, relevant, accepted, criteria (yardsticks of efficiency, effectiveness, or results) to support judgmental conclusions and recommendations. The practitioner may derive relevant standards of performance from (1) internally generated measurement yardsticks, such as stated goals, objectives, historical results, policies, procedures, pronouncements, commitments, budgets, corporate plans, and capacities; (2) externally generated measurement yardsticks, such as legislative language, contractual terms, industry standards, productivity studies, trends and comparative performance, and authoritative publications; and (3) previous engagements involving similar operations. Depending on the circumstances, the practitioner may agree with the engaging party to rely on either internal or external criteria alone. It is preferable to use objective, documentable standards, since these give the findings a more authoritative foundation and enhance credibility and acceptance.[8]

---

[8]AICPA, *Operational Audit Engagements* (New York: AICPA, 1982), pp. 11–12.

Generally, it is advisable to reach agreement with the management of the activity being reviewed, and with the engaging party if different, on appropriate performance criteria before extensive work is done to develop specific findings and recommendations.

Review of Administrative and Related Controls

Earlier in the chapter, two broad categories of internal control were explained—accounting control and administrative control. The distinction between the two broad categories of control was developed to highlight the controls that are relevant for a financial audit. Concern with controls is also an important factor in an operational audit, but the operational auditor is more likely to be interested in administrative controls. However, the operational auditor is concerned with any controls that have a bearing on the achievement of the goals of the activity under review.

The operational auditor is concerned with the following aspects of control:

- Whether the policies of the organization comply with its basic charter, grant of authority, or assignment of responsibility
- Whether the administrative controls designed to carry out those policies and activities are conducted as planned by management and in an efficient and economical manner
- Whether the administrative and accounting controls provide adequate safeguarding of the organization's resources, revenues, and expenditures

In assessing the administrative and other relevant controls, the operational auditor should be alert to the following conditions or circumstances:

1 The failure by management to establish criteria for judging accomplishment, productivity, or efficiency
2 Lack of clarity in written instructions that may result in misunderstandings, inconsistent applications, or deviations
3 Lack of capability of personnel to perform their assignments
4 Failure to accept responsibility
5 Duplication of effort
6 Improper or wasteful use of financial resources
7 Cumbersome organizational arrangements
8 Ineffective or wasteful use of employees and physical resources
9 Work backlogs

The existence of these conditions or circumstances indicates problem areas to be investigated further in the development of specific findings and recommendations.

Development of Specific Findings and Recommendations

The development of specific findings and recommendations requires analysis of the information obtained in the prior steps and gathering of evidence to corroborate that information. Generally, the operational auditor should take the following approach:

1 Identify specifically what the problem is—that is, what is deficient, what is defective, what is in error, and the like.
2 Determine whether the condition is isolated or widespread.
3 Determine the significance of the deficiency in terms of costs, adverse performance, or other effects.
4 Ascertain the cause or causes for the condition.
5 Identify the persons in the organization responsible for the deficiency.
6 Determine possible lines of corrective or preventive action and formulate constructive recommendations.[9]

The operational auditor should discuss the findings with management officials responsible for the area being reviewed so that he or she will have the opportunity to obtain as much information as possible bearing on the problem and formulate recommendations in the light of the knowledge of those responsible for the performance being reviewed. Note that the GAO standards include the views of responsible officials in every audit report. Even in engagements for which these standards do not apply, including management's views is often valuable.

Preparation and Submission of Operational Audit Report

The final step in an operational audit is to organize and draft the report on specific findings and recommendations. Generally, the form and content of the report will be as described earlier in this chapter in the section on the framework of an operational audit.

EXAMPLES OF OPERATIONAL AUDITS

This section describes one example each for the type of operational audit that might be conducted by an independent CPA, a governmental auditor, and an internal auditor.[10]

Independent CPA

The organization involved is a mass transit corporation owned by a city that receives substantial funding from the state and the federal government. Under state law, the regional transportation planning agency is responsible for ensuring that operational audits are made of state-funded transit operators. The regional transportation planning agency issues a request for proposal and several independent CPA firms submit responses. An independent CPA firm is selected to conduct the operational audit.

Purpose and Scope of Engagement   The purpose of the operational audit engagement is to assess the performance of the mass transit corporation and provide an evalu-

---

[9]Morse, Ellsworth H., Jr., "Performance and Operational Auditing," *The Journal of Accountancy,* June 1971, pp. 43–44.
[10]These examples are adapted from Appendices A, B, and F of AICPA, *Operational Audit Engagements* (New York: AICPA, 1982).

ation of the efficiency and effectiveness of operations during 1 year of operation. The operations of the functional areas of (1) maintenance, (2) safety management, and (3) claims management are to be studied in some depth. The operations in other functional areas of service, planning, transportation operations, fare structure, marketing and public relations, budgeting and financial planning, management reporting, purchasing, and personnel administration are to be reviewed in less detail.

Development of Criteria and Conduct of Engagement   The independent CPA firm conducted interviews and reviewed documentation to identify the key performance measures for each functional area. The performance measures were derived from a transit operators' operational audit guide that was prepared for the regional transportation agency. For those functional areas selected for detailed study, additional interviews and tests were conducted to probe compliance with the performance measures in greater depth. The state had defined performance indicators intended as overall measures of transit operators' efficiency and effectiveness. The engagement included reviewing the operator's performance for each of the following indicators:

Efficiency:
> Cost per vehicle service hour
> Cost per vehicle service mile
> Cost per passenger
> Service hours per employee

Effectiveness:
> Passengers per vehicle service mile
> Passengers per vehicle service hour

Features of the Operational Audit Report   The report is addressed to the board of directors of the mass transit corporation and the regional transportation planning agency (the engaging party). It presents findings and recommendations for each of the functional areas enumerated earlier. The three functional areas studied in depth are presented in a separate section. There is also a separate section on performance criteria.

The section of the report presenting performance criteria notes that the amounts are based on data provided by the transit company. It also notes the limitations of using such criteria in comparing the performance of one organization to another. The report identifies a number of factors to be considered in the comparison—service area population, service area miles, age of systems, number of vehicles, and types of service—and concludes that a numerical comparison of the performance indicators of the transit operators in the geographic region does not afford a valid comparison of their relative efficiency and effectiveness. The report does not contain an overall opinion on the efficiency or effectiveness of the transit company.

Governmental Auditor

The organization involved is a federal agency that provides loans to individuals and organizations that meet specific qualifications. The agency was requesting additional personnel. The Office of Management and Budget (OMB) questioned the necessity and requested a study to determine whether the loan servicing functions and activities were efficient and effective.

Purpose and Scope of Engagement   The purpose of the engagement is to assess performance and identify opportunities for improvement and to determine whether existing loan servicing procedures are appropriate in light of private industry practices and standards. The review included a significant sample of agency regional office activities and the activities of a sample group of private industry lenders.

Development of Criteria and Conduct of Engagement   Agency loans files were reviewed, practices were discussed with loan officers, a questionnaire on servicing activities was completed, and activities were observed. Private-industry lenders were interviewed and they completed a questionnaire on their servicing activities. The performance criteria were based on a comparison of the activities performed by the government agency to those performed by private industry. This approach required a subjective evaluation by the review team, based upon their background and experience.

Features of the Operational Audit Report   The report was addressed to the management of the federal agency and the OMB. Generally, the study confirmed the high quality of agency procedures and their implications for additional staff. However, the appropriateness of the agency maintaining certain loan programs was questioned and suggestions for improvements were made.

Internal Auditor

The organization involved is a segment of a financial institution—the data processing department. The senior management of the financial institution was concerned that the data processing department was not operating effectively and requested the internal audit department to make an operational audit of data processing.

Purpose and Scope of Engagement   The purpose of the engagement is to assess the adequacy of data processing operations in meeting the needs of the organization, including assessing performance, identifying opportunities for improvement, and outlining recommendations for improvement.

The scope of the review included administration, organization, user evaluation, planning and operations, hardware utilization, data communication, and information resource management.

Development of Criteria and Conduct of Engagement   Key users in the organization were interviewed. Data processing documents were reviewed, including plan budgets and employee training records. Actual operations were observed on a random basis. Hardware records on usage were analyzed.

In this case, the internal auditor was able to identify performance criteria from an independent source—the AICPA publication, *Operational Reviews of the Electronic Data Processing Function.*

Features of the Operational Audit Report   The report was addressed to the president, executive vice president, and vice president of data processing. Findings and recommendations for improvement were presented in five major categories: Administration, Organization, Planning, Hardware Utilization, and Information Resources.

CHAPTER 15 ASSIGNMENTS

OBJECTIVE QUESTIONS

15-1 For the following statements indicate whether the statement is true or false.

T F **a** Operational auditing is a type of auditing that is performed only by governmental auditors and internal auditors.

T F **b** Third-party reliance on audit results is a common characteristic of operational audits and financial audits.

T F **c** An operational audit is more in the nature of a systematic review than an examination to gather sufficient, competent evidence to support assertions in accordance with professional standards.

T F **d** The identification or development of performance standards is an important aspect of every operational audit.

T F **e** To conduct operational audits it is necessary to obtain a license to practice as an operational auditor.

T F **f** The objective of an operational audit engagement is to express an opinion on the overall efficiency or effectiveness of an organization.

T F **g** An operational audit report on a governmental entity must include a description of material weaknesses in administrative control, if any, but in an operational audit of a business organization, such disclosure may be described but is not required.

T F **h** The first step in an operational audit engagement is usually a preliminary survey to identify problem areas.

T F **i** It would be inappropriate for an operational auditor to use performance criteria developed within the organization under review.

T F **j** A review of controls is not usually important in an operational audit.

T F **k** An operational audit report usually describes the objectives, scope, and approach of the engagement and presents specific findings and recommendations, but does not have a standardized form or content.

15-2 The following questions relate to aspects of operational auditing. Select the *best* response.

a Governmental auditing often extends beyond examinations leading to the expression of opinion on the fairness of financial presentation and includes audits of efficiency, effectiveness, and:

1 Internal control structure

2 Evaluation

3 Accuracy

4 Compliance

b A typical objective of an operational audit is for the auditor to:

1 Determine whether the financial statements fairly present the entity's operations

2 Evaluate the feasibility of attaining the entity's operational objectives

3 Make recommendations for improving performance

4 Report on the entity's relative success in attaining profit maximization

AICPA

DISCUSSION QUESTIONS

Discussion questions require the application of the concepts explained in the chapter to specific facts, issues, or problems. They are classified by the primary topic to which they relate. However, responses should not be confined to primary topics but should include all relevant implications.

The Framework of Operational Auditing

15-3 An internal auditor states:

> I view operational auditing as a natural extension for my traditional responsibilities. My operational audit work is built on and integrated with my financial auditing. In a given area, say purchasing or data processing, if I believe more attention is necessary to operational aspects, I'll expand that work and reduce the financial auditing emphasis.

Required:
a Compare this view of the internal auditor with the likely view of an independent CPA. In what ways would the independent CPA's view be expected to differ?
b Why does the independent CPA's view differ; what are the reasons for the differences you have identified?

15-4 The Veterans Administration agency rents to its employees government-owned housing at its field stations. GAO auditors examined the rentals being collected for about 15 percent of the quarters and found that they were too low by nearly $600,000 a year. The standard of comparison in this case was the rental rates for comparable private housing in the same communities. The standard is prescribed by the federal OMB. Recommendations for improving the situation were agreed to by agency officials.

Required:
a Why did GAO auditors conclude revenues were too low; was there a diversion of funds?
b Compare the approach used by GAO auditors in examining revenue in this case to the approach that would be used by an independent CPA in auditing the agency's financial statements to express an opinion.

15-5 Financial auditing and operational auditing have several similarities and differences. List the important similarities and differences of an operational audit and an audit of financial statements.

The Conduct of an Operational Audit

15-6 A city government's mayor engaged an independent CPA firm to conduct an operational audit of city services for sanitation (garbage collection) and maintenance of streets and sewers. The purpose of the engagement was to evaluate the efficiency and effectiveness of delivery of services.

Required:
a Outline the general approach and procedures the CPA firm would use in conducting the engagement.
b Describe the CPA firm's likely approach to developing performance criteria.

15-7 The president of a manufacturer of plastic containers questioned the efficiency of current office procedures. The internal audit department was requested to conduct an operational audit of the activities of the office staff of eight personnel. The purpose of the engagement was to identify ways to improve the efficiency and effectiveness of the activities.

Required:
Outline the general approach and procedures that would be used in conducting the engagement.

15-8 A state government funds nursing homes operated by cities within the state. The county board is concerned because the nursing homes are experiencing significant budget overruns. The state auditor conducts annual financial audits of the nursing homes. The county board requests the state auditor to also conduct an operational audit of the nursing homes this year to assess the efficiency and effectiveness of delivery of services.

Required:
a Is the auditor independent in the audit of the financial statements of the nursing homes in accordance with generally accepted auditing standards?
b Must the operational audit report to be issued this year comply with the GAO standards?
c What performance criteria would the state auditor be likely to use in conducting the operational audit?

15-9 A state public service commission requests an operational audit of the efficiency and effectiveness of a state-owned public utility.

Required:
a What type of auditor might be engaged to conduct the operational audit?
b What performance criteria would be used in conducting the operational audit of the utility?
c To whom would the operational audit report be addressed?

INDEX